# The Complete HyperCard Handbook

## Second Edition

DANNY GOODMAN

BANTAM BOOKS
Toronto · New York · London · Sydney · Auckland

*For my father*

*The Complete HyperCard Handbook, 2nd Edition*
*A Bantam Book/October 1988*


*Interior design by Nancy Sugihara*
*Production by Inter Text Productions,* Inc.



*ISBN 0-553-34577-X*

*Published simultaneously in the United States and Canada*

Bantam Books are published by Bantam Books, Inc. Its trademark, consisting of the words "Bantam Books" and the potrayal of a rooster, is registered in U.S. Patent and Trademark Office and in other countries. Marca Registrada. Bantam Books, Inc. 666 Fifth Avenue, New York, New York 10103

PRINTED IN THE UNITED STATES OF AMERICA

BH 0 9 8 7 6 5 4 3 2 1

# Contents

*Acknowledgments* xv
*Foreword by John Sculley* xvii
*A Conversation with Bill Atkinson* xxi
*How to Use This Book* xxxiii
*Preface to the 2nd Edition* xxxiv

Introduction Coping with the Information Revolution 1

The Historical Chain of Information 1 • Information Today 4 • Information Threads and Links 5 • Program Information 7 • The Database Software Heritage 8 • HyperCard and the Databases 10 • The Center of Your Macintosh World 11 • Programming for Poets 12 • Three Points of View 13

PART ONE
*Browsing Through HyperCard* 15

Chapter 1 The Browsing Building Blocks 17

User Preferences 17 • The Basic Elements 19 • Stacks 20 • Backgrounds 23 • Cards 24 • Fields 27 • Buttons 27 • The Home Stack 28 • Recent 32 • The Message Box 34

Chapter 2 Finding and Entering Information 41

Finding Information in the Real World 41 • Retrieval Environments 42 • Using the Browse Tool 43 • Flipping Through Cards 45 • Where Do I Click 47 • Finding Text 47 • Entering Text Information 56

Chapter 3 HyperCard Linking and Printing 65

Cross-Reference Information 65 • HyperCard Printing 68

PART TWO

*HyperCard's Authoring Environment* 83

Chapter 4 Introduction to Authoring 85

What Authoring Means to You 85 • Authoring Scenarios 86 • Accessing HyperCard's Authoring Tools 89 • The HyperCard Screen 92 • HyperCard Menu Types 93

Chapter 5 All About Stacks 97

Two Stack Types 97 • Making a New Stack 100 • Protecting a Stack 105

Chapter 6 All About Layers 109

Object Layers 109 • Background and Card Layers 111 • What the Browser Sees 112 • Layers and Heterogeneous Stacks 116

Chapter 7 All About Backgrounds 119

Backgrounds and the Browser 119 • Blank Backgrounds 120 • Background Info... 121

Chapter 8 All About Cards 123

Card and Background Interaction 123 • Card Properties 125 • Selecting Cards 126

Chapter 9 All About Fields 129

Fields vs. Graphic Text 129 • Accessing the Field Tool 130 • Field Layer Properties 131 • Field Visual Properties 138 • Font Properties 143 • HyperTalk Properties 148 • Creating New Text Fields 149 • Customizing Field Properties 151 • Cloning Fields on the Same Card 152 • Changing a Field's Domain 156 • Copying and Pasting Fields Between Stacks 158

Chapter 10 All About Buttons 161

What Buttons Do 161 • Accessing the Button Tool 162 • Button Layer Properties 163 • Button Visual Properties 165 • HyperTalk Button Properties 175 • Creating New Buttons 175 • Cloning Buttons on the Same Card 177 • Changing a Button's Domain 180 • Copying and Pasting Buttons Between Stacks 182

Chapter 11 Basic Linking 185

The Essence of a HyperCard Link 185 • Instant Link Scripts 188 • New Button Strategies 191

Chapter 12 Introduction to HyperCard's Painting Tools 193

The Role of HyperCard Art 193 • Macintosh Painting 194 • Graphics Overview 196 • Undo—The Savior 199

Chapter 13 HyperCard Painting Palettes 201

The Selection Tool 201 • The Lasso Tool 205 • The Pencil Tool 207 • The Paintbrush Tool 209 • The Eraser Tool 212 • The Straight Line Tool 214 • The Spraypaint Tool 219 • The Rectangle Tool 221 • The Rounded Rectangle Tool 224 • The Paint Bucket Tool 224 • The Oval Tool 228 • The Curve Tool 230 • The Text Tool 232 • The Regular Polygon Tool 236 • The Irregular Polygon Tool 240 • The Patterns Palette 242

Chapter 14 The Paint Menu 245

Select 246 • Select All 246 • Fill 246 • Invert 246 • Pickup 249 • Darken and Lighten 250 • Trace Edges 251 • Rotate Left and Rotate Right 252 • Flip Vertical and Flip Horizontal 252 • Opaque and Transparent 253 • Keep 254 • Revert 256

Chapter 15 The Options Menu 259

Grid 259 • FatBits 262 • Power Keys 266 • Line Size 268 • Brush Shape 268 • Edit Pattern 268 • Polygon Sides 274 • Draw Filled 274 • Draw Centered 274 • Draw Multiple 275

Chapter 16 Painting Strategies 277

Borrowing from Others 277 • The Sequence of Things 278 • To Menu or Not To Menu 279

Chapter 17 Building a HyperCard Stack 281

Overview 281 • Part One: Creating the New Stack 284 • Part Two: Modifying Background Graphics 293 • Modify Background Fields 316 • Delete Background Buttons 321 • Add Background Buttons 321 • Making the Cards 328 • Using the Stack 337

PART THREE

*HyperCard's Programming Environment* 339

Chapter 18 Introduction to HyperTalk 341

Programming and Personal Computers 341 • HyperTalk, The Language 345 • What You Can Do with HyperTalk 346 • What HyperTalk Cannot Do 347 • HyperTalk Modularity 348 • Using the Script Editor 349 • Structure of a Script 350 • Pieces of a HyperTalk Script 352 • The "It" Local Variable 364 • Other Terms 365 • Foreign Language HyperTalk 366

Chapter 19 Messages, Hierarchy, and Inheritance 367

Messages, Again 367 • Hierarchy 368 Message Entry Points 376 • System Messages 383 • Where to Place Message Handlers 393 • External Resources 394 • Inheritance 395

Chapter 20 Introducing HyperTalk Commands 397

Notation Conventions 398 • Containers 400 • Container Components 402

Chapter 21 Navigation Commands 407

Go 407 • Find 409 • Push 411 • Pop 411 • Help 413

Chapter 22 Action Commands 415

Put 415 • Get 419 • Delete 420 • DoMenu 420 • Wait 422 • Dial 424 • Send 427 • Do 428 • Choose 429 • Click 430 • Drag 431 • Type 433 • Sort 434 • Open 436 • Open Printing 439 • Print 439 • Close Printing 439

Chapter 23 Arithmetic Commands 441

Add 441 • Subtract 442 • Multiply 444 • Divide 445 • Convert 446

Chapter 24 Object Manipulation Commands 449

Hide 449 • Show 451 • Get 454 • Set 454 • Global 457 • Edit Script 458

Chapter 25 Screen Manipulation Commands 461

Visual 461 • Answer 463 • Ask 465 • Ask Password 465

Chapter 26 Sound Commands 469

Beep 469 • Play 470

Chapter 27 File Manipulation Commands 475

Open File 475 • Close File 475 • Read 476 • Write 478 • Print 480

Chapter 28 HyperCard Properties 483

Global Properties 484 • BlindTyping 484 • Cursor 485 • DragSpeed 486 • Edit-Bkgnd 487 • Language 487 • LockScreen 488 • NumberFormat 489 • PowerKeys 490 • UserLevel 491 • Window Properties 492 • Location 492 • Rectangle 493 • Visible 494 • Painting Properties 494 • Brush 494 • Centered 495 • Filled 495 • Grid 496 • LineSize 497 • Multiple 497 • MultiSpace 497 • Pattern 498 • PolySides 499 • TextAlign 499 • TextFont 499 • TextHeight 499 • TextSize 499 • TextStyle 499 • Stack, Background, and Card Properties 500 • Name 501 • Script 502 • Field Properties 503 • Location 503 • LockText 504 • ShowLines 504 • WideMargins 504 • Name 504 • Rectangle 505 • Script 506 • Scroll 507 • Style 507 • TextAlign 508 • TextFont 508 • TextHeight 508 • TextSize 508 • TextStyle 508 • Visible 509 • Button Properties 510 • AutoHilite 510 • ShowName 510 • Hilite 510 • Icon 511 • Location 512 • Name 513 • Rectangle 514 • Script 514 • Style 515 • TextAlign 516 • TextFont 516 • TextHeight 516 • TextSize 516 • TextStyle 516 • Visible 517

Chapter 29 Introducing HyperTalk Functions 519

Functions 520 • Using Functions in Scripts 520

Chapter 30 Time and Date Functions 523

The Date 523 • The Abbreviated Date 523 • The Long Date 523 • The Time 524 • The Long Time 524 • The Seconds 525 • The Secs 525 • The Ticks 526

Chapter 31 Keyboard and Mouse Functions 529

The MouseH 529 • The MouseV 529 • The MouseLoc 529 • The CommandKey 531 • The OptionKey 531 • The ShiftKey 531 • The Mouse 534 • The MouseClick 534 • The ClickLoc 535

Chapter 32 Text Functions 537

The Length 537 • Offset 538 • The Number 540 • The CharToNum 541 • The NumToChar 541

Chapter 33 Math Functions 545

The Random 545 • The Value 546 • SANE Functions 548 • Abs 548 • Annuity 548 • Atan 549 • Average 549 • Compound 549 • Cos 549 • Exp 549 • Exp1 550 • Exp2 550 • Ln 550 • Ln1 550 • Max 550 • Min 550 • Round 551 • Sin 551 • Sqrt 551 • Tan 551 • Trunc 551

Chapter 34 Miscellaneous Functions 553

The Number of Cards/Buttons/Fields 553 • The Result 555 • The Sound 556 • The Target 557 • The Param 558 • The ParamCount 558 • The Params 558 • User-Defined Functions 561

Chapter 35 Mathematic Operators 563

Plus 563 • Minus 564 • Multiply 565 • Divide 565 • Is, Is Not 566 • Comparison 567 • Div 568 • Mod 568 • Miscellaneous Operators 570 • And 570 • Or 570 • Not 570 • Concatenate 572 • Contains 573 • Is In 573 • Comment 574 • Precedence 575

Chapter 36 Constants 577

True 577 • False 577 • Up 577 • Down 577 • Empty 579 • Quote 579 • Return 580 • Space 580 • Tab 580 • FormFeed 580 • LineFeed 580

Chapter 37 HyperTalk Control Structures 583

If-Then Decisions 584 • If...Then 586 • If...Then...Else 587 • Nesting If-Then Decisions 589 • Repeat Constructions 590 • Repeat For 590 • Repeat Until 591 • Repeat While 592 • Repeat With 593 • Modifying Repeat Execution Order 594 • Next Repeat 594 • Exit Repeat 595 • Exit If 595 • Exit 595 • Pass 596

PART FOUR

*Applying HyperCard and HyperTalk* 599

Chapter 38 Introduction to Applications 601

A Useful Utility Script 602

Chapter 39 A Corporate Directory 605

Overview 605 • Scripts and Properties 608 • Further Ideas 615

Chapter 40 A Telephone Logbook 617

Overview 617 • Scripts and Properties 619 • Further Ideas 624

Chapter 41 A Time Sheet 625

Overview 625 • Scripts and Properties 627 • Further Ideas 633

Chapter 42 A New and Improved To Do List 635

Overview 635 • Scripts and Properties 638 • Further Ideas 649

Chapter 43 A Conversion Calculator 651

Overview 651 • Scripts and Properties 654 • Further Ideas 662

Chapter 44 A Visual Outliner 663

Overview 663 • Scripts and Properties 667 • Further Ideas 682 • A Final Note 683

PART FIVE
*HyperCard 1.1 and 1.2* 685

Chapter 45 Making the (Up)Grade 687

The Importance of Upgrades 687 • Update Chronology 688 • How to Upgrade 692

Chapter 46 New HyperCard Features 697

TextArrows Property 697 • HyperCard and MultiFinder 699 • New Find Commands 700 • Auto Tab 702 • Keyboard Shortcut Change 705 • Working with Write Protected Disks 705

Chapter 47 New HyperTalk Features 707

Abbreviations and Synonyms 707 • Two Old System Messages 709 • New System Messages 710 • Keyboard Shortcuts 713 • Peeking at Objects 713 • Peeking at Scripts 714 • Testing for the HyperCard Version 716 • Locking and Unlocking Screens 717

• Target and Me 718 • Other Improvements 718 • Bug Fixes to HyperCard 1.2 721 • XCMD Enhancements 722

Chapter 48 HyperTalk Expressions 725

Everyday Expressions 725 • Expressions in HyperTalk 726 • Evaluating Expressions 727 • Expression Types 728 • Expression Notation 732 • "Do" and Expressions 732

Chapter 49 HyperTalk Commands Update 735

Exit to HyperCard 735 • Reset Paint 737 • Select <object> 738 • Select <text> 740 • Hide 743 • Show 743 • Lock Screen 744 • Unlock Screen 744 • Find Whole 746 • Find String 746

Chapter 50 HyperTalk Functions Update 749

The HeapSpace 749 • The StackSpace 749 • The DiskSpace 750 • The ClickH 751 • The ClickV 751 • The SelectedText 752 • The SelectedChunk 752 • The SelectedLine 751 • The SelectedField 751 • The FoundText 754 • The FoundChunk 754 • The FoundLine 754 • The FoundField 754 • The Number of Cards of <Background> 756 • The Version of HyperCard 757 • The Long Version of HyperCard 757 • The Version of Stack 757 • The ScreenRect 759

Chapter 51 HyperTalk Properties & Operator Update 761

LockMessages 761 • LockRecent 762 • Size 763 • FreeSize 763 • Left 764 • Top 764 • Right 764 • Bottom 764 • TopLeft 764 • BottomRight 764 • BotRight 764 • Width 764 • Height 764 • Cursor 766 • CantDelete 767 • CantModify

768 • UserModify 769 • AutoTab 770 • ShowPict 771 • Within 772

Chapter 52 New HyperTalk Features at Work 775

Search-and-Replace 775 • An Efficient Spreadsheet 779 • Multiple Scrolling Fields 780 • Field Bugs 785 • Turning Lines into Spreadsheet Cells 786 • Adding it All Up 789

Chapter 53 Using HyperCard on Locked Media and Networks 791

What Exactly is CD-ROM? 792 • CD-ROM and HyperCard 793 • Getting a Stack onto CD-ROM 794 • HyperCard on a Network 794

Chapter 54 Introduction to External Resources 799

Resources—the Building Blocks 799 • About ResCopy 800 • Resources and Copyrights 807

Chapter 55 Interpreting "HyperCard Helper" Messages 809

Appendix A Tips on Importing and Exporting Data 835

Text Transfers to HyperCard 835 • Exporting Text 836 • Graphics Transfers 837

Appendix B HyperCard 1.2 Quick Reference 839

Index 849

# Acknowledgments

Although I use many metaphors throughout this book to describe various aspects of HyperCard, I'd like to use a HyperCard metaphor to thank the many people who made my participation in this important project possible and so rewarding. You'll pardon me, then, as I choose Recent from the Go menu to review in historical order the faces of those who played key roles.

In the very first position is Jane Anderson. While my contact with her was for other Apple-related purposes, Jane ultimately became the critical link to the rest of my journey with HyperCard.

Next in the Recent dialog is John Sculley. For reasons still unknown to me, he took me into Apple's confidence early in 1986 and revealed the wonders of HyperCard, while suggesting I write a book on the product. He was also kind enough to contribute the Foreword.

If the Recent dialog box showed a minicard for each visit to that card, the dialog would be almost completely filled with Bill Atkinson cards. The experience of watching him for a year and a half mold HyperCard into its present shape has been a privilege I will never forget. He instructed me, he listened to what I had to say, he made me feel very much a part of his vision of HyperCard.

Next comes Chris Espinosa, who had to put up with many hand-wringing messages and conversations as various deadlines came and went. He was far more supportive of my "outsider" HyperCard efforts than I thought possible.

As I near the end of the Recent dialog box, I see the friendly face of Dan Winkler. As the caretaker of HyperTalk in its development, he volunteered a great deal of extra time to check the HyperTalk parts of this book for accuracy. He turned HyperTalk scripts for my stack applications in Part Four into some of the cleanest, most elegant HyperTalk code I can imagine.

I also wish to express gratitude to Olivier Bouley, Ted Kaehler, and Julie Lieber at Apple for giving my projects special attention. My thanks also go to Kenzi Sugihara and Jono Hardjowirogo of Bantam Books for their faith in my early estimate of HyperCard's importance to personal computing.

To my many friends and colleagues who couldn't get me to reveal the Big Secret for such a long time, well, This Is It. Thanks for putting up with my tight-lip policy.

Finally, I'm lucky to have a place here to express my appreciation for Linda's love and understanding over the last ten-plus years of our life together— so much of which I've spent putting words to disk. Your eternal patience is a great comfort.

# Foreword

John Sculley
Chairman and CEO
Apple Computer Inc.

Hypermedia. It's a new word for most of us. Yet this term and its definition will become increasingly important the more we rely on personal computers to store, manage, and retrieve information.

In broad terms, hypermedia is the delivery of information in forms that go beyond traditional list and database report methods. More specifically, it means that you don't have to follow a predetermined organization scheme when searching for information. Instead, you branch instantly to related facts. The information is eternally cross-referenced, with fact linked to fact, linked to fact.

Hypermedia is particularly true to its name when it links facts across conventional subject boundaries. For example, when studying chemistry, you may wish to study the life of a chemical compound's creator. One hypermedia link would connect that compound to the chemist's biographical information located in an entirely different reference work. Another link might connect the chemical compound to a listing of grocery store products that incorporate the compound, or to long-term health studies on the compound. We can focus more on content, while ignoring the organization.

Until recently, there has been little need to address hypermedia on personal computers, largely because of the limited amount of information most computers could manage "on line" at any one time. But as high capacity magnetic hard disks become nearly standard equipment on computers like the Macintosh, established methods of finding related pieces of information become cumbersome. At the same time, we've scarcely begun to take advantage of new magnetic and optical mass storage technologies that place on our desktops more information than the largest mainframe computers managed ten years ago.

The hardware that holds the information is only one side of the hypermedia equation. The balancing side—and unquestionably the most difficult part—is the software that lets us function in a hypermedia environment. By "function," I mean working with linked information in an intuitive and interactive way. And not putting information delivery just into the hands of computer professionals, but giving everyone sufficient power to bring information to life. Bill Atkinson's HyperCard puts hypermedia into the hands of nearly every Macintosh owner.

I should stress that HyperCard is not an application, like a word processing, spreadsheet, or database program. It is, rather, a software engine—a hypermedia toolkit, if you will. With HyperCard, virtually anyone can become a software author, producing an information-based application that looks like a professionally designed Macintosh application. HyperCard is also like a tape player on which you run HyperCard applications written by others.

The key to HyperCard's authoring environment is HyperTalk, a marvelously simple programming language built into the engine. Within a very short time after HyperCard's release, I foresee the development of thousands of applications not now available on the Macintosh. These applications will not come from the ranks of experienced Macintosh programmers, but from non-programmers who are otherwise intimidated by the complexity of serious programming. Danny Goodman, the author of this book, is a case in point.

Over the course of several years, Danny developed in his mind's eye a dream application to help him manage his time, writing projects, and deadlines. Even though he had a firm idea of what the program should do, Danny didn't have the time to master computer programming to make his program do what he needed. Even the relational database programs for the Macintosh didn't offer the flexibility he required. But working in the HyperCard environment, Danny was finally able to turn his dream into a practical program. Then he discovered that other people liked it as well. Thus was born Focal Point™, one of the first third-party stackware products.

This story will be repeated by many authors for many applications in the years ahead. This, I believe, is a major strength of HyperCard: it shatters the barrier between a person's information handling dream and its realization. The expertise embodied in HyperCard applications will be the expertise of businesspeople, professional people, and educators—in short, the people who work with information daily.

Information publishing may also take a new turn with the advent of HyperCard. Since HyperCard is ready today to act as a familiar "front end" to mass storage devices like CD-ROMs, interactive videodiscs, and future optical storage technologies, anyone with information to distribute can design toward a unified software interface for all Macintosh models. Once a user has access to this information, HyperCard stacks are empowered to work far more interactively with the information than the traditional "search and sort" routines of a read-only database.

Potentially, HyperCard can be as important for the Macintosh in the late 1980s as AppleSoft BASIC was for the original Apple II in the late 1970's. AppleSoft BASIC allowed dedicated enthusiasts to put a new computer technology to work for them. HyperCard puts far more powerful tools into the hands of virtually everyone who knows how to use a Macintosh. Like so much of what we at Apple have been doing for our first decade— enabling people to use personal computers productively— HyperCard in our second decade presents a new software technology platform on which many more people can build.

HyperCard and the wonderful opportunities it presents for personal computing would not have been possible without the genius of Bill Atkinson. When I first saw a prototype in late 1985, it was clear to me that Bill was brewing a software revolution. Since then, he has solved enormous technical difficulties and added more features and ease of use than anyone thought possible. In the land of Apple Computer, Bill Atkinson is a national treasure.

Now that the IBM compatible world recognizes the Macintosh human interface style as a mainstream idea— and a desirable idea at that— Apple Computer must push even harder to maintain meaningful differences between the IBM and Macintosh worlds. I believe HyperCard stands as a perfect example of Apple's commitment to that goal.

# A Conversation with Bill Atkinson

Bill Atkinson, the creator of HyperCard, took time out during the last weeks of HyperCard development to talk with me about many issues surrounding the program's development and his aspirations for the product. The interview took place in what I would call a HyperCard community: his home in the hills at the far south end of the San Francisco Bay area. As he and I talked into a tape recorder in one part of the house, Dan Winkler, Bill's chief co-programmer, was in another part of the house making the HyperTalk language work faster. In yet another room, Marge Boots, a Macintosh artist, was busy exploring card and icon designs that would be included with the program. It was Memorial Day, but when Apple deadlines approach, it's "business as usual" seven days a week at this HyperCard colony.

DANNY GOODMAN: A lot of people have different ways of describing HyperCard. How do you describe HyperCard?

BILL ATKINSON: HyperCard is an authoring tool and an information organizer. You can use it to create stacks of information to share with other people or to read stacks of information made by other people. So it's both an authoring tool and sort of a cassette player for information.

GOODMAN: Where did the idea for HyperCard come from?

ATKINSON: There were a lot of roots to it. One of the early contributors was the Magic Slate project that I worked on for a while, but that was later cancelled. Magic Slate was a laptop computer that had a full-page display and an all-graphical interface. We worked out some neat paradigms for breaking down the barriers to applications.

Goodman: Why was Magic Slate dropped?

Atkinson: It couldn't really happen in a short time frame. It wouldn't be cost effective for a lot of people. It would be too expensive for many people to get their hands on it.

Goodman: What happened then?

Atkinson: So I backed down to saying, "How much of what I've learned or dreamed about here in Magic Slate could I do on today's generation of computers?"

I started thinking that many more people would have a use for a computer if it did some different things than it does now. Right now, they're used mostly for word processing and spreadsheets and, I guess, lately, some graphics applications. But, I thought, in order to use one of those applications, you have to see yourself as being a creator of information. What do you do about the consumer of information? There are maybe twenty times as many people who want to read information.

Goodman: Was that a major turning point?

Atkinson: That's when I started thinking about gradually unfolding a path that starts with clicking and browsing– something that anybody could do and that would be useful for a lot of things. Then up to some painting, which isn't that much harder if you've used something like MacPaint before. And then onto cutting and pasting buttons and making some authoring tools in a kind of erector set approach. You're really making a program. But you're making it just by cutting and pasting little pieces. And then, finally, all the way up to teaching what I do, which is programming. The HyperTalk language is sort of a humane starting language for people who want control of their computer. They are not interested in programming per se. The language is something that can be a good first introduction to programming and will provide enough power that most people don't have to go into Assembler language and what not.

Goodman: HyperCard seems like many different programs in one. You have a graphics program, you have a programming environment, and you have the ability to do a lot of things with those tools.

Atkinson: A lot of its multiple facet is because you're looking at things made with HyperCard. The HyperCard program itself is an authoring tool, but the things that it creates are applications in their own right. So you look at HyperCard as it comes. It comes with an address book and an appointment calendar, and a dozen stacks that are like applications. One part of the multiplicity comes because you're looking at some sample tapes that came with your cassette player. The other part of it is just that it is an authoring tool, with graphics and text intermixed.

GOODMAN: From the authoring standpoint, when someone looks at the manual that comes with HyperCard, the program doesn't seem that complex. But then they heft this rather thick book and they see an enormous program with a lot of depth. Is that going to frighten some people away?

ATKINSON: Well it's very important that one's first interaction with HyperCard be a positive experience. You've got to have success right away or you'll never go on to growing into some of the more powerful features. That's why, in fact, I've gone to great lengths to hide some of the power in the early stages. It's like prerequisites for courses in college. In the same way, I hope that beginners can come into this with the idea of, "Well, I can just click to browse around, and I can click and type to add cards," and they can use it right away. There are a number of good strong resting points that let you say, "Okay, I understand browsing now," or "I understand typing now, and I can rest there for a while. Later I'll learn how to work all the painting tools."

Even in the language, when you get more into HyperTalk, there's this gentle gradual progression from typing things into the Message Box. You type 5/6 and press Return, and it calculates some number. And you say, "Okay, that's not much harder than a calculator, I think I can figure that out." But then you can type little things like *go "Clip Art"* and you learn that whatever command you type in there HyperCard will do. You learn one little step at a time. You say *the date*, carriage return, and there's today's date. You learn that before you learn about *put the date into field 3.* And you learn all that before you learn, "Oh you can get other things to type in these commands for you."

GOODMAN: How long have you been at HyperCard?

ATKINSON: About two and a half years, almost three.

GOODMAN: Over that time, how have the basic features of HyperCard evolved? How have they evolved from your original plan?

ATKINSON: My initial mockup was done with MacPaint documents and a text file that described the relationships between them. A button would have three attributes basically: a visual effect, a sound effect, and a destination. And that was initially all the buttons could do. But there was no language, because it was just a matter of choosing which of those attributes you wanted. But still the very quick branching from one place to another by touching hasn't changed much since then.

The card size changed, it used to be the same size as a MacPaint window, which is about one-half of the area of the card we're doing now. As HyperCard became more of an authoring tool, it became obvious that people really needed to be able to take over the whole screen, including the menubar, in order to control the complete look of what their application behaved like.

GOODMAN: Didn't you have some breakthroughs in handling graphics?

ATKINSON: It went from being the card-specific graphics just being OR'ed on top of the background— where all you could do was add more black bits: You couldn't add more white bits— to a strategy of actually having mask and data so that the bit maps are all two bits deep and you can have opaque white. That was a major step and a major hurdle to get over. That was the point when I had to come up with the bit map compression because things just got totally out of hand. But I really wanted the flexibility and artistic ability of bit maps rather than using structured graphics, which just couldn't express the richness that I want for a user interface.

At one point, there were two completely different environments. There was the painting environment and the authoring environment, and I literally bank switched a whole hunk of code out, another hunk of code in. Those two were not integrated at all. They were very, very different palettes and very different behaviors. We've worked a lot toward integrating them now so that going back and forth isn't so painful and it's much more integrated. In fact, the latest stages of integration, as one of the last things along that line, is this business about actually being able to control the painting tools from the language, which gives a tremendous power for its memory cost. Now you can algorithmically compute things that you want to draw: charts and drawings and various plots and stuff like that.

GOODMAN: Any other evolutions?

ATKINSON: When we went to full size and mask in data, there were big performance hits. Suddenly things got about fifteen times slower than

MacPaint, and I had to figure out some whole new algorithms and ways to handle that. In fact, I took a room at a hotel near the beach and just camped out there in seclusion, away from anybody else, while I cracked getting the graphics stuff working. That was pretty nice when I got that working.

GOODMAN: For the painting tools, then, you've done far more than just carry over the MacPaint code.

ATKINSON: You bet! It has disapointed me how little other programmers have done with the additional RAM that they've got. A lot of the shortcomings of MacPaint were strictly because I had to squeeze it into 128K bytes, when there was 22K of that on the screen and another good chunk in the system heap. But the whole resident code for MacPaint was 25K bytes. The resident code for HyperCard is more on the order of 250K. With more code, if you have more memory, you can do a lot more. Some of the things I wanted to do in the original MacPaint I was able to do here, like having infinite Undo, and being able to select the last thing you just drew. They seemed like obvious things to me, and I don't know why other people haven't done them. Being able to operate on a lasso selection as a first class citizen means that you can really do everything to a lasso selection that you could do to a rectangular selection.

It costs memory when I'm in the Painting tools. It costs me seven additional buffers, each of which is the full size of a card. So seven times 22K on top of the six buffers that I normally have, that's where a lot of the memory is going. But these days, memory is cheap compared to the power that it gives. You can get a non-Apple upgrade from 512K to a megabyte for something like $200. If you were to buy a program for $200, you wouldn't be that put out. But I have really struggled trying to get this thing to run on a 512, not because of the cost, but because of the number of machines that are out there that are still 512s, and the hassle of going in and getting it upgraded. I just wasn't able to do it for the painting tools. I may still be able to do it for a browse-only kind of thing.

GOODMAN: As far as the functionality of the program goes, has the function or the scope of the program changed over this period, in light of the way the Macintosh has been accepted or perceived by different categories of users?

ATKINSON: Not because of what's happening with the Macintosh, but it certainly has changed a lot. The initial intention was for it to be an authoring system, but not necessarily a programming system. Through

HyperTalk, it has really gained much more generality and has became much more of an erector set for building applications.

GOODMAN: For the programmers in the audience, how was your software development environment different for HyperCard as compared to MacPaint?

ATKINSON: Well, I wrote MacPaint on a Lisa. I compiled and ran on a Lisa on a Profile. I would always then download to a Macintosh and try it. The first year and a half of doing HyperCard, I did on a Mac Plus with a hard disk. And that was pretty nice that I could actually take my whole working environment with me to a hotel and hide out there, because all I needed to take was a hard disk and a Mac. Then I got hooked on this faster Mac II prototype that cut my compile time. As the program got bigger, a forty-five minute compile was a killer. If I could cut that down to about six minutes, then I figured I'd marry myself to the big clunker.

GOODMAN: What about the personal environment?

ATKINSON: Well, when I was working on QuickDraw, that was all mine. I wrote it all myself. I didn't let anybody look at my sources. I listened to what people needed in the labs, but it was my call on everything. Then I went from that to MacPaint, which was more of a shared thing, because I would accept a lot of kibitzing from people who would use it as I was developing it. Still, I wrote every line of code. Nobody saw the source until after we had shipped.

What I'm finding with HyperCard is that this trend in the way I work is progressing. I'm working more with other people. There are twenty people who've got their fingers in the pie on HyperCard. There are four that are writing serious chunks of the code. It's still basically my baby. I insist that everything be right, and I read all the code. I probably have written 70 percent of the code that's in there. Dan Winkler is the next major contributor to the code. I needed somebody who could keep up with me, who would go with my style. Dan was willing to learn from me and pick up my style. We work back and forth, we hand code back and forth. We both work here at my house, and I see, in general, I'm able to accomplish a lot more by working with other people.

That's good because I think what HyperCard is all about is sharing information. A program's soul has a lot to do with the people who are making it and what they're thinking about as they're making it. We're not making this to make money. We're not making this to make Apple happy. We're making this because we want to share something. One of the things that I find myself sharing is my understanding of programming. I find that I'm a very good programmer and that I know something about computer graphics. Those two things I think I can teach by example in HyperCard.

GOODMAN: HyperCard was almost not an Apple product. What's the real story behind that?

ATKINSON: Well, Apple has felt a lot of pressure from third-party developers to not ship application software because it competes with the third-party developers. And there are aspects of HyperCard that are application-like. It comes with an address book. That's like an application. There are other aspects of it that are clearly a tool to build things with— the authoring aspects of it. But as Apple saw it as potentially application-like, there was this big question: If Apple sees itself as system software people and this thing is somewhere between system software and application software, what happens to it?

This came up at the time that they unbundled MacPaint from inside the Macintosh box. After telling me, "Don't worry, we're not going to unbundle it," and then telling me, "Oh, it's too late, it's *fait accompli* now," I felt that somebody wasn't dealing with me fairly. The relationship that I had with Apple was going downhill fast. I have a very special relationship with Apple, it's a relationship of trust and cooperation. I need them and they need me, but it's never been one of an arms-length contract relationship. I don't work very well that way. I'm not good at that kind of thing. I like to work with people who are rooting for me and helping me. So at a certain point I said, "I see you unbundling MacPaint. I see Donn Denman, who wrote this beautiful BASIC for Mac, not being able to publish his beautiful work that he put three years into."

I could see something coming for HyperCard. I went to John Sculley and said, "I'm leaving. I have to leave Apple at this point because I want to write a really great program for Macintosh. I can do Apple a lot of good, but I want to make sure that it gets out." John was very supportive, and was enthusiastic about the potential of HyperCard. He talked it over with the executive staff and let me give a presentation. I said, "What I want is to bundle it. If you want to bundle it, I'll write it for Apple. You can have the exclusive proprietary rights and all that stuff, but if you don't want to bundle it then it's time for me to graduate from Apple and go on and be an independent developer myself. I'm going to get this out to people whether I give it away or whether I get Apple to give it away." To this day, Apple is not required to bundle it. They only have an option that if they choose to accept it, then they have to bundle it. They could say no to me right now, but at least then its ownership reverts to me so that I can give it away, which I would do. You see, I want it to be given away so that it can be a base for people to share.

What I will be really excited about is the stacks that come back to me that other people have done. The Apple II when we first put it out was sort of a wrench that we didn't say what it was good for. People would use it for the most amazing things. We'd be kind of flabbergasted when we'd see this Apple II controlling some oil drilling rig. I think that HyperCard has that same flavor to it. The reward of sharing it will come right back and I will get amazing stacks from people who have information but don't have the tools to get it out now.

GOODMAN: If you were a software reviewer in the magazines, what would you try to compare HyperCard to?

ATKINSON: HyperCard is an authoring tool, and as such I would compare it with authoring tools like Owl's Guide, like Plato, like Pilot, like Logo. Those are the fairest comparisons, I think. It's an authoring tool. It's kind of a personal organizer, too, but that comes as a result of the authoring tool rather than as the motivating factor. You can use it as a hub for launching documents and applications. In that sense, it's almost like a Finder.

GOODMAN: Where do you think you'll find these people starting to apply it first? Where do you expect the first applications?

ATKINSON: Education will pick it up right away. There is a growing number of Macintoshes in lower education, but higher education already has lots of Macintoshes and it's so easy to whip together a teaching application.

GOODMAN: What kinds of things do you expect them to be doing?

ATKINSON: For example, in the Exploratorium Science Museum in San Francisco, I would expect them to be using Macintoshes and HyperCard to give hands-on interactive demonstrations of physics principles they are trying to teach, where you poke at something and try this, sort of a little HyperCard lab.

The people at Stanford have been a very early seed for HyperCard. It's being used in a film-editing class where they go out with a video camera and shoot all the scenes for a movie. Then they put them on a video disk. Students come in and use a HyperCard stack that has a storyboard, one little miniature picture for each sequence that was shot. They build the movie out of it. You splice it and lay it together by touching on things in HyperCard and play it back and edit it, make this shorter or make that longer, or move this scene out of here and put it over there.

The end result is that each student has a diskette with a HyperCard stack on it that represents his editing of that film. Nobody's ever had to actually get his hands wet in a darkroom or do any acetate-splicing or videotape-editing and everybody's got the same stuff to work with, so you're concentrating on the editing job rather than the cinematography. Now it's very interesting to see the different renditions different people can come up with because of their own artistic tastes. You can take the same raw stuff and come up with very different pieces based on it.

GOODMAN: Let's move on to HyperTalk. Programming languages all seem to come down an ancestral path. What are the language ancestors of HyperTalk?

ATKINSON: The first one is English. I really tried to make it English-like. It also borrows some concepts from SmallTalk— the inheritance concepts. If you send a message to the card and the card doesn't understand it, it falls through the background of it. If the background doesn't understand it, it falls through to the stack, and if the stack doesn't understand it, it falls through to HyperCard. That inheritance is similar to what they have in SmallTalk. HyperTalk has some background in Pascal just because that's what I speak a lot of. HyperCard itself is about 80 percent Pascal and 20 percent Assembly language.

GOODMAN: How did HyperTalk evolve?

ATKINSON: The first design of the HyperTalk language I did in a five-day period. I had an outline that's still basically what it does now: the way you name things— buttons, fields, cards, backgrounds, stacks, the Home Stack— and they way you name things— card one, first card, last card, any card— those kinds of things. Then Dan Winkler came into the picture. He took this rough mockup and breathed life into it and made it real. He's developed a full language out of it, and we worked together back and forth, kibitzing a lot. But Dan has certainly done the bulk of the work of making it real. He's done a lot of thinking on how to implement it well and how to make it cleanly organized inside.

GOODMAN: Who were some of the other key players on Apple's HyperCard team that helped put HyperCard together?

ATKINSON: Ted and Carol Kaehler were really big players. Carol did the on-line help system. Here was an author, not a programmer, who, in the course of working with HyperCard, had to use all the features. She had to become a HyperCard programmer. I often find that I design by pull. In the HyperTalk language and in HyperCard, the capabilities were really determined by what people wanted to do with it, so Carol has been a big pull there.

Ted has been kind of a kibitzer to me. We talk algorithms and we talk about what we really want, and stuff like that. Adam Paal has been a major contributor. He's been Mr. Printing and has solved the really difficult problem of how to get a LaserWriter that's running Adobe software, which doesn't like bit maps, to not only take bit maps, but go quickly. He's dealt with that, he's dealt with, well, what are the different ways that people would like to print the stuff. It would be safe to say that I wrote all of HyperCard except for the language and the printing and the sound manager. The language is Dan's, the printing is Adam's, and the sound manager is Ted's.

That's the breakdown of who contributed to the code. Lots of people contributed to shaping it. You know, I asked people what they wished they had. The biggest thing is to get people to try to build something with it. Then they run into what they really need, not just what they think they need.

GOODMAN: Was anybody at Apple running interference for you while you coded?

ATKINSON: Yes. Chris Espinosa has been a godsend. He's my product manager and he's been with Apple for a long, long time. I think I've been there nine years and he's one of the few people who has been there longer. I've worked with marketing types before, and it's always grating because they didn't understand the technical side of things. Chris has been real good and he "gets it." He really sees what HyperCard can do for the world. And there aren't enough people at Apple who see that. They may see it more as it gets out and as people start doing stuff with it and they start reaping the benefits, but Chris really has that vision and can see what HyperCard is going to do to people's lives and to Apple's future.

GOODMAN: What parts of HyperCard are you most proud of?

ATKINSON: Well, I'm really proud of the fast search. I worked out a way to make searching about 200 times faster than a more obvious way. I'm proud of the bit-map packing. Bit maps are packed about 30 to 1, and it's really tough to get them that tight. The dominating factor in the size of stacks is how big the bit maps are. So it's something I'm always chewing on in the back of my mind: Is there a way to get the bit map smaller?

Overall, the thing that I'm most excited about in HyperCard is its "opening up" potential. You know, we talk about open architecture hardware. Well, this is open architecture software where, really, you can go inside a stack that somebody else wrote and look and see how it was done and modify it and tweak it a little to tune it for your uses and learn from what someone else has done.

GOODMAN: What's the chance that someone from the MS-DOS or OS/2 worlds will replicate HyperCard?

ATKINSON: Oh, 99 percent. Something like that. I think it's a good enough tool that people will say, "Of course," and start working on clones. It will take them a while to get anything as smooth. You know, I've had a couple years jump on them. When that starts to happen, I hope that they'll do one that's data compatible, so we can exchange stacks between "PC Card" and HyperCard. To that end, we intend to make all the file formats public. We won't actively go out and help people get it up on the PC, but we're helping them an awful lot just by giving all the details of the file format. I'd like to see Apple get an edge, but I'm really more interested in the worldwide sharing of information. That will happen much better if there is a compatible program on all the different machines. I'd like to see one on the Apple II, which doesn't have any conflict for Apple, and so I will be helping a programmer at Apple make an Apple II version of HyperCard.

GOODMAN: Is there still a lot of proprietary technology built into HyperCard?

ATKINSON: Well, what's proprietary? You know, you get a great idea, you use it. There's no idea that's totally original. The question is, can you get a patent on it? Sure, there's stuff in there we could easily get patents on. What's really right in terms of your long-term goals? What are you trying to do? Yes, we want to keep Apple in business so they can do other great stuff, but we also want to make an environment for sharing.

GOODMAN: Do you have future plans for HyperCard?

ATKINSON: Oh, do I have anything else? Yes. I have many, many future plans. I've got a big laundry list of features. I know what they all are, and I know which ones are most pressing. I'd rather not tell everybody what they are because I want to have a little bit of jump when those features come out.

GOODMAN: But we can expect to see additions?

ATKINSON: Lots of improvements. This is not going to be abandoned like MacPaint was. Pretty much Apple put me on something else and gave the maintenance of MacPaint to someone else and then kept shuffling that from one person to another, and MacPaint never got maintained. My full-time schedule for the next couple years is improving Hyper-Card. I have a lot in front of me that I need to do.

# How to Use This Book

By now, you have probably started HyperCard at least once to see what it is all about. Some of the HyperCard applications delivered with the program have obvious utility for nearly every Macintosh owner– the name and address card file, the calendar, and the appointment book. But HyperCard is far more than these examples demonstrate. So much so that this book is divided into four sections, each exploring additional features and powers of HyperCard. Each section will also bring you to a higher level of HyperCard proficiency.

There are few prerequisites for this book. All we ask is that you be familiar with basic Macintosh operations, such as pointing and clicking, pulling down menus, choosing menu items, and the basic "feel" of the Macintosh Finder. This information is readily available in the owner's manual of the Macintosh model you use. If you are not fully acquainted with these concepts, take some time now. Exploring the Finder for fifteen or thirty minutes now– moving file icons around the screen, opening folders, selecting an icon, and choosing Get Info from the File menu– will save you much time later when you'll have to call upon that experience. Fortunately, it doesn't take long to become comfortable with basic Macintosh operations.

Like HyperCard, this book is structured to let you reach increasing stages of proficiency without having to devour the entire work at once. Move through each part at your own pace. Don't rush it.

Most importantly, read this book while sitting in front of your Macintosh with HyperCard ready to go. You will learn HyperCard much faster if you follow the experiments and step-by-step instructions throughout the book. All in all, it should be an enjoyable experience.

# Preface to the 2nd Edition

The release of Version 1.2 presented an excellent opportunity to update *The Complete HyperCard Handbook*. The quick acceptance of the First Edition, which became the best-selling Macintosh book ever produced, caught everyone, including me, off guard. It is most gratifying that many experienced HyperCard authors today still regard the *Handbook* as the primary reference and instructor for the program and the HyperTalk language.

In this Second Edition, I have made minor corrections to the First Edition's main text. Some of these corrections appeared earlier, starting with the third printing of the original book.

At the end of this edition is an eleven-chapter supplement, which details all new features of HyperCard 1.1 and 1.2, plus a few items that crept into HyperCard 1.0.1 after the *Handbook* went to press. I believe that with this edition, I have met the responsibility of the book's title: it is the most complete reference and instructional tool for HyperCard and HyperTalk.

As you'll learn in my interview with Bill Atkinson, HyperCard is still under construction. As HyperCard evolves, so will the *Handbook* evolve to match its new powers.

# INTRODUCTION

# Coping with the Information Revolution

LONG BEFORE MY HANDS TOUCHED A COMPUTER KEYBOARD OR MY EYES PEERED INTO a computer monitor, I saw television advertising for worldwide computer companies that talked about "moving information." The screen showed colorful, mystical interconnections linking New York with New Delhi, via dozens of stops in Europe, Asia, and everywhere. When I watched these commercials, I had great difficulty visualizing "information" and why anyone would want to "move" it.

The problem was my failure to understand how all-encompassing the term "information" can be, and how many forms information can assume. Nor, I think, was I the only one unsure about what information is.

Our inability to grasp the concept is largely the result of information's intangible nature. It can be printed, spoken, and drawn, but these forms are mere representations of information. The marks on a page or screen, the sounds of speech and music—none of this is information unless it conveys meaning to yourself or others. Yet human history demonstrates a long-standing need for information and the skills to manipulate it.

## *The Historical Chain of Information*

The earliest surviving evidence of information recording (other than the artistic expressions of cave painting) comes from the ancient Sumerian civilization in the Middle East, dating back to 3000 B.C. Clay tablets bearing pictographic impressions of a wedge-shaped stylus record the movement of commodities through the marketplace. Unlike the oral tradition, which was responsible for great epic poetry like the stories of Gilgamesh and Odysseus, writing provided a medium for accurate and lasting information. Even 5000 years ago, civilization and its commerce placed information burdens on its participants greater than their ability to manage solely by memory and word of mouth.

Eventually, pictographic Indo-European languages evolved into phonetic languages, in which combinations of alphabet letters spelled out sounds. Written information spread to include not only business transactions but also literature and personal correspondence. We have much archaeological evidence from the ancient Egyptian, Greek, Roman, and Oriental cultures to demonstrate the growing diversity of information through the millennia.

## INFORMATION'S EARLY SPEED LIMITS

The movement of information from person to person, however, remained at the mercy of the transportation systems available. For centuries after Gutenberg's printing press, goods and information traveled no faster than animal- and natural-powered transport. The speed at which information flowed, even well into the nineteenth century, is considered intolerably slow today. American farmers in rural sections of Atlantic seaboard states had no direct way of knowing what the prevailing market prices were for their goods, especially if those products were purchased by overseas buyers and their agents in the port cities. Information that made the journey back to the farm was hopelessly out of date.

To offset this information bottleneck, levels of sales agents, brokers, jobbers, wholesalers, and credit systems intervened. Control over information was essentially handed to others who worked closer to where the information changed hands. Cumbersome though it was, this form of distributed information handling worked adequately in its time, especially since goods themselves moved slowly, drawn overland by horse or across oceans by wind-powered sailing ships.

## THE EARLY INFORMATION AGE

In the 1830s, applications of two powerful technologies— steam power (for transportation and manufacturing energy) and the telegraph—signaled radical changes in information quantity and distribution. According to contemporary reports of comparative travel times between major cities, steam-powered locomotives increased the throughput of goods three to ten times during the first quarter-century of steam railroads. For example, the trip from New York to Chicago shrank from a horse-drawn three weeks to a railroaded two days.

Railroad companies adopted the telegraph as a means of controlling their spreading empires (indeed, most telegraph lines ran along railroad rights of way). But telegraphy quickly became a major information pipeline for commercial, as well as personal, data, as goods and people moved through the steam-powered rail and water transportation systems at great speeds and with predictability.

With the spread of these transportation and communications systems— infrastructures, they're called— came an increased need for controlling the systems themselves. Timetables, fee schedules, collecting of ticket fees from passengers, monitoring the location of rolling stock, and similar controls became more important as the infrastructures became larger than one person could manage. The word *control* implies that information proceeded outward, from a "central office" to the extremities of the infrastructure. Actually, control requires a two-way movement of information: control going out and *feedback* returning home as a means of measuring the effectiveness of the outgoing control. This was the beginning of a class of workers whose sole job was gathering and manipulating information, rather than processing energy or materials.

As the decades passed into the twentieth century, the spiraling codevelopment of technologies (energy utilization and communication, in particular) increased the speed at which goods, services, and people moved throughout the world. With each increment of the transportation speedometer came an increased need for control.

The controlling mechanisms themselves required additional information gathering and processing for adequate feedback. For example, consumer advertising was an established method of controlling the buying patterns of consumers even in the late nineteenth century. By 1910, advertising agencies widely employed information workers whose jobs were to compile statistics on the effects of advertising— feedback on the control, if you will. Later, as advertisers discovered radio, they sought information about their audiences with the help of feedback innovations such as Archibald Crossley's telephone surveys of radio audiences (1929) and A.C. Nielsen's audimeter, which recorded a radio listener's station preferences throughout the day (1935). (A detailed history of these spiraling developments is chronicled in *The Control Revolution* by James R. Beniger, published by the Harvard University Press in 1986.)

## *Information Today*

The process of harnessing energy and devising ways of controlling it continues today, except that the energy most often singled out is that of the microprocessor, rather than steam or electricity. This difference is not insignificant, because in harnessing earlier powers, the effects were first applied to goods, services, and people; the informational backdrop developed slightly later. But with the application of the microprocessor and related integrated circuit chips, the power under harness immediately affects the informational part of our lives. A chip doesn't move goods or people from one town to another; it manipulates information. The result is a speedup in the quantity of information passing before our eyes and around us.

### FROM BATCH PROCESSING TO REAL TIME

Not many years ago, it was commonplace for a small business equipped with a centralized computer system to print reports in "batches." Every Tuesday at 3 P.M., the Computer Department would distribute printouts of the previous week's sales activity and finished goods inventory. That, of course, was a vast improvement over the gathering of quarterly inventory counts and seat-of-the-pants tallying of sales. But today a weekly printout is often insufficient. We virtually demand instantaneous access to the information. Instead of batch processing, the computer is now responsible for tracking numerous parts of the business in "real time," with video terminals on the desks where tons of printouts had once dropped regularly.

Personal computers contribute to the increasing need for up-to-the-second information. If you are active in the stock market, for example, you can retrieve real-time stock exchange data with the computer and a modem, then perform calculations on that data with the help of a spreadsheet or other analysis program. Similarly, you can maintain a database of information that is particularly useful to you, even if the corporate computer department doesn't have time to think about your application.

Personal computer software, in general, encourages the creation of "new" information, even if "new" means a different way of viewing existing data. For instance, you may have always had to prepare a quarterly budget forecast for your division or department. Without a computer, the budget was probably prepared on a columnar pad (with many erasure marks) and then transferred to a typewritten spreadsheet. With a personal computer and spreadsheet software, you have the chance to analyze the budget from different perspectives in less time than it took to create a draft of the manual budget. You might even chart the results as bars or pie wedges for the forecast meeting— perhaps to get a competitive leg up over your colleagues in nearby office cubicles.

## INFORMATION OVERLOAD

The rapid increase in information throughput is not without its problems. All it takes is a casual look through virtually any business computer magazine to see that a primary concern today is passing personal computer information from machine to machine. Even within the confines of a particular computer brand and model, it is often difficult (if not impossible, at times) to pass information between two software programs. For example, if the maker of a particular Macintosh word processing program doesn't make a concerted effort to allow transfer of files between his program and others already on the market, you, as a purchaser of that product, won't be able to share your nicely formatted word processing files with colleagues, except in printed form. Worse yet, if you have information files stored on floppy disks and attempt to read or modify those files on someone else's Macintosh, that other machine must have the identical software you used to create the files in the first place.

The Macintosh, with its propensity to mix text and graphics into the same document, actually complicates matters of file compatibility among programs and between Macintoshes and other computer makes, such as the IBM Personal Computer and Personal System/2 families. While users of the Macintosh technology benefit from this convergence of text and graphics modes, the complexity of storing, sharing, and distributing such information for everyone to use demonstrates the absence of what I call an information infrastructure.

Just as transportation spread across the United States first with an infrastructure of rail lines, then with highways, and most recently with flight paths linking airports, so will computer information become prevalent around the world when an information infrastructure is established. It will entail many computer companies reaching agreements on storage standards, file formats, graphics layouts, and several other technical aspects of personal computing. The technologies are perhaps too immature for such a universal standard to emerge in the near future, but steps can be taken in that direction. HyperCard is very likely one of those steps.

# *Information Threads and Links*

If you've performed any kind of research, like preparing a term paper, you may have recognized that hardly any fact exists in a vacuum. For example, Julius Caesar was assassinated on March, 15th in 44 B.C., yet it's difficult to consider that bit of information entirely on its own. You probably have other questions relating to the incident that require additional information: who were the assassins, what was their motivation, on what literature is the actual date based, what was the political and social climate of the time, what happened after the assassination?

The trouble is, if you find an information source for the event, that source likely won't have the additional information you require. You need to branch away from a strictly date-based collection of facts to other collections, such as information bases centered around literature of the time or historical observations made many centuries later. What this points to is that information very often consists of threads emanating in many directions from a single fact. At the end of each thread is a fact that itself, has additional threads running in yet other directions, and so on.

You may have found yourself making such threaded connections in a research project. Visualize a large bulletin board filled with index cards. Each card contains a fact or quotation extracted from a research source. No matter how you label the cards by subject, a card may relate to more than the card positioned next to it. To help you visualize the relationships from a distance, you link two distant cards by a strand of colored yarn, thumbtacked to the board. After a while, you may have many different colors crisscrossing the board.

## EVERYDAY LINKS

Even in our personal lives, we are surrounded by interrelated facts. For example, if you buy a major appliance, the transaction has many implications on your personal information management. You have to make sure you have the money to pay for the item or have an amount set aside from a monthly budget to make payments. You have to adapt your schedule to accommodate delivery, making sure someone will be home to meet the truck. The value of the new appliance may affect your insurance coverage. Record of the sale must also be maintained for possible tax deductions when you next file your income tax. And on it goes.

If all this is for a relatively simple transaction, consider all the information generated and managed by each individual in a lifetime. This phenomenon is best summed up in an excerpt from Alexander Solzhenitsyn's *Cancer Ward*:

> As every man goes through life, he fills in a number of forms for the records, each containing a number of questions.... There are

thus hundreds of little threads radiating from every man, millions of threads in all. If these threads were suddenly to become visible, the whole sky would look like a spider's web....

### RESEARCH LINKS

As those webs grow, whether they contain threads of personal or business information, it becomes increasingly difficult to locate a particular item. For example, if you are researching a topic, you might start the search in the *Reader's Guide to Periodical Literature*, an index to articles that have appeared in 200 popular consumer magazines. But if the subject might also be covered in technical journals, you will have to check reference works similar to the Reader's Guide that cover the subject. If you're not familiar with those reference works, you must take an additional step away from the material you seek and look into something like The *New York Times Guide to Reference Materials*. In other words, even the number of information cross-references is so large that we need a "guide to the guides."

Each information level we are forced to transcend in search of a fact lessens the desire to perform the search, in an inverse square proportion. If a related fact is two levels away, we're one-fourth as likely to make the effort to track it down; for three levels, it's one-ninth as likely.

It's one thing to be thwarted in a search for "external" information, such as that found in libraries and electronic information services, because of intervening information levels. It's quite another to experience that same difficulty with the information you work with daily on the computer.

## *Program Information*

Any applications program you use that saves files on the disk is an information handler. A word processing program, for example, is often the tool for turning ideas into something a bit more tangible for printing or communicating over the telephone. A spreadsheet program, on the other hand, might be more often used as a transitional information tool, transforming existing figures into presentation graphics or extrapolated forecasts. Even a drawing program, like MacPaint or MacDraw, is an information handler. Any picture you save on the disk (whether created with the program or captured by way of a video digitizer) is information.

Owing to the way we've been brought up on computers and their programs, we too often consider each document as a stand-alone hunk of data. And unless we're working in an integrated applications environment, we probably look at a particular kind of document as having no implications beyond the current program.

It's important to recognize, however, that very few saved documents exist in their private vacuums. More often, a document is only one piece of information within a larger context. A business letter, for instance, may be one point along a communications continuum comprising a much larger project. Part of the letter, such as the addressee's name, address, and greeting, may be merged from a database; another part may contain an excerpt from a job-costing spreadsheet. Even among your own documents, then, invisible colored yarns stretch from file to file.

## *The Database Software Heritage*

One type of information management software you may already know about is a category called database management software (DBMS). For decades, DBMS has been the cornerstone of information management on large computers. It has also been adapted for use with the personal computers that are common today. Within the personal computer category, there are two broad types of database management: file management and relational database management.

### FILE MANAGERS

File management software is the simplest kind of database software. The file part of its name does not refer to the kinds of files your applications generate. Rather, the file is like a finite collection of information, usually replicating a drawer full of filled-out forms. For example, one database file may consist of a collection of names, addresses, and telephone numbers for your business contacts. Before you can use the database, you essentially create an on-screen form to be filled out each time you add a new contact to the file. The form probably has blanks for the person's name, title, company, street address, city, state, ZIP code, and phone number, and perhaps a blank for additional notes.

Once you have designed the empty form, you can begin entering information. As with its paper counterpart, you fill in the blanks on a given form with information for one contact. You wouldn't type in Sarah's phone number on Tom's form, of course. In other words, all the information you deem important about that contact will be viewable on a single form.

It is the additional duty of the file management software to offer you ways of sorting the forms so that you can "thumb through" forms in any order you see fit. Therefore, while you might keep a paper version of this file in alphabetical order by the contact's last name, the file management software allows you to sort the forms by ZIP code. The information on the forms hasn't changed, just the order in which the forms are stored.

An important function of file management software is the search. If you wish to look at only those contacts in Chicago, you can instruct the software to display only those forms whose "city" blank is filled in with the word "Chicago."

From there, you should be able to have the file management program print out a report that lists information on the forms of all contacts you selected with the search criteria. Good file management software will give you multiple search criteria, with which you could select all contacts whose "city" blank says Chicago, and whose "notes" blank contains the word "prospect." You can then use the printed report as a way of following up on leads.

## RELATIONAL DATABASES

A much more sophisticated type of database management is called "relational," because it extends links between individual files. For instance, if your name and address database also has a blank for a consecutive serial number for each form you filled out, a relational database will let you use that number to link the name and address database to a different database.

Let's say you wish to keep a record of orders placed by companies whose names are stored in the name and address database. When designing the order form, you would set up a blank into which you will eventually type the serial number of the customer. You would then establish links between name and address blanks in the order form and the database that actually holds that information. As soon as you type a serial number into an order form, the relational database program looks up the name and address information from the name and address database, and displays the relevant data in the blanks. In other words, you establish threads between forms.

Relational database programs also have the same kind of sorting, searching, and reporting features that file managers do. But with the ability to retrieve information from multiple databases, the job of filling in potentially redundant blanks is greatly simplified.

Both types of database management programs are valuable applications for their intended jobs. By and large, current database management programs for the Macintosh are text-oriented, despite their abilities to incorporate graphics elements in places. Moreover, database programs generally work by themselves: there is little interactivity between a database and the rest of your Macintosh work.

## HyperCard and the Databases

The above introduction to database management software was an important prerequisite to talking about HyperCard because the two environments may appear to do the same kinds of things. In some respects that's true, but HyperCard is not intended to replace database management software as we know it today. In fact, there will likely be many cases in which a Macintosh owner will use a database management program and HyperCard together. We'll see exactly how that works much later in the book.

Let's look at HyperCard in comparison with database management software.

You can use HyperCard quite simply to perform certain operations found in file management software. For example, you use HyperCard to design information input forms on the screen, insert information into the forms, sort the filled-out forms, and search for a particular form. But in this context, you should notice some significant differences. First, you have total control over the appearance of your forms with HyperCard. In fact, you are encouraged to design on-screen forms that resemble noncomputerized objects as much as possible. And by "form," we mean a much wider range than something you fill out like an application form. A HyperCard "form" can be virtually anything that you can recreate inside the area of a standard Macintosh screen: a rolodex-type file card, a calendar page, a weekly appointment book, and so on. In other words, you can use HyperCard to recreate computerized versions of real-life objects, as well as environments impossible in the physical world of paper and ink.

HyperCard also has what a database management devotee would call "relational capabilities." That's because information stored in one stack of HyperCard forms can be retrieved by forms in other stacks. HyperCard takes quite a large additional step, however. Unlike a relational database, HyperCard actually lets you zip over to other stacks to view the full context of related information. Thus, while a relational database generally restricts its relational capabilities to simply retrieving information from elsewhere, HyperCard lets you hop around as your information needs require. You can also use HyperCard to establish generic links between forms to speed the search for related information.

For example, if a generic link exists between a monthly calendar and a daily appointment book, you can click on a day in the calendar to have HyperCard pick out the card in the appointment book file for that day.

Nor are the links you establish finite or rigid. You can adjust the links as you please or create new ones as additional files of related information are added to your collection. The threads, in other words, can keep growing and weaving, like an ever-expanding spider web.

A major distinction between HyperCard and DBMS software is in the way retrieved information is displayed and printed. A raison d'etre for DBMS programs is the ability to generate reports. A report usually consists of columnar data that lists some or all elements of a form. The reporting software then usually performs various math functions, such as providing a total count of items in the report or creating subtotals and totals of numeric information in the report.

HyperCard, on the other hand, is not designed for generating reports of that nature (although it is capable of simpler report printing). Instead, it is optimized for quickly looking through existing cards— browsing— in search of desired information. Therefore, while a DBMS program might produce a report listing based on desired selection criteria (presuming you have already set up the report format), HyperCard very quickly finds cards matching your criteria.

## The Center of Your Macintosh World

It should be clear by now that your Macintosh—with or without HyperCard— is a machine that thrives on information. It lets you create fresh information, it stores old information, and it transforms one information type into another. Even the process of managing the computer's applications and files is an informational task. I call this Macintosh-centered concentration of personal and other information your *Macintosh World.* Every application or document file, every font, every desk accessory— they are all parts of your Macintosh World.

At its most basic level, HyperCard gives you the power to take control over your Macintosh World. It can be the very nucleus of your Macintosh World. From HyperCard, you will have access to every application and file; you'll be able to reach personal and business information you feel important enough to store on a disk or file server; you'll use HyperCard to access new information bases.

This last feature is an important one. Because HyperCard is included with every Macintosh beginning in August 1987, its power will be available to every new Macintosh owner. Because of its mass distribution, HyperCard will serve as a medium through which Apple and third-party publishers will be able to distribute information of any kind, because most Macintosh owners will have access to that information.

It's true that information could be distributed in plain Text Only format, which every Macintosh word processor can load, but that medium strips away key elements, such as the relationships among points of information and the graphical base for which the Macintosh is well-known. HyperCard, then, will certainly serve as a critical step in establishing a long-term information infrastructure for all Macintoshes. HyperCard will become the familiar "front end" to information access not only on our own disk drives, but in network file servers, on compact disc read-only memories (CD-ROMs), on videodiscs, and in mainframe computers linked by cable, telephone, or satellite. We won't have to worry about the storage medium or tricky commands to access remote computers: HyperCard, with the help of third-party publishers, will take care of that for us.

By expanding our reach for information, we extend our Macintosh World. No matter how big that world gets, HyperCard will allow us to keep control over our information.

## *Programming for Poets*

A major barrier between potential computer users and the machines has been the lack of software tailored to narrow applications. Most commercial software tries to appeal to as broad a user spectrum as possible. Specialists, users who could truly benefit from a computer like the Macintosh, simply haven't had the tools to use a machine profitably.

In the past, educators and business people dedicated to putting computers to work for them studied to become nearly professional programmers. They wrote the custom software that no publisher or commercial developer would bother with. That was difficult, but not impossible, on simple computers like the Apple II and the early IBM PC. But today, as computers like the Macintosh become easier to use, they become extremely difficult to program. It can take an experienced programmer a year or more to begin writing quality programs based on visual desktop environments such as the Macintosh.

HyperCard significantly narrows the gap between the nonprogramming specialist and the sophisticated program he or she needs. As you'll learn in later stages of this book, HyperCard handles the hard parts of programming for the Macintosh. You'll spend more time on applying your ideas than on technical issues. Or, as Bill Atkinson says, "It's programming for 'the rest of us'." HyperCard will spawn a new cottage industry of HyperCard developers who have a clear idea of specialty needs and who now have a way to fulfill those needs for themselves and for others in the same fields.

## *Three Points of View*

HyperCard may appear to be a simple program. That is mostly because of its structure, which shields new users from its more fully featured inner workings. If you've started HyperCard and have clicked on an icon or two, you have participated in only one of its three stages of complexity, the *Browsing/Typing level.* Its second stage, which is hardly obvious (and purposely so), is its *Painting/Authoring* level, which is followed closely by its third stage, the *Programming* level. Let's use an automotive analogy to distinguish the three levels.

For the majority of us, an automobile is a convenient, if not necessary, method of transportation. We buy an auto because we have a desire to get from point A to point B. Through driver training classes, we've learned how to start, stop, and maneuver the vehicle in traffic. When the fuel needle nears E, we head for a gas station to refill the tank. And when things don't sound right or, as with tires, appear to be worn, most of us take the car into a service shop for the appropriate repairs. Our main concern, in other words, is using the vehicle as a reliable means of transportation. Our choice of model is usually dependent upon budgetary and aesthetic considerations.

But many of us also see more to an automobile than just its utility or its aesthetic appeal. Curiosity about what lies under the hood leads many of us to take a peek. After overcoming trepidations about opening the hood, we might check a fluid level or tug on a belt to make sure everything is secure. We may then progress to doing minor maintenance jobs like adding a quart of oil. Suddenly we're concerned with grades of oil, trying to determine which is best for the type of engine and climate. Even at this relatively simple level of auto maintenance, we're getting our hands dirty while influencing the performance and longevity of the vehicle.

At the far end of the scale are dedicated weekend mechanics—"hackers" of the grease pits, if you will. They are likely to spend more energy on improving a vehicle's performance or rebuilding carburetors than thinking about its utilitarian function. They see an automobile in terms of what makes it run rather than where it's going.

Using HyperCard's Browsing/Typing level is analogous to driving the auto as a driver only. You use HyperCard to find or enter information. You need not know anything else about the program. In fact, you may see HyperCard set up in browsing and typing applications that virtually disguise the fact that they are running inside HyperCard. The applications are there to help you get from point A (needing information) to point B (having information).

In contrast, HyperCard's Painting/Authoring level gives you the power to peek and tinker "under the hood" to design simple, though useful, applications. HyperCard comes with a remarkably powerful set of design tools, which you can use to modify existing applications or develop your own.

Lastly, the Programming level allows you to modify the performance and operation of HyperCard applications, or design entirely new applications from scratch. This level is built around an English-like language called HyperTalk. While it's true that you can be a HyperCard author without programming in HyperTalk, I believe that anyone with a desire to write an application won't be satisfied, ultimately, unless he investigates HyperTalk's possibilities.

Use Part One of this book first to learn how to drive HyperCard. Then in Part Two take a peek under the hood to perform simple maintenance and repairs. Graduate to Part Three, in which you'll don overalls and learn how to dismantle, rebuild, and create HyperCard applications with HyperTalk. Finally, in Part Four, you start working on real vehicles, applying your newly found knowledge to real information-handling problems. You'll then know HyperCard well enough to mold it into the master of *your* Macintosh World.

# PART ONE

# Browsing Through HyperCard

# CHAPTER 1

# Browsing Building Blocks

YOU CAN USE HYPERCARD STRICTLY IN ITS BROWSING ENVIRONMENT AND STILL BENEFIT greatly from the experience. You are likely doing that already if you are availing yourself of some of the HyperCard template applications—called *stacks*— that come with the program. You've probably seen how easy it is to store and retrieve personal information in familiar forms, like the name and address card file or the daily appointment book. A well-designed stack makes information storage and retrieval painless, if not fun and inviting.

## *User Preferences*

Very much aware that HyperCard's advanced features may overpower newcomers, the program's design team established five levels of complexity. As you grow comfortable with each level, you can graduate to the next, with HyperCard revealing more menus, commands, and internal facilities that you'll need for each level.

The user level is set in a special card in the Home Stack called User Preferences, shown in Figure 1-1. From the Home card you have many ways to get there. The sure-fire way is to choose Home and Last from the Go menu or to type Command-H and Command-4 (the Command key is the one with the ⌘ symbol— press this key and the H or 4 key simultaneously).

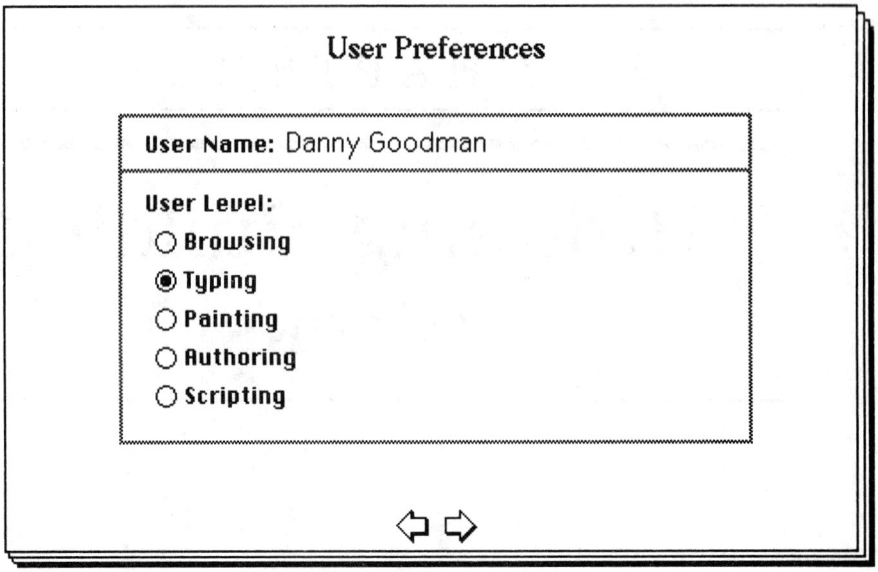

User Preferences

User Name: Danny Goodman

User Level:
- Browsing
- Typing
- Painting
- Authoring
- Scripting

*Figure 1-1. The User Preferences card in the Home Stack set to Typing level*

Each level adds powers to the abilities of the previous level. The five levels and their respective powers are as follows:

| Level | Powers and Abilities |
|---|---|
| Browsing | Find information only; no text entry or editing. |
| Typing | Adds text entry and editing on cards. |
| Painting | Adds access to the Painting Tools. |
| Authoring | Adds access to Button and Field Tools. |
| Scripting | Adds access to HyperTalk scripts. |

To continue with this book, be sure your user level is set at least to the Typing level (there's little need for the Browsing-only level unless a HyperCard author doesn't want you to change text in his stack). At the Typing level, the menus are kept to a minimum for newcomers. If you select a higher user level now, some of the menu illustrations in these first three chapters may be different than on your Macintosh. That's OK with us, as long as you are aware of the potential differences.

We believe that the Browsing and Typing levels are so intertwined that for the balance of Part One, we will refer to the Typing level as the *browsing environment*. In most HyperCard applications, like the Address and Datebook stacks supplied by Apple, browsing and typing really go hand in hand.

When you use HyperCard for simple information storage and retrieval, you are approaching the program with a browser's point of view.

You need know very little about the inner workings of HyperCard to use a well-designed stack productively. Still, you can significantly enhance your experience as a HyperCard browser with an appreciation for a few fine points of a stack's basic structure and how you interact with it. Our immediate goal in these first chapters is to help you browse— find and store information— efficiently. The concepts will also be essential for further exploration about HyperCard's authoring powers later.

The only assumptions we make about your HyperCard expertise is that you have looked through the HyperCard manual and have completed the tutorial. We won't be showing you how to use the stacks provided with HyperCard (the manual and tutorial do that nicely), but we will use those stacks frequently to demonstrate features and concepts. In many places throughout this book, you'll be given the opportunity to type and mouse along to step-by-step instructions. Following along will help you master HyperCard much more quickly— we strongly suggest it.

## *The Basic Elements*

Working through HyperCard's browsing environment will be much easier once you acquaint yourself with its nine major elements:

- Stacks
- Backgrounds
- Cards
- Fields
- Buttons
- The Home Stack
- Recent
- The Help Stack
- The Message Box

The first five items are the basic building blocks of any HyperCard application; the next three are navigation aids that are always available to help you out of a jam; and the last element is an important communication medium between you and HyperCard. Once you know what these elements are, you should have a firmer understanding of what you see on the screen while browsing.

As HyperCard's name and many items in the above list imply, the program is largely a metaphor for collections of information stored on cards, much like a card catalog at a library. We'll use the card catalog model to describe the functions of the major HyperCard elements.

## Stacks

A HyperCard *stack* is usually a homogeneous *collection* of information. We can liken a HyperCard stack to a drawer in a card catalog, provided we limit the contents of the drawer to one subject. For example, if a card drawer were labeled "Trees," you would expect its contents to consist of references to arboreal subjects. The HyperCard version of that drawer would be a stack, also labeled "Trees."

Each stack in HyperCard is a separate Macintosh disk file, which you can see as a HyperCard document icon in the Finder. Document icons resemble the HyperCard program icon sufficiently to remind you of their association, but the two icon types are, indeed, different (Figure 1-2).

Thus, when you insert the HyperCard program disk into your Macintosh disk drive and open the folder labeled "HyperCard Stacks," you will see several HyperCard stack icons (Figure 1-3). Each icon represents a file that stores all the information you would store in a comparable card catalog drawer.

A stack can be empty— it can be there in name and in icon but be devoid of information— or it can be chock full of information to the limit of the disk device you use to store it.

### OPENING A STACK

You open a stack by one of three methods. First, if you are at the Finder level, you may double-click on the desired stack icon. The Macintosh automatically starts HyperCard and opens the stack at the same time. Second, once you are in HyperCard, you can choose Open Stack... from the File menu (Figure 1-4). This brings up what is called a *standard file dialog box* (Figure 1-5), which lets you access the stack name as you would any Macintosh document in a program. Select the stack name and click the Open button (or double-click the stack name) to open the stack. Third, a HyperCard stack may have a button on the Home card (described below) or on another card that opens the stack with a single click.

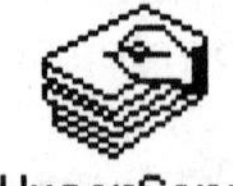

*Figure 1-2. HyperCard application and document icons*

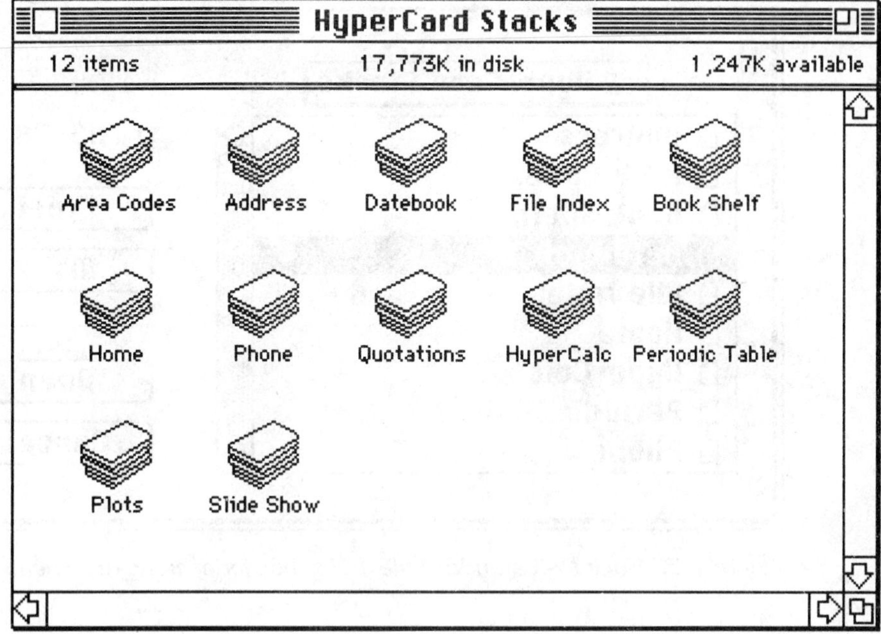


*Figure 1-3. Stack icons in a folder*

*Figure 1-4. HyperCard File menu with Open Stack... selected*

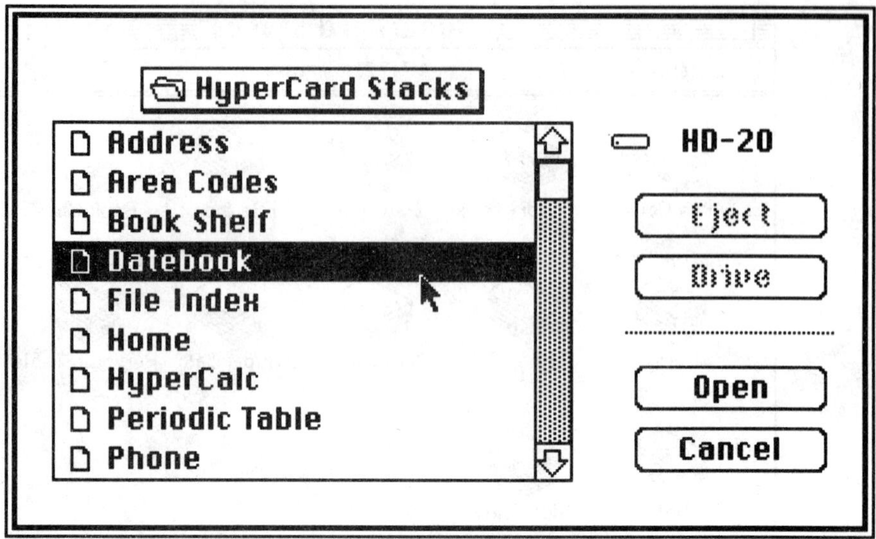


*Figure 1-5. Macintosh standard file dialog box for opening documents*

HyperCard must be able to find a stack that you open by clicking a button. HyperCard might not find a stack if the stack file is nested in a folder or located on a disk other than the one(s) to which it has ready access. If HyperCard cannot immediately find a desired stack, it displays the standard file dialog box for you to show HyperCard where the stack is.

In the case of stacks nested in folders, you can instruct HyperCard to automatically search through specific folders (by folder name) for stacks and other kinds of files. We'll describe how to do this in detail in the section on the Home Stack in this chapter.

You don't really close a stack, per se. By opening one stack, you essentially close the previous stack. When you're through with your HyperCard session, choose Quit HyperCard from the File menu. This action closes the current stack and brings you back to the Desktop.

## ABOUT SAVING STACKS

As you'll learn in more detail later, information entered into a HyperCard stack is automatically saved to the stack file for you. But you can store a copy of the current stack on disk by choosing Save a Copy... from the File menu. You'll be prompted in a standard file dialog box for a file name, although HyperCard suggests the current stack name preceded by the words " *Copy of* ", as shown in Figure 1-6. This is a good way to make a copy of a stack on a floppy disk to give to a friend or colleague.

*Figure 1-6. Macintosh standard file dialog box for saving documents. The only saving needed in HyperCard is saving copies of existing stacks.*

## Backgrounds

Let's say you pull out a library catalog drawer labeled "Trees." If this drawer were in a regular library, you'd expect to see it loaded with cards, perhaps of the index card variety, with horizontal lines printed on them. In other words, before any information was entered onto any card, the card had a *background* of horizontal lines preprinted on it. Those lines will be on every card in the drawer, regardless of the other information entered onto a card.

Let's also say that some cards in this "Trees" drawer contain miniature pictures of various tree species. You wouldn't want to draw the pictures on cards filled with preprinted lines. Instead, you'd want a blank card or one with a rectangular area on one half of the card, set aside for the picture, and horizontal lines on the other half, for a written description. In other words, you'd want two preprinted backgrounds, or formats, available in this drawer to accommodate two different kinds of information (Figure 1-7).

A HyperCard stack accommodates this need quite readily. You can design a HyperCard stack to have as many different backgrounds as the information in the stack requires.

More often than not, a HyperCard stack will have only one background. The Address stack provided with HyperCard is a case in point. Its background consists of a rolodex-like card surrounded by a grey fill pattern. A few other graphic elements, like the arrows and telephone

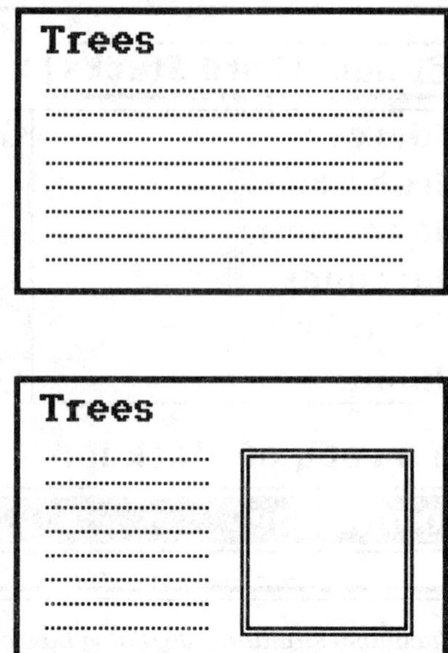


*Figure 1–7. Two different backgrounds may be needed for the same information "drawer."*

icon, are also present on this background (Figure 1–8). They appear on every card in this stack, as if the cards came preprinted.

At the user levels of Painting, Authoring, and Scripting, you can always filter out foreground elements to see what a card's background is at any time. Simply choose *Background* from HyperCard's Edit menu (or type Command-B). HyperCard temporarily hides everything in the foreground (*hides*, not erases). To restore the foreground, choose Background once again.

Some stacks may appear to have no background: When you choose Background, the background turns all white. This is perfectly natural for some stacks, whose cards contain a full screen of graphic information. Even though the background appears empty, that empty space is, nonetheless, considered a HyperCard background. *Every HyperCard stack has at least one background*, even if it is blank.

## Cards

When you pull open a card catalog drawer, you usually see many cards— 3" x 5" cards in most libraries. Typically, a single card contains

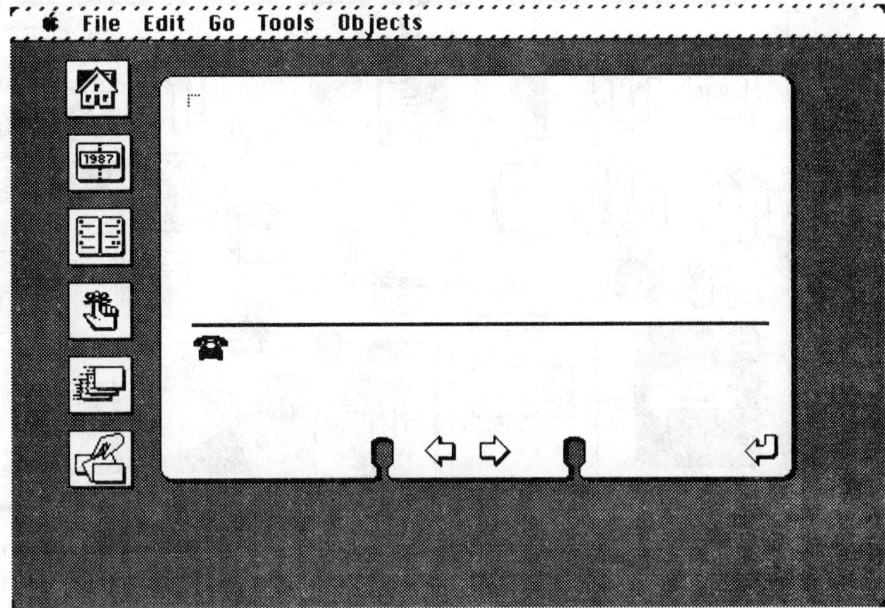


*Figure 1–8. The Address stack has one background, which includes the grey fill pattern, the representation of a card, and other graphic elements.*

one piece of information related to the content of the entire drawer. The content of one card is different from that of any other card in the drawer.

Such is the case with a card in a HyperCard stack. A card is added to the stack each time a new piece of information is added to the collection, as when a newly filled-out form is to be filed away.

A card may contain text information, graphics information, or both. A card in the Address stack, for instance, contains strictly textual data, like names, addresses, and phone numbers (remember: the card picture, arrows, and icons are in the card background). In contrast, the stack called "Art Ideas" on HyperCard's Ideas disk contains text and graphics information on each card: This information changes from card to card in the stack (Figure 1–9). The white, drop-shadow "card" area, its surrounding grey fill pattern, and icons are in the background.

A card is not restricted to carrying only one piece of information. You'll see applications in which a stack is actually a long list of words (as in a dictionary). But to keep the size of the stack file on the disk to a minimum, each card contains as many consecutive words in the list as will fit while remaining readable (Figure 1–10).

*Figure 1-9. An Art Ideas stack card has text data in the upper left corner and graphics data below the heavy line. The picture of the white card, grey fill pattern, and icons at the upper right are in the background.*

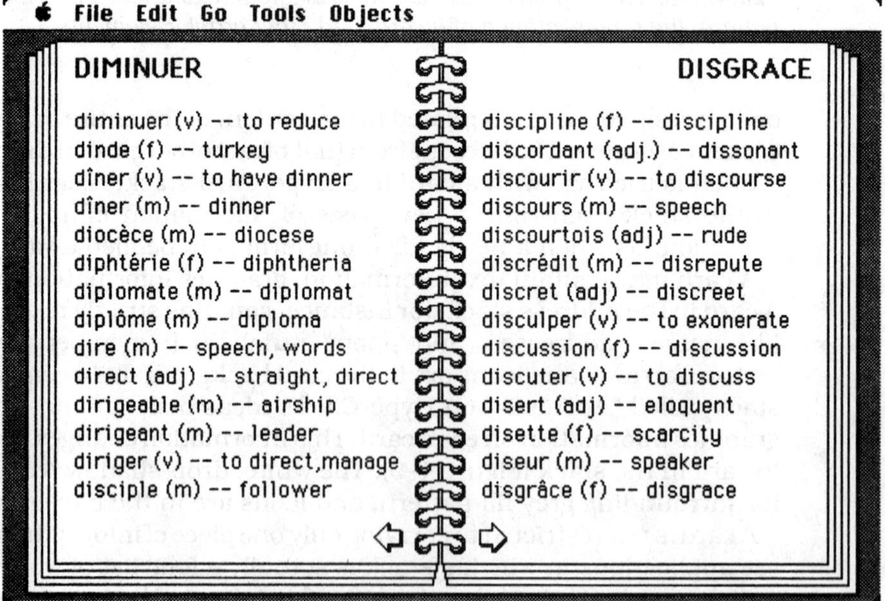


*Figure 1-10. Stacks consisting of lists often contain many pieces of information on a single card, like this French dictionary.*

## *Fields*

Cards in the library card catalog are loaded with textual information, the "stuff" for which you are looking. This is the information that usually changes from card to card. For example, every card in a stack may be imprinted with the name of the library system (for example, Smallville Public Library) in the background. While that bit of information is helpful, it is not the information for which you are likely to browse through the stack. The important information on the card is the content, such as a book title, its call number, and so on.

Textual information that changes from card to card in a HyperCard stack almost always exists in fields. Fields shouldn't be anything new to you. If you've used your Macintosh to save a new document in virtually any application, you've used a text field without realizing it. When you choose Save As... from a program's File menu, you usually see a dialog box like the one in Figure 1–6. The rectangular area at the lower left corner of the box is a text field, into which you are to type the name you wish to assign to the document.

Fields in a HyperCard card may be only a few characters wide or many lines deep, depending on the nature of the information carried on the card. The size of a text field is established by the person who originally designs the card in the stack. We'll have more to say about the dynamics of fields in chapter 2 when we discuss entering information into a card.

## *Buttons*

Of the nine basic elements of HyperCard listed earlier, *buttons* have no direct analog in the world of card catalogs, at least not in the real world. So let's imagine that we're reading a card in a drawer labeled "Trees." Amid the textual information on the card is a reference to an important botanist of the early twentieth century. If you get the urge to learn more about this person, you would normally have to go to another drawer containing biographies, and flip through the cards until you find the desired card. But what if the original card had a magic button you could press that instantaneously pulled out the biography drawer and flipped to the botanist's card? That's the kind of action a HyperCard button can perform.

On a HyperCard card, a button can have one of many forms. Sometimes they'll look like the buttons you commonly see in dialog boxes (Figure 1–11). At other times, a button will look like an icon whose picture indicates the kind of action that results from a press of the button. Still other kinds of buttons will be situated atop text fields or

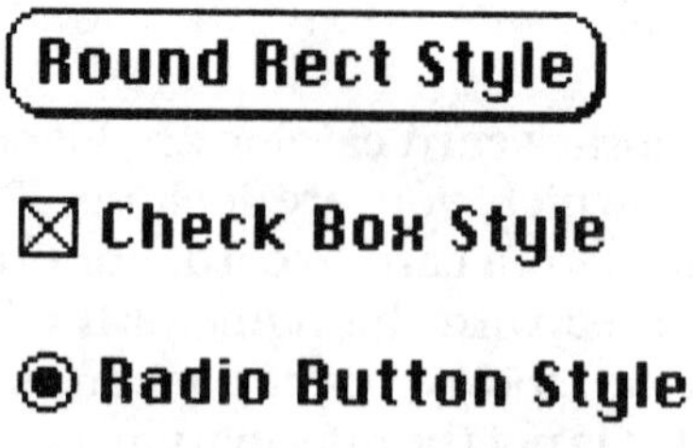

Round Rect Style

☒ Check Box Style

◉ Radio Button Style

*Figure 1-11. HyperCard stacks often have these familiar-looking button styles.*

may be entirely invisible, depending on the aim of the application author. No matter what the design, however, a button is activated by simply using the mouse to move the pointer atop the button and pressing the mouse button once. In HyperCard, there is no need to double-click on a button. One click, and the button's action begins.

Notice that we've been using the word "action" when referring to the result of clicking on a button. We can't emphasize this enough: Clicking on a HyperCard button in a predesigned HyperCard stack will *cause something to happen.* You may zip to a different stack, hear a musical tune, or go to another card. A well-designed stack should let you browse through its information (or find related information) simply by clicking buttons.

Buttons, therefore, are your primary navigational tools as you browse through a HyperCard stack. In more powerful roles, they will help you locate related information in the same or different stacks, helping you thread your way through a vast quantity of stored information.

## *The Home Stack*

The old saying "There's no place like home" holds ever true in Hyper-Card. "Home," however, is actually a stack that has special properties of particular interest to those who pursue HyperCard authoring. For browsers, however, the Home stack is best described as a kind of master index to all the stacks your Macintosh can access. As you get more comfortable with HyperCard, the physical makeup of your Home stack may change from what HyperCard initially comes with. But it is a good idea to stick with the original setup for a while, until you gain confidence as a HyperCard author.

Unless you have changed the HyperCard program, it will display the first card in the Home stack whenever you start HyperCard from the Finder. The first card in this stack which is called the Home Card, usually displays icons representing each stack to which you desire quick access. You could think of the Home card as a small replica of the drawer fronts of an entire library card catalog cabinet. Clicking on a drawer's icon pulls open the drawer, giving you access to its cards and information.

A stack need not have an icon on the Home card for you to open that stack. You can always choose Open Stack from the File menu, and select the desired stack file from the standard file dialog box.

In HyperCard terms, the Home card normally contains many buttons. A click of a particular button sets in motion the necessary actions to open and display the stack that is "linked" to that button. Later we'll show you how to transfer a button and its icon from a stack to a Home card to speed the opening of that stack (that is, obviating the File menu operation).

Incidentally, the actions associated with buttons on a Home card can range from simple to more powerful than you might imagine. On the simple side, for instance, a Home card button can open a stack and display the first card of the stack. A more powerful button might open the stack and search for the card that contains today's date in one of its text fields (the Datebook stack on your HyperCard disk does this, for example).

## FILE PREFERENCES

The Home Stack also contains three special cards that help HyperCard find stacks and other fields that may be nested in disk folders. The cards are labeled:

Look for Stack in:
Look for Applications in:
Look for Documents in:

These cards, like the Stacks card in Figure 1–12, list *pathnames*, which guide HyperCard in its search through your disk(s) for stacks. Because the concept of pathnames may be new to you, an explanation is in order.

When you wish to open a Macintosh application or document from the Finder, you go through a subtle search procedure to find the icon so that you can double-click it. By opening a disk icon, you can see the topmost level of files and folders stored on that disk. This level is called the *root* (or *root directory*), because all disk organization starts from this level.

As you open folders to see the desired document icon, you are essentially cutting a pathway from the root to the icon. Behind the scenes the Macintosh, meanwhile, traces your steps down the path, building a list of folders through which you reach your iconic destina-

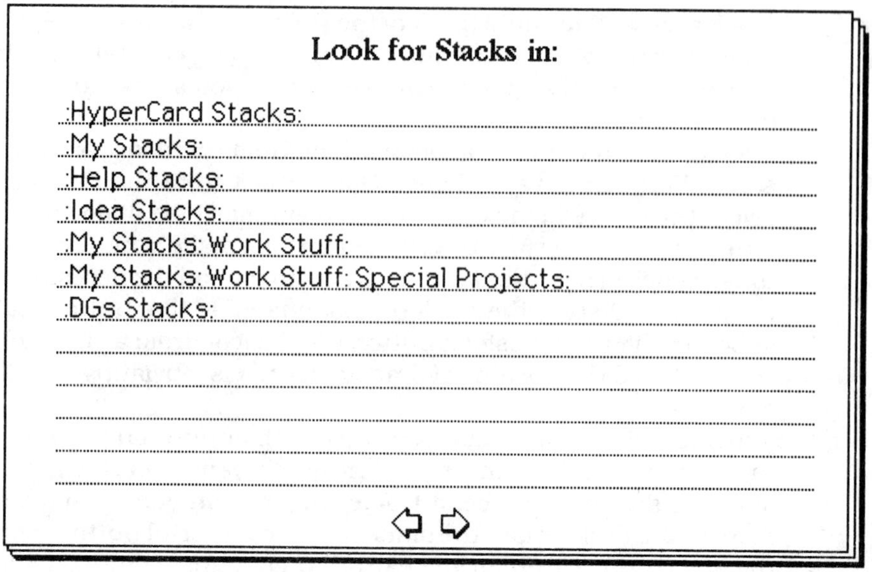

**Look for Stacks in:**

:HyperCard Stacks:
:My Stacks:
:Help Stacks:
:Idea Stacks:
:My Stacks:Work Stuff:
:My Stacks:Work Stuff:Special Projects:
:DGs Stacks:

*Figure 1-12. The Stacks card in the Home Stack establishes folder pathnames HyperCard should search through to locate and open stacks.*

tion. That list, including the icon's file name, is called the pathname of the file.

## PATHNAME NOTATION

The notation for a pathname places colons between folder and file names. Therefore, a pathname HD-20:Applications:Word Processing:MacWrite indicates that the disk (also called a volume) name is HD-20, which contains a folder called Applications; this folder, in turn, contains a folder called Word Processing; the Word Processing folder contains the application file MacWrite. This pathname and folder organization is illustrated in Figure 1-13.

A notational shortcut lets you omit the disk (volume) name by beginning a pathname with a colon. The Macintosh assumes you mean the current volume. If you use only one hard disk all the time, this method works fine.

Back to the Stacks card in HyperCard: You can list the pathnames HyperCard should use to search for a stack. If all your stacks are stored in a folder called HyperCard Stacks, then that's the only pathname you'll need to list. As your collection of stackware grows, however, you'll start building other folders and pathnames to organize them.

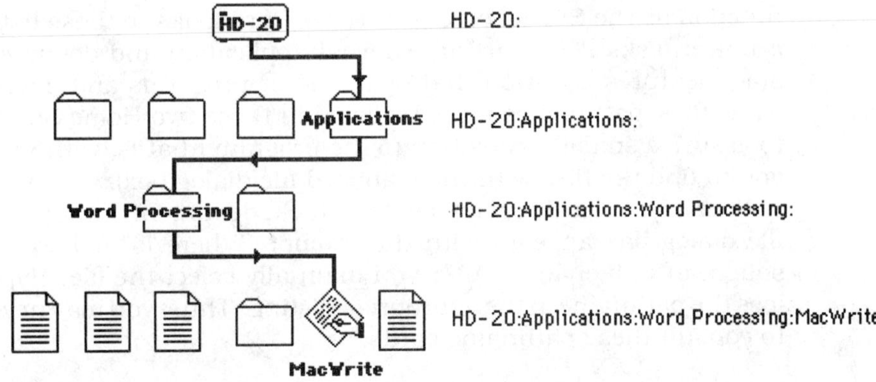


*Figure 1-13. Pathnames reveal names of the disk volume and folders opened on the way to the desired file.*

If you aren't sure about a pathname, you can use the Find File desk accessory to get the details. Use the accessory to search for the stack name. Then click on the file name. Its folder pathway will be spelled out in the lower right corner (Figure 1-14). Build the pathname *from the bottom to the top.* You can omit the disk name, but in that case be sure to start the pathname with a colon.

Find File
HD-20
Search for: ResEdit
1.0
ResEdit 1.0

Created: Thu, Sep 4, 1986; 7:00 PM
Modified: Thu, Sep 25, 1986; 11:14 PM
Size: 157875 bytes; 154.5K on disk

Utilities
Pascal
Programming
HD-20

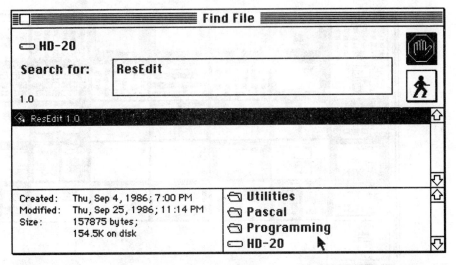

*Figure 1-14. Use the Find File desk accessory to determine a stack's full pathname (lower right corner). Then assemble the name from the bottom up.*

The Applications and Documents pathname cards perform the same function as the Stacks card, but HyperCard looks to these lists when a button asks it to start an external application and document. If a stack features a button that opens other programs and documents, these files' pathnames must be listed in these two Home Stack cards to assure a smooth transition to the program (that is, without asking you to find the files with the standard file dialog box).

When HyperCard cannot locate a stack, document, or application, a file dialog box appears with the prompt "Where Is" followed by the sought after filename. After you manually select the file, HyperCard logs the pathname in the appropriate listing. Thus, you may never have to consult these pathname cards.

## *Recent*

HyperCard does its best to stay in the background while you search for information. The program tries to be subservient to a variety of searching methodologies, described later. Recent offers you a way to quickly find a card you saw "recently," without forcing you to figure out which stack that card may have been in and how to navigate to it. In the library card catalog model, Recent would be like tagging the last forty-two different cards you browsed through, even if they were in

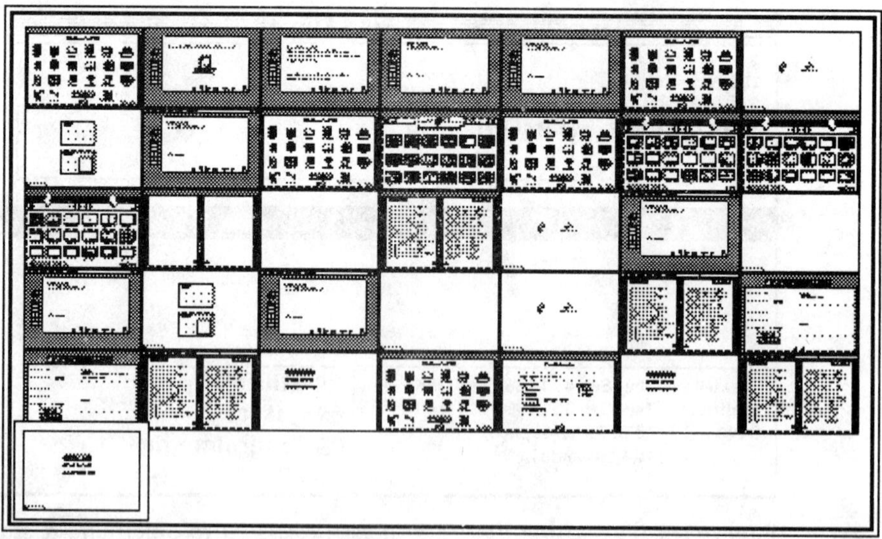

*Figure 1-15. Recent shows miniatures of the last forty-two cards for instant access back in time.*

many different drawers. When you needed to look at a recent card, you could find the tag and immediately go to the card.

As you step through cards in a stack or jump from one stack to another, HyperCard maintains a kind of photo album of your moves. Miniature representations of the last forty-two unique cards you viewed on the screen are stored in Recent (Figure 1-15). Only one representation of a card appears, no matter how often you go that card. To look at any one of those cards, simply choose Recent in the Go menu, or type the keyboard shortcut, Command-R. Then click on the screen you wish to see.

You can also step back in time without going to the Recent screen. Whenever you are browsing through cards (that is, navigating by way of the mouse), you can choose Back from the Go menu or press the keyboard key sdesignated as the Go Back keys. On the Macintosh 512E and Macintosh Plus keyboards, it's the tilde (~) key, located at the upper left corner of the keyboard (Figure 1-16a). On keyboards designed for the Macintosh SE and Macintosh II, you may use either the tilde key (located immediately to the left of the spacebar) or the Escape key

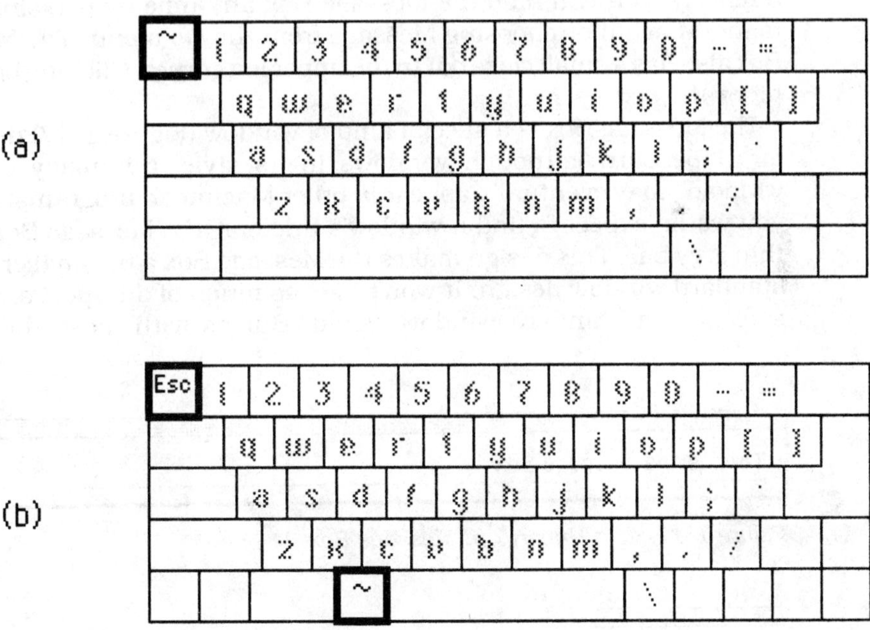


*Figure 1-16. Command and tilde key locations on the Macintosh keyboards: (a) Macintosh 512E and Macintosh Plus; (b) the "Apple Keyboard" for the Macintosh SE and Macintosh II.)*

(Figure 1-16b). On any keyboard with arrow keys, you may also press the down key to go back one screen (and the up arrow key to go "forth"). Issue the command again, and you'll take a second step back.

Note that going back (and forth) retraces your precise steps, including repeated vists to the same card. Going back, therefore, differs from Recent.

Back and Command - ~ come in very handy when you accidentally click on a button or just want a quick referral to a recent card. Think of it as a multiple step Undo command.

## The Message Box

The last item in our list of essential HyperCard elements is the *Message Box*. It has many functions, but we can characterize its underlying purpose as being the primary communications avenue between you and HyperCard or between you and a HyperCard stack.

If the Message Box is not showing on your screen, you can make it appear by typing Command-M or choosing Message from the Go menu. Similarly, you can hide the Message Box any time by pressing Command-M again or choosing Message from the Go menu. The Message Box also has a small *close box* in the upper left corner. Clicking here also hides the box.

The Message Box is a special kind of window (Figure 1-17) designed for HyperCard (although windows in its style, informally called a windoid, may eventually appear in other Macintosh programs). Where you would expect to find a window's title bar, the Message Box has a thin grey bar. This design makes the Message Box a bit smaller than a standard window design. It won't hide as much of a HyperCard stack screen as a standard window would. But as with most Macintosh

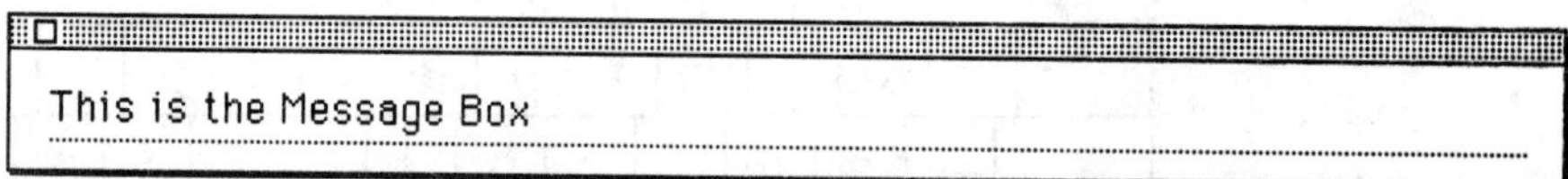


*Figure 1-17. The HyperCard Message Box*

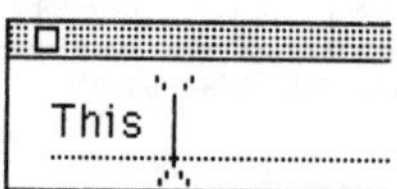


*Figure 1-18. When you type into the Message Box, the flashing text insertion pointer shows where the next typed character will go.*

windows with title bars, you can drag the Message Box around the screen by placing the mouse pointer anywhere on the top bar (except in the close box), holding down the mouse button, and rolling the mouse around your desk. When the box is in its desired location, release the mouse button. You are free to move the Message Box as often as you like, anywhere on the screen. HyperCard won't let you accidentally drag the box entirely off the screen, out of reach.

Another special property of the Message Box is that it has a single line for text display. When you wish to type into the Message Box, you should be aware of the condition of the flashing text insertion pointer (Figure 1–18). If there is no flashing text pointer in the Message Box or elsewhere in the card, then the next characters you type go into the Message Box, automatically erasing whatever text was there previously. This erasure is not as frightening as it may sound; in fact, it turns out to be rather helpful, as you'll see shortly.

At the entry of your first character, the text pointer appears. That means that you can edit the Message Box text line, just as you would any piece of Macintosh text, including backspacing, cutting, copying, and pasting. The text pointer disappears after one of the three following actions: 1) pressing the mouse button with the cursor in any text field *outside* the Message Box; 2) pressing the Return key; and 3) pressing the Enter key. Pressing either of the two keys tells HyperCard to perform specific tasks with the text in the Message Box (detailed next). With the flashing text pointer gone, you can start typing into the Message Box again.

If you wish to clear the Message Box of its contents, press the Clear key, which is located on the numeric keypad section of Macintosh Plus, Macintosh SE, and Macintosh II keyboards. You needn't dwell on the detailed actions and reactions to typing in the Message Box. You'll learn its operation quickly enough by forgetting the rules and observing its response to situations in which you will find yourself often.

Now let's look at the kinds of "messages" that appear in the Message Box.

## SAMPLE MESSAGES

First of all, you can type *commands* into the Message Box. Commands are actually words in the HyperTalk language vocabulary. You certainly don't need to be an experienced HyperTalk user to issue useful commands in the Message Box. For example, one of the simplest commands is the *go* command.

*Go* is the most-often-used HyperTalk command, because it helps you navigate through HyperCard or a HyperCard stack. We'll demonstrate a simple *go* command to navigate from stack to stack. Follow along on your Macintosh.

1. Start HyperCard.

   The Home card should appear. If the Message Box is not showing, type Command-M.

2. Type *go to Address* into the Message Box.

   If other text is already in the Message Box, it will be replaced by this command. This command tells HyperCard to open up the stack named Address, which is probably already familiar to you.

   Incidentally, here are two useful shortcuts. First, the "to" is optional after the *go* command. You can also type *go Address* to achieve the same effect. Also, HyperCard is not finicky about capitalization. You can type in all lower case, all upper case, or any mixture you wish.

3. Press the Return or the Enter key.

   HyperCard brings you instantly to the first card of the Address stack. Note that you may use either the Return key or Enter key to send the command to HyperCard.

While it's true that you would probably go from the Home card to the Address stack by clicking on the Address stack's icon, you might use the *go address* command when you are in a different stack. Instead of finding your way back to Home to click on the Address stack icon, you could type *go Address* into the Message Box. HyperCard would bypass all intermediate steps and bring you to the Address stack instantly.

As a final demonstration of Message Box commands in this chapter, we'll show you the one command that always gets you out of a navigational jam: the *go home* command.

1. From any stack, type *go home* into the Message Box.

   You can also type *go to home.*

2. Press the Return or Enter key.

   You instantly return to the first card of the Home stack.

The *go home* command is the same as choosing Home from the Go menu.

You also type into the Message Box when you want HyperCard to search a stack for textual information. We'll examine this in great detail in the next chapter.

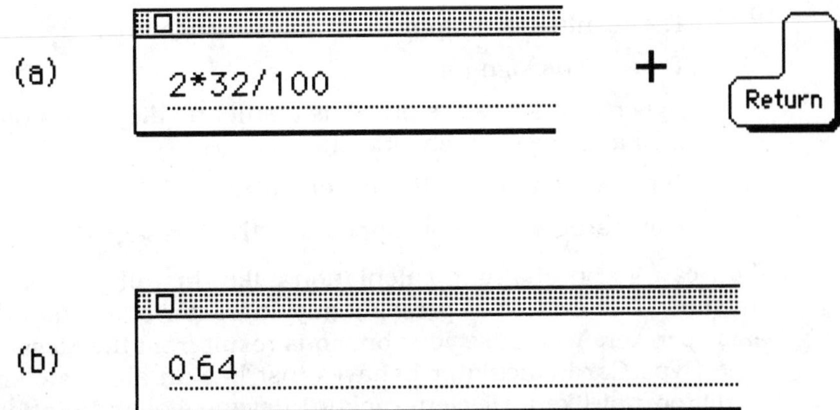


*Figure 1-19. The Message Box can be used as a quick calculator. Enter a problem and press Return or Enter.*

## THE MESSAGE BOX AS CALCULATOR

The Message Box also functions as the digital display of an electronic calculator. This built-in feature of HyperCard can be used with any HyperCard stack.

To use the calculator, simply type in the problem you want to solve, as shown in Figure 1-19a). Then press the Return or Enter key. HyperCard instantly produces the result in the Message Box (Figure 1-19b). Do not type an equal sign (=) at the end of the formula; just press Return or Enter.

The Message Box breaks its rule about automatically replacing its contents at the press of the next key when that next key is one of the four basic arithmetic operations. After the HyperCard calculator presents the result of a calculation, you can type +, -, *, or / to perform an additional calculation on the result. Try it now.

1. Type the formula *25 * 40* into the Message Box (Figure 1-20).

   Spaces between numbers and operator signs are optional, so

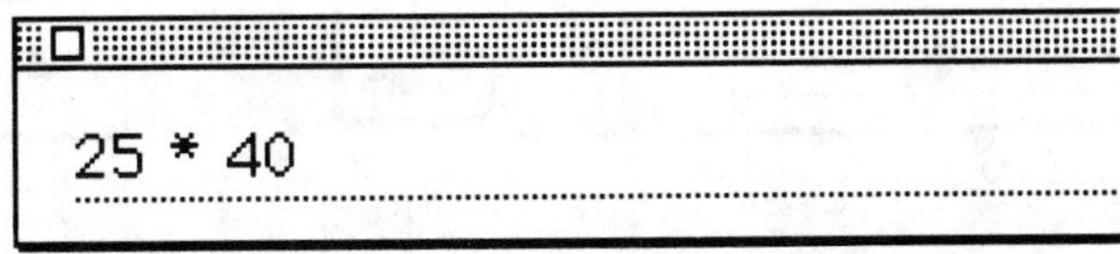


*Figure 1-20. Spaces between numbers and operators are optional.*

2. Press the Return or Enter key.

   The result, 1000, appears in the Message Box.

3. Type a plus sign (+).

   HyperCard saves the previous result and displays a plus sign, with a space on each side of it.

4. Type *500* and press Return or Enter.

   The result, 1500, now appears in the Message Box.

You can go on chaining calculations like this all you want. Just remember, however, that pressing any character *other* than the four basic operators will erase your previous result from the Message Box.

The HyperCard calculator behaves just like an algebraic scientific calculator, not like a Hewlett-Packard Reverse Polish Notation (RPN) type. This means that you can add parentheses around expressions to make sure the proper operations are performed as you expect.

For example, if you wish to add two numbers and multiply their sum by a third number, you would enter the formula as shown in Figure 1–21a. If you don't put the parentheses in, HyperCard calculates the multiplication first, and then the addition, giving you a different result (Figure 1–21b).

HyperCard's calculator adheres to a standard hierarchy of algebraic calculations. In other words, when facing a string of calculations, the calculator will solve operations in the following order:

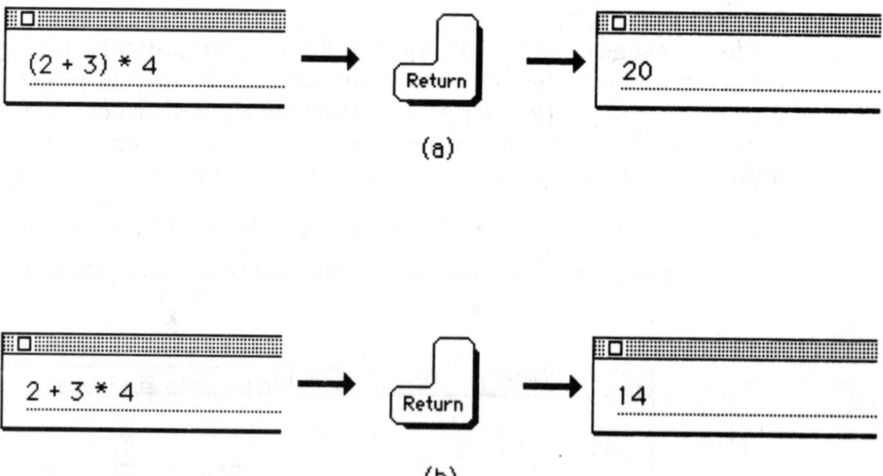


*Figure 1–21. Message Box math is algebraic in nature. Parentheses play a vital role in some calculations.*

functions
multiplication/division
addition/subtraction

Only by placing parentheses around operations in lower levels of the hierarchy (for example, addition and subtraction) will you be assured the desired result.

The calculator comes equipped with a couple of "preprogrammed" functions and constants to give you more than simple arithmetic. Although HyperCard calculates with greater than 16-digit precision (that is, 16 places to the right of the decimal), Message Box results are displayed to six decimal places.

Type the following problems into the Message Box and press Return after each one to see the results:

| | |
|---|---|
| 3^2 | (three to the second power; three squared) |
| 3^3 | (three cubed) |
| pi | (pi) |
| pi * 12^2 | (pi times twelve squared) |
| sin (45) | (sine of 45 radians) |
| cos (75) | (cosine of 75 radians) |

With the basic HyperCard building blocks under our belts, we can now move on to techniques for finding existing information and entering new.

# CHAPTER 2

# Finding and Entering Information

THE BULK OF THE TASKS YOU'LL PERFORM AS A HYPERCARD BROWSER WILL INVOLVE finding and entering information. In this chapter, you'll learn about vitally important text search techniques, how to enter and edit text information in cards, and how to create and delete cards in an existing stack.

## *Finding Information in the Real World*

Few things are more frustrating for a computer user than needing a piece of information stored on a disk—someplace. Locating that information usually requires exiting the program you're in, starting another program, opening the information file, and then performing the search. By the time you find what you're looking for, you've forgotten why you needed the information in the first place.

Consider what this scenario would be like in a noncomputer environment. Let's say you're drafting a report on a pad of lined paper when you realize you need to include some numbers from a budget you wrote out on a columnar pad the previous day. Following the computer example above, you'd have to put the report pad away in a drawer, pull out the budget sheets, and then look for the figures. Putting those figures into your report would require jotting down the numbers on a scratchpad, putting away the budget sheets, and then retrieving the report pad from the drawer. Of course, no one would do that in a noncomputer environment. So why should we have to do it with a computer?

## *Retrieval Environments*

HyperCard solves that problem for the majority of information retrieval needs on your Macintosh, particularly those involving information stored in a HyperCard application. It actually solves the problem in two ways, depending on which is more accommodating to the way you use your Macintosh. You can use HyperCard as a stand-alone application or in a multiple-application environment, like Switcher or programs of its type.

### STAND-ALONE HYPERCARD

Running HyperCard as a stand-alone application means starting the program from the Finder. In other words, HyperCard becomes the main program in your Macintosh. For many people, this will be a quite appropriate way to use the program. You have full access to every nook and cranny of the program, both the browsing and authoring structures.

Before you think this too restrictive because it separates you from your applications, HyperCard has a feature that lets you open external programs and documents. In essence, you will have access to any application program and any document created by your applications directly from HyperCard. The importance of this is that you can use HyperCard as the center of your Macintosh World in a way that the Finder is not empowered to do.

### HYPERCARD WITH MULTIFINDER

Because HyperCard will likely become the major repository of your day-to-day information, as well as a highway to archival information stored elsewhere (on a file server, an optical mass storage device, or an on-line database, for example), you will want ready access to it while you are using applications. For example, if you are writing a letter and need the full address of the recipient, you'll want quick access to your HyperCard name and address card file without quitting your word processing program.

In a computerless world, you would simply lay your address book atop your writing pad, look up the address, copy it to the pad, close the address book, and continue writing. Interruption is kept to a minimum.

You can use HyperCard in almost the exact same way if your Macintosh has more than one megabyte.

When you install HyperCard in MultiFinder, you can summon its browsing powers any time you are in another application program. MultiFinder keeps more than one application open at once, although only one program is usually active at a time. Therefore, in the address example, you might be typing the top of the letter in your word processing program and come to the spot where you need to type in the address. Switch to HyperCard. Then use HyperCard's searching abilities (described below) to locate the name and address card of your addressee. Use the standard Macintosh editing techniques to select the address lines and copy them into the Clipboard. Next switch back to your word processing document, where the text pointer is in the exact spot you left it before switching to HyperCard. Because the address is still in the Clipboard, you can simply choose Paste from the Edit menu (in most word processors) to insert the address. It takes longer to explain it in words than to actually do it with your Macintosh.

The significance of having HyperCard available as a second application in MultiFinder is that it is far less disrupting to your train of thought to branch to HyperCard for information the instant you need it. In fact, you will see more and more Macintosh software products provide HyperCard stacks for their on-line documentation to be used in MultiFinder or similar environments, such as Andy Hertzfeld's Servant.

(Note: HyperCard requires an application memory size of nearly 750K. With the amount of memory reserved for the System File, this doesn't leave enough room to use HyperCard with another program in one megabyte of MultiFinder memory. If you upgrade your Macintosh to more than one megabyte of memory, you'll be able to assemble a highly integrated software setup along with HyperCard.)

## *Using the Browse Tool*

When we described buttons earlier, we said that you need to click the mouse pointer on a screen button to set that button's actions in motion. To respond to the click, however, a button requires that the mouse pointer be in the form of the *Browse tool* (Figure 2–1). In fact, when you are in search of HyperCard information, you will always want to have the Browse tool showing.

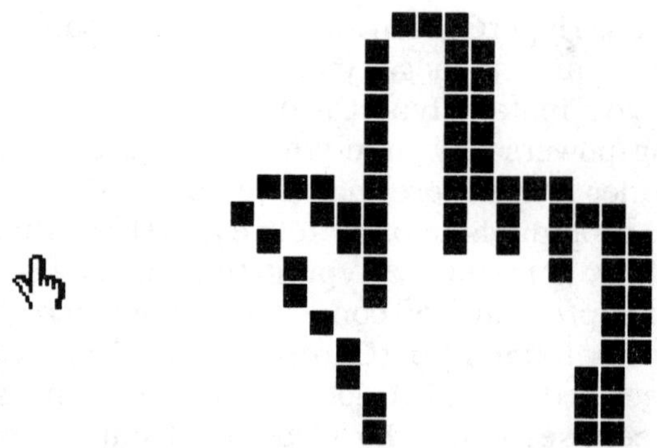

*Figure 2-1. The Browse tool, in normal size (left) and magnified (right)*

In the Browsing and Typing user levels, you will never find yourself out of the Browse tool. At higher user levels, however, you may need to get back to the Browse tool from any of the other tools available at those levels.

While most HyperCard stacks automatically hand you the Browse tool when you need it to click on a button, you should know how to reach for it, in case a different tool is showing. Pull down the Tools menu (Figure 2-2). You will see a palette of eighteen tools. The only one we're concerned with right now is the one at the upper left corner, the one that looks like a hand with its index finger extended. This is the Browse tool. If this tool in the palette is highlighted, as in Figure 2-2, you already have the Browse tool available. If another tool is highlighted, simply use the mouse to click the Browse tool. When the Tools menu disappears, the mouse pointer on the screen will become the Browse tool.

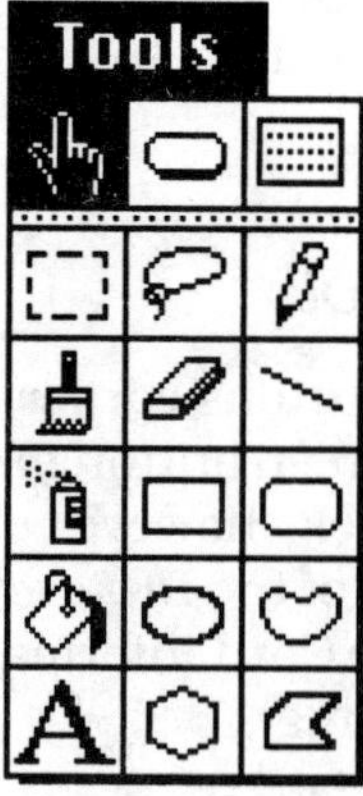


*Figure 2-2. The Tools palette. Selected in the upper left corner is the Browse tool.*

## *Flipping Through Cards*

One way to find information once you are looking at a HyperCard stack is to flip through cards one by one, just as you might in a card catalog drawer. This may seem to be inefficient in light of HyperCard's advanced search capabilities, which we'll see in more detail in just a moment. But as you know if you've ever done research involving leafing through a series of cards or references, it is often beneficial to look at information that may be sorted in the same category. Therefore, HyperCard gives you ways of looking one card ahead or behind the card you're looking at.

### ARROW KEYS

If you have a Macintosh keyboard with arrow keys, the task is quite simple. The left- and right-facing arrow keys bring up the previous and next cards, respectively (Figure 2–3). HyperCard also gives you keyboard access to the previous and next cards, in case you're using a Macintosh keyboard lacking arrow keys. Press Command-2 and Command-3 to go to the previous and next cards, respectively. These keyboard commands perform the same actions as Prev and Next in the Go menu. That menu also contains selections for the first and last cards in the stack.

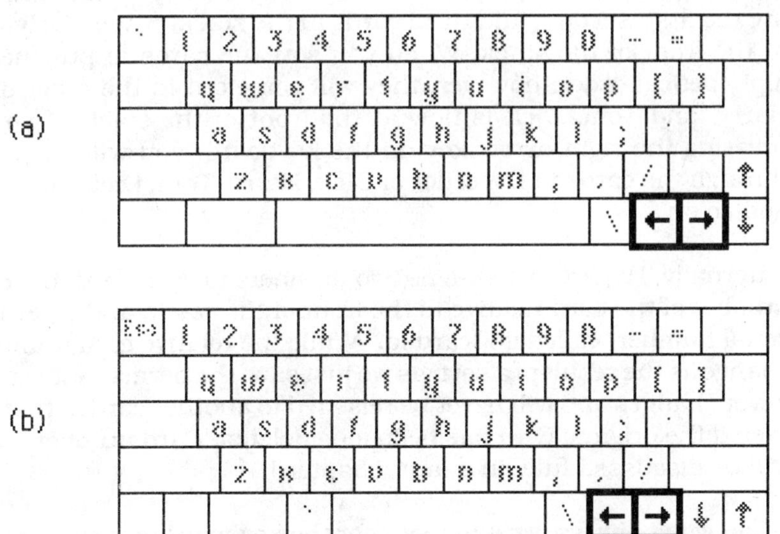

*Figure 2–3. Left and right arrow keys bring up previous and next cards in the stack: (a) Macintosh 512 and Macintosh Plus keyboards; (b) Macintosh SE and Macintosh II keyboards.*

When you hold down the Option key and press the left or right arrow keys, you zip straight to the first and last cards in the stack, respectively. These actions are identical to the First and Last items in the Go menu.

## 'ROUND AND 'ROUND

HyperCard stacks are, by their nature, cyclical. In other words, when you flip through the cards in a stack, there is no stop mark at the end of the stack. Therefore, if you are viewing what you consider to be the last card in the Address stack (Stanley Zzyzx), a press of the right arrow key or card button leading to the "next" card will bring you to the front of the stack.

The "front" of the stack is determined by the order in which cards are created in a stack. Each time you create a new card in the stack, it is placed *behind* the card you were viewing when you created the card. Therefore, the first card you fill out in a new stack becomes the front of the stack. When you create a second card, it will be inserted behind the first card. Then, no matter which card you're looking at when you create the third card, the first card you created stays at the front of the stack.

The order can change, however, with the help of the sorting powers of HyperCard. For example, if you create three cards in your name and address stack in the order of Tom, Dick, and Harry, these three cards are the first, second, and third cards in the stack, respectively. Tom is at the front of the stack. When you sort the cards to put them into alphabetical order, however, they will come out in the order of Dick, Harry, and Tom. Dick is now at the front of the stack. If you keep pressing the right arrow key on the keyboard, you will keep cycling through the cards in the order of Dick, Harry, Tom, Dick, Harry, Tom, and so on.

(Internally, HyperCard assigns two numbers to each card: the current number of the card relative to the front of the stack, and a permanent serial number, called its "card id." While the relative card number can change as the result of a sort, as we just saw, the permanent ID number never changes and will never be reissued to another card in that stack, even if the original card has been long deleted. Card numbers and ids will be discussed fully in a later chapter.)

You won't always want to reach for the keyboard to view an adjacent card, however. Many HyperCard applications will be almost entirely mouse-driven, particularly during information retrieval tasks. Most stacks provide buttons that let you leaf through cards one at a time. For example, on the Address card stack, clicking the Browse tool on the fat left-facing arrow "flips" one card one so you can see the previous card; clicking the right-facing arrow flips forward to the next card (Figure 2–4). In case a stack does not automatically provide this kind of navigation, you will be able to modify its cards to include such buttons. Instructions for doing this will be provided in Part Two.

## *Where do I Click?*

If you're ever at a loss about where to click on a card, you can look at the locations of all buttons on the card, even if the buttons are completely transparent ("see-through"). Press the Command and Option keys at the same time. Outlines of all buttons will appear on the screen. You may discover buttons you never knew were on a card.

## *Finding Text*

A much more sophisticated way of finding desired information is to let HyperCard search all the cards in a stack for a particular series of text characters– a text *string.* HyperCard can search text in any text field on any card in a stack for a match to a string you specify. HyperCard's blindingly fast searching capability actually encourages this kind of search.

For HyperCard to search for text, it must, of course, be told what text characters it is to look for. That's where we again meet the Message Box.

### FINDING AND THE MESSAGE BOX

To make HyperCard look for a match to a text string, you must enter the *Find* command into the Message Box, plus the string, which must be inside quotation marks. Fortunately, HyperCard provides a shortcut for typing the find command. By choosing Find... from the Go menu, or

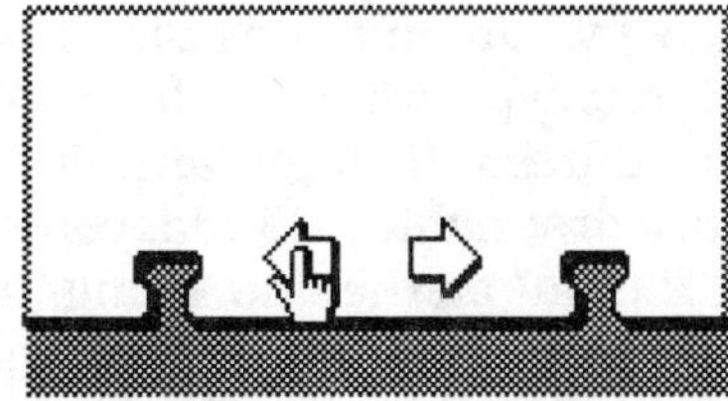

*Figure 2–4. Many cards have buttons to get to previous and next cards with the mouse.*

by typing Command-F, HyperCard automatically enters the Find command and the two quotation marks into the Message Box (if the Message Box is hidden when you issue the Find menu command, it shows itself). Moreover, the flashing text insertion pointer is preset between the quotation marks. All you do is start typing the text string you wish to find. The text between the quotation marks is called the *find string.* Then, as with any command, press Return or Enter to carry out the search.

HyperCard searches every field in the *current stack* (that is, the stack you're viewing at the moment) for the first occurrence of the find string. Upon finding a match, HyperCard displays that card and draws a box around the text in the card that matches the find string. Figure 2–5 shows the results of a search in the Address stack for the find string "Andrew."

In the time it takes HyperCard to find a match, the cursor changes from the Browse tool to the Beachball cursor (Figure 2–6). The ball appears to spin as the search progresses. You'll also see the Beachball when the program is busily churning away on certain other HyperCard operations.

HyperCard starts its search with the card you're viewing when you type text into the Message Box. If you have just opened the Address stack from the Home card and entered a Find command into the Message Box, HyperCard begins its search with the first card of the stack. But if you issue the Find command without changing the find string (that is, by simply pressing Return with an existing Find command already there), then the search begins with the card following the one you're viewing. Let's explain.

HyperCard is aware that a search for text may result in more than one match. Once you've built up your own name and address stack, for instance, a search for the common name John will surely turn up multiple matches. To speed your way to viewing all possible matches for a find string typed into the Message Box, you can continue to press the Return or Enter key. Each press causes HyperCard to carry out the same Find command it just performed, but starting with the next card in the stack.

You can use this knowledge of HyperCard's inner search workings to your advantage if you're in a hurry to find a particular card and don't want to spend time typing in the full text for which you're searching. If your name and address stack contains 200 cards, and three of them are for people whose first name is Linda, you can cut your typing chore by simply typing "Linda" as the find string, instead of Linda's full name. HyperCard will begin its search for a text match. If the first match is not the one you want, simply press the Return or Enter key again. Keep

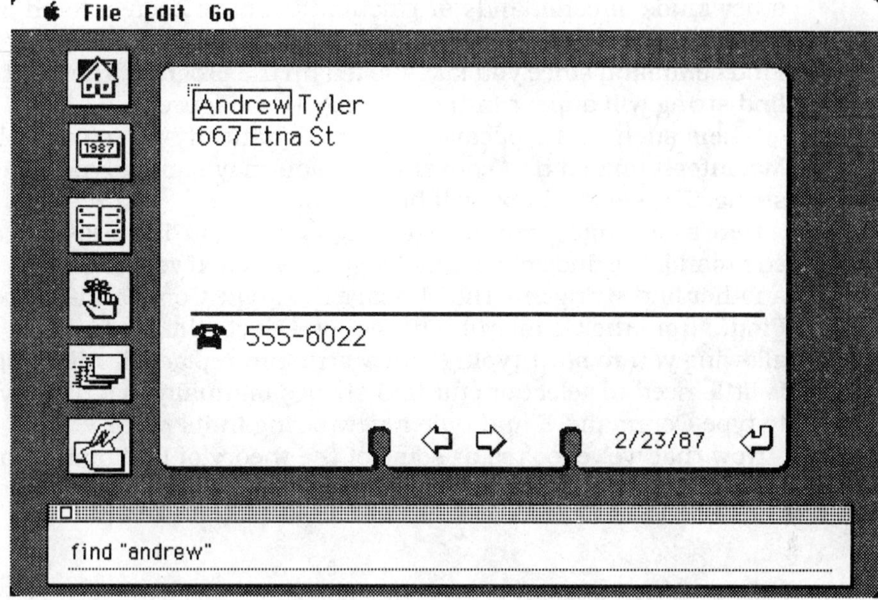


*Figure 2-5. When HyperCard finds a match, it draws a box around the matching text.*

*Figure 2-6. The Beachball cursor*

pressing either of these keys until the desired card appears. By drawing a box around each "Linda" found in various cards, HyperCard draws your eye to the appropriate information in the card to help you more readily identify the correct card when you land on it. HyperCard searches the stack quickly enough to make this both a time and typing shortcut.

## HYPERCARD REMEMBERS FIND STRINGS

If you've opened stacks that have built-in Find commands (that is, Find commands are carried out in scripts behind the scenes), you may discover text already inserted into the find string when you choose Find... from the Go menu or type Command-F. The reason for this is that HyperCard remembers the last find string it searched for, even if other kinds of commands or calculations have been entered into the Message Box in the meantime. If HyperCard has performed any kind of Find command since you last started up the program, the most recent find string will appear in the Message Box (Figure 2–7).

When such text appears, it is automatically selected. Following Macintosh text editing conventions, you may simply type a new find string. The selected text will be erased.

Here's one more related shortcut. Once you have issued a Find command, the find string is no longer selected. If you then want to type another find string into the Message Box, type Command-F (or choose Find... from the Go menu). This action selects the current find string, allowing you to start typing a new string to replace it. All in all, there is little need to select or edit find strings manually. It's usually faster to type Command-F and type a new string in its place.

Now that we've looked at some of the theory of finding information, let's look at specific examples.

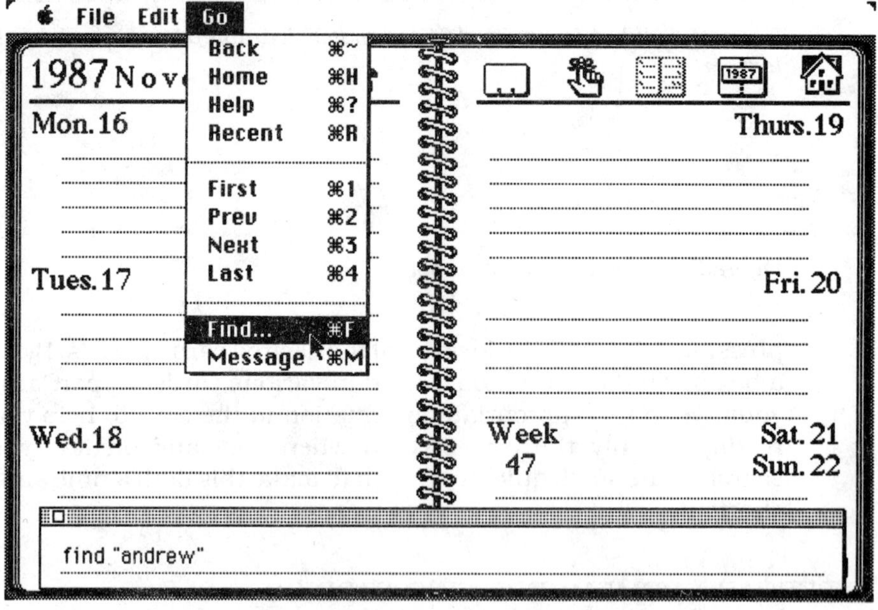


*Figure 2–7. HyperCard remembers the last find string it searched for, even if the find was done by a script. Don't be alarmed when find strings already appear*

## EXPERIMENTING WITH FIND

To bring our examples to life, we'll use a hypothetical stack that resembles the Address stack on your HyperCard disk. In this stack are five cards with friends' names on them, plus a cover card, similar to the one in Address. A representation of the stack and the five names on its cards is shown in Figure 2–8.

We've sorted these cards according to the last name in the first line of the text field, precisely the way the Address stack's Sort button does it. Since there is no text on the first line of the cover card, it sorts out as being first. John Atkins is the next card in the stack. When we start this stack from the Home card, the cover card is the first we see (Figure 2–8), along with the Message Box poised to receive a find string.

If we wish to see if there are any other cards with the name "John," we type the name into the find string and press Return (or Enter). HyperCard begins searching with the current card and flips to John Atkins' card, drawing a box around John Atkins' first name (Figure 2–9). Pressing Return again sends HyperCard on a search through the stack. Since HyperCard is looking for a match for any group of text starting with the letters J-O-H-N, the search stops on Tom Johnson's last name, with a box drawn around the full word (Figure 2–10).

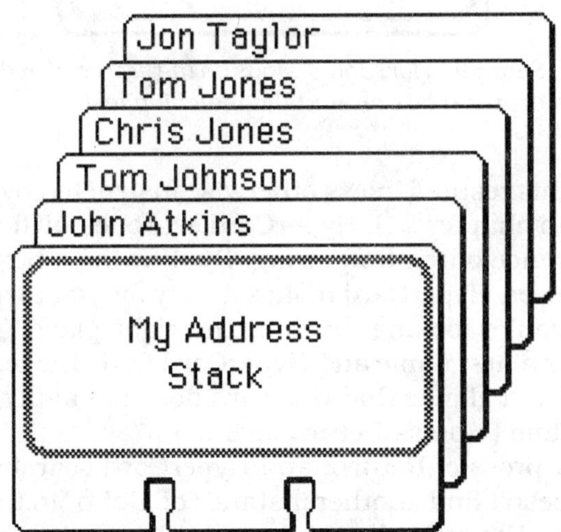


*Figure 2–8. Simple stack setup for a FIND experiment*

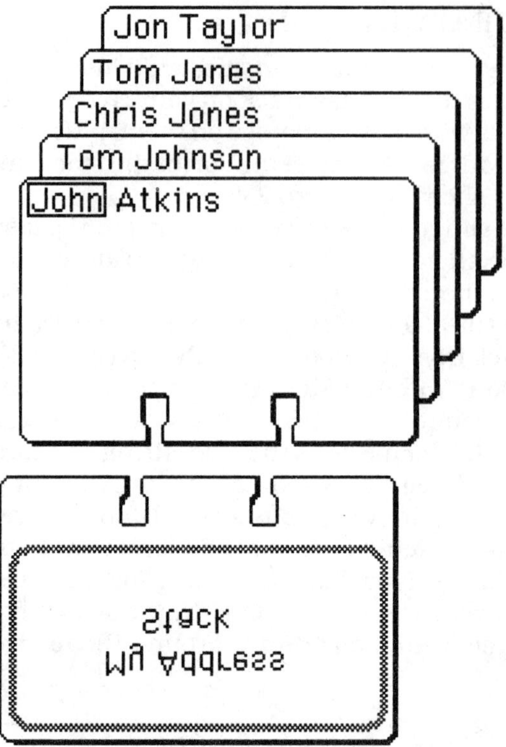


*Figure 2-9. Searching for "John" stops on the first card in the stack with a match. HyperCard draws a box around the matching text.*

Notice this result. Unless otherwise instructed by way of a command (covered in chapter 21), HyperCard searches *all* fields of the stack for an occurrence of the find string. By drawing a box around the found text, however, HyperCard makes it easy for you to quickly see whether the text you're looking for is in the right place. Therefore, if you're looking for a first name and HyperCard finds the text in the last name, you'll see at a glance that this card does not apply to your immediate search. Time to press Return again.

Another press of Return, and HyperCard searches once more. This time, it doesn't find another instance of "John" in the remaining cards. But, since a HyperCard stack is cyclical, it continues its search through the stack again, stopping on John Atkins' card (Figure 2-9).

To demonstrate this further, let's say you want to find the card with Jon Taylor's name on it. The spelling of his first name precludes searching for "John," although if you forgot that Taylor's name had this variant spelling, you may have difficulty searching for his first name. If you knew how to spell Jon's name, you could search for "Jon." Doing

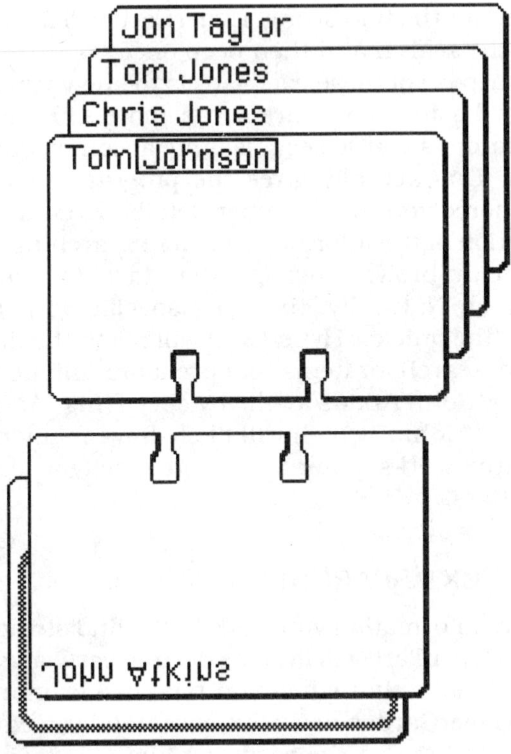


*Figure 2-10. Another press of Return, and HyperCard finds the next instance of "John" in the name "Johnson."*

so, however, will cause HyperCard in this stack to stop on three different names, two of which have "jon" as part of their last names, the Joneses (Figure 2–8). You could search for just "jo," but in this stack, HyperCard would stop on each card.

At the other extreme, you can be as specific as you want to find text in a card. Note that in our sample stack, two cards have the first name of Tom. The easy way to find Tom Jones, would be to type "Tom" into the find string and continue to press Return until his card appeared on the screen. But if you're not afraid of typing more letters into the find string and prefer to race immediately to the desired card, you can type the full name into the Message Box. HyperCard won't bother stopping until it finds a match for the entire content of the find string. Continually pressing Return in this case will cause HyperCard to search the entire stack again, winding up at Tom Jones' card each time.

One other case we haven't explored yet is searching for a name that is not in the stack. If you searched the above stack for "Steve," HyperCard wouldn't find any cards to match. To confirm that it searched for the find string, HyperCard will flash the Beachball cursor during the search and then beep once.

The purpose of these exercises is to show you that the more specific you can be in your search, the more efficient the search will be. HyperCard, as you've seen, is quite accommodating if you prefer to be general. This actually gives the program enormous power, since it doesn't force you to remember details. Even if you have only a slight recollection of the information you're searching for, HyperCard will let you quickly browse through the stack to find exactly what you're looking for. Naturally, the more specific you can be in your search request, the quicker HyperCard will reach the desired card. Whenever possible, search for items that are more unique than general, such as searching John Atkins' name by specifying "Atkins" as the find string instead of "John," which will likely have many matches. HyperCard's text search works faster when you specify a search string of three or more letters.

## NARROWING TEXT SEARCHES

The more information you place in the find string prior to a search, the quicker HyperCard will find the desired card, as we've shown. But what isn't obvious is that when you type two or more words into the find string, HyperCard is actually searching for a card that contains both words anywhere on the card, not just side by side. You can use this feature to narrow a search by looking for the occurrence of words in different fields.

Suppose you return to your office and find a badly garbled answering machine message waiting for you. About the only words you can pick out are the last name, Johnson, and the area code of the number to call, 312. If you want to check for all the Johnsons in your name and address file located in the 312 area code, you would type the following search message into the find string:

Johnson 312-

If you had typed *Johnson* only, HyperCard would stop on every Johnson in the stack; typing only *312-* would make it stop on every phone number in the 312 area code. But by specifying both names separated by a space, you instruct HyperCard to stop only on cards that meet both criteria. If both words are at least three letters long, then HyperCard performs its fastest search.

This may also explain those rare occurrences when you can't figure out why a HyperCard search displayed a card that didn't appear to match. For instance, if you search your name and address stack for someone named John Street, HyperCard will find all occurrences of cards with both "John" and "Street"— which could be a lot of cards. In practice, this shouldn't happen too often, but this aspect of HyperCard multiple-word searches may explain some apparently anomalous behavior.

## PICKING UP TEXT

You may also enter information into a find string directly from text already in a HyperCard text field. The procedure is called *picking up text.*

Normally, when you position the Browse tool atop a text field, the cursor turns into the I-Beam text cursor. If you hold down the Command key at the same time, the I-Beam turns back into the Browse tool, whose hand "picks up" text when you press the mouse button. With the Command key held down, click on a single word. HyperCard flashes a box around the whole word and places that word into the Message Box (Figure 2–11). Click and drag across a few words, and the box around the text grows as each word is added to the Message Box.

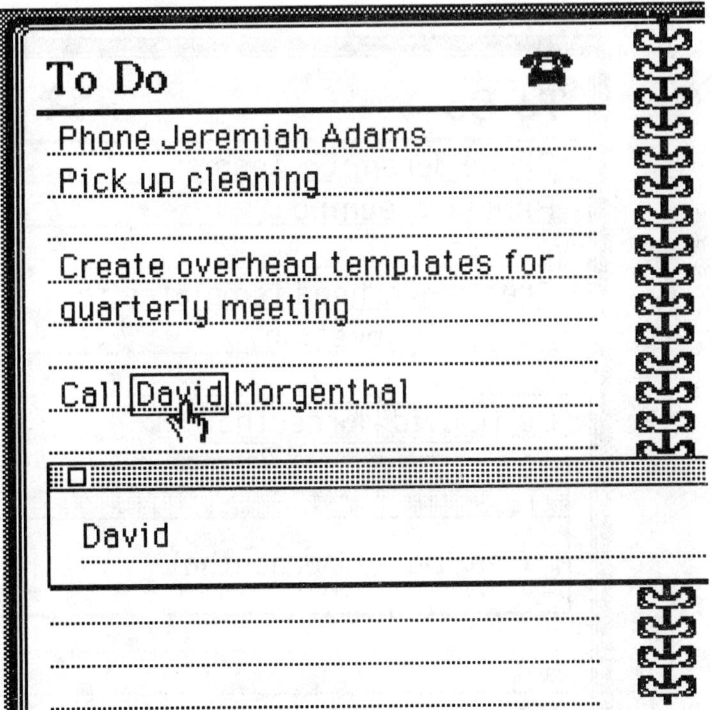


*Figure 2–11. Picking up a single word by Command-clicking it*

The efficient way to use this technique for finding text already in a text field is to type Command-F and pick up the desired text. It goes directly into the find string.

Typically, text pick up is used to find the occurrence of a text string in a different stack or background. Therefore, if you find a name on a To Do List, you can pick it up, navigate to the name and address stack, and press Return to find that person's phone number (Figure 2–12). Similarly, you may also pick up the phone number and click a dial button, which sets in motion auto-dialing of whatever number is in the Message Box.

## *Entering Text Information*

While you'll probably use HyperCard more for browsing and retrieving information than any other action, it will also become a repository for new information you wish stored in your computer. After all, what good is a name and address type of file if you can't add names and addresses to it?

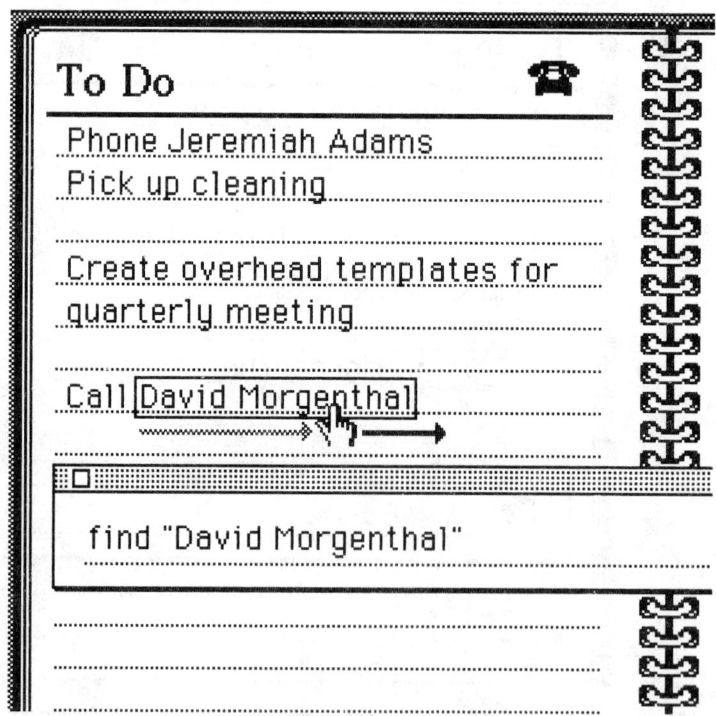


*Figure 2–12. Command-drag over the text to pick it up prior to a search.*

## FIELDS, AGAIN

Earlier we described how a field fits into the big picture of HyperCard. Fields are strictly for text entry and storage. A card may contain only graphic information, such as a piece of clip art, so there is no law that says a card *must* contain fields. But practically every card in your stacks will contain at least one field. Even a clip art stack will probably have a field with a text description of the object. That way, you'll be able to have HyperCard search a potentially huge clip art file for images in a particular category or images of a particular item.

As we'll see in chapter 9, specifications about a card's fields are established in HyperCard's authoring mode. Field specifications that will be obvious to you as you enter information into a card are such things as the location on the screen, the horizontal dimension (how "wide" it is on the screen), the number of text lines, the font type, and the font size. If you are using a stack that has been authored by someone else, these decisions have been made for you, although you will probably be able to adjust fields as you see fit.

## THE TEXT CURSOR

To help you enter text into a field, HyperCard automatically changes the Browse tool to an I-Beam cursor (Figure 2–13). This is identical to the cursor you have probably seen in other Macintosh text applications.

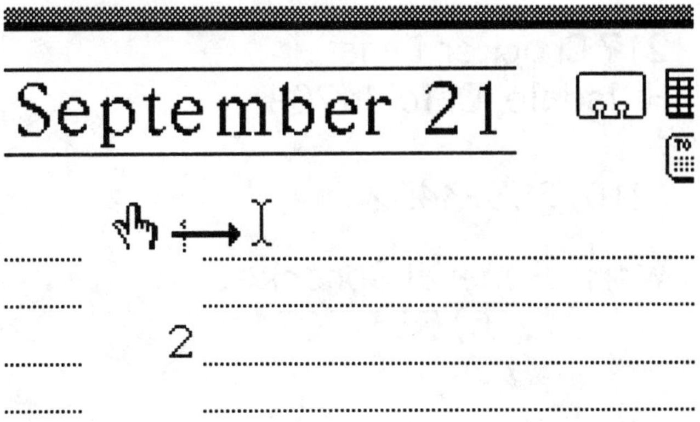

September 21

2

*Figure 2–13. The Browse tool turns into the I-beam when it enters a field. Upon leaving the field, the tool returns to the Browse tool.*

## FINDING A CARD'S FIELDS

Unlike a paper form, which usually has a blank line or box that you are to fill in, a HyperCard field may not be so obvious when you are just looking at the card. For example, when you look at a blank card from a stack, it is not immediately clear how many fields have been created for the card or exactly where they are on the card (Figure 2–14). Nor can you be certain that text you see on a card is in a field or text in the background, like the preprinted portion of a form. Fortunately, you have a couple of ways of finding where a card's fields are.

The simplest way to get started in your search is to watch the cursor as you move it around the screen. Wherever there is a text field to which you have access, the Browse tool turns to the I-Beam.

Click the mouse button anyplace the cursor is the I-Beam. The text insertion pointer will appear and flash at the left margin of the field in the same line of the field as you clicked (the text pointer may also flash in the center or at the right margin, however, if center and right alignment had been assigned to the field when it was created). You may type text if you wish.

To find other fields in the card, simply press the Tab key a few times. If no text has been entered into any field, you will see the text insertion pointer flash at the beginning of each field on the card. Fields, as you will discover in chapter 9, have an order on the card, just as cards have

*Figure 2–14. How many fields are there on this card? How many lines are there in each field?*

an order in a stack. As you press the Tab key, each field *in its order* becomes activated and is ready to accept text typed from the keyboard. Because the order of fields does not have to follow any prescribed geographic order on the card, it is possible that as you press Tab, the fields activated in turn will be all over a card.

If text already occupies a field, then a press of the Tab key that activates that field selects the entire text in the field. Following the Macintosh text editing conventions, selected text means that it is ready for cutting or copying into the Clipboard. It also means that a press of any key will replace the original text with that new key (reversible by choosing Undo from the Edit menu).

A second way to find the fields of a card requires us to skip ahead for just a moment to another tool on the tool palette: the Field tool (Figure 2–15). You can access the Field tool only when the user level is set to Authoring or Scripting. When you choose the Field tool from the Tools menu, HyperCard shows outlines of every field on the card (Figure 2–16). If a field has more than one line, the field is shown with the locations of its multiple lines and the spacing allocated for each line, according to the font size defined for that field.

## ENTERING AND EDITING FIELD INFORMATION

If you've done the least amount of word processing or text entry in another Macintosh application, you'll feel right at home entering and editing text in HyperCard fields. Wherever the text insertion pointer flashes in a field, the next character you type will go into that spot (Figure 2–17).

When you've finished typing text for one field in a card, you can proceed to the next field either by pressing the Tab key or by using the

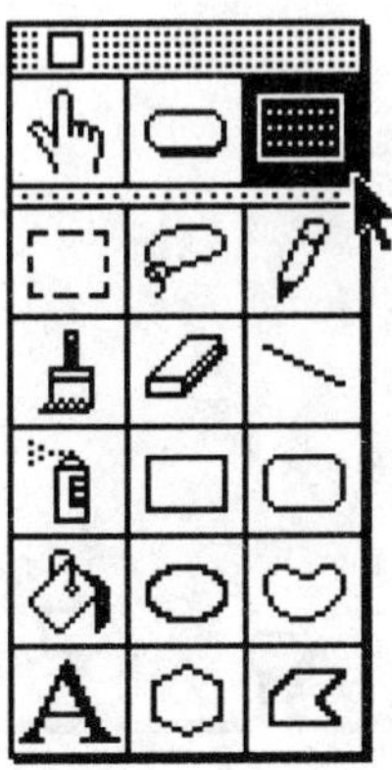

*Figure 2–15. The Field tool*

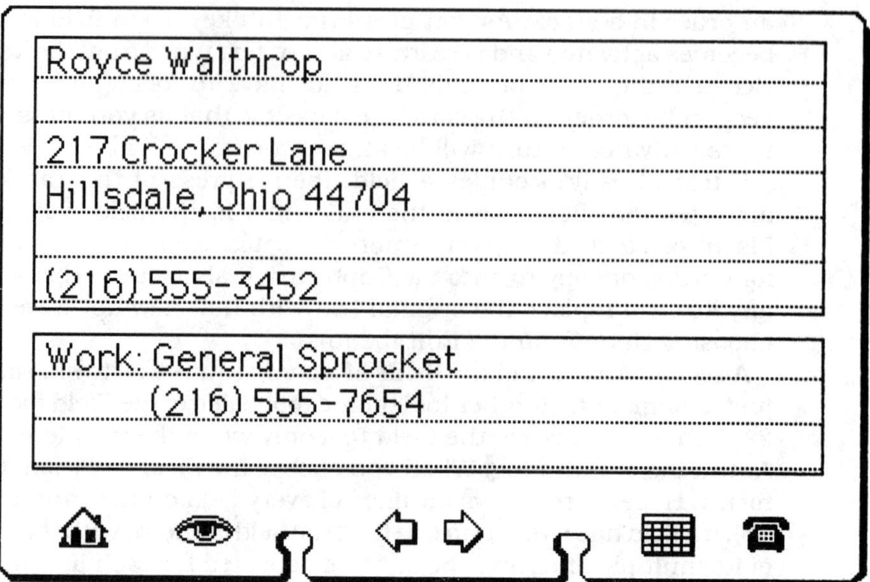


*Figure 2–16. With the Field tool selected, each field's outlines and text lines appear.*

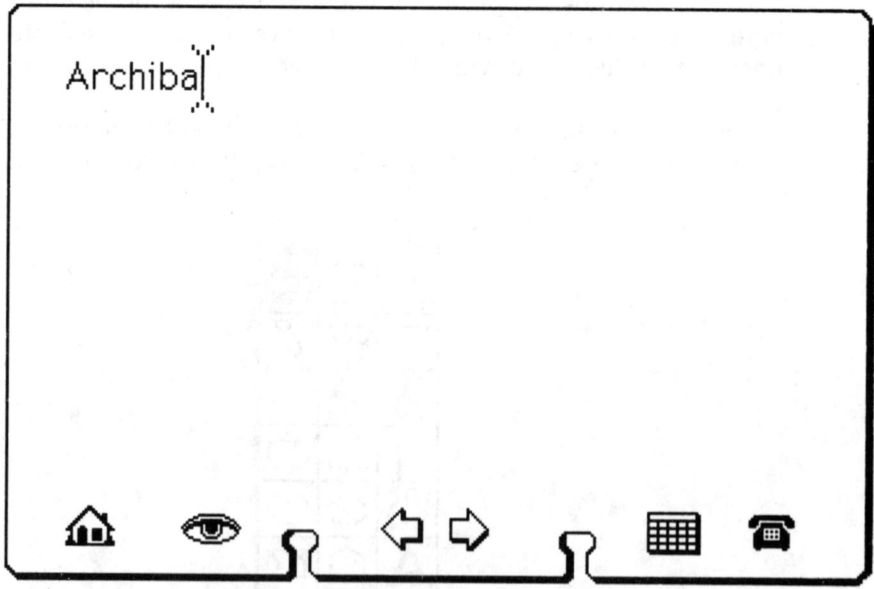


*Figure 2–17. The flashing text insertion pointer shows you where the next character you type will appear in the field.*

mouse to point to the next field and clicking. Since text entry is by keyboard, it is far more efficient to progress through fields using the Tab key.

HyperCard text fields follow most editing conventions of the Macintosh user interface, as described in your Macintosh owner's manual. Selecting text for cutting and copying to the Clipboard, pasting from the Clipboard, and undoing your last operation hold true for HyperCard fields.

Note, however, that the font type, font size, and style (for example, bold, italic) are fixed for an entire field. You cannot, for instance, italicize one word in a field.

## CREATING A NEW CARD

Except for those cases in which you need to modify text in an existing card, most of your HyperCard text entry will be into new cards. Creating a new card is a simple task in HyperCard. Open the stack in which you wish to create a new card. Find a card that has the same background you wish the new card to have (some stacks may have more than one background). On most stacks, you can use the first card that appears when you open the stack. Next, choose New Card from the Edit menu or type Command-N (Figure 2–18).

HyperCard displays a card without any text or any foreground graphics (for example, a piece of clip art). If the card has a text field, the stack may automatically place the text insertion pointer at the first field of the card, but this is not true for all stacks, depending on the stack author's ideas.

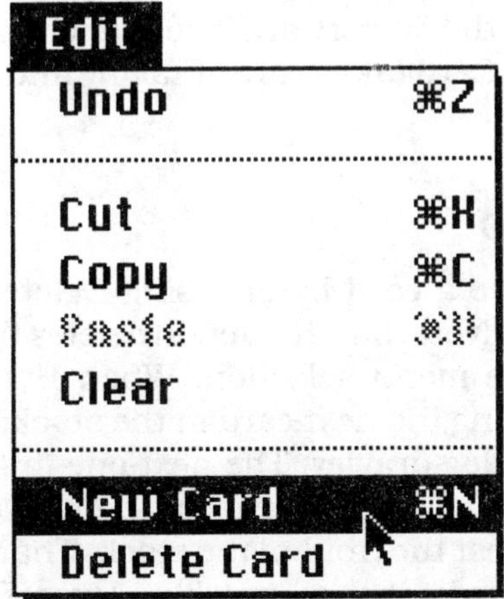


*Figure 2–18. Create a new card with New Card in the Edit menu.*

The card just created was placed in the stack in order right after the card you were viewing when you created the new card. If the stack provides a sort button, it's not critical that you create a card in its final place in the stack's cycle.

It's quite possible that until you develop a routine for creating new cards in your stacks you will accidentally create a number of new cards that carry no text. This will be especially true if you are accustomed to entering information into more traditional database programs on the Macintosh or other computers. The reason is that you will feel as if you must "enter" the information for it to be duly recorded and saved on the disk. In database programs, this action usually entails pressing the Return or Enter key, which clears the form on the screen. That's not the case with HyperCard.

HyperCard automatically saves your card's freshly typed information to disk the minute you do one of the following:

- press the Enter key
- advance the text pointer to the next field with the Tab key or mouse
- click the Browse tool outside the text field
- change the cursor to any tool other than the I-Beam
- make a menu selection
- press a left- or right-arrow key on the keyboard to view an adjacent card in the stack
- click the mouse pointer inside the Message Box
- create a new card

Therefore, HyperCard covers you by saving your information whenever you risk losing it. In fact, you'll notice that there is no Save command in the HyperCard File menu, unlike other Macintosh programs. HyperCard takes care of saving and updating for you automatically.

## DELETING A CARD

You can delete a card by choosing Delete Card from the Edit menu (Figure 2–19). Note that this action deletes the card you're viewing when you make the menu selection. When HyperCard removes the card, you'll be viewing the next card in the stack, just as if you pulled a card in a card catalog drawer: The next one in line would be visible.

If you need to delete several consecutive cards in a stack, start with the card nearest the front of the stack. That way you'll be able to delete successive cards rather quickly. HyperCard intentionally has no keyboard command for deleting cards. You must make a conscious menu choice to get rid of each card.

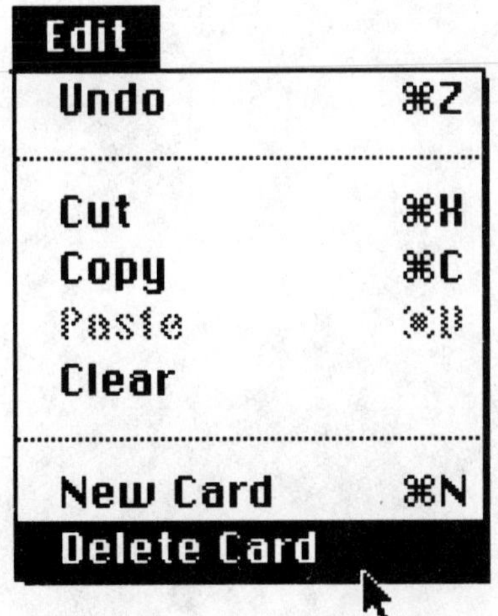


*Figure 2-19. Delete a card with Delete Card in the Edit menu.*

CHAPTER 3

# HyperCard Linking and Printing

WE FINISH OUR GUIDE TO THE HYPERCARD BROWSING ENVIRONMENT BY DEMONSTRATING more sophisticated methods of finding information that may be built into stacks provided by Apple and others. We'll also explain in some detail how to take the fullest advantage of HyperCard's extensive printing functions.

## *Cross-Reference Information*

As we discussed in the Introduction, there are many cases in which a search for information must branch away from the current, specialized body of knowledge. Buttons, as we hinted in chapter 1, give you that kind of branching power in HyperCard. When you combine text, the Message Box, and buttons, you have an incredibly powerful browsing capability at the tip of your mouse finger.

Buttons, of course, can be instructed during the authoring process to perform many different tasks. Not all buttons are joined with find strings in the Message Box, but we'll look at one such combination to demonstrate effortless searching among seemingly unrelated stacks.

Our demonstration falls under the broad guise of linking stacks. We'll have much more to say about linking in chapter 11. For now, however, you can think of a link as one of those colored yarns that jumps across traditional boundaries of groups of information. Actually, a link

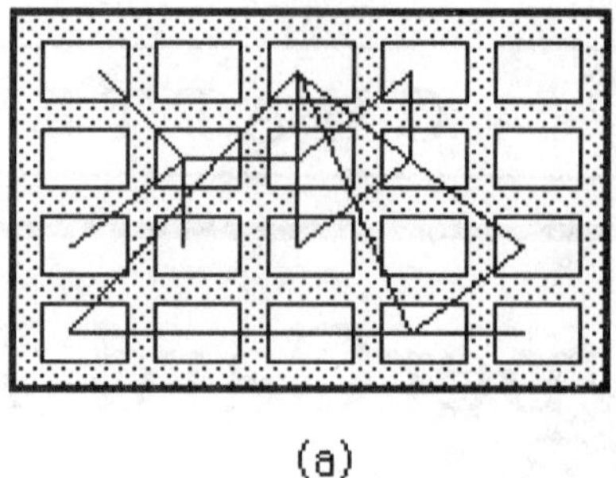

(a)

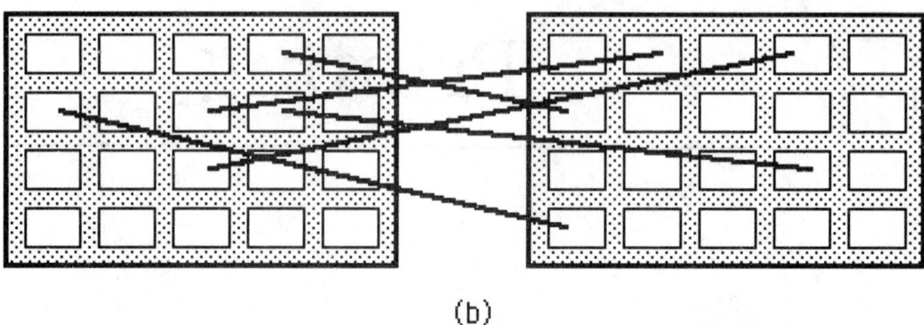

(b)

*Figure 3–1. Links are like yarns between cards in a single collection (a) or between cards in different collections (b).*

between stacks is more like a yarn between two different bulletin boards, each board consisting of cards detailing a separate body of knowledge (Figure 3–1).

## THE MESSAGE BOX AND LINKING

When a card contains a button that links to another stack, it often needs some search text in the Message Box before it jumps to the other stack and begins its search. As you may recall, if you hold down the Command key and click the Browse tool atop any text in a field, it picks up the text and copies it into the Message Box.

You should be aware that the Message Box is very much alive, even when it is not displayed on the screen. HyperCard keeps the content of the Message Box intact at all times the program is running. As an extra level of feedback that things are, indeed, working as you expect, the Message Box shows itself the instant you begin picking up text.

As a result of the automatic placement of text into the Message Box and find string, a search into another stack can be accomplished with the mouse, provided the button that branches to the other stack has been given the proper instructions during its authoring session. A button so empowered will usually perform the following actions:

- open the other stack
- start a search for the text in the find string

In essence, then, the button switches stacks, inserts the Message Box text into the find string and does the equivalent of pressing the Return key to commence the search. HyperCard takes over from there. If a match is found, HyperCard brings that card into view and draws a box around the matched text. If it's not the exact card you expected, you can continue pressing Return as HyperCard checks further through the stack for the text originally placed into the Message Box.

## INTELLIGENT LINKS

Another style of card linking is exemplified in the HyperCard stack called Datebook. This stack is represented on the Home card by three icons: To Do, Weekly, and Calendar (whose background is named, "Six Monthly"). These three applications are actually combined into a single stack with three backgrounds. Still, there is a sophisticated structure established to link the Weekly and Calendar parts of the stack.

In the Calendar application, for example, you can click the Browse tool on any week of any month showing in the six-month spread (Figure 3-2). A rather complex script calculates which week you've clicked on and then proceeds directly to the weekly appointment card for that week. These two applications could just as well have been in two separate stacks, yet the operation would not be affected by that file arrangement.

Links of this nature not only bring two applications together but take the extra steps to eliminate manual searching on the user's part. The more a link action anticipates your next moves and appears almost magical, the more care has gone into designing the link.

## OTHER LINKING POSSIBILITIES

In later chapters, you will see that linking is one of the powers of HyperCard that makes the program behave unlike any other software. For example, HyperCard can send along information during a link-up. Your Address stack, for instance, has a button on it with an icon of a telephone. When you click the phone icon in an Address card, HyperCard jumps to the Phone stack where a special-purpose card instructs a telephone modem to dial the number in your Address card. Thus you have an automatic dialer at your fingertips.

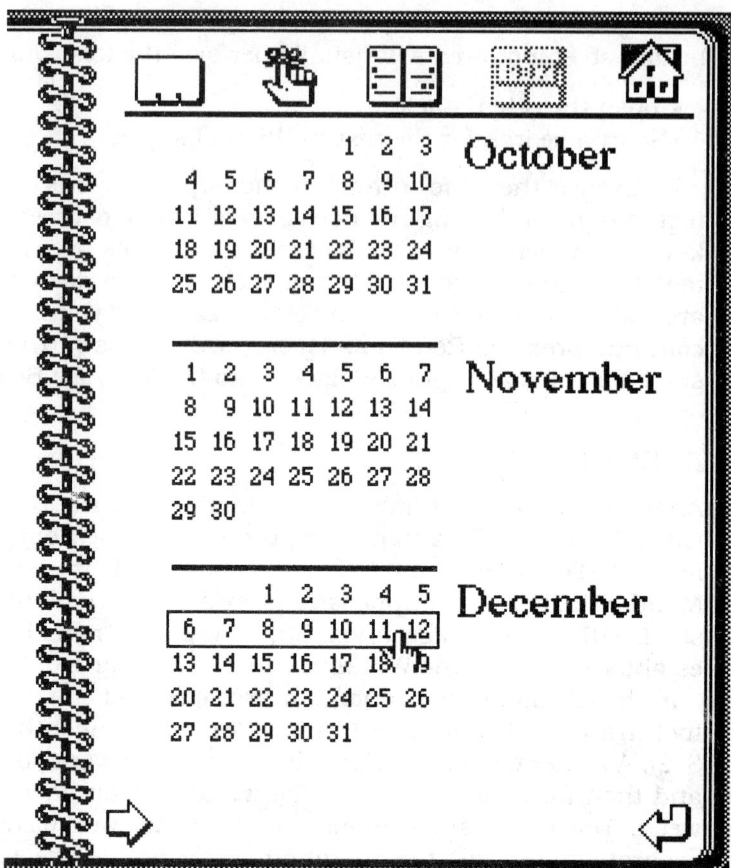


*Figure 3-2. Clicking atop a week in the calendar (above) links to the weekly appointment book card for that week.*

## HyperCard Printing

Even in the browsing environment, you have full access to HyperCard's extraordinary printing variety. You can print cards, stacks, or even lists of the information stored in text fields. Many of the options available to you will be self-explanatory in the various dialog boxes presented with most printing menu commands, but we'll spend some time here explaining what your options are. All print menu items may be found in the File menu.

## PAGE SETUP

Most Macintosh applications provide a Page Setup dialog box in which you specify important issues related to the way your printer should handle the program's output. Choices available depend on the printer you use. For example, if you select the ImageWriter with the Chooser (in the desk accessory menu), the Page Setup Dialog box looks like the one in Figure 3–3. In it you may choose paper type, horizontal or vertical orientation, or any one of three special effects. For most HyperCard printing applications, the settings you use for other programs will work well.

You have many more Page Setup choices when you use a LaserWriter (Figure 3–4). The paper sizes and orientation shouldn't need additional explanation. In other Mac applications you may reduce or enlarge the image on a pageby specifying the percentage in the small text box. Normal size is considered 100%. If you wish to reduce the image by approximately 5%, you would type *95* into the box. Similarly, you can bump up the size 10% by typing *110* into the box. This feature does not work in HyperCard.

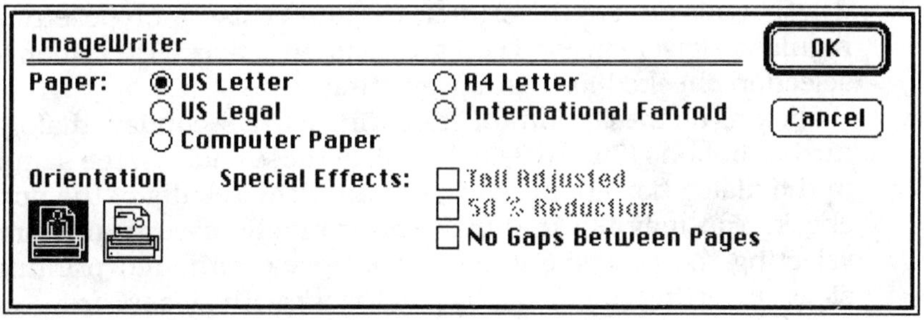

*Figure 3–3. Page Setup dialog box for the ImageWriter*

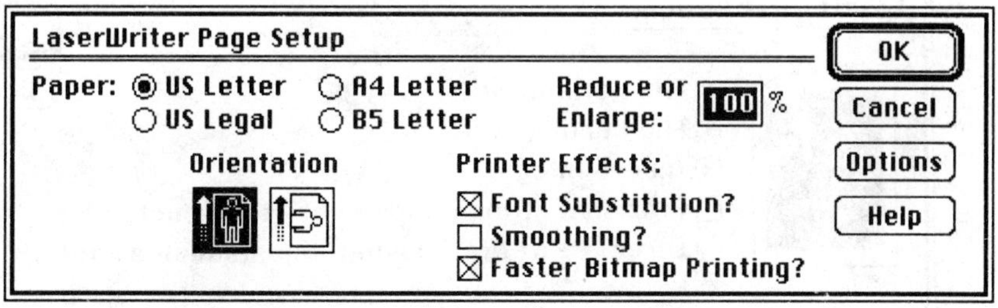

*Figure 3–4. Page Setup dialog box for the LaserWriter*

Printer effects in the LaserWriter Page Setup are often confusing, so we'll spend a moment on them before getting to the HyperCard-specific options. Selecting Font Substitution tells the LaserWriter to do its best to substitute built-in laser fonts for nonlaser fonts you use on your Macintosh screen. In the most frequent examples, the New York font on the screen becomes Times on the LaserWriter; Geneva becomes Helvetica; and Monaco becomes Courier. Because these font pairs are related in appearance, they are natural substitutions. But be aware that letting the printer do the substitution won't necessarily give you the optimum letter spacing or line lengths that you'd get if you use the laser fonts on the screen, too. If you do not check Font Substitution, the printer treats the text as graphics images. For some fonts, like Chicago, this is a good solution.

Smoothing affects all graphics images. If selected, Smoothing attempts to make the jagged lines of the screen resolution print out much more smoothly, since the printer is capable of much higher resolution. It is recommended for graphics, unless the desired effect is to print an exact replica of the screen, complete with square dots at regular screen resolution. Printing speed, however, will be very slow.

Faster Bitmap Printing affects the speed at which the LaserWriter driver sends data to the printer. Certain Postscript typesetting devices require a slower speed. If you are using the LaserWriter, then leave this selection checked for regular printing.

Clicking on the Options button brings up a secondary dialog box with further options (Figure 3–5). For all of these choices, the sample image in the dialog box changes to dramatize the results of the options you check. You may flip the image horizontally or vertically (or both) by selecting the corresponding check boxes, although printing will be slow. Inverting the imagedoes not work with HyperCard.

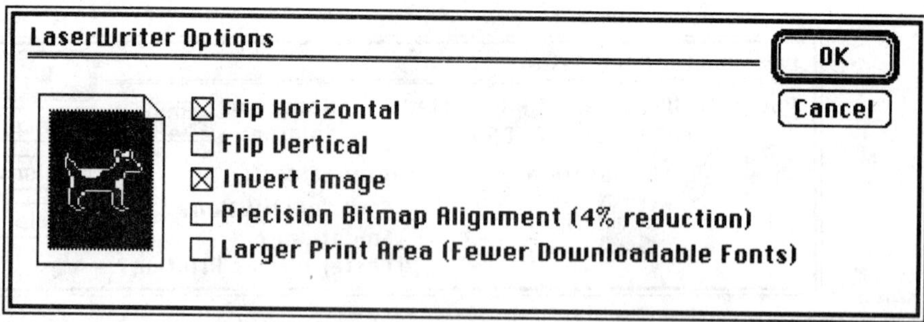


*Figure 3–5. With a LaserWriter, you have many additional printing options available.*

Precision Bitmap Alignment helps the LaserWriter avoid minor distortions in graphics images that occasionally occur. This distortion happens when the LaserWriter tries to convert the Macintosh 72-spot-per-inch graphics resolution to the printer's 300-spot-per-inch resolution. To compensate for this uneven multiple, a 4% reduction in the printed image results in a density of 72 screen spots being converted to 288 spots on the LaserWriter, an even multiple of four. The LaserWriter is still printing in 300 spots-per-inch, but one inch of screen image is taking up 4% less space on the paper.

If you are concerned with printing an image closer to the edges of the paper than the LaserWriter normally allows, then select Larger Print Area. This choice takes some of the LaserWriter's internal memory for storing the page information while the printer assembles a page. The tradeoff is that you will have less memory available for downloadable fonts. If you use standard laser fonts, this should not affect your printing.

## PRINT CARD

The Print Card menu choice is the only one of the printing commands that does not lead to a dialog box. That's because this command simply prints the current card according to settings in the Page Setup dialog box. With this command, you get only one full-size card per printed page.

## PRINT STACK

When you wish to print all cards in a stack, the Print Stack... menu choice is where you start. The resulting dialog box has many options governing the number of cards on the page, their layout, and other important information (Figure 3–6).

Two check boxes in the upper left corner control your printer. For both the ImageWriter and LaserWriter, you may check the Manual paper feed box if you intend to load paper one sheet at a time. If you are using an ImageWriter, the second check box, Darker Printing, is similar to the Best print quality setting on other programs' print dialog boxes. Output quality will be higher, but the printing speed slower. When you are printing on a LaserWriter, the second check box is labeled Fast Laser Printing. This item is automatically checked because you should use the enhanced speed setting most of the time. Some Postscript-based typesetters and LaserWriter print spoolers, however, require that laser printing be slowed to regular speed. If you print to these environments and encounter difficulties with the fast setting, turn off Fast Laser Printing.

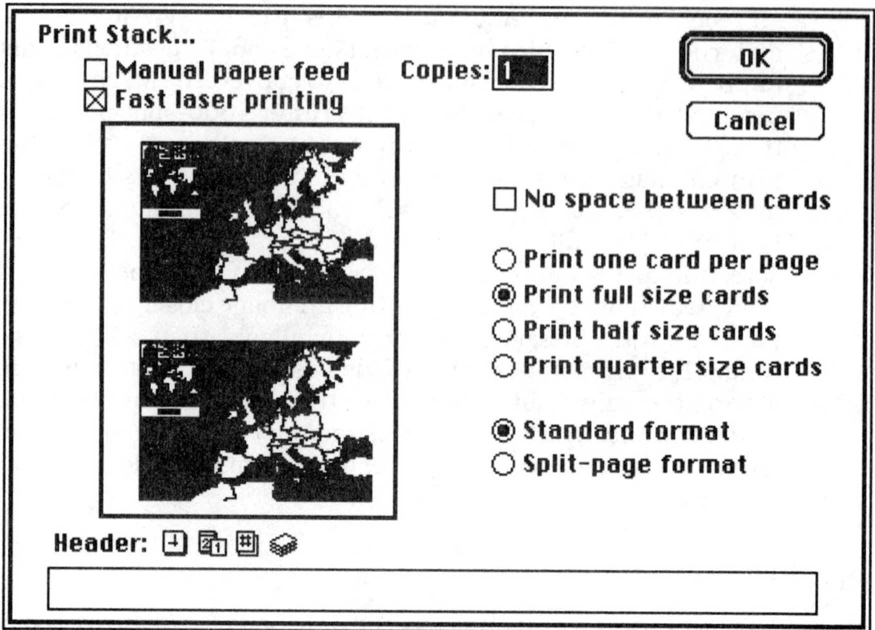


*Figure 3-6. The Print Stack dialog box*

The most important choice is whether you wish one card per page, full-size, half-size, or quarter-size cards. Full-size cards print two cards per page (Figure 3-6). Half-size cards leave enough space on the page for eight cards (Figure 3-7). If you have a LaserWriter, you might also want to try quarter-size cards to display thirty-two cards per printed page (Figure 3-8). Because of the high resolution of the LaserWriter, 12-point text in the card fields is still readable in quarter-size cards. This choice is most convenient if you wish to print a lengthy stack for quick reference when you're away from the computer.

You may also choose between a standard and split-page format. The difference between the two is subtle, but quite important (Figure 3-9). In standard format, the card images are placed on the page with a slightly wider margin on the left edge of the page, leaving ample room for loose-leaf binder holes. In the split-page format, however, the card images are carefully positioned so that you can fold and punch pages to fit into most personal directory binders (sometimes called "executive organizers") sold in stationery stores. When you choose this format, HyperCard shows you where the fold line will be (the dotted line in Figure 3-9). To get a better idea of the fine differences between these two choices, alternate between the two selections and watch where the card images appear on the page.

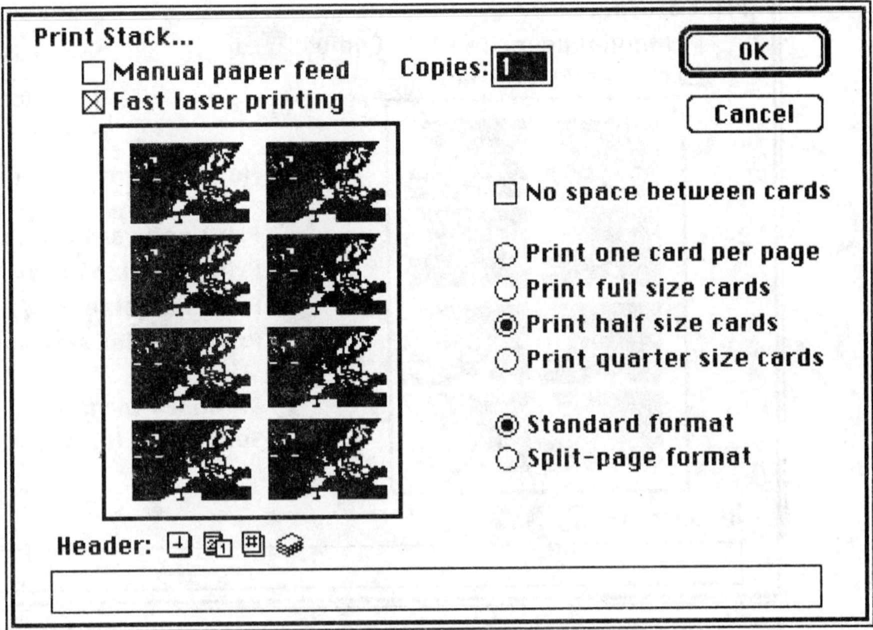


*Figure 3-7. Specifying half-size cards produces eight cards per printed page.*

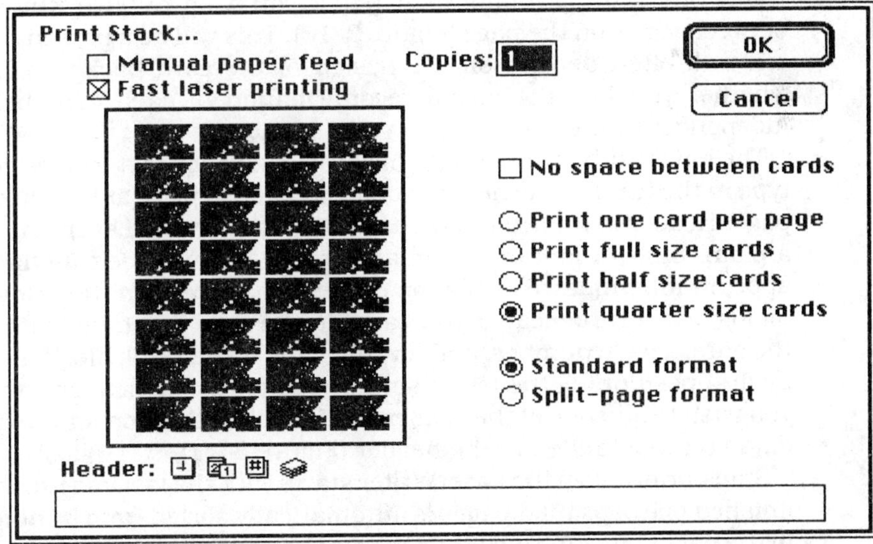


*Figure 3-8. Specifying quarter-size cards on the LaserWriter produces thirty-two readable cards per page.*

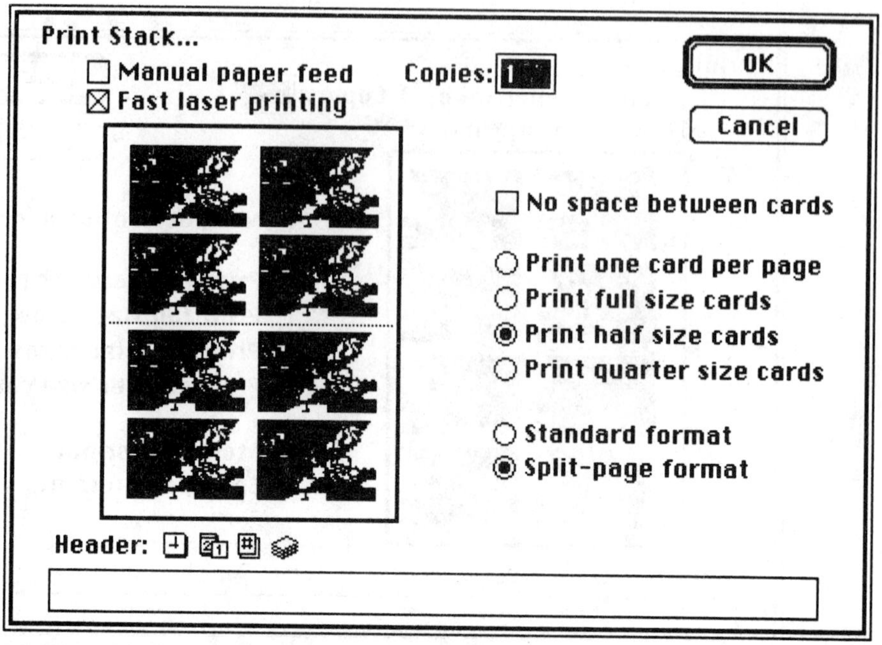

Print Stack...
☐ Manual paper feed   Copies: 1   OK
☒ Fast laser printing   Cancel
☐ No space between cards
○ Print one card per page
○ Print full size cards
◉ Print half size cards
○ Print quarter size cards
○ Standard format
◉ Split-page format
Header:

*Figure 3-9. Split-page formatting leaves room for hole punching and insertion into loose-leaf executive organizers.*

One other format option is whether you wish to have white space between cards on the page (Figure 3-10). This will be a personal choice and will often depend on the design of the card backgrounds and whether you like the visual reconfirmation of each card being an independent unit.

The long text box at the bottom of the dialog box is the place you can type in the text for any header you would like to print at the top of each page. Header text prints in the Helvetica font on the LaserWriter or in a plain, built-in font on the ImageWriter. All text is left-justified and appears in miniature at the top of the sample page in the Print Stack dialog box. To the header you can add the time (the time of printing), the date, a page number, and/or the name of the stack file. You do this by first positioning the text insertion pointer in the header box where you wish to add one of the elements. Then click the icon for the desired data you wish added to the header (Figure 3-11).

Stack printing on the LaserWriter starts with the last page so that the finished pile of printed pages is automatically sorted from front to back in the paper output tray. While the stack is printing, you can cancel the process at any time without having to finish the entire stack.

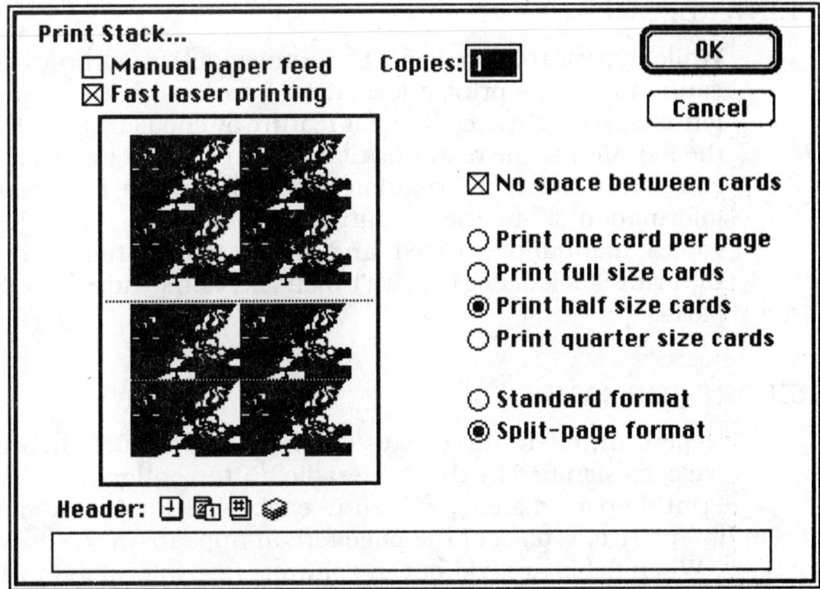


*Figure 3-10. Selecting no white space between cards scrunches the cards together on the page.*

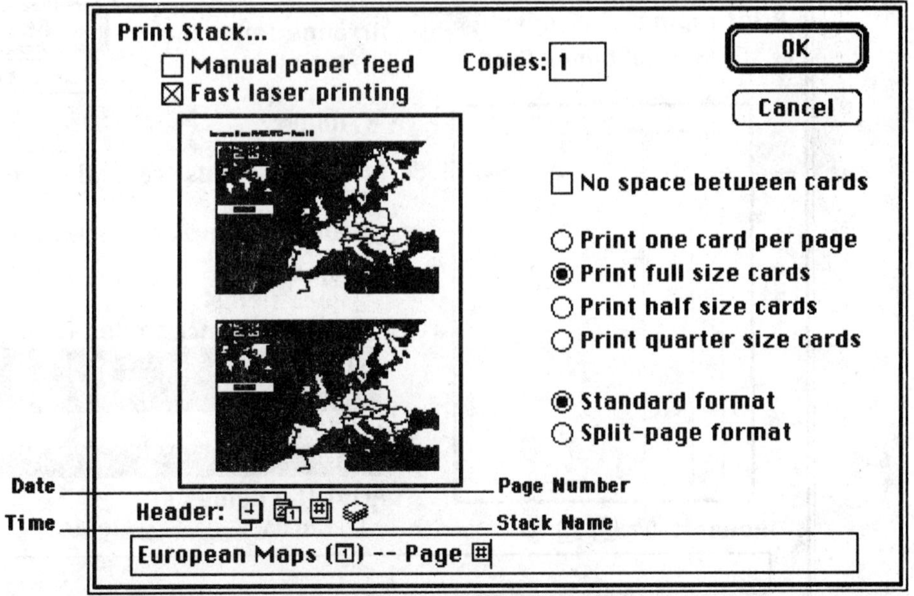


*Figure 3-11. Enter header text into the text field and click on the time, date, page number, and stack name icons where you want the information in the header.*

## PRINT REPORT

While HyperCard should not be confused with reporting databases, you can nonetheless print information from text fields in various report formats. You gain access to this feature by choosing Print Report... from the File Menu. The resulting dialog box contains many choices to help you select which information you want in the report and how the information should be formatted (Figure 3–12). Since the number of copies, manual paper feed, and header information is the same as in the Print Stack dialog box, we'll focus here, instead, on the box's unique parts.

## REPORT FORMATS

HyperCard offers three ways of formatting the field information on a page, as signified by the three radio button options near the top of the Print Report dialog box. With each selection, a miniature, often interactive, replica of the page format appears in the dialog box.

When fields are laid out in columns, the information will appear in what you'd more likely recognize as a database type of report (Figure 3–12). You can choose which of the current stack's background fields you

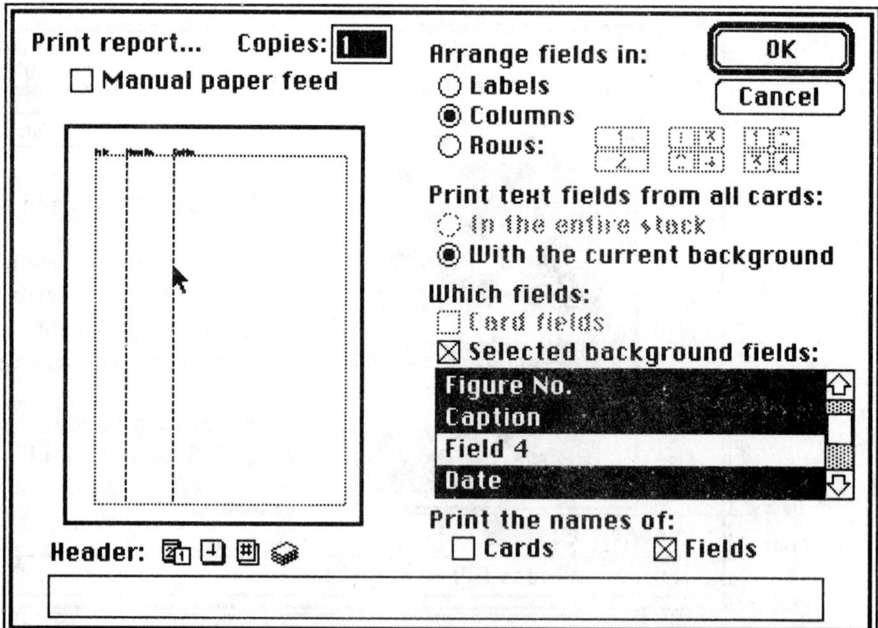


*Figure 3–12. Print Report dialog box set to print fields in columns*

wish to be included in the report. If the fields are named (most fields in Apple's stacks and third-party stacks are named), the field names will appear in the field listing. When a field lacks a name, its place is held by the word Field and a number indicating its order among all the fields. To choose individual fields but not all fields, hold down the Shift button and click on each field name you wish in the report (Figure 3–12). Importantly, field information will appear in the report in the same order as you Shift-click their names in the scrollable field name box.

HyperCard initially allocates equal width for each column, based on the number of fields in the card. You can, however, drag the dotted dividing lines left or right to make columns as wide or as narrow as needed. If information in the field is longer than the column is wide, the text "wraps" to the next line in the same column during printing. Two additional options let you print card names (which adds an extra column— see Figure 3–13) if the cards in the stack have different names (most of the time they don't have any name) and print field names. If the field names in the scrolling box have real names (instead of Field 1, Field 2, and so on), printing the field names will probably be a good idea, because the names become headings for the columns. As you select background field names to be included in the report, their names appear in the miniature replica.

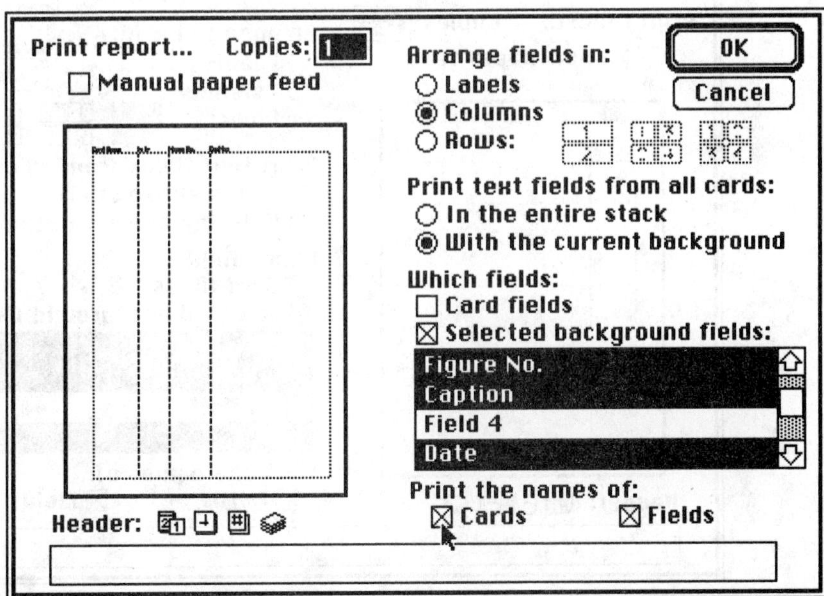


*Figure 3–13. When you print card names along with fields, HyperCard prints an extra column for those names.*

If you specify that the fields be arranged in rows, each card's information is grouped together, as indicated in Figure 3–14. You can print card names and field names if you wish, although field names are probably the more common selection when the fields are named descriptively. If the field names are long, you can drag the dotted dividing line in the miniature page to make appropriate room. An example of the printout of a couple of cards is shown in Figure 3–15. Another choice is to print in rows and in two columns, as shown in Figure 3–16. When you make this selection, you have yet another choice to make: the layout order. The middle and right-hand schematic layout diagrams (next to the Rows button) indicate in which order card information will be assembled on the page. Numbers in the diagrams stand for the order of cards. The left diagram indicates that the cards' data will be printed first down the left column and then down the right column. The right diagram indicates that the printing layout order will be from left to right. Figure 3–17 demonstrates the difference.

You may also choose whether the report should extract text fields from all backgrounds in the entire stack or from only the background you were viewing when you chose Print Report in the menu. If you elect to print the entire stack, you lose a great deal of your report format control, because HyperCard won't know what fields to expect in other

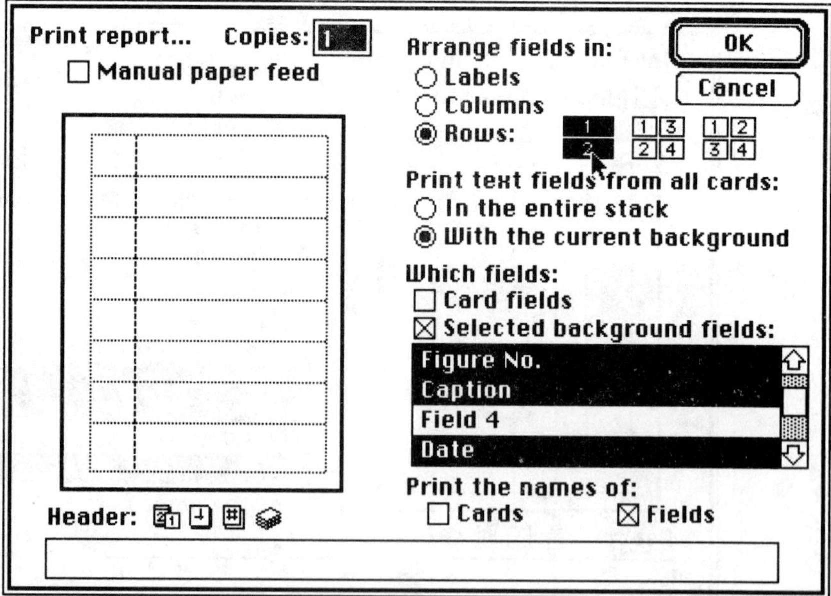


*Figure 3–14. Laying out fields in rows gives the information an entirely different look and organization on the page.*

My Address Book — Page 4

| | |
|---|---|
| Name and Address: | David Ogborn<br>2119 Runnymede St<br>Tempe, Arizona |
| Phone Number: | (602) 555-6692 |
| Name and address: | Edmund Reid<br>6080 Nicole Place<br>Monterey, California |
| Phone Number: | (408) 555-0406 |
| Name and Address: | Beverley Richie<br>1250 Washington Avenue<br>Gettysburg, Pennsylvania |
| Phone Number: | (717) 555-8454 |

*Figure 3-15. Sample printout of a vertically oriented report.*

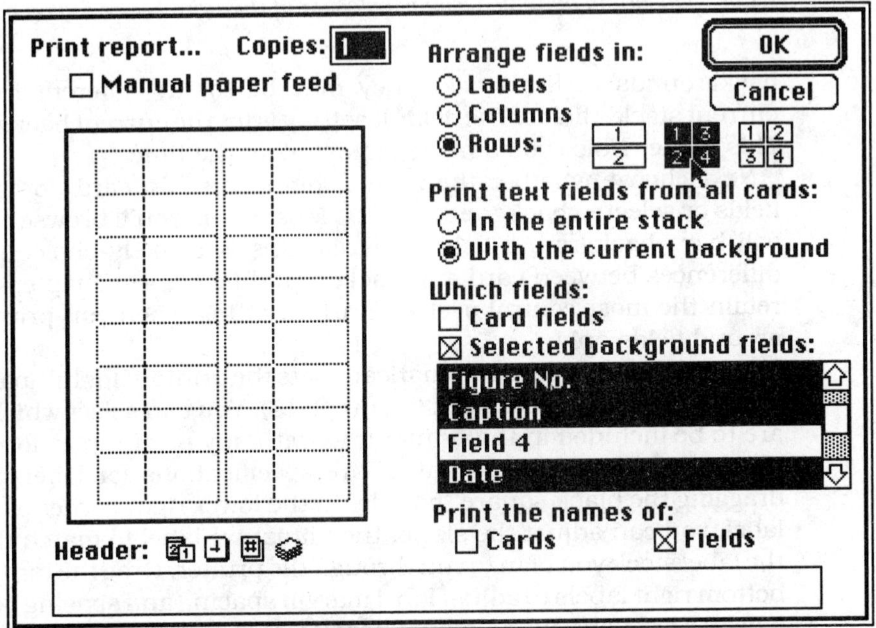


*Figure 3-16. Row format also allows printing in two columns.*

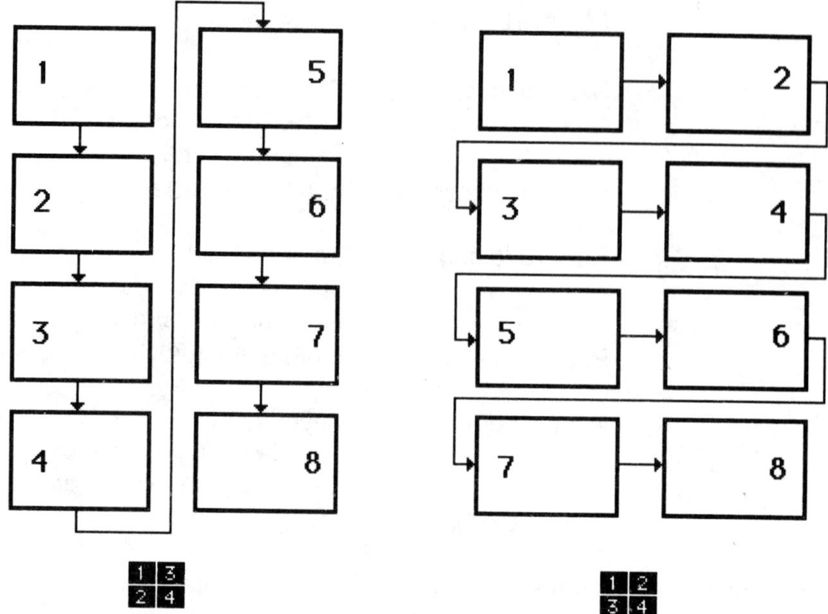


*Figure 3–17. Row printing in two columns may be organized in two different ways, depending on which icon is selected in the Print Stack dialog box.*

backgrounds in the stack. They may be totally different from the current stack's fields. The default setting is for the current background. This is the choice you'll make almost all of the time.

Next choose whether the report should contain card (foreground) fields or selected background fields. Most cards you'll browse through will have background fields only, so this is a likely choice (for the differences between card and background fields, see chapter 9). You retain the most control over report formatting when you print background fields only.

A third report format automatically sets the printout for full-page self-adhesive mailing-label stock (Figure 3–18). You can select which fields are to be included in the printout, as with any print report format. In place of the header information are specifications for label size. By dragging the black square "handle" in the lower right corner of the top label, you can adjust the size of the miniature label to match those of the label stock you plan to run through the printer. Drag the top left and bottom right labels to adjust label margin spacing and spacing between labels. There should be adjustment to accommodate most standard label stocks measured in inches or centimeters.

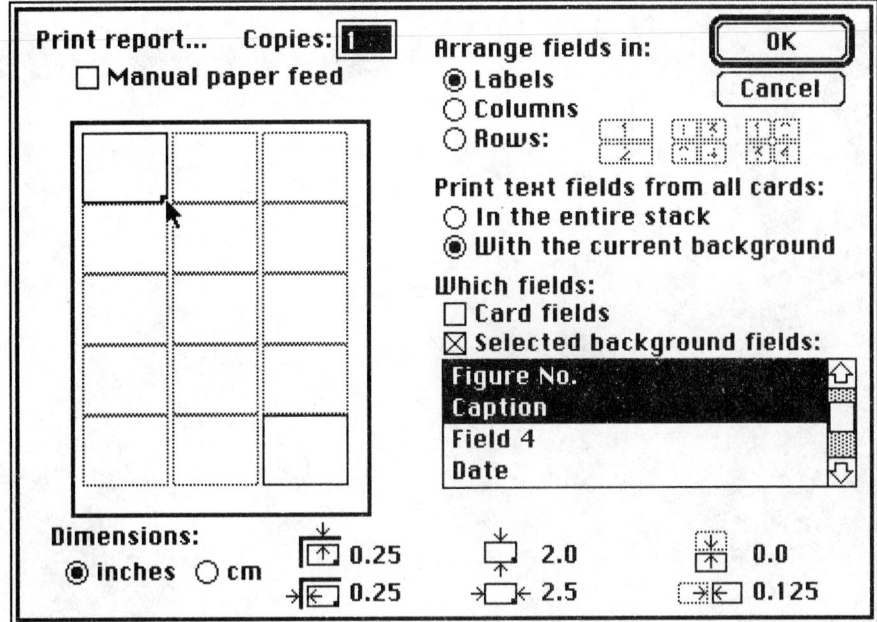


*Figure 3-18. Formatting for adhesive mailing labels is provided. Drag the handle in the upper left label to adjust printout to actual size of labels. Drag the labels to adjust label spacing and margins.*

Thus ends a whirlwind tour of the browsing environment of HyperCard. Even without writing your own HyperCard stacks, you have quite a bit of power available to you. But after using the stacks supplied by Apple and understanding the fundamental concepts behind HyperCard described so far, we hope that you'll be interested enough to pursue developing your own stacks. That's where Part Two begins.

# PART TWO

# HyperCard's Authoring Environment

# CHAPTER 4

# Introduction to Authoring

IF YOU DO NOTHING MORE THAN USE THE HYPERCARD STACKS THAT COME ON YOUR HyperCard disks, you will certainly gain productive use of the program. But you will have only scratched the surface of what HyperCard is all about. True, it is a program that gives you fast access to a variety of information. More importantly, however, HyperCard lets you build the kind of information world that makes the most sense for your work and your life.

## *What Authoring Means to You*

By combining card backgrounds, fields, and buttons into meaningful stacks, you can determine the precise contours of your Macintosh World. HyperCard provides many tools for the creation of on-screen graphics that may be metaphors of a familiar, noncomputer world, or you can create useful graphics environments that would be impossible without a computer.

With HyperCard you can also establish relationships among numerous collections of information. The powers of linking stacks to one another goes much further than what commercial relational database programs can deliver.

Finally, HyperCard offers the dedicated user the ability to bring his or her information to life. By applying HyperCard scripts to stacks, cards, fields, and buttons, you dictate what operations are to take place with each navigational step through HyperCard. If you've been disappointed that a commercial program does not exist for an information management application you have in mind, there is a good possibility that you can mold HyperCard into that very application.

Access to the fundamental building tools—painting, fields, and buttons—is what we mean by the authoring environment of HyperCard.

Despite the vast powers built into HyperCard, you shouldn't be frightened by them. HyperCard's designers paid special attention to simplifying your access to these powers, even building in a bit of forgiveness here and there to ward off frustration. Still, it may seem that there are many things to learn at first. Just remember that you don't have to learn them all at once. The weekend mechanic more than likely started out as a simple user of the transportation. Only by gradually digging deeper under the hood from one weekend to the next did he learn the impact of various adjustments and maintenance chores.

So, too, you began by using HyperCard in the browsing environment, which we've already covered. Now you'll begin to learn little by little what goes on under the HyperCard hood. By the time you're finished with Part Two of this book, you'll know how to build applications from the many prepared cards and buttons on your HyperCard disks. In Part Three, we'll dig still deeper into the programming tools built into HyperCard, while learning the basics of HyperTalk and scripts. Part Four will be the advanced course for those who can't wait to get dirt under their fingernails while building impressive HyperCard applications.

## *Authoring Scenarios*

There are many reasons why you should actively pursue HyperCard as an authoring system. The three most likely reasons are: building your Macintosh World; creating an easy-to-access information source for colleagues and family members; and developing applications for general consumption.

### YOUR MACINTOSH WORLD

As we mentioned in the Introduction, your Macintosh World consists of not only the kind of information you are likely to store in a computer database but also information you frequently retrieve from outside sources and the documents you create with other Macintosh applications. You should use HyperCard as a way of extending the reaches of your Macintosh World.

Prompted by the Address and Datebook stacks supplied with HyperCard, you will probably begin assembling personal information—names and addresses, your daily schedule—in HyperCard stacks. These are practical and among the most obvious applications for HyperCard. But then start using HyperCard as a quick repository for random thoughts and ideas that shoot into your mind. Instead of reaching for the notepad to jot something down that you hear in a telephone conversation, type it into a stack designed for that purpose.

Also, start thinking of collections of personal information which you need quick access to. Perhaps it's a list of hotels and restaurants in cities you visit, complete with notes that remind you of their high and low points. HyperCard is the place you should store the "mental notes" you always make but tend to forget about after a time. Later, use HyperCard's full text search abilities to track down that thought. Let HyperCard do the remembering, while you make decisions based on the information stored and retrieved. The more you use HyperCard for these kinds of tasks, the more you will find for HyperCard to do. Gradually you may develop "systems," like tickler files, logs of client phone calls, client meeting notes, and so on. Where you have probably failed to start or maintain a paper system in the past, you will have a much greater likelihood of success with its HyperCard equivalent.

## STACKS FOR COLLEAGUES AND FAMILY

You can perform a great service for people you work with, for classmates, or for others in your family with HyperCard. By creating a HyperCard stack that eases their access to information, you may help computerphobes overcome their fears.

A HyperCard stack can be as narrowly focused as needed to accomplish an information storage and retrieval task. Therefore, if you can convert budget figures from a spreadsheet into HyperCard cards, and reduce the chore of accessing the information to a series of mouse clicks. Those who normally shun computers may find your HyperCard stack application to be rewarding—even fun. It may encourage computer use.

In college coursework, an energetic student or professor can create a HyperCard application containing specialized information pertaining to the course or a particular topic. A well-conceived stack of this type, especially with HyperCard's linking and searching capabilities, will likely encourage further exploration through the HyperCard information base, well beyond finding the simple answer to a problem or question.

If you use a Macintosh at home, the family can also benefit from HyperCard applications. The graphical environment is more inviting to storing and searching various inventories. Record collections, books, appliance maintenance schedules, warranty information— these and many other household records are suited for HyperCard archival. And since you, as HyperCard author, are in control of the way the application looks, strive for simplicity and graphic appeal to encourage its use by everyone who is allowed access to the machine.

## GENERAL CONSUMPTION

A logical extension of authoring stacks for yourself and others close to you is designing stacks for distribution as public domain, user-supported, or commercial offerings.

*Public domain* HyperCard stacks will likely be available from most Macintosh user groups. An author of a public domain HyperCard stack essentially shares his or her work with the rest of the HyperCard community, expecting no remuneration in return. This is in the best spirit of the early days of personal computers and is quite popular today for all kinds of software on all popular personal computers. If you've designed a stack that you find useful, you may wish to share it with others by uploading via telephone modem to a Macintosh user group bulletin board or by sending a disk to user groups.

Another category that relies heavily on user groups and bulletin boards is called *user-supported* software. Such offerings are freely distributed to the user community. The author of a user-supported program usually asks users to try the program at no charge. In a HyperCard stack, this request may be on the first card of the stack. The message also states that if the program is useful, the user should send the stated sum (usually a low price compared to commercial products). In return, the user often gets a printed manual, free program updates for a period of time, and telephone support. Authors of user-supported software have met with varying degrees of success with this method of distribution.

A third option for distributing a stack to the computing community is to publish it as a software product, either through an established software publisher or on your own. HyperCard offers many opportunities for nonprogramming Macintosh enthusiasts to get into the software business. Specialized information stacks will appeal to many "vertical markets," which are often best approached by self-publishing. Apple predicts, and rightly so, that HyperCard will spawn a cottage industry of stack publishers. Prior to HyperCard, you had to be almost a programming wizard to produce a Macintosh application. HyperCard raises every dedicated user to wizard status with much less work and frustration.

Remember, too, that you can use HyperCard to create stacks for general consumption that benefit the community. Bill Atkinson (HyperCard's creator) and several colleagues are donating equipment and time to help the Los Gatos, California, Public Library put its entire card catalog into HyperCard. With the help of an optical character reader (OCR), Bill and friends will scan the printed cards and convert them to HyperCard cards. Library patrons will be able to perform full-text searches of the entire card catalog in seconds. Although this application won't be performing many sophisticated button tricks, it will be using HyperCard to its fullest speed-searching capabilities while providing researchers with a way of scouring the entire catalog for needed reference material.

The authoring possibilities of HyperCard are rather extensive, ranging from the most private to the most public. It's all up to you and your inventiveness. As we proceed through the various authoring tools in HyperCard, we hope you will be thinking about potential HyperCard applications in your world.

## *Accessing HyperCard's Authoring Tools*

Back in chapter 1, you saw the User Preferences card of the Home stack and learned that it controls access to various levels of tools. Just as we combined the Browsing and Typing levels into a single browsing environment, so, too, will we combine two more User Levels. This time we join the Painting and Authoring levels into one *authoring* environment. More often than not, you'll want both sets of tools available to you whenever the authoring Muse inspires.

In the browsing environment, you had three pull-down menus available, as shown in Figure 4–1. For the rest of this book, however, you should boost your user level setting all the way to Scripting. You might get by in the next several chapters by setting the level to Authoring, but we'll be sneaking in some preliminary exposure to HyperTalk programming when you're not looking, and the Scripting setting will be necessary.

The menu structure changes when you reach the Painting level. First of all, the File and Edit menus gain several items (Figure 4–2). You also get the Tools menu, as shown on the left of Figure 4–3 (when you choose any of the painting tools, three additional menus— Paint, Options, and Patterns— come into view). At the Authoring level, the Objects menu appears (Figure 4–3, right). These are the menus you'll be using for the remainder of the book. The Scripting level doesn't affect the menus in any way: Its changes are more subtle. Still, set your user level to Scripting now (Figure 4–4). For the time being, ignore the Power Keys and Blind Typing boxes. We'll get to those later.

| File | |
|---|---|
| New Stack... | |
| Open Stack... | ⌘O |
| Save a Copy... | |
| Page Setup... | |
| Print Card | ⌘P |
| Print Stack... | |
| Print Report... | |
| Quit HyperCard | ⌘Q |

| Edit | |
|---|---|
| Undo | ⌘Z |
| Cut | ⌘X |
| Copy | ⌘C |
| Paste | ⌘V |
| Clear | |
| New Card | ⌘N |
| Delete Card | |

| Go | |
|---|---|
| Back | ⌘~ |
| Home | ⌘H |
| Help | ⌘? |
| Recent | ⌘R |
| First | ⌘1 |
| Prev | ⌘2 |
| Next | ⌘3 |
| Last | ⌘4 |
| Find... | ⌘F |
| Message | ⌘M |

*Figure 4-1. HyperCard's browsing environment menus.*

| File | |
|---|---|
| New Stack... | |
| Open Stack... | ⌘O |
| Save a Copy... | |
| Compact Stack | |
| Protect Stack... | |
| Delete Stack... | |
| Page Setup... | |
| Print Card | ⌘P |
| Print Stack... | |
| Print Report... | |
| Quit HyperCard | ⌘Q |

| Edit | |
|---|---|
| Undo | ⌘Z |
| Cut | ⌘X |
| Copy | ⌘C |
| Paste | ⌘V |
| Clear | |
| New Card | ⌘N |
| Delete Card | |
| Cut Card | |
| Copy Card | |
| Text Style... | ⌘T |
| Background | ⌘B |

| Go | |
|---|---|
| Back | ⌘~ |
| Home | ⌘H |
| Help | ⌘? |
| Recent | ⌘R |
| First | ⌘1 |
| Prev | ⌘2 |
| Next | ⌘3 |
| Last | ⌘4 |
| Find... | ⌘F |
| Message | ⌘M |

*Figure 4-2. Two of the three browsing environment menus change when you graduate to the authoring environment.*

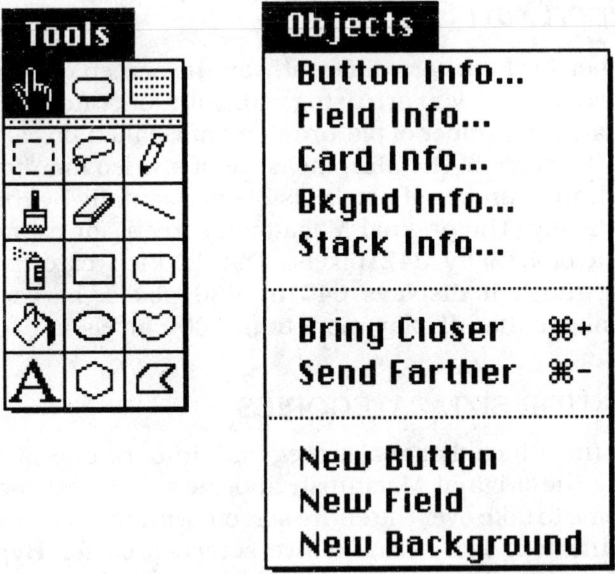


*Figure 4-3. Two more menus, Tools and Objects, also come to life in the authoring environment.*

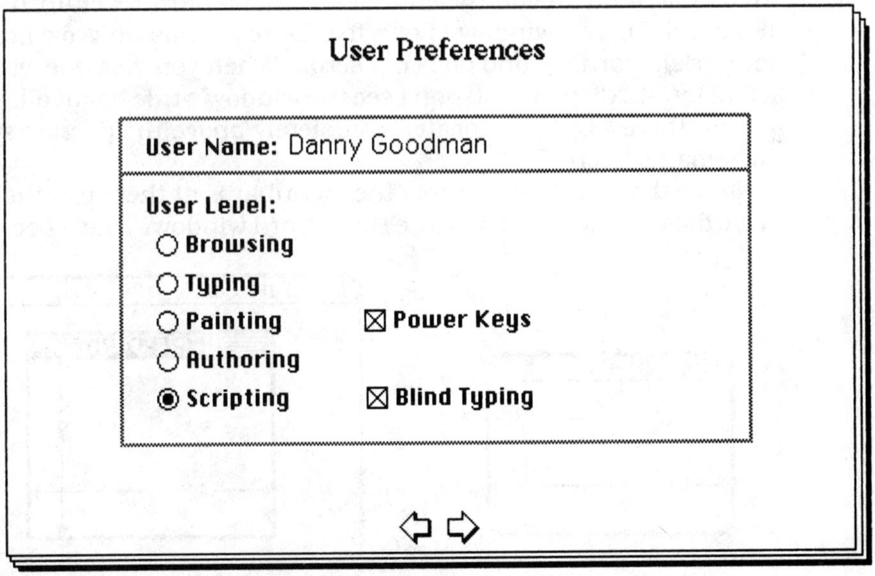

User Preferences

User Name: Danny Goodman

User Level:
- ○ Browsing
- ○ Typing
- ○ Painting ☒ Power Keys
- ○ Authoring
- ◉ Scripting ☒ Blind Typing

*Figure 4-4. Setting the user level to Scripting*

## The HyperCard Screen

HyperCard appears differently on the screen depending on the size of video monitor you are using with your Macintosh. By monitor size, we mean the number of picture elements, called *pixels*, or dots, that show on the screen. The pixel measure of a video monitor is usually stated with the number of pixels visible horizontally by the number of pixels vertically. The original Macintosh screen, for example, has a display area of 512 by 342 pixels. The 12-inch external monitor for the Macintosh II displays 640 by 480 pixels. Larger screens are also available that display more than 1000 pixels in each dimension.

### TWO MONITOR SIZE CATEGORIES

On the 9-inch diagonal screen built into the one-piece style Macintosh (like the original Macintosh and its direct descendants), HyperCard seems to take over the entire screen, with the exception of the menubar at the top. The actual active screen area for HyperCard, however, extends underneath the menubar to the full 512 by 342 pixel display area. This allows HyperCard applications to hide the menubar from view, if desired, and take over the whole viewing area of the 9-inch screen.

On larger screens, you will notice that the active HyperCard screen area is actually inside the confines of a standard Macintosh window (Figure 4–5). The window is of a fixed size— it has no grow box at the lower right corner— and does not scroll. When you view the window on a 512 by 342 display, you don't see the window's title bar at all. The title bar is "there," but it is located completely above the display space on the small screen.

Notice that on large screens, the menubar is at the top of the screen, regardless of the location of the HyperCard window. That's because the

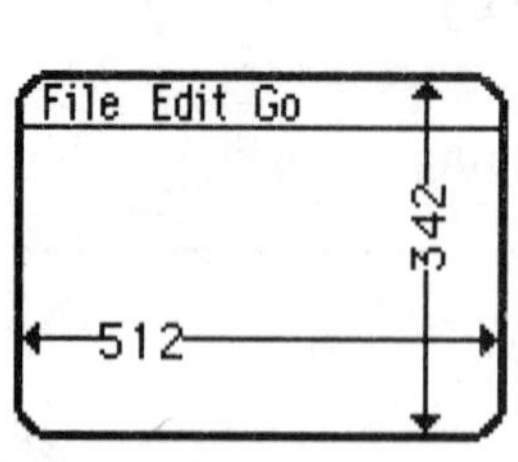


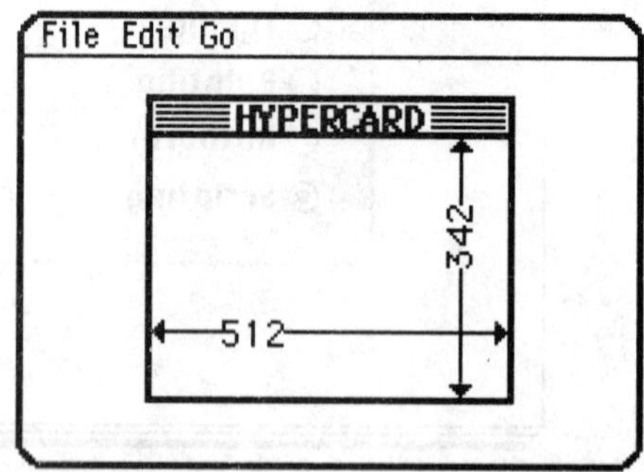


*Figure 4–5. The HyperCard screen takes up the full 512 x 342 pixels of the 9-inch Macintosh screen, but it is really a 512 x 342 window, as seen on larger Macintosh monitors.*

programmer's toolbox inside the Macintosh automatically places menus across the top of the screen. This may help you better visualize what is happening on the 9-inch screen when menus seem to overlap the very top of the HyperCard active screen area. The menubar belongs to a top layer on the screen that does not interact with the HyperCard window's content in any way.

As a HyperCard author, especially if your stacks will be distributed to other Macintosh users using a variety of screens, you should be very aware of the two ways HyperCard displays its content on both the 9-inch monitor and larger monitors. For example, if you design a stack using a big screen monitor and place important information, such as a field or button, near the very top of the HyperCard window, another user with a 9-inch screen may have part of that information obscured by the menubar. As a rule, you are safer designing stacks for the smaller displays, because they are the predominant style in circulation,and should be so for several years to come.

## *HyperCard Menu Types*

While authoring a stack, you will make heavy use of the standard HyperCard menus. Most of the menus contain commands that assist you in building your application. We'll gradually cover the commands in detail as we begin building sample applications later in the book.

### STANDARD MENUS

Most of the menus in the menubar behave just like menus you've encountered in other Macintosh applications. A number of choices in the menus are available from the keyboard by pressing the Command key and a character key (Figure 4-6). You don't have to learn the keyboard shortcuts right away. As you start using HyperCard more frequently, you will notice certain commands that you use often. If these commands have keyboard equivalents, try performing the commands from the keyboard when you remember to do so. Slowly, you'll find keyboard commands to be practical shortcuts, particularly if you are in the middle of a lot of keyboard work.

### TEAR-OFF PALETTES

HyperCard also introduces a new kind of menu to the Macintosh repertoire of user interface issues: the *tear-off palette.* Two HyperCard menus, Tools and Patterns, are of this new type. To begin with, these menus pull down like other menus, except that they reveal choices of

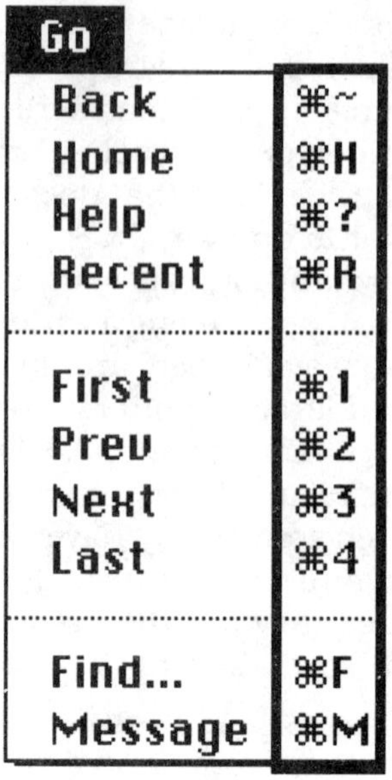

| Go | |
|---|---|
| Back | ⌘~ |
| Home | ⌘H |
| Help | ⌘? |
| Recent | ⌘R |
| First | ⌘1 |
| Prev | ⌘2 |
| Next | ⌘3 |
| Last | ⌘4 |
| Find... | ⌘F |
| Message | ⌘M |

*Figure 4-6. Many menu commands may be activated by typing the Command-key equivalent listed in the menu.*

graphics items instead of text items. You pull down the palette from the menubar, make your selection, and release the mouse button to remove the menu from the screen. But since you are likely to make frequent selections of tools and patterns while authoring, HyperCard lets you "tear off" the palettes from the menubar and drag them as free-standing windows anywhere on the screen where it's convenient. To do this, simply pull down the menu as usual, but then drag the mouse pointer completely off the palette that dropped down from the menubar. As you drag the pointer, you will see an outline of the palette follow the cursor (Figure 4-7). When the outline is in a suitable location, release the mouse button. The palette will shift from below the menubar to that new location (Figure 4-8).

Tear-off palettes turn into small windows when they are detached from the menubar. To remove palettes from the screen, just click the mouse pointer in the close box on the window's title bar (Figure 4-9).

If one or both palettes is already detached from the menubar and you reach for the palettes from the menubar, HyperCard will oblige, showing you both the menubar and detached palettes at once (although you won't be able to tear off two copies of the same menu). Use the palette that is most natural at any given moment.

Next we examine key HyperCard components from the author's perspective.

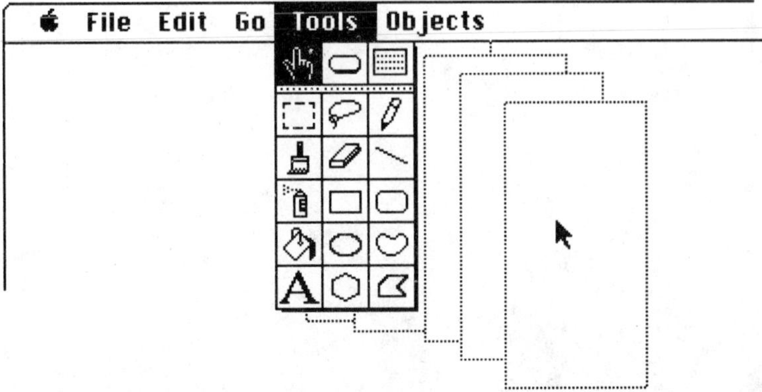


*Figure 4-7. Drag the menu away from the menubar, and an outline of the palette follows the cursor.*

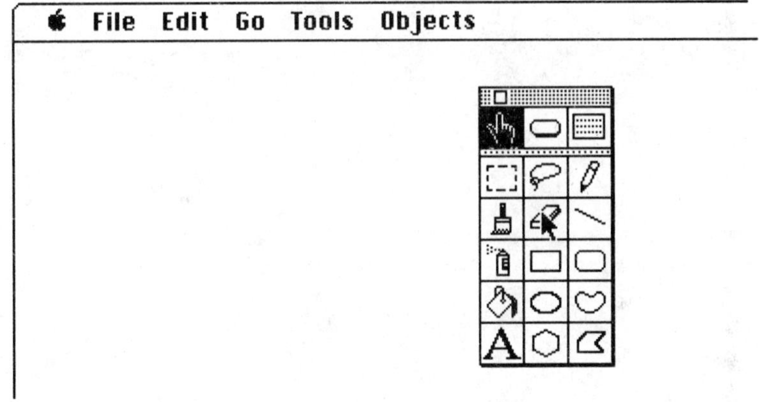


*Figure 4-8. The free-standing palette may be moved around the screen to a convenient place for frequent tool selection.*

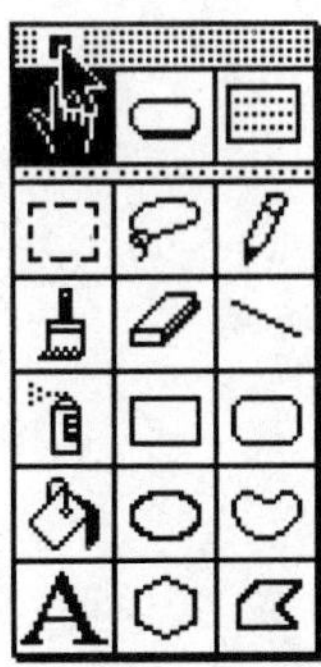

*Figure 4-9. Click on the close box to remove the Tools palette from the screen.*

CHAPTER 5

# All About Stacks

IN CHAPTER 1, WE DESCRIBED THE BASIC PROPERTIES OF A HYPERCARD STACK FROM the browser's point of view. But we must spend more time discussing the stack concept now, because your perception of stacks changes when you are the author. This is true also for the other basic elements of HyperCard: backgrounds, cards, fields, and buttons.

Rest assured that your time in the first chapter was well spent. A HyperCard author must be aware of the browser's point of view for all HyperCard elements when developing new stacks— especially if the stacks will ultimately be used by other people. It's just like a writer who must also be a reader of his own work. While practicing the craft of transferring ideas into words on paper (or screen), the writer also takes the reader's point of view, questioning each phrase: "Is this stating the idea clearly enough for the reader to understand?" or "Am I conveying the desired emotions to the reader?" Consequently, as we begin our look at the basic HyperCard elements from the author's perspective, we'll also remind you from time to time about the browser— your audience.

## *Two Stack Types*

Our first stop is the HyperCard stack. While we've seen that, technically speaking, a HyperCard stack is a single collection of information, the way you design that collection will vary, depending on the way you present information in the stack. The two methodologies are what we call *homogeneous* and *heterogeneous.*

## THE HOMOGENEOUS STACK

Probably the most common type of stack you will create at first falls into the homogeneous category. As the term implies, a homogeneous stack consists of a single entity. In the HyperCard environment, that means that the stack has one card background that pervades the entire stack or system.

Perhaps the best example of a homogeneous stack is the Address stack provided with HyperCard. As you flip from the first to last cards, the background "look" remains the same. Only the information you store on each card changes.

This homogeneity closely resembles the kinds of "stacks" we're accustomed to in the noncomputer world. The physical name and address book or the daily desk calendar have the same background look to each card or sheet, no matter how large the collection. Only the information that is specific to a card or sheet— a phone number or the date— changes.

A homogeneous stack is most often created and saved on the disk as a single HyperCard stack file. This is not a prerequisite by any means. For example, you may have a very large homogeneous collection that ends up being too large for distribution on a single floppy disk. If that's the case, you will have to break up the collection into smaller files strictly for ease of distribution, even though the backgrounds of all component files are identical.

Another reason to divide a homogeneous stack is for the sake of modularity in design. The HyperCard on-line help system is an example. Even though the backgrounds of the Help and Help Index stacks are the same, the system is divided into two stack files. To the browser, however, the help system appears as a single unit. The division between stack files is completely *transparent* to the browser.

The bottom line, then, is that a homogeneous stack appears to the browser as a single stack with a single background, regardless of its underlying stack and file structure.

## THE HETEROGENEOUS STACK

A feature of HyperCard that is potentially of great importance to an author is its ability to combine multiple backgrounds into a single stack. There aren't many examples of this in the noncomputer information world (which tends to be homogeneous). But consider a textbook that consists of many pages of textual information and a section that consists of color photographs. While the text is printed on a thin paper in black only, the photographs are printed in four colors on a glossy paper. The "backgrounds" here (thin paper and thick glossy paper) are combined in a single collection (the book). Moreover, the kind of information presented on each background type is quite different. The presentation is a mixed one, heterogeneous in nature.

A heterogeneous stack is perhaps best characterized as being more than a simple information collection. Rather, it is an environment consisting of two or more card backgrounds. Typically, the information stored on multiple backgrounds in such an environment is interrelated. For example, you may design one background that best conveys the feeling of a table of contents. A second background you designed for the stack contains the actual information cards. Clicking on a button next to a table of contents item calls up one of the information cards (Figure 5-1); a click on a Contents button located on an information card brings you back to the table of contents. The browser has a sense of a single information environment, yet in HyperCard terms, the collection is a heterogeneous one.

HyperCard stacks can be quite heterogeneous. There is virtually no limit to the number of backgrounds you can design into a stack.

One of the decisions you will have to make when designing a HyperCard stack that requires more than one background is whether the information collection is better served by being divided into multiple

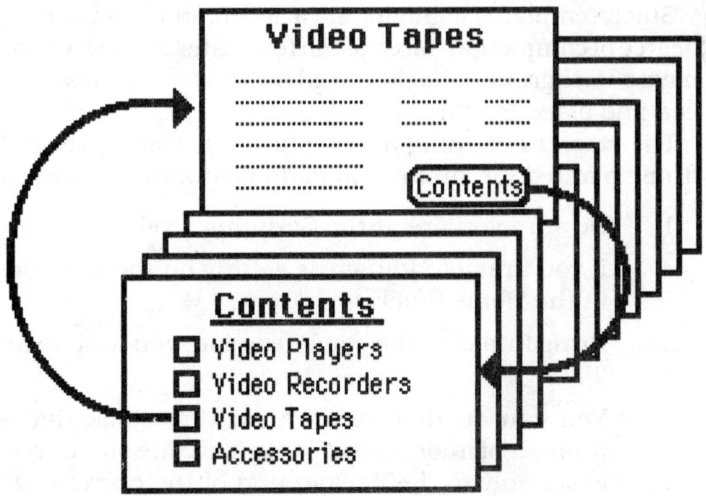


*Figure 5-1. A heterogeneous stack contains two or more backgrounds built into a single stack file. Buttons link cards in the different backgrounds.*

homogeneous stacks (that is, separate stack files) or a single heterogeneous stack. If you plan to distribute the environment to others—especially via an electronic medium such as a user group bulletin board—a single, heterogeneous stack makes the most sense. Conversely, if one or more of the stack backgrounds you supply may grow to a large collection (such as a name and address background), it may become a disk management burden to lump so many potentially large stacks into one disk file. You should do your best to anticipate the way you and your stack users will work with your stack over time and choose the optimum stack strategy accordingly.

## *Making a New Stack*

The prospect of creating a new stack may be a terrifying one the first time out. Fortunately, Apple softens the blow for your early experimentation by providing you with a number of predesigned stacks, which you can borrow directly.

What makes this kind of new stack so simple is the way HyperCard generally creates a new stack. It assumes that for most of the new stacks you will create—especially when you need one in a hurry—you will use either an existing stack or a stack template of some kind as a starting point. HyperCard comes with several such templates on the disk that contains art, card, and stack ideas. Additionally, HyperCard experts will surely be placing their templates into the public domain via user groups and electronic bulletin boards.

Stack templates come in all varieties, in terms of content as well as degree of completion. Most of the templates in the HyperCard ideas disk have a background, background buttons, and background fields. This is a fine place to start.

The steps in creating a new stack—at least getting the foundation firmly planted for later editing and customizing—are simple and few:

1. Be sure you are at the Scripting level.

   If you are not, adjust the setting on the User Preferences card in the Home Stack.

2. Bring into view the stack template you wish to adopt (Figure 5-2).

   You can do this from an existing stack that already has a number of information cards in it. The stack creation operation looks only to the background of the current card. HyperCard won't disturb the existing stack or its information in any way.

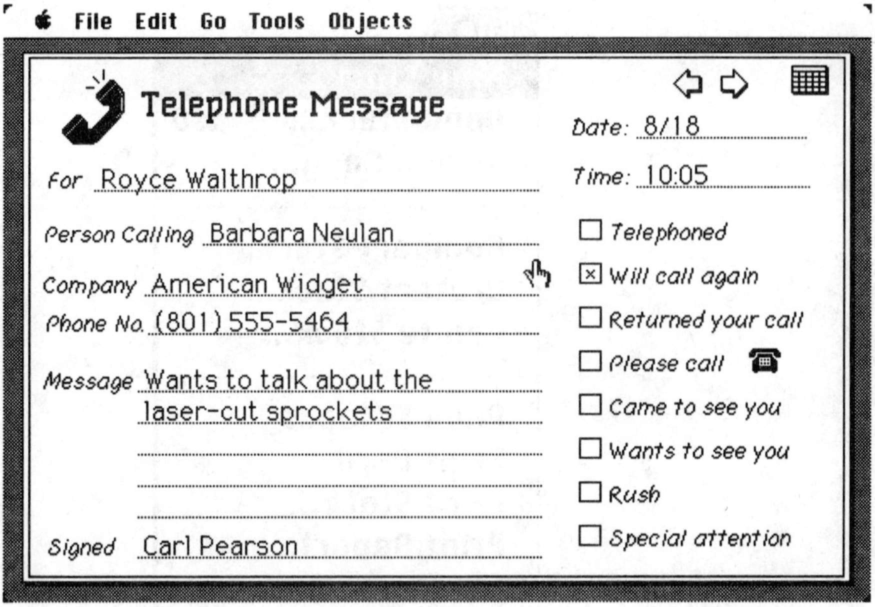

*Figure 5-2. To make a new stack from a template, first bring the template card into view.*

3. Pull down the File menu and choose New Stack... (Figure 5-3).

   A standard file dialog box appears on the screen, requesting a name for the stack you are about to create (Figure 5-4). Unless you have performed some file manipulation previously in this HyperCard session, the dialog box will indicate that the stack you are about to create will be saved in the same disk and folder as your Home Stack. It also offers a choice of whether you want to copy the current background or start from scratch. For now, copy the current background.

4. Type in a name for the stack and press the Return key.

   This action creates the stack file on the disk for your new stack. Unlike many other Macintosh applications, HyperCard creates the disk file when you start a new document so that it can automatically save any changes you make to it. HyperCard automatically saves your work, most of the time when you don't even realize it.

That's all there is to creating a new stack. You may not notice anything different on the screen than what you saw when looking at the template, unless the template had sample text typed into its fields.

*Figure 5-3. Choose New Stack from the File menu.*

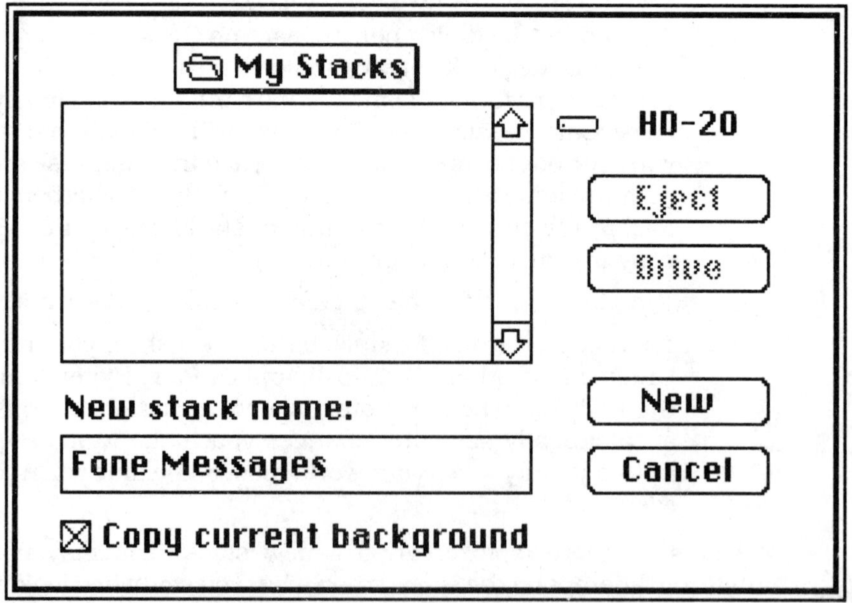


*Figure 5-4. Type in a name for the new stack you are creating.*

Such text does not go into the new stack. To prove to yourself that you are looking at your new stack, you can check the Stack Info... dialog box. To do this, pull down the Objects menu and choose Stack Info... (Figure 5–5).

This dialog box displays all relevant information about the stack you just created (Figure 5–6). First, it shows the stack name and the folder

*Figure 5–5. Choose Stack Info... from the Objects menu to see the Stack Info dialog box.*

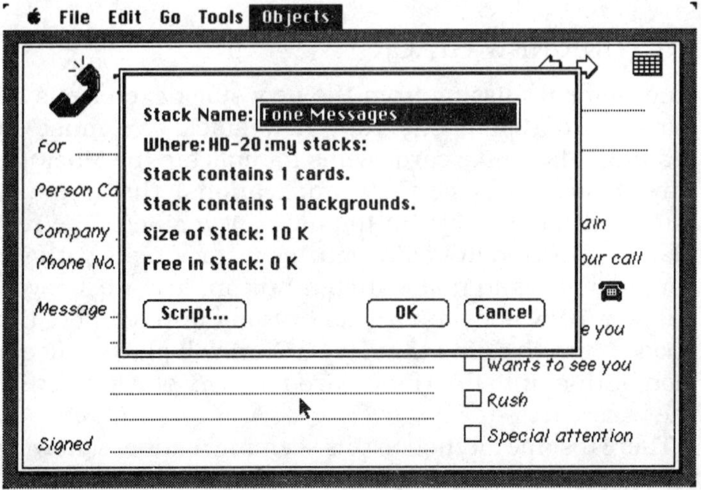


*Figure 5–6. The Stack Info dialog box reveals data about the stack's backgrounds, cards, name, and stack size on the disk.*

pathway to that file. Next, it details the number of backgrounds and cards in the stack. In a brand new stack, both numbers will be one. This dialog box can be very helpful when you begin designing complex stacks, particularly heterogeneous stacks, by giving you a peek inside the structure of the stack. You can summon the Stack Info dialog box any time you are in the stack whose "insides" you wish to inspect, including the Home Stack. To get used to the information that comes in this dialog box, open a few stacks already on your HyperCard disk and choose Stack Info... from the Objects menu.

Also in the dialog box is a button labeled Script... (if you had set the user level to Authoring instead of Scripting, this button would have been dimmed, denying you access to the script). You can inspect stack scripts this way on any stack you encounter. Until we have more to say about HyperTalk, however, "look but don't touch" the scripts in these dialog boxes.

## WORKING WITH YOUR NEW STACK

If the design of the stack you just cloned suits your needs, then you can begin entering information into its text fields right away. Use the techniques you learned earlier as a browser to add new cards and enter text into the fields. You may reduce the user level to Typing, if you prefer.

Regardless of the user level selected, you also have available to you menu navigation commands in the Go menu. The most important to remember, perhaps, is the Home command, particularly if your new stack does not have a button that brings you to the Home card.

## OPENING YOUR NEW STACK

One element missing from the new stack exercise is a button on the Home card that opens your new stack. We must emphasize that although the Home card seems to replicate the Macintosh Finder as a way to access HyperCard applications, the Home card does not automatically receive buttons to a new stack. The responsibility for placing a button linked to your new stack rests with you. There are a couple of ways to make such a button, and we'll cover them later in chapter 10, when we discuss buttons in more detail. It's easy to get spoiled into thinking that HyperCard will place a nice button, like an icon button, into the Home card for every stack we create. Such is not the case.

There is some method to this seeming madness, however. If the Home card were to display icons or buttons for every stack on your disk, the card would lose its simplicity. Moreover, you would be forced to look at buttons for stacks that don't need them. For example, the HyperCard help system consists of three stack files. It's much better to have only one icon button to summon help, and then let the help system drive us around to the various stack files as needed. As you develop more of your own stacks, you will find many cases in which a button to a stack belongs only inside another stack, and not at the Home card level.

Endeavor to keep your Home stack as simple as possible. Put only essential buttons on it. The result will be a much less confusing environment in which to grow.

## *Protecting a Stack*

As a HyperCard stack author, you may have reason to prevent your users from modifying, deleting, or inspecting the scripts of your stacks. HyperCard provides many ways of locking out users from the insides of your stacks if you feel it necessary to make those restrictions. For example, in an application set up as a HyperCard stack running continually in an open environment, like a library or self-service counter, you will probably want to prevent users from deleting or entering information. Such a stack should be limited to "read-only" status. Or you may wish to limit access to browsing and entering information, but prevent access to authoring and scripting tools. All of this can be controlled via the Protect Stack... menu choice in the File menu.

The Protect Stack dialog box (Figure 5-7) first lets you determine whether the entire stack (that is, the current stack you are in) can be

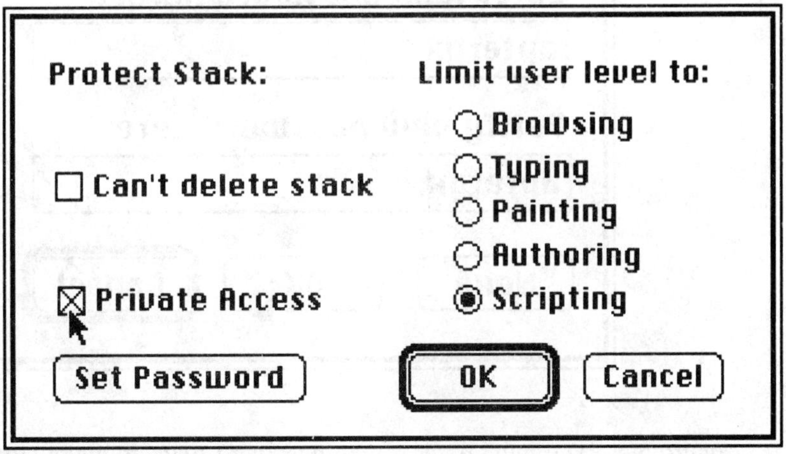

Protect Stack:
Can't delete stack
Private Access
Set Password

Limit user level to:
Browsing
Typing
Painting
Authoring
Scripting
OK
Cancel

*Figure 5-7. Protect Stack dialog box*

deleted. If this item is checked, a small dialog box reminder appears whenever the user tries to delete the stack.

You may also set the user level for the current stack by clicking one of the five radio buttons next to the list of levels. This setting will not affect the user level setting on other stacks. If you are regularly at the Scripting level, for instance, and open a stack set to the Typing level, the user level changes only while you are in that stack. The instant you leave that stack, the user level as set in the Home Stack's Preferences card takes over.

An important feature to remember is that when you set a stack's user level to Browsing or Typing, the Protect Stack... menu entry does not appear in the File menu. That would seem to leave you without any way of getting back to the Protect Stack dialog box to make adjustments you might need. The trick, however, is to hold down the Command key and then pull down the File menu. You'll see the full File menu, complete with Protect Stack.

If you set the modify, delete, or user level buttons in the Protect Stack dialog box, chances are that you don't want the user to be able to get to this box and make changes on his own. To prevent access to the dialog box, you can password-protect it. Click on the Set Password button in the Protect Stack dialog box. This brings up another dialog box requesting you to type the password of your choosing twice (Figure 5-8). It asks for two entries of the password to make sure you don't mistype it accidentally. Passwords are case insensitive, which means

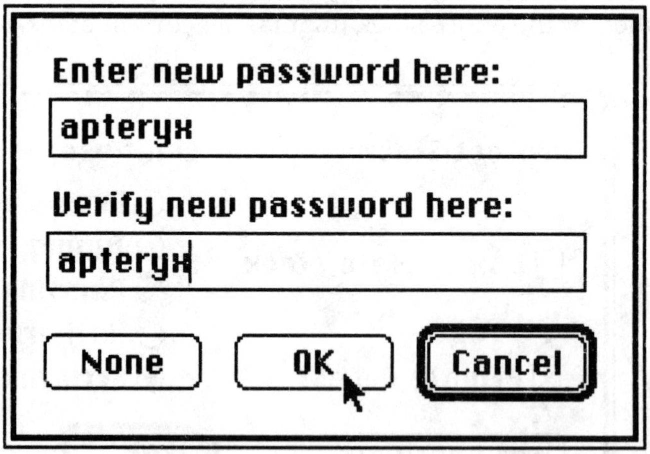

*Figure 5-8. You must enter a new password twice to make sure you type it correctly.*

that HyperCard does not distinguish between uppercase and lowercase letters. Therefore, the passwords "Webster," "WEBSTER," and "webSTer" are identical in HyperCard's eyes. You may change your password as often as you like by clicking the Set Password button in the Protect Stack dialog box again. Once you click the password box's OK button, you will no longer be granted access to the Protect Stack dialog box unless you type in the password (Figure 5–9).

IMPORTANT: DO NOT FORGET YOUR PASSWORD UNDER ANY CIRCUMSTANCES. IT IS THE ONLY KEY TO THE LOCK. EVEN BILL ATKINSON CAN'T HELP YOU RECOVER YOUR PASSWORD. STORE AN UNLOCKED COPY OF A VALUABLE STACK ON A FLOPPY DISK BEFORE PASSWORD-PROTECTING THE ORIGINAL.

## LIMITING ACCESS TO THE STACK

HyperCard provides a way of preventing casual browsers from accessing a stack you wish to keep private (although a network-oriented privacy setup will be available in a future release of HyperCard). Here's how it works.

In the Protect Stack dialog box is a check box labeled Private Access. When you check this setting, you don't immediately protect the current stack from access by others. This privacy level works only the first time you try to open the stack in a new HyperCard session (that is, after start-up from the Finder). When opening the stack for the first time, the password request dialog box asks for the password (the same password you set to limit access to the Protect Stack dialog box). Once you type in the correct password, however, you will not be asked again the next time you open the stack during the session. HyperCard, in essence, remembers the last password you type into the password request dialog box and applies it to the Private Access system. Note that this does not apply to accessing the Protect Stack dialog box: That is always password-protected if a password is in effect.

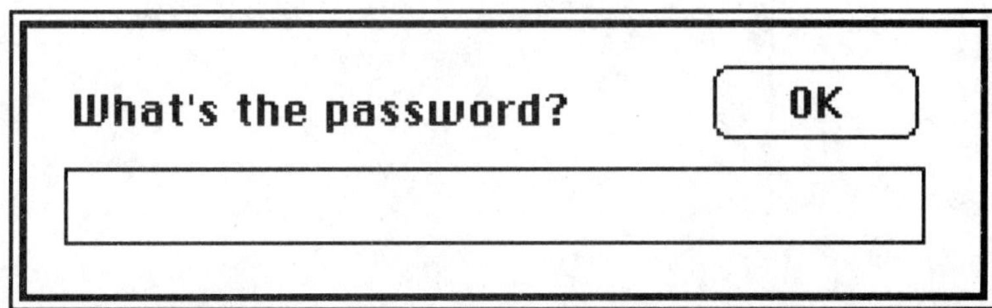


*Figure 5–9. Protected stacks request a password before allowing access to the Protect Stack dialog box.*

The reasoning behind this password remembrance scheme is that once you have successfully accessed a protected stack, you won't want to be prompted for a password each time you Go Back to or need a quick browse through that stack. In that situation, the Private Access system would be more of an impediment than a help.

To try out the Private Access feature, click the Private Access checkbox and set a password. Quit HyperCard. Then restart HyperCard and try opening the stack. You'll be prompted for the password. Once you type it in, you'll be given free access to the stack until the next time you quit HyperCard.

## FURTHER PROTECTION

HyperCard offers one more rather powerful means of protecting a stack, although it requires knowledge of HyperTalk programming to get it going. By way of HyperTalk scripts, a HyperCard author can intercept any or all menu commands that a user might invoke. By carefully filtering out menu commands, an author may allow users to add new cards but prevent them from deleting existing cards (intercepting the Delete Card menu option). Similarly, the author may allow the printing of individual cards but prevent printing the entire stack or a report of the stack's contents (intercepting Print Stack and Print Report).

We'll have more to say about how to protect stacks in this manner in Part Three.

# CHAPTER 6

# All About Layers

PERHAPS THE MOST DIFFICULT CONCEPT A HYPERCARD AUTHOR MUST MASTER IS THE layering of HyperCard elements. The problem may stem from the usual way we see layers in the real world: from the side, like strata in geological layers or the moist tiers of a seven-layer chocolate cake. In HyperCard, however, we see the layers not from the side, but from above, looking *through* the layers.

A HyperCard browser, who knows nothing about authoring HyperCard stacks, is never conscious of the layering process that has gone into the design of the stacks he uses. But as a stack author, you must be intimately familiar with layering. We'll start by explaining the two layering worlds of HyperCard: object layers and background-and-card layers.

## *Object Layers*

Each HyperCard element— called an object— is applied in its own layer. If the object is transparent ("see-through"), then we can see through it to layers beneath it; if the object is opaque (solid), like a familiar-looking clickable button, then that opaque object obscures our view of objects directly beneath it all the way down to "bedrock."

One way to visualize HyperCard's object layers is to make believe that even the smallest HyperCard object is drawn on a full-screen-size sheet of crystal clear plastic. (If you've been exposed to the preparation of advertising artwork or cartoon animation, think of each layer as an acetate sheet.) Each object you add to the stack– a button or text field– adds one more sheet to the top of the pile (Figure 6–1). Whatever object you designate as opaque will be visible through all the layers; if the object covers only a tiny portion of the screen, the rest of the clear plastic sheet will let other opaque objects below it be seen. If you apply another opaque object atop the previous one, then the object lower in the pile will be hidden from view (Figure 6–2).

Transparent objects may be harder to conceptualize, but fortunately their transparency is primarily for the benefit of the browser. The author can "see" where transparent objects are located while creating

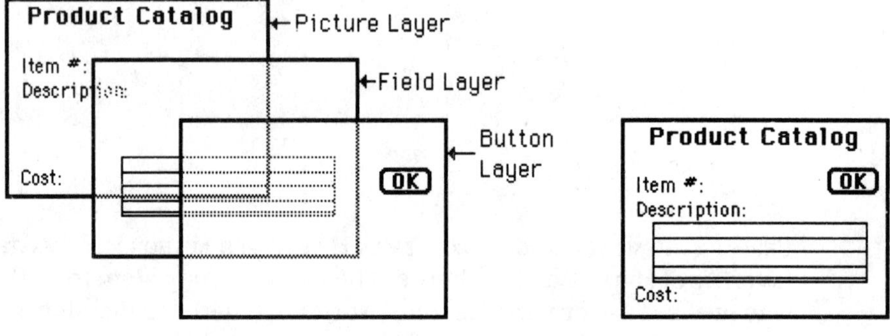


*Figure 6–1. Each object resides in its own layer.*

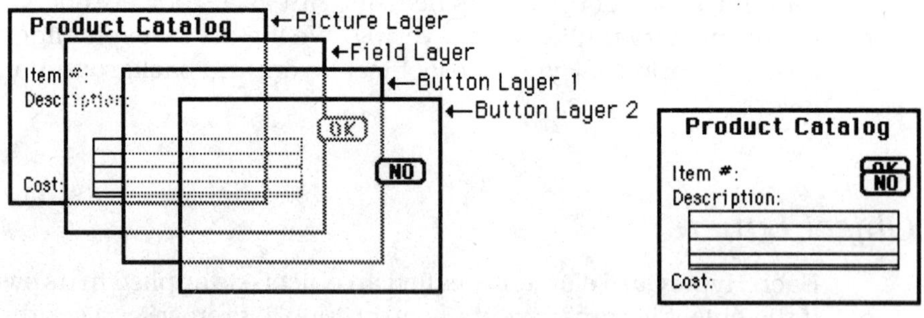


*Figure 6–2. What the browser sees. An opaque object in a layer closer to the viewer (the No button, above) obscures an object in a layer farther away from the viewer (the OK button).*

and modifying a stack. Nevertheless, a transparent object allows opaque objects beneath it to show through, even though the property of the transparent object— like a text field's ability to accept typed text— is on top.

This brings up an important distinction between an object's visible properties and its action properties. As examples of action properties, text fields accept and display text; buttons react to the click of the mouse button when the cursor is on the button. These action properties are independent of their visual properties. A button, for example, reacts to a mouse click whether it is transparent or opaque.

If an opaque button is beneath a transparent button, the topmost button— the transparent one— is the one that recognizes the click of the mouse. It's not the number of layers atop a button that prevents it from recognizing a mouse click, it's whether any other object (transparent or opaque) lies between it and the cursor (the cursor is the topmost object without fail). Therefore, a button could be situated near the bottom of a 50-layer card, and it will react to the click of the mouse button provided no other object is in its way; the button essentially looks upward through all the clear plastic sheets to see the cursor.

## *Background-and-Card Layers*

In addition to the principles of object layers just discussed, a HyperCard author must also recognize the difference between objects in the background and card (foreground) domains. Everything that you assign to the background domain will be visible and active on every card of a homogeneous stack. In other words, graphics, text, buttons, and text fields that go into a background design appear to be copied onto every card you or the browser creates in that stack. We refer to objects assigned to the background domain as "background" objects, such as background buttons and background fields.

You can, however, also assign graphics, text, buttons, and text fields to a specific card. These objects are assigned to the card domain. In keeping with the clear overlay paradigm established earlier, all objects in the card domain rest on top of background objects (that is, closer to the browser's eye). You might call card objects "foreground" objects, but it's better to remember that they are part of a single card. Therefore, if you assign an opaque button to one card, it will be visible and active only on that one card. We refer to such objects as "card" objects: card buttons and card fields.

As you'll learn in a later chapter, you can use HyperCard's layering abilities to your advantage to simplify card and stack design. As a hint of what's to come, imagine you have assigned a background button to perform a task when the user clicks on it. It may be that you don't want the user to access that button on a particular card— maybe you don't want to encourage the user to proceed to the next card in the stack from the last card. On the last card in the stack, you could assign an opaque card button that has no action written for it. The button's card-domain opacity covers up the background-domain button that brings up the next card. Moreover, the empty script for the card-level button assures that HyperCard won't do anything if the user unexpectedly clicks the mouse button with the cursor on that card button. The net result is that you don't have to worry about assigning individual "next card" buttons to every card but the last one; just place the button in the background and cover it up on cards that don't require the action.

## *What the Browser Sees*

Now we'll take what we've learned about layering to see how the browser sees various pieces of the layering puzzle. In the next few chapters, we'll have more to say about the specific objects we'll be showing here. For now, study the layering construction.

To demonstrate the effects of additional layers, we'll graphically show an exploded view of the layers as well as a head-on view as if looking at the screen. We'll use the building of a simple name and address HyperCard stack as an example.

### STARTING IN THE BACKGROUND PICTURE

First we start with a background picture, the "bedrock" of any card. The background picture is the lowest possible layer (Figure 6-3). Here, we'll put the picture of a rolodex-type card and a grey fill pattern around the

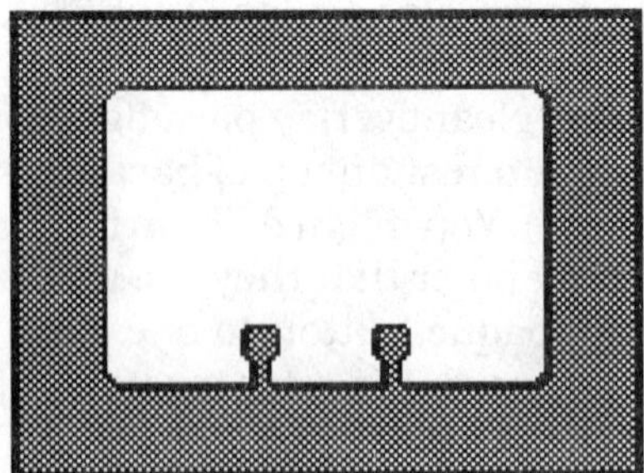

*Figure 6-3. The background graphics layer is the "bedrock" of what a viewer sees as a card.*

*Figure 6-4. You can add any kind of graphic to the background, including art that underlies a transparent button, like the Home button art added here.*

card. Since the card and grey fill pattern are on the background layer (indeed, they *are* the background, as you'll see later), they are actually all on the same layer.

We can add any kind of artistic element to the background (see chapters 12-16), including art that simulates a button. Note that we're talking about the button art, not the actual button object. For the sake of demonstration, let's say that we want to add a custom piece of art that will serve as the art for a button that will take us back to the Home card. Using HyperCard's painting tools (or perhaps by cutting and pasting art from another HyperCard card, MacPaint document, or other Macintosh source), we can add a house painting to the background (Figure 6-4). This house is on the same layer as the rolodex-type card and grey fill pattern, because we are adding the art to the actual background picture.

## BACKGROUND BUTTON LAYERS

Next we can add the background buttons that we want on every card (there is no prescribed order for adding background or card objects: They may be added or modified at any time, even after a stack has been used for some time). For this kind of stack, we'll just put two buttons that help us navigate to the previous and next cards in the stack.

For these buttons, we'll use some special buttons that come with HyperCard. These buttons, called icon buttons, already have art attached to them and scripts that perform the actions we need. Following HyperCard design conventions, the button art for previous and next card actions are left- and right-facing buttons respectively. We copy and paste them into the bottom corners of the card (Figure 6-5).

You can create only one button at a time. When you create a button, it establishes itself in its own layer. Therefore, even though we're creating these two icon buttons right after each other, the first one we

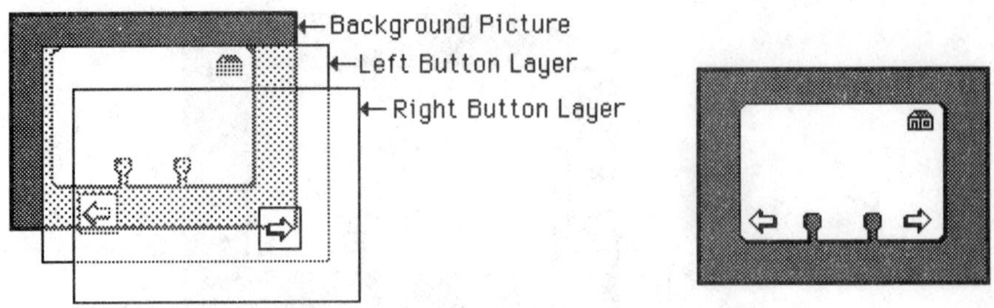


*Figure 6-5. Each object is its own layer, which is like a transparent acetate sheet laid atop the background. Here, two buttons are added to the card's background domain.*

create is in one object layer below the second one. To the browser, however, these two buttons look like ordinary buttons that happen to appear on every card in this stack.

## BACKGROUND TEXT FIELD LAYERS

Next we add a text field to the background to eventually hold the name and phone number (Figure 6-6). Although we're bunching all the information into one text field for simplicity of demonstration, we could also divide the information into multiple text fields. As you become more accustomed to designing HyperCard stacks, you'll be able to quickly determine whether many single-line fields or one or more multiple-line fields better suit your stack design. The text field layer is

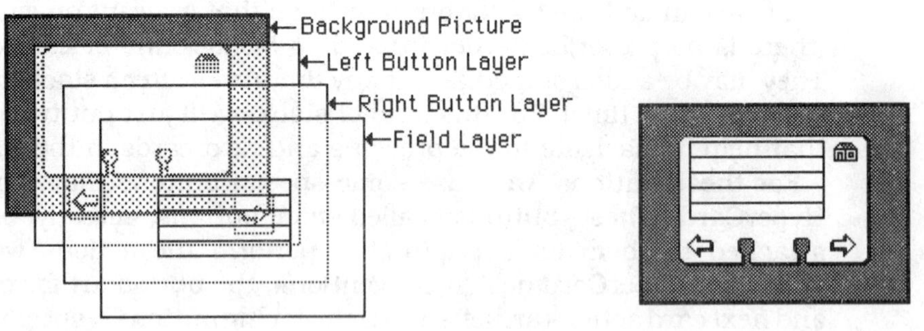


*Figure 6-6. A field object layer is added here atop the buttons. As long as the field does not cover the buttons, the buttons will be visible to the viewer.*

the last of our background layers. This is the blank card that the browser will see when he calls for a new card from the Edit menu.

In Chapter 2, we covered how text information typed into a background text field "belongs" to the card in which it was typed, even though the field is in a background layer. With each new card, the browser gets a new blank field with font and other attributes established when it was assigned to the background layer. The text becomes part of the card layer— a very special relationship between a background object (text field) and a card-level object (the card itself) that we'll examine later.

## CARD LAYERS

It is also possible to add graphics, text fields, and buttons to the card domain. They heap atop the object pile, but "belong" to the one card to which they are added. Let's see how that affects the name and address stack we've watched grow so far.

Let's say we want to add a button to Tom's card. We'll later train that button to jump to another stack that contains a map to Tom's house. This calls for a card button, since we have a map only for Tom's house, and it's not likely we'll add too many more maps for people in this name and address stack (if nearly everyone had a map, it would be more efficient to add such a button to the background and cover it up on cards that don't need it).

When we add the button, we must be careful to place it on the card so that it does not obscure the background buttons or background field (Figure 6-7). To the browser, the card looks like all the others in the

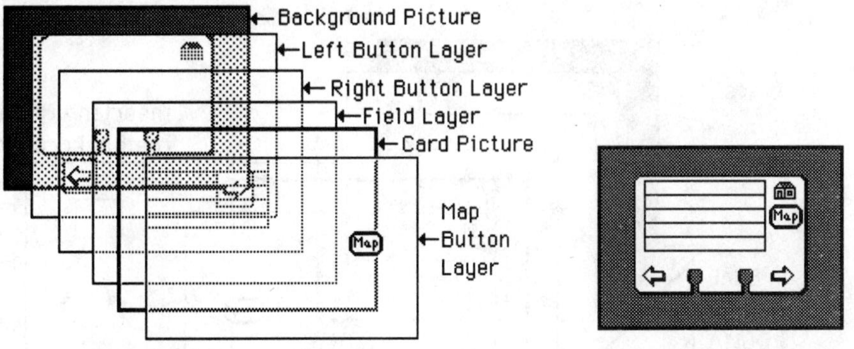


*Figure 6-7. All cards have a card picture layer (the nearer heavy-outlined card above), which may or may not contain graphics. Object layers may also reside in the card domain, like the Map button above. No other card in the stack will have that button.*

stack, but with one extra button. The browser, unaware of the background and card layering, sees all buttons as if they were on one level.

We could go back at any time and modify a layer or add a layer as the application requires. If we wanted to add another background button, we would instruct HyperCard that we wish to work in the background. HyperCard obliges by temporarily hiding all card-level objects. The new button we add would go on top of the background domain, but beneath the card domain, no matter how many background objects we insert (Figure 6–8).

Similarly, we can add graphics or objects to the card level. For instance, if we had a small MacPaint sketch of Mary's face, we could paste it into her card. This graphic is considered card-domain information, just like the text typed into the text field blank on the card. Therefore, the graphic "belongs" to the card— it is part of the card object.

## *Layers and Heterogeneous Stacks*

We've come to know, now, that in a homogeneous stack, all the background objects are in a sense grouped together and remain in view at all times. A card and its objects are also grouped together. When you view a card, therefore, the card's information and objects essentially overlay the background. Flipping through a stack simply overlays each card's information atop the static background.

The principles are the same in a heterogeneous stack, but the stack's multiple backgrounds throw a little twist into the story. Recall that a

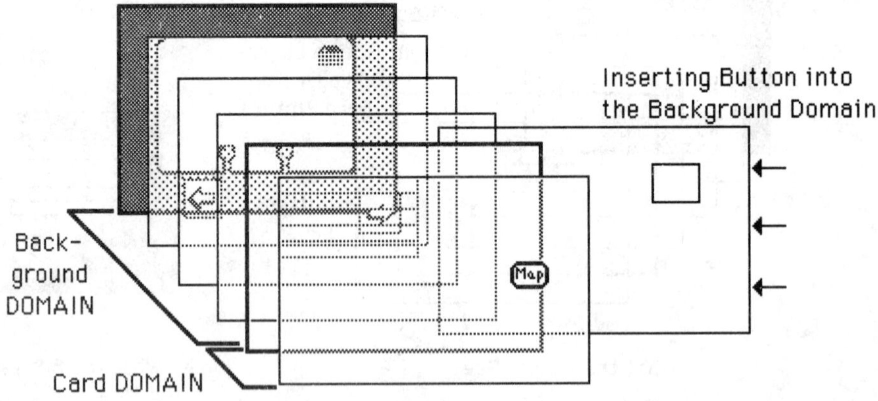


*Figure 6–8. When you insert an object to the background domain, it is added as a new layer closest to the viewer, but just behind the card graphics layer.*

homogeneous stack has one background. As you flip through the cards, that background never changes, even as the cycle of cards begins anew (that is, proceeding from the last card in the stack to the first card). In contrast, flipping through a heterogeneous stack will eventually lead you through the multiple backgrounds.

A convenient way to organize a heterogeneous stack is to group together all cards that share the same background (Figure 6-9). Therefore, if you have fifty cards with background A and 100 cards with background B, you can start at the first card of background A, proceed to the next card forty-nine times, and view only cards with that background. But if you are looking at the last card of background A and ask to view the next card, you will see the first card of the background B group.

With regard to layering, you should remember that a background is the "bedrock" of a card. Therefore, elements of two distinct backgrounds will not interfere with one another. A background's art, buttons, and text fields are said to be "private" to that background: They are not shared with any other background.

That means, therefore, that if you wish two backgrounds in a heterogeneous stack to have identical features in places— such as the next and previous card buttons— you must specifically design those buttons into each background. Don't expect a second background in the same HyperCard stack file to automatically inherit any attributes of the first one you designed. Fortunately, HyperCard does simplify manually borrowing objects from one background to another, as described in the next several chapters.

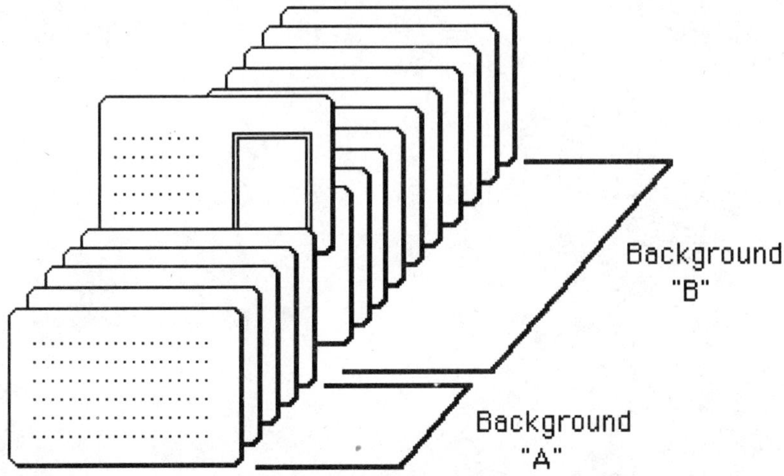


*Figure 6-9. Cards created by the New Card menu item in a heterogeneous stack are automatically grouped in such a way that all cards sharing the same background are contiguous in the stack.*

# CHAPTER 7

# All About Backgrounds

WE WILL BE LIMITING DISCUSSION IN THIS SECTION TO THE BACKGROUND PICTURE layer– the "bedrock" layer, as we've called it. Background buttons and fields will be covered in their respective chapters.

In all our illustrations about backgrounds so far, we may have given the impression that every stack has some kind of graphical background. It's true that most stacks do have such a background, but it is not a prerequisite that a stack have a graphical background to be an official stack. Every stack, of course, has a background picture layer. In its pristine form, a background picture layer is completely blank– white on the screen. If you ever design an entirely custom stack, this is where you will start building– a frightening thought, perhaps.

## *Backgrounds and the Browser*

What the browser sees as graphics in the background of a card is nothing more than a careful arrangement of dark spots on the white background, just as a newspaper photo upon close inspection consists entirely of black ink dots on a white paper. The design that results is entirely up to the HyperCard stack author.

As stack author, especially for stacks that will be used by others, your responsibility is to make backgrounds appealing and intuitive. When a browser encounters your background, its purpose should be obvious, or should at least offer an obvious way for the browser to get help in some fashion.

The background graphic is important. The browser will adopt a third-party stack initially for its information content; the degree of enjoyment that person derives from the stack, however, is much more dependent upon the design of the background. A stack with a well-designed background will have a much higher perceived value than the same stack with an amateurish or awkward background design.

### BACKGROUND STRATEGIES

A common design theme running through most of the stack and card ideas provided on HyperCard's ideas disk is that a card background should be an on-screen metaphor for something in real life, like a note card, an appointment calendar page, or some other paper form. These may be fine ideas to start with, but don't let them influence you into thinking that this is the only way to design a card background. Sometimes an entirely new way of representing a familiar form is more appropriate. Additionally, unchain your imagination from the confines of traditional forms and explore new ways of using the Macintosh screen.

As you see other Macintosh applications and screens, remember that it is a simple process to capture the art from a screen onto disk and paste it into a background of a stack you design. You can also cut and paste sections of one HyperCard card background into another. As a result, you can achieve remarkably professional-looking card backgrounds even if you are not an accomplished artist.

(A word of caution, however, if you plan to offer a stack you design for resale. Copyrighted background and icon art may not be used as component parts of stacks for redistribution to others unless you obtain permission from the copyright holder. Personal use of such art, however, is a common practice among Macintosh users.)

## *Blank Backgrounds*

Surprisingly, there are cases in which your HyperCard stack design may prescribe a background picture that is completely blank (white). In fact, the stack may not even have any background fields or buttons, either.

An example of such a creature might be a stack of one card whose content is a graphic chart, like the Periodic Table of Elements. There is only one periodic table, so there is no need to put the table's art into the background for additional cards to share. The art can be pasted, instead, into the card layer. Underneath the card layer, the background layer is blank.

Another example, this time with a stack of many cards, might be a stack consisting of clip art. The art is pasted, card by card, into the card layer. If the art may extend to full screen size, you won't want any kind of decorative border in the background to run underneath the card's content. Therefore, it may be best to keep the background blank. In such a stack, there may still be background buttons and fields, but the bedrock background layer is empty.

## *Background Info...*

At any time while in Authoring or Programming levels, you can see information about the background of the card you are viewing. Pull down the Objects menu and choose the Background Info... item. You will see a dialog box similar to the one you get for Stack Info (Figure 7-1).

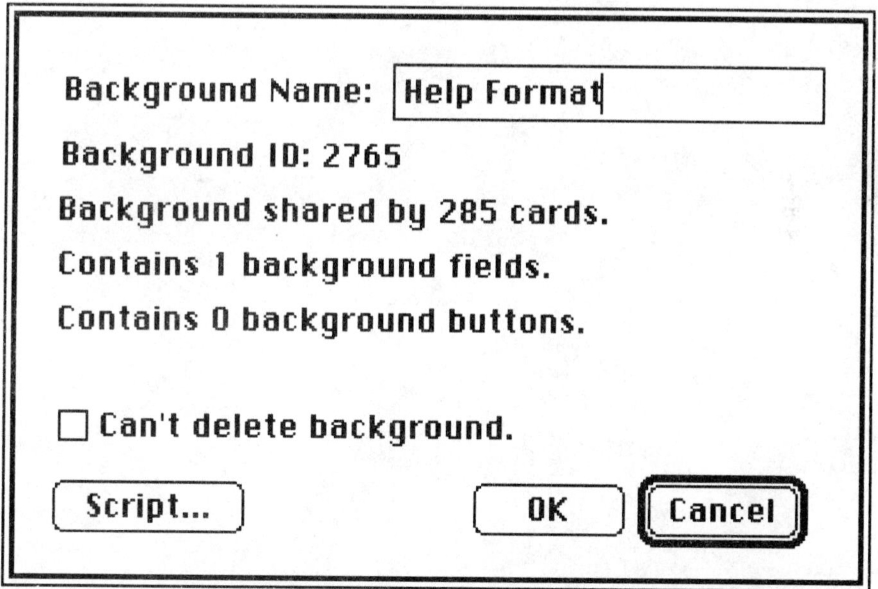


*Figure 7-1. The Background Info dialog box tells you about the number of objects in this background, the number of cards, and the background name. An additional setting allows for a level of protection against or deletion.*

Notice that the first item in the box is a blank for a name. You can assign any name you please to the background. For now, this may not seem particularly helpful. But when you begin programming in HyperTalk, object names (backgrounds, cards, fields, and buttons) will prove to be very practical. Therefore, it is not a bad idea to get in the habit of assigning names to objects you create.

Other information about the background in this dialog box includes its unique ID number and the number of cards, fields, and buttons assigned to this background. You are also given the opportunity to protect backgrounds from modification or deletion in case you wish to protect only one background in a stack. This background status report will prove helpful in future design of HyperCard stacks.

Like stacks and other HyperCard objects, a background may have a script attached to it. You are free to inspect the script by clicking on the dialog box's Script... button. If there is a script there, look but don't touch until we've had a chance to acquaint you with the essentials of the HyperTalk language.

# CHAPTER 8

# All About Cards

As we did for the background discussion in the last section, our coverage of cards in this section is restricted to the actual card picture layer, not to buttons and fields that may exist in this "foreground" layer.

## *Card and Background Interaction*

An intriguing property of the card picture layer is that it is transparent. But the card layer is a layer just the same, and as such may be the recipient of graphical elements, just like the background layer.

What makes this relationship between background and card pictures so interesting is that a stack designer can perform visual tricks by orchestrating the interaction between the two layers. For example, if a section of background art applies to all but a few cards, that section can be covered by different art in the card layer. Even if the background element art is surrounded by the white of the background, the card layer can cover it. But to do so, the author must paint a white patch on the card layer to match the background's white field. As you'll see in the discussion of painting tools, this might feel funny, because to your eye it appears as if you're painting with "nothing"— the paint blends with the background white.

Another kind of interaction may involve overlaying a card layer pattern atop a background layer pattern. Again, we'll have more to say about patterns in our discussion of the painting tools, but look at Figures 8-1 and 8-2 to see how a card layer pattern interacts with a background map to create a striking day/night contrast.

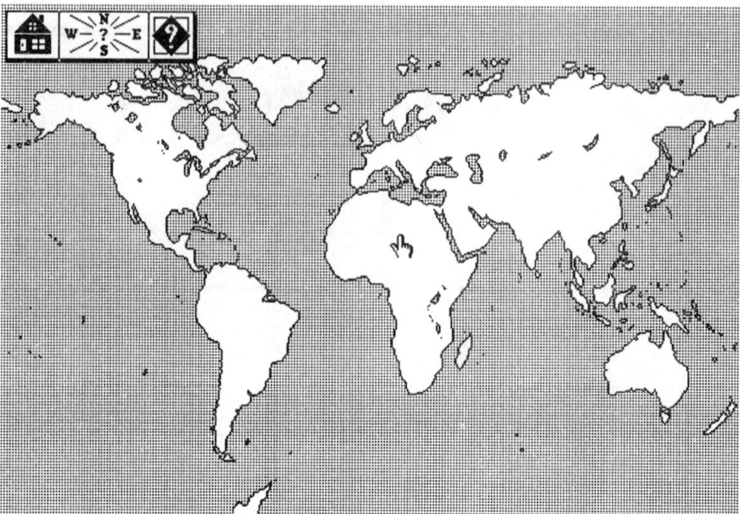

*Figure 8-1. This world map is a background. Land areas are white, while ocean areas are filled with a dotted pattern.*

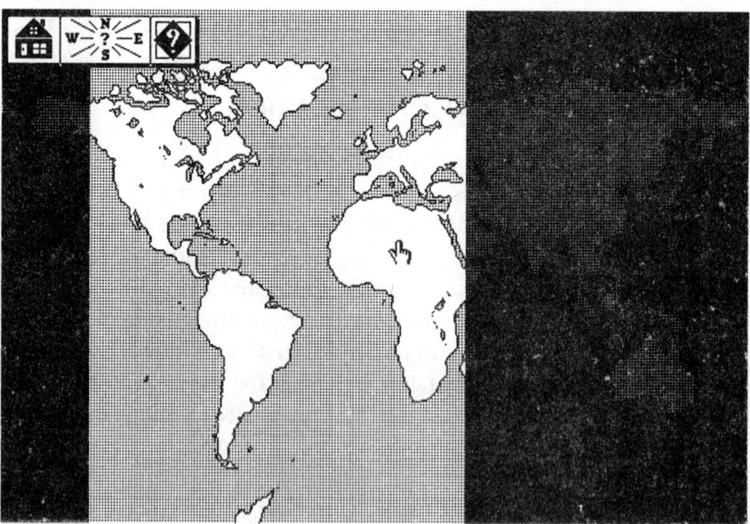

*Figure 8-2. A card layer graphic consists of a cross hatch pattern that complements the ocean pattern in the background. The result is black for the night oceans, and the crosshatch pattern for night land areas. (Reproduced from Business Class, a stack published by Activision, Inc.)*

## *Card Properties*

We've said it before, but it bears repeating at this stage: The information you type into a text field "belongs to" the card in view at the time, even if the text field is a background field. It's just like the note card in the library card catalog. The spot on the card designated for the book's title is determined by the placement of that blank in the background (that is, it is the same for all cards in the drawer), but a particular book's title is actually entered onto the card. Wherever that card goes, so goes the information typed onto it.

To help hammer this point home, HyperCard automatically assigns numbers to cards in a stack. There are actually two numbering systems imposed on cards in a stack.

### CARD NUMBERS

First of all, cards in a stack are recognized by their place in the stack. A card in a stack has a number relative to the start of the stack. That is, HyperCard counts cards, one by one, from the first card in the stack. If you know the precise location of a card relative to the beginning of the stack, you could issue a command in the message box like "Go to card 22."

The problem with relying on this numbering system to locate a card (other than the first and last card in a stack) is that the number of a card can change during the life of a stack. For instance, if you delete card number 2, all the cards above that number slip down a number to fill the gap left by the card yanked from the number 2 slot. Even more hazardous to this numbering system is the way HyperCard adds a new card to a stack. Unless instructed otherwise, HyperCard slips a blank card after the card you're viewing, ready for you to fill out. If you're not at the last card in the stack, then the numbering system for cards above the new card will be off by one.

Fortunately, HyperCard comes through with a much more reliable numbering system that works automatically for you each time you generate a new card in a stack. Immediately upon creation, a new card receives a unique identification number, called its card ID. A card maintains its card ID virtually forever. No other card in that stack will ever again be given that ID number, even after a card is deleted. Like the jersey numbers of famous professional baseball and football players, a card's ID number is retired upon the card's deletion.

### CARD NAMES

A HyperCard author also has the option of assigning names to individual cards. For most stacks, particularly homogeneous stacks that may grow to be quite large (name and address or daily calendar stacks, for instance), naming cards won't be of much value. Card names will be important, however, if you start writing HyperTalk scripts, especially in heterogeneous stacks. We'll see much more about card-naming in later chapters covering HyperTalk.

Because a card is an object, you can obtain information about it by choosing Card Info... from the Objects menu. The dialog box that results is very much like ones we've already seen (Figure 8–3). It offers a blank for entry of a card name, followed by its sequence number in the stack and its unique ID number. Next the number of card domain fields and buttons assigned to that specific card are listed, as well as a protection setting for deleting an individual card. Cards, too, can have HyperTalk scripts, and the Script...button is the portal to the script dialog box.

## *Selecting Cards*

There is one special case in which the card terminology may seem to be confused with that of the background. It has to do with the Edit menu choices labeled Cut Card and Copy Card (Figure 8–4).

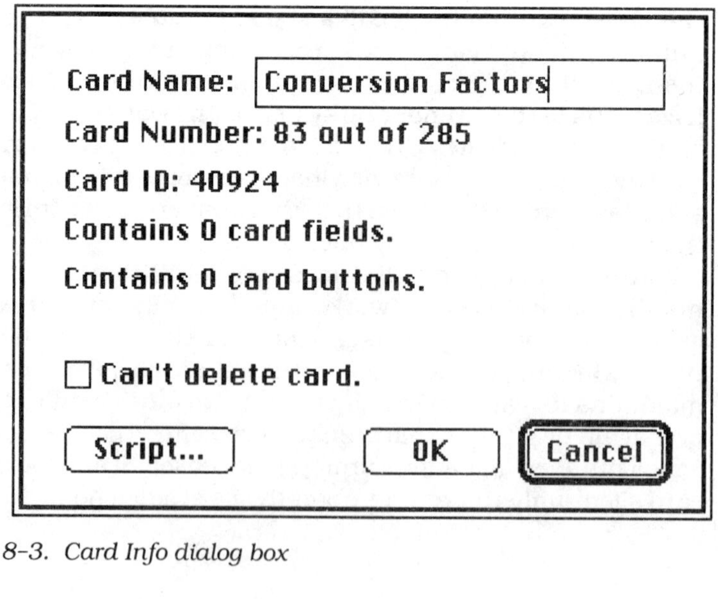

Card Name: Conversion Factors

Card Number: 83 out of 285

Card ID: 40924

Contains 0 card fields.

Contains 0 card buttons.

☐ Can't delete card.

Script... OK Cancel

*Figure 8–3. Card Info dialog box*

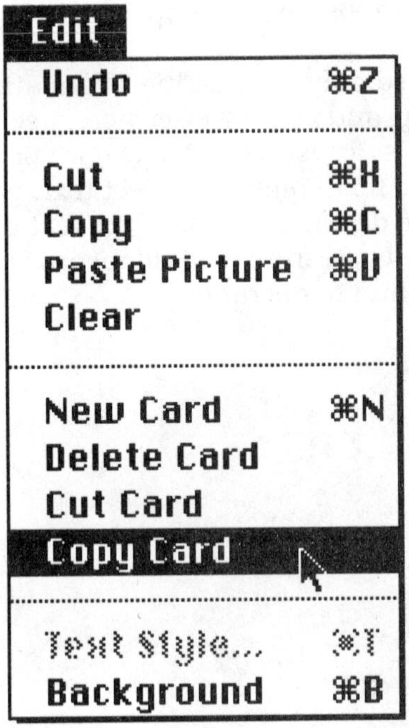

*Figure 8-4. Copy Card and Cut Card menu choices*

When you make this menu choice, HyperCard cuts, or copies, the complete card you're viewing at that instant. By "complete card," we mean the background, all background objects, the card layer (with the information stored in that card), and card objects. Both commands place this card into the Clipboard (Cut also removes it from the stack).

Once the card is in the Clipboard, you can then go to another stack and paste this complete card into that stack. The moment you do that, however, the stack gains not only an additional card but an additional background. In other words, if you were to check the Stack Info dialog box before and after the paste, you will see that both the number of backgrounds and the number of cards has increased by one.

This is a very handy feature for a very specific purpose: building heterogeneous stacks from homogeneous stacks. In fact, it points up a good strategy for developing heterogeneous stacks. Work first with the building blocks as separate stacks to prevent getting mixed up between multiple backgrounds in a developing stack. When the basic blocks are all set, then make one of the stacks the recipient of the other backgrounds. Go to each of the other stacks, copy a card, go to the target stack, and paste the complete card (card and background) into the target stack. Now you can connect the workings of the diverse backgrounds by establishing appropriate links with buttons (discussed later).

If you are interested only in selecting information stored in a card's text fields for copying and pasting elsewhere, use the standard Macintosh text editing tools, as you would in a word processing program. In other words, use the text pointer to select text, choose Copy from the Edit menu, go to the destination, place the text pointer in the desired location, and choose Paste from the Edit menu. Do *not* use Cut Card or Copy Card for this kind of operation.

# CHAPTER 9

# All About Fields

TEXT FIELDS ARE, BY AND LARGE, THE INFORMATION HOLDERS OF HYPERCARD CARDS. Except for stacks designed to hold different graphics images on each card (as in a clip art stack), the practical value of a stack you create will first be evaluated by the textual information it stores for the browser.

## *Fields vs. Graphic Text*

We should make one important distinction at this point: Text fields are not used when you wish to display fixed text in a card (or every card in the stack), as in a uniform card title. Text fields are predominantly of the fill-in-the-blank variety. When you wish cards in a stack to display fixed text, the most efficient way will be to make the text as part of the background picture layer. HyperCard's painting tools (chapters 12–16) provide a facility for typing text into these layers. If you type some text into the background graphics layer, that text will appear on every card, just like the rest of the background graphic. A background text field, on the other hand, will show up blank with the creation of each new card in the stack. Therefore, this section refers strictly to the fill-in-the-blank type of text entry.

## *Accessing the Field Tool*

To work with text fields, you must select the Field tool from the Tools palette. Here's how:

1. Make sure you are at the Authoring or Scripting user level.
2. Pull down the Tools menu.

   This action reveals the Tools palette (Figure 9–1). As you recall from our discussion in chapter 4, you may drag the pointer off the palette to "tear" it from the menubar.
3. "Tear off" the Tools palette.

   Place it anywhere on the screen.
4. Click on the field tool icon in the upper right corner of the palette (Figure 9–2).

   Depending on the construction of the card you are viewing when selecting the Field tool, the card's appearance may change slightly, as the borders of all text fields become highlighted or, in the case of transparent fields, suddenly visible.
5. When you are finished with the Field tool, return to the Browse tool by clicking on its icon in the upper left corner of the palette.

   You may dispose of the Tools palette at any time by clicking on its close box (Figure 9–3).

Unlike the HyperCard objects discussed so far in this part of the book, fields have many more properties at the discretion of the stack author. We'll divide these properties into layer, visual, font, and HyperTalk properties.

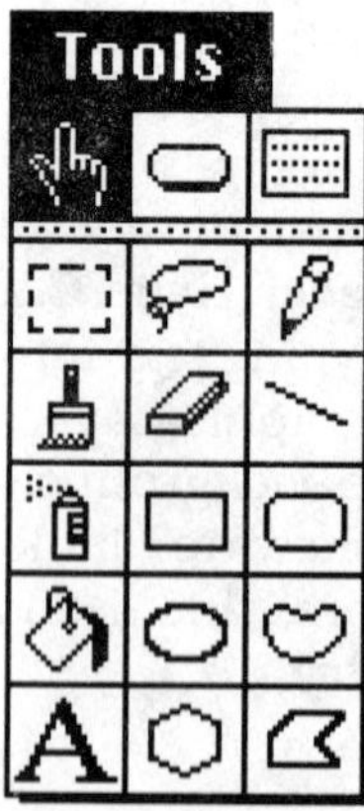


*Figure 9–1. The Tools palette*

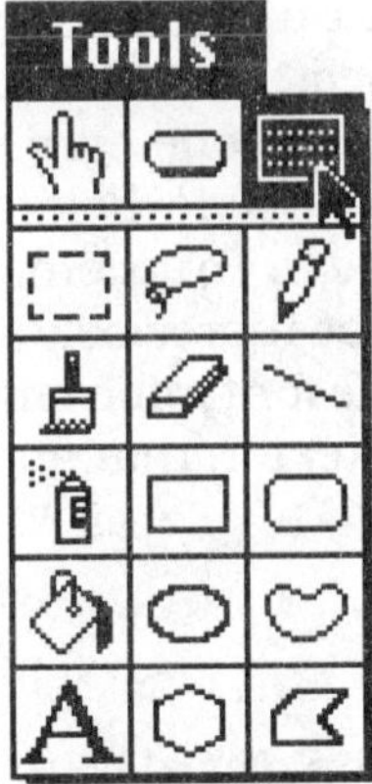


*Figure 9-2. The Field tool is in the upper right corner of the palette.*

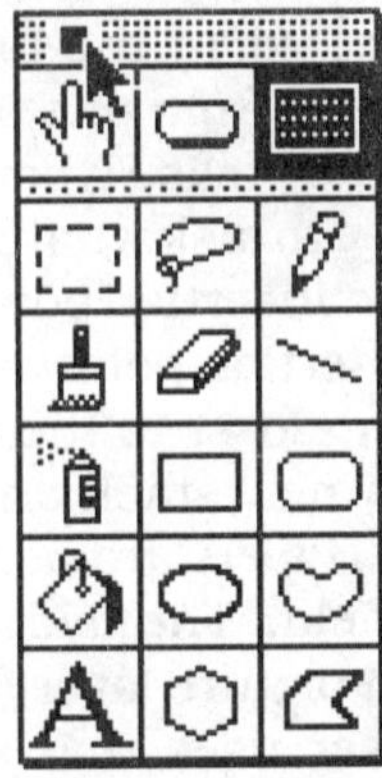

*Figure 9-3. Close the palette by clicking the close box in the upper left corner.*

## Field Layer Properties

We've already covered the difference between background and card fields with respect to the way HyperCard applies individual layers to each object. The nature of most HyperCard stacks calls for practically all fields to be background fields: They are shared with all cards in a stack, but instances of card fields are easy to dream up.

For example, if one card in a stack is a kind of reference card, perhaps with tabular data to which other cards in the stack frequently refer, you may create that card's table art and information-containing text fields in the card layer. This card layer essentially masks the stack's primary background. By putting the text fields in the card domain, while other cards in the stack use background fields, the tabular data fields won't interfere with the background field information.

Another case might utilize the layering properties that let you place a card domain object directly atop a background domain object. Therefore, there may be one card whose text fields you would like to display in a font or font style (boldface, perhaps) different from the rest of the cards in the stack. To accomplish this, you would add a card field to that card, and place it precisely atop the corresponding background field. By adjusting the font information (see below), you will assure that the browser will see text in that spot in a different style than the other cards.

## FIELD ORDER

Since each text field on a card is its own layer (remember, like the clear acetate sheets), fields assume an order based on the way the layers stack atop one another. The order of fields can be quite important to the browser, although he doesn't realize that field order is due to layering. It becomes important when the browser is pressing the Tab key to advance the text cursor from one field to the next.

A press of the Tab key tells HyperCard to carry out two main tasks. The first task is to save to disk whatever new information was typed into the field where the text insertion pointer is now located. The second task is to move the text insertion pointer to the field next in line, that is, the field in the next layer closer to the browser's eye. Let's explain.

When you create a new stack and begin creating new background fields for that stack, HyperCard assumes that the first field layer you lay down is the "first field." The field in the next layer (building out, away from the background picture layer) becomes the "second field," and so on. When the browser uses that stack, he presses the Tab key to advance the text cursor from the first field, to the second field, and so on, until he reaches the frontmost field in the card. The next press of the Tab key starts the cycle all over again, starting with the first field, on the very bottom of the layers.

## A FIELD EXPERIMENT

We're going to experiment with this field ordering in the next couple of pages. To really see how this works, let's make a new stack from one of the stacks provided with HyperCard that has several text fields on it. We'll make a temporary new stack from the weekly appointment book background in the Datebook stack rather than mess up the one that came with HyperCard. Let's make the new stack first:

1. From the HyperCard Home card, click on the Weekly icon (Figure 9–4).

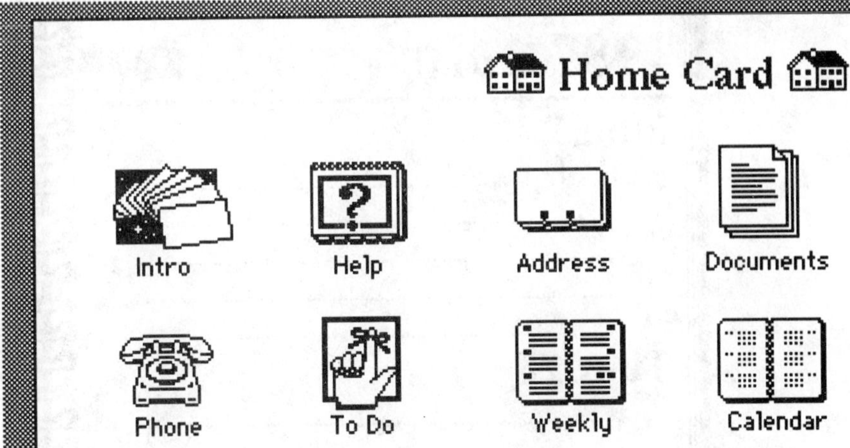


*Figure 9–4. Clicking the appointment book icon in the Home card.*

2. With the appointment book on the screen, choose New Stack... from the File menu.
3. At the standard file dialog box prompt, type the name "Field Explorer" as the new stack's name, and press Return.

Now we're ready to experiment with the text fields on the card. As you move the screen cursor over various parts of the card, you'll notice that whenever it is atop what looks to be text field, the Browse tool changes to the I-beam text cursor.

1. Click the I-Beam cursor at the upper left corner of the top left text field (Figure 9–5).
2. Press the Tab key once.

   Because of the way the text fields were laid out by the author of this stack, the text pointer advances to the next logical field, the one for the second day of the week.
3. Press the Tab key a few more times.

   As you do so, watch the progression of the text pointer from one day to the next.

The progression from day to day was no accident. The author planned it that way because it was what the browser would expect.

Now, you may think that this places an exorbitant burden on the author to make sure the design of text fields is nailed down well in advance of actually building a stack. In practice, a card design evolves through trial and error. The author may sketch out on paper the basic

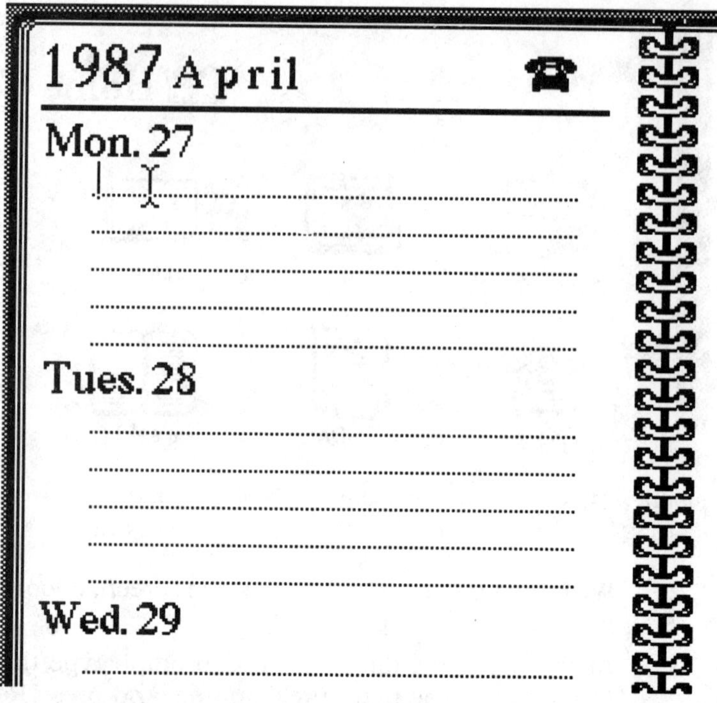


*Figure 9–5. Clicking the I-Beam cursor at the top left corner of the Monday field sets the text insertion pointer flashing.*

function of a card and then start assembling the pieces on a real stack. After working with the stack for a while, the author can see what "works" and what doesn't.

## MODIFYING FIELD ORDER

What if the author discovers that he must insert a text field to the card in such a way that the browser tabs to it between the fields originally designated as the first and second fields? Does he have to start from scratch, assembling the layers in the new order?

Fortunately not. HyperCard gives you the ability to modify the order of text fields (and button objects) within either the background or card domains. The commands that accomplish this, found in the Objects menu, are called Move Closer and Move Farther. Let's see how they work.

We'll use our Field Explorer stack to experiment with manipulating field layers.

1. With the Field Explorer stack in view, choose Background from the Edit menu.

   The menubar displays short diagonal marks along its top and bottom edges, indicating that you are in the background editing mode.

2. Pull down the Tools menu and choose the Field tool in the palette's upper right corner.

   Outlines of the text fields on the card become visible.

3. Click once anywhere within the first text field, that is, the field that contains appointments for Monday.

   This actions *selects* the field. Its outline turns into what is called the marquee or the marching ants, giving you visual feedback that this field is, indeed, selected and that your next action will affect this field only.

4. Pull down the Objects menu and choose Move Closer (or bypass the menu entirely and press the keyboard shortcut, Command-+, the +/= key).

   Nothing much happens on the screen when you do this, but there has indeed been a change in the order of the text fields.

5. Pull down the Tool menu and choose the Browse tool.

   The outlines to the fields disappear, and the menubar returns to its normal appearance, indicating that you have also come out of background editing mode.

Before we look at the results of this maneuver on the screen, let's examine what happened schematically. When we started, the six text field layers in this stack were in the order shown in Figure 9-6. Then

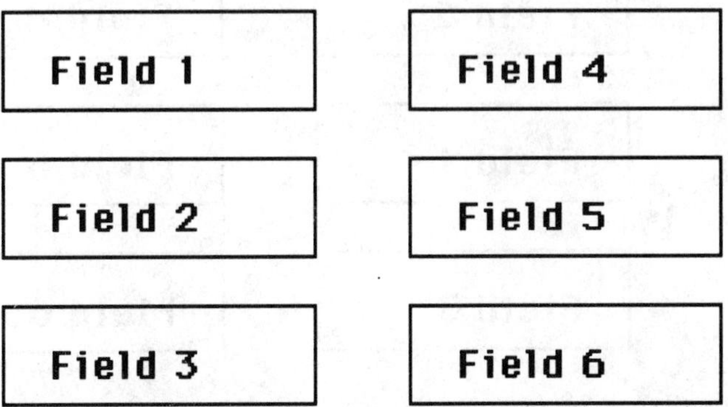


*Figure 9-6. The original order of the six fields allows orderly advancement through the week by pressing the Tab key.*

we selected the bottom field layer and moved it closer by one layer. This means that the field originally in the number 2 slot has now become number 1; the field originally in the number 1 slot has now become number 2 (Figure 9-7). The order of fields 3 through 6 have been unaffected by our single-layer shift. Let's see if it worked:

1. Click the I-Beam cursor at the upper left corner of the Tuesday text field.

   This field, if our calculations are correct, should be the first field in the order of the six.

2. Press the Tab key once.

   The text pointer now advances not to Wednesday but to the field considered number 2, the Monday field.

3. Press the Tab key once more.

   Now the pointer advances to field number 3, Wednesday.

Subsequent presses of the Tab key advance the pointer to the appropriate days until it is time to start the cycle over again. At that time, the pointer advances to the first field—Tuesday, in our mixed-up week of fields.

The action of the Move Closer and Move Farther commands, then, works on one selected layer at a time, and shifts that layer in the desired direction one layer at a time. "Closer" means closer to the eye of the viewer; "farther" means farther away from the viewer's eye. You should also be aware that when you select a text field layer, for instance, and start moving it in one direction, you are moving it not only with respect to other text field layers, but to button layers as well. Let's examine this more closely.

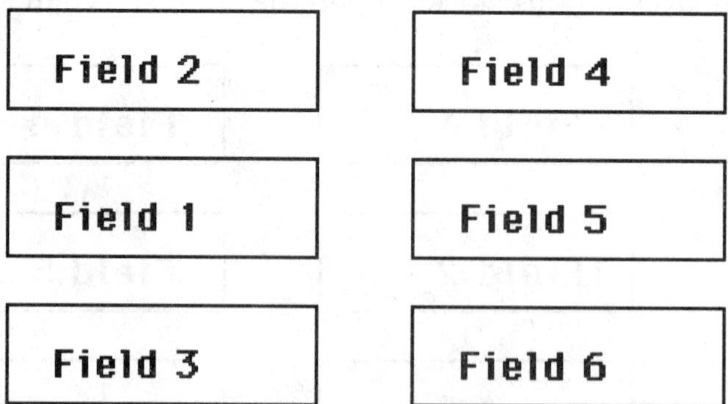


*Figure 9-7. After bringing the first field closer by one layer, the Tuesday field is now the first in field order. Tab key cursor advancement follows the new order: Tuesday, Monday, Wednesday, Thursday, Friday, Saturday/Sunday.*

Recall that in the background domain, you can have many text field and button layers (one layer per object) sitting above the actual background graphic layer (Figure 6–7). If you had created the layers in the following order,

picture
field A
button 1
button 2
field B

HyperCard sees the background picture and four object layers in that order. The Move Closer and Move Farther commands treat all object layers within a domain as equals. Therefore, if you wish to change the order of the text fields so that field B is the "first" field for this card, you would have to select that field and issue the Move Farther command three times. At each step of this process, the order would look like this:

| Move Farther (1) | Move Farther (2) | Move Farther (3) |
|---|---|---|
| picture | picture | picture |
| field A | field A | **field B** |
| button 1 | **field B** | field A |
| **field B** | button 1 | button 1 |
| button 2 | button 2 | button 2 |

It is only after the third issuance of the Move Farther command that field B actually moved ahead of field A as far as the browser would notice with the way the text pointer responds to the press of the Tab key. During the first two commands, the field B layer was working its way through two button layers. What you must observe as an author, therefore, is how object layers are laid out in case you need to change their order. On a card that has a couple dozen objects, it may take many presses of Command-+, for example, to move an object to the layer closest to the viewer's eye. In our discussion a bit later about buttons, we'll set up a multilayer system of easily visible overlapping objects and shift them freely from layer to layer to demonstrate the effect.

Moving text field layers with Move Closer and Move Farther works only within the confines of the domain in which the field was originally created. In other words, if you create a background field, the Move Closer command will not bring that field into the card-level domain. The card picture layer acts as a kind of barrier to shifting layers around. Layers created in the background cannot come any closer than one layer immediately below the card picture layer. Conversely, card object layers cannot be pushed away from the viewer any further than one layer immediately above the card picture layer. There are facilities for cutting and pasting fields from one domain to the other, as we'll see in a moment.

## *Field Visual Properties*

Text fields give the author many options for their appearance on cards. These choices are made by clicking various buttons on the Field Info dialog box (Figure 9–8). You can choose from one of five field styles: transparent, opaque, rectangle, shadow, and scrolling. Moreover, you can turn on any of the following three options: lock text, show lines, and wide margins.

Text fields, in general, are rectangular areas on the screen. Except for scrolling fields, the only limit to the number of lines a field may display on the screen is the size of the HyperCard screen. The same goes for the width of a text field. A text field could, if your card design dictated, fill the entire screen. The actual number of text lines a field will display on the screen at any one time is also dependent upon the font size and line spacing you select for the field (see below).

Text fields may be created fresh (discussed below) or may be copied and pasted from other cards in other stacks. Text fields you copy and

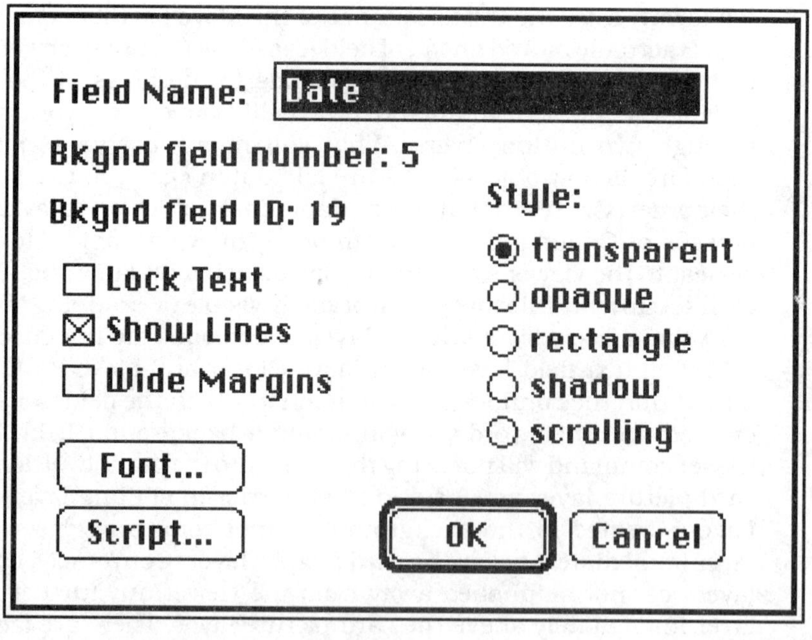

*Figure 9–8. The Field Info dialog box*

paste from other sources may be resized to suit the needs of the stack you create.

Visual attributes of any field are set by various buttons in the Field Info... dialog box (Figure 9–8), which you can see by first selecting a field (remember, you must choose the Field tool from the Tools palette first) and choosing Field Info... from the Objects menu. As a shortcut, you may also double-click on a field with the Field tool selected to see the dialog box— a procedure you will quickly come to follow after designing a few stacks.

## FIVE FIELD STYLES

Of the five field styles (transparent, opaque, rectangle, shadow, and scrolling), you may choose only one at a time.

A transparent field appears invisible to the browser. That is, there is no discernible outline to the field area on the screen. The only clue HyperCard provides to the browser that a transparent field exists is that the Browse tool changes to the I-Beam when it is in the text field's territory. You would specify a transparent text field primarily when something in the background graphics layer gives a visual clue to the browser that a text field sits ready to receive or display textual information. For example, the background design may call for a fancy border around the text entry area. The border would be executed in the background graphics layer. The transparent text field would overlay the graphics area (Figure 9–9). To the browser, the combination looks like a fancy text entry box.

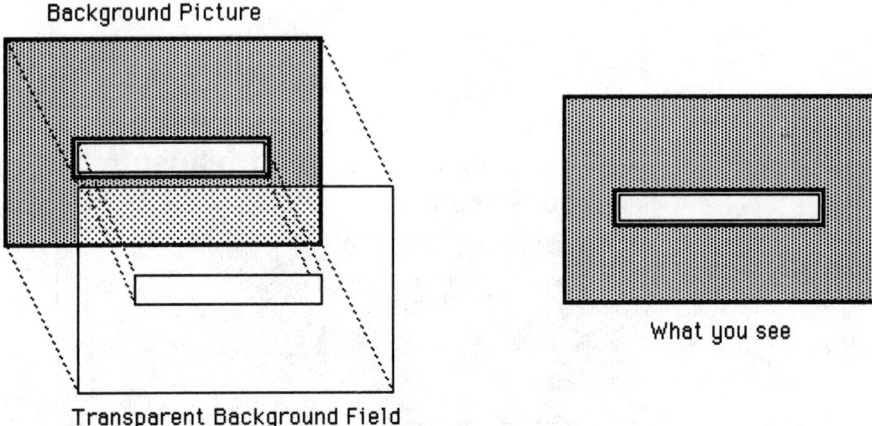


*Figure 9–9. A transparent background text field combined with an intricate background picture creates an interesting entry field for the user.*

You should be careful in your use of the transparent field atop a graphically rich background layer. The rectangle of the field is, as its name implies, completely transparent, revealing all graphics beneath it. If the background coming through the field is too "busy," you run the risk of making the text hard for the browser to read (Figure 9–10).

If you have a rich background and want the text field to be a plain white area without any border imposed on it, then choose an opaque field style from the Field Info dialog box. An opaque field overlays the background graphics layer with a white rectangular region. You are assured that text typed into the field will be readable, regardless of the visual interference coming from the background layer (Figure 9–11).

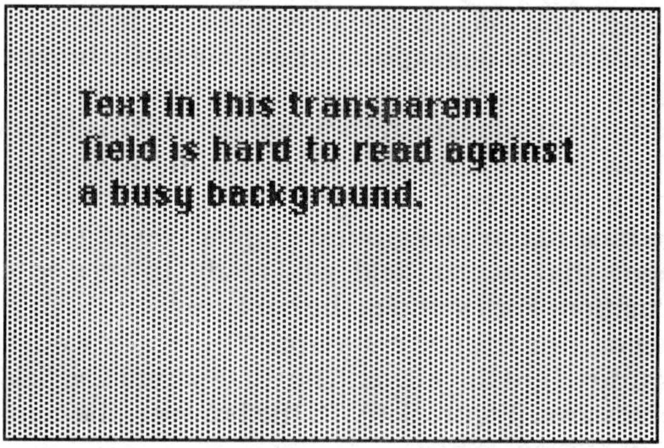

*Figure 9–10. When applying transparent fields, be careful that text is readable atop the background or surrounding graphics.*

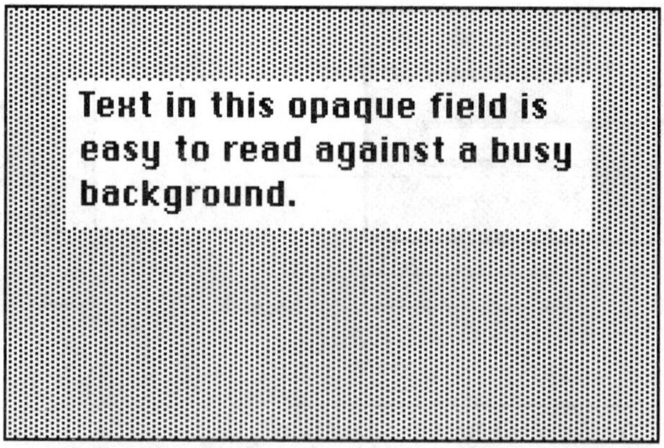

*Figure 9–11. An opaque field obscures a busy background picture, making text very readable.*

A very common field style is the rectangle. With this choice, you get an opaque rectangle surrounded by a single black border line. The rectangle style will be most familiar to those browsers who have experience working with Macintosh database programs, which often display entry fields as black-bordered rectangles. Typically, a rectangle field will be accompanied by background art that contains text titles of the kind of information that should go into the rectangular text area (Figure 9-12).

The shadow style presents an opaque rectangle drawn with a black border and a graphic technique called the drop shadow (Figure 9-13). The drop shadow adds a feeling of depth to an ordinary text box.

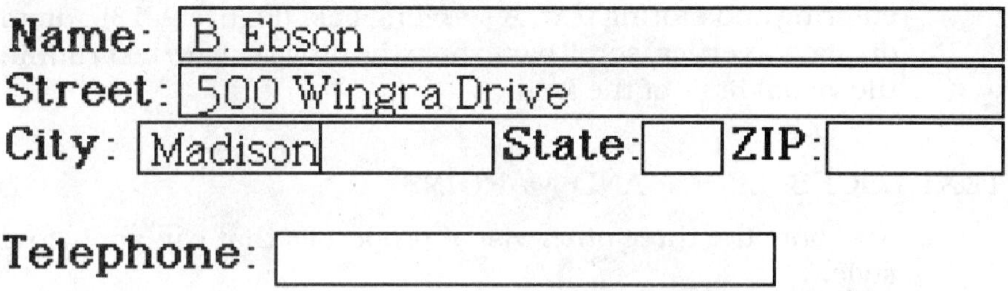

*Figure 9-12. Rectangle fields are frequently used to designate text entry areas on a form.*

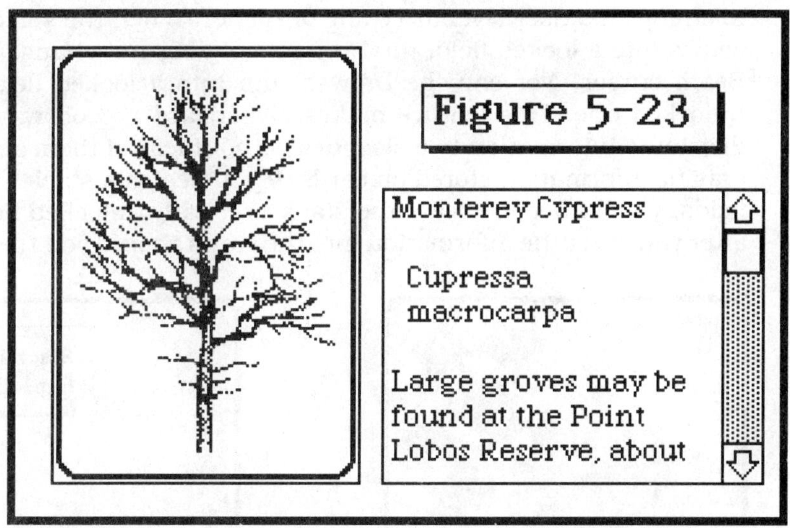


*Figure 9-13. Shadow fields, like the one with the figure number above right, are opaque and appear with a drop shadow around their borders. They can be used for dramatic effects when needed. Scrolling fields, bottom right, may be used where text may run longer than allotted space on a card.*

Experienced Macintosh screen designers encourage sparing use of drop shadow devices, since the technique is often overused. That's good advice.

In the HyperCard environment, shadow-style text boxes are perhaps best used in those designs that call for a text field to be hidden (that is, completely invisible, including the content of the field) until the browser clicks on a button. The shadow text field then appears, providing some additional information or assistance. A click on another button or on the text field itself causes the shadow field to once again disappear (Figure 9–14). Its three-dimensionality works well in presenting this kind of overlapping note metaphor.

The last field style, the scrolling field, extends the card boundaries for entering and storing text. A scrolling field (Figure 9–13) automatically displays a vertical scroll bar to help the browser view text running below the visual limit of the field.

## TEXT LOCKS, LINES, AND MARGINS

Now onto the three other visual properties that can apply to any field style.

The first, Lock Text, is a valuable option for the HyperCard author who intends to present read-only textual information in stacks for others to use. When you specify that a field's text is to be locked, the browser cannot accidentally change the text, even if he knows enough to change his user level to Typing or higher. When the screen pointer comes into a locked field, the Browse tool does not change into the I-Beam cursor. Nor can the browser tab into a locked field from an unlocked one. This feature makes HyperCard a good way to safely distribute information to colleagues without fear of them accidentally erasing information stored on cards. If you design a stack with locked fields, you'll have to create the stack first with unlocked fields. Only after you enter the information into the cards should you then lock the

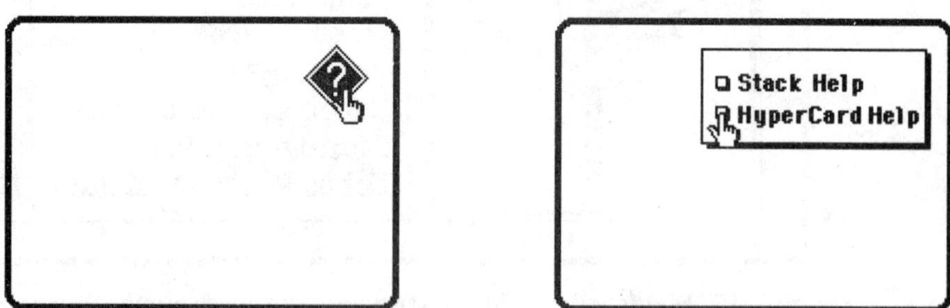


*Figure 9–14. Use shadow fields for notes that are normally hidden from view. The drop shadow effect looks like an overlay atop the rest of the card layers.*

fields. Fortunately, by placing the field in the background, you can lock one background field and lock the text in that field for all the cards in the stack.

Another option is the Show Lines property. When you engage this option, HyperCard displays a dotted line across the full width of the field (although not in scrolling fields). If you size the field for multiple lines, HyperCard shows as many dotted lines as the space allows. The vertical distance between the lines corresponds to the font size and line spacing specified in the field's Font dialog box (below).

The ability to show dotted lines in fields is a most useful card design element. For one thing, it eliminates the need for you to emulate dotted lines in the background graphics layer— not an easy task when trying to align graphic lines with text in an overlaying text field. More importantly, if the user of your stack prefers a larger font size for greater readability, HyperCard automatically adjusts the field's dotted lines with the font. If the lines had been graphically done in the background, the user would be confronted with the substantial task of digging into the painting tools and carefully aligning more widely spaced dotted lines to the larger line spacing. Showing lines also gives more solidity to transparent and opaque fields, which, by themselves, are virtually amorphous to both browser and author.

The last design choice is Wide Margins. With this option, you have a measure of control over the formatting of text in a text field. Depending on the design of your card and the size of your text fields, it may be desirable to have more white space between the characters in the field and the edges of the field. The Wide Margin selection increases the width of both left and right margins by approximately one character and the top margin by about one-half line. Generally speaking, very large text fields often look better with wide margins, but this is not a steadfast rule. As you design your cards, try your fields with both standard and wide margins. Then judge for yourself which does the best job.

## *Font Properties*

If you've done any word processing on the Macintosh, you've probably become quite familiar with the ability to change typefaces ("fonts" in the Macintosh lexicon), character sizes, and character styles at will. HyperCard text fields give you most of that power with one important exception. Unlike the word processing environment, the font, font size, and font style you select for a text field applies to the entire field. You cannot, therefore, adjust one word in a field to be boldface, while the rest of the text in that field is in plain text. Similarly, when you specify

*Figure 9–15. The Font dialog box, accessible via the Field Info dialog box.*

that a text field is to be the 12-point Times font, the entire field is in that font and size.

Font attributes are adjusted by controls in the Font dialog box, which is accessible via the Field Info dialog box (Figure 9–15). These are no different from most word processing program font selection dialogs, although you may be used to having many of these choices available as menu options. Two attributes— alignment and line height— should be explained in some detail.

Text alignment— left, center, right— pertains to the alignment of text in the selected text field. The default setting (the setting HyperCard automatically gives to a new field unless you tell it otherwise) is left alignment. This is how most word processing text is aligned. How you align text in a HyperCard text field will depend largely on where you position the field on the screen. For example, if the design calls for a text field comprising the title field for a card to be placed along the right edge of the screen, then it may make excellent sense to specify right-aligned text.

One attribute you may not be accustomed to seeing— line height— is at times a crucial measure when designing your HyperCard cards. The measure, analogous to *leading* in the typesetting world, is the distance in points (1 point, or 1/ 72 inch) between baselines of text (Figure 9–16). HyperCard offers default line spacing that may be too large when you are trying to squeeze many lines of text into a small area on the

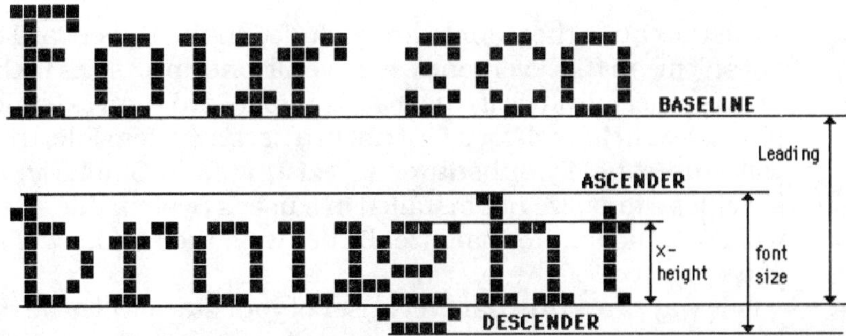


*Figure 9-16. Font size is measured in points (1 point = 1/72 inch) between ascender and descender; leading is measured between baselines of adjacent lines.*

screen. When that happens, you can adjust the line spacing to a smaller size. A typical closely spaced setting is two points larger than the font size. When experimenting with line spacing and font sizes, be sure to test combinations on actual text, especially on letters that have descenders (like j, y, and g) to assure good readability.

## FONTS AND THE SYSTEM

If you are planning to distribute a stack to other Macintosh owners, be aware of an important factor that may limit the variety of fonts you incorporate into the stack. Even though your System File may contain many elaborate fonts, the System File of the users of your stack must also contain those same fonts for their text fields to look just like yours. For example, if you like the LaserWriter font called Garamond and design text fields in a stack around this font, other users without this font installed on their system will get another font in its place— perhaps New York. The results may be artistically disastrous.

There are two ways to prepare for this eventuality. The simplest is to design your text fields around the standard fonts in the System included with HyperCard. The list is as follows:

| | Font Size | | | | |
|---|---|---|---|---|---|
| Font Name | 9 | 10 | 12 | 14 | 18 |
| Chicago | | | • | | |
| Courier | | • | • | | |
| Geneva | • | • | • | • | • |
| Helvetica | | • | • | | |
| Monaco | • | | | | |
| New York | • | • | • | • | • |
| Times | | • | • | | • |

Just because these fonts are included in the HyperCard System File doesn't mean that everyone will have all fonts in all sizes in their system. This is especially true if a user adds HyperCard to an existing hard disk. If your text fields call for a font not in a user's System File, the Macintosh will automatically substitute an existing font. Similarly, if your field specifies a font size not installed in a user's System File, the Macintosh will *scale* the font to that size. Either way, the results will not be what you expected.

One way to assure that every user of your stack will have the fonts you specify is to use a small font set called *system fonts*: Geneva-9 and -12, Monaco-9, and Chicago-12. No one can remove these fonts from the System File with the Font/DA Mover, because the Macintosh needs them for the Desktop. It may be cramping your style to very few fonts and sizes, but you are assured that this lowest common denominator of fonts is in every Macintosh.

## FONTS AND THE STACK

A second method to obviate this font concern is to include the desired font in your application. This technique, not for beginners, requires the aid of a utility program called a resource editor. One such program, ResEdit, is commonly available from Macintosh user groups and on-line bulletin boards.

But before you get too many ideas about attaching fonts to your stacks for distribution, you should be aware of copyrights that protect most fonts. The copyrights prohibit your distributing the fonts with your HyperCard stacks without permission from the copyright owner. Technically speaking, if you wished to make sure an Apple font, such as Venice, were available on your distributed stacks, you would need permission from Apple Computer. Therefore, unless you design your own font for your stacks, the attachment of a font to a stack is probably not a good idea.

Everything we've been saying about fonts applies only to text fields that hold textual information. As a stack author, you may use any font you wish when placing text in the background or card graphics layers. When you use the appropriate painting tool (described in chapters 12–16), HyperCard is not placing the text into a text field, but is instead laying down a series of black spots on the white or transparent layer. The ultimate user of the stack does not need that font installed in his System File to see the font you painted on the graphics layer. So feel free to choose from a variety of fonts in designing fixed backgrounds.

## FONT TECHNIQUES AND SHORTCUTS

Before finishing our discussion about font properties of text fields, we'd like to share a technique you may find useful in designing cards that stand out from the ordinary. The effect we're after is white text field lettering on a black background—reverse lettering, as it's known in printing circles. Although we haven't yet gotten to the painting tools, just watch for now as we create the illusion of a black text field showing white characters.

To accomplish this feat, first paint a black rectangle in the background graphics layer where you want the text field to be on the card. Then create a transparent text field atop the black rectangle. The field may be either a background or card field, but you'll probably want it to be a background field so that it shows up on all cards in the stack. With the Field tool selected on the Tools palette, double click on the text field. At the resulting Field Info dialog box, click on the Font... button. No matter what font you specify for the field (Chicago works very well), also click on the Outline check box (Figure 9–17) and then OK. Now, when you type into the text field, all characters will look white on the black background (Figure 9–18).

Finally, here's a useful shortcut whenever you are in the Font dialog box of a field. You can double-click on a couple places to both make a selection and do the same as clicking on the OK button. For example, if you change the font from Geneva-12 to Geneva-10, you can simply

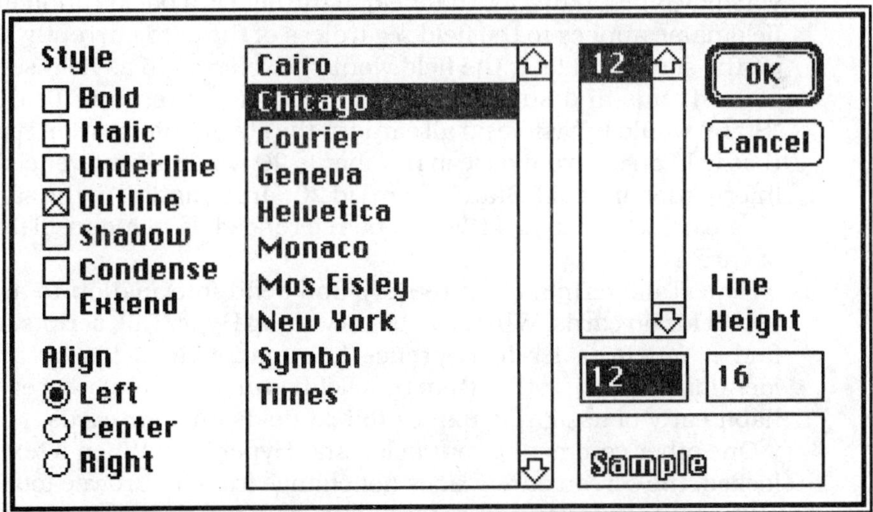


*Figure 9–17. The Outline check box in the Font dialog box*

*Figure 9–18. Outline characters on a black background look reversed.*

double-click on the 10 in the list of font sizes inside the Font dialog box. That action will both select the 10-point font and close the dialog box. This double-click shortcut works when selecting a font or font size. A double-click on the selection is all you need to select and return to regular display.

## *HyperTalk Properties*

It's really too early in this book to get deeply involved with HyperTalk. But we think it is important at this stage to explain the importance of assigning names to text fields.

In the Field Info dialog box, the first entry is a small text box into which you may type a name for that field. If the field is a background field, the field name applies to the field regardless of the card currently showing on the screen. In fact, the field would be referred to as field so-and-so of card thus-and-such. In a real stack, a background field named "State" would be visible on all cards in the stack. Information typed into that field on a card whose ID number is 20 would be referenced by the information in "field 'State' of card id 20." Information in the same field on a card whose ID is 41 would be referenced as being in "field 'State' of card ID 41."

HyperTalk scripts often retrieve and send information to and from text fields on cards. When you begin writing HyperTalk scripts, you will find it much easier to reference information in fields by a readily identifiable name rather than by a field number. Therefore, get into the habit early of assigning names to text fields on your cards.

One other comment about fields and HyperTalk. When a text field is locked, the screen cursor does not change from its Browse tool cursor. This means that you can essentially turn a text field into a button that performs some action when you click the mouse button with the cursor in the text field. We'll see how to do this in a later chapter, but you may want to keep this in the back of your mind as you begin dreaming up HyperCard card designs.

## *Creating New Text Fields*

HyperCard provides two distinctly different ways to create a new field. The steps involved in each method are quite simple. The trickiest part is remembering to place the new field in the correct domain: background or card. Most of the time you use HyperCard, you are in the card domain, yet most of the fields you will put into a card design are background fields. It is easy to forget to choose Background from the Edit menu (or press Command-B) before planting the field in the stack.

To create a text field the easiest way, follow these steps:

1. Since this is an authoring task, be sure you are in either the Authoring or Scripting user level.
2. Select the desired domain: background or card.
3. Pull down the Objects menu and choose New Field (Figure 9–19).

   A five-line text field appears in the center of the screen. The marching ants indicate the field is selected and that HyperCard has automatically selected the field tool.

*Figure 9–19. The New Field choice in the Objects menu*

The second field-creation method is a little longer but may be preferred by some HyperCard authors. Here are the steps:

1. Pull down the Tools menu and select the Field tool.
2. Hold down the Command key.

   When you do this, the cursor changes to a "plus" sign. This is like a drawing cursor.
3. Position the cursor at the upper left corner of the location on the screen where the field is to appear.
4. Click and slowly drag the pointer to the right and down (Figure 9-20).

   As you do, the outline of the field rectangle shows you the extent of the rectangle you are dragging.
5. When the field is the desired size, release both the mouse button and the Command key.

Regardless of the method you use, HyperCard creates the default style of text field, which is transparent, with no lines showing and with narrow margins. The default font is Geneva-12. If those properties are acceptable, you can choose the Browse tool in the Tools menu (which also automatically brings you out of background editing mode, if you're there to start) and begin entering text into the field.

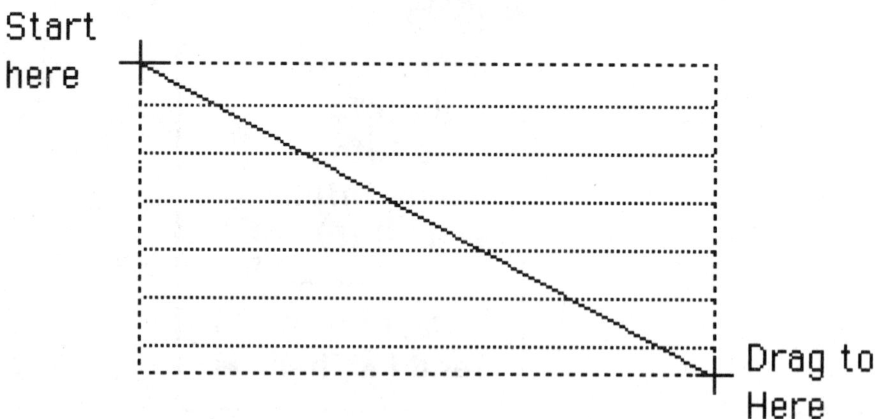


*Figure 9-20. Clicking and dragging on a selected field lets you resize it to suit your needs. The dotted text baselines show you how many text lines will be available at the chosen font size.*

## *Customizing Field Properties*

More than likely, however, you will want to adjust the location, size, visual properties, font, and perhaps script for the field. In a moment, you'll see how to "clone" the field if you wish to add more fields of the same type to the card. Before you do your cloning, however, it is advisable to set all the properties. That way, they'll all be set in future clones, so you can deal simply with the fields' locations and names. If you clone the fields first, you'll have to adjust the visual and/or font properties field by field.

We should emphasize that you are free to make any adjustments to fields at any time, even after information has been typed into them. For example, if you use a stack for a while and discover that a field should be in a larger font size and not quite as long, you may edit that background field for those attributes. The information typed into the field in the stack's cards will not be damaged. The next time you look at the previously entered cards, your old text will have the new attributes you assigned in the editing process.

To change any attributes other than size and location, you'll need the Field Info dialog box. With the field selected, choose Field Info from the Objects menu. Alternatively, you can double-click on the object. You may then make any adjustments, as described earlier.

### MOVING AND RESIZING FIELDS

Changing the location and size of a text field will be familiar processes to anyone with experience in object-oriented graphics programs, such as MacDraw, Cricket Draw, and the object layer of SuperPaint. Even if this is new to you, it won't be difficult to understand.

Before you can edit a field in any way, you must first select the Field tool. Selecting this tool makes all fields visible (except those that have been "hidden" by way of a HyperTalk command in a script or in the Message Box). Even transparent fields, which are essentially invisible when you view a card as a browser, are visible when the Field tool is selected. You see both an outline of the field and dotted lines representing base lines for text (to let you know how many lines will be visible in the current font and font size). If you are adjusting a brand-new field, the field is already selected for you.

To move a field on the screen, place the cursor in the center of the rectangle, hold down the mouse button, and drag the rectangle. The field follows the pointer as you drag it around the card. Release the mouse button when the field is in the desired position.

To resize a field, place the cursor on one of the field's four corners. The corner you choose depends on the direction in which you wish to stretch or reduce the field's dimensions.

Precise dragging and placement of objects on the screen is an acquired skill. Some users adapt to it quickly, while others need considerable practice. As an aid for all users, HyperCard lets you constrain (limit) the motion at any one time either vertically or horizontally on the screen. Even an experienced artist finds constraining to be a useful shortcut when an object is properly aligned in one axis and needs minor adjustment in the other: Constraining the motion prevents the correctly aligned axis from getting out of alignment.

You constrain the direction of an object drag by holding down the Shift key prior to clicking and dragging the mouse button. With the Shift key down, HyperCard watches the direction you drag the object. If you start dragging it to the left or right, HyperCard constrains movement to those two directions only. No matter how you move the cursor from top to bottom, the object will move only to the left and right. Conversely, if you hold down the Shift constrain key and make your first dragging movement up or down, all motion of the object will be in those two directions only.

Constraining also works for resizing fields. For example, if you hold down the Shift key and drag the bottom right corner of a field first to the right, you will be constrained to left and right motion only. A good strategy in resizing fields is to first size its vertical dimension accurately, paying close attention to how its lines of text will display. Once the vertical dimension is correct, constrain resizing motion to the horizontal, dragging the field to the desired width without harming the carefully adjusted height set earlier.

## *Cloning Fields on the Same Card*

Chances are that if your card design has more than one field, the font and visual properties will be identical— at least good taste usually dictates this idea. Exceptions exist, of course. For example, if you have text fields in a card that are prefilled-out for the browser (and perhaps cannot be adjusted by the browser), they may be opaque rectangles without borders; fields in which the browser is encouraged to enter information may then be bordered rectangles. Still, the font and font size will probably be the same.

To simplify the creation of multiple fields of the same style on a card, you can readily clone— "peel off" if you will— copies based on the first field you create. Let's try it.

1. Pull down the Go menu and choose Home to return to the Home card.
2. Pull down the File menu and choose New Stack...
3. At the standard file dialog box prompt, type *Clone Home* as the name of the new stack, and click OK (or press Return).

   This creates a new stack based on the card design of the Home card.
4. Pull down the Edit menu and choose Edit Background, or type Command-B.

   The foreground art of the card disappears temporarily as we see the blank background graphics layer, one background field, and two background buttons.
5. Tear off the Tools palette and place it in a lower corner.
6. Choose the Field tool on the Tools palette.
7. Double-click on the background field that was on the card when you created the new stack. Change the field style from transparent to rectangle, and click the Show Lines checkbox.

   The Field Info dialog box shows this field to be background field number 1.
8. Click the OK button in the Field Info dialog box.
9. Choose New Field from the Objects menu.
10. Double-click on this new field.

    The Field Info dialog box shows that the new field we just created is background field number 2, which puts it in a layer somewhere closer to our eye than field number 1.
11. Click the Shadow style button and then click OK to close the dialog box.
12. Hold down the Option key (the cloning key), then click and drag the new field we just created (field number 2) to an area under field number 2. Release the mouse button (Figure 9–21).

    A copy of the field traces the motion of the cursor, leaving the original field in place.
13. Double-click on the field you just cloned.

    The Field Info box shows this field to be field number 3, which is in a layer one level closer to you than field number 2. The box also shows that the shadow style is in force for this new field.

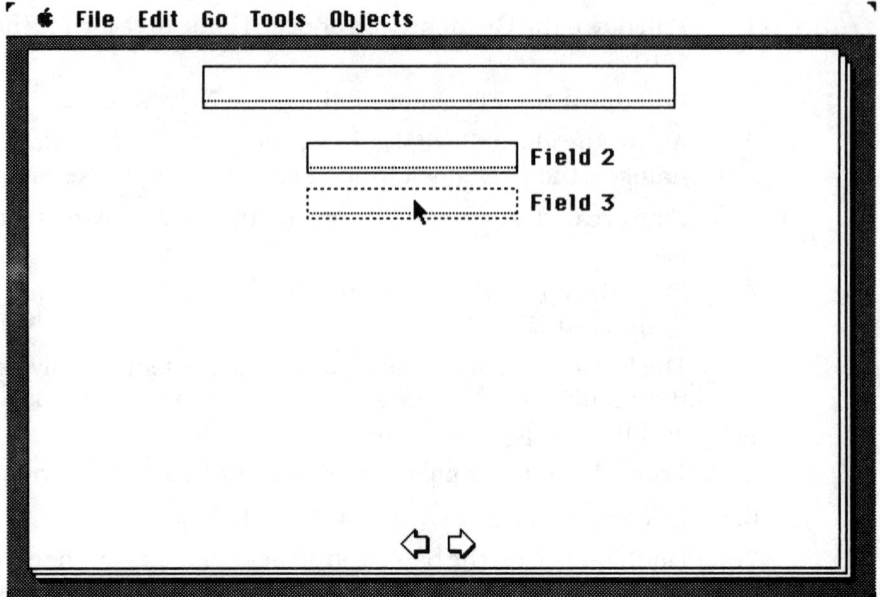


*Figure 9-21. Cloning a field makes an exact duplicate of the original. Clone by holding down the Option key, clicking on the original, and dragging the copy.*

If you wish to add another field with the same attributes, you can clone either field number 2 or field number 3. In practice, the most convenient method is usually to clone the most recent field—number 3 in this case.

## COLUMNS OF FIELDS

Constraining also functions during the cloning process, greatly simplifying alignment of multiple fields that are to be in a column or on the same horizontal plane. Let's do some more cloning to demonstrate:

1. In the background editing mode and with the Field tool selected on the Tools palette, click on field number 3.

   Its border will turn into a marquee (or marching ants, if you prefer).

2. Now, simultaneously hold down the Option key (for cloning) and the Shift key (for constraining) simultaneously.

3. Click and drag on field number 3 in a downward motion.

   A copy of field number 3 (this one will be field number 4), will follow the cursor on the screen.

4. Place the new field directly beneath field number 3 (Figure 9–22). Release the mouse button, but keep holding down the Option and Shift keys.
5. Now click and drag from field number 4 to the right.

   Yet another clone (field number 5) peels off, following the cursor (Figure 9–23).
6. Position this last field directly next to field number 4 and release the mouse button and all keyboard keys.

Cloning text fields, particularly with constraining, is a fast way of setting up columns consisting of many fields. While you clone the fields, too, you can dictate the order of tabbing that the browser will encounter— without you having to go back into the background layers later and adjust the layers closer and farther. Therefore, before you start cloning fields on a many-fielded card, plan out the order in which you wish your browsers to tab through fields.

In a two-column arrangement, for example, you may want the tab progression to be down the left-hand column, then down the right-hand column. To keep the fields in this order from the very beginning of your

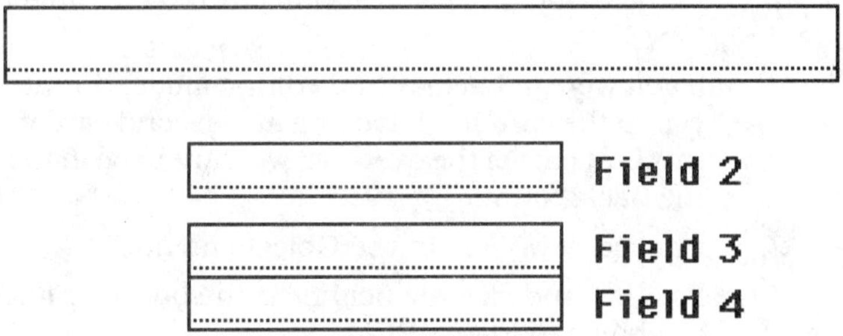

*Figure 9–22. Option-Shift-dragging a cloned field constrains the movement to either the vertical (above) or horizontal axis.*

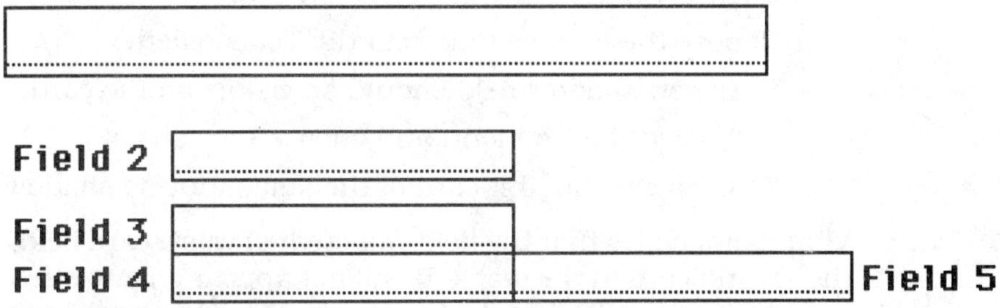

*Figure 9–23. Use constrained cloning to align fields in forms.*

design process, you would create the first field at the top of the left column and begin cloning vertically, using the vertical constrain to keep the fields in columnar alignment. Then clone the top left-hand field again, but constrain for horizontal motion only. Drag it into position at the top of the right-hand column. Continue cloning vertically down the right-hand column with the constrain key in force. Remember: Each time you clone a field, that new field is added as the topmost layer of the domain in which the original lives (that is, background or card).

## *Changing a Field's Domain*

The greatest hazard in creating a new text field is making sure you are in the correct domain: background or card. If you discover that you've placed a field in the wrong domain— especially after carefully sizing it, positioning it, and perfecting its attributes— all your work will not be in vain. Fortunately, you can cut the entire field from one layer and paste it into the other in precisely the same location.

We'll use our new stack, Clone Home, as a scratchpad to work with.

1. In the Clone Home stack, pull down the Edit menu and choose New Card.

   If you were in background editing mode, this action will return you to the card level, looking at a second card in the stack. For this first part of the exercise, we want to be in the card level, not the background.
2. Choose New Field in the Objects menu.
3. Position and size the field near the bottom right of the screen, as shown in Figure 9–24.
4. Double-click on the new field to bring up the Field Info dialog box.
5. Click the Shadow style button and OK.
6. Choose the Browse tool from the Tools palette.

   Your new shadow field should be visible on the card.
7. Pull down the Go menu and choose Previous.

   You will see the first card of the stack, but no shadow field.

What happened is that the field you created was a card field, specific to the second card in the stack. It will not appear on any other card in the stack. If you want that field to be on all cards, then you must cut

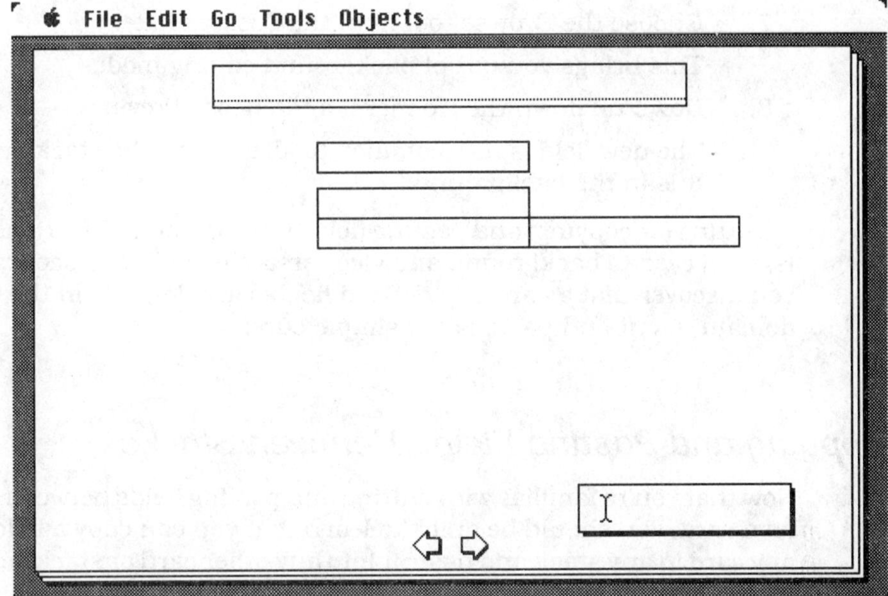


*Figure 9–24. Adding a shadowed card-domain field. This field will not appear on any other card in the stack.*

it from the card it's on and paste it into the background. Here's how you do it:

1. Pull down the Go menu and choose Next.

   You should be looking at the card with the shadow field you created.

2. Choose the Field tool from the Tools palette.

3. Click once on the field.

   The outline will turn into the marquee.

4. Pull down the Edit menu and choose Cut Field.

   The field will disappear from view, but it is safely in the Clipboard in memory.

5. Pull down the Edit menu and choose Background.

   The menubar will show its diagonals to confirm that you are in background editing mode.

6. Pull down the Edit menu and choose Paste Field.

   The field you just cut now appears in exactly the same spot on the screen from which you cut it.

7. Choose the Browse tool from the Tools palette.

   This brings you out of background editing mode.

8. Now Pull down the Go menu and choose Previous.

   The new field is now common to all cards in the stack because it is in the background.

Cutting (or copying) and pasting fields works in both directions, that is, from card to background and vice versa. So don't be discouraged if you discover that a carefully defined field is accidentally in the wrong domain. A cut and paste is the simple cure.

## *Copying and Pasting Fields Between Stacks*

Now that you're familiar with cutting and pasting fields between layers on a card, you should be quick to learn that you can copy a field from any card in any stack and paste it into any other card or stack. You use the same commands and procedures that we've already discussed for changing layers.

It's not likely that you'll be copying fields between stacks, but one case that may prove useful is when you discover a nicely designed stack with a carefully measured boundary, special font attributes, and other properties that would take you some time to replicate by way of the Field Info dialog box on a new field. If you encounter such a field and wish to import it into a stack you're creating, follow these steps.

1. With the Field tool (in the Tools palette) selected, click once on the field you wish to copy.

   You must also be in the same card or background domain as the field.

2. Choose Copy Field from the Edit menu.

   This puts a complete copy of the field into the Clipboard.

3. Choose the Browse tool from the Tools palette and navigate your way to the new stack you're creating.

   You may issue a Go command in the Message Box, use Recent to find the miniature card of the new stack you were working on earlier, open the new stack via the File menu, or any other method you see fit.

4. When you are in the appropriate domain for the new field, choose Paste Field from the Edit menu.

HyperCard automatically pastes the field into the card (or background) in exactly the same screen location as it was when you copied it.

When you paste this field, it acquires the next higher field number for the new stack and is therefore added as the layer closest to your eye within the background or card domain.

This wraps up our discussion about fields. It was a comparatively long one, but many of the properties of fields also apply to our next subject: buttons.

# CHAPTER 10

# All About Buttons

WHILE TEXT FIELDS ARE THE INFORMATION HOLDERS OF HYPERCARD CARDS, BUTTONS are the "movers and shakers" that can carry quite remarkable powers. As you have probably observed in your explorations in the stacks provided with HyperCard, a button may be a simple navigation aid, directing your view to a neighboring card in the stack or to a specific card in another stack. A button also has the potential of finding, retrieving, posting, and manipulating information stored in text fields on any card in any stack.

## *What Buttons Do*

Buttons perform *actions*. The action that a particular button carries out is determined entirely by the content of the HyperTalk script assigned to that button. That a button "runs" on HyperTalk may cause alarm at this stage, since we're still a bit away from beginning our discussion of the language. Fortunately, a HyperCard author does not need to know a syllable of HyperTalk to give the most common power assigned to a button: linking one card to another. This action can be assigned to buttons by way of dialog box selections and a special card-linking device we'll describe in this section.

## *Accessing the Button Tool*

To work with buttons, you must select the Button tool from the Tools palette. Here's how:

1. Make sure you are in the Authoring or Scripting user level.
2. Pull down the Tools menu.

   This action reveals the Tools palette (Figure 10–1).
3. For convenience, tear off the Tools palette from the menubar, and place it anywhere on the screen.
4. Click on the Button tool, which is the middle icon in the palette's top row (Figure 10–2).

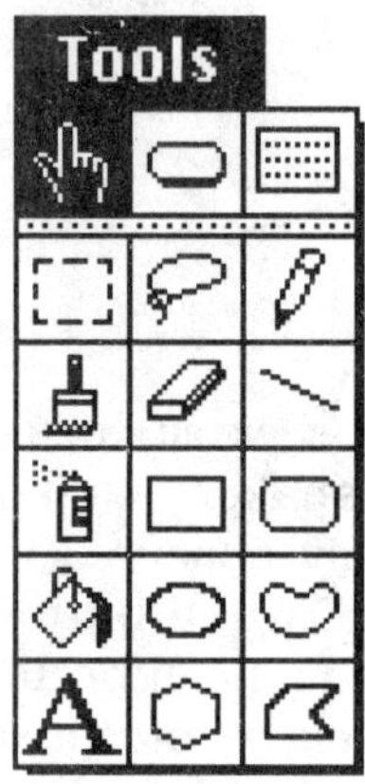


*Figure 10–1. The Tools menu*

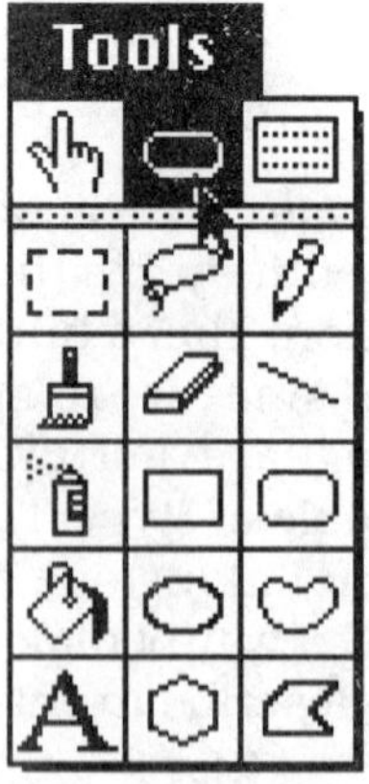


*Figure 10–2. Selecting the Button tool*

Depending on the construction of the card you are viewing when selecting the Button tool, the card's appearance may change slightly, as borders of buttons become highlighted.

5. When you are finished with the Button tool, return to the Browse tool by clicking on its icon in the upper left corner of the palette or typing Command-Tab (Figure 10-3).

   You may dispose of the Tools palette at any time by clicking on its close box.

As a HyperCard author, you have many options regarding button properties. The properties we'll concern ourselves with in this section are the layer, visual, and HyperTalk properties of buttons. Linking choices will be covered in the next chapter.

## Button Layer Properties

HyperCard buttons can be assigned to either the background or card domains. Like text fields, each button is itself a separate layer– like the acetate sheet metaphor we mentioned earlier. The browser, of course, perceives all buttons on a card to be essentially in one plane. As author, however, you are aware that what the browser sees may be made up of several background layer buttons and additional card layer buttons.

Background buttons are those that you wish to be available on every card in the stack. They "show through" all the layers and can also "see" the Browse tool when you press the mouse button. That means, of course, that for a background button to respond to the click of the

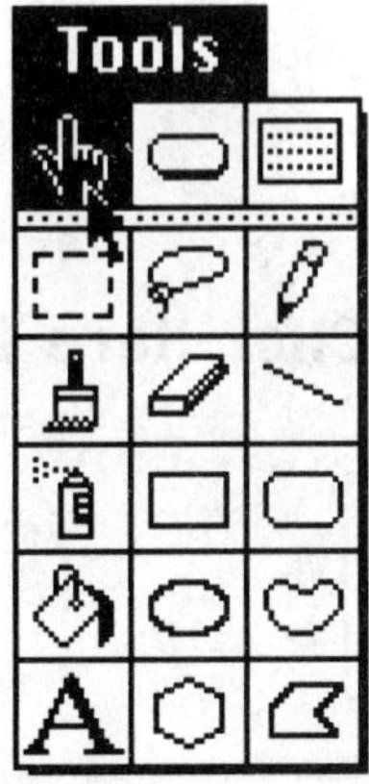


*Figure 10-3. Selecting the Browse tool*

mouse, the button cannot be obscured by buttons in layers closer to the viewer's eye nor by text fields or the card graphic layer. The button must be in the clear.

## CARD BUTTONS

A button in the card domain will be visible and available to the browser only in the card in which it was created or into which it was pasted. An example of the need for a card button would be a name and address stack. If, on a card elsewhere in your stacks, you have a graphic image of a map to someone's house, you could create a button on that person's address stack card, linked to the card bearing the map. There would be no need for a button on any other card in the address stack if you had only the one map. Therefore, it makes good sense to create a card domain button for that card only. The instant you advance to any other card in the address stack, that button will not be there. You are much more likely to create card domain buttons than card domain text fields.

As long as the buttons on a card are not obscured by other objects in their same domain (background or card), the precise order of button layers is not particularly important. With fields, you'll recall, the order of field layers affects the order in which the cursor advances from field to field at the press of the Tab key. Buttons do not react to the keyboard; so, in nearly all cases, their exact order is inconsequential.

You may have occasion, however, to design buttons in such a way that they overlap or rest atop each other (Figure 10-4). If so, you may have to change the order of buttons to suit your scheme. For example,

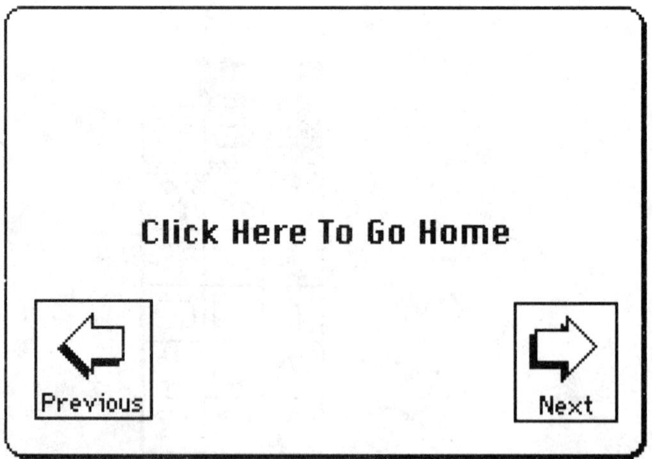


*Figure 10-4. Overlapping buttons*

in Figure 10–4, the large button (which takes you Home) must be farther away from the viewer than the two arrow buttons. If you create the arrow buttons first, the large button will cover them up when you create it. To rectify such a situation, you'd change the button order to make the large button number one in the ranks. To change the layer of a button within a domain, you use the Move Closer and Move Farther commands in the Objects menu. We explained in detail how these commands work on adjusting layers of text fields. The principle is identical for button layers. The Move Closer command brings a selected button one layer closer to the viewer's eye; the Move Farther command pushes a selected button one layer farther away from the viewer's eye.

### BUTTON NUMBERS AND ORDER

Each button, when it is created, is assigned both a sequence number and a unique ID number. The sequence number is its order within the domain. Therefore background button number 1 is closer to the "bedrock" background picture layer than button number 2. If you change the buttons' orders with the Move Closer or Move Farther commands, their sequence numbers may change. Consequently, it is often risky to refer to buttons (in HyperTalk scripts) by button number: The number may change as the design of the stack evolves. A button's ID number, however, stays with it, even after a button is deleted from a stack. Once an ID number is handed out, it will never be given to another button in the same domain in the same stack. ID numbers, therefore, are safe ways of referring to buttons.

An important point to remember about button layers is that they are, indeed, there. Because their order does not affect perceived card properties, an author may forget that adjusting a text field layer means that it must also pass through button layers. For example, if you assign field A and buttons A through F, and then add field B, it will take seven Move Farther commands to push field B below the field A layer (Figure 10–5).

The Move Closer and Move Farther commands work only within one domain; that is, you do not use these commands to shift a background to the card domain or vice versa. To do that, you cut and paste between layers, as we'll describe in detail later in this section.

## *Button Visual Properties*

Buttons are rectangular areas on the screen. Beyond that unalterable feature of buttons, a wide choice in the visual presentation of a button awaits the HyperCard author. All visual properties of a button are

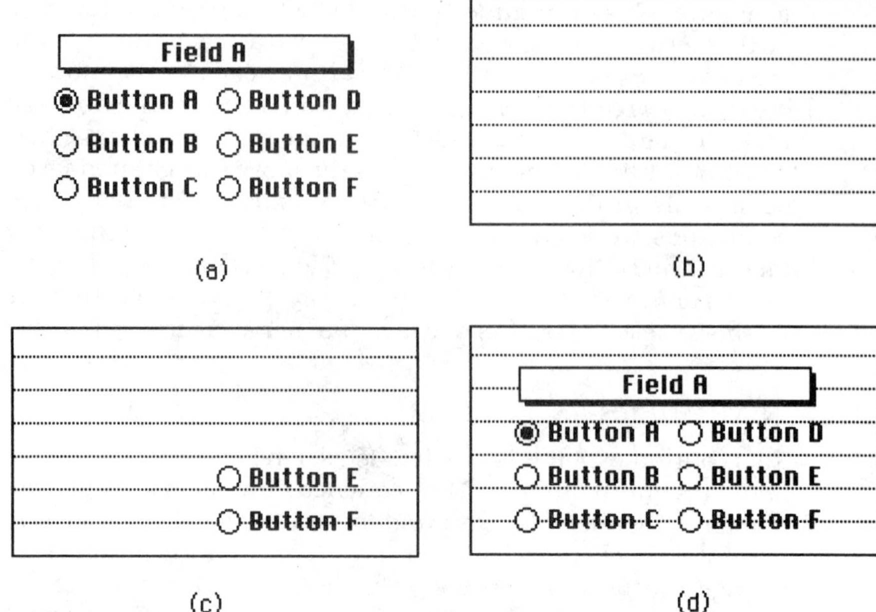


*Figure 10–5. Starting with one field and six buttons (a), you can add a new field, which automatically goes to the topmost layer of the selected domain (b). After two Move Farther commands, the new field moves back 2 layers (c). After a total of seven commands, the field is number 1 (d).*

defined in the Button Info box (Figure 10–6). There are seven button styles (transparent, opaque, rectangle, shadow, round rectangle, check box, and radio button), plus the choices of attaching icon art to a button, showing the button name on the screen, or having the button highlight when you click it.

## OVER TWO DOZEN BUTTON STYLES

By the time you apply the icon and name combinations to the seven button styles, you end up with twenty-eight ways to show a button on the screen. These variations are displayed in Figure 10–7. Since the icon and name options affect the way each of the four button styles shows up on the screen, we'll discuss these options first.

## ICON BUTTONS

Anyone who has used the Macintosh for some time is well acquainted with icons. Even casual users can't miss them: Turning on the computer without any disk drive attached or diskette inserted brings

File Edit Go Tools Objects

Button Name: Button A

Card button number: 1

Card button ID: 1

☒ Show name

☒ Auto hilite

Icon...

LinkTo...

Script...

Style:

◯ transparent
◯ opaque
◯ rectangle
◯ shadow
◉ round rect
◯ check box
◯ radio button

OK Cancel

*Figure 10-6. The Button Info dialog box*

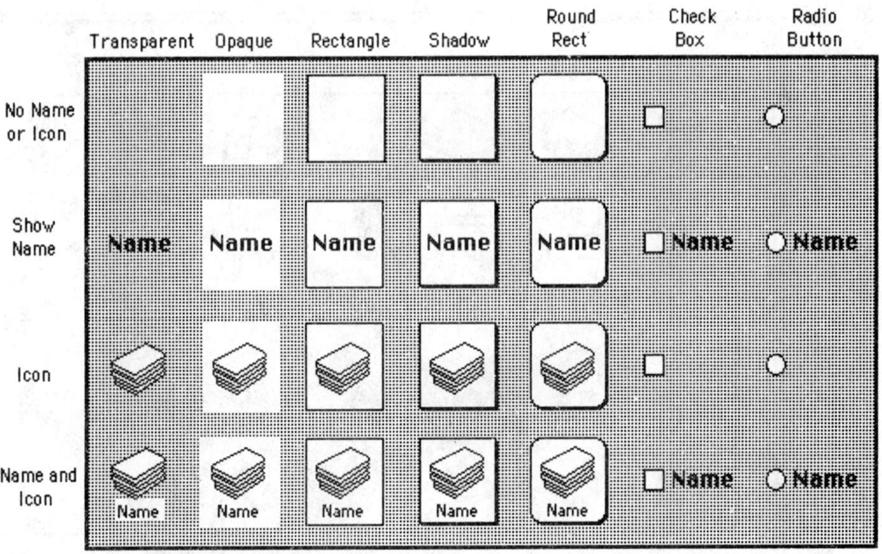


*Figure 10-7. Samples of possible button style and property combinations available to HyperCard authors*

up a Macintosh icon with a flashing question mark. Everyone is familiar with clicking and dragging icons in the Macintosh Finder. The browser of your stacks, then, will feel right at home with the idea of an icon button.

For the HyperCard author, the primary benefit of an icon button is that this is the only kind of button that has any graphics attached to it. In other words, you cannot simply draw a graphic on the screen with the HyperCard painting tools and turn it into a button that you copy, paste, or drag around the screen along with the action attributed to the button. Art for an icon is stored in a part of the stack file, the Home stack file, or in the HyperCard application file itself. This special part of the file is called the Resource Fork. Not particularly a place for beginners, the Resource Fork also contains information any program needs for such things as dialog boxes and their contents, fonts, and the application's icons.

HyperCard makes it rather simple to assign icon art to a button. From the Button Info dialog box, click the Icon... button. You then see another dialog box that presents a visual catalog (Figure 10–8) of all the icons the current stack could find (in the resource forks of the stack itself, the Home Stack, and the HyperCard program file). Icons have both an ID number and optional name. When you click an icon in the

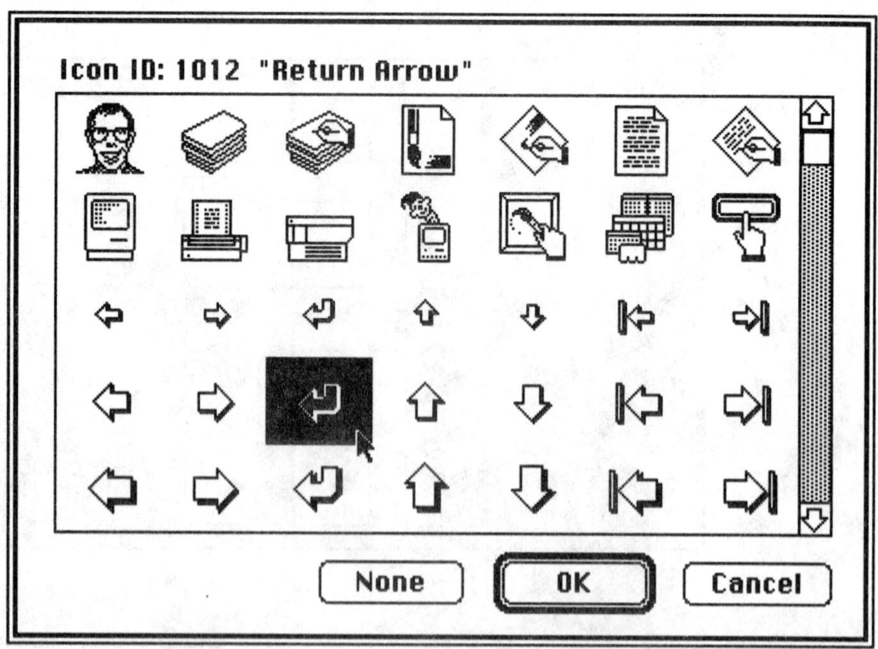


*Figure 10–8. The Icon dialog box presents a visual catalog of icons available for use in buttons.*

dialog box, its ID and name are assigned to that button. You may change the icon by clicking on another icon picture. If you change your mind and don't want an icon button, click None in the Icon dialog box.

You have probably noticed that very few icons are perfect rectangles, which may seem on the surface to violate the rule stated earlier that all buttons are rectangular. The rule holds, even for icon buttons, no matter how irregularly shaped they are. That's because the button area that contains the icon art is still a rectangle. Therefore, the active area of a button is not just atop the individual picture elements of the icon, but every spot within the rectangle around the icon. That rectangle, incidentally, can be literally as large as the HyperCard screen, but the icon will remain only one size.

## ICON ART AND MACINTOSH RESOURCES

HyperCard comes with a number of icons already installed into the HyperCard application file's Resource Fork. The full set of icons and IDS is shown in Figure 10–9.

If you design icon art for an application to be distributed to other HyperCard users, you will have to follow several steps to convert the art into an icon resource and install that resource in your HyperCard

| | | | | | | | | | |
|---|---|---|---|---|---|---|---|---|---|
| 2002 | 1000 | 1001 | 1002 | 1003 | 1004 | 1005 | 1006 | 1007 | 1008 |
| 1019 | 26884 | 18814 | 27056 | 15420 | 16560 | 6720 | 16692 | 3584 | 24317 |
| 29903 | 1014 | 1013 | 1012 | 29019 | 2730 | 30557 | 26865 | 9301 | 27009 |
| 2162 | 32488 | 2335 | 5472 | 766 | 902 | 26425 | 29114 | 4895 | 6724 |
| 21449 | 24830 | 17779 | 8419 | 7417 | 26020 | 15279 | 19381 | 22308 | 14953 |
| 6460 | 6179 | 3835 | 29484 | 9120 | 19162 | 1016 | 32650 | 1011 | 11045 |

*Figure 10–9. Icons and their ID numbers already installed in HyperCard for your immediate use*

| 20098 | 21700 | 20689 | 21847 | 1017 | 10610 | 30696 | 17481 | 3430 | 11645 |
|---|---|---|---|---|---|---|---|---|---|
| 4432 | 20965 | 17357 | 21209 | 8961 | 22855 | 4263 | 15972 | 20186 | 32670 |
| 26635 | 25002 | 32462 | 21060 | 2507 | 31685 | 1020 | 23078 | 19678 | 2478 |
| 14767 | 1018 | 1015 | 1009 | 8538 | 9761 | 7012 | | | |

*Figure 10-9. (continued)*

stack file. This brings up an important concept, however. The concept, called hierarchy, revolves around an underlying structure of the way HyperCard performs many of its tasks internally. We'll get more into the theory and practice of hierarchy in the chapters on HyperTalk. In the meantime, we'll look at the role hierarchy plays in making icon buttons visible at various places throughout HyperCard.

When you click on an Icon dialog box icon (thus attaching an icon ID number to that button) the button has a prescribed series of places it can look for the icon artwork. First stop on its search is in the file of the stack in which the button lives. If there is no match for the Icon ID in that file, it looks to the Home stack's resources. Finally, when all else fails, the button looks into the HyperCard application file's resources. The direction of search– from current stack to Home stack to HyperCard– is fixed. The implications of this hierarchy of resource searching are many.

Right off the bat, you should recognize that if you attach an icon resource to your stack file, a Home stack button can not display that icon's art. Resource searches go in only one direction: from the specific to the general, or, in HyperCard terms, from the application stack to Home to HyperCard. A button in the Home stack will not know to look in any other stack file for icon art. It looks only in its own stack file and in HyperCard itself. Fortunately, if you copy and paste an icon button from one stack to another, HyperCard copies and pastes the icon resource along with all other button properties. Then, even if you delete the button from the second stack, its icon resource stays there for use later on.

If you are developing a stack for distribution to other people, and the stack uses custom icons of your design, be sure to put the resources for your icons in the stack file. Leaving the resources in your Home Stack or in your copy of HyprCards won't help the people receiving your stacks.

It's important that the ID number assigned to your icon is not used by any other icon. Unexpected results may crop up. If, for example, you assign an ID number of 1000 to an icon you design for a stack, you might logically install it in the Home stack. To do so, however, will conflict with buttons in other stacks that were designed to display the HyperCard stack icon, which also has an ID OF 1000. The HyperCard stack icon resource is in the HyperCard application file, but when a button starts looking for a match to the Icon ID number assigned to it, it will look up through the hierarchy in its prescribed order. The instant it finds a match, it looks no further. Therefore, if your icon ID 1000 is in the Home stack, all buttons in all other stacks expecting to find the HyperCard stack icon will display your new icon instead. Since the icon resource consists strictly of art for the icon, the original button style and script assigned to the buttons are not affected by the icon art. But a browser could be mightily confused to encounter your custom icon when the HyperCard stack icon should be in a particular button in another stack.

## BUTTON NAMES

A second visual attribute that affects all button styles is the choice of showing the button name. The name is the one you type into the Name blank in the Button Info dialog box (Figure 10–6). As shown in Figure 10–7, the name displays differently depending on the button style you choose. Showing the name on a button is optional when the button is associated with icon or background art. Usually, the graphic image of either the icon or background button art is enough to convey the meaning of the button. But when there is doubt, or when the button style dictates that some textual explanation of the button's action is in order, showing the name is the best way. We'll have more to say about naming buttons when we cover a button's HyperTalk properties.

## TRANSPARENT BUTTONS

Now we come to the first of the button styles, the transparent style. Without showing the button's name or icon, the transparent button style is, for all practical purposes, invisible to the browser. There are no borders or even any cursor indication that a transparent button exists on the screen. When, then, would you use a transparent button?

Actually, there are many instances in which a transparent button is the ideal choice. The most obvious one is when another object in a lower layer—a text field or a graphics layer—implies the message "Press Here." That message need not be grossly obvious. For example, if you wish someone to click on one of several locations on a map, you might place transparent buttons strategically atop a map's graphics layer. When the browser clicks on those transparent buttons, the stack may branch to detail screens about the locations on the map. Figures 10-10 and 10-11 show what the browser and author see in a card from Activision's *Business Class* stack.

Another example would be in a predominantly textual card. If you have further explanations about key words on the card, you may mark them with an asterisk or other character in the text field. Then overlay transparent buttons atop the asterisks or atop the word and asterisk. Clicking on these buttons brings the user to a different card with the detail text. This kind of instant expansion and linking of text is in the tradition of the concept *hypertext*, pioneered by Ted Nelson.

So, you see, transparent buttons can be quite useful, even though the browser doesn't "see" the button per se. It's up to the stack author to make the browser perceive a button when there is none to see.

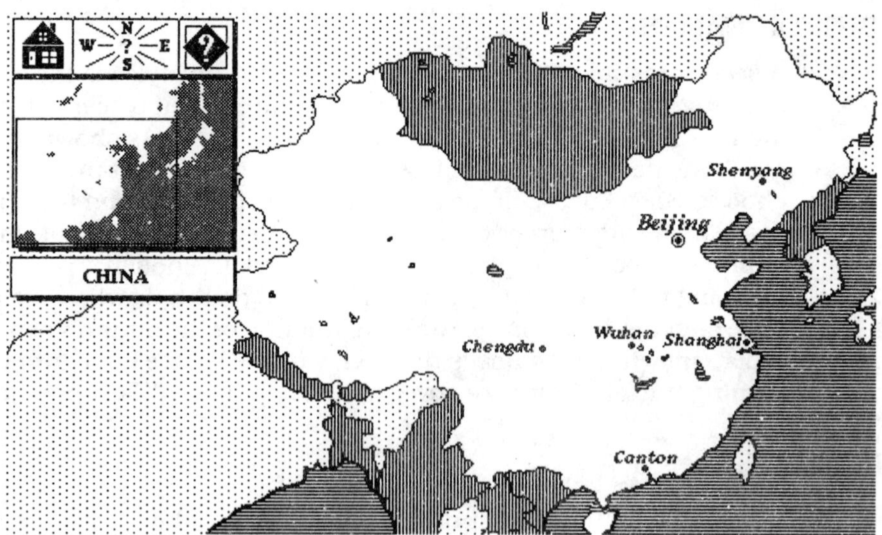


*Figure 10-10. This map has many transparent buttons atop it, each leading you to an adjacent country's map.*

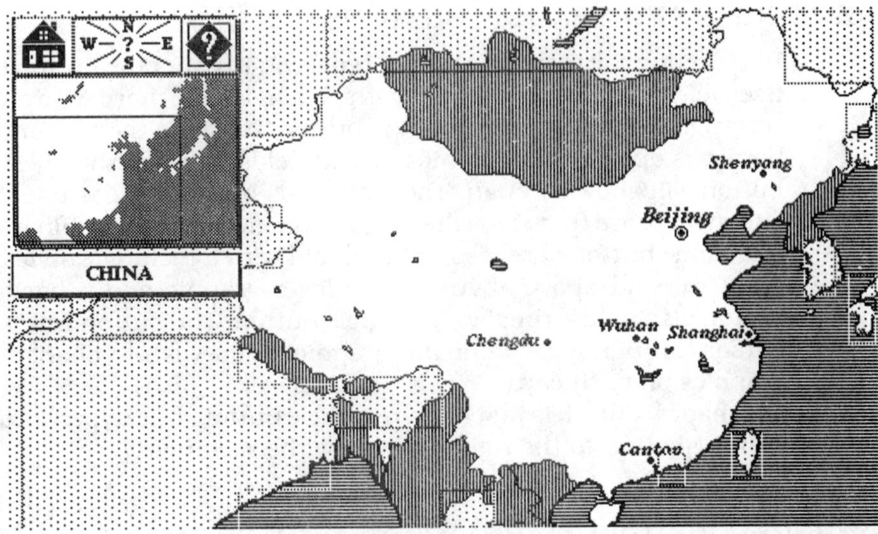


*Figure 10-11. Holding down the Option and Command keys reveals the locations of all the transparent buttons on the map.*

## OPAQUE BUTTONS

An opaque button appears to the browser as a rectangle that doesn't let any objects behind it show through. Without any background graphic to invite the browser to "click me," this button style begs for the Show Name attribute to be checked, an icon, both the name and the icon, or, surprisingly, a graphic in a layer between the button and the viewer's eye. Let's explain this last idea.

In all our discussions about the interaction between background and card domains, we've made it sound like anything in the card domain graphic layer obscures objects beneath it, that is, in the background domain. *Visually*, that's correct. But buttons have a kind of X-ray vision that lets them look at the surface level cursor through the card picture layer. Therefore, if you have an opaque button in a background layer, you can put a card level graphics image directly between the button and the viewer's eye. To the browser, the graphic may appear to be a background graphic under a transparent button or like an icon button altogether. But what the arrangement of background opaque button and card layer graphic gives you is a consistent button action from card to card, while the graphic associated with the button changes from card to card. If that is a desired effect, then the opaque button is the right choice.

## RECTANGLE AND SHADOW BUTTONS

By selecting the rectangle button type, you instruct the button to show itself clearly to the browser with a single line border around the rectangle defining the area of the button. Because the area inside the border is opaque, no graphics or text fields beneath the layer of that button will show through. Therefore, this button style is usually best suited for those that show the button name. Icon and combination icon and name buttons are also not unusual with a rectangle style button. What we said above about a card layer graphic and a background button also holds true for a rectangle button. The button will "see" the cursor through a card domain graphic if you wish to change button graphics on each card.

A shadow button is just like a rectangle button, but HyperCard draws a drop shadow to the right and below the rectangle.

## ROUNDED RECTANGLE BUTTONS

The round rectangle style draws a shadowed round rectangle inside the rectangular area of the button. This button style will look familiar to most Macintosh users, since it and versions closely related to it are used commonly in dialog boxes. Buttons that show the button name look particularly appealing in this button style. Round rectangle buttons are also opaque, and observe the same layering properties as opaque, rectangle, and shadow buttons, detailed above.

## CHECK BOX BUTTONS

A favorite button style from Macintosh dialog boxes is the check box. Use this button when you wish the user to turn features on and off. According to published Macintosh user interface guidelines, check-box buttons do not interact with other buttons (as radio buttons do), so each one should control a toggled selection of some kind.

While a click of an unchecked check-box button should place an X in the box, this action must be carried out by the button's script. Therefore, until you learn about HyperTalk, you'll have to limit your check-box ventures to copied and pasted varieties from other stacks.

In almost every case, you'll want to show the name of the button to tell the user its purpose on the card.

## RADIO BUTTONS

According to the Macintosh interface guidelines, radio buttons are usually grouped together in sets of two or more. They should behave in a way that lets only one button in the group be engaged— set with a black center dot— at a time. Hence its derivation from the old car radio pushbutton model.

The actions that highlight and unhighlight buttons in a group are controlled strictly by scripts— and carefully conceived scripts at that. As one button is clicked, its script must unhighlight the others and highlight itself. It's not as difficult as it sounds, but it's also not something you're likely to do before diving into HyperTalk.

A radio button, like a check box button, should show the button name to help identify its meaning. Always check the Show Name property in this style of button's Button Info dialog box.

## HyperTalk Button Properties

Without getting into specifics about HyperTalk at this stage, we can say that HyperTalk scripts may frequently refer to specific buttons in a HyperCard stack. For example, you may find yourself writing a script that includes a statement to essentially click on a card's button. That is, the script will perform several operations on your behalf, one of which is clicking on a particular button to effect that button's action. For this to happen, the button needs a name, whether you show it with the button or not.

You may not start writing these kinds of scripts right away, but it would be a good idea to get in the habit of assigning names to buttons. Chances are that the exercise will actually help you in your card design by forcing you to think through exactly what purpose each button has on the card. To the best of your ability, assign a one- or two-word name to the button that closely describes the action that the button performs.

## Creating New Buttons

If you were with us when we created new text fields, creating new buttons from scratch will be a breeze. The techniques are identical. As with fields, the biggest trap to watch for is being in the desired domain (background or card) before creating a button. In the haste to make buttons, it's easy to forget to choose Background from the Edit menu when you desire background buttons.

Here, then, is one of the two ways to create a button:

1. Creating a button is an authoring task, so be sure you are at the Authoring or Scripting user level.
2. If you wish to make a background button, choose Background from the Edit menu, or type Command-B.

3. Choose New Button from the Objects menu.

   A default rounded rectangle-style button appears in the center of the screen. The marquee is already swirling around it, indicating that the button is selected and the Button tool is in force.

The other button creation method takes these steps:

1. Pull down the Tools menu and select the Button tool.
2. Hold down the Command key.

   When you do, the cursor changes to a "plus" sign. This is like a drawing cursor.
3. Position the cursor at the upper left corner of the location on the screen where the button is to appear.
4. Click and slowly drag the pointer to the right and down (Figure 10–12).

   As you do, the outline of the button's rectangular area shows you the extent of the button you are dragging.
5. When the button is the desired size, release both the mouse button and the Command key.

The default button style for the New Button method is a rounded rectangle, with no icon, but showing the New Button name. If that's the kind of button you want, simply select the Browse tool in the Tools palette to return you to the card layer (if you were in the background). For the Command-drag method, HyperCard dishes out a transparent style button with neither name nor icon properties set.

Of course, no matter which method you follow, you haven't instructed the button to do anything, so clicking it with the Browse tool results in no action. We'll show you how to give the button life in the next chapter, on linking.

Rarely will the default button style be the one you want, nor will your first attempt at dragging the button always be successful at placing and sizing the button as you had planned. It's then time to edit the button.

## MOVING AND RESIZING BUTTONS

As far as the button's size and location goes, you can adjust them most simply right after you create it, before selecting the Browse tool. When you create a button, the new button is selected, as noted by the marquee (or marching ants) around the button's rectangle. When a button is selected, you can drag it around the screen and resize it.

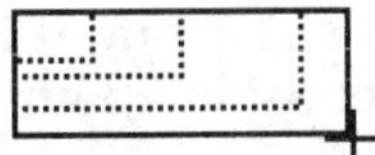

*Figure 10-12. To create a new button from scratch, select the Button tool, hold down the Command key, and drag the button to the desired size.*

To drag the button while it's selected, place the screen cursor in the center of the button's rectangle, click, and drag the button. As with text fields, you have the ability to constrain movement along one axis. Before clicking and dragging the button, hold down the Shift key. If you start dragging the button up or down, you will be restricted to movement in the vertical direction only, no matter how you move the mouse cursor; similarly if you drag the button first to the left or right when the Shift key is pressed, your drag motion will be constrained to the horizontal axis.

Resizing the button is a similar process, except that you click the cursor on one of the corners of the button's rectangle and drag that corner like a rubberband. Release the mouse button when the button is the desired size. Constrained movement with the Shift key is also available when resizing buttons, in case you have carefully adjusted one dimension and need to adjust the other without disturbing the first. Hold the Shift key down before clicking and dragging the button's corner.

When the button style is checked as Round Rectangle, the Shift constrain on resizing performs one special feature that aids in uniformity of button size on a card. By holding down the Shift key and grabbing a corner of the button's rectangle, HyperCard automatically sizes the vertical dimension of the button to one size for all round rectangle buttons. That should ease the design burden for those not steady with the mouse.

If you change your mind, and don't want that button there at all, you can delete the button two ways. First, select the button and choose Cut Button from the Edit menu (or type Command-X). Second, select the button and press the Backspace key.

You may move, resize, and remove buttons at any time, even after you've used the stack for some time.

## Cloning Buttons on the Same Card

If you've sized a button and assigned visual properties to it, you may wish to duplicate it one or more times on the same card. As with text fields, you may clone, or "peel off," copies of a button with the aid of the

Option key. To demonstrate how this works, use the Clone Home stack you made in our discussion about text fields.

1. Pull down the File menu and choose Open Stack...
2. In the resulting standard file dialog box, select the file Clone Home and click Open (or double-click on the Clone Home file name as a shortcut).
3. When the stack appears on the screen, choose Background from the Edit menu or type Command-B.

   The menubar will display its identifying background hash marks. You should see outlines for the fields originally in the stack and those we made in the last section. At the bottom of the card are two buttons, whose actions point to the previous and next cards in the stack.
4. Tear off the Tools palette and place it in a lower corner.
5. Choose the Button tool from the palette.
6. Hold down the Command key and drag the outline for a new button in an open area on the screen (Figure 10–13).
7. Double-click on the new button's outline to bring up the Button Info dialog box.
8. Select the Round Rectangle button style, and click on the Show Name checkbox.
9. Type the name "Button 1" into the name blank (Figure 10–14), and press the Return key to close the Button Info dialog box.

When you return to view the card, you'll see the round rectangle button with its name in the center, and the marquee around the button's rectangle. If you wish to see what the button looks like to the browser, select the Browse tool in the Tools palette. Then reselect the Button tool, because we are about to edit the new button we just created.

10. If the new button's outline is not a marquee, click once on the button to select it.
11. Hold down the Option key, and click and drag on the new button to the right of the first button (Figure 10–15).

    An exact copy of the first button peels off the first, ready for you to place anywhere you wish. This second button is in a separate layer, actually the topmost layer in the background domain, since it is the most recent object added to that domain.

Notice something quite important: The exact copy of the button includes an exact copy of the button's name. If you double-click on the

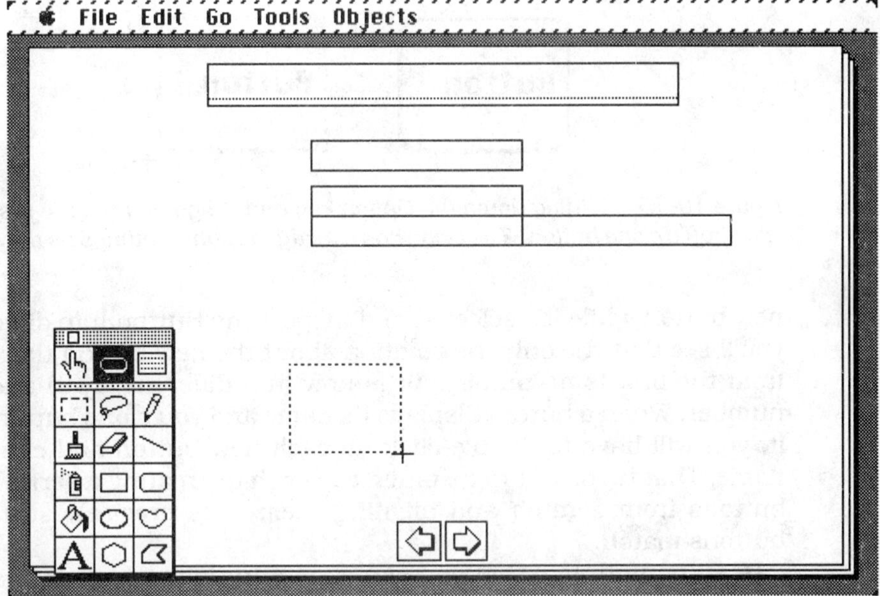


*Figure 10-13. Command-dragging a new button*

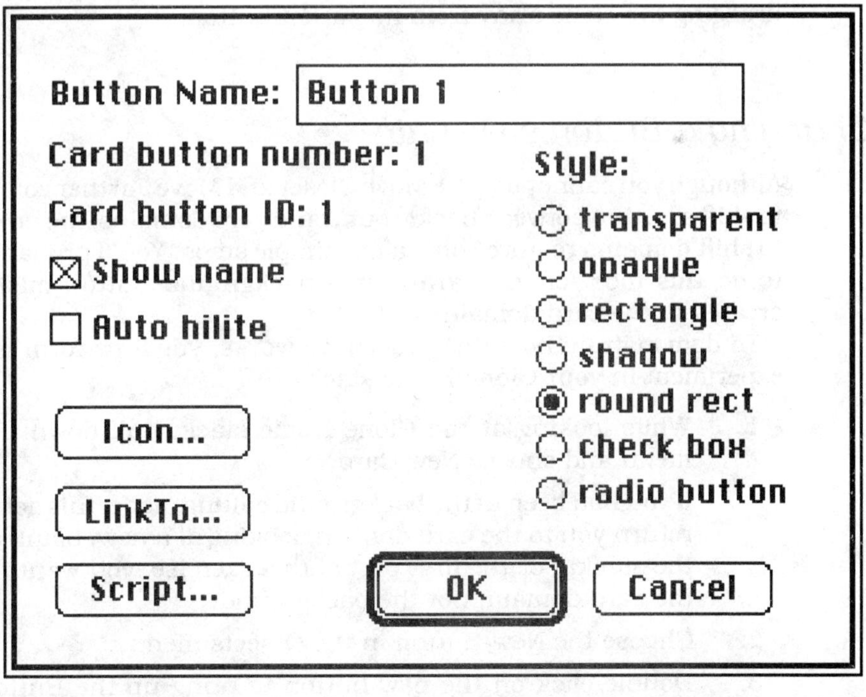

Button Name: Button 1

Card button number: 1

Card button ID: 1

☒ Show name

☐ Auto hilite

Icon...

LinkTo...

Script...

Style:

- transparent
- opaque
- rectangle
- shadow
- round rect
- check box
- radio button

OK

Cancel

*Figure 10-14. Assigning the name Button 1 in the Button Info dialog box. Note that the Round Rect style and Show Name property are selected.*

*Figure 10–15. Holding down the Option key and dragging from the first button "peel" off a clone button. The clone has exactly the same settings as the original.*

new button while it's selected and inspect the Button Info dialog box, you'll see that the only information about the new button that differs from the first is its number (it is now in a different layer) and its ID number. When a button displays its name and you clone buttons from it, you will have to double-click on each new button and change its name. That turns out to be much easier than creating a series of new buttons from scratch and aligning their sizes precisely so that all buttons match.

Bear in mind, too, that you can constrain the movement of a clone when you are peeling it from its parent. Therefore, if you wish to place a pair of buttons in precisely the same horizontal or vertical axis with each other, you can hold down the Shift and Option keys before dragging the clone away from its parent button.

## *Changing a Button's Domain*

Although you cannot use the Move Closer and Move Farther commands to shift a button between background and card domains, the procedure to shift domains requires only a few simple steps. You'll probably need to do this most often to transfer a background button mistakenly created in the card domain.

To demonstrate how this procedure works, you'll perform one last experiment in your Clone Home stack.

1. While looking at the Clone Home stack, pull down the Edit menu and choose New Card.

   If you had been in the background editing mode, this action will return you to the card domain, looking at a new, blank card in the stack. For the first part of this exercise, you want to be in the card domain, not the background.

2. Choose the New Button in the Objects menu.
3. Double-click on the new button to bring up the Button Info dialog box.

4. Click the Icon... button and choose the HyperCard stack icon from the icon dialog box.
5. Now select the Browse button on the Tools palette.

   You see the icon button you just created.
6. Click on the left-facing arrow button at the bottom of the card.

   This action takes you to the previous card in the stack.

Notice that your new card level button is no longer visible. As a card button, it exists only on the card in which it was created. If you want that button to appear in every card, then you must transfer it to the background. Here's how:

1. Click on the right-facing arrow button to bring the card with your new button into view.
2. Choose the Button tool from the Tools palette.
3. Click once on the button.

   The button will display a marquee outline.
4. Choose Cut Button from the Edit menu (or type Command-X).

   The button disappears from view, but it is safely in the Clipboard in memory.
5. Choose Background from the Edit menu (or type Command-B).

   The menubar will show its hash marks to confirm you are in the background editing mode.
6. Choose Paste Button from the Edit menu (or type Command-V).

   The button from the clipboard is pasted into the background, in precisely the same spot from which we cut it.
7. Select the Browse tool from the Tools palette (or type Command-Tab).

   This brings you out of background editing mode.
8. Click on either the right or left arrow buttons to move through our short stack.

   The new button appears on all cards. Even if a background field from your earlier experiments is in the location of your button, the button is a newer and, therefore, closer layer to your eye, so the button will be seen over the text field.

This cut and paste procedure for buttons also works in the opposite directions. If you wish to transfer a button from the background to only one or two cards, you can cut it from the background and paste it into the desired cards' card domain.

## *Copying and Pasting Buttons Between Stacks*

Until you become familiar with HyperTalk, the prospect of building button actions may sound a bit forbidding, especially because button actions rely entirely on HyperTalk scripts. Anticipating this fear on the part of beginning HyperCard users, Apple has supplied a library of button ideas on the ideas disk, which accompanies the HyperCard program. There are also dozens of buttons located in the stack and card ideas stacks on the same disk. You can use the familiar copy and paste techniques to borrow liberally from these existing buttons.

The collections include numerous icon buttons, round rectangle buttons, and others. If the action associated with a particular button in these libraries is not clear from the button's name, you will probably learn something about it from the script, even if you're not fluent in HyperTalk. HyperTalk is, after all, practically all in plain English. If you read aloud the script behind a button in these libraries, you will probably get an idea of what this button can do for your stack.

To inspect the script for a button, you'll first have to be in the Scripting user level. Then do the following:

1. Bring into view the card with the button whose script you wish to explore.
2. Choose the Button tool from the Tools palette.
3. Double click on the button to bring up the Button Info dialog box for that button.
4. Click on the Script button.

   Incidentally, there is a shortcut to reach button scripts. After you choose the Button tool, hold down the Shift key and double-click on the button. This brings you directly to the script dialog box for that object.

Most of the buttons in Apple's libraries contain short scripts, no more than ten lines each. In the script shown in Figure 10–16, for instance, the actions are to bring the next card into view whenever you release the mouse button and the cursor is atop this screen button. If you would like this button to be in a stack you are creating, copy it into the Clipboard (select it first with the Button tool, then choose Copy Button from the Edit menu), navigate to your stack under construction, choose the desired domain (background or card), and choose Paste Button from the Edit menu. All it takes is a handful of steps and no knowledge of HyperTalk.

Between the button libraries supplied by Apple and the buttons sure to become available in the public domain through user groups and bulletin boards, you will be able to incorporate quite powerful buttons

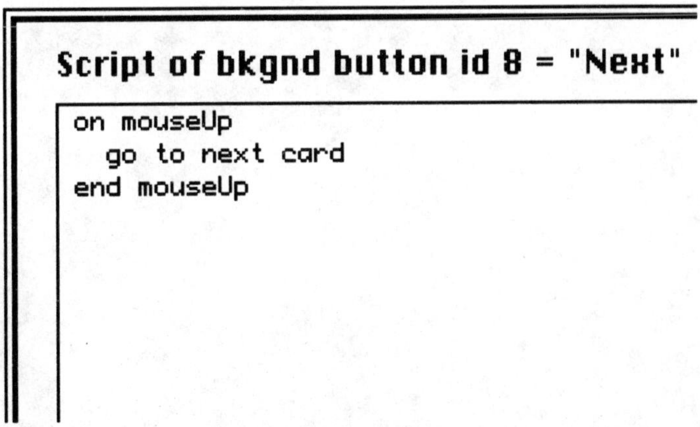

**Script of bkgnd button id 8 = "Next"**

```
on mouseUp
  go to next card
end mouseUp
```

*Figure 10-16. Most button scripts are short. This one advances the view to the next card when the mouse is pressed atop this button.*

into stacks you design. HyperCard is very open-ended in this regard. The intent behind these libraries is to encourage you to build applications around these many building blocks.

In the next chapter, we progress to the linking abilities of HyperCard and how you can have HyperCard actually write button scripts for you that link information, whether the cards be next to each other in a stack or in entirely different stacks.

# CHAPTER 11

# Basic Linking

HYPERCARD GIVES THE NONPROGRAMMING AUTHOR A CHANCE TO CREATE AN IMPORTANT button action without having to learn HyperTalk. With the help of the Link To button in the Button Info dialog box, you'll actually be writing HyperTalk scripts for your buttons.

## *The Essence of a HyperCard Link*

At the core of most HyperCard button activity is the link. A link ties together two cards, just like the colored yarns on the wall of index cards to which we referred in the Introduction. More precisely, a link is a one-way path from one card to another. It says, "Go from the card we're at to a different card." That "different card" may be:

- the next card in the stack
- a previously viewed card in the same or different stack
- the first card in another stack
- a specific card in another stack

### SIMPLE LINKS TO ADJACENT CARDS

Notice that we said that the link is one-way. If you wish to devise a two-way link, you would create a one-way button on each card pointing to the other. For example, in most stacks you see left- and right-facing buttons that link you to the previous and next cards, respectively. An instruction in the left-facing arrow's button script says, "Go to previous card." That's the extent of the link instruction. When you click on that button, you follow the "colored yarn" to the previous card in the stack order. To provide a button action that gets you back to the card from which you came, you need one that has a script saying, "Go to next card." That's exactly what the instruction in the right-facing arrow button's script says.

## LINKS TO DISTANT CARDS

When the link instruction is supposed to send the browser to a more distant card, the instruction must be more specific about the destination.

To zip to a distant card in the same stack you're browsing through, the instruction must refer to the destination card by number, ID number, or name. As we've already discussed, referring to any object by its sequence number is risky business, since the order of objects in a stack (or on a card, for that matter) can change with any addition, deletion, or reordering of objects. A card sort, for instance, will likely change many card numbers.

The best way to refer to a distant card is by either its unique ID number or its name. Names can be tricky because there is nothing stopping you from accidentally assigning the same name to two or more cards in a stack. The card ID number, however, is a sure thing. An instruction to link to a specific card by name would be something like,

```
Go to card "Index Page 1"
```

in the button script. A link instruction to a card's ID number would be something like

```
Go to card ID 5010
```

in the script.

## LINKS TO DIFFERENT STACKS

The link instruction that goes to a different stack must know the name of the stack to which the link is connected. When you specify only the name of the stack, HyperCard opens the stack and displays the first card of that stack— the card in the number 1 position in the card order. The instruction to go from a card to the first card of a stack named Proposals would be

```
Go to stack "Proposals"
```

HyperCard is also smart enough to know that if you don't specify objects, like buttons and fields in a Go instruction, then you must mean go to a stack. A Go instruction also does not need the word "to" added after it. Therefore the instruction could also be, simply,

```
Go "Proposals"
```

instead of explicitly mentioning the word "stack."

To link a card with a card in a different stack, the instruction must contain information about the card and stack. Following the kind of English instruction you might give to a friend to go to "the pizza place on Main Street," the HyperCard link instruction would be,

```
Go to card "Index Page 1" of stack "Proposals"
```

You could also use the card's ID number, which would make the instruction read,

```
Go to card ID 122 of stack "Proposals"
```

In other words, the link instruction contains something like a roadmap to the destination card, no matter where that card is.

## HARD LINKS

You might call these kinds of links "hard" links, because they simply take the browser from one card to the other, without performing any other kind of action. Once the hand-off to the destination is made, there is no connection with the information on the card of origin. Not that there's anything wrong with hard links— they form the cornerstone of a HyperCard stack's button actions. Most of the links in the rather extensive HyperCard Help system are hard links, so don't be led into thinking you can't do anything practical with only these simple links. Your stacks will need hard links. Lots of them.

As you'll see in a moment, it's quite easy to establish a hard link between cards, even without knowing about HyperTalk scripts. Depending on the kind of stack you're designing and the stack to which these links go, however, the hard link may seem like a burden to you, the author. One such cumbersome hard link environment would be a monthly calendar. Let's look at a hypothetical calendar and see what the link situation is.

We'll assume that the monthly calendar is to be linked to a daily appointment book stack, one in which there is a card for each day of the year. Ideally, we should be able to reach the daily appointment card for whatever day we click on the monthly calendar. There are two basic ways we can accomplish that link.

One way, using hard links, would be to create card domain buttons for each of the days of the month on each month's card. The day's numbers in the monthly calendar could be either in card domain text fields or in the card graphics layer. Each button would contain a hard link to the corresponding day's card in the appointment book stack. That means, however, that we would have to create twenty-eight to thirty-one card domain buttons per monthly calendar card and establish the links one by one— 365 of them for a year.

### SOFT LINKS

There is an easier way, although it means establishing a "soft" link. For this setup, you would create the monthly calendar stack with a small background text field in each daily square of a blank calendar form. Now, you can fill in the numbers for each day in the small fields of your calendar stack— one card for each month. After that, change the properties of the background fields in such a way that they are Locked Fields. This turns a field into an ad hoc button.

Instead of the hard link between monthly calendar day and the appointment book, you would then write a short HyperTalk script that performs a soft link. The script would combine the date number inside the field you click with the name of the month and year for that card into a full date, such as September 11, 1990. Next, the script would perform the hard link part of the operation, going to the first card of the appointment stack. Finally, the soft link part plays its hand, as the script orders HyperCard to find the full date among the cards in the appointment book stack.

The convenience of this kind of soft link to an author should be obvious. You need write only as many links as there are squares in the monthly calendar form, not one for every day of the year. Moreover, as time marches on, you can add months to the calendar without adding one letter of HyperTalk script to accommodate links to the new dates.

Admittedly, soft links require knowledge of HyperTalk. We unashamedly present this example at this relatively early stage in your HyperCard learning as enticement. We hope you don't stop short of getting into HyperTalk.

## *Instant Link Scripts*

We've come to the part that shows you how to have HyperCard make button scripts that link one card to another— automatic hard links, if you will. The procedure revolves around the one button in the Button Info dialog box we haven't yet covered: the Link To... button.

When you create a new button and double-click on its outline, you get that button's Button Info dialog box, in which you set its visual

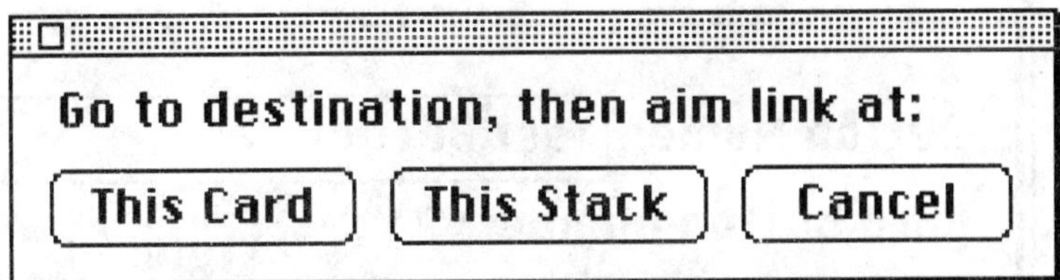


*Figure 11-1. The Link To button produces a small window to help you establish the link.*

properties. At that point you can also establish a hard link action for the button. The outline of the process is covered in three simple steps:

1. Click on the Link To... button, which displays a small window with instructions (Figure 11-1).
2. Navigate your way to the card to which you wish to link.
3. Click the This Card button on the overlaying window.

With the click of that This Card button, HyperCard generates a "Go to" entry in the button's script, complete with the exact designation of the destination card. If the destination is in the same stack, it signifies the card by its ID number. No stack name is entered, because the current stack is implied in the script when no stack name is provided. If the destination card is in a different stack, the line of the script identifies the card's ID number and the stack's name. Let's experiment with this power.

1. Go to the Home card.
2. Choose New Button from the Objects menu.
3. Double-click on the new button, which should still have the marquee around it.
4. Type the name Test Button into the Name box.
5. Click the Round Rectangle radio button in the list of styles (Figure 11-2).
6. Now click the Link To... button.

   A mini window appears on the screen, advising you to go to the card to which the current button should be linked.
7. Click on the Weekly icon in the Home card (Figure 11-3).

   HyperCard will bring the Datebook stack into view and advance to the current week.
8. Click twice on the right facing arrow, bringing into view the card of two weeks ahead of the current week.

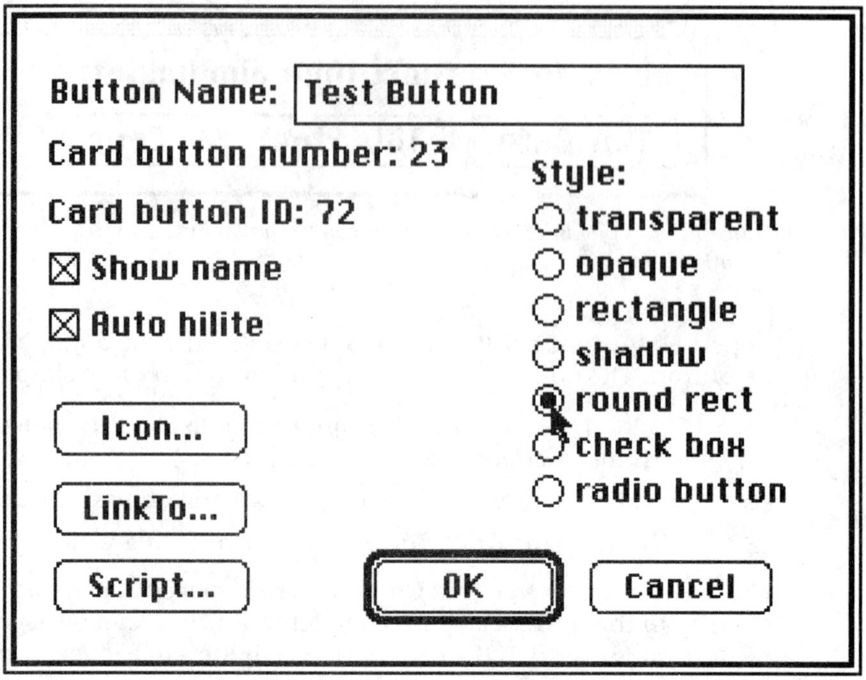

Button Name: Test Button

Card button number: 23

Card button ID: 72

☒ Show name

☒ Auto hilite

Style:

○ transparent
○ opaque
○ rectangle
○ shadow
● round rect
○ check box
○ radio button

Icon...

LinkTo...

Script...

OK

Cancel

*Figure 11-2. Clicking the round rect button style for Test Button*

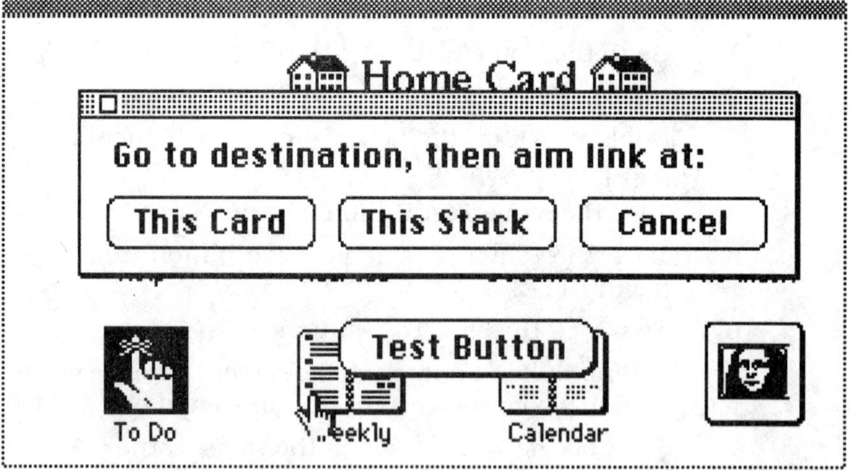


*Figure 11-3. Clicking on the weekly appointment book icon on the way to establish the link between the Test Button and a card in the Datebook stack*

9. Click the This Card button in the mini window.

   This tells the button named Test Button where it should "go to" when you click on it in the Home card. After specifying the link, HyperCard brings you immediately back to the card with the new button on it for further editing or additions.

Before we try the button, let's see what HyperCard did for us in this button's script.

1. Choose the Button tool from the Tools palette.
2. Double click on the new button.
3. Click on the Script button in the Button Info dialog box.

Notice that the script now contains a line that says "Go To card ID 4012 in stack 'Datebook'" (the ID number in your script may be different). HyperCard will perform this action whenever the cursor is atop this button when you release the mouse button.

Now, click Cancel in the Script dialog box, and choose the Browse tool in the Tools palette. Click once on Test Button. In a flash, you are looking at the card in the Datebook stack to which you linked.

As we mentioned, there is no link created for you in the other direction. You can, of course, go Back (in the Go menu) step by step, in case you want to see where you have been.

If you're not happy with the link you have made, you can change it, using the same Link To...button in the Button Info dialog box and procedure we just walked through. The new link you establish will replace the first one written into the script. In a way, then, you can edit the button script without even opening the script dialog box.

## New Button Strategies

Now that we've seen the component parts of what goes into a button, including a hard link, we present a prescription for creating new buttons most efficiently. You don't have to follow our orders, but we've found this procedure to be the least time-consuming.

If you are Command-dragging a new button, don't be too concerned about accurate placement or sizing at first. Just get any kind of button outline on the screen.

With either button-creation method, double-click on the button, since it is still selected (has the marquee around it) when you release the mouse button from creating it in the first place. Go to work on items in the Button Info dialog box.

Assign a name to the button (optional, but recommended). Now grab the mouse and start selecting the remaining visual attributes.

First, if the button is to show its name, click the check box. Then set the button style from the list of seven on the right of the dialog box.

Now we come to the automatic scripting. Click the Link To... button. Follow the directions on the mini window, as we described above. When you're finished, you'll automatically come back to the card, ready to use the button.

Now that the button is in its proper style and is correctly linked, you can select it and adjust its location and size to suit. Remember to use constraining for fine-tuning both location and size. Also, since so many of the button's attributes are already set, you can clone the button if needed. The only adjustments you'll need to make to the Button Info dialog box for each cloned button are the button name and in the Link To... button. Follow the mini window's directions for each button to make sure it links to the desired card.

You're now ready to accomplish quite a lot with new buttons of your own creation. The only area we really need to cover for all HyperCard authors (HyperTalk and non-HyperTalk) is what all those painting tools are about.

CHAPTER 12

# Introduction to HyperCard's Painting Tools

WITH THE HELP OF THE STACK, CARD, AND BUTTON IDEAS INCLUDED ON YOUR HyperCard disks, you can go far creating your own stacks that have a great deal of visual appeal and information storage power. But there will be times when you'll want to modify the background art on one of those stacks. After all, the purpose of the "ideas" files provided with HyperCard is not just to give you "canned" stacks that you adopt blindly. They are intended as starting points to stimulate your thinking about the way you can use HyperCard to manage information. It probably won't be long before you'll want to take that grander step and design a new stack from scratch.

## *The Role of HyperCard Art*

What you'll begin to appreciate with your first explorations in HyperCard stack design is that no matter how powerful the button actions you assign to a card or how interactively cards link with each other, the overall "look" of the card will have a pervasive impact on the stack's appeal. To that end, HyperCard provides the author with a very complete set of artistic tools— the same kinds of tools that professional Macintosh artists have been using since the Macintosh became available in January 1984.

We would be leading you on if we said that these tools turn anyone into an accomplished artist. As with any tool, the quality of the work resulting from the application of that tool is directly proportional to the skill of the user. Someone using a hammer for the first time will more than likely drive a nail in askew or perhaps miss the nail's head and damage the wood surface. With practice, however, you get a feel for how a nail responds to various pressures of the hammer's head in different types of wood; you learn, for instance, when to stop hitting a wood finishing nail before its head reaches the wood surface and then to carefully recess the nail with the aid of a tamp.

What this means is that you can expect to gain a comfortable skill level by practicing with the HyperCard graphics tools. They'll give you a headstart in many graphical areas. If you can't draw a straight line on paper with a ruler and pencil, don't fear: One HyperCard tool draws straight lines, no matter how crookedly you drag the mouse pointer. Other tools help you draw perfect circles and squares. Still others fill areas on the screen with intricate patterns and shades.

Practice is the best way to gain mastery of the graphics tools. But you are also free to examine the techniques of those who have gone before you to create the screens of existing stacks. We'll show you in chapter 15 how to literally put a magnifying glass on their work to see how they accomplished various graphics effects. If *they* did it, so can you.

## *Macintosh Painting*

The basis of the HyperCard graphics tools is known by a couple of terms among Macintosh users. One term you'll see sometimes in this regard is "bit-mapped graphics." Bit-mapping is a term borrowed from the programmer's lexicon, meaning being able to turn on or off each tiny dot on the screen. We won't be using this term much, because it tends to get confused with the Macintosh's nature as a bit-mapped graphics computer. Not all Macintosh graphics programs give you direct control over each dot on the screen, but the Macintosh nevertheless draws everything on the screen dot by dot.

### PAINTING VS. DRAWING

We prefer to call the HyperCard graphics tools *painting* tools, as distinct from *drawing* tools. Both terms are derived from two early graphics programs that Apple released for the Macintosh. The first was MacPaint, written by the same Bill Atkinson who designed HyperCard. The other was MacDraw, adapted by Mark Cutter from his LisaDraw, a program on Apple's earlier Lisa workstation computer. By examining the difference between these two environments, you'll understand quite a bit about HyperCard's graphics environment.

MacPaint, which is still a popular graphics program on the Macintosh, gives you control over each dot on the screen (a dot is better known as a picture element, or pixel). When you draw a rectangle in a "paint" environment, you are actually laying out a pattern of black pixels atop a white background. The graphics document you store on the disk doesn't recognize the pattern of pixels as being any kind of graphics object. It simply stores the locations of black pixels on the page— a map, if you will, to the on and off bits on the page. Since the rectangle is only a set of pixels, you cannot "pick it up" to adjust its size or line thickness.

MacDraw, on the other hand, treats graphics shapes as objects instead of a collection of dots. For instance, when you draw a rectangle in a "draw" environment, the program stores information about the shape as an object. A rectangle has a screen coordinate for its top left and bottom right corners, a certain width of the line that makes the rectangle's four sides, and a certain pattern that may fill the rectangle. You can select and "pick up" an object at any time after you draw it on the screen and change any of its attributes: its size, location, line thickness, or pattern. Draw objects, then, have layers, just like HyperCard's text field and button objects have layers. What you can't do with a draw program, however, is adjust individual pixels on the screen for certain artistic touches, such as gradation of shading or fine-tuning complex graphics one pixel at a time.

Each kind of program has had versions produced by third-party software developers. In the paint environment, FullPaint (Ann Arbor Softworks) has been popular. Cricket Draw (Cricket Software) improves on MacDraw. One program, SuperPaint (Silicon Beach Software) combines both the paint and draw environments into one, each environment getting its own layer domain in a document.

## HYPERCARD PAINTING

HyperCard's graphics tools are in the paint tradition. Everything you create with the graphics tools will be painting pixels on the screen. You can apply the tools equally to the background and card picture layers. The layers can even interact with each other for some special effects you can't get with regular paint programs.

If you've had experience with paint programs such as MacPaint, FullPaint, or SuperPaint, HyperCard's painting tools will be familiar to you. There are a number of enhancements over MacPaint, however, so don't think you're getting old stuff in this program.

If you're new to Macintosh graphics, you're in for a treat. Paint graphics are fun on the Macintosh. You'll be surprised at the results you'll be getting in a short time. The best part, though, is that there is no penalty for trying any kind of drawing or technique. If it doesn't work, then erase it and try again. Experiment freely.

After an overview of the HyperCard painting environment, we'll present each of the HyperCard paint tools, commands, and shortcuts. As we discuss each one, try it out on your Macintosh. Only by practice will you become proficient with HyperCard's painting tools.

## *Graphics Overview*

In all your HyperCard painting, you'll be turning pixels on and off. Since a HyperCard graphics layer can be the size of the entire HyperCard window, the maximum area is 512 pixels across and 342 pixels vertically. The exact number isn't particularly important, unless you're trying to figure out how many pixels wide to make a certain number of recurring elements so that they all fit on the screen.

Macintosh screen pixels are square. This accounts for their remarkable clarity, especially on the monochrome Macintosh screens. Round pixels, as found on many other computers' screens, tend to create fuzzy edges on graphics and text characters. Most of the time, you will be working with the pixels at a density of approximately 72 pixels per inch. At this density, individual pixels are distinguishable, but quite small. Don't expect to work with individual pixels at this scale right off. Your ability to work with single pixels at this level will grow with experience. For more detailed work, you'll be able to zoom into your work in a scale made for single-pixel work—FatBits, it's called. Still, at the regular scale, you'll be able to use HyperCard's painting tools to draw polygons, circles, lines, free-form shapes, and text. You'll use FatBits for any fine-tuning you deem necessary.

### BACKGROUND VS. CARD LAYERS

While it's true that you're painting with pixels on both the background and card graphics layers, the two blank layers are very different. This difference will affect the way you paint on each layer.

The background layer, as "bedrock" for the entire card the browser sees, comes up looking like a white layer. In other words, it is a blank layer of 512 by 342 white pixels. Images you paint on this layer will be blackening whatever pixels are necessary to convey your graphics image.

In the card graphics layer, however, the blank card is actually transparent—a 512 by 342 grid of clear pixels. Sitting atop an all-white background graphics layer, the card graphics layer appears white.

What you're seeing, however, is the white of the background graphics layer showing through the transparent card graphics layer.

This means that if you wish to have a card layer graphic contain white area when the entire background graphics layer is shaded grey, you would have to paint that white area in the card layer. We'll have more to say about this later but the concept is a fundamental one you should be aware of right now. When you get an unexpected result with a paint tool, it is usually attributable to the differences in the properties of these two graphics layers.

## PAINTING MENUS

HyperCard strives to keep the complexity of menus to a minimum at all times. Therefore, the menus associated with the painting tools are hidden until the instant you select one of those tools. To activate the painting menus, pull down the Tools menu and select any of the painting tools below the dividing line in the palette (Figure 12-1). The Objects menu disappears, and three new menus appear in the menubar: Paint, Options, and Patterns (Figure 12-2). The instant you select one of the three object tools at the top of the Tools palette (Browse, Button, or Field), the painting menus disappear, and the Objects menu reappears.

You will find it most convenient to tear off the Tools palette when working extensively with the painting tools. Place the small palette window in a spot on the screen where it will be out the way of your painting. You can drag it around during any paint operation.

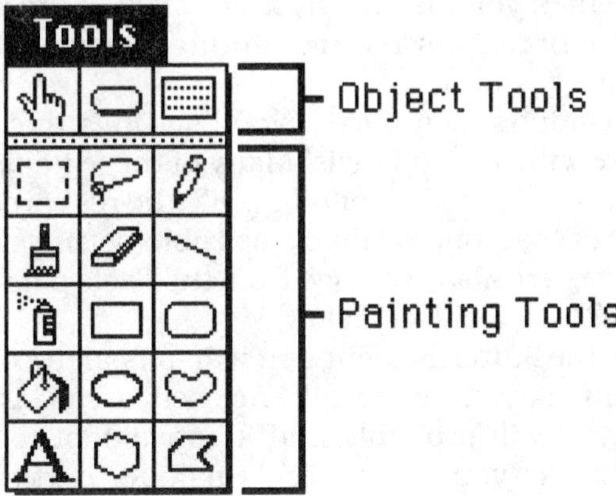


*Figure 12-1. Below the object tools in the palette are fifteen painting tools.*

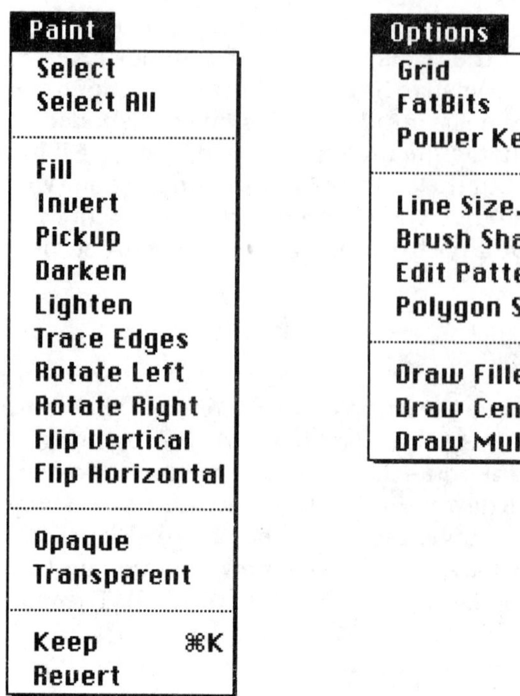

*Figure 12-2. When you select a painting tool, the Objects menu disappears and three painting menus appear in the menubar.*

The Paint menu contains a long list of items that enhance the painting work in which you may be involved. Most of the items are actions that affect items or regions in your painting that you've selected for a specific alteration.

In the Options menu are several settings that affect future actions you'll take with various tools. Many of these items are switchable (that is, they can be turned on or off), while the rest produce graphical dialog boxes to choose one of many possible settings. Those that produce dialog boxes are also accessed from the Tools palette by double-clicking on the affected tool (see below).

Finally, the Patterns menu is a tear-off palette of all the patterns with which you may draw or fill enclosed areas. In an active graphics session, you will probably find it convenient to tear off the Patterns palette just as you do the Tools palette, particularly if you need to experiment with various patterns to achieve a desired graphics effect.

## *Undo — the Savior*

HyperCard's painting environment would be anything but inviting if you couldn't easily undo experiments with the tools. Despite HyperCard's tendency to save changes to the disk at every turn, it is far more forgiving when you are using the painting tools. You can try different effects and undo those that don't work. Perhaps you want to try filling an area with different patterns to see which one looks the best; or perhaps you would like to compare the effect of different paintbrush styles when embellishing a graphic. HyperCard's painting Undo command gives you that freedom.

Whenever you are in the painting tools, HyperCard remembers the last action you took— cutting, rotating, filling, anything. If you see that an action brought you unexpected results, or at least results you don't want to live with, you can immediately undo the action three different ways.

One way to undo is to choose Undo from the Edit menu. A slightly more convenient way for the more experienced Macintosh user would be to type Command-Z, which is the keyboard equivalent of the Undo command.

The fastest way, however, is to press a special Undo key— the tilde key. On the Macintosh 512K Enhanced and Macintosh Plus, the tilde key is located to the left of the 1 key at the upper left corner of the keyboard (Figure 1–16). On the Apple keyboard for the Macintosh SE and Macintosh II, the tilde is located to the left of the spacebar. Pressing this key is the same as choosing Undo from the Edit menu. Pressing it again brings your erroneous action back onto the screen. You can use this toggling action to your advantage when you are trying to compare two techniques. When you decide on the choice you wish to stay with, just leave it on the screen and proceed to your next action.

This particular kind of Undo— a single action— remembers only the last action. If you make a boo-boo and perform another action after it, you won't be able to undo the boo-boo.

We've divided coverage of HyperCard's painting powers into three chapters: The first deals with the choices in the Tools and Patterns palettes, the second with the actions in the Paint menu, and the third with the choices available in the Options menu. We'll then finish our tour of painting with a chapter on painting strategies within HyperCard.

# CHAPTER 13

# HyperCard Painting Palettes

WE'LL START OUR TOUR OF ALL HYPERCARD PAINTING TOOLS WITH THE TOOLS IN THE Tools and Patterns palettes. The presentation for each tool will be as complete as possible, including all variations for using the tool with Option, Command, and Shift keys, where applicable, and any shortcuts that accrue to the tool. In this way, you'll end up with a reference work to which you can refer when designing your own stacks. If at all possible, work through this chapter in front of the computer, so that you can try these tools and their variations.

## *The Selection Tool*

One of the early techniques you learned with your Macintosh was selecting text to do things like cutting, copying, and changing font properties. The paradigm was 1) select the material to be changed, and 2) make the change with a menu command (or keyboard equivalent). That same paradigm also applies to HyperCard painting work. What's different, however, is the way you select the material to be altered.

Instead of dragging a black area over the material, you surround it with a selection outline. This kind of outline is very noticeable on the screen because it looks like the lights flashing around a theater marquee or, as some have suggested, marching ants. Everything inside the selection outline is selected; the next menu command that affects a selected item will work on everything inside that outline.

There are two types of selection outlines in HyperCard: the Selection tool and the Lasso. Our discussion here focuses on the Selection tool (the Lasso is covered next).

With the Selection tool, you can select a rectangular area on the screen. To do so, follow these steps:

1. Choose the Selection tool from the palette by clicking once on its icon.
2. Place the screen cursor at the top left corner of the rectangular area you wish to select.
3. Click and drag to the right and down from that spot.

   The marquee will expand to follow the mouse pointer (Figure 13–1).
4. When you are at the bottom right corner of the desired rectangular area, release the mouse button.

   The marquee will still "sizzle."

   Everything in that rectangle, including white background around the target shape, is selected. The next menu action you take— if it acts on a selection— will affect every pixel inside that rectangle. We'll see what most of those actions are in our discussion of the items in the Paint menu in chapter 14.

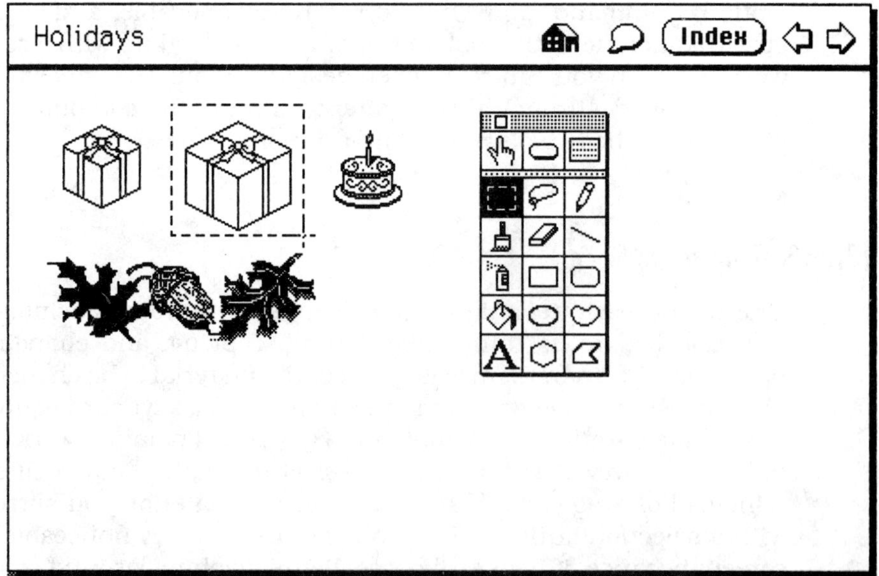


*Figure 13–1. Enclose shapes and regions with the selection rectangle to move, copy, cut, or perform other operations.*

The Edit menu also contains a few items that can act on a graphics selection. Cut, Copy, and Clear perform the same actions on a graphics selection as they do on a text selection. Cut and Copy, in particular, place a duplicate of the entire rectangle into the Macintosh Clipboard for pasting elsewhere. You would cut and paste, for example, if you accidentally begin creating a graphic in the card layer but wish to transfer it to the background graphics layer. First select the graphic, cut it, choose Background from the Edit menu, and paste it.

After you perform an action on a graphic selection, the selection rectangle stays in force. Thus, if you need to perform multiple actions on a selection, you are assured that the exact same rectangular area is selected for each operation.

## COMMAND KEY ENHANCEMENT

You won't always want to select the entire rectangular area around a graphics image. If that's the case, you can force the Selection tool to "hug" the graphic image that would be inside its rectangle. To do this, hold down the Command key before and during the dragging of the Selection tool. When you release the mouse button, the selection marquee will snap to a rectangle defined by the image's outermost pixels (Figure 13-2).

There are some rules you need to follow to make this feature work. First of all, it is intended ideally for those times when an image is in a white background. If the image is in a pattern of any kind, the selection rectangle won't be able to snap to the image because it will run into black pixels of the pattern (Figure 13-3). That, therefore, is the key: The rectangle collapses around the nearest black pixels inside the selection rectangle.

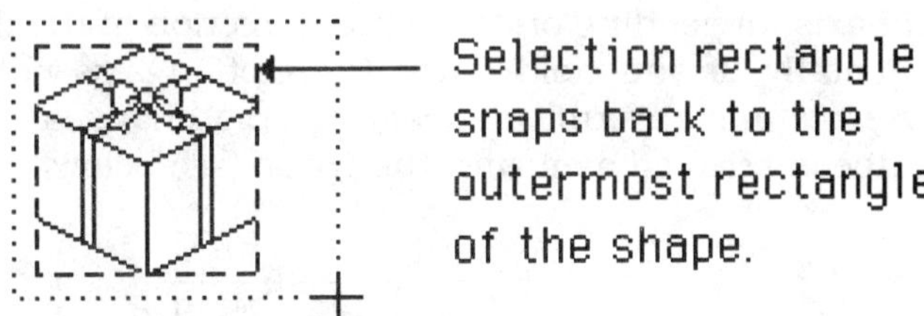
Selection rectangle
snaps back to the
outermost rectangle
of the shape.

*Figure 13-2. When you hold down the Command key when dragging the selection rectangle, the marquee will snap to a rectangle defined by the outermost pixels of the enclosed shape.*

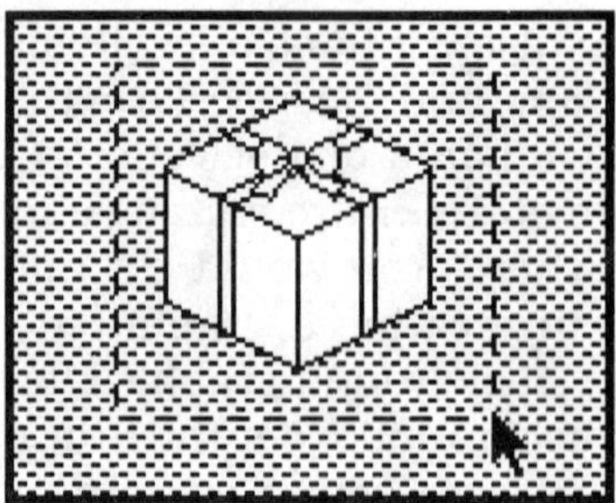

*Figure 13-3. Using the Command key enhancement with the selection rectangle on a shape in a pattern results in the rectangle snapping to the pattern's pixels.*

## SHIFT KEY ENHANCEMENT

Once you've selected an area or image, you are free to move it about the screen. To move it in any direction, simply place the mouse pointer within the selected area, click, and drag. But if you wish to move the image in a strictly vertical or horizontal motion, press the Shift key before dragging to constrain motion to one axis. This constrain action works identically to the way it does when moving fields and buttons around the screen.

## OPTION KEY ENHANCEMENT

You may also clone a selected image. This, too, is like cloning fields and buttons. After you've selected the image, hold down the Option key, click, and drag. The original image remains in its original position, while an exact duplicate follows the cursor around the screen (Figure 13–4). A combination of the Option and Shift keys allows cloning an image while constraining the movement of its copy to the horizontal or vertical axis, depending on the initial direction of the drag motion.

Incidentally, if you hold down the Option key while you drag a selection rectangle around an image, the tool changes to the Lasso, and the shape is selected as if with the Lasso (see below).

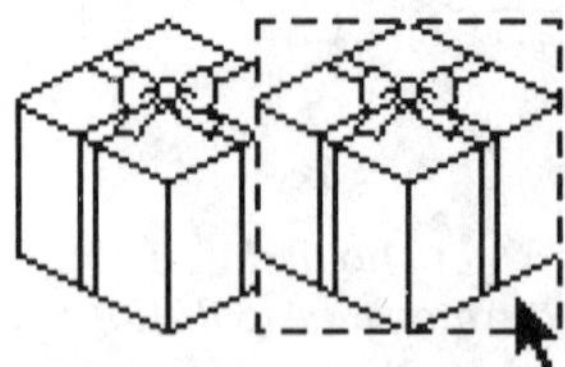

*Figure 13-4. The Option key enhancement to the selection rectangle lets you clone shapes or regions enclosed by the rectangle.*

DOUBLE-CLICK SHORTCUT

There will be times when you'll want to select and copy (or cut) the entire graphics layer, whether background or card, to paste in another stack or on another card. A quick way to do that is to first be sure you are in the desired domain (background or card) and double-click on the Selection tool in the palette. This selects the entire 512 by 342 rectangle of the graphic layer. Once the screen is selected, you may then cut or copy as you see fit. Remember, this selection and copying affects only the graphics layer, not the fields or buttons in the graphic layer's domain.

## *The Lasso Tool*

Like the Selection tool, the Lasso selects an image for further action. In fact, any action you can do following application of the Selection tool can be done with the Lasso. The only difference between these two selection tools is that the Lasso lets you select images that you can't initially surround with a selection rectangle.

We said earlier that the Selection tool grabs everything inside its four corners. If you wish to select irregularly shaped images amid other irregular images, a selection rectangle will invariably select pieces of the surrounding images and throw off your next action. With the Lasso tool selected in the Tools palette, you can use the mouse to draw an irregularly shaped selection edge (Figure 13-5). Simply hold down the

*Figure 13-5. Use the Lasso to select irregularly shaped objects or objects not selectable inside a selection rectangle.*

mouse button and begin drawing the edge around the image. When you release the mouse button, the marquee automatically "hugs" the images within the lassoed area, even if there is more than one item in the area. Notice that the Lasso hugs the items tightly, not within a rectangle as in the Command key enhanced selection rectangle, above.

One nice feature of the Lasso is that it automatically finishes the loop of the selection for you when you release the mouse button. In other words, you don't have to be precise in joining the two ends of your loop together. In fact, if you are trying to draw a lasso through a narrow gap and experience difficulty, you can let the tool do it for you.

In Figure 13–6, we want to select the octagon, which is so close to the diagonal line that it would require meticulous care to drag the Lasso tool through the narrow gap. If we start the lasso on the left side of the gap, drag it around the octagon, and release the mouse button on the right side of the gap, the tool will finish the job for us.

## SHIFT KEY ENHANCEMENT

As with the selection rectangle, the Lasso selects images that can be moved around the screen. Pressing and holding the Shift key prior to dragging a lasso-selected image constrains movement to the same axis as the first motion.

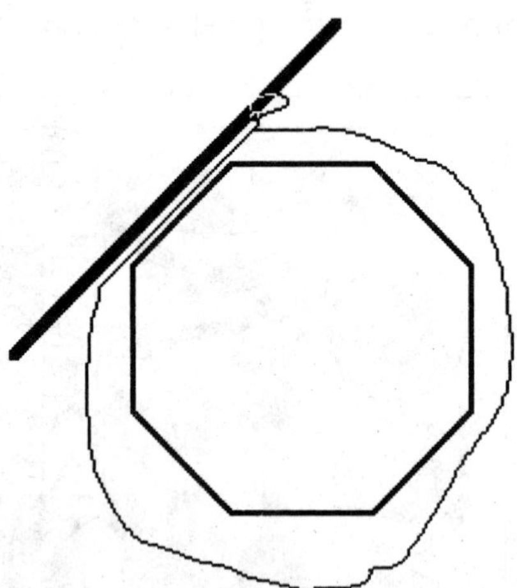

*Figure 13–6. The Lasso automatically closes the loop with a straight line between the starting point and the point at which you release the mouse button. This technique helps you select objects in tight places, like the octagon next to the line, above.*

### COMMAND KEY ENHANCEMENT

HyperCard's Lasso gives you an alternate solution to the problem shown in Figure 13–6. Instead of dragging the lasso around the octagon, you can also hold down the Command key and click the Lasso tool anywhere inside the octagon. The tool then selects the contiguous black pixels nearest the click point, plus any adjacent pixels. That means you can Command-click in a black object, and the entire object will be selected as if lassoed.

### OPTION KEY ENHANCEMENT

When you hold down the Option key and drag the Lasso, you'll notice that the marquee appears a bit thicker. This signifies that the entire lassoed area—including the white pixels—is selected. Once an area is lassoed (enhanced or otherwise), the Option key serves to let you clone the image. Hold down the Option key prior to dragging an image, and a duplicate will peel off. Holding both the Option and Shift keys constrains the movement of the clone.

### DOUBLE-CLICK SHORTCUT

You may perform the equivalent of dragging the Lasso around the entire perimeter of a graphics layer by double-clicking on the Lasso tool. The result will be a selection of all items in the layer, "hugged" by the selection marquee if there is white space in the layer. If the layer is filled to the edges with a pattern (as with a grey pattern) then the entire 512 by 342 screen will be selected.

## *The Pencil Tool*

The one graphics tool you will probably use more than any other is the Pencil. When you hold down the mouse button and drag, the Pencil leaves a trace on the screen exactly one pixel in height and width. The "color" of the trace may be black or white, depending on the condition of the pixel under the Pencil when you clicked the mouse button. If the pixel was white, the Pencil will leave a black trace; if the pixel was black, the Pencil will leave a white line. In other words, the Pencil has the power to turn pixels on and off, one at a time.

Notice that the Pencil stays in the same color as long as the mouse button stays down. If you start a black line in a white area and drag the Pencil through a black area, the line the Pencil draws will remain black—indistinguishable from the black background (Figure 13–7). The reverse is true for a white line reaching a white background area.

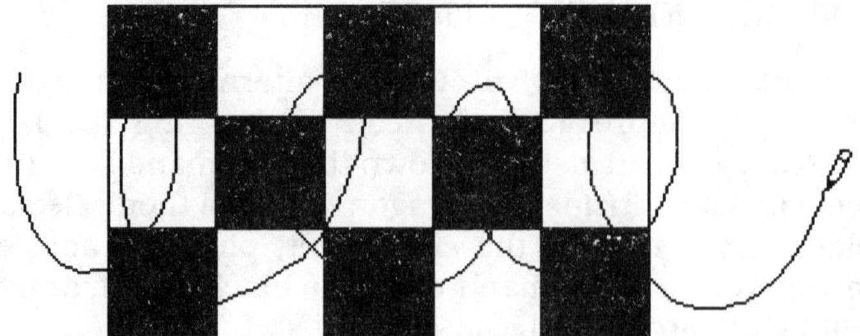

*Figure 13–7. When the Pencil starts drawing in black, it stays in black, even when drawing over black pixels. Similarly, if it starts drawing in white pixels atop a black background, it continues to draw white as long as the mouse button is held down.*

The Pencil works differently from other painting tools in one important regard: It transcends the usual barrier between background and card picture layers. When you click the Pencil in the card picture layer, the tool draws the opposite color of whatever appears on that pixel, no matter which layer's pixel is showing at that spot. Thus, if the background picture shows a black pixel, the Pencil will draw a white pixel in the card picture layer. That white pixel is on the card picture; the background picture layer is undisturbed. Because the other painting tools don't have this black-to-white or white-to-black pixel property, those tools operate in one layer at a time, completely independent of what's happening in the other layer.

## SHIFT KEY ENHANCEMENT

You can constrain the motion of the Pencil by holding down the Shift key before drawing. While there are better tools for drawing straight lines, there are times when the Pencil constrained by the Shift key is a convenient way to paint a straight white vertical or horizontal line in a field of black (Figure 13–8).

In practice, the Pencil is rarely used in the standard, 72-dot-per-inch drawing environment of HyperCard, except by the very skilled— those who have one-pixel acuity at regular size. The Pencil is used predominantly in a HyperCard painting mode called FatBits. We'll show you how to use FatBits in chapter 15. The reason we bring it up here is that

*Figure 13–8. The Shift key constraint is particularly helpful in drawing straight white lines in a black background.*

the Pencil tool on the palette offers two shortcuts to zoom you into FatBits.

### DOUBLE-CLICK SHORTCUT

When you double-click on the Pencil tool in the palette, HyperCard immediately goes into FatBits. The close-up look of the card layer you're working in is automatically set to the center of the screen. You are able to scroll within FatBits, as detailed later.

### COMMAND SHORTCUT

An even faster way to get into FatBits, looking directly at the part of the graphics you wish to adjust in this mode, is to hold down the Command key and click the Pencil cursor on the very spot of the normal-size graphic. We'll have more to say about this shortcut and other related ones in the section on FatBits.

## *The Paintbrush Tool*

Perhaps the most versatile painting tool in the palette is the Paintbrush. Many painting novices avoid the Paintbrush, fearing it is a tool only for the experienced artist. While it is admittedly best applied as a freehand painting tool, even beginners can obtain accomplished effects.

The Paintbrush merges two graphics concepts into a single tool: the pattern and the brush shape. You can think of the pattern as the "paint" that the brush applies to the graphics layer. If the pattern is a grey pattern, the "paint" that comes from the tip of the Paintbrush is that very pattern.

The brush shape defines the apparent surface of the tip of the Paintbrush. A brush tip that is only a couple of pixels tall and wide will leave a thin trail of the selected paint pattern; a calligraphic brush tip shaped in a diagonal line leaves a different width trace of the paint pattern, depending on the direction of travel of the brush (Figure 13-9).

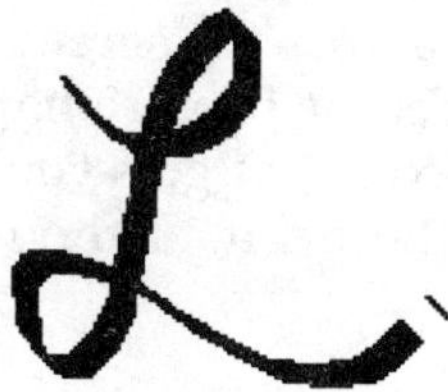

*Figure 13-9. A calligraphic brush style*

You draw with the Paintbrush just as you do with the Pencil. First select the Paintbrush tool in the Tools palette. The cursor becomes the shape of the brush. Place the cursor on the screen where you intend to begin painting. Then hold down the mouse button and draw with the mouse. It may be a single "dab" of paint by clicking and releasing the mouse button without moving the mouse, or it may be a more elaborate stroke. If the first attempt at a dab or stroke doesn't work, undo it, and try again.

## SHIFT KEY ENHANCEMENT

Constrain painting motion by holding down the Shift key before clicking the mouse button at the beginning of the stroke. The first direction you move locks you into either the vertical or horizontal axis.

## COMMAND KEY ENHANCEMENT

Whereas the Pencil automatically inverts the color of the pixel on which it starts drawing, the Paintbrush always paints in the pattern selected in the Pattern palette, even if it means painting over other material or patterns already on the graphics layer in which you're working. Remember that when we're talking about painting on the graphics layer, there is no layering within that layer. Thus overpainting completely replaces whatever graphics layer pixels are in the way of the Paintbrush. HyperCard does, however, provide an option to use the Paintbrush to *erase* in the pattern you've selected. Just hold down the Command key before painting. The tool will turn all black pixels into white (or transparent in the case of the card level graphics). Note that it does not invert white into black: It just erases black pixels in the same swath that its brush would normally paint in the pattern.

When you start HyperCard's painting tools, the paint pattern automatically selected for you is all-black. Altering the paint pattern is as simple as selecting a different pattern from the Pattern palette (see below). You may also edit a pattern for a custom paint job (also see below).

The default Paintbrush shape in HyperCard's painting tools is a small round tip. It presents a line of uniform width, regardless of the direction you drag the brush across the screen (Figure 13–10). HyperCard comes with thirty-two different brush shapes from which to choose. While there is a menu choice that gets you to the brush shape selection box (described later), there's a faster way via one of the Paintbrush's shortcuts.

## DOUBLE-CLICK SHORTCUT

By double-clicking on the Paintbrush tool in the Tools palette, you bring up a dialog box that shows all thirty-two brush shapes (Figure 13–11). The shape with the small box around it is the one that is currently selected. To choose a different one, simply click on it in the dialog box. When you do, the dialog box disappears, and the new brush shape is in effect until you either change the shape or exit HyperCard's painting tools. When you return to the painting tools next time, the default round dot will be in effect.

The number of combinations of Paintbrush shapes and patterns applied to those shapes is enormous: 1280, in case you really wanted to know. And then there's the opportunity to design your own patterns.

*Figure 13–10. The default brush style is a small circle.*

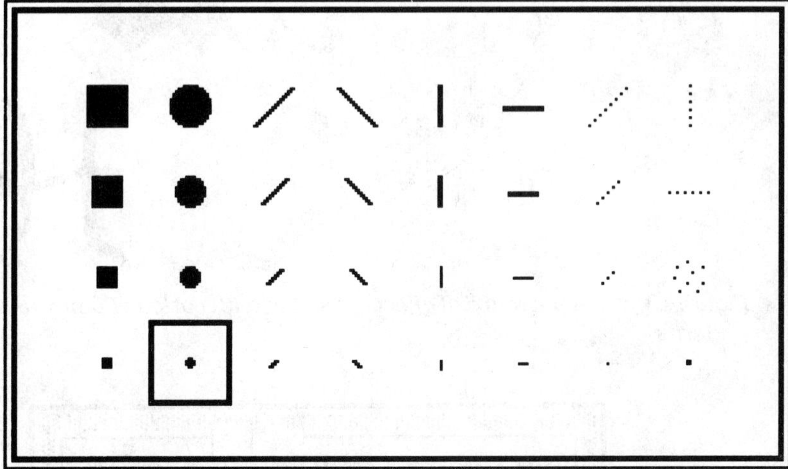

*Figure 13–11. Double-click on the Paintbrush tool, and you'll get the menu of brush styles available in HyperCard.*

The possibilities are staggering. We wouldn't presume to give you anything claiming to be even a representative sample of what you can do with these combinations. We've collected a few scribbles, however, in Figure 13-12. You'll have to experiment on your own to see how flexible the Paintbrush tool can really be.

## The Eraser Tool

With so many HyperCard painting tools putting black pixels on the screen, there must be a tool to get rid of them. That's the Eraser.

When you select the Eraser tool from the Tools palette, the screen cursor turns into a white square. Wherever you touch that square and press the mouse button, the black pixels will turn white in the background picture layer (Figure 13-13) or transparent in the card picture layer. You can also drag the Eraser around the screen to erase wide swaths of black pixels or patterns.

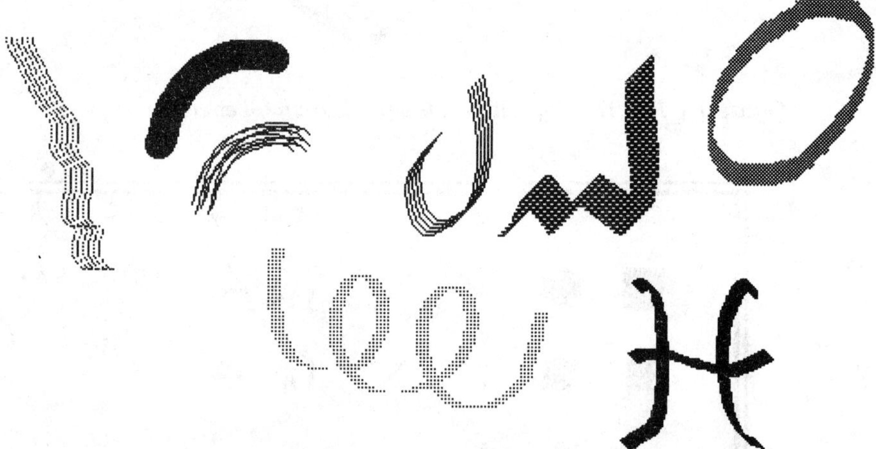

*Figure 13-12. A potpourri of effects possible with various Paintbrush styles and patterns.*

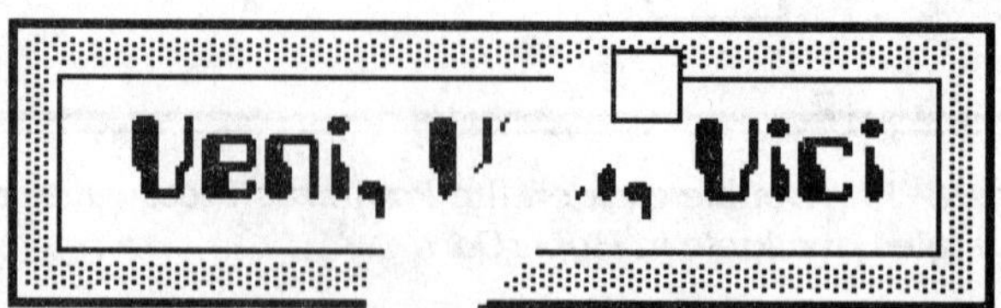


*Figure 13-13. The Eraser tool turns black background pixels into white.*

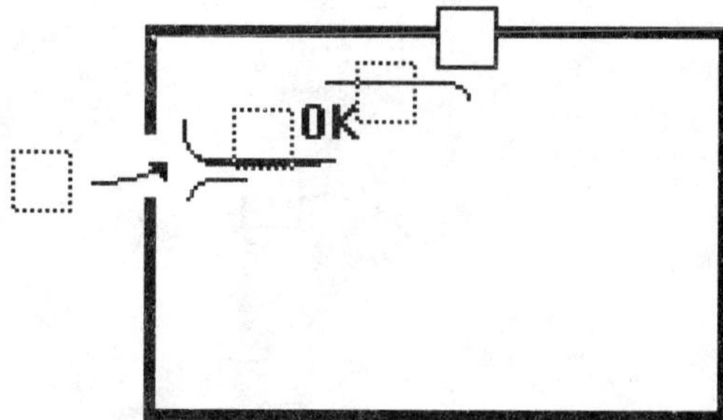


*Figure 13-14. Erasing in the card graphics layer also erases the layer's white pixels. If a background graphic is underneath, it will show through in the wake of the eraser.*

In the card picture layer, the eraser sometimes seems to take on an almost magical property. That's because the card layer sometimes has white pixels covering up a background graphics layer full of images. The effect seems like the opposite of erasing when background domain graphics and objects appear in the wake of the card layer Eraser (Figure 13-14).

Be on the lookout for accidental remnants of card layer graphics that may obscure background domain objects. Sometimes you'll be flipping through a stack and see the text in a background field mysteriously covered with lines or white blotches. Chances are, there is a card domain white remnant overlapping the background information. To get rid of the errant white material, select the Eraser in the card graphics domain, and wipe over the affected area. The white will disappear to let the background show through without any interference.

## SHIFT KEY ENHANCEMENT

As with most tools, the Shift key constrains motion of the Eraser to either the vertical or horizontal axis. This can be most useful when you need to erase graphics in a straight line. Simply hold down the Shift key, click, and drag. No matter how askew the pointer moves on the screen, the eraser action stays on the straight edge.

## COMMAND KEY ENHANCEMENT

We've been saying that the Eraser turns black pixels into transparent ones on the card layer. If you want to erase black pixels and leave white pixels in their place, you can hold down the Command key prior to erasing. The eraser will turn card layer graphics pixels (even those that started out transparent) into opaque white pixels. This is one way to

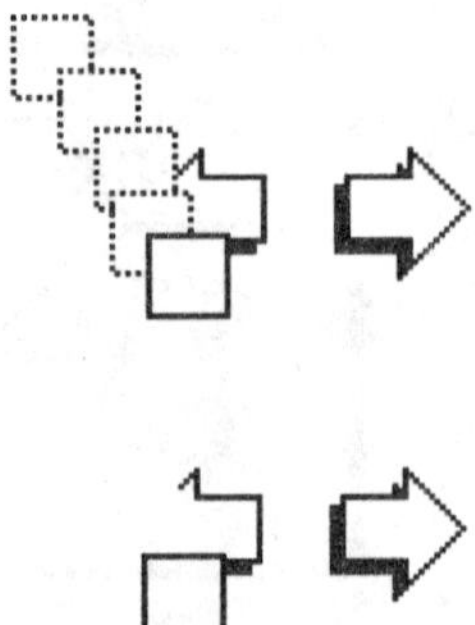

*Figure 13–15. With the Command key pressed, the Eraser turns card layer pixels to white. Use this effect to cover unwanted background graphics.*

effectively cover up a background graphic on selected cards (Figure 13–15).

### DOUBLE-CLICK SHORTCUT

The expression "back to the drawing board" sometimes applies to a graphics layer you're trying to create. It isn't uncommon to try one approach and discover that it just won't work out the way you anticipated. When it's time to start over, you may as well use the stack file you've already created and just erase the entire graphics layer. That's what double-clicking on the Eraser tool in the Tools palette does for you. It affects only the graphics layer currently in force (background or card), and not the fields or buttons in that domain.

Erasing the entire graphics layer is a last resort. There is usually something worth salvaging from an attempt at design. If so, select that part of the graphics layer with the Selection tool or Lasso and copy it. Then double-click on the Eraser to wipe the layer clean. Finally, paste the contents of the Clipboard onto the clean slate. You'll have a foundation on which to build, clear of the clutter you didn't like from the previous attempt.

And don't forget Undo. If you accidentally double-click on the eraser or do so when the wrong graphics layer is up, undo the damage immediately.

## *The Straight Line Tool*

You don't need a straight edge to draw a straight line with HyperCard's painting tools. When you select the Straight Line tool from the Tools palette, the cursor turns into a cross marker (Figure 13–16). The center

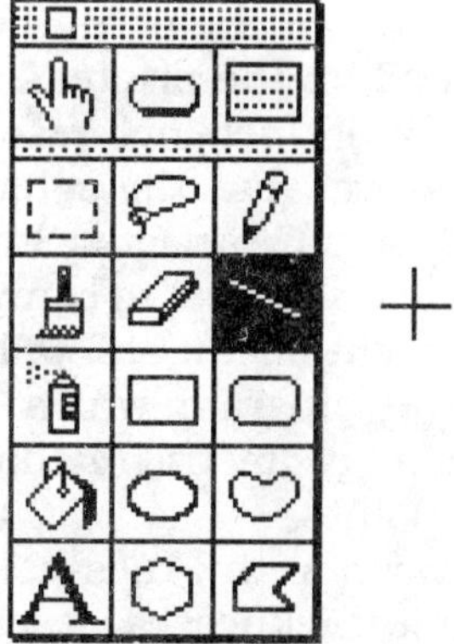

*Figure 13-16. The cross cursor of the Line tool*

of that cross is where the "ink" comes from when you click and drag the cursor across the screen. End points of the straight line you draw are defined by the pixel on the screen where you first click the mouse button and the pixel on the screen where you release the mouse button.

The straightness of the line depends on the angle you choose for the line, which is at the mercy of the 72-dot-per-inch resolution of pixels on the screen. While for many tasks, this resolution is quite good, it results in a ragged line when the angle of a line requires a stair-step effect to best fit the true geometric line between the line's two end points (Figure 13-17). Because of the nature of the screen, you will have the appearance of a true straight line only at angles in multiples of 45 degrees. Therefore, strictly horizontal and vertical lines will look smooth, as will 45 degree diagonal lines. All others may have what appear as breaks in their straightness. Still, in a full-screen painting, the overall effect of the straight line will more than likely come across to the viewer.

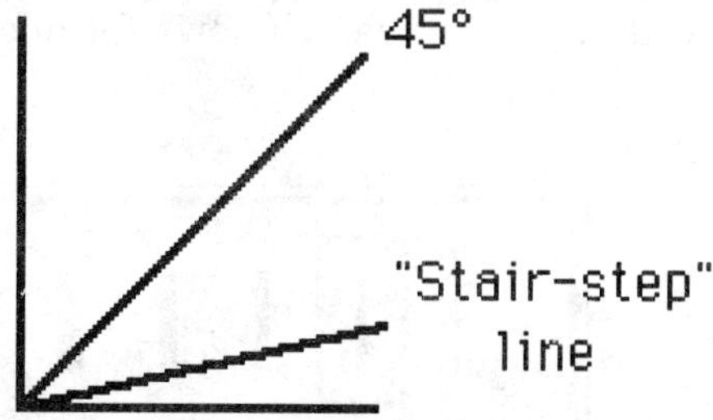


*Figure 13-17. At many angles, the Line tool produces ragged, "stair-stepped" lines on the screen and on printouts. The LaserWriter smooths the rough edges somewhat. Forty-five-degree lines are smooth on the screen.*

If the viewer prints out the card, the straightness of the line in the printout will depend on the printer's resolution. An ImageWriter will imitate the same 72-dot-per-inch resolution as the Macintosh screen. A LaserWriter, however, has the potential of printing in 300-dot-per-inch resolution. If you have selected Smoothing in the Page Setup dialog box, the printer will do its best to convert the 72-dpi stair-stepped line into a smooth, straight line. It still will not be as smooth as you would get from a draw-type program, which instructs the printer to generate lines in a much more geometric method: a line being a series of points between two end points.

Lines may be drawn in thicknesses of 1, 2, 3, 4, 6, and 8 pixels. As you select larger line thicknesses (described below), the thickness of the cross cursor increases to match that size. The cursor helps you place the start and end points of the line as accurately as possible.

## DOUBLE-CLICK SHORTCUT

There is a menu option that lets you change the line thickness for several tools that generate lines on the screen, including the Straight Line tool. You can bypass the menu by double clicking on the straight line tool's icon in the Tools palette. You go immediately to the dialog box that presents the possible choices for line size (Figure 13–18). A small box surrounds the size currently in effect. To select a different size, simply click on its representation in the dialog box. The new thickness remains in effect for all line-generating tools (like the rectangle and oval, discussed below) until you change it again or exit the painting tools. Whenever you start the painting tools, the one-pixel-wide line thickness is in effect.

## SHIFT KEY ENHANCEMENT

Shift key constraining offers a bit more flexibility with the Straight Line tool than with others. Instead of simply constraining the line in the horizontal and vertical axes, it allows for accurate angling of lines in

*Figure 13-18. Double-click on the Line tool to get the line size dialog box. You have six line thicknesses to choose from.*

multiples of 15 degrees— a total of 24 fixed angles around a circle. Let's see how this works.

In either the background or card domain, select the Straight Line tool from the Tools palette. In a clear area on the screen, drag a short line from a starting point and keep the mouse button down. Drag the line around the starting point in a roughly circular motion (Figure 13-19) to see how you normally draw a line to any angle. Before releasing the mouse button, press the Shift key. This turns on constraining. Now twirl the line around its starting point. You'll see that the line snaps into place every 15 degrees around the circle (Figure 13-20). Watch closely how straight the line is on the screen at each of the 15 degree increments. Only the lines at degrees 45, 90, 135, 180, and so on appear perfectly straight on the screen.

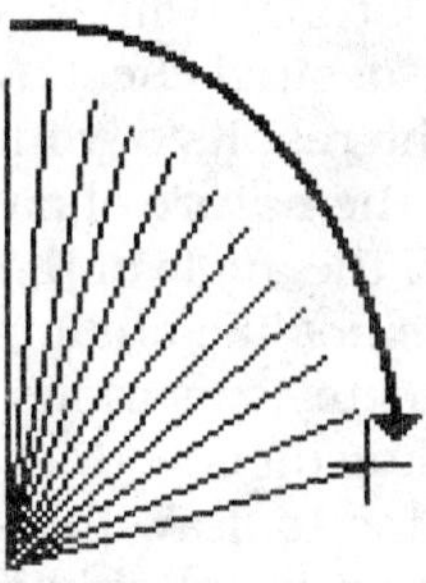

*Figure 13-19. Freehand drawing with the Line tool may be difficult to replicate if you need to have the same angle line in another part of a drawing.*

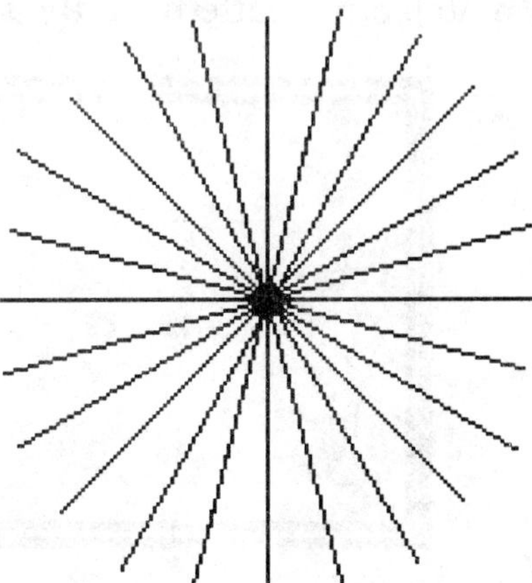

*Figure 13-20. Shift-constraining the Line tool limits line angles to increments of fifteen degrees for easy replication in other parts of a drawing or other drawings.*

Chances are that you'll use the constrained Straight Line tool to draw horizontal and vertical lines most of the time, but there are also other occasions to use it, particularly with the angled lines. If you are creating a three-quarter-view image, you'll want to maintain the same angle for all lines that connect various planes of the drawing. Once you determine which constrained angle works best, you can recreate the identical angle for the rest of the connecting lines in your drawing.

## OPTION KEY ENHANCEMENT

Black isn't the only ink your lines can be. You can also draw straight lines with any pattern in the Patterns palette (or pattern of your own design). To accomplish this, select a pattern from the palette and hold down the Option key before drawing your straight line.

Drawing straight lines with patterns takes experimentation to achieve the desired effect. As we'll see in more detail when we discuss patterns, the results of your patterned lines may not be as you expect because of the nature of pattern generation on the Macintosh screen. Essentially, the angle of the pattern does not change with the angle of the line: It's *not* like angling a wallpaper roll, as you might expect. So be prepared to try various patterns, particularly irregular patterns, before settling on one. Just hold down both the Option and Shift keys when starting to draw the straight line.

One very practical application of Option key pattern drawing is to draw white lines atop black or patterned areas. In card borders, for instance, you can select the all-white pattern and paint Shift-constrained straight white lines as insets to heavy black borders of someone else's design (Figure 13-21). You might also try drawing with a grey pattern atop other patterns in the same manner.

*Figure 13-21. Using the Shift-constrained, Option-enhanced Line tool lets you draw straight-edged patterns (including the white pattern) in whatever thickness you select from the line size dialog box. Above, two thicknesses of white lines ornament an otherwise dull border.*

## The Spraypaint Tool

Even if you claim to have no artistic talent when using these HyperCard painting tools, the Spraypaint tool will give you a sudden feeling of artistic power. With this tool, you can use any pattern in the palette to produce subtle gradations of shading on the screen. The metaphor of a spraypaint can is most apropos.

Painting with a real can of spraypaint lets you apply varying textures of the paint, depending on how quickly you pass the nozzle over the surface and how many times you cover the same area. HyperCard's Spraypaint tool works in much the same way, with the added advantage that the "paint" doesn't run when you apply too heavy a coat in one spot.

When you select the Spraypaint tool from the Tools palette, the cursor turns into a nozzle of sorts (Figure 13-22). The dots you see are where the paint comes from as you pass the cursor atop the graphics layer of your choice. As you can see, they're spread fairly far apart. If you simply click the Spraypaint cursor and quickly release, paint will come through whatever dots line up with black segments of the selected pattern. On a black pattern, all dots will issue paint; on a very thin grey pattern, only a few dots will likely splash paint onto the surface.

Paint doesn't come through those dots in a steady stream. It pulses, albeit quickly. But if you drag the cursor along the surface very quickly, the pulsing action will leave definite blotches along the trail of the cursor, not connecting lines (Figure 13-23). Therefore, the speed at which you drag the Spraypaint cursor in the painting area greatly influences the thickness of coverage the pattern will have. Likewise, if you go over the area a second time, it is highly unlikely that the dots of the cursor will be in exactly the same spot. Therefore, you will get

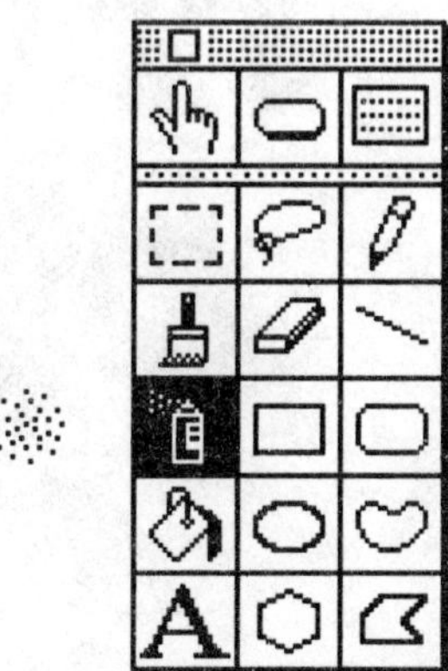


*Figure 13-22. The Spraypaint tool uses a "nozzle" cursor to indicate the density of paint that pulses from it as you drag the tool.*

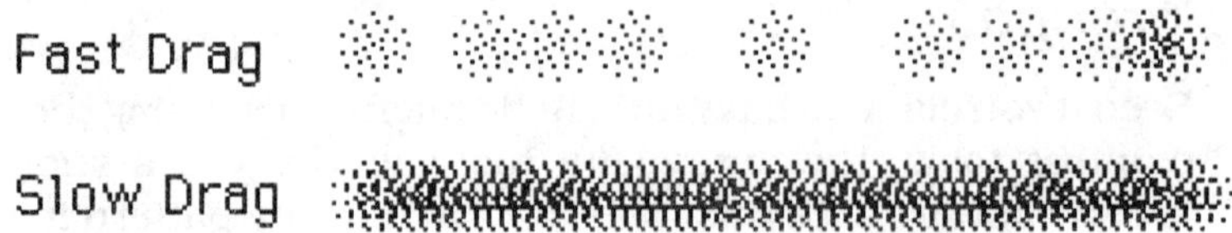


*Figure 13-23. Paint pulses from the Spraypaint nozzle as you drag the tool across the screen. Coverage on the screen is directly related to the speed at which you drag the tool.*

additional coverage by the pattern on succeeding passes. The slower the pass, the greater the coverage.

There is certainly no hard-and-fast rule about which patterns make the best paints for the Spraypaint tool. It's something you'll have to experiment with for each application. Surprisingly, some of the textured patterns provide very nice effects when used in a light coat, just lighter than revealing the actual pattern. Therefore, don't be fooled into thinking that only black and grey patterns are for shading (Figure 13–24).

## SHIFT KEY ENHANCEMENT

Constraining action is available for the Spraypaint tool. Holding down the Shift key prior to painting keeps the tool active in either the horizontal or vertical axis, depending on the direction of your very first

*Figure 13-24. Use the Spraypaint tool for shading effects you cannot get from filling patterns.*

move with the tool. Typically, the Spraypaint tool is used freehand, but there may be times when you want to constrain this tool.

### COMMAND KEY ENHANCEMENT

An unexpected property of the Spraypaint tool comes to life when you hold down the Command key prior to painting. Instead of leaving a sprayed trail of a particular pattern, the tool erases whatever is beneath it, but in the same thin coverage as when the tool sprays paint. Therefore, you can work in the reverse of shading a white area with black. Start with a black area, like a circle, and start erasing "shades" of black until you make the circle appear as a sphere, complete with white highlights (Figure 13-25).

## *The Rectangle Tool*

Painting rectangles in HyperCard is a breeze. When you select the Rectangle tool from the Tools palette, the cursor becomes the cross pointer (the same as Straight Line tool). Place the cursor on the screen where the upper left corner of the rectangle is to appear. Then drag the cursor to the right and down. The outline of the rectangle expands as you drag the bottom right corner. When you've placed the bottom corner where you want it, release the mouse button. Remember that because this is a bit-mapped graphics environment (instead of an object-oriented one), the "rectangleness" of the shape is only in the eye of the beholder. HyperCard sees it only as a series of black pixels on the screen. You won't be able to resize a rectangle once it is drawn. If you make a mistake, undo it and try again.

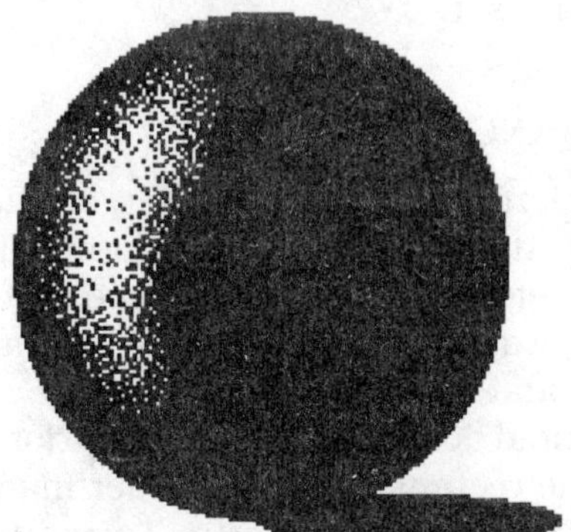

*Figure 13-25. Gradations of shading on a dark object can be achieved with the Command-key enhancement to the Spraypaint tool.*

You do, however, have control over several properties of a rectangle: The thickness of the border line, the presence or absence of a fill pattern (and what that pattern will be), whether the border should be a black line or the same as the fill pattern, whether the rectangle should be drawn as a perfect square, and whether the rectangle should be drawn from corner to corner or around a specific center point.

When you start up the HyperCard painting tools, the standard settings for a rectangle specify a black border of one pixel in width, no fill pattern, and drawing from corner to corner when you drag its outline with the rectangle tool cursor. If you change the thickness of the border line, the tool's cursor takes on a size commensurate with the line thickness. This property has nothing to do with the type of ink used to draw the border, merely its thickness.

## DOUBLE-CLICK SHORTCUT

While it is always possible to fill a rectangle with a pattern at a later time (see the Paint Bucket tool, below), you can also draw it right away with a pattern. There is a menu option to turn on painting filled images, but the shortcut is to turn this setting on by double-clicking the rectangle tool in the Tools palette. When you do this, the rectangle in the palette turns grey, indicating that the filling option is turned on. That grey does not represent the pattern it will be filled with. The actual pattern is determined by the selection in the Patterns palette. Now when you draw the rectangle on the screen, it automatically draws filled with the selected pattern. You can't change a pattern once it fills a rectangle, so if you don't like the results, undo it, and try drawing the rectangle again with a different pattern. If you can't find one right away that does the job, paint the rectangle without a fill pattern and experiment later with patterns and the Paint Bucket (below), once all the other elements in the graphic are set.

## OPTION KEY ENHANCEMENT

In some designs, the black border of the standard rectangle may interfere with the look you're attempting. The most common example would be a preference for a dotted line instead of a solid black line for a rectangle border. That's a perfectly normal request. And HyperCard will accommodate it with the Option key.

When you hold down the Option key prior to dragging a rectangle, the tool draws the rectangle with a border made from the current pattern selected in the Patterns palette. To make a dotted line border, for instance, you would select one of the grey patterns in the palette and then draw the rectangle with the Option key in force (Figure 13–26). Because of the way HyperCard draws patterns on the screen, the result

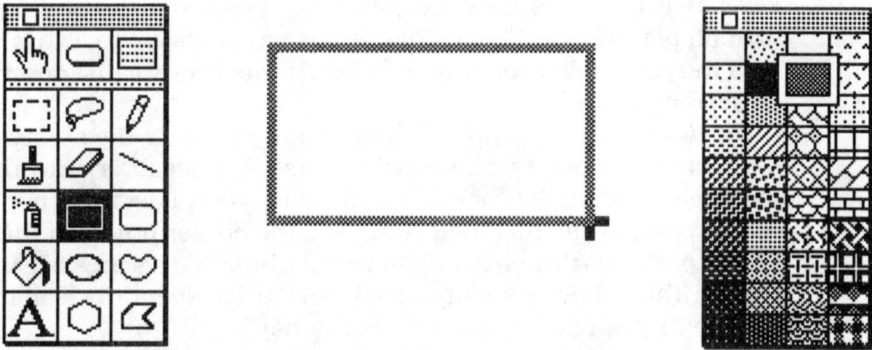

*Figure 13-26. With the Option key pressed, the Rectangle tool draws the outline with the currently selected pattern.*

may not always meet the expectation, particularly with the more irregular patterns in the palette. Be prepared to experiment a bit until you find the right combination. With some patterns, for instance, you may have to select a thicker line to make the border be seen with any regularity around the perimeter of the rectangle.

Keep this enhancement in mind when you wish to draw a kind of filled patch on the screen with the appearance of no border. What you'd do is draw a filled rectangle with the Option key held down. The result is a rectangle bordered by the same paint pattern as the internal fill (Figure 13-27).

## SHIFT KEY ENHANCEMENT

Unless you have an excellent eye at the 72-dpi resolution of the Macintosh screen, you'll be hard pressed to drag a rectangle that is a perfect square, if that is your goal. To help you in this regard, the Shift

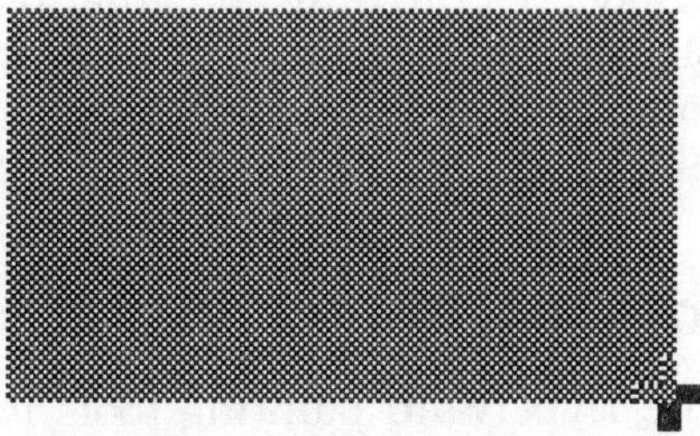

*Figure 13-27. With the Option key pressed and Draw Filled selected, you get the effect of a borderless rectangle, although the border is being drawn with the same pattern as the filled center.*

key constrains rectangles into perfect squares. Use the Shift key along with fill patterns and the Option key when you wish to create squares with the pattern border or "borderless" properties we just described for all rectangles.

The last rectangle property under your control is the ability to draw the rectangle from its center point. That is, instead of drawing a new rectangle from one corner to its opposite, you place the cursor at the center point of the rectangle and drag the cursor out from the center. This is particularly helpful when you are building a series of concentric objects (this property works with HyperCard's other drawn objects, like rounded rectangles, ovals, and polygons).

To turn on this feature, choose Draw Centered from the Options menu. A checkmark will appear next to this menu item when it is in force.

One way to put this feature to use is to first establish a center point in the area where the concentric shapes are to be. Click the pencil tool there once to designate one pixel as the center point, just as you might on a piece of paper. Then place the drawing cursor atop that point. The centerpoint of the cross will turn white when it is atop the pixel (Figure 13–28). Then drag the cursor away from the centerpoint until the shape is the desired size. Repeat this procedure for each of the shapes, even if they have different border thicknesses (Figure 13–29).

## *The Rounded Rectangle Tool*

Every property we discussed for rectangles applies to rounded rectangles, including all shortcuts and enhancements. Therefore, we won't repeat them here.

Rounded rectangles are often preferred for such things as HyperCard background designs. Their appearance is less harsh than a regular rectangle (Figure 13–30). The roundness of the corners may be too much for certain graphics applications, however. In small rectangles or squares, you may prefer to draw a regular rectangle shape and modify the corners slightly with FatBits (demonstrated below) rather than use the level of rounding the Rounded Rectangle tool provides.

## *The Paint Bucket Tool*

After using the HyperCard painting tools for a while, you'll come to think that the Paint Bucket is the most powerful tool in the palette. With one click of the mouse, you can instantaneously influence the appear-

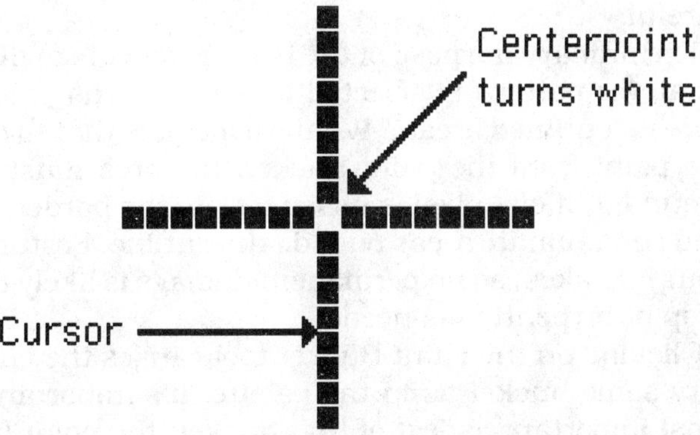


*Figure 13-28. To draw concentric shapes, establish a centerpoint with one dot. Then place the cross cursor directly above the dot before dragging each shape. The center spot of the cross cursor turns white when it is directly above the centerpoint dot.*

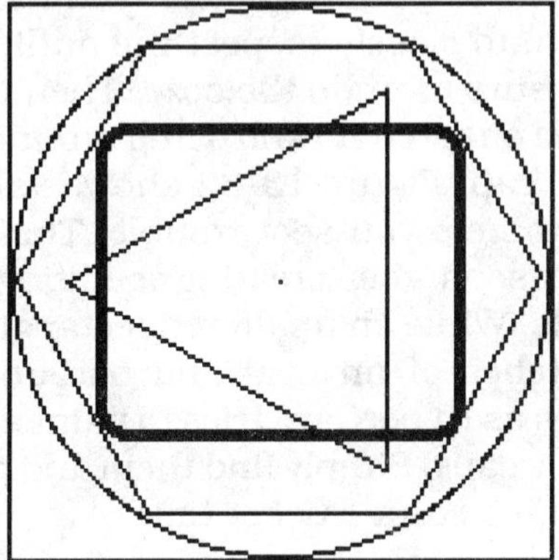

*Figure 13-29. You can use the same centerpoint to draw different kinds of concentric shapes.*

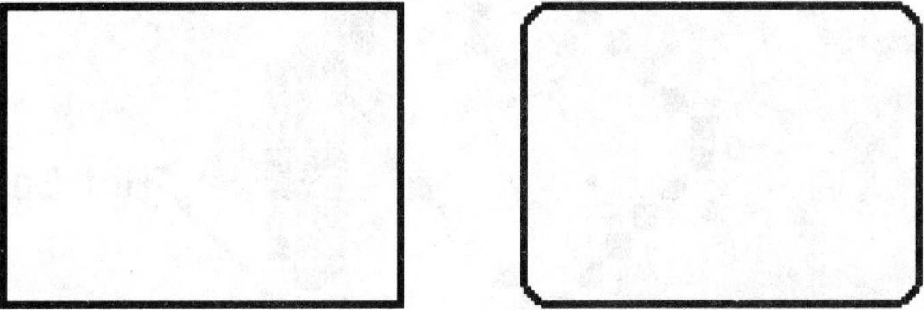

*Figure 13-30. Rounded rectangles (right) are often preferred over regular rectangles (left) because of their softer look.*

ance of a huge area of the screen— or the whole screen, if you're not careful.

The primary purpose of the Paint Bucket is to fill outlined areas with whatever pattern is selected in the Patterns palette. The key phrase here is "outlined areas." What we mean is that to contain the spread of the paint from the paint bucket, the area must have a solid border around it. If one pixel is missing from the border, paint will "ooze" out and contaminate areas outside the outline. Fortunately, you can undo your mistakes, so no permanent damage is likely to occur (and not one drop of turpentine is needed).

Clicking on the Paint Bucket tool causes the cursor to turn into the very same bucket as in the palette. It's important to understand the most important aspect of that bucket: the point from which the paint spills onto your graphic. The bucket cursor's "hot spot" is one pixel below the tip of the paint that appears to be spilling out of the bucket (Figure 13-31). When you're working in close quarters on the screen, this is the spot of the cursor that you want to be located inside the outlined area before clicking the mouse button to fill with the pattern.

When paint oozes out from what you thought was a solidly outlined area, it's time to closely inspect the outline. Before you do anything, however, be sure to undo the ooze. Then invoke FatBits (explained in more detail in chapter 15) and scroll around the entire outline. Look for the smallest gap. Figure 13-32 shows valid outlines and samples of tricky gaps to help you spot trouble. These gaps can happen for any number of reasons when creating or editing shapes with the HyperCard painting tools. While an unaltered rectangle should not have any gaps, certain stretches of an oval and odd-angled lines can easily have multiple gaps as HyperCard tries to paint a best fit on the screen. Don't be alarmed by gaps. Simply find them and plug them to the best of your ability. Then it's Paint Bucket time.

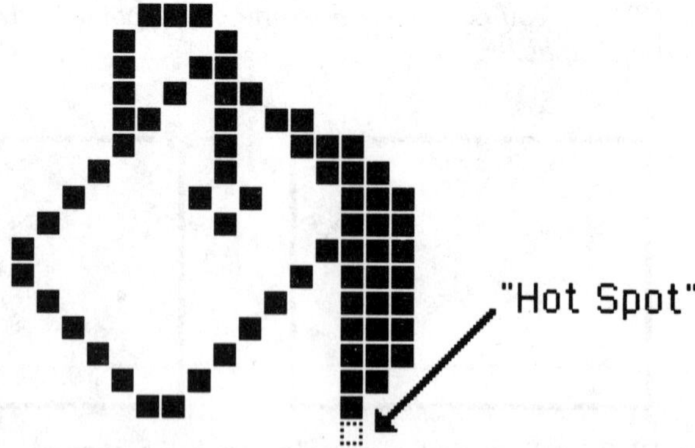


*Figure 13-31. The Paint Bucket tool's "hot spot" is where the paint pours from.*

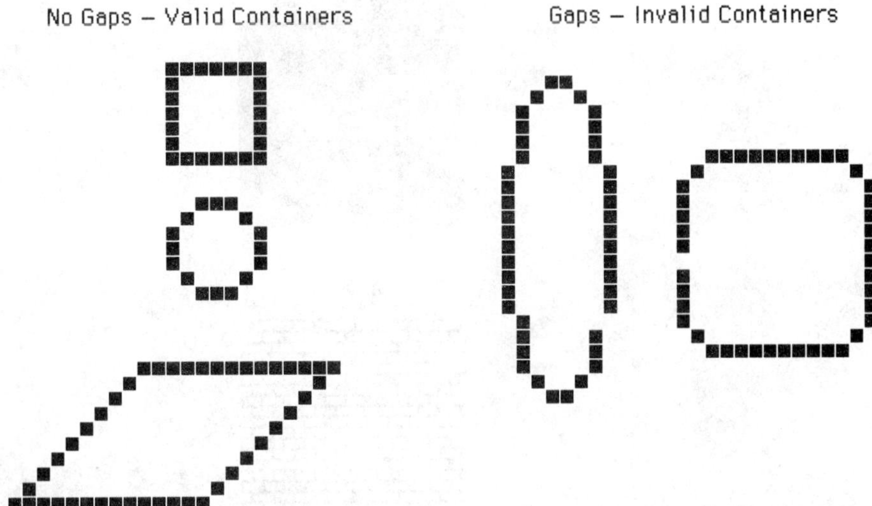


*Figure 13–32. Closeups of valid and invalid outlines that contain and ooze Paint Bucket paint, respectively.*

The Paint Bucket has another property that might not be self-evident, given its definition above. When you apply the Paint Bucket to a shape that may be filled with another pattern or all black, you can alter the appearance of the pattern— provided there is the equivalent of a solid outline around the area. In an all-black square, for example, you can touch the paint bucket to any place in the square and it will change into the pattern selected in the Patterns palette (Figure 13–33). The pattern extends only as far as the outer edge of the square, which the tool interprets as being the solid outline.

One application of this technique is to change painted text (see below) from its regular black into a pattern, perhaps a grey "ink." To make this happen, you type the text in the desired font and font size. Then select the Paint Bucket and a pattern. Carefully touch the hot spot of the paint bucket cursor to each letter in the text (Figure 13–34). It may take a while if the text is extensive, but the result will be striking, depending on the font, font size, and pattern chosen. Experiment with this feature.

## DOUBLE-CLICK SHORTCUT

The Paint Bucket tool offers a most convenient shortcut in anticipation of your desire to change the selection in the Patterns palette. Double-click on the Paint Bucket tool in the Tools palette and the Patterns palette automatically appears, already detached from the menubar.

*Figure 13-33. Use the Paint Bucket to change black objects to patterned objects.*

Arma virumque cano

*Figure 13-34. By touching the Paint Bucket tool to painted text, you can turn the text characters into a pattern selected in the Patterns palette.*

Double-click a second time to hide the palette (or close the palette by clicking on its close box).

## The Oval Tool

Sometimes it seems that ovals and circles are the hardest regular shapes to draw on paper, even with the help of compasses and templates. Not so with HyperCard's painting tools. They're as easy to draw as rectangles. In fact, all of the enhancements and shortcuts that apply to rectangles apply to ovals. With the Oval tool, the shape may be different, but the concepts are the same. Therefore, constraining with the Shift key produces perfect circles with the Oval tool, just as it produces perfect squares with the Rectangle tool. Because of the consistency of these enhancements and shortcuts, we refer you to the rectangle discussion for details. If you're already familiar with the properties of rectangles, you already know ovals inside and out.

About the only property of ovals you should be aware of is that they may leave gaps in their outlines, wreaking havoc with the Paint Bucket tool. Of course, if you draw the oval (or circle) with the Draw Filled choice in the Options menu turned on, HyperCard will hold the pattern within the confines of the outline, even if there is a gap in it (Figure 13-35).

Concentric circles of the same or varying line thicknesses are effects you may wish to try. Just use a center point and choose Draw Centered from the Options menu. Trying this effect without the benefit of the Draw Centered option can be a frustrating endeavor.

If you need a semicircle as part of a drawing, use the Oval tool to draw the entire circle. Then erase the half you don't need. The coffee cup in the HyperCard help system's description of ovals is an excellent example of what you can do with ovals and semicircles both shaded and hollow. Study this picture on your HyperCard screen and try to replicate it on your own. You'll learn quite a lot from this one picture.

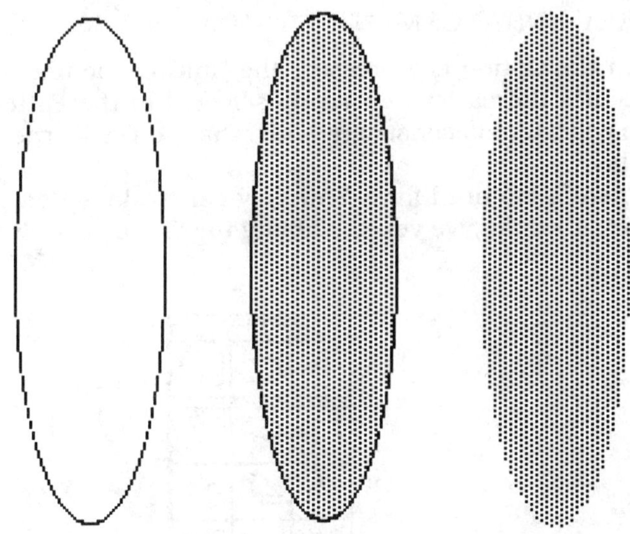

*Figure 13-35. Ovals may leave gaps in their outlines when stretched to extreme proportions. If you draw a filled oval, however, the pattern remains within the border, even if gaps appear. Option-dragging creates a border with the same pattern as the fill pattern, as if no border existed.*

## *The Curve Tool*

The Curve tool is perhaps inappropriately named, since it is more of a freehand drawing tool with a hybrid set of properties from the pencil and other shape tools. From the pencil comes the ability to draw any freehand shape you wish. From the other shape tools comes the ability to draw with a thicker line, draw with a pattern as the ink, and, optionally, to have the tool automatically fill with a pattern whatever area the freehand shape encloses. Let's see how these various properties work.

First, we'll look at the Curve tool's raw drawing ability. When you select the Curve tool, the cursor changes into the same cross that draws other shapes (Figure 13-36). The center of the cross is the point from which the "ink" flows as you drag the cursor around the screen. You are free to drag it in any direction and to the maximum of your skill in this department.

If you change the thickness of the line, the cross cursor changes thickness to match. This is consistent with the behavior of the shape-drawing tools.

### OPTION KEY ENHANCEMENT

With the Option key pressed, the "ink" of the line left by the cursor becomes the pattern currently selected in the Patterns palette. This behavior, too, is consistent with what you've learned for other shape tools.

There is no need for a Shift key constrain action with this tool. At most, it would give you the ability to draw a solid or patterned line in

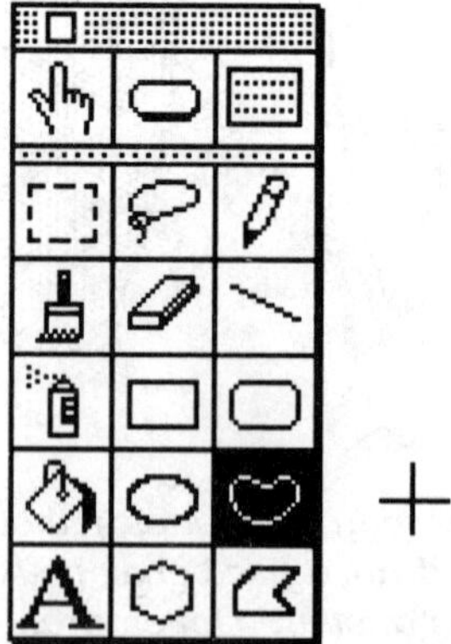

*Figure 13-36. The Curve tool uses the cross cursor shared by most tools.*

the vertical or horizontal axis. You've already seen how to do that with the Straight Line tool.

## DOUBLE-CLICK SHORTCUT

As with the other shape tools, when you double-click on the Curve tool, it turns on the Draw Filled option in the Options menu. You might wonder, though, how the tool can possibly draw a filled shape when the shapes this tool creates are so freeform. The answer lies in a special feature of the Curve tool that is in effect when the Draw Filled option is in force. The tool automatically draws the line that connects the start and end points of your drawing and then fills the enclosed area with the selected pattern (Figure 13-37).

As far as the automatic closing up of the loop is concerned, it follows the same principles used by the Lasso as it finishes the job for you. Therefore, it's up to you if you wish to try to bring the drawn line all the way back to the starting point or let the tool finish it.

You can combine the Draw Filled choice with the Option key enhancement to draw custom filled shapes with what appears to be no border. Actually, the border is in the same pattern as the internal fill (Figure 13-38).

This tool is fun to experiment with, because you can create rather complex shapes and observe how HyperCard fills the nooks and crannies according to its rules about filling to the outline.

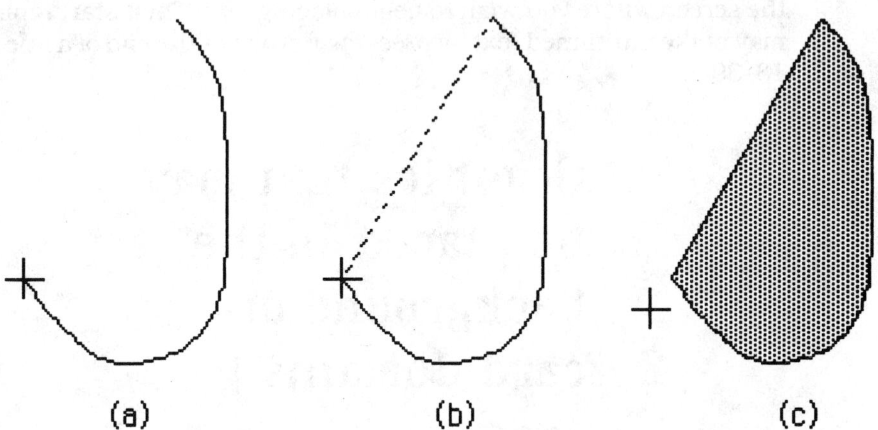


*Figure 13-37. Drawing a filled curve means that HyperCard automatically closes the gap between the start and end points of the curve and fills the area inside.*

*Figure 13-38. Drawing filled and with the Option key creates the appearance of borderless shapes, some of which may surprise you.*

## *The Text Tool*

The kind of text we'll be discussing here has no relation to the text that goes inside text fields— the information that cards hold. This text is the kind that goes into the background or card picture layer and can be altered only with the painting tools. You'll use painted text primarily in the background graphics layer as card headlines and as labels for text fields you or the browser will fill with information. The text will appear on all cards sharing that background.

Clicking on the Text tool in the palette— make sure you differentiate this in your mind from the Field tool in the upper right corner of the palette— causes the cursor to change into an I-Beam cursor. To use the default font and font size (Geneva 12), simply click the text pointer on the screen where you wish to begin placing text. Then start typing. You may make multilined text by pressing Return at the end of a line (Figure 13-39).

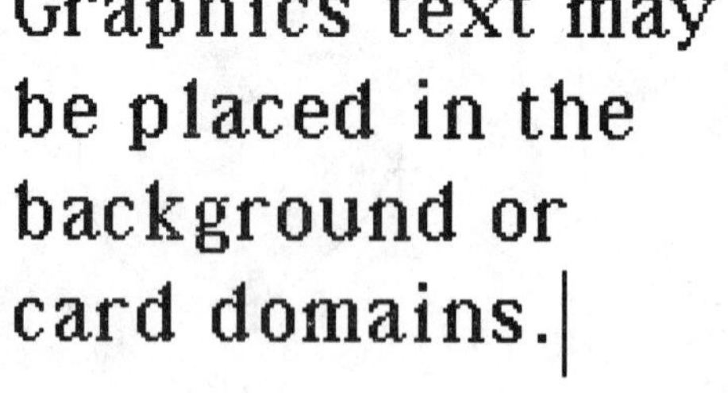

Graphics text may
be placed in the
background or
card domains.

*Figure 13-39. Create multilined graphics text by pressing Return at the end of a line.*

## DOUBLE-CLICK SHORTCUT

Text may be typed in any font installed in your System File. To change the font attributes of text prior to typing the text, either choose Text Style from the Edit menu or, more conveniently, double-click on the palette's Text tool icon. Either way, you'll get the font dialog box (Figure 13–40). It's the same font dialog that you get with the Field tool (chapter 9), so there's no need to spend more time on it here.

There is one very important difference between text in the paint layer and in fields if you or your browsers plan to print cards from your stack on the LaserWriter. Text in fields will be sent to the printer as separate characters that are turned into laser fonts, like Helvetica and Times. Print quality of that text will be very good— as good as a LaserWriter user expects from text. Paint layer text, however, is not sent to the LaserWriter as separate text characters for translation into laser fonts. Paint text goes to the printer as a bit map, just like the boxes and drawings in the paint layers.

If the user prints the card without checking Smoothing on the HyperCard's Page Setup dialog box, then the paint text will be printed with the same resolution as displayed on the screen. If, on the other hand, the user prints with Smoothing in force, the LaserWriter will do its best to smooth over the bumps of the text characters, but it will not print them with the clarity of laser fonts. In fact, sometimes smoothing

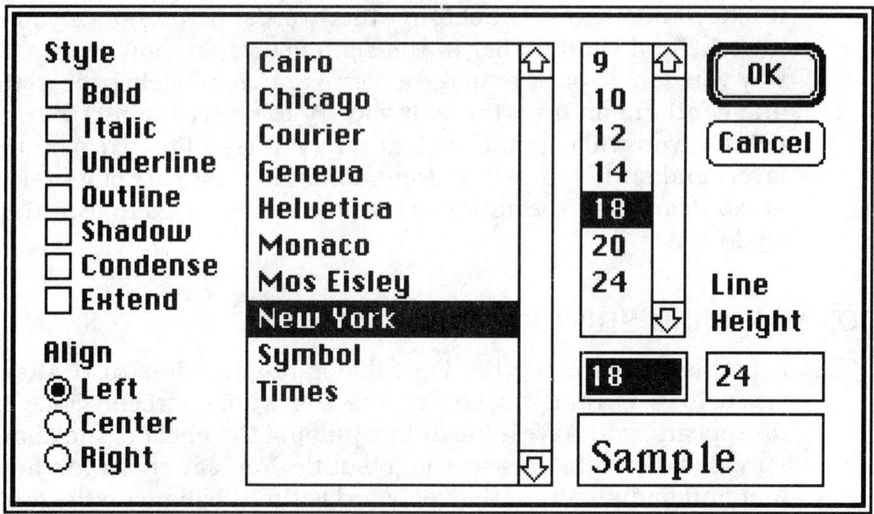


*Figure 13–40. Font dialog box*

does an injustice to a nicely designed screen font. We also recommend that you choose Precision Bitmap Alignment in the LaserWriter's Page Setup Options screen to reduce possible distortion.

Believe it or not, there is a good side to this loss of laser resolution on paint layer text. You can use any screen font you like in designing paint layer text without worrying about the browser having the same fonts installed on his Macintosh System File (a concern with text in text fields). This is because, just like shapes, the text characters essentially lose their identity once they are typed onto the paint layer: They become simply a layout of pixels in what we recognize as text. Therefore, if you find a public domain font or purchase one that looks particularly good for your stack design, you have the confidence that what you design on your screen will be there when browsers from all walks of System File life start using your stack.

While you're typing text into the paint layer, it stays in a somewhat active mode until you click the mouse elsewhere. Until you click the mouse, however, you can still adjust the font characteristics of the text you just typed. Therefore, select the Text tool, plant the text pointer on the card where you want text to begin, and start typing. Before you click anywhere else on the card or on any other tool, double-click on the Text tool to bring up the font dialog box. The current settings for the text you just typed will be highlighted. Change any settings you wish and click OK. The changes will be made to the text. Even now, you can go back and make additional changes to the font attributes.

One thing you may *not* do to text you type into the paint layer is edit it like you do text in a field. In other words, if you notice you made a mistake in a word earlier in the sentence you're now typing, the only way you can go back to make a correction is to backspace to the error and continue on from there. If you try to select the text with the text pointer, you will commit the text that you typed to pixels on the paint layer, and shut yourself off from adjusting any part of its text or font attributes. This aspect may take some getting used to. But that's why Undo exists.

## COMMAND AND SHIFT KEY SHORTCUTS

A problem with using the Font dialog box to adjust text after you've typed it in is that the box covers the whole screen. Once the box disappears, you have a hard time judging the effect of the change you specified. Font changes are often subtle. You can, however, adjust the font and font size from the keyboard without calling up the font dialog box.

First of all, it's important to understand that you can do this only while you are entering text or after you've entered the whole chunk of text but before you've clicked the mouse button anywhere. In other words, the text must be sitting there ready for you to type in more text if you have any.

When you're at that stage and ready to experiment with font and font size, hold down the Command key while pressing the comma and period keys (it may be easier to think of these keys as the < and > keys). With the Command key down, these keys adjust the size of the font of that active text to the sizes of that font installed in your System File. If you typed the text originally in Geneva 12, pressing Command-< twice will bring the text down to Geneva 9. From there, you can press Command-> three times to bring the text up to Geneva 14. Remember, the sizes available in this shortcut are only those installed on your System. Therefore, if you typed the text in Chicago, these two Command-key shortcuts will not change the text in any way, since only Chicago 12 is installed on most Systems.

By holding down both the Command and Shift keys, you can try other fonts installed in your system on the current text. Type Command-Shift-< to try a font whose name is earlier in the alphabet than the current font; type Command-Shift-> for a font whose name is later in the alphabet. What is going on here is that each press of the magic keyboard combination shifts the selected font one slot in the corresponding direction up and down the list of fonts in the Font dialog box. Because fonts are listed alphabetically in this dialog, that's how they change when you press the Command-Shift combination.

You can use these two shortcuts together to find the right font and size for a piece of text you are putting into the graphics layer. Type it first in the default font. Use the Command-Shift combination to try different fonts. When you find an acceptable font, use the Command-key shortcut to try different sizes in that font. This system turns out to be an efficient way of selecting the right font for each graphics layer text job.

## TEXT STRATEGIES

Choosing fonts for the background, card, and field layers should be taken seriously. Newcomers to the Macintosh often get so caught up in the flexibility of offering many fonts that screens (and even word processing documents) become cluttered with too many fonts. There is rarely reason to use more than three fonts on the same card. If more are used, the font potpourri may distract the user from the information content. Remember that readability of the information should be your first priority.

There are many techniques for entering paint text and manipulating it on the screen. Chances are that you'll find it easier to type paint text in an open area on the screen and then select it like any image and move it into the precise position you choose. That's a fine strategy, and often an efficient one.

If you find that you need to piece together a line of text from disparate pieces or make sure corresponding lines in multiple columns are on the same horizontal base line, you can use the Straight Line tool to help. First position the starting piece of text on the screen. Then select and drag the next piece as closely into position as your eye will allow (Figure 13-41). Next, select the Straight Line tool and draw a constrained horizontal line to create an artificial base line for the text (Figure 13-42). Compare how the first and second chunks of text look with respect to the base line. If the second chunk is too high or low, estimate how many pixels (it will probably be just one or two) and immediately undo the straight line. Select the second chunk of text and drag it the appropriate distance. Repeat the straight line trick until both chunks of text are on the same horizontal.

## *The Regular Polygon Tool*

The Regular Polygon tool is so much fun that you'll catch yourself playing with it for long stretches, trying to grasp all its potential. We'll only scratch the surface in this discussion. Experienced MacPaint users should also pay close attention, because this tool is new.

A polygon is a shape with many ("poly") sides. A regular polygon is a polygon all of whose sides are of an equal length. The number of sides is unspecified. It can be anywhere from two to infinity. In HyperCard, a regular polygon can have three, four, five, six, eight, or infinity sides. In geometric terms, these shapes are the isosceles triangle, square, pentagon, hexagon, octagon, and circle, respectively.

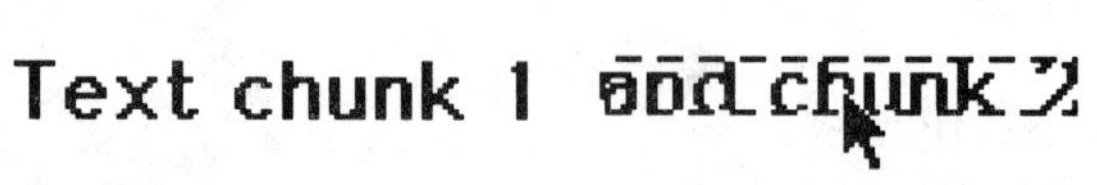

*Figure 13-41. To align different groups of text, bring them into position as well as you can.*

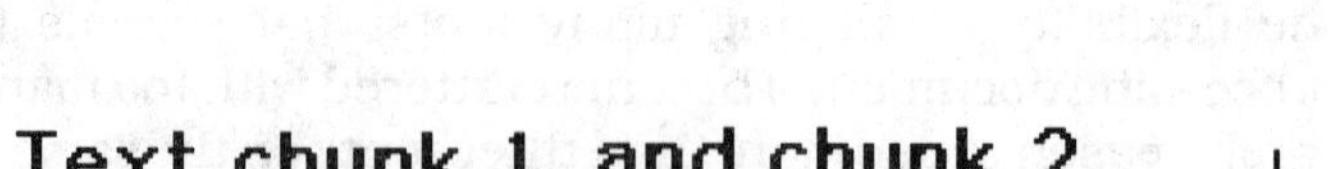

*Figure 13-42. Then draw a temporary baseline to see if the two text chunks are on the same horizontal. Immediately Undo the line and make adjustments to text groups as needed. Repeat the temporary line to make sure all text is aligned.*

A special feature about regular polygons in HyperCard is that you can rotate them as you create them. When you select the Regular Polygon tool from the Tools palette, the cursor becomes the now-familiar cross cursor. You click on the location on the screen where you want the centerpoint of the polygon to be. As you drag the cursor away from the centerpoint, the polygon grows and is free to rotate to follow the cursor as you control it with the mouse (Figure 13–43).

## SHIFT KEY ENHANCEMENT

Rotation can be constrained to 15-degree increments when you start creating a regular polygon with the Shift key held down. Depending on the number of sides the polygon has, this constraint may help you choose an orientation of the polygon that best displays each side's straight lines with the least amount of distortion.

Note that when you rotate a polygon, its border line may have one or more gaps that must be plugged before you can fill the area with the Paint Bucket tool. The alternative is to draw the polygon filled from the start, as noted below.

## DOUBLE-CLICK SHORTCUT

When you select the Regular Polygon tool, HyperCard automatically preselects the square shape for you. To choose one of the other shapes, you can choose Polygon Sides from the Options menu or, more conveniently, double-click on the Regular Polygon tool in the Tools palette.

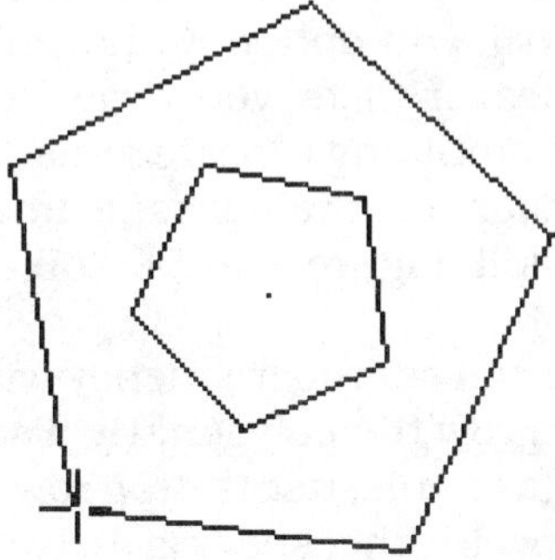

*Figure 13–43. Regular polygons are always dragged from their centerpoints and can be rotated freely until you are satisfied with their orientation.*

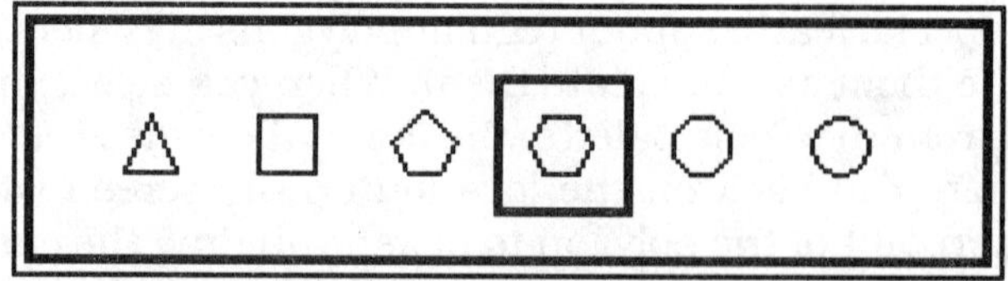

*Figure 13-44. Regular Polygon dialog box.*

In return, you see a dialog box featuring outlines of all six polygon shapes offered by HyperCard (Figure 13-44). A small box surrounds the current selection. To choose another shape, click the mouse pointer on it. The dialog box disappears, and that shape can now be drawn with the Regular Polygon tool.

The thickness of the border may be altered by changing the line-thickness choice in the line size dialog box. As you've come to expect of tools that offer varying border line thickness, the cross cursor of the regular polygon tool thickens with the selected line thickness.

## OPTION KEY ENHANCEMENTS

Similarly, you can draw the border with a pattern by holding down the Option key just prior to drawing the polygon. The border pattern will be in the thickness specified by the line size.

If you wish the polygon to be drawn initially with a pattern fill, choose Draw Filled from the Options menu and select a pattern in the Patterns palette. With this menu item turned on, you can draw the polygon with what appears to be no border when the Option key is also pressed, since the border of the shape and its filled pattern are identical.

Regular polygons, probably more than any other shape in the Tools palette, benefit from an option we haven't yet said much about: Draw Multiple. This feature lets you draw repeated images of a polygon automatically. Combining repeated images and the polygon's ability to rotate can make for some remarkable images that don't require a great deal of artistic skill (Figure 13-45). You can turn on Draw Multiple by typing Option-M.

Moreover, you can set the frequency with which images are repeated as you rotate or grow the polygon. By also typing the Option key and a digit from 1 to 9 (as a rule, use the top row of keys instead of the numeric keypad), you specify the spacing between images. The smaller the number, the denser the repetition; the higher the number, the more widely spaced the repeated images are. If you then hold down the

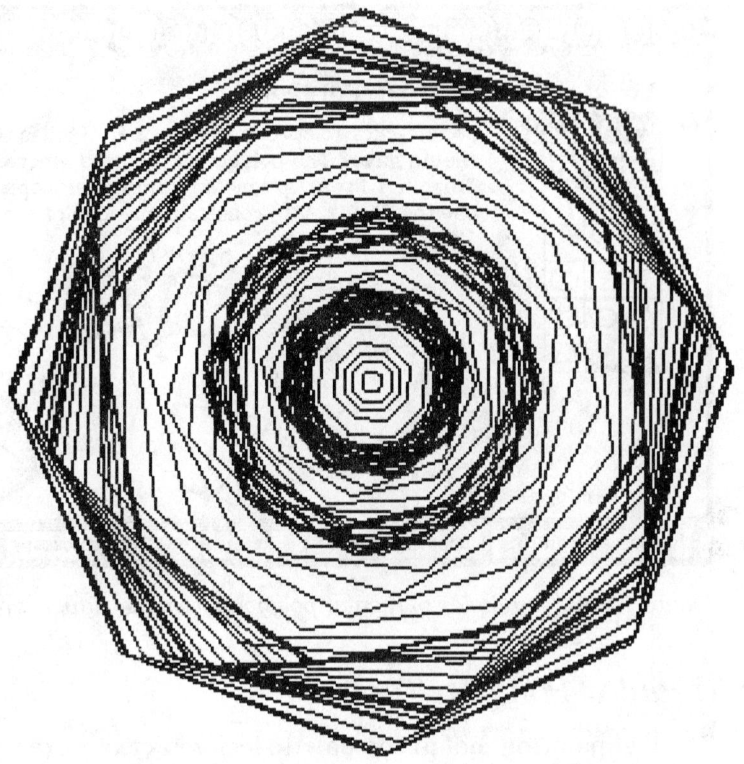

*Figure 13-45. The Regular Polygon tool makes it easy to draw rather complex drawings.*

Option key when drawing the polygon, the repetitions are of a polygon whose border is of the same "ink" as the currently selected pattern.

What this all comes down to is a vast variety of possibilities using the Regular Polygon tool. As a starter, study closely the examples in the HyperCard help system that demonstrate examples of regular polygons (shown in Figure 13-46). Then plan to spend time experimenting with the combinations of various settings. You might even want to create a stack of polygon ideas that you've created. Do all your drawing in the card graphics layer of the stack and conduct one experiment on each card in the stack. Set up a background text field, as well, to make room for notes that will remind you about which settings were in effect when the sample polygon effect was made. Then you'll have a record of your experiments for use later on, when creating yet other stacks.

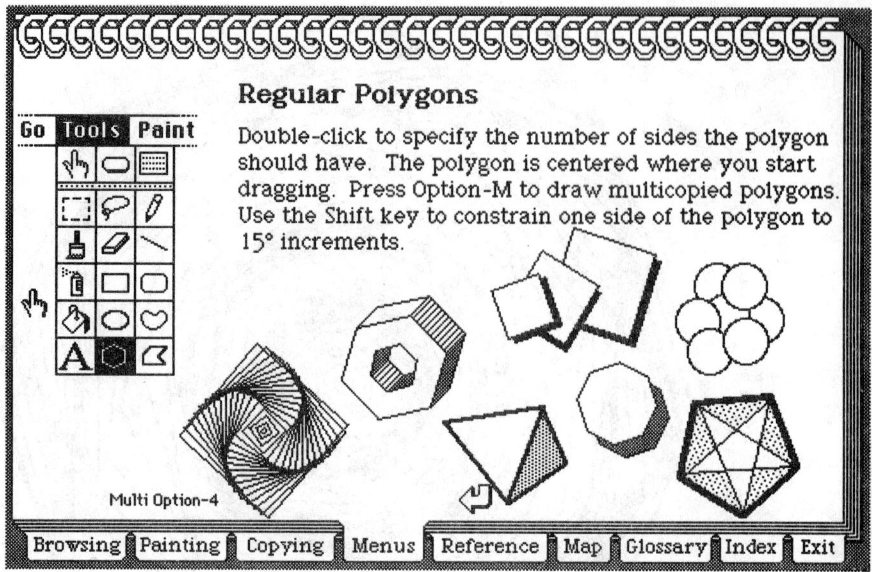


*Figure 13-46. Examples of regular polygons from the HyperCard Help system*

## *The Irregular Polygon Tool*

The last painting tool in the palette lets you create irregular polygons on the screen. An irregular polygon is a many-sided object whose sides are not necessarily of equal length. Each side, however, is a straight line, no matter how long or short.

Like most of the other shapes, you can draw irregular polygons with borders of varying thickness. When you draw the shape, however, the behavior of the lines you draw will seem very different. First you position the cross-hair cursor at the beginning point of the polygon with a click. You may then release the mouse button, but the tool is not only still active, it stretches the first side of the polygon from the starting point, like a rubber band. You determine the second point of the polygon and click the mouse button. Again, the second side stretches between the second point and the cross-hair cursor. You keep up this plant-and-stretch process for as many sides as your polygon needs (Figure 13-47).

One way to close off the polygon is to click the final point on the same point as the starting point. Another way is to click a point twice on the same pixel. This halts the polygon drawing (this is good to remember if you find yourself getting carried away and unable to find the starting point).

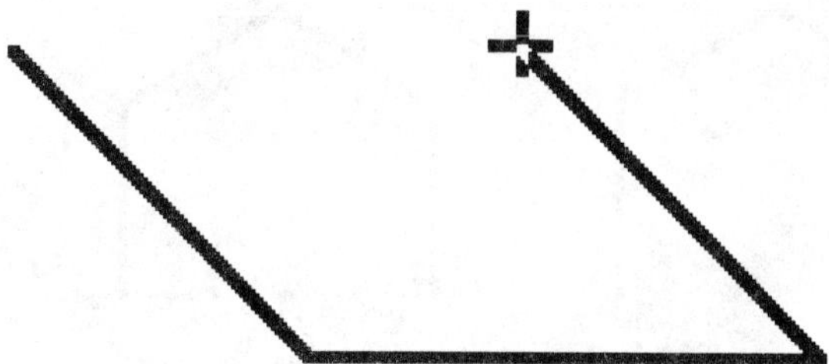

*Figure 13-47. Irregular polygons are defined by stretching each side, clicking where the side ends, and stretching the next side. A double-click at any point ends the polygon definition.*

## OPTION KEY ENHANCEMENT

To draw an irregular polygon with a pattern border rather than black, hold down the Option key when you click the starting point of the polygon. You may release the Option key after that, while you carefully position each point of the polygon.

## SHIFT KEY ENHANCEMENT

You can constrain the angle of each side of an irregular polygon to multiples of 15 degrees by starting the polygon with the Shift key down. This choice tends to make more polished polygons, but you'll have to evaluate the look and how it compares with the graphics concept you're striving for. Holding down both the Option and Shift keys when starting the polygon gives you 15-degree constraint of patterned border lines.

## DOUBLE-CLICK SHORTCUT

Irregular polygons can also be automatically filled upon completion, if you like. The Draw Filled option (in the Options menu) can be turned on by double-clicking the Irregular Polygon tool icon in the Tools palette. When you close up the polygon, the tool fills the area within the border with the currently selected pattern. If instead you double-click on one pixel, thus ending the polygon creation process, the tool will draw a line between that double-click point and the starting point of the polygon. Then it will fill the interior with the selected pattern (Figure 13-48). This behavior is consistent with the filling that the curve tool performs.

If you are unsure about a particular pattern prior to building an irregular polygon, draw it without a fill pattern and use the Paint Bucket to fill it later. Be on the lookout, however, for sides of the polygon

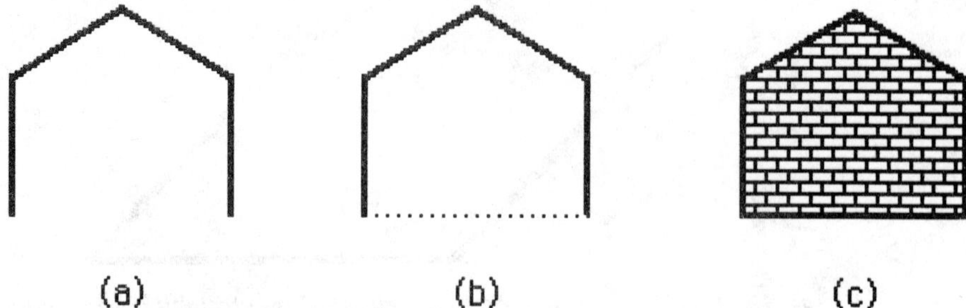


*Figure 13-48. If you end the polygon definition while drawing filled, HyperCard automatically closes the gap between start and end points, filling the interior with the currently selected pattern.*

that may have gaps because of odd angles. If paint oozes out of the polygon, undo the damage, and plug the gap(s) with FatBits (described in chapter 15).

## The Patterns Palette

By now you've seen that the Patterns palette may be torn from the menubar just like the Tools palette. You may also show the Patterns palette (already detached) by pressing the Tab key whenever you're in the printing tools.

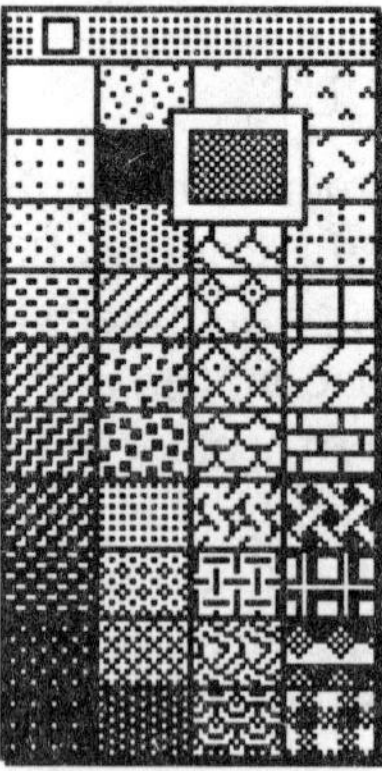

*Figure 13-49. The Patterns palette*

HyperCard comes with forty predefined patterns. The Patterns palette displays small samples of them. When you first select a paint tool, HyperCard preselects all-black as the pattern. A selected pattern has a white border around it in the palette (Figure 13–49). To select a different pattern, click on the sample in the palette.

## DOUBLE-CLICK SHORTCUT

You are free to edit any pattern in the palette. While you can reach the pattern editing facility via the Options menu, you may also double-click on a pattern in the palette to reach the editing facility. See the discussion about the Edit Pattern choice in chapter 15 for complete details about patterns and pattern editing.

That wraps up the detailed discussion of the painting tools and palettes. But there is a lot more to the HyperCard painting environment than just those tools. Next, we'll dive into the selections on the Paint menu.

# CHAPTER 14

# The Paint Menu

IN OUR INTRODUCTION TO THE PAINTING TOOLS, WE DREW A DISTINCTION BETWEEN THE bit-mapped characteristics of paintlike graphics environments and object-oriented environments of the MacDraw variety. The graphics environment of HyperCard is bit-mapped, but some of the features we're about to show you may make you wonder if HyperCard doesn't have a bit of the object orientation in its graphics tools.

What is really going on is that HyperCard devotes a portion of the Macintosh's memory to monitoring the things you draw on the screen. Every time you click the mouse to drag a new rectangle, rotate a new polygon, or type some paint text, the program stores the steps you went through. It knows which was the most recent "thing" you painted on the screen. But what it can do with this knowledge is exciting. It can select the shape or text— even if it consists of a complex pattern-filled shape atop a previously painted shape with yet a different pattern. You get the feeling that the last item you drew on the screen is in a kind of middle ground between bit-mapped shape and drawn object: not quite in the real bit map of the graphics layer you're working on, but hovering perilously close. That may not be a bad way to think about the most recently drawn shape. You need to remember that the last shape is always available for instant selection or modification by many Paint menu selections. The instant you click the mouse to draw another shape, the previous one is fixed into the bit map of the graphics layer. If you're new to painting programs, this shouldn't be too difficult a concept. For MacPaint users, it's a whole new ball game.

With this understanding, we can now progress down the Paint menu to see what goodies lie in store for HyperCard authors working on the graphics layers. All these features work in both the background and card graphics layers, but most of the time, you'll be working in the background graphics layer to create consistent card environments throughout a stack.

## Select

You'll recall the discussions we had when looking at the actions of the Selection and Lasso tools in the Tools palette. The point of selecting any piece of graphics is to alert HyperCard which pixels we want some action to work on, whether it be as simple as moving the item around the screen or as complex as rotating it.

It turns out that a majority (not all, to be sure, but a majority nonetheless) of the actions we want to perform on a shape occur immediately after creating that shape. This is one reason HyperCard takes great pains to remember the last shape (including paint text) we draw on the screen. Rather than messing with the Selection tool or Lasso, we can tell HyperCard with the Select command to select the item just painted on the screen.

When we issue the Select command, the "thing" we just added to the screen is selected as if we had lassoed it. In other words, the marquee "hugs" the perimeter of the shape. We are now free to do whatever we'd normally do with a selected section of graphic.

## Select All

When you want to capture the entire graphics layer— every pixel of the 512 by 342 HyperCard window— Select All is the command for you. It is the same as dragging the selection rectangle from one corner to the opposite corner.

The primary reason this command exists is that, with HyperCard graphics running under the menubar of built-in Macintosh screens, it is sometimes not easy to determine if dragging the selection rectangle from, say, the bottom left to the top right corners encompassed every pixel. Select All removes any doubt.

Be aware that this command works on the graphics layer only. It does not select field or button objects. If you want to pick up all those items for pasting into another stack, for example, use the Copy Card option in the Edit menu when the painting tools are not in force.

Once you've selected the entire graphics layer, you can copy it into the Clipboard for pasting elsewhere: in a clean, new background layer of a stack, for instance. If you're building a new stack with a background imported this way, you'll then have to start creating fields and buttons to give the cards some life.

## Fill

While the Paint Bucket tool fills the area within an outline, the Fill command on the Paint menu fills the entire shape that is selected or that was the last item drawn. As usual, the pattern this command uses is the currently selected pattern in the Patterns palette.

Use Fill with caution, particularly on shapes that contain internal detail. If, for example, you lasso the rectangle with the detail graphic shown in Figure 14-1 and then Fill it, the pattern will write over the detail graphic inside. If you intended another effect, then don't use Fill for this task. Undo a Fill as you would any errant paint command.

## Invert

The Invert command turns black pixels into white and white pixels into black within the area of the selection (Figure 14-2). This is a most practical tool for the design of certain shapes. It is sometimes easier to draw with a black pen and then invert the drawing to produce a white shape on a black background.

Inverting can sometimes be tricky when the area you've selected for inversion is surrounded by a black line. The results of the inversion will vary, depending on whether you've selected the black line or an area one pixel inside the outermost black line. In Figure 14-3a, the selection is one pixel outside the border. In Figure 14-3b, the selection is on the

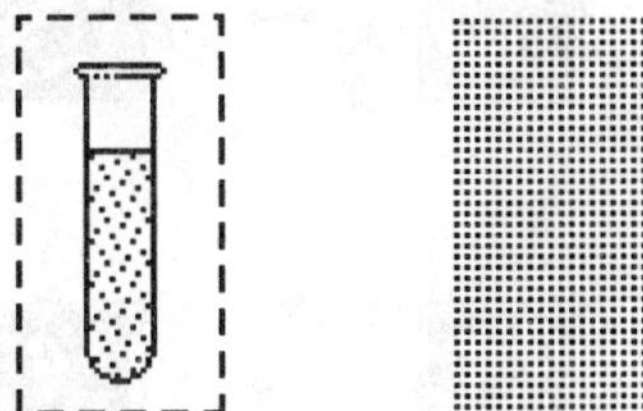

*Figure 14-1. Use Fill with caution, since it may overwrite a detail graphic within a selection.*

border. Notice that inversion worked on all pixels inside and under the selection rectangle. Because the outer border of the graphic in Figure 14-3c was not selected, it was not inverted, whereas the white lines under the selection rectangle were. The result is a doubly thick black border. In Figure 14-3d, only the original outer black line remains. The border is one pixel farther out from the center than Figure 14-3b.

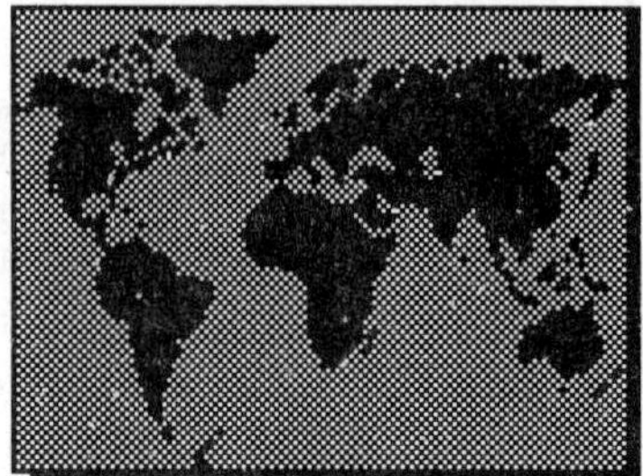

*Figure 14-2. Invert turns black pixels to white, and vice versa, within the selection.*

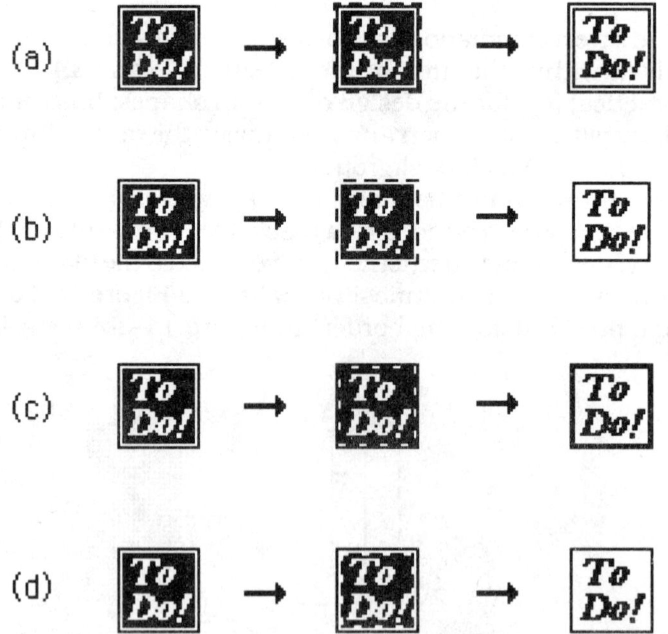


*Figure 14-3. Exercise care when placing the selection rectangle around an area to be inverted. Invert affects all pixels within and under the selection rectangle.*

## *Pickup*

The Pickup concept may be a bit difficult to grasp at first, but it turns out to be a powerful tool in a bit-mapped graphics environment like HyperCard. In essence, it allows you to pick up a copy of an existing graphic in the shape of a selected object (or the last shape you drew).

One of the best ways to demonstrate this feature is to establish a scenario in which you have a detailed piece of art—perhaps from a commercial clip-art file—from which you would like to snip out an oval-shaped area for use in another card. Without the Pickup tool, you'd have to copy a rectangular section of the art and paste it into a new card for some painstaking erasure to leave the oval shape. The Pickup tool makes achieving your goal much easier.

First you bring into view the clip art from which you want to copy. Then with a solid-filled oval tool, draw the oval on top of the area you wish to copy (Figure 14–4). Remember that until you click the mouse someplace else in the graphics area, the oval is not quite on the same layer as the clip-art graphic, so the oval has not obliterated the original art. Now choose Pickup from the Paint menu. The oval has picked up a copy of the clip art and is selected. You can now cut it into the Clipboard. Use HyperCard's navigation tools to get to the new stack you're building and paste the picture into it. You'll get the oval tracing of the original clip art (Figure 14–5).

There are many other uses for this tool. In the HyperCard help system, there is a suggestion about using it to trace text from an irregular pattern. That's a good one. Other ideas will come when you discover a need for complex outline shapes of complex drawings or patterns.

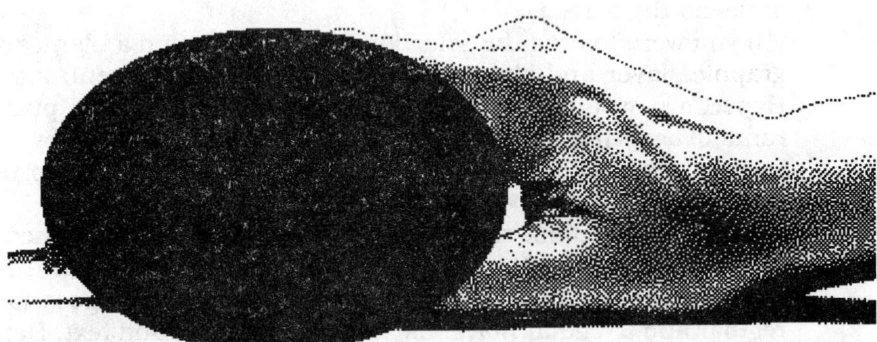

*Figure 14–4. To pick up an oval section of the graphic, first draw a filled oval atop the desired area.*

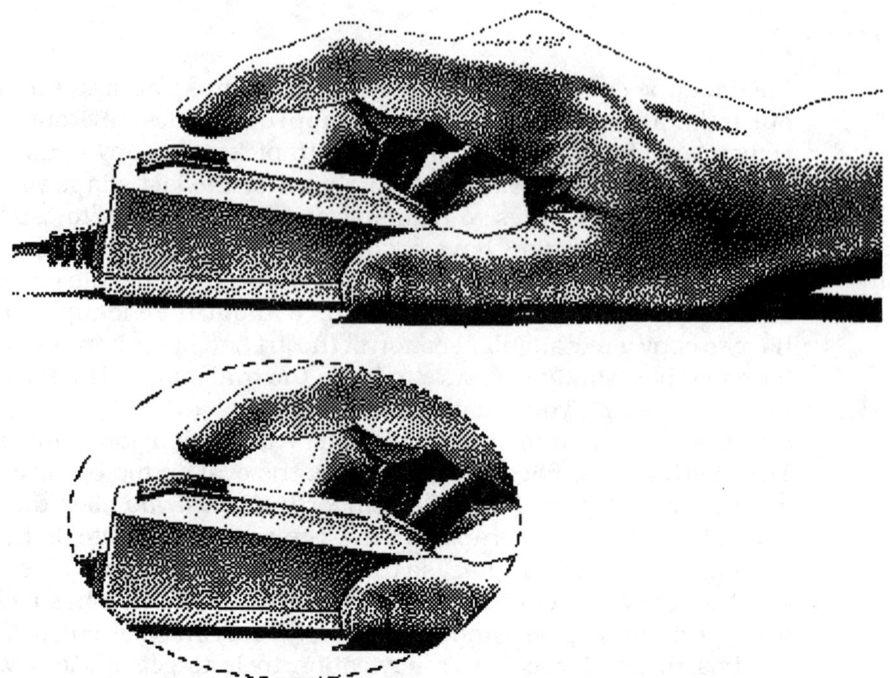

*Figure 14-5. When you choose Pickup from the Paint menu (or type the P Power Key), the filled oval picks up the underlying graphic in the oval's shape. You can then drag, cut, copy, or paste the oval section wherever you need it.*

## Darken and Lighten

We'll discuss these together because they do the opposite of each other. Both tools can be helpful in creating shading effects in carefully defined areas on the screen.

If you were to drag the selection rectangle around a blank area on a graphics layer and choose Darken from the Paint menu repeatedly, HyperCard would gradually fill in the area with black pixels on a random basis (Figure 14–6). You could reverse the process by choosing Lighten repeatedly. This command turns random black pixels into white pixels within the selected area.

You need not limit the affected area to a rectangle defined by the selection rectangle. Remember that all the commands in this menu work on the last "thing" drawn on the screen. That goes for ovals, regular and irregular polygons, free-form curves, and text. Depending on the resulting look you're in search of, the random "pattern" created by Darken and Lighten may be more desirable in some places than the very regular patterns that come from the Patterns palette.

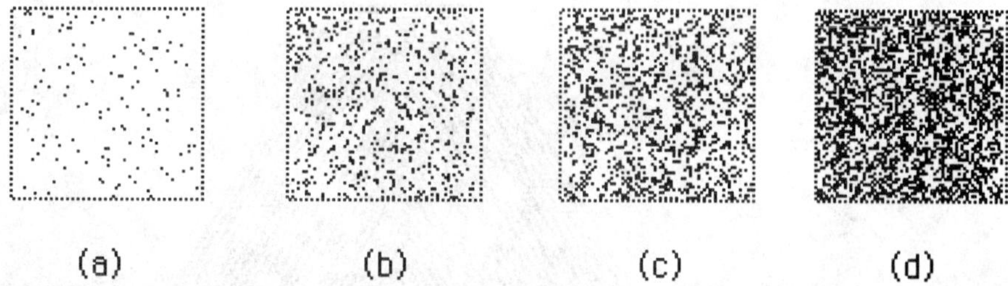


*Figure 14-6. Darken fills the selected area with black pixels on a random basis. It takes many Darken commands to turn an area completely black. These are the results of darkening a square one time (a), five times (b), ten times (c), and twenty times (d).*

## Trace Edges

A fun command to experiment with is Trace Edges. The premise behind this tool is that it turns the black pixels of a selected shape into white, while turning the pixels just inside and just outside the original pixels into black (Figure 14-7). This works on all shapes and sizes and can change the appearance of a shape substantially.

On some objects, Trace Edges adds a certain body or thickness to the original shape that can be pleasing. You can also issue the Trace Edges command repeatedly in such a way that with each succeeding command, HyperCard traces the edges created by the previous Trace Edges command, and so on. The effect can be quite striking when used on the right objects (Figure 14-8).

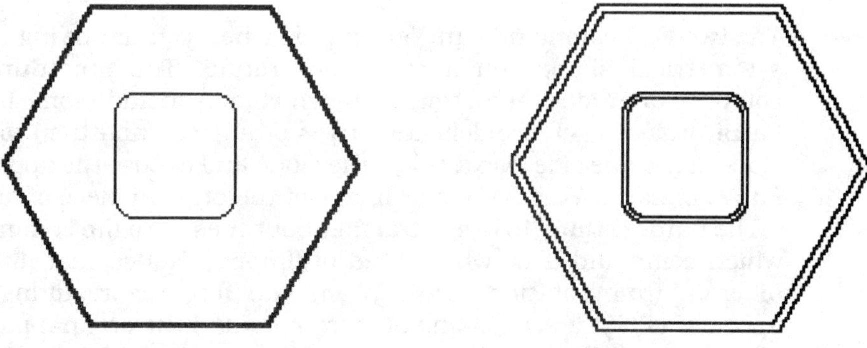

*Figure 14-7. Trace Edges acts as if tracing the edges of shapes within a selected area. Black pixels become white and vice versa.*

*Figure 14-8. You can issue several Trace Edges commands in succession, for striking effects.*

## Rotate Left and Rotate Right

While you might be spoiled by the intricate rotations possible during the creation of regular polygons, the Rotate Left and Rotate Right commands shift the selected images only in 90-degree jumps (Figure 14-9).

Arrows and pointers of all kinds are frequent targets for the rotate commands. Even though the commands work in 90-degree chunks, you can start with arrows that point at 45-degree angles and rotate them to 135, 215, and 305 degrees (Figure 14-10).

## Flip Vertical and Flip Horizontal

The two Flip commands are very handy when you are trying to draw symmetrical shapes on a card background. The procedure is to complete one side of the symmetry— which may include some intricate FatBit work to achieve delicate curves or angles— and then to drag a clone of the one side. Next, select the clone and choose the appropriate Flip command. Voilà: a mirror image of the original piece of art.

The hardest thing to keep straight about these two flip commands is which command does which kind of flipping. Notice that flipping is different from rotating twice. When you flip, the resulting image appears as if you are looking at it from behind the original page. The page has been flipped, like turning a transparent page in a book. When you flip an image vertically, the "book" containing the pages has its spine along the top or bottom of the page; when you flip horizontally, the "book" has its spine along the side, as in a traditional book. Figure

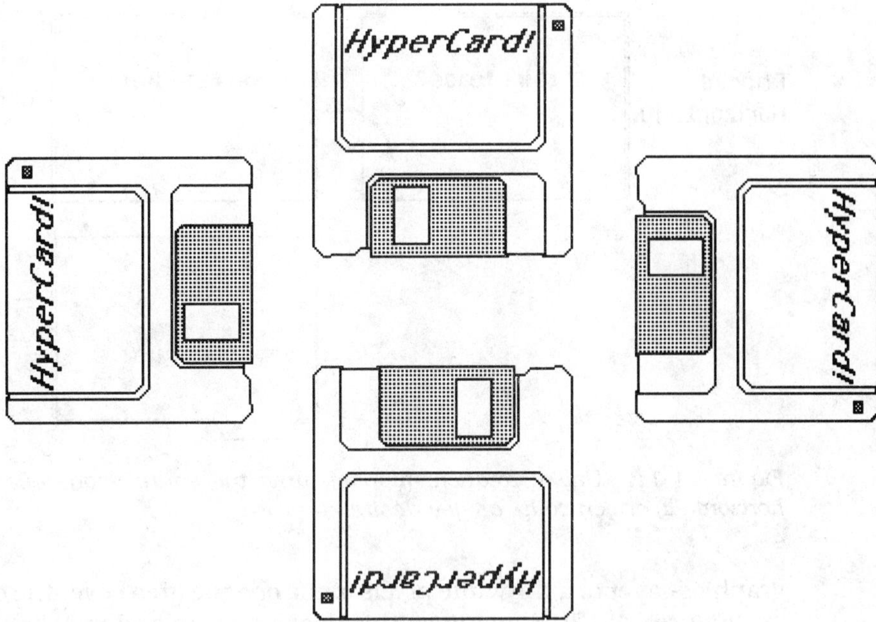


*Figure 14-9. Rotation works in 90-degree increments.*

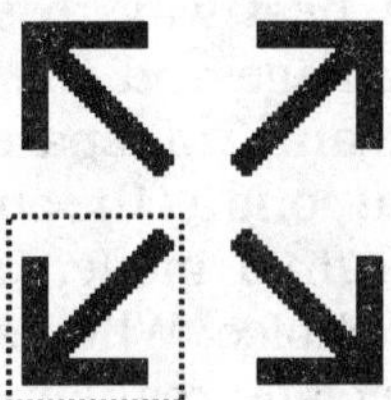

*Figure 14-10. If the original image is pointed in a 45-degree direction, rotation will angle the image to 135, 215, and 305 degrees.*

14-11 demonstrates the difference between the vertical and horizontal action of flipping a selected image.

## *Opaque and Transparent*

The two commands Opaque and Transparent affect a selected image, including images you paste from the Clipboard.

The default setting of most images pasted from the Clipboard is Opaque. This means that any area inside the shape's outlines is filled with white pixels. If the selected image is dragged atop existing

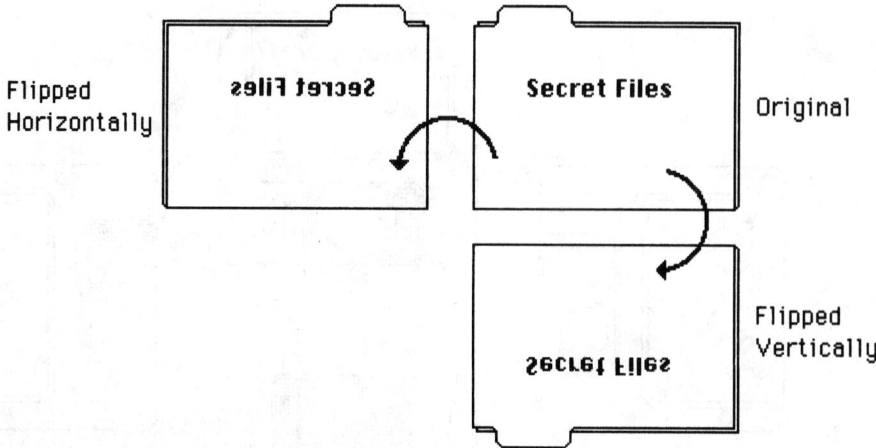


*Figure 14-11. Unlike rotation, flipping turns the entire image over, either horizontally or vertically, as you desire.*

graphics-layer art, the white pixels of the opaque area cover the existing art (Figure 14–12). Sometimes this does no harm and may be desired.

At other times, the desired effect is for all space inside the lines of a selected image to be clear, to let the original graphic layer show through (Figure 14–13). The best way to test which is the best effect for a particular selected image and the background graphic is to "toggle" between the Opaque and Transparent settings. These two menu items let you do just that, as long as the object is still selected. When choosing Transparent as the final mode, be especially careful to study the implications of that choice. When an image is made transparent atop some patterns, especially regular grey fill patterns, angled lines are sometimes partially or completely disguised by the pattern (Figure 14–14). Be on the lookout for this kind of visual interference, which may make the final background art hard to read.

## Keep

HyperCard's automatic save feature behaves differently when the painting tools are active than when any other tool is in force. Changes you make to a background or card domain picture are not saved until one of three things happens: 1) you exit the painting tools; 2) you go to a different card; or 3) you choose Keep from the Paint menu (or press Command-K).

Behind this behavior is the belief that you should be free to experiment with the graphics layer without damaging art that has been safely

*Figure 14-12. Most images pasted into a graphics layer start out opaque, that is, with white pixels blocking the underlying image from showing through.*

*Figure 14-13. If you want the underlying image to show through a pasted image, choose the Transparent command from the Paint menu (or type the T Power Key). You can toggle between Transparent and Opaque to test which version suits the picture you are creating.*

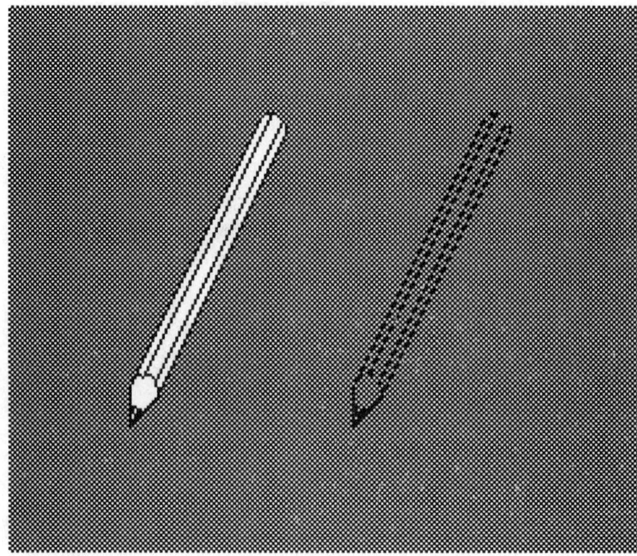

*Figure 14-14. Transparency atop filled patterns may sometimes obscure or distort the lines of the overlaying graphic.*

stored on disk. You should be able to undo a number of changes in a session (with the Revert command). Therefore, as long as you stay in the painting tools, no changes become completely final.

But there will be times, in modifying a graphics layer, when you'll want to save the changes made so far, and any further changes kept in memory. When you are ready to save your work to disk, choose Keep from the Paint menu. This command "keeps" the current state of the graphics on disk. Additional modifications will not be recorded to disk until the next time you give the Keep command, go to a different card, or exit the painting tools. A Keep command now and then also guards against loss of changes due to power failure or system error.

## *Revert*

With changes to the graphics layer maintained in memory until they are specifically stored to disk, you may undo all your changes by issuing the Revert command in the Paint menu. This command reaches back to the disk and loads in the graphics layers as they were previously saved to disk. The time to hit Revert is when the changes you're making to a graphics layer are making things worse. Revert gets you back to where you started.

This ends the discussion of items in the Paint menu. As you have seen, these items perform much of the action "after the fact," that is, after a shape or text has been painted on the screen. There should be enough in the way of tools in this menu alone to let you create virtually any graphics effect you have in mind.

Our next stop is the Options menu, which holds some of HyperCard's real painting powers.

# CHAPTER 15

# The Options Menu

IN CONTRAST TO THE HEAVILY COMMAND-ORIENTED PAINT MENU, THE OPTIONS MENU contains items that you either switch on and off or that lead to dialog boxes offering a choice of settings. Every item on this menu, then, ultimately lets you set a switch that affects future graphics operations.

Those items that simply turn on and off display a checkmark next to the item's name when the option is in force (Figure 15–1). If an item brings up a dialog box with multiple choices, the menu item displays three periods after it, indicating that it leads to something else. We've already seen the effects of a couple of items in the menu, but we'll examine each one in more detail here.

## *Grid*

Unless you've seen the effects of a grid on other painting programs, you may have the wrong expectation about what HyperCard's Grid does for your painting. In a paper environment, a grid usually helps you line up objects along vertical and horizontal axes. It helps you keep everything nicely aligned.

What may disturb you about turning on the HyperCard Grid is that when you do so, nothing seems to happen, and you certainly don't see any grid lines or ruler on the screen to help you line up shapes. That's because the grid is invisible. How, you may wonder, can you line up objects against an invisible grid?

Options
Grid
FatBits
✓Power Keys
Line Size...
Brush Shape...
Edit Pattern...
Polygon Sides...
✓Draw Filled
✓Draw Centered
Draw Multiple

*Figure 15-1. Many choices on the Options menu are toggles. When a feature is turned on, HyperCard places a check mark next to its name in the menu.*

The answer lies in the fact that something has changed in the painting environment, but it is a subtle change at first. After turning on the Grid, select a painting tool like the Rectangle tool. Watch closely how the cross-hair cursor seems to jerk on the screen, snapping to invisible lines. Then drag a rectangle on the screen, and watch how its size grows, not smoothly but in steps, as you drag the cursor away from the starting point. No matter how hard you try, you won't be able to size the rectangle to dimensions other than the ones imposed by the way the cursor snaps to those invisible lines.

Those invisible lines are in the HyperCard Grid. If you could see them, they'd be spaced 8 pixels apart in both the horizontal and vertical axes (Figure 15-2). Whenever Grid is turned on, it guarantees that starting and ending points for drawn shapes will be on the grid.

For very regular shapes—lines, rectangles, circles, regular polygons—the Grid is often a time saver when you need to create different shapes in identical proportions. For example, if you create a square on the grid and wish to create a triangle with sides the same length as the square, the grid's 8-pixel spacing lets you see quickly when the triangle is the desired size (Figure 15-3). You could even count the number of grid squares as you create each object to double-check the dimension.

The Grid imposes a kind of linearity that doesn't work well when you are doing free-form drawing with tools like the pencil and curves. And

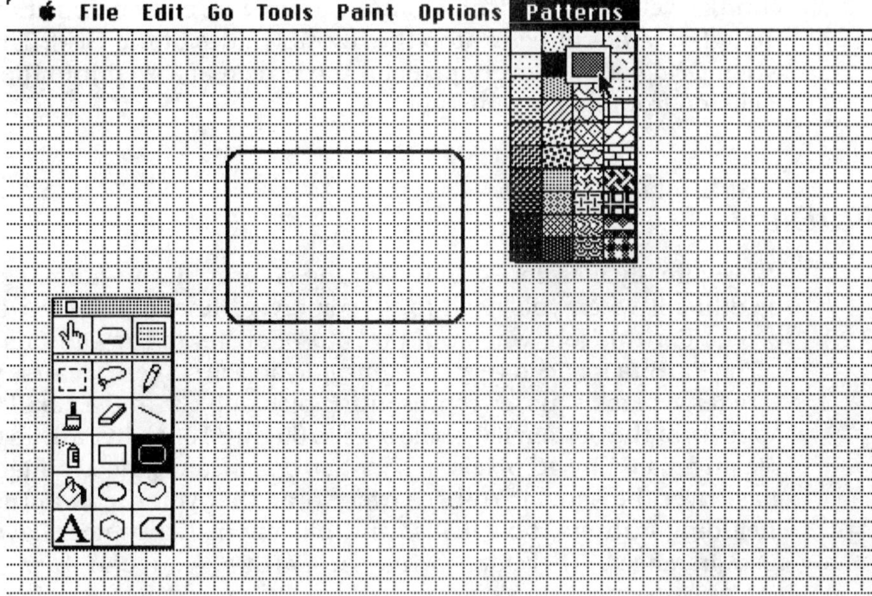


*Figure 15-2. If you could see the Grid, this is what it would look like. When the Grid is on, cursors and drawn object "snap to" the nearest grid intersection.*

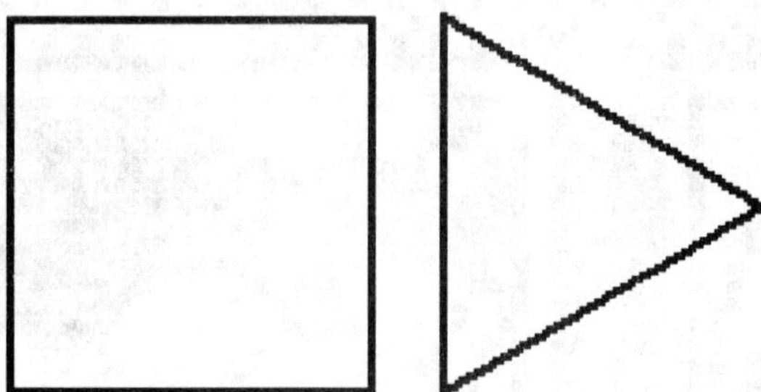

*Figure 15-3. The Grid helps you align objects and draw different objects with identical line lengths, such as this square and triangle.*

sometimes, you just need to maneuver a shape in a smaller increment that 8 pixels. Just turn off the Grid. You can always turn it on again later for other drawing.

You should be aware of one aspect of Grid that may throw you at first. You'll notice it most if you create a shape with the help of Grid, turn Grid off to move the shape a few pixels, and then turn Grid back on. When you turn Grid back on, the shape does not snap back to the nearest grid line— that would be disastrous. But if you select the object with the grid on and begin to drag it around the screen, it will move only in 8-pixel chunks vertically and horizontally from the current position, even though it is not directly atop the invisible lines of the Grid. Therefore, when Grid goes on, every pixel on the screen is frozen into the 8-pixel lockstep from its current spot.

## FatBits

We've already mentioned that working on graphics in normal size can be difficult when you need to do some very fine adjustment of a few pixels. For this job, you would turn on FatBits in the Options menu.

The FatBits mode is very recognizable on the screen because you see very large black squares representing black pixels, and a small window appears at the bottom left of the screen (Figure 15–4). In FatBits you can see an area 64 by 43 pixels. It's just as if someone placed a magnifying glass over the screen. You see everything that you see in normal size, including buttons, text fields, and bit-mapped graphics. Layering is also in effect. Therefore, while in FatBits, you can turn on the

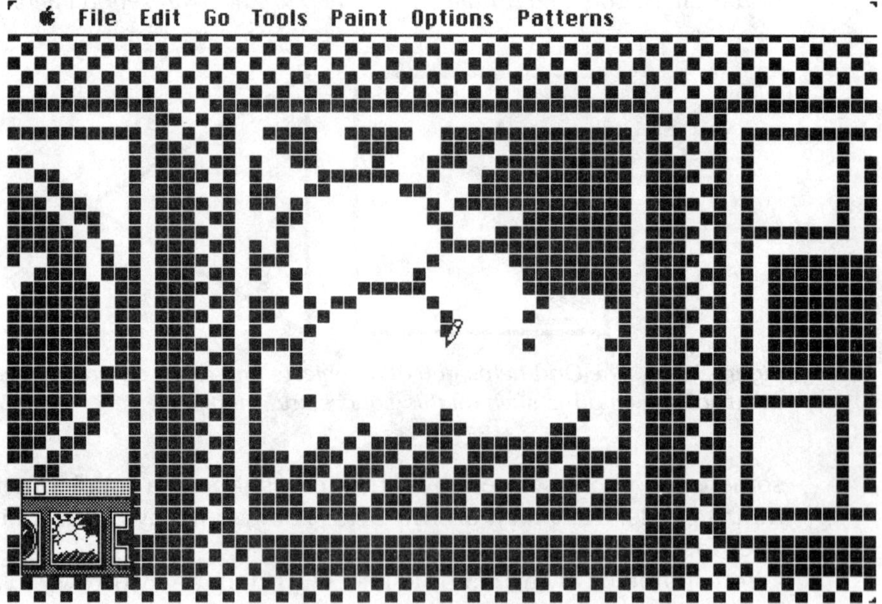


*Figure 15–4. FatBits magnifies graphics eight times, giving you pixel-by-pixel manipulation powers. A small draggable window in the lower left corner of the screen shows you the actual size of the area you're working on under the microscope.*

Background mode to see only what's in the card's background picture. Otherwise, you see what the browser sees: the full interaction of background and card domains.

Since FatBits is a painting tool, you'll have influence only over the bit-mapped graphics in either the background or card domains. Adjusting buttons and fields in FatBits is out of the question. When FatBits is in force, you may choose any painting tool. The cursor changes to the tool's regular-size cursor. You use the Pencil tool to point to a pixel and click the mouse button to turn black into white or white into black. Remember, however, that because of layering effects, you won't be able to turn background pixels on and off unless you are specifically editing the background. But you can turn transparent card picture pixels to white, which gives you the false impression that you're editing the background picture.

The small window on the FatBits screen contains a normal-size view of the detailed area covered by the screen in FatBits. That way, you can see how your FatBits fine-tuning will impact the normal-size painting without having to turn FatBits on and off repeatedly. Notice, too, that the mini window is, indeed, a window. You may move it around the screen by dragging its thin title bar, or you may close it (without turning off FatBits) by clicking its close box.

## SWITCHING ON FATBITS

There are three ways to turn on FatBits and four ways to turn it off—that should satisfy everyone. Let's see how to turn it on first.

1. Choose FatBits from the Options menu.

   The first time you turn on FatBits this way after starting up the painting tools, the FatBits window magnifies the center of the screen. If there are no black pixels or HyperCard objects in this area of your card, then the FatBits screen and the mini window with the normal-size graphic will appear to be blank. If you want to work on an area of the card other than the center, you'll have to scroll over to it (described below). Once you've scrolled to another location, HyperCard remembers that spot and will show up there the next time you start FatBits this way. When you exit the painting tools, however, the location will be forgotten, and FatBits will come up in the center of the card the next time.

2. Double-click the Pencil icon in the Tools palette.

   This action is the equivalent of choosing FatBits from the Options menu. They're completely interchangeable actions.

Therefore, if you start FatBits once with the menu selection and scroll the FatBits view to another location on the screen, a double-click of the Pencil tool will bring you to that second location.

3. Press Command and click on the card with the Pencil tool cursor.

   This is the preferred way to start FatBits if you're in a hurry. In this one action, you not only start up FatBits, but you also position the FatBits magnified view to the spot at which you're pointing the pencil tip. You bypass the need to scroll the FatBits view. This Command-key shortcut works only with the Pencil tool, but usually it is still more efficient to change tools and Command-click into FatBits. Scrolling in FatBits can be a trying experience if the destination is far from the current location (see below).

## SWITCHING OFF FATBITS

Now on to the four ways to leave FatBits. As with all good Macintosh design, the way out is the opposite of the way in, plus one extra shortcut.

1. Choose FatBits from the Options menu.

   The item will be checked when you pull down the Options menu this time. Choosing this item turns off both FatBits and the checkmark next to its menu item.

2. Double-click on the Pencil tool in the Tools palette.

   This is same as choosing the item in the menu. The check mark in the menu will be turned off for you.

3. Press the Command key and click with the Pencil tool cursor.

   There is no positional advantage to using this method over the first two. When you leave FatBits this way, you come to the full screen. It's here as a convenience for those who prefer this method of getting into FatBits.

4. Click any tool pointer in the mini window.

   This method is the simplest and requires no preplanning on your part. You don't have to worry about which tool you're using when you leave FatBits. Any tool, including the Eraser, will safely turn off FatBits without drawing or erasing on the graphic.

Scrolling in FatBits is a different experience from the kind of scrolling you may be used to in other programs. The FatBits view has no scroll bars. Therefore, you need to use a "grabber" tool, which magically appears when you hold down the Option key while in FatBits. Any tool from the Tools palette turns into the grabber, which you use with the mouse button pressed to slide the view around the screen until you see the area on which you wish to work.

Because of the level of magnification that FatBits produces on the screen, it may not always be easy to find your way. Use the mini window as much as possible to help you get your bearings. If you still have trouble, then exit FatBits and re-enter it using the Command-click-and-pencil method to zoom right to the desired spot.

While you are in FatBits, you can use all the tools in the Tools palette, including the selection tools and the Eraser. Moreover, the Shift key constraints and other enhancements are also in effect for those tools, even in FatBits. You'll find this feature particularly handy when you need to select a very small shape or a shape in a tightly spaced area. In Figure 15-5, for instance, we use the selection rectangle in FatBits to close up the spacing between letters in a small font.

FatBits will be a frequent friend when you start designing your own graphics layers.

*Figure 15-5. You can use all painting tools even while in FatBits. Selecting text characters, for example, gives you pinpoint precision for placing items on the screen.*

## Power Keys

As you have probably noticed by now, HyperCard's painting tools are loaded with shortcuts. Well, there are many more. Called Power Keys, they are turned on by choosing Power Keys in the Options menu.

You may also recall a Power Keys check box setting in the Home Stack's User Preferences card. When that box is checked, HyperCard automatically turns on Power Keys when you enter the painting tools (Figure 15-6). We suggest you keep that box checked if you're doing any stack authoring.

With Power Keys turned on, you can issue twenty-two different commands with the press of a single keyboard key. Most of the commands you'll recognize as coming from the Paint menu, whose items we've already discussed. Others come from the Options menu, giving you the ability to turn items on and off with a single keystroke.

The reason these Power Keys work is that when you're using any painting tool other than the Text tool, you really don't need keyboard keys other than Shift, Option, and Command. So HyperCard puts character keys to work for us (at our option) while painting. Obviously, when we're in the Text tool, Power Keys are temporarily disabled. In certain cases, Power Key commands require that the Message Box not be visible. When working in the painting tools, there is almost no need for the Message Box, so it's better to close it anyway.

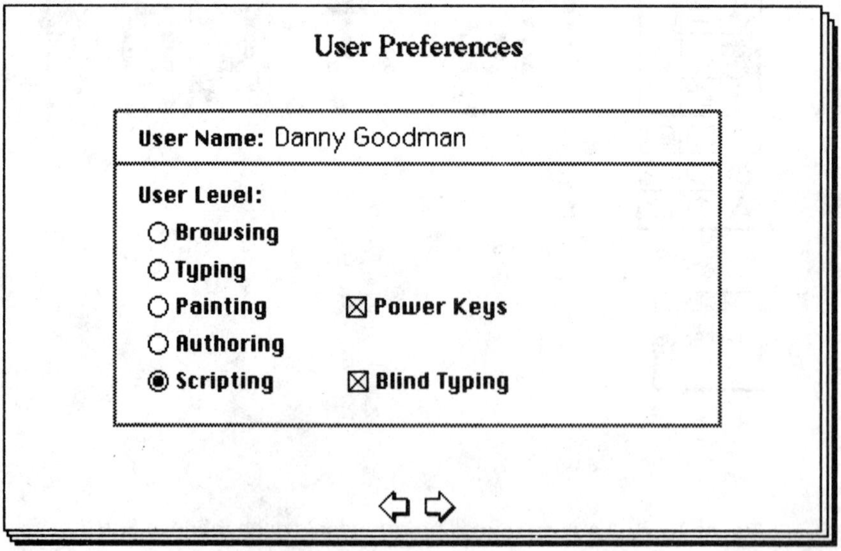

*Figure 15-6. To set Power Keys as a default setting when you start up HyperCard, click the Power Keys check box on the Home Stack's Preferences card.*

## POWER KEYS LIBRARY

What follows is a complete list of the keys and their corresponding commands. Wherever possible, the letter of the key is the first letter of the command.

| Key | Command |
|---|---|
| A | Select All (use Command-A when Message Box is visible) |
| B | Select the Black pattern in the Patterns palette |
| C | Turn Draw Centered on/off |
| D | Darker |
| E | Trace Edges |
| F | Fill with the current pattern |
| G | Turn Grid on/off |
| H | Flip Horizontally |
| I | Invert |
| L | Lighter |
| M | Turn Draw Multiples on/off |
| O | Opaque |
| P | Pick Up |
| R | Revert |
| S | Select (Command-S selects the current text when the text tool is active; also use Command-S when Message Box is visible). |
| T | Transparent |
| V | Flip Vertically |
| W | Select the White pattern from the Patterns palette |
| 1 | Set line thickness to 1 pixel |
| 2 | Set line thickness to 2 pixels |
| 3 | Set line thickness to 3 pixels |
| 4 | Set line thickness to 4 pixels |
| 6 | Set line thickness to 6 pixels |
| 8 | Set line thickness to 8 pixels |
| [ | Rotate Left |
| ] | Rotate Right |
| Backspace | Clear the current selection |

Power Key commands that control Paint menu choices require that a shape or screen region be selected first. If you forget to select a shape, an alert box will tell you so. After the alert box, you'll still be able to select with the S Power Key the last shape you painted.

For some Power Key commands, repeated pressing of their Power Key is the same as toggling back and forth between two views, as in the Flip commands. Other commands, like Lighten and Darken, are very practical as Power Keys because they require many activations to make a significant visual difference. Pressing the D key ten times is much more convenient than choosing Darken from the Paint menu ten times.

## *Line Size*

We've seen the dialog box that this menu selection gives us (Figure 15–7). Whatever line thickness you choose in this graphical dialog box applies to the lines drawn by all tools except the Pencil.

## *Brush Shape*

Here is another way to get to the brush-shape dialog box for selecting one of the thirty-two possible shapes (Figure 15–8). Your selection here affects only the Paint Brush tool.

## *Edit Pattern...*

Previously we've hinted at the possibility of editing the patterns in the Patterns palette. Well, it's true, and the Edit Pattern... command in the Options menu is one place of entry to do just that. When you choose this item, HyperCard presents a small dialog box with a FatBit-style editing window (Figure 15–9). In this box are both a magnified version of the pattern and a square area in normal size to show you what the pattern looks like in its typically repeated setting. It's time we took a minute to explain patterns in more detail.

### INSIDE PATTERNS

A Macintosh pattern is determined by the black and white pixels in an 8 x 8 square. At first glance, that may seem hard to believe, considering some of the intricate patterns you see in the Patterns palette. But all of those patterns consist of a repeated 8 x 8 pixel pattern. Examine them

*Figure 15-7. Line Size dialog box*

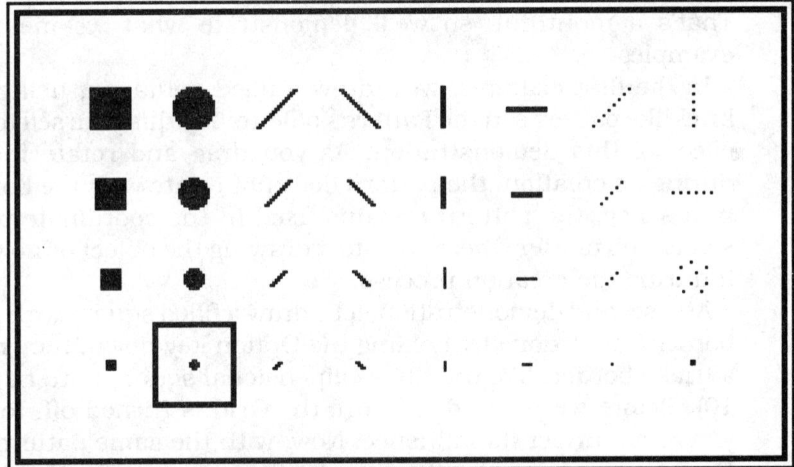

*Figure 15-8. Brush shape dialog box*

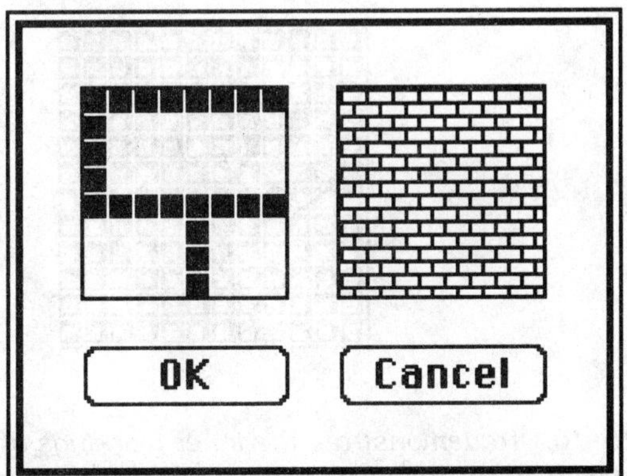


***Figure 15-9. Edit Pattern dialog box. You can edit patterns here in FatBit style, with a representative sampling of the resulting pattern in the right-hand window.***

yourself. Select a pattern in the palette and then choose Edit Pattern from the Options menu (you can also double-click on the pattern in the palette to bypass the menu). The patterns in the palette were carefully designed so that the top edge of one 8 x 8 square blends into the bottom of the 8 x 8 square that would appear above it on the screen.

You may use FatBit techniques to edit a pattern pixel-by-pixel. As you do, the change in the pattern is immediately reflected in the sample on the right. The number of combinations is large enough to keep you busy for weeks.

An important point to remember about patterns is that *as you draw a filled object* and *when you fill an outline with the Paint Bucket tool*, the pattern is fixed within the coordinate system of the Macintosh screen. That's a mouthful, so we'll demonstrate what we mean with two examples.

In the first example, we'll draw a filled pentagon, using one of the bricklike patterns in the Patterns palette. Try this yourself to get the full effect of this demonstration. As you drag and rotate the pentagon during its creation, the pattern does not rotate with the border shape. In a sense, the pattern remains fixed in the coordinate plane of the screen, no matter where you start drawing the object or how you rotate it during the creation process.

As a second demonstration, let's draw a filled square with a patterned border (that's done by holding the Option key down, remember?) with a tricky border, like the three-dimensional square pattern (Figure 15–10). Before we proceed, be sure the Grid is turned off, to prove that you're not under its influence. Now, with the same pattern, select the Oval tool and draw a filled oval with a pattern border (Option key enhanced) on top of the square (Figure 15–11). Notice that the patterns merge perfectly. Undo the oval and try again in a different spot. The

*Figure 15–10. To demonstrate the inner workings of patterns on the painting screen, begin by drawing a filled, patterned border square with a complex pattern.*

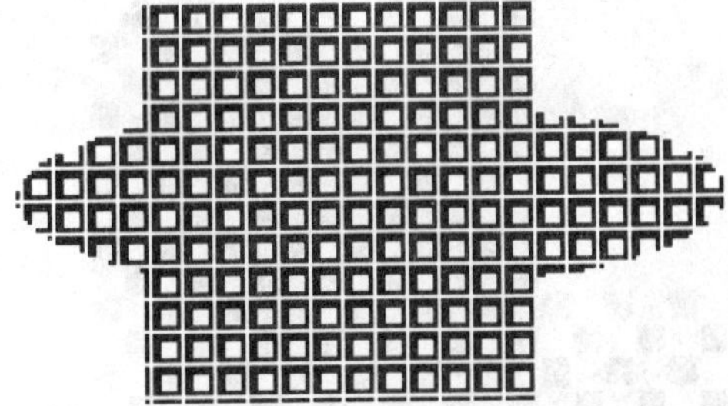

*Figure 15-11. Then draw another filled shape, also with a patterned border. The location of the pattern remains constant with respect to the screen. The minute you select and drag the shape, however, the pattern may lose its registration.*

results will be the same, because the pattern drawn for the square and oval is "nailed down" to the same coordinate plane.

## PATTERNS AND BIT MAPS

The situation gets a bit more complicated, however, when you select a filled area and move it around the screen. Recall that we said text characters become mere black pixels on the screen once we click the text pointer elsewhere. The same principle applies to patterns. As soon as we release the mouse button when drawing a shape, the pattern becomes a bit map, no longer tied to the original coordinate plane of the starting pattern. Therefore, you could shift a filled shape on the screen a couple pixels and be out of registration with the same pattern when it is used to draw or fill a new shape.

You will probably encounter this registration problem first when trying to match a grey fill pattern cut and pasted from another picture. Because of the tightly knit, repetitive nature of the pixel pattern that makes the grey pattern, you have a 50% chance of placing the pasted grey pattern in precisely the same orientation as the existing material (Figure 15-12). With the marquee swirling around the pasted selection, it's often difficult to see where it's "safe" to accept the paste procedure. For patterns with a less tightly knit pixel arrangement or a less-regular pattern, the chances can be much less than 50%. It may take several attempts at pasting and careful positioning before you get it just right.

If you move a filled shape in such a way that it comes off the registration of the live pattern, you still have a way to use the Paint Bucket tool to fill with the same off-registration pattern. It entails editing a pattern to match the new one— something you can do with a single click of the mouse.

In a typical setting, you may copy a piece of a card background or other Macintosh program screen to use as a foundation for a stack

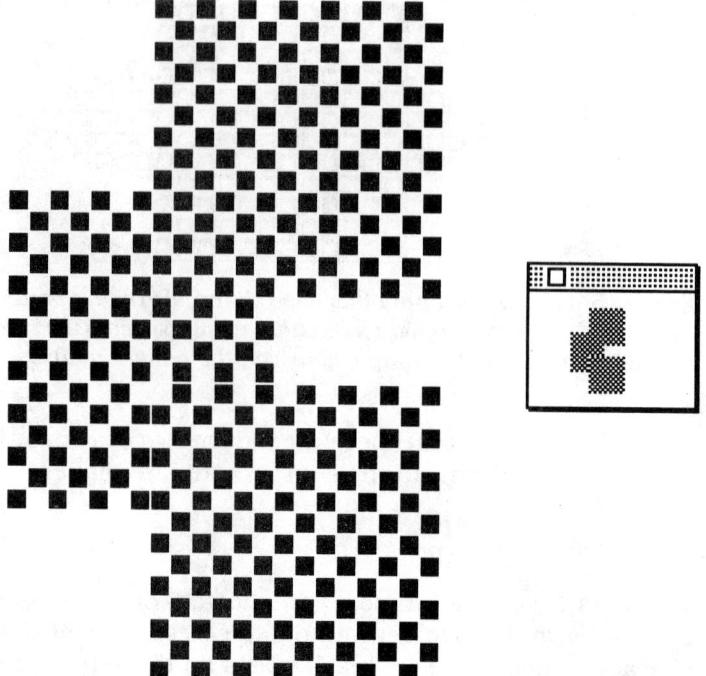

*Figure 15-12. Two squares of the same grey fill pattern were pasted atop the original. The top square happened to maintain full registration with the original; the bottom was off by one pixel. This tight pattern gives you a 50-50 chance of perfect registration the first time.*

you're building. Let's say that piece has a grey fill pattern around it, and some of that pattern is included in the section you paste into your new background (Figure 15-13). When you're finished adding your own touch to the graphic, you then want to fill the rest of the screen with the grey pattern. Applying the Paint Bucket, however, reveals that the grey you pasted is slightly off registration from the live pattern that HyperCard uses for drawing and filling (Figure 15-14).

What you need to do is edit a pattern to coincide with the pattern as you pasted it. Pull down the Patterns menu and select a pattern you won't be using during this HyperCard session. Then choose Edit Pattern... from the Options menu. The dialog box with the FatBitted pattern will appear. Now, simply click on any spot of the background grey pattern that you're trying to match. HyperCard will read that pattern and devise a live pattern that matches it. For the moment, this new pattern has taken the place of the unused one in the Patterns palette (this won't survive the exit from the painting tools). You can now

*Figure 15-13. Pasting a selection copied from another card and then dragging it on the screen may put the pattern out of registration.*

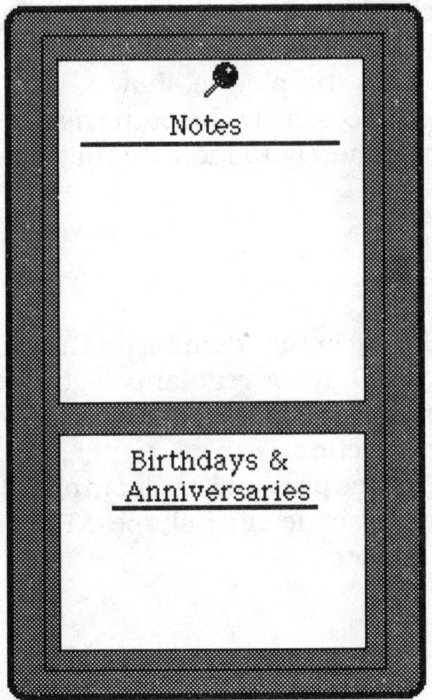


*Figure 15-14. When later filled around the pasted shape, the pattern is indeed off registration by one pixel. You can edit a pattern to match the off-registration one.*

fill the rest of the screen with the Paint Bucket and your new, temporary pattern (Figure 15–15).

This has been a crash course in Macintosh patterns, but all the details are here for you to study and experiment with at your leisure. As with fonts, keep the number of patterns on a screen to a visually appealing few. As professional artists will tell you, sometimes empty white space around elements makes a stronger statement than patterns.

## Polygon Sides

The dialog box summoned by this menu item shows the six types of polygons you can choose (Figure 15–16). A more efficient way of reaching this box, as noted earlier, is to double-click on the Regular Polygon tool in the Tools palette.

## Draw Filled

The Draw Filled item is an on/off switch, which is uniformly accessible by double-clicking on all shape-drawing icons except the regular polygon. As extra feedback to show you that Draw Filled is turned on, the tool icons in the palette show a grey fill pattern. Note that this pattern is not necessarily the pattern selected in the Patterns palette; it fills the tools merely to indicate that Draw Filled is turned on.

## Draw Centered

We've seen the effect that turning on Draw Centered has for most of the regular shapes. Only the regular polygon automatically draws from the center. All others— lines, rectangles, and ovals— must have this switch turned on to function.

Follow directions provided earlier in our discussions about rectangles and ovals to draw concentric shapes. The centerpoint technique is one you should master.

*Figure 15-15. After editing a pattern to match, the new fill pattern blends seamlessly with the pasted pattern.*

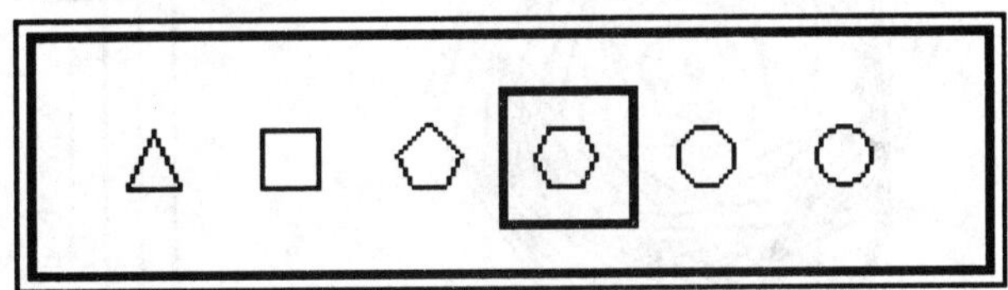

*Figure 15-16. Regular Polygon dialog box*

## *Draw Multiple*

In our discussion about regular polygons, we indicated the kind of effects you can attain when the Draw Multiple feature is in force. It also works when drawing other shapes, including rectangles and circles.

Once you turn on Draw Multiple, you can set the interval between repeated images by pressing the Option key and any number from 1 through 9. Figure 15–17 demonstrates some repeated drawings.

In the next chapter, we'll close our painting discussions with comments about painting in general.

*Figure 15–17. Examples of what you can do with the Draw Multiple feature engaged*

# CHAPTER 16

# Painting Strategies

NOTHING CAN BE MORE FRIGHTENING THAN A BLANK PAGE, ESPECIALLY IF YOU'RE expected to work in a medium— graphics— that is foreign to you. Using the painting tools built into HyperCard should ease the pain considerably, but you may not know where to begin.

## *Borrowing from Others*

Perhaps the easiest way to begin designing a stack background graphic is to borrow ideas from existing Macintosh programs whose looks appeal to you. The Macintosh actually provides you with the tools to copy and paste part of a Macintosh screen into a new background you're creating. Here are the steps:

1. With the screen you wish to adapt showing on the screen, press Command-Shift-3.

   This three-key combination saves the entire screen, including menubar, as a MacPaint document file on the disk with the name Screen 0. Each time you press this key sequence, a new file is created, with the number in the file name increasing automatically by 1 until it reaches 9. After that, the Macintosh won't let you do any more "screen dumps" until you change the names of the existing Screen files.

2. Enter HyperCard and bring up the blank background you wish to start work on.
3. Select any painting tool from the Tools palette.
4. Determine which domain's picture layer is to receive the graphic and make sure you are in that domain (for example, background).
5. Pull down the File menu and choose Import Paint...

   With a painting tool selected, HyperCard will look to the disk and find only MacPaint or similar graphics files for importing. The standard file dialog box will be presented, from which you can choose the desired file.
6. Choose the file Screen 0.

   HyperCard will place a copy of the picture in Screen 0 into the graphic layer of your choice, overwriting whatever was in that layer.

You're now ready to use the HyperCard painting tools to erase those parts you don't want and modify those that you'd like to keep. If you plan to import several background or card MacPaint documents, be sure to create a new background or new card prior to importing the pictures. That way you'll avoid overwriting existing graphics.

CAUTION: Commercial program screens are usually copyrighted by their authors or publishers. If you intend to resell your stack in the open market, consult with legal counsel regarding the copyright of the source material pasted into your stack.

## *The Sequence of Things*

It's difficult to recommend a precise order in which to build a stack from scratch. A lot depends on the type of buttons and fields you intend to use.

One methodology dictates that you design the background graphics layer first, at least elements such as basic outlines and background text. Then add the button and field layers, as your application requires.

A second methodology focuses first on the placement of text fields and buttons, particularly buttons that are copied from other stacks and pasted into yours. You might call this a functional approach, because you spend initial energy on the information and action elements of your stack— making sure they work— before making the stack look nice. The way a stack's function evolves may greatly influence the artistic design for the background behind it.

It will be the rare stack that is designed the first time without any changes needed during the break-in or testing phase. Be prepared to make many adjustments to all elements of a stack. In that regard, avoid locking yourself into certain graphics features that will make fine-tuning difficult. For example, the very last task should be the filling of the background graphics layer with a pattern, like the grey pattern. In fact, you might even wait a couple days or weeks before filling in the grey pattern. That way, if you find you need to make changes to other elements, you won't have to erase the pattern already there. Especially if you find that you need to move elements around, registration problems with a background fill pattern could end up being more trouble than it was worth to make the first edition good-looking. So, hold off filling in the background until you're satisfied with the overall card design and have lived with it for a while. Then fill the area in one convenient spill of the Paint Bucket tool.

## *To Menu or Not to Menu*

One design decision you'll have to make early on is whether you need the menubar visible while your HyperCard application runs. The effect this choice has pertains primarily to those who use your stack on the Macintosh models with the self-contained 9-inch monitor. On these screens, you'll recall, the menubar covers the top part of the active HyperCard screen.

If you plan to hide the menubar on your application (a HyperCard script in your stack can hide the menubar for you), you can design the background graphic to take up the entire screen without any interference. Those who use your stack on a large external monitor on any Macintosh will have the entire screen anyway, so there is no difference between the two monitor styles.

But if your stack uses the menubar for navigation purposes (especially to help the browser find the Home stack and Help), then you must be mindful of how the card will look to those who use large screens on their Macintosh. If you design the card on a 9-inch internal Macintosh screen with the menubar showing, the area under the menubar will probably be all white. On a large Macintosh screen, this will look like a white bar across the top of your cards— probably not what you would want.

To prepare for the eventuality of someone using your stack on a large screen, be sure to check the card design with the menus turned off (press Command-Spacebar to toggle the menubar). You might consider filling the area under the menubar with black so as not to call attention to the area on a large screen.

So far, we've covered many of the tools you need to create a practical stack in HyperCard. In the next chapter, you'll apply what you've learned to create a new stack based on one of the samples provided on the HyperCard disks. You'll also get a chance to practice with some of the painting tools to add custom touches— not a simple cut-and-paste exercise.

# CHAPTER 17

# Building a HyperCard Stack

IT'S TIME TO APPLY THE KNOWLEDGE GAINED SO FAR TO BUILDING A PRACTICAL STACK. We'll start with one of the ideas on the HyperCard ideas disk, but we'll make some cosmetic changes to the graphics layer and add a number of objects to increase the power of the stack. By "increase the power," we mean making it easier to use and more functional in managing time and information. We strongly encourage you to follow along, step by step, as we build this stack. The stack that we develop will also be at the core of some future examples when we apply HyperTalk scripts in Part Four.

## *Overview*

Before designing a stack, it's a good idea to map out– at least in your mind– what the stack will be doing when it's finished. There should be a kind of statement of purpose that leads you in a certain direction. Concepts and details may change along the way– that's fine. But without a starting idea of what you want to accomplish, you'll find yourself hung up, staring at the blank screen, wondering how to proceed.

## OUR PURPOSE

In a sense, the exercise we'll be going through in this chapter is artificial, because it implies not only that we had a very clear vision of what the final stack would look like, but that we pursued that vision unswervingly. In reality, nothing could be further from the truth. The stack that we'll be building together here went through many variations and changes before it found its way into the book. By necessity, we will show you the steps along a rigid path, only because the real development process will differ with everyone who designs a stack. We'll explain certain design decisions, and even relate some alternatives, but the actual evolutionary process was too fragmented and helter skelter to narrate in a cohesive tale.

The real purpose of this exercise is to demonstrate many of the object and graphic techniques discussed earlier in the book. We want you to have hands-on experience with them in a real stack environment. Even if you don't use the stack we end up with, you'll have applied the tools successfully and can then apply them to your future stacks.

## THE FINISHED STACK

With these warnings in mind, here's the idea we'll be designing toward: a stack that manages a To Do list, that is, a list of tasks we need to accomplish each day. A To Do list is different from an appointment book. An appointment book dutifully lists items that must be accomplished at a certain time. A To Do list, on the other hand, lists items that must be accomplished on a given day, but not at any particular time. Our days are frequently filled with these two kinds of tasks.

A To Do list can have a few different approaches. One would be a single card stack that lists tasks for today only. When tomorrow rolls around, you inspect that card, erase those items completed yesterday, and enter new items for today. That's not much of an improvement over a paper note pad and pencil, so this system doesn't qualify as one worthy of translating into HyperCard.

A second type would consist of a very large stack, with a To Do sheet for every day of the year. That way, you could jot a note of something you need to do on a particular day next week and find it there when it comes time to update the list for that day. The difficulty for this kind of stack, however, is that to make it effective, you'd have to make up 365 cards for the next year. Without the help of HyperTalk, that could be a tedious process at best.

For our exercise, we'll choose a middle ground. Our stack will have seven cards in it, one for each day of the week, Sunday through Saturday. It will be a kind of "rolling" To Do list. For example, when we're looking at the Tuesday card, the previous card in the stack, labeled

Monday, is actually the To Do list for the following Monday. Therefore, we can use this To Do list to plan tasks one week ahead.

The stack will have cards that look like the one shown in Figure 17–1. Each card's day of the week will be plainly visible in a large font. To assist in quick navigation from one day to another, there will be a set of seven buttons corresponding to each of the seven cards. When we're viewing a card, that day's button will be highlighted by a surrounding dark square. There will be icons that bring us directly to some other existing stacks, like the weekly appointment book and the name and address stack. This will allow us to zip straight to these related stacks without having to go via the Home card. We'll also need a button that our browsers can copy and paste in other stacks if they wish to zip straight to the To Do stack. Finally, the card will have two text fields set up in columns. We could have made one wide text field, but since most tasks can be described in a handful of words, we'll end up with better screen utilization for people with lots of things on their To Do list. As another idea, you may want to use the left column for items that change on a daily basis and the right column for long-term projects that will stay in the card perhaps for weeks until completed.

## THE PLAN OF ATTACK

We'll start by borrowing one of the stack ideas in the ideas disk supplied with HyperCard and making several changes to it. The changes will involve modifications to the background and card graphics layers, the

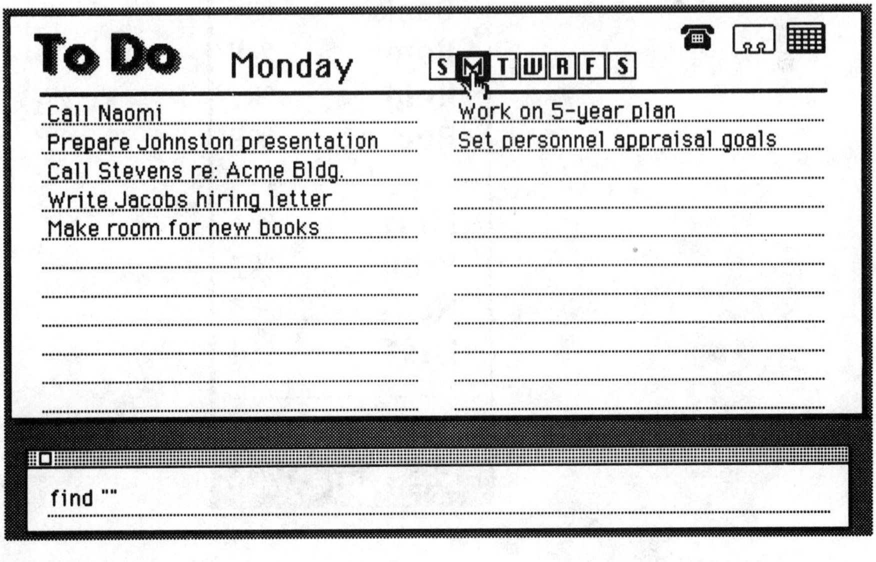

*Figure 17–1.*

resizing and addition of text fields, and the addition of different types of buttons. All of the new buttons will have links to other cards or other stacks, so you'll get to practice basic linking skills as well.

Give yourself about an hour to work with this exercise if you're still unsure about some of the techniques. It is better to work this entire exercise in one sitting with an occasional break so that you get the rhythm of creating or adapting a stack. Let's go.

## *Part One: Creating the New Stack*

The card we'll use to begin is in the stack named Stack Ideas. Use the Go command in the Message Box to get directly to the card.

1. Wherever you are in HyperCard, make sure the Message Box is showing on the screen. If it is not, choose Message from the Edit menu or type Command-M (Figure 17-2).
2. Type the following command into the Message Box:

   Go to card "To Do Today" of stack "Stack Ideas"

   The card and stack names must be in quotation marks. As a shorter, alternative way of issuing this command, you can leave

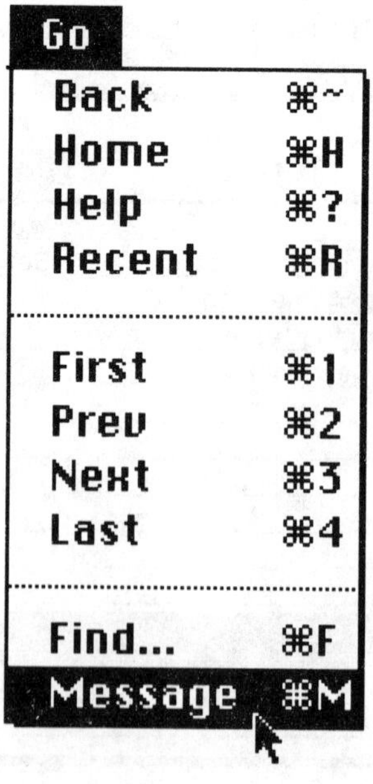

*Figure 17-2.*

out the *to.*

Depending on how you have set up your HyperCard files on disks, HyperCard may not find this stack right away. If HyperCard cannot find the stack file, it will display a standard file dialog box. Use it to find the stack file (or insert the floppy disk with the file and open the file). When the stack is open (it shows a cover card with instructions), type *Go to card "Do Today"* into the Message Box.

3. With the sample To Do card in view, select New Stack from the File menu (Figure 17-3).
4. In the resulting standard file dialog box, be sure you are in the desired folder and disk. Type *My To Do List* into the blank for the file name (Figure 17-4). Either press Return or click OK to continue.

   There will be no change on the screen, except that the sample text in the original card's field will disappear. A dialog box asks whether you wish to extend the stack. Click the Cancel button. You are now looking at the first card of the new stack, My To Do List.

*Figure 17-3.*

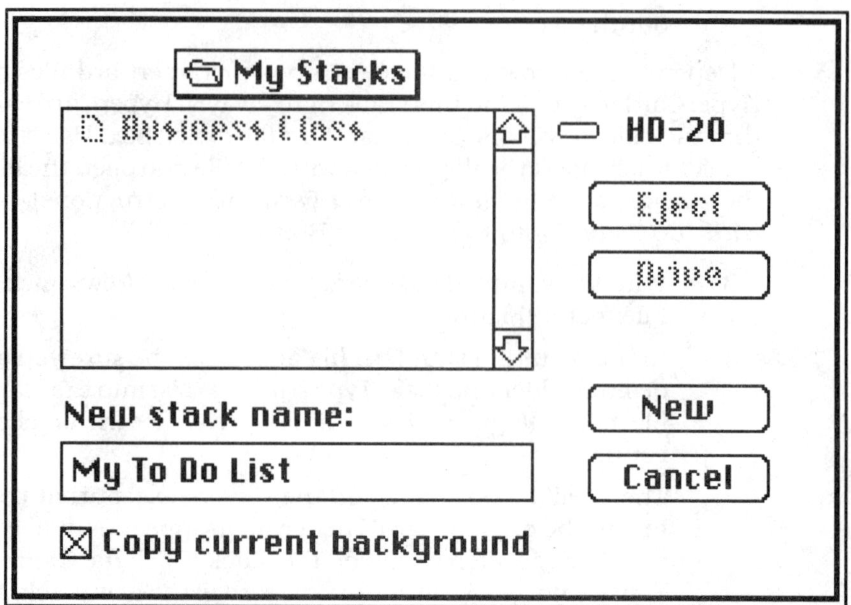


*Figure 17-4.*

What you've just done is to create a new stack with the card background, field, and buttons that were in the card from the Stack Ideas stack. Therefore, the button at the upper right corner of the card, which contained a script linking to the Calendar stack while this card was in the Stack Ideas stack, has the identical script in your new stack, My To Do List.

A good idea at this point is to inspect the object information dialog boxes for the stack, background, card, and some of the fields and buttons. This will provide an overview of the current status of the various parts of this stack before you start working with it.

5. Pull down the Objects menu and choose Stack Info....

   The Stack Info dialog box comes up (Figure 17-5). Information about the stack's location will probably be different on your disk, but the rest of the information should be the same. At this point, it says, there is one card and one background in the stack. Click OK when you're finished.

6. Pull down the Objects menu and choose Background Info....

   The Background Info dialog box appears (Figure 17-6). The background ID number will be different for your stack. Other pertinent information should be the same, including the fact

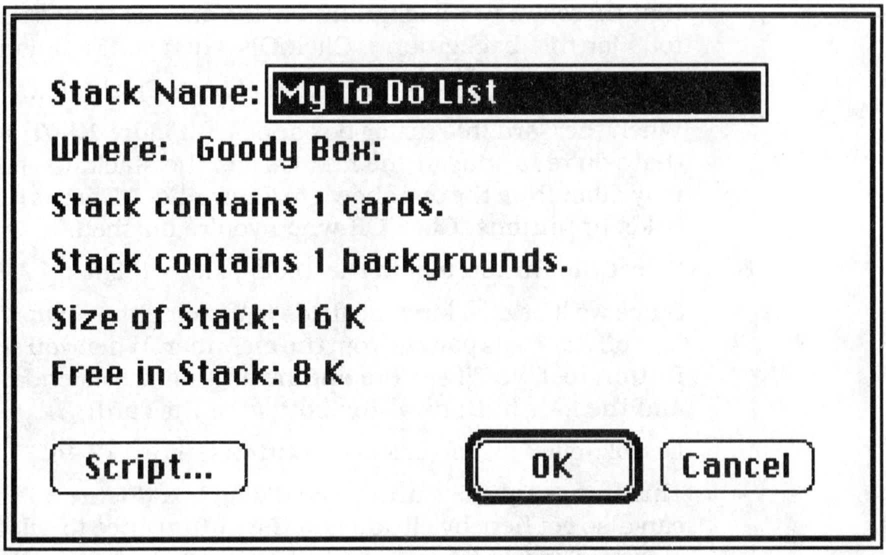

Stack Name: My To Do List

Where: Goody Box:

Stack contains 1 cards.

Stack contains 1 backgrounds.

Size of Stack: 16 K

Free in Stack: 8 K

Script... OK Cancel

*Figure 17-5.*

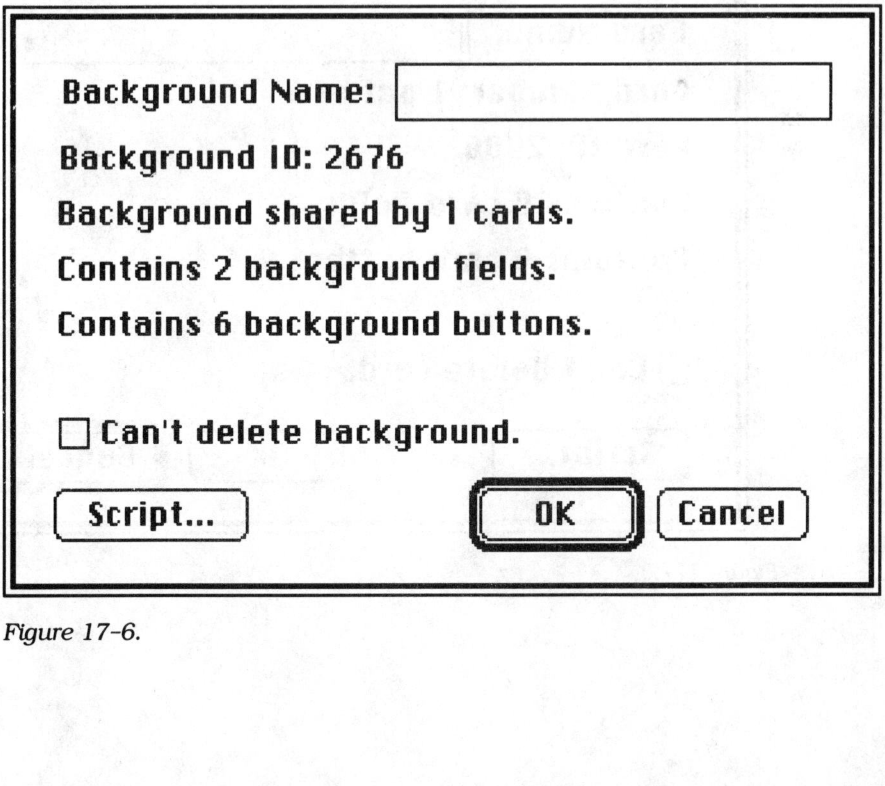

Background Name:

Background ID: 2676

Background shared by 1 cards.

Contains 2 background fields.

Contains 6 background buttons.

☐ Can't delete background.

Script... OK Cancel

*Figure 17-6.*

that there are two background fields and six background buttons for this background. Click OK when you're finished.

7. Pull down the Objects menu and choose Card Info....

   When the Card Info dialog box appears (Figure 17-7), you'll see that you're looking at the first card of the stack. Its ID number may differ from the one shown in Figure 17-7. There are no card fields or buttons. Click OK when you're finished.

8. Select the Button tool in the Tools palette (Figure 17-8).

   Since we'll be checking the fields in a moment, you may wish to tear off the Tools palette from the menubar. When you select the Button tool, you'll see the outline around the calendar button and the four buttons at the bottom of the card.

9. Double-click on the calendar button (Figure 17-9).

   This brings up the Button Info dialog box (Figure 17-10). You can also get here by clicking on the button once to select it (the marquee swirls around the button) and choose Button Info... from the Objects menu. We see that the button has a name and is transparent.

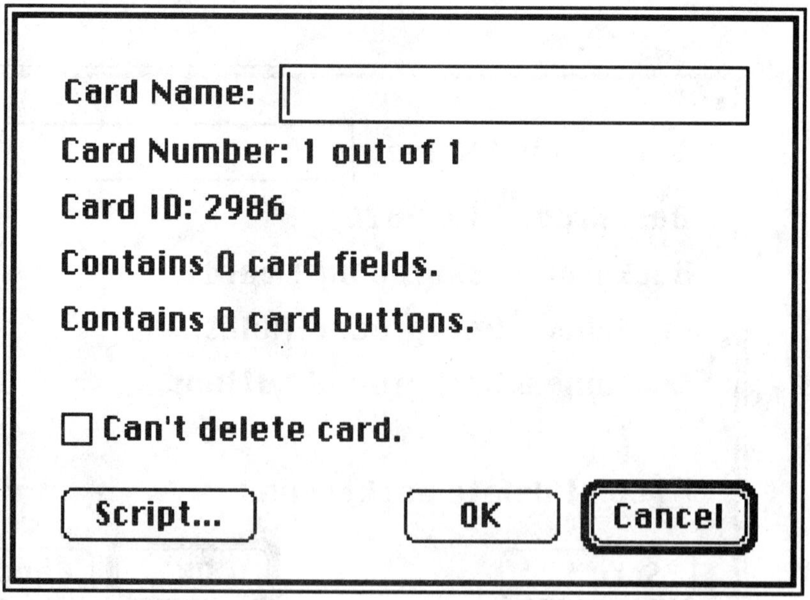

*Figure 17-7.*

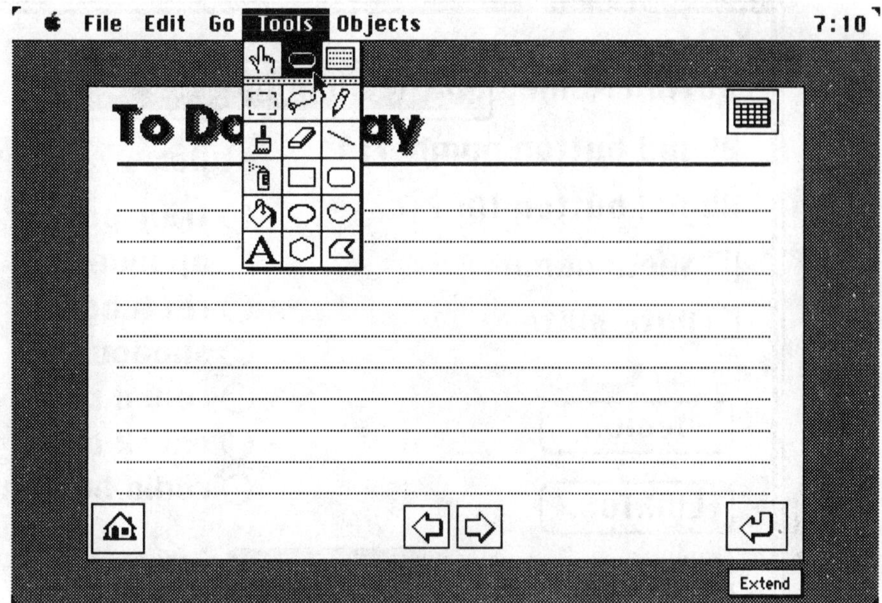


*Figure 17-8.*

*Figure 17-9.*

10. Click the Script... button.

    Although you may not know HyperTalk scripts yet, it is still helpful to see if you can recognize anything in the button script to understand what that button's purpose is. In this case, the script performs some date calculations and then tells HyperCard to go to a stack named Datebook whenever the mouse button is released (on mouseUp) atop this button (Figure 17-11). Click OK when you're finished.

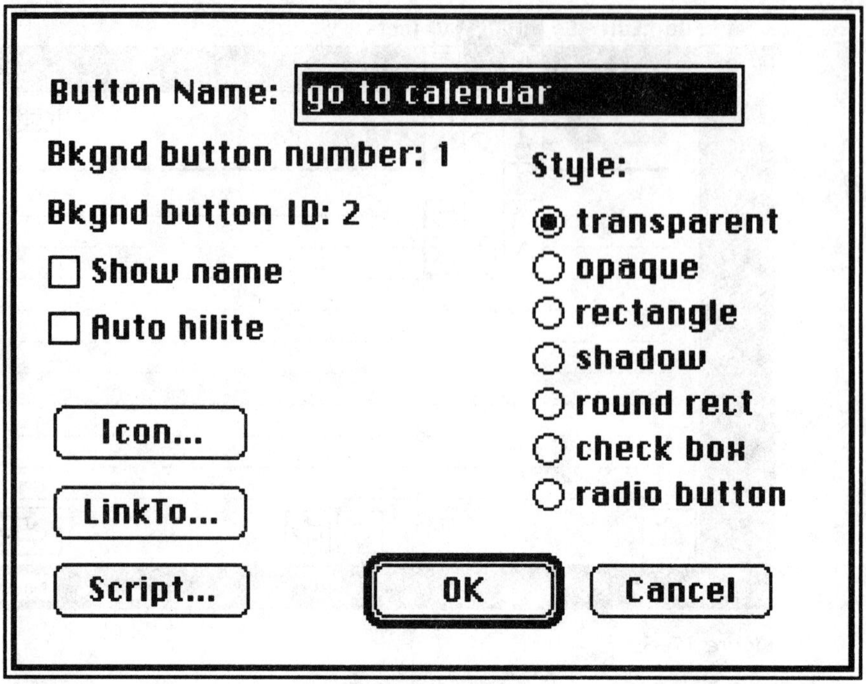

Button Name: go to calendar
Bkgnd button number: 1
Bkgnd button ID: 2
Show name
Auto hilite
Icon...
LinkTo...
Script...
Style:
transparent
opaque
rectangle
shadow
round rect
check box
radio button
OK
Cancel

*Figure 17-10.*

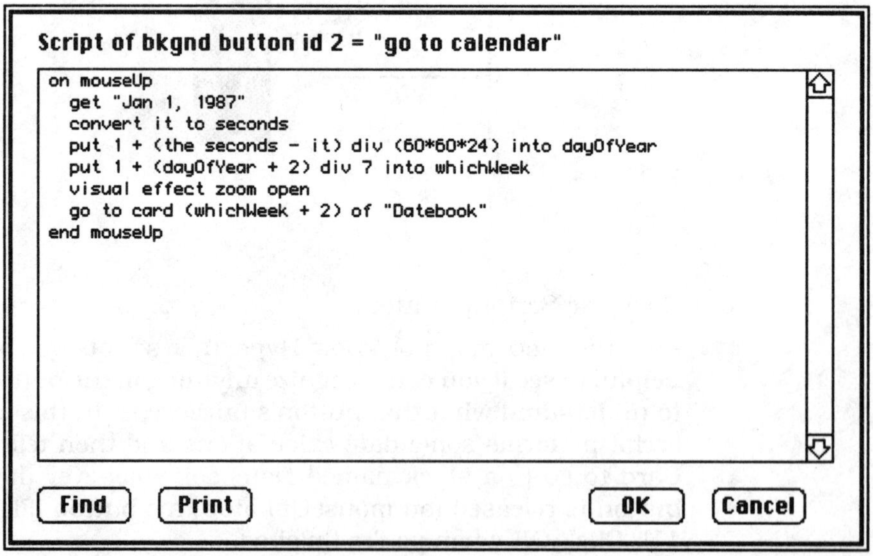

Script of bkgnd button id 2 = "go to calendar"

```
on mouseUp
  get "Jan 1, 1987"
  convert it to seconds
  put 1 + (the seconds - it) div (60*60*24) into dayOfYear
  put 1 + (dayOfYear + 2) div 7 into whichWeek
  visual effect zoom open
  go to card (whichWeek + 2) of "Datebook"
end mouseUp
```

Find Print OK Cancel

*Figure 17-11.*

11. Double-click on the right arrow button.

    This brings up the Button Info dialog box (Figure 17–12). Information for this button is the same as the calendar button except for the name.

12. Click the Script... button.

    The script for this button is different (Figure 17–13), but the go command could have been written using the Link To feature of the Button Info dialog box. Click the Cancel button.

13. Select the Field button in the Tools palette.

    Now the borders around the card's fields are visible. There are two fields on this card.

14. Double-click with the cursor anywhere in the large field in the middle of the card.

    You can also click once inside the field to select it (the marquee will swirl around its border) and choose Field Info... from the Objects menu. In the Field Info dialog box that results (Figure 17–14), you see that this is a transparent field with Show Lines

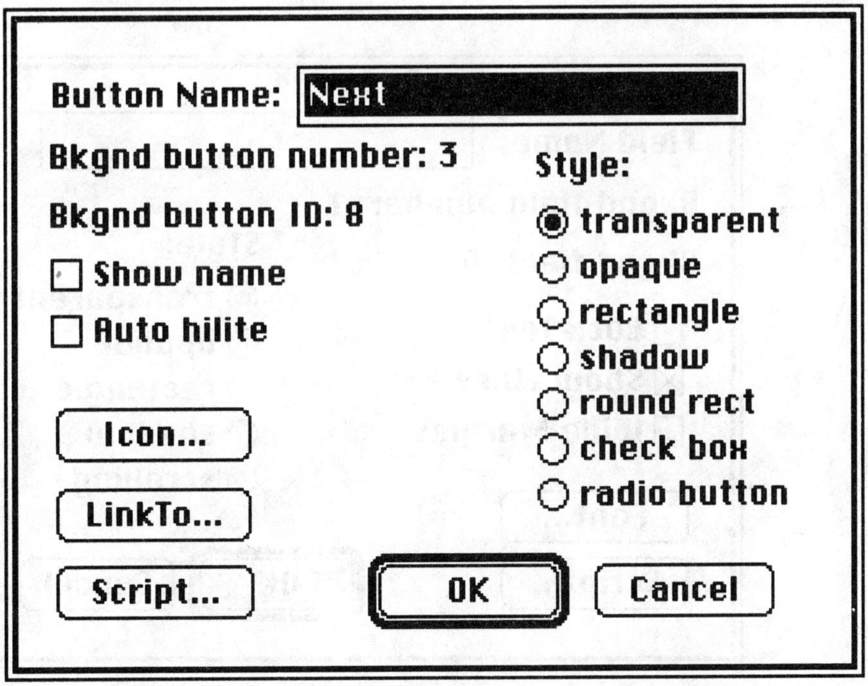

Button Name: Next
Bkgnd button number: 3
Bkgnd button ID: 8
Show name
Auto hilite
Icon...
LinkTo...
Script...
Style:
transparent
opaque
rectangle
shadow
round rect
check box
radio button
OK
Cancel

*Figure 17–12.*

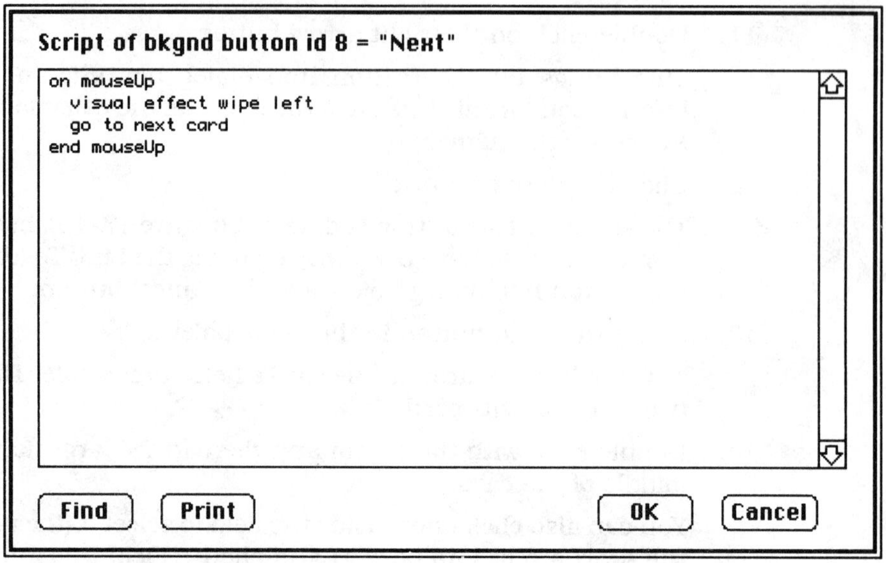

Script of bkgnd button id 8 = "Next"

```
on mouseUp
  visual effect wipe left
  go to next card
end mouseUp
```

Find Print OK Cancel

*Figure 17-13.*

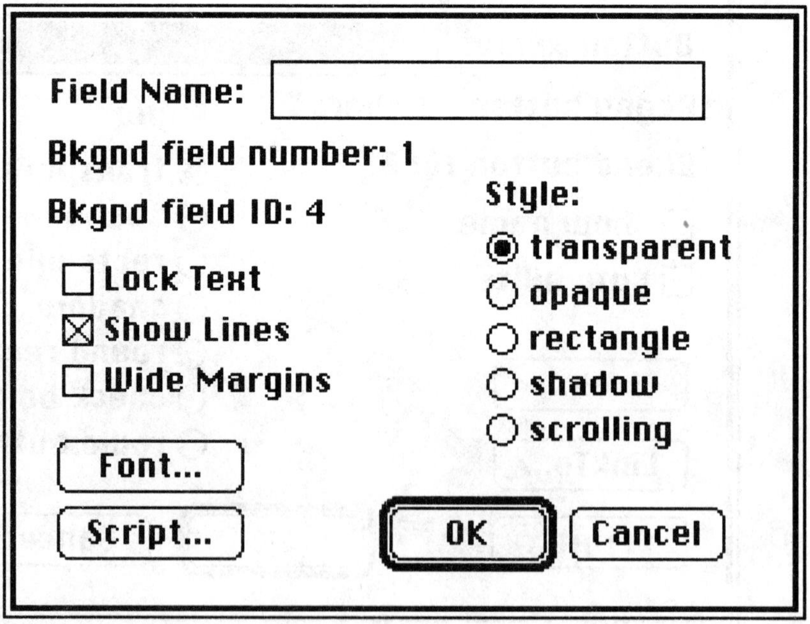

Field Name:

Bkgnd field number: 1

Bkgnd field ID: 4

☐ Lock Text

☒ Show Lines

☐ Wide Margins

Style:

◉ transparent

○ opaque

○ rectangle

○ shadow

○ scrolling

Font... Script... OK Cancel

*Figure 17-14.*

activated. That's where the dotted lines on the card come from. Click OK when you're finished.

15. Finally, select the Browse tool and choose Background from the Edit menu.

    Now you'll be able to see how much of the graphics you see is actually on the background graphics layer. Since there was no difference between the original view and the background view, you can deduce that the entire graphic is in the background.

16. Type Command-B to come out of background editing mode.

## *Part Two: Modify Background Graphics*

In the background graphics department, there are five changes we will make to the card.

The first is to adjust the depth of the card on the screen. Since you may wish to search the stack for text words and phrases typed into it, the card design should accommodate the Message Box, without it looking like the Message Box is slapped atop the card. Therefore, we'll shorten the depth of the card.

Second, we'll make the card wider to take advantage of the space currently available to the left and right of the card. This will give us back some of the field space we take when shortening the card.

While we're working on the card outline, we'll also show you how to add a drop shadow to the card, giving it a feel of three-dimensionality. This simple technique is a basic skill all Macintosh painters should know (but not abuse).

The last two background graphics tasks involve the card content. One is to remove the word "Today" from the card background. This will be replaced later in the card graphics layer by the names of the days of the week. The other will be to apply the background art for some special navigation buttons.

In all these tasks, we'll be editing the background. If you have to leave HyperCard or if you look into another stack in the middle of this part of the exercise, be sure to return to the background editing mode upon your return.

### REDUCING THE CARD DEPTH

The basic plan for this task is to erase much of the grey fill pattern currently surrounding the card. This will also help us in the next task when we widen the card. There are a couple of ways we could accomplish the removal of all or some of the grey fill pattern. The technique we'll use here will give you practice with the Eraser tool.

1. Choose Background from the Edit menu.

   The menubar hash marks will appear to confirm that you are editing the background domain.

2. If the Message Box is showing, press Command-M or click on its close box to hide it.

3. Tear off the Tools palette from the menubar.

   We'll be using a lot of its tools in the next several tasks, so we'll want it handy.

4. Select the Eraser tool.

   The cursor will turn into the white square eraser.

5. Place the Eraser tool immediately next to the right edge of the card, as shown in Figure 17-15.

   Pay special attention to the way the black line around the Eraser tool interacts with the black line of the card. Without pressing the mouse button, move the Eraser slowly from right to left and back again in the vicinity of the card edge. We want the Eraser to erase only those black pixels *outside* the card edge, not the

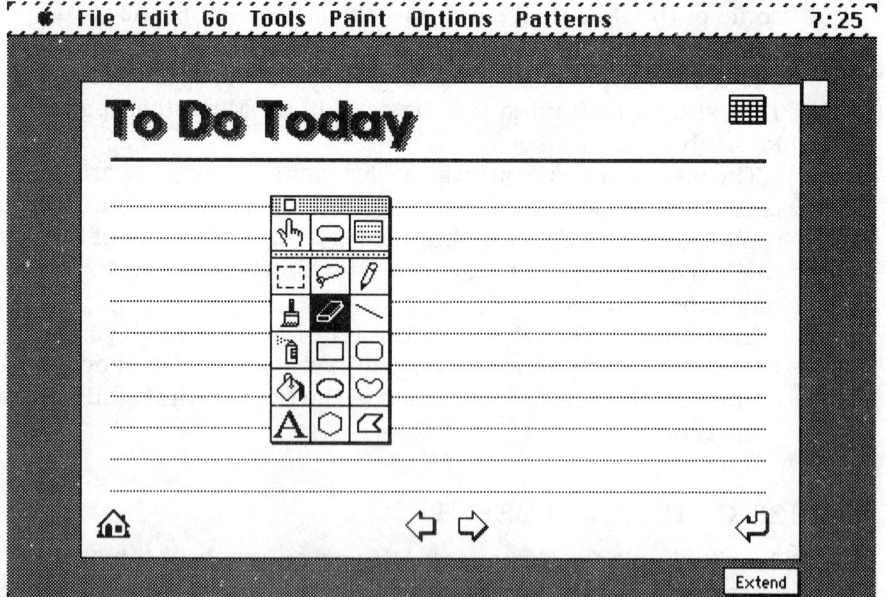


*Figure 17-15.*

edge itself. Since the Eraser erases everything under it (including under its own black edges), you must place the edge of the tool so that it is just outside the edge of the card. You're in the right spot when the meeting of the card edge and Eraser tool edge look like a double-thickness line (Figure 17–15).

6. Hold down the Shift key and drag the Eraser down to the bottom of the screen (Figure 17–16).

   The Shift key constrains movement of the tool to the axis in which you first drag the tool. If you accidentally dragged to the left or right first and erased part of the card, undo the erasure (pressing the tilde key is the fastest way) and try again. The same goes if the Eraser moved away from its proper place right next to the card and you erased the border edge of the card. Simply undo and try again. And if you erased a pixel or two too far away from the card, leave the erasure where it is, and try the erasure again to get those last remaining grey pattern pixel columns.

7. Repeat the erasure for a second and third swath down the right side. Then repeat the Shift-erasures for the left edge of the card (Figure 17–17).

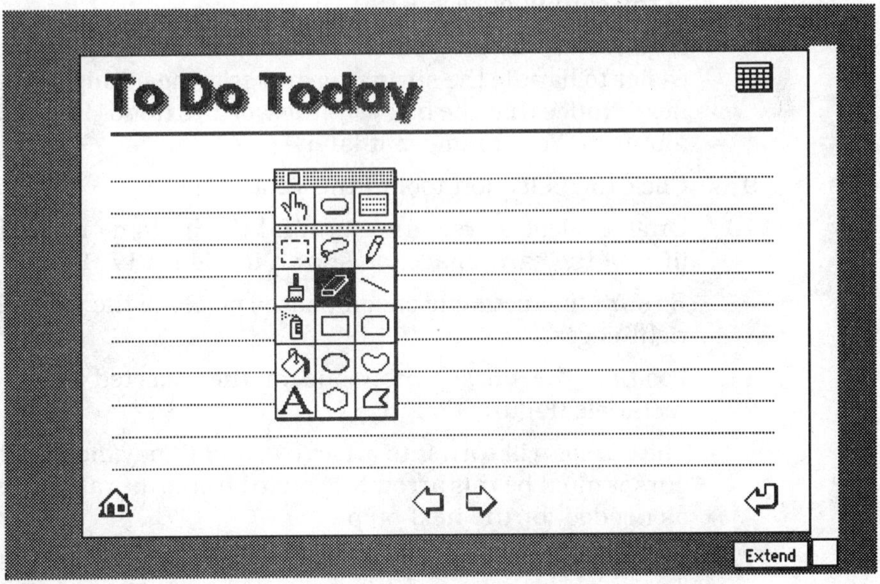

*Figure 17–16.*

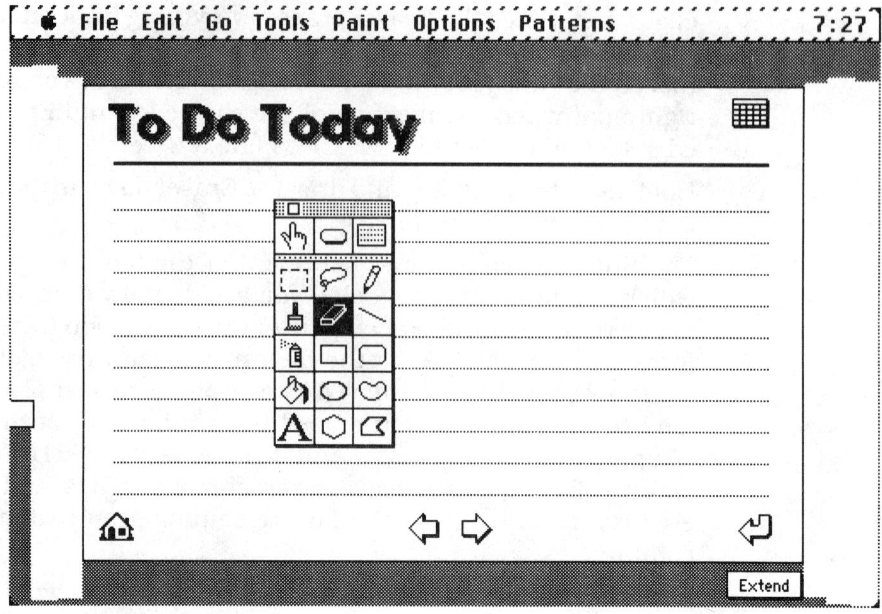


*Figure 17-17.*

8. Repeat the erasure twice more, Shift-erasing horizontally just under the bottom edge of the card and just above the top edge of the card (Figure 17-18).

   By clearing the grey pattern around the card, it will be much easier to handle the shrinking and growing in this task and the next. Notice that the box with the word "Extend" in it is actually a button. You'll remove it later.

9. Click the Selection tool in the Tools palette.

10. Drag a selection rectangle around the bottom one-half to one inch of the card image, as shown in Figure 17-19.

    Be sure the rectangle encompasses pieces of the card's left and right edges.

11. Position the cursor atop one of the selected edges of the rectangle (Figure 17-20).

    The cursor will turn into an arrow, and it may flicker a bit. The cursor must be this arrow for you to be able to grab the selection as needed for the next step.

12. Hold the Shift key down (to constrain movement), and drag the selected image up approximately one inch (Figure 17-21).

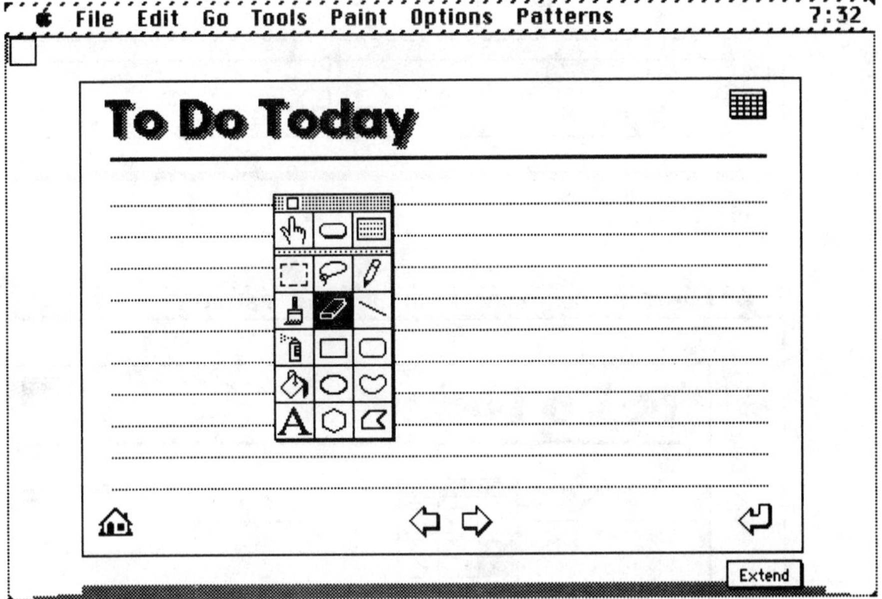


*Figure 17-18.*

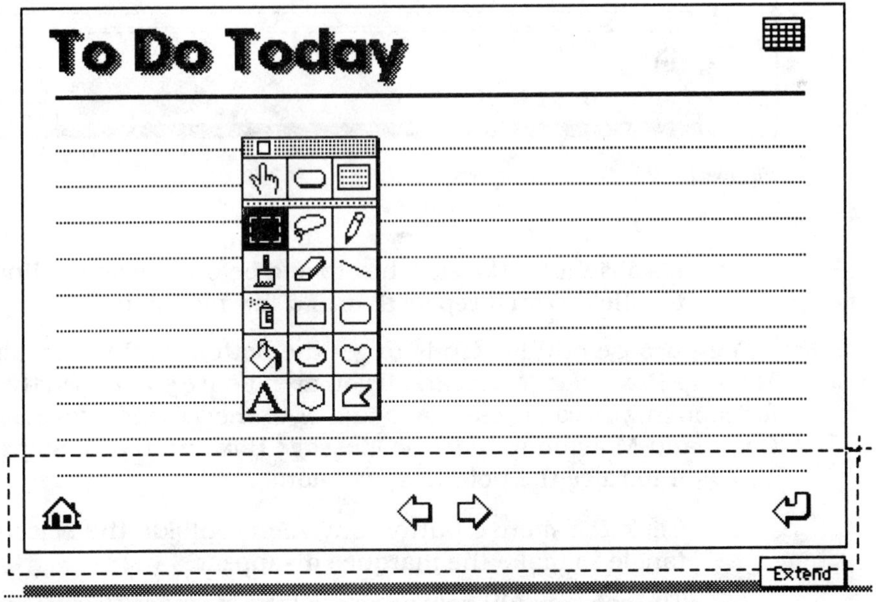


*Figure 17-19.*

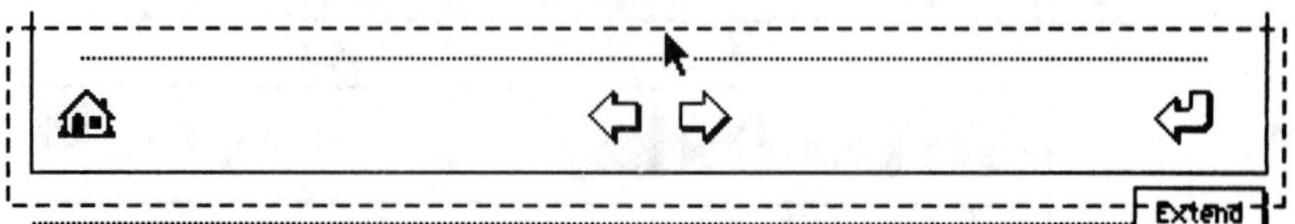


*Figure 17-20.*

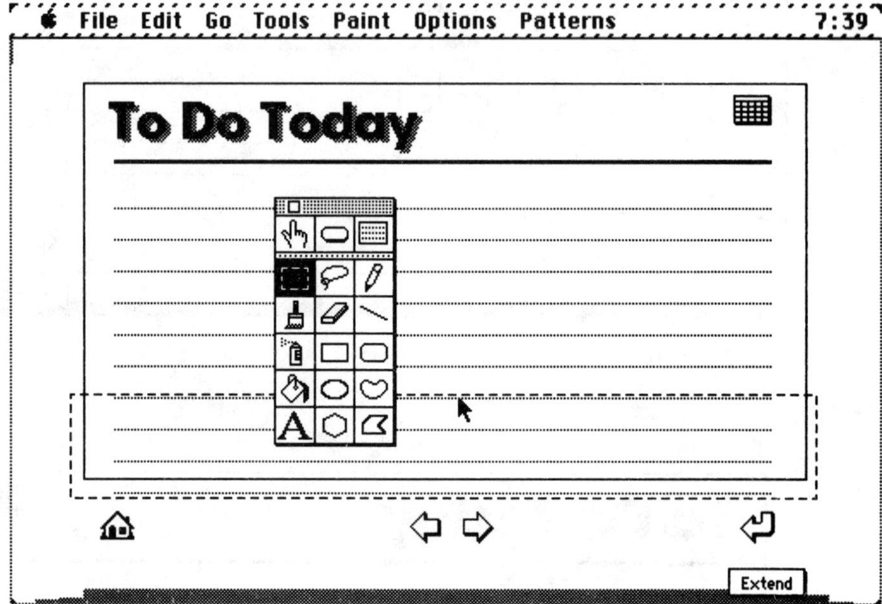


*Figure 17-21.*

It's alright for the card box to end before the dotted lines of the text field. You'll repair that in a few moments.

The purpose of this step is to get the bottom of the card above the Message Box when it appears. If you aren't sure you raised the bottom far enough, you can press Command-M to show the Message Box. Press Command-M again to hide the Message Box and repeat steps 10 and 11 again to raise the bottom some more.

13. Click the mouse button anywhere outside the selection rectangle to make the marquee disappear.

    The card should now be clear of the Message Box whenever the box is visible.

## WIDENING THE CARD

In this task, we'll be widening the card by extending both the left and right sides. The technique is not much different from the one used to shorten the card, but because you want to extend the card easily, you need a way to leave a trace of the top and bottom edges as you drag the sides away from the card. Using the selection rectangle alone, as you did above, would leave gaps in the top and bottom edges as you drag the sides away. Here's where the Option key enhancement to the selection rectangle comes in very handy.

1. Drag a selection rectangle around the left edge of the card, including the words "To Do" at the top of the card (Figure 17-22).
2. Position the cursor over one of the card's lines inside the selection rectangle so that the cursor changes into the arrow.

   Remember, when the cursor changes to the arrow, you can drag the image.
3. Hold down the Shift and Option keys together.

   Not only do you want to leave a trace of the image, but you want to do it in a perfectly straight horizontal line. The Shift key constraint is the right tool for that.

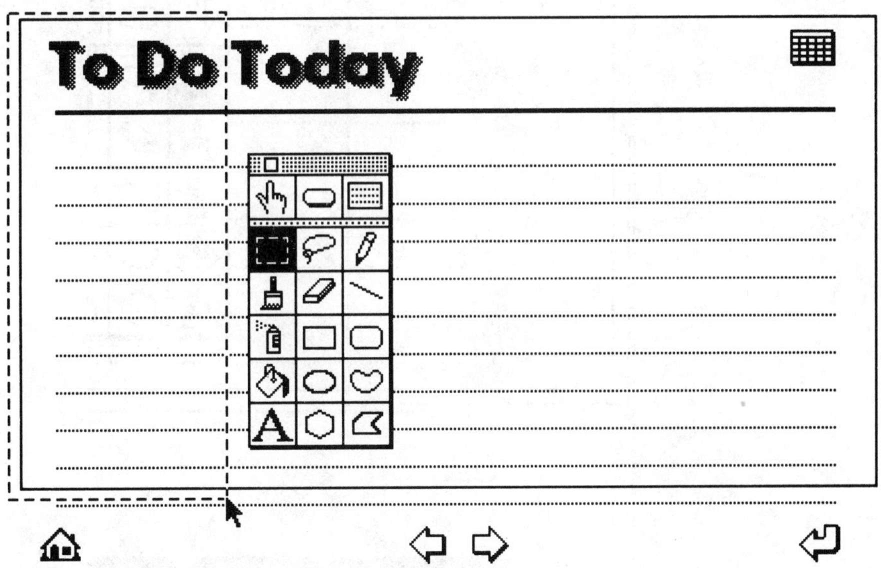


*Figure 17-22.*

4. Click and drag the selection to the left about one-half inch (Figure 17-23).

   As an exercise, you should also drag the selected image to the right for a moment to uncover what's really going on. Under the selection rectangle, the original image of the card's left edge is intact. You're actually dragging a copy on top of the original. By dragging it only a small way to the left, the copy covers up the original left edge, but also leaves some of the original top and bottom edge lines. The net effect when you're dragging to the left is that the top and bottom edges are leaving "tire tracks," when in reality you're seeing the original lines.

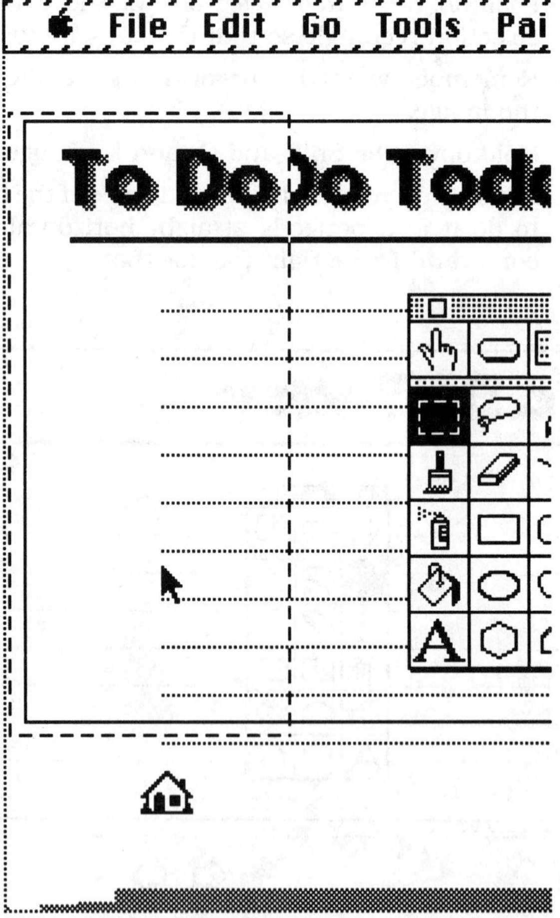


*Figure 17-23.*

5. When you're satisfied with the position of the new left edge, click the mouse pointer outside the selection rectangle to turn off the marquee.

   When you release the marquee, the new bit map completely covers up the original left edge (although you can undo the action immediately if you need to).

6. Repeat steps 1 through 5 with the right edge of the card, but don't include the card heading text in the selection rectangle.

   Use the distance between the card edges and the screen edges as a visual guide to make the left and right sides of the card as equidistant from the screen edges as possible (Figure 17-24). Because the art for the calendar button is an icon, rather than background art, the selection tool won't affect it.

## ADD A DROP SHADOW

Most viewers of Macintosh applications sense a certain depth or three-dimensionality to many of the images that appear on the screen. Even the pull-down menus have an overlapping feeling when they appear on the screen.

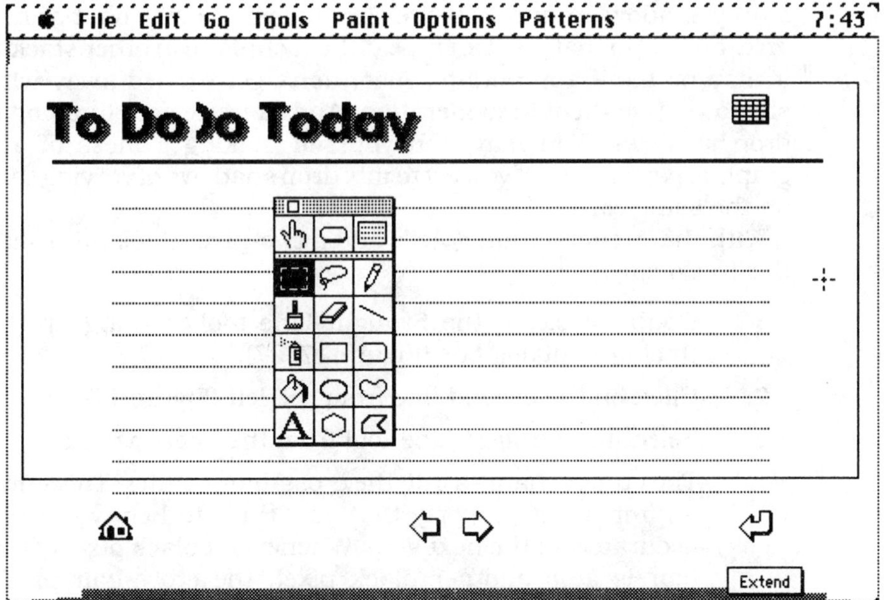


*Figure 17-24.*

Most of the time, this effect is caused by what is called a drop shadow. Pull down a menu and examine the right and bottom edges closely (Figure 17–25). Notice that these two sides are thicker than the one exposed on the left. Not only that, but look very closely at the missing pixels at the top of the right line and at the left of the bottom line. The net effect is that the eye is tricked into thinking there is a light source up and to the left of the screen that is casting a shadow behind the menu.

You'll see this drop shadow effect on many Macintosh devices, including windows. All standard Macintosh windows have a drop shadow. This was designed into the toolbox that programmers use to generate screen windows. The purpose of drop shadow windows is particularly evident when you have multiple windows open at one time. Drop shadows give each window a feeling of depth and tangibility. We forget that the screen is a combination of dots; instead, we see three-dimensional "layers."

Drop shadows don't have to be limited to single-pixel thicknesses. Sometimes a more dramatic drop shadow effect can be achieved by a very wide shadow, as shown in Figure 17–26. The thickness of the shadow and its distance from the top right and bottom left edges affect two visual factors: 1) the angle of the light source; and 2) the distance of the primary object from the perceived backdrop.

Not every card, window, or other screen object needs a drop shadow to be effective. In fact, even our To Do card could survive nicely without a drop shadow around it. We're showing you how to do it primarily as an exercise, so that you can repeat the technique in other stacks where it may be more appropriate. Also, don't get carried away with drop shadows. Use them in moderation. And exercise care in using thicker drop shadows. You may find yourself making a mess of a simple graphic, particularly if you try to mix drop shadows of varying thickness on the same card.

With that understanding, let's add a two-pixel-thick drop shadow to the To Do card.

1. Double-click on the Straight Line tool to bring up the line-thickness dialog box (Figure 17–27).

2. Click on the second line from the left (Figure 17–28).

3. Select the Straight Line tool from the Tools palette.

   The cursor changes into the cross-hair pointer. This cursor has an important property that you'll use to help you position it accurately in the next step. Whenever a black pixel of the cross hair is atop another black pixel, the cross-hair pixel turns white. Therefore, when it is atop a vertical line, the vertical of the

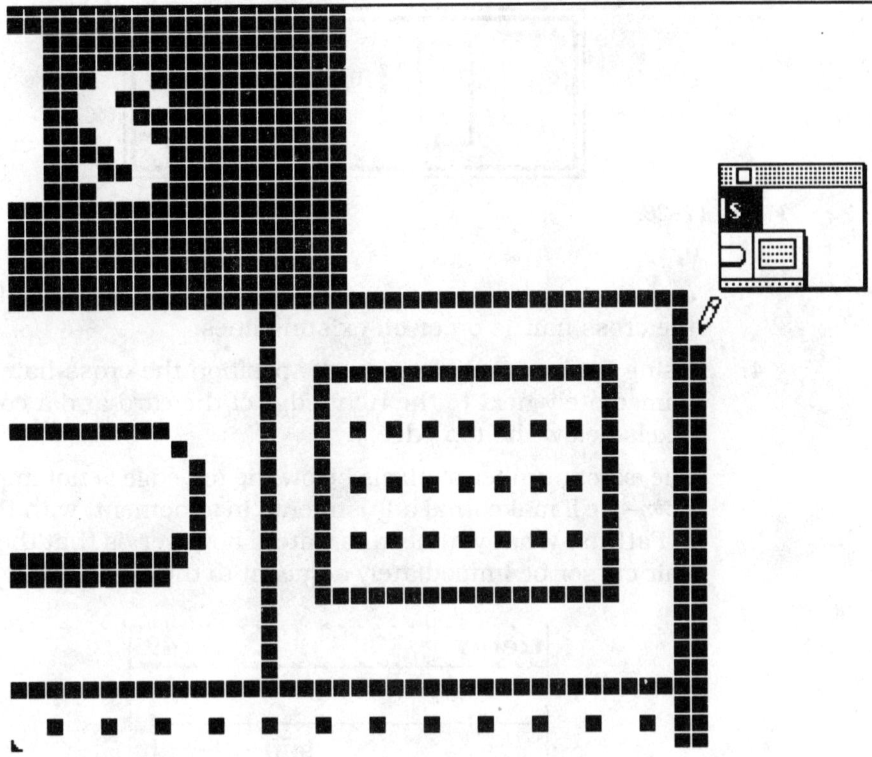

Figure 17-25.

Figure 17-26.

Figure 17-27.

*Figure 17-28.*

cross hair turns white. You can use this property to make sure the cross hair is on or off existing lines.

4. Using Figure 17-29 as a guide, position the cross-hair cursor immediately next to the right edge of the card and a couple of pixels below the top edge.

   The exact number of pixels below the top edge is not important now—we'll make final adjustments in a moment, with the help of FatBits. What you need to watch, however, is that the cross-hair cursor be immediately adjacent to the card's edge. Gently

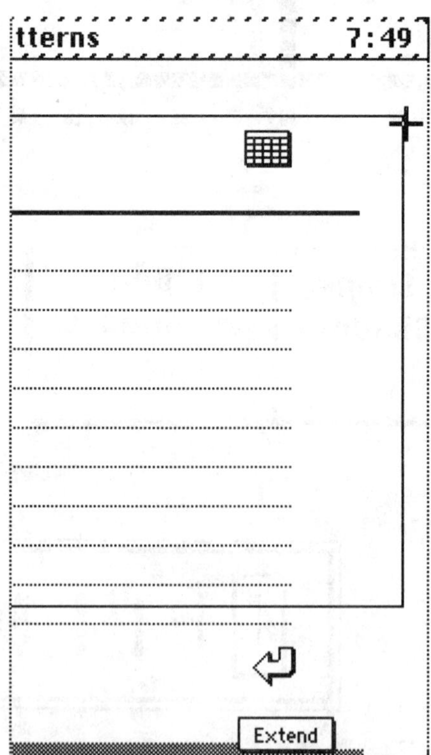


*Figure 17-29.*

move the cursor to the left and right. Notice how one vertical strip of the cross hair's pixels turn white when it is atop the card's edge (Figure 17–30). For the drop shadow, you want the cross hair to abut the card edge, but not be on top of it (Figure 17–29).

5. Hold down the Shift key and drag the cursor down to just below the bottom edge of the card (Figure 17–31).

   The exact measure below the card is not important now.

6. Repeat steps 3 through 5, but starting at the left end of the bottom edge of the card (Figure 17–32).

   When you Shift-drag the line to the bottom right corner of the card, you can extend the line beyond the edge for now.

7. Select the Pencil tool from the Tools palette.

   The cursor changes into a pencil cursor.

8. Place the pencil cursor near the spot where you began drawing the vertical line (Figure 17–33).

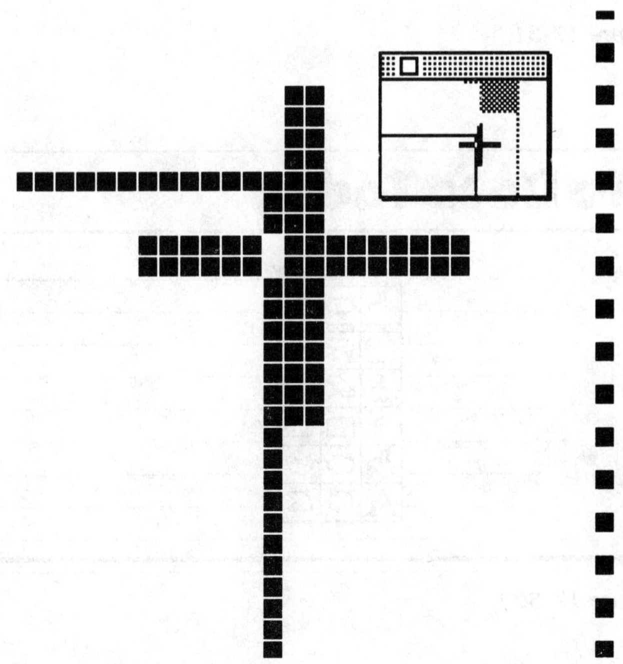

*Figure 17–30.*

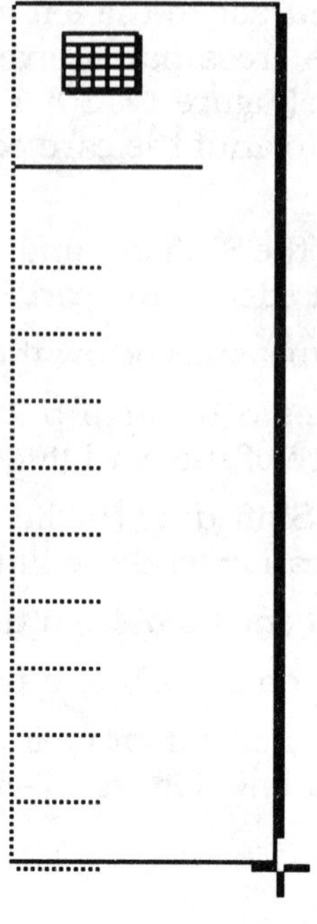

*Figure 17–31.*

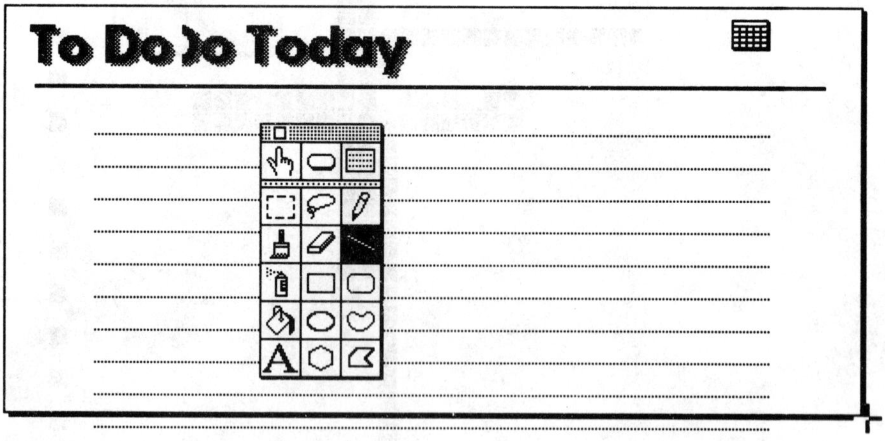

*Figure 17–32.*

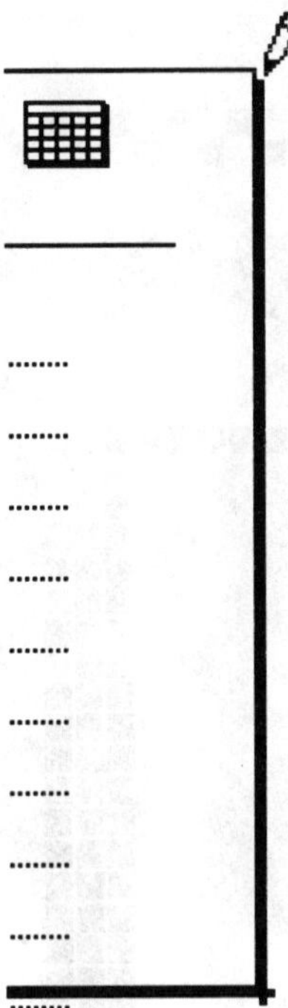

*Figure 17-33.*

9. Hold down the Command key and click the mouse button.

   This brings you into FatBits, looking at the place where the drop shadow begins.

10. Where necessary, add or remove black pixels in such a way that the start of the heavy drop shadow line is on line with the third pixel down the card's left edge, as shown in Figure 17–34.

    Notice the instant change to the normal-size drawing in the mini window as you change each pixel.

11. Hold down the Option key (the pencil turns into the grabber cursor), and with the mouse button also held down, scroll to the lower left corner of the card inside FatBits.

    It will take several drags across the screen to reach the opposite corner. This exercise should give you the feel for scrolling within FatBits. You could have also exited FatBits and re-entered, repeating steps 8 and 9 at the opposite corner.

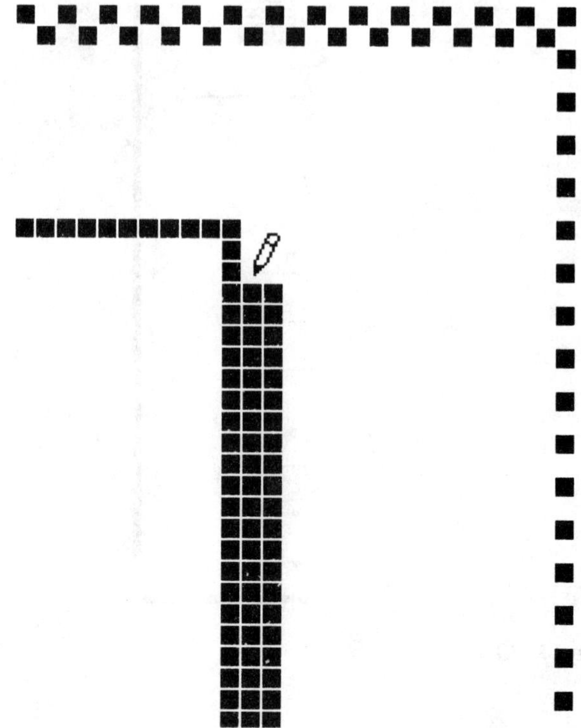

*Figure 17-34.*

12. Where necessary, add or remove black pixels from the drop shadow line, so that it starts at the third pixel of the card's bottom edge, as shown in Figure 17-35.
13. Exit FatBits (there are four ways to do this, remember) and re-enter FatBits by placing the pencil cursor at the bottom right corner of the card, holding down the Command key and clicking the mouse button.
14. Add or erase black pixels on the drop shadow line until the corner looks like the one in Figure 17-36.
15. Exit FatBits once more.

    That's all there is to making a drop shadow. It may seem like a lot of steps here, but it all goes rather quickly after you've done a few.

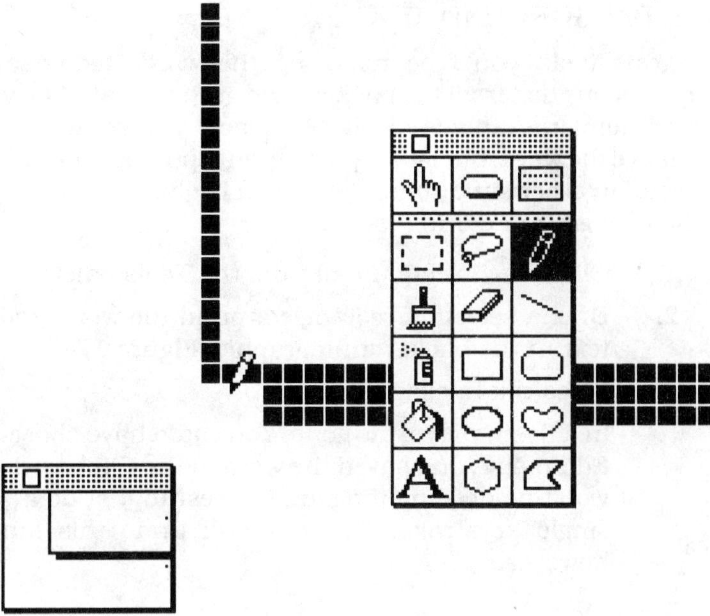

Figure 17-35.

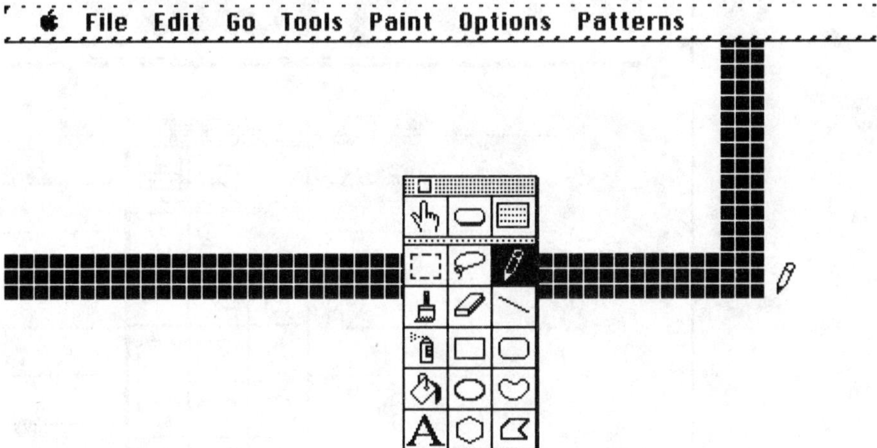


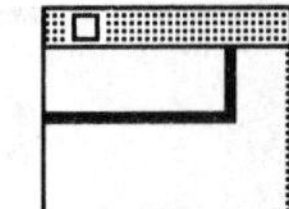

*Figure 17-36.*

## REMOVE BACKGROUND TEXT

In this task, you'll be removing the word "today" and any other extraneous text from the background graphic. Later on, you'll add some card-domain graphics to take its place. You could use the Eraser to remove the word, but let's try a different approach, one that you will find useful in other situations. Before you begin, make sure you are still in the background editing mode.

1. Click the Selection tool from the Tools palette.
2. Drag a selection rectangle around the word "today" and other text in the background graphic (Figure 17-37).
3. Press the Backspace key.

   In a flash, the text is gone. You could have chosen Cut from the Edit menu, and saved the word in the Clipboard. But since you won't be needing it again, it's best to just do away with it in a single keystroke. You can still undo this kind of erasure, however.

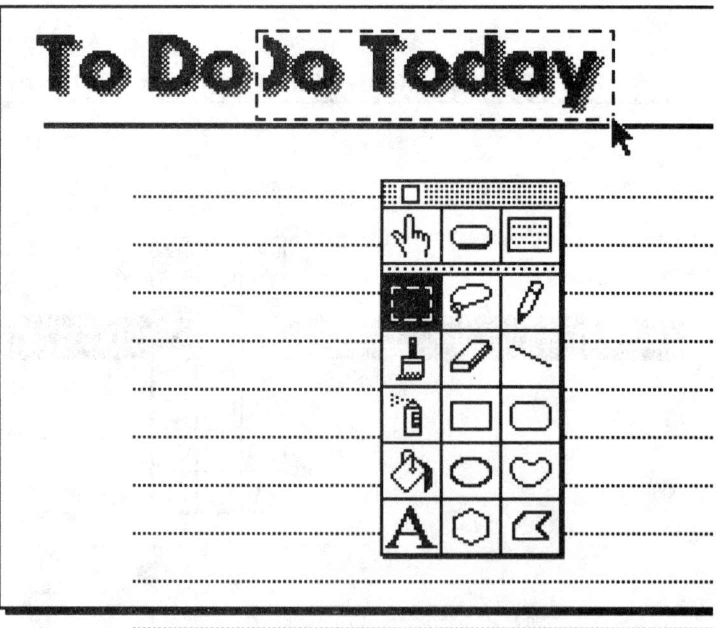


*Figure 17-37.*

## ADD DAILY BUTTON GRAPHICS

A major addition to the functionality of this To Do stack rendition is a series of buttons across the top of the card that will let you zip immediately to the To Do card of any day of the week. In other words, you won't have to flip card after card to advance several days. You'll just click on a button for the desired day.

The buttons will be fairly small and labeled with the first letter of each day of the week: S M T W T F S. You'll put the graphic design for the buttons in the background graphic layer, while the button link actions will be included in transparent background buttons that you'll add later.

How you design a button graphic is a personal choice. In this exercise, the design is a simple square with the day's letter inside it. The letters will be in the Chicago font, which has a nice bold feel to it and is one of the most readable fonts in the standard font library. Later in this chapter, we'll show you how to add a highlighting feature to the buttons so that when you are viewing Wednesday's card, the W button will have a heavy border around it.

Since most of the drawing of these buttons will be on a relatively small scale, a lot of the work will be done in FatBits. Among other things, you'll see how to work with several tools while in FatBits. Again, be sure you are editing the background for this task.

1. Select the Pencil tool from the Tools palette.
2. Position it approximately in the center of the card, near the top edge (Figure 17-38).

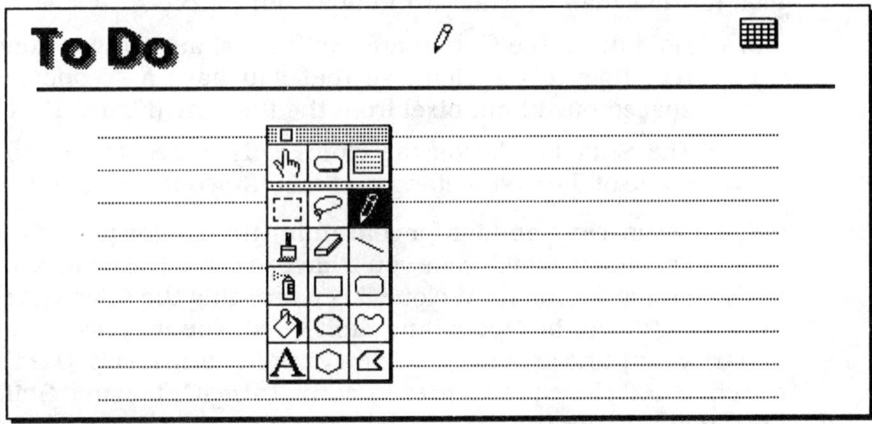


*Figure 17-38.*

We'll start working up here. If we find we need to move the results, we can do so later for all the buttons we draw.

3. Hold down the Command key and click the mouse button to enter Fat Bits at this location.
4. Double-click the Straight Line tool and select the single-pixel-thickness line.
5. Select the Rectangle tool from the Tools palette.

   The cursor changes to a cross hair.
6. Place the cross-hair pointer near the upper left corner of the screen and drag a rectangle, as shown in Figure 17–39.

   For the best results, draw the rectangle with the same number of pixels on each side, as shown in the Figure— 16 pixels across and 16 pixels down, including the one already in place from drawing the horizontal line.
7. Select the Selection tool from the Tools palette.
8. Hold down the Command key and drag a selection rectangle around the rectangle you just drew.

   The selection rectangle snaps to the rectangle you drew, so when we clone the rectangle in the next step, we won't get any superfluous white pixels with it.

When you're in FatBits, the selection rectangle is also in FatBits, so it may seem odd at first to be working at such a large scale. But it turns out that you have far more control over the selection rectangle (or any tool, for that matter) when working within FatBits.

9. Hold down the Option and Shift keys, and drag a clone of the rectangle to the right, so that you have a second rectangle spaced one blank pixel from the first one (Figure 17–40).

   The Shift key keeps the clone constrained to the horizontal plane of the first rectangle, eliminating one alignment concern.

You now have two options for continuing the cloning process. You can do it in FatBits, in which case you'll have to scroll the images to the left to make room for the third clone (keep dragging the selected rectangle by holding down the Option and Shift keys). You may also exit FatBits and try your hand at some precision work in normal size. Use the same selection and clone procedures in normal size (Option and Shift before dragging), and use the distance between the first and second rectangles as a guide to the spacing between the remaining rectangles.

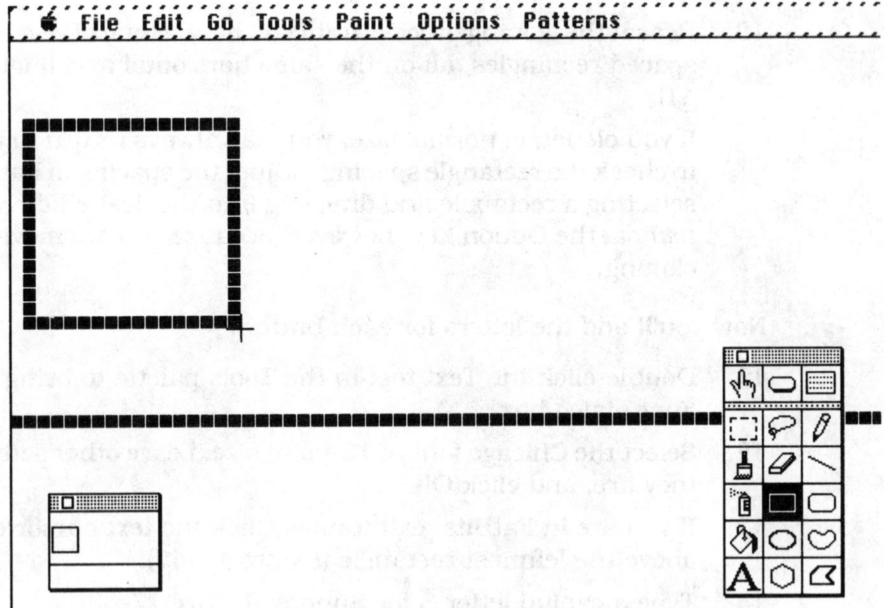


*Figure 17–39.*

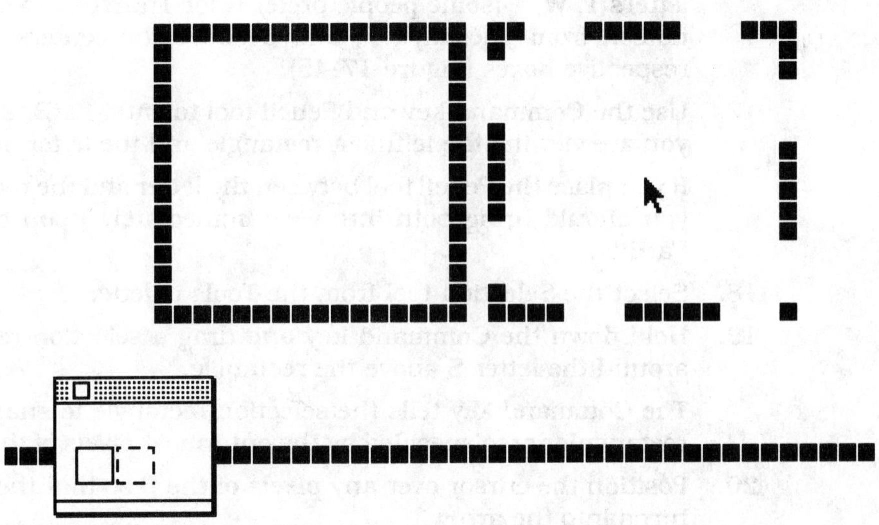

*Figure 17–40.*

10. Repeat the cloning process until you have a total of seven evenly spaced rectangles, all on the same horizontal axis (Figure 17–41).

    If you cloned in normal size, you may always return to FatBits to check the rectangle spacing. Adjust the spacing in FatBits by selecting a rectangle and dragging it in the desired direction—*without* the Option key, however, because you are moving, not cloning.

Now you'll add the letters for each button.

11. Double-click the Text tool in the Tools palette to bring up the Font dialog box.
12. Select the Chicago font in 12-point size. Leave other settings as they are, and click OK.
13. If you are in FatBits, exit it now. Click the text cursor directly above the leftmost rectangle (Figure 17–42).
14. Type a capital letter S for Sunday (Figure 17–43).
15. Press the Spacebar twice, so that the flashing text point is approximately centered over the second rectangle and type M for Monday (Figure 17–44).
16. Continue this process for each day of the week, typing the letters T, W, T (some people prefer R for Thursday to differentiate it from Tuesday), F, and S above the centers of their respective boxes (Figure 17–45).
17. Use the Command key and Pencil tool to enter FatBits so that you are viewing the leftmost rectangle and the letter above it.

    If you place the Pencil tool between the letter and the rectangle, you should bring both into view immediately upon entering FatBits.

18. Select the Selection tool from the Tools palette.
19. Hold down the Command key and drag a selection rectangle around the letter S above the rectangle.

    The Command key tells the selection rectangle to snap to the rectangular area specified by the outermost pixels of the letter.

20. Position the cursor over any pixels of the S so that the cursor turns into the arrow.
21. Drag the letter into the center of the rectangle (Figure 17–46).

    Notice that the rectangle was sized to allow the letter to be centered vertically with two blank pixels above and below the

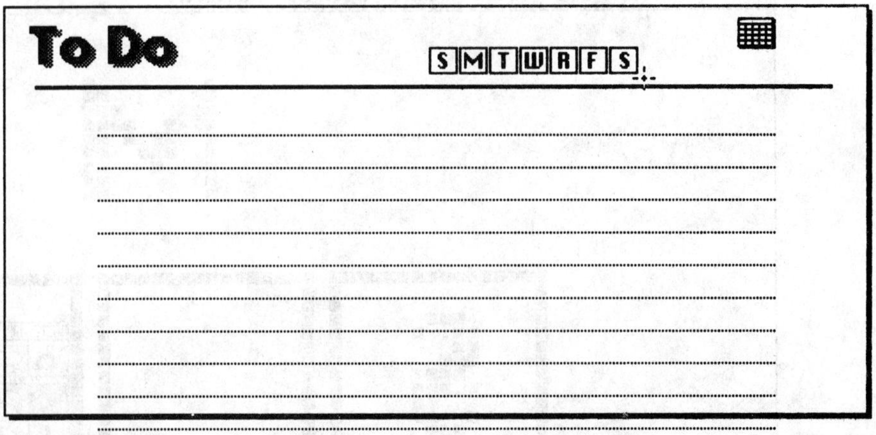

*Figure 17-41.*

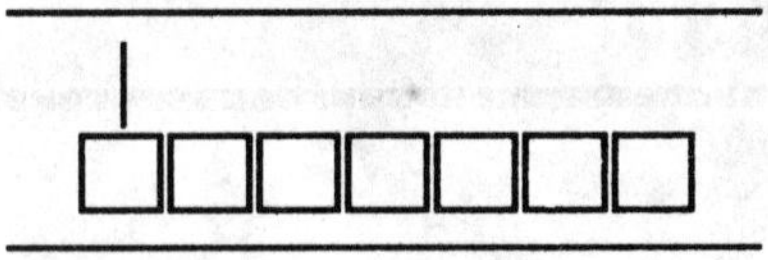

*Figure 17-42.*

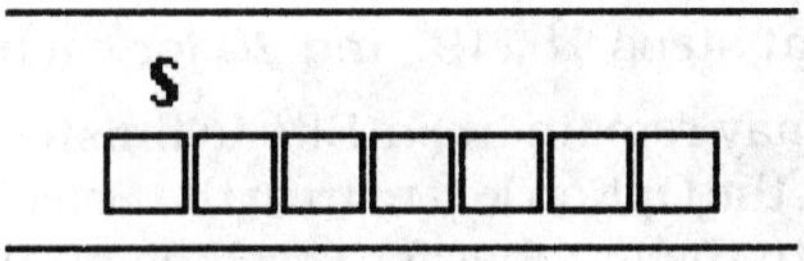

*Figure 17-43.*

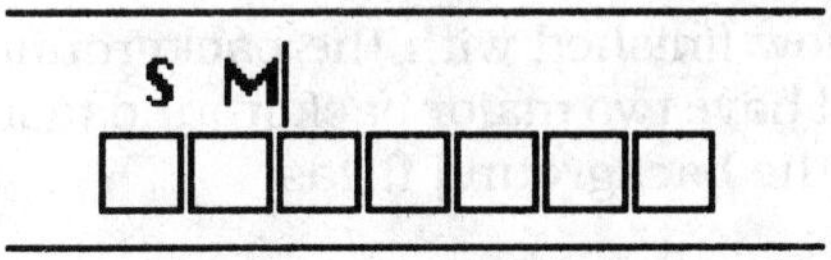

*Figure 17-44.*

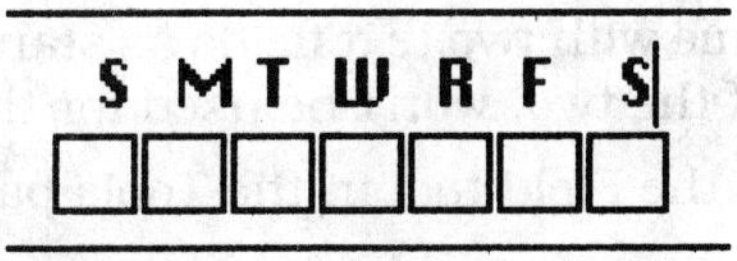

*Figure 17-45.*

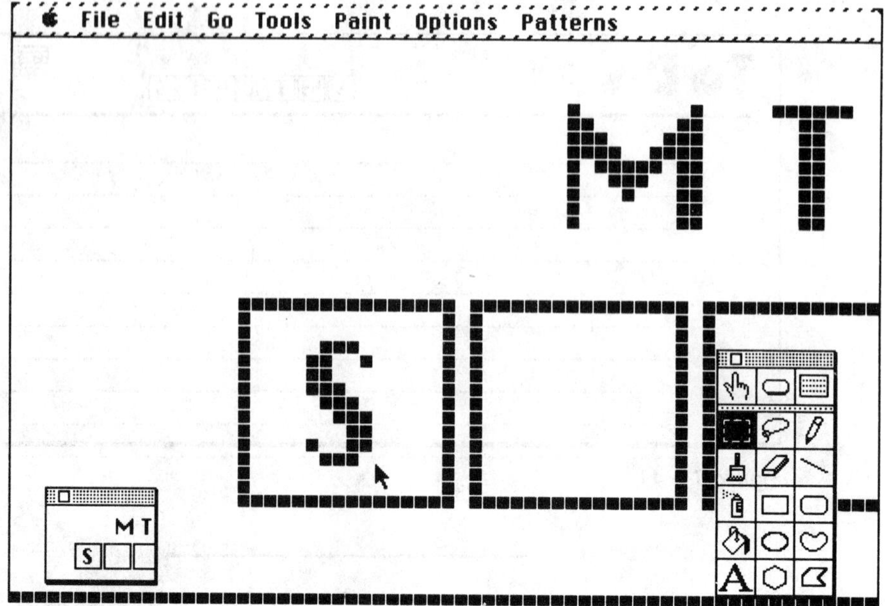


*Figure 17–46.*

letter. Also be sure the letter is centered between the left and right sides of the rectangle.

22. Repeat steps 18, 19, and 20 for each of the letters.

    You may remain in FatBits to finish the job. Remember to hold down the Option key to turn the Selection tool cursor temporarily into the grabber for scrolling around inside FatBits.

23. When you are finished placing the letters, exit FatBits (Figure 17–47).

You are now finished with the background graphics modifications. But you still have two major background tasks to complete. The first is to work on the background fields.

## Modify Background Fields

This stack came with two text fields as standard equipment. One field, the smaller of the two, won't be used for this stack. Delete it now.

1. Select the Field tool in the Tools palette.

   Outlines surround both background fields.

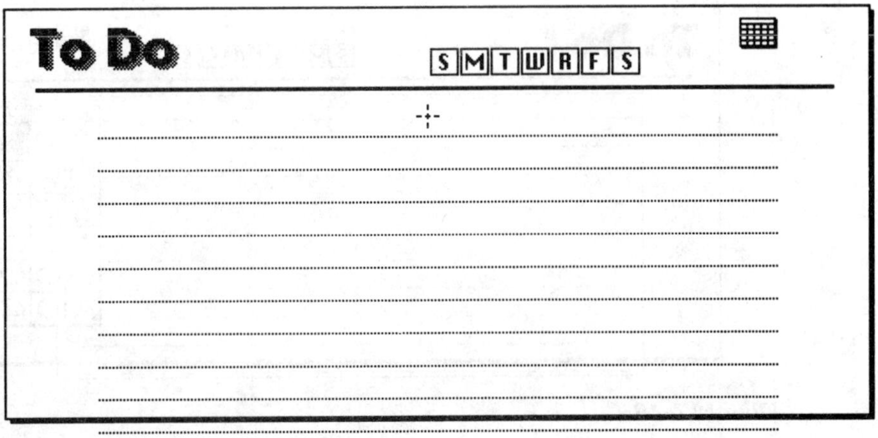

*Figure 17-47.*

2. Click on the small field just below the calendar button.

   The field outline turns into a marquee.

3. Press the Backspace key.

   The field disappears.

Now you can focus on the large text field. Because of the graphic changes made to the size of the card, the available text area is too wide to make a single field practical. Considering that most items on a To Do list will be less than ten words, the space on the right side of the card would be wasted. Why not turn that space into a second column? Then you can divide your To Do tasks into two categories, such as items that must be accomplished on a certain day, and long-term items that need gradual or protracted attention.

Shrinking the depth of the card reduced the number of lines you can have in the column. But since the font of the field as copied from the Stack Ideas stack is in a 14-point New York, we can choose a different font and font size to squeeze more lines into less space.

With our overall target in mind, let's begin this task.

1. Select the Field tool at the top of the Tools palette.

   The border around the single large field will become visible (Figure 17-48).

2. Double-click on the field to summon the Field Info dialog box (Figure 17-49).

   A quick glance at the field's attributes reveals that it will show its own lines and is transparent. That's fine for our purposes.

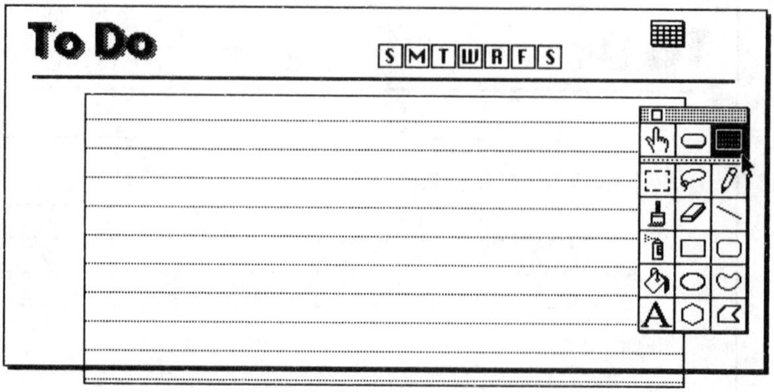

*Figure 17-48.*

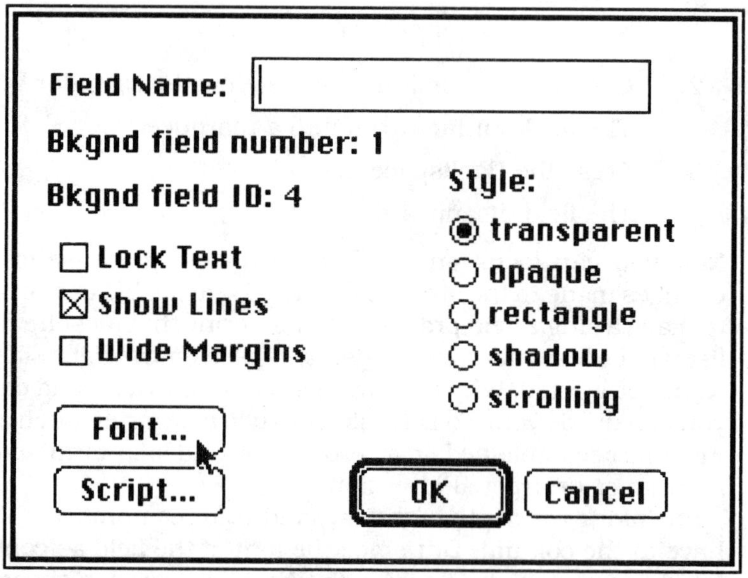

*Figure 17-49.*

3. Click on the Font... button to change the font attributes of this field.
4. Select Geneva in 12 point, and click OK (Figure 17-50).

   You return to the card view, with the field selected.
5. Grab the field near its center and position the top left corner, as shown in Figure 17-51.

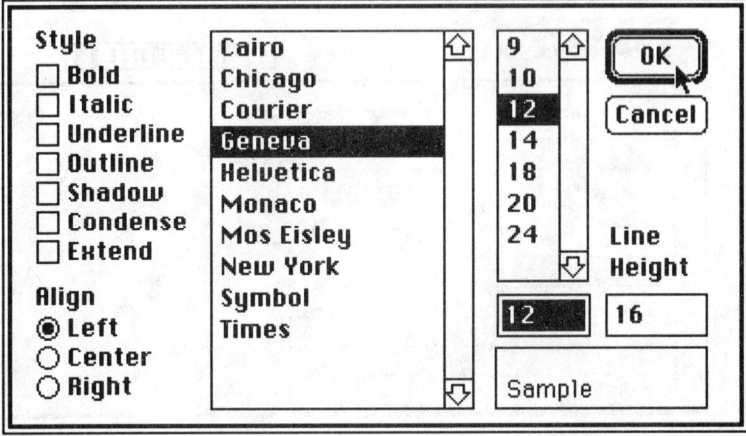


*Figure 17-50.*

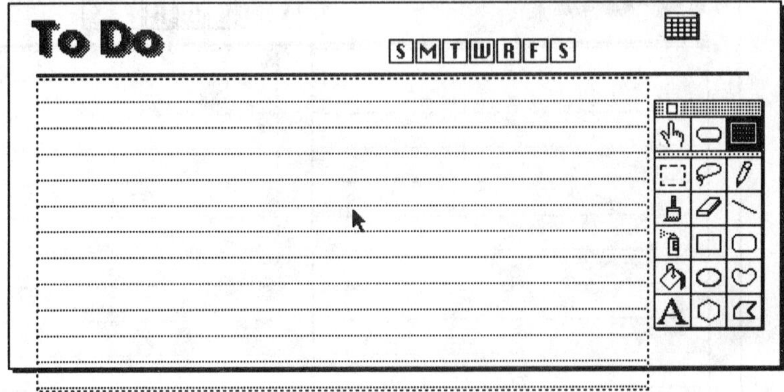


*Figure 17-51.*

6. Grab the lower right corner of the selected field and drag it up and to the left so that it takes up approximately one-half of the card area, as shown in Figure 17-52.

   Use the text lines as a guide to lining up the bottom of the field with the bottom of the card area.

7. Clone the field by holding down both the Option and Shift keys and dragging a copy to the right, positioning it as shown in Figure 17-53.

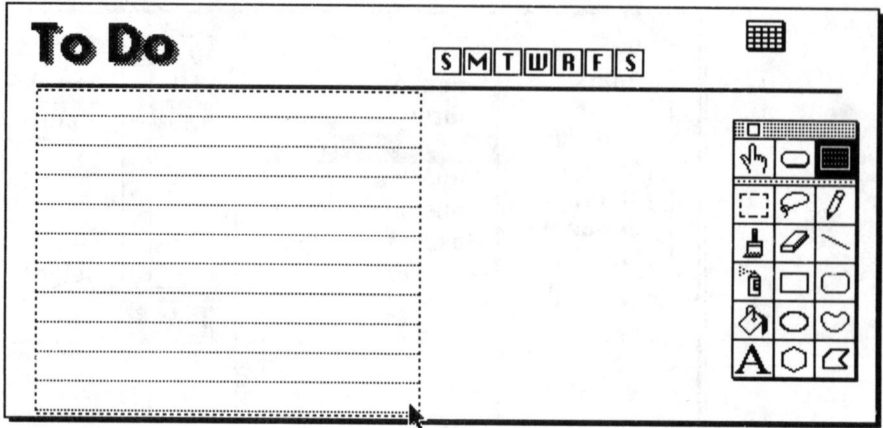


*Figure 17-52.*

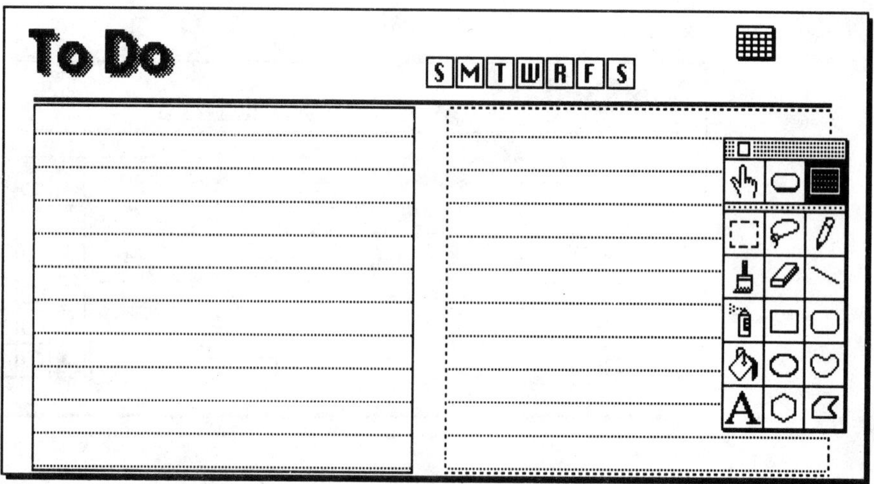


*Figure 17-53.*

Since you have set the font and other attributes in the first field, the clone will have identical settings.

8. Select the Browse tool to see how the text lines will look in every card.

That completes the field modification for this stack. Simple enough, wasn't it? Now to the buttons.

## *Delete Background Buttons*

Five of the six buttons provided with this stack— all but the calendar button— won't be needed. You'll delete these buttons now.

1. Select the Button tool.

   All but the Extend button show their outlines. The outline of the shadow style Extend button blends with its own border, so you can't see it.
2. Click once on the Home button at the lower left to select it.
3. Press the Backspace key.
4. Repeat steps 2 and 3 on the four other buttons at the bottom of the screen, including the Extend button.

You're now ready to add some new buttons.

## *Add Background Buttons*

The remaining button links the stack to the Calendar stack supplied with HyperCard. You're about to give your new stack substantially more linking power to other cards in this stack and to other stacks.

The first task will be to add an icon button linked to the Name and Address stack. Then you'll create the buttons that go atop the seven-day button art you just created. Finally, you'll create one more icon button that you'll be able to copy and paste in other stacks (including the Home stack and weekly appointment calendar) to gain immediate access to your To Do list at the click of a button.

### MODIFYING AN EXISTING BUTTON

The existing button with which you'll start is in the background. While you could make some adjustments to this button whether or not you are officially in the Background editing mode, you will be cloning the button and creating some new ones in the background. Therefore, make sure you are in the Background editing mode before you begin.

1. Select the Button tool from the Tools palette.

   A rectangle around the Calendar button indicates that you are in the button editing facility at the moment.
2. Click once on the Calendar button to select it and drag it closer to the upper right corner of the card.

3. Hold down the Option key and drag a clone of the Calendar button to the left (Figure 17-54).

   Behaving dutifully as a clone, the second button retains the icon, name, and script of its forebear. You need to change a few things about it.

4. Double-click the clone button to bring up its Button Info dialog box.

5. Type a new name, such as "To Name/Address," for the button.

6. Click the Icon... button and select the icon representing a rolo-file address card (the one we use has the ID number 3430).

   All other attributes of the button are fine, except for the script, which we'll handle right now.

7. Double-click the new button to see its info dialog box, and click the Link To... button.

   The Link window appears, instructing you to go to the card this button should link to.

8. The Browse tool is automatically selected, so navigate your way back Home and into the Name and Address stack.

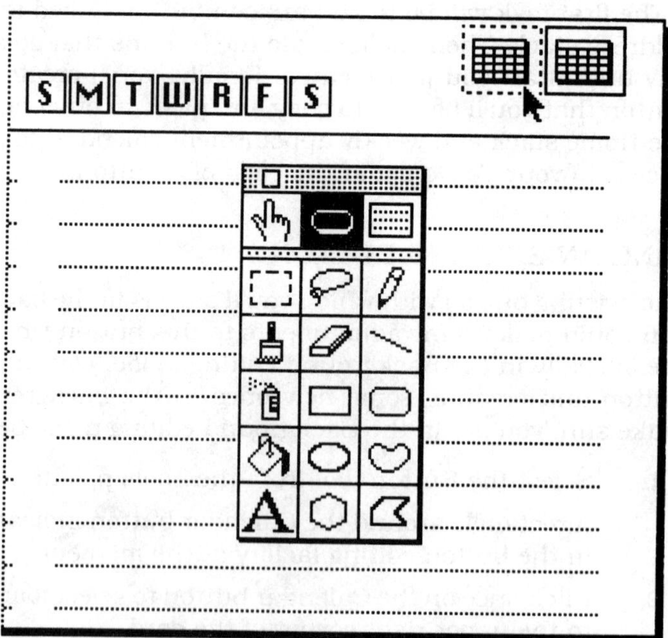


*Figure 17-54.*

9. When the first card of the Name and Address stack is on the screen, click the This Stack button in the Link Window.

   The link is automatically established in the button's script, and you are brought back to the To Do card.

You can try your button now, if you like. Click on it with the Browse tool (Figure 17–55). If you followed the steps above correctly, you will go immediately to the Name and Address stack with the zoom open visual effect. If you get different results, repeat steps 7 through 9, above.

Your next task is to copy a button from one of HyperCard's button idea stacks and paste it into your new stack.

10. Type Command-M to show the Message Box.
11. Type *Go "Button Ideas"* into the Message Box and press Return.
12. Use the stack's Index to find a button for Telephones or type *Go card ID 6144* into the Message Box to go directly to the card.
13. Select the Button tool from the Tools palette, and click once on the telephone button, shown in Figure 17–56.

    This button contains a script that dials a telephone number.

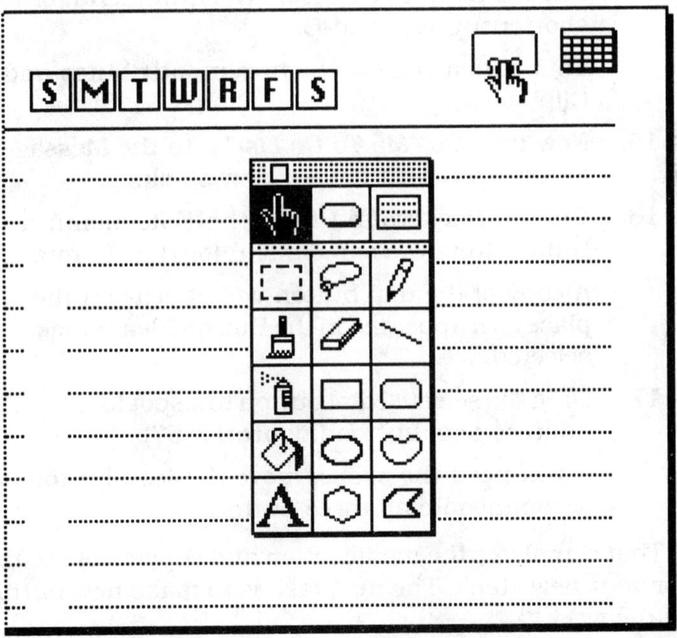


*Figure 17–55.*

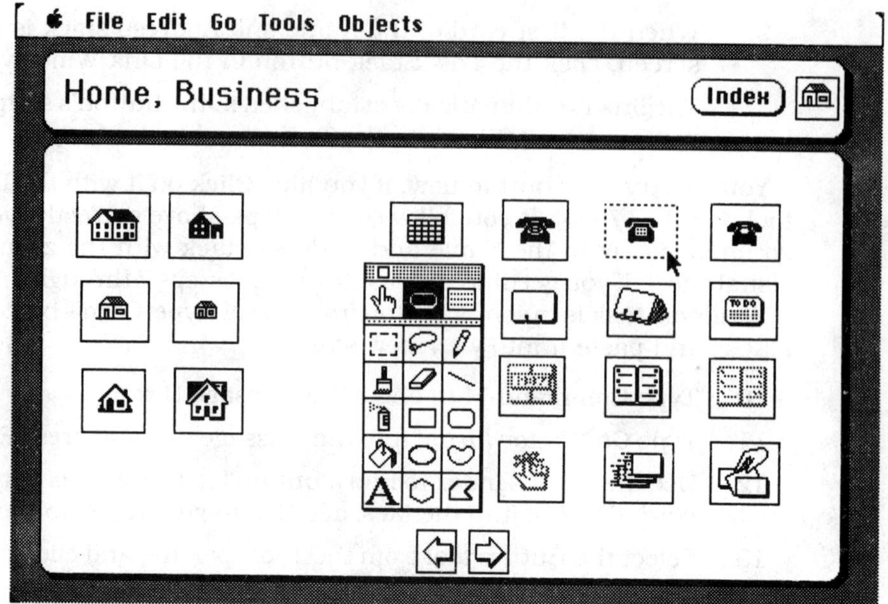


*Figure 17-56.*

14. Choose Copy Button from the Edit menu, or use the keyboard shortcut, Command-C.

    This puts a copy of the button (attributes and script) into the Clipboard.

15. Now type *Go "My To Do List"* into the Message Box and press Return to return to your new stack.

16. Choose Background from the Edit menu, and choose Paste Button from the same menu (or type Command-V to paste).

    A copy of the dial button will appear on the card in the same place as it appeared in the Button Ideas stack. The button is still selected.

17. Drag the selected dial button to a spot to the left of the Name and Address icon button (Figure 17-57).

    If you need the space, move the icon buttons around a bit to accommodate all three buttons.

That completes the modification and copying of existing icon buttons for your new stack. The next task is to make new buttons for the days of the week.

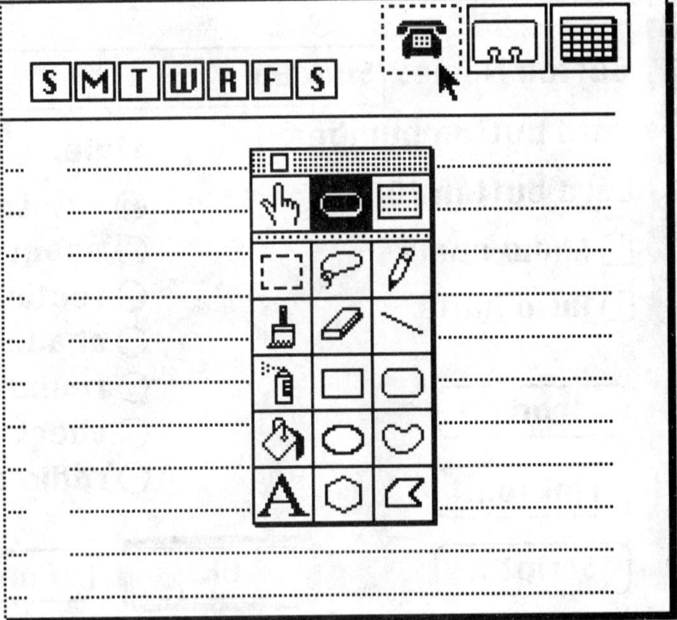


*Figure 17-57.*

## CREATING NEW BUTTONS

You'll need seven buttons. Recall that the best strategy for this installation is to create the first button and set as many attributes as possible. Then clone that button for the others.

1. Make sure you are in the background editing mode before proceeding.
2. Choose New Button from the Objects menu.

   A named, round rectangle button appears selected in the center of the screen. A number of attributes need changing before you begin cloning.
3. Double-click the new button.

   This brings up the Button Info dialog box for the new button.
4. Change the name of the button to *Sunday.*
5. Uncheck the box next to Show Name.
6. Click the radio button for the Transparent button style (Figure 17-58).

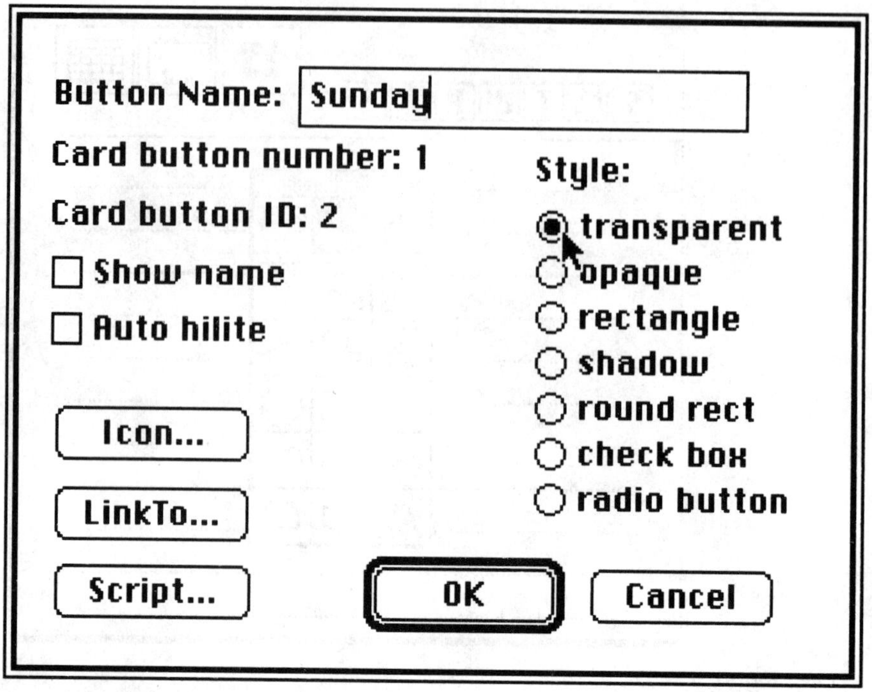

*Figure 17-58.*

7. Click OK in the dialog box.

   The new button has lost its visual attributes but is still selected on the screen.

8. Drag the button to the row of day button graphics in such a way that the upper left corner is directly overlaying the upper left corner of the Sunday button graphic (Figure 17-59).

9. Grab the bottom right corner of the selected button and shrink the button so that the swirling marquee completely covers the outline of the Sunday button (Figure 17-60).

10. Hold down the Shift and Option keys, and "peel off" a clone of the Sunday button to the right. Place it carefully atop the Monday button (Figure 17-61).

11. Continue cloning with the Shift and Option keys until all seven buttons are created (Figure 17-62).

12. Select each of the buttons in turn and assign the name of their respective day to the name of the button, as you did for Sunday in step 4, above.

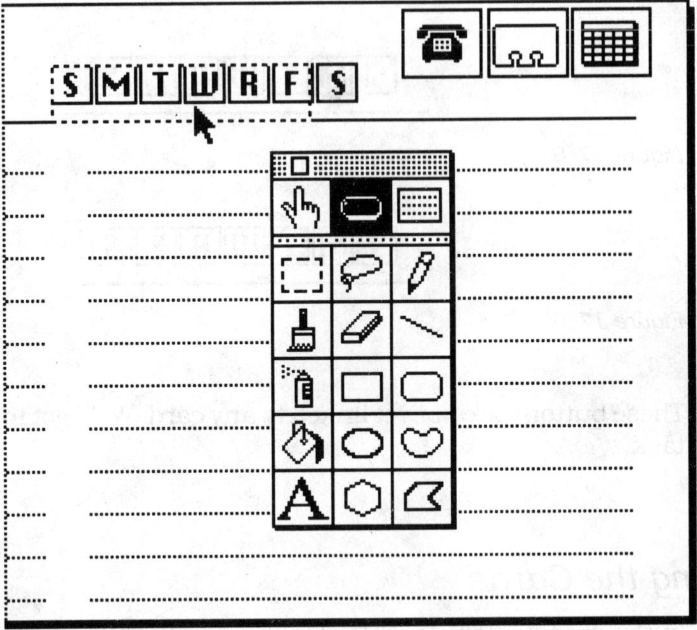


*Figure 17-59.*

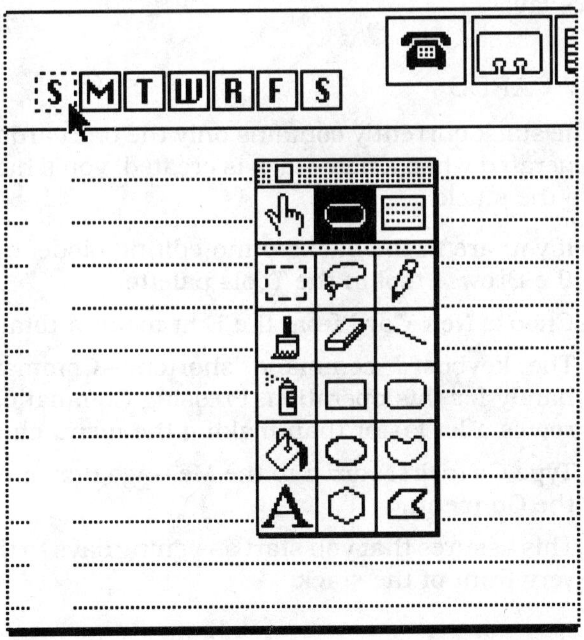


*Figure 17-60.*

*Figure 17-61.*

*Figure 17-62.*

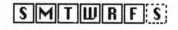

These buttons are not yet linked to any card. We'll get to that in the next task.

## *Making the Cards*

In the card domain for this stack, the only layer you'll be dealing with is the graphics layer. All buttons and fields are in the background. But the graphics layer of each card will interact with the background graphics layer.

### ADDING NEW CARDS

Since the stack currently contains only the one card that is automatically generated when a new stack is created, you'll have to add six new cards to the stack.

1. If you are in the background editing mode, exit it by selecting the Browse tool in the Tools palette.
2. Choose New Card from the Edit menu a total of six times.

   The keyboard command shortcut—Command-N—comes in handy for this operation. Pressing Command-N six times in a row is a lot faster than making the menu choice six times.
3. Type *Go to first card* into the Message Box or choose First from the Go menu.

   This assures that you start assigning days to the cards from the very front of the stack.

At this point, you should decide which card you want to be the first one in the stack. It won't matter while you use the stack, but the first card is the one that HyperCard displays when you open the stack from the File menu or from the To Do icon that may be on another stack. Even though we've set up the daily buttons to start with Sunday, that is no reason to make Sunday the first card. Since Monday is usually the shocker of the week, perhaps that's the one to make the first card.

4. Select the Text painting tool from the Tools palette (Figure 17–63).
5. Double-click on the tool to bring up the fonts dialog box.
6. Select Geneva 18.

   You're about to add some card layer text to run on with the background text.
7. Click the Text pointer about one and a half inches to the left of "S" button, and type *Monday* (Figure 17–64).

   Don't worry if the word doesn't line up with the buttons. That's what the next steps are for.
8. With the Command key down, drag a selection rectangle around the word *Monday*.
9. Carefully adjust the location of the "Monday" so that it is on the same base line as the day buttons and has enough room to the right to accommodate the longest day name, Wednesday (Figure 17–65).

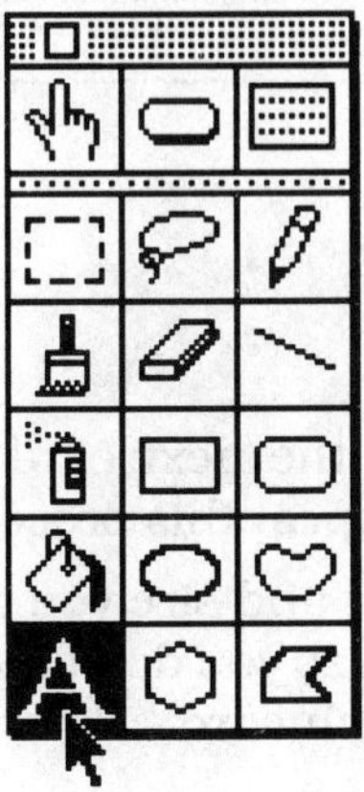

*Figure 17-63.*

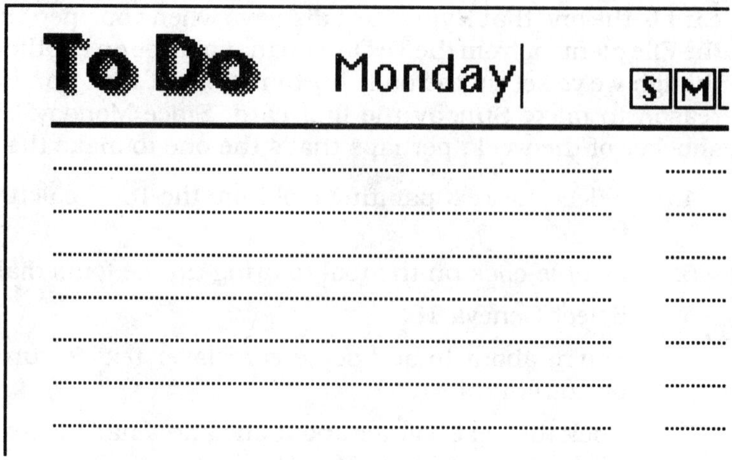

*Figure 17-64.*

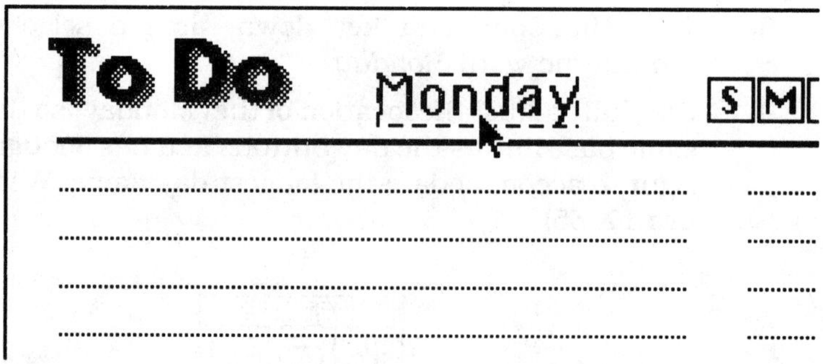

*Figure 17-65.*

10. Advance to the next card and repeat steps 7 through 9 for Tuesday. Repeat this procedure for each card through Sunday.

    The text font and size you selected for the entry of "Monday" is still in force, so you don't have to get to the fonts dialog box prior to typing each card's day name.

From here you go to another graphics task: placing the highlight rectangles on each day's card.

## ADDING A CARD LAYER GRAPHIC

With a separate card for each of the seven days in the rolling To Do stack, you have the luxury of adding custom graphics to each day's card. In this exercise, you'll be adding a highlight—a heavy border—around the daily button of the day whose card you're viewing. Thus, the Monday card will have a heavy black rectangle around the M button.

1. Be sure you are *not* in the background editing mode, because these graphics go into the card graphics layer.
2. Starting with the Monday card, enter FatBits and bring the M button into view near the center of the screen (Figure 17-66).
3. Double-click on the Straight Line tool to summon the line thickness dialog box.
4. Choose the third line from the left (Figure 17-67).

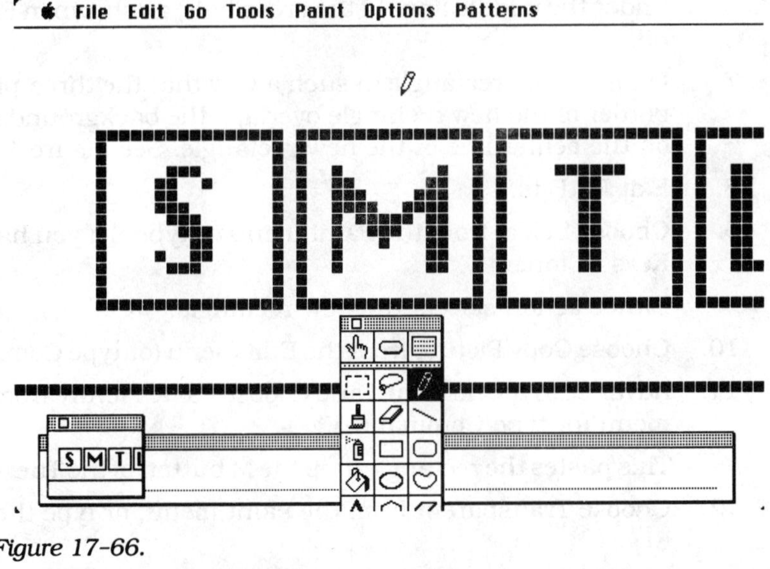


*Figure 17-66.*

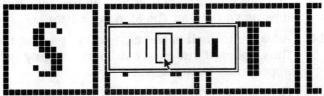

*Figure 17-67.*

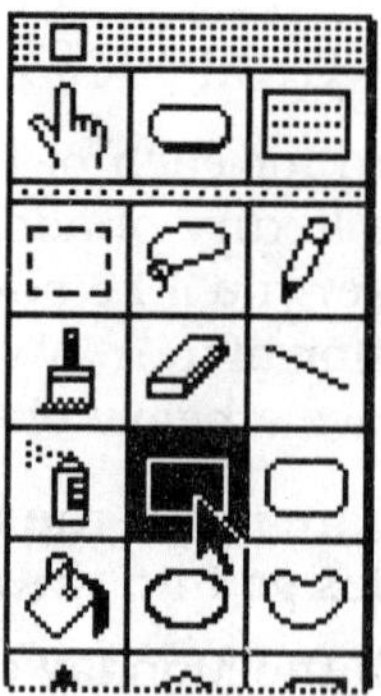

*Figure 17-68.*

5. Select the Rectangle tool from the Tools palette (Figure 17–68).
6. Carefully position the cross-hair cursor in such a way that the single-thickness outline of the background button outline is under the middle lines of the cross hair, as shown in Figure 17–69.
7. Drag a small rectangle in such a way that the three-pixel-thick border of the new rectangle overlaps the background rectangle on the center line of the new rectangle. See Figure 17–70.
8. Exit FatBits.
9. Choose Select from the Paint menu or type S if you have Power Keys in force.

   Either action selects the new rectangle.
10. Choose Copy Picture from the Edit menu (or type Command-C).
11. Advance to the next card and choose Paste Picture from the Edit menu (or type Command-V).

    This pastes the rectangle atop the M button of the Tuesday card.
12. Choose Transparent from the Paint menu, or type the T Power Key.
13. While the square is still selected, drag it to the T button graphic and place it directly overlapping the background graphic outline, as you did for the Monday button.
14. Advance to each of the next cards, pasting the rectangle from the Clipboard into each card and dragging the rectangle to the appropriate button graphic.

    Remember: only one highlight rectangle per card.

*Figure 17-69.*

*Figure 17-70.*

15. When you've finished with all seven buttons, hold down the right or left arrow keys to cycle through the stack. Ideally, you should see the effect that the heavy highlighting rectangle has as it inches its way down the row of buttons smoothly with the change of each card.

The next step is to enable the links between the daily buttons and the cards in the To Do stack.

## LINKING THE BUTTONS AND CARDS

By making the daily buttons background buttons, we can make all necessary links by using the Link To... button for each of the seven buttons. You can begin carrying out the following steps from any card in the stack.

1. Select the Button tool from the Tools palette.
2. Double-click on the Sunday button and then on the Link To... button in the Button Info dialog box.

   The mini window will appear with instructions to bring the destination card into view.
3. Use the keyboard's left and right arrow keys to bring the Sunday card into view (the one with the word "Sunday" in the card layer graphic).
4. Click the This Card button on the mini window.

   This action writes the script for the Sunday button; that is, every time you click on this button, it will bring the Sunday card into view, as you would expect.
5. Continue double-clicking on each button and repeating the Link To... mini window technique.

   Before clicking the This Card button in the mini window, be sure you are viewing the card whose daily button you're editing— the Monday card for the M button, and so on.
6. When you're finished making the links, select the Browse tool and try out the daily buttons.

   Click them at random, checking your results with the expected results. If you click a daily button and get the wrong day, then somewhere you erred in establishing the link. Try it again.

A final graphics task is to fill in the grey pattern around the card.

1. Double-click on the Paint Bucket tool in the palette.

   This action brings the pattern palette into view.

2. Select the grey fill pattern immediately to the right of the black pattern (Figure 17-71).
3. Choose Background from the Edit Menu.
4. Click the Paint Bucket's hot spot in the white areas surrounding the card.

   It may take two or three fills, depending on the pixels you erased in the early stages.
5. Choose Background again to leave background editing mode.

We now come to the last construction task, which is to create an icon button linked to the To Do stack.

## MAKING A STACK BUTTON

For a stack like a To Do stack, to which you may wish to refer from other stacks, you should create a button of some kind. That way you can copy the button and paste it in any other stack for an instant switch to your To Do stack.

1. Type *Go to first card* into the Message Box and then choose Background from the Edit menu.

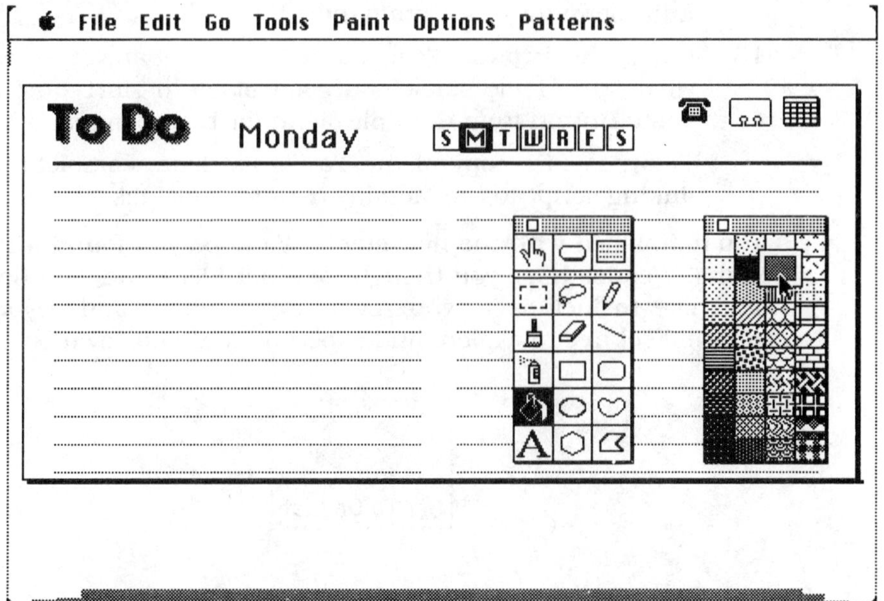


*Figure 17-71.*

2. Choose New Button from the Edit menu.

   A default button appears in the center of the screen, already selected.

3. Double-click on the new button to bring up its Button Info dialog box.
4. Change the name to "My To Do."
5. Click the Icon... button and select the HyperCard stack icon. Click OK.
6. Double-click the new button again to bring up its info box.
7. Click the Transparent style button.
8. Click on the Link To... button.
9. Click the This Stack button in the mini window.

   Until you can write a more complex script, this icon button will open the stack and show the first card of the stack, Monday's.

10. Back in the card background, grab the lower left corner of the selected new button and resize it so that the icon is clearly visible (Figure 17–72).
11. Drag the button to an unused area of the card.
12. While the button is still selected, choose Copy Button from the Edit menu (or type Command-C).
13. Using the Browse Tool, maneuver to whatever stacks you wish—the Home stack is a good place to start—and choose Paste Button from the Edit menu (or type Command-V).

    This pastes a copy of the To Do list icon, complete with its linking script to the Monday card in the stack.

You're finished with the new stack. We hope you found it fun and inviting. We also hope you thought of other ideas and variations you would like to include in your own edition above and beyond this exercise. Feel free to explore and experiment at your own pace.

*Figure 17–72.*

## *Using the Stack*

Now that the stack is complete, you may begin using it. Into the left column, type activities that should be accomplished on a specific day. Put longer-term projects and goals into the right-hand column. As you accomplish an item, use the Macintosh text editing tools to erase its line from the field.

At the end of each day, select the remaining items from the left column and choose Cut Text from the Edit menu. This removes the items from the day's listing and places them into the Clipboard. Then advance to the next day's card, place the text pointer at the first empty line in the left column, and choose Paste Text from the Edit menu.

When you plan a task for a day several days from now, click on that day's button. When the day's card appears, type the item into the appropriate column. It will be waiting there for you when the day comes along, and you carry over unfinished items from the previous day.

So far, we've made this stack very functional. But we can also give it considerably more "life" and "intelligence" with the help of simple scripts written in the HyperTalk language. In the next part, we begin to reveal the wonders of the HyperTalk language. It will be worth the trip. In Part Four, you'll embellish this stack with some powerful scripts.

## Using the Stack

# PART THREE

# HyperCard's Programming Environment

# CHAPTER 18

# Introduction to HyperTalk

THE FEW PEEKS AT HYPERTALK YOU'VE HAD SO FAR IN THIS BOOK PROBABLY DIDN'T make a lot of sense to you beyond their immediate purpose. For example, when you inspected the left and right arrow button scripts in the last chapter, it was easy to follow our lead. But left on your own, you surely wouldn't have known where to look for these scripts or how to modify them. You'd need a working knowledge of HyperTalk to even know that you could make such modifications. By the time you're finished with this book, you'll have that knowledge, as well as much hands-on experience in making your stacks do far more than just link card to card.

## *Programming and Personal Computers*

In the early days of personal computing, in the mid-1970's when you could finally buy a fully assembled computer instead of having to build one from a kit, computers were so new that very little applications software existed for them. Even though these computers were meant to get into the hands of general consumers, there was little you could do with them. Among the most popular computers of that day were the original Apple II, the Commodore PET, the Radio Shack TRS-80 Model 1, and a host of machines whose makers are no longer in the personal computer business (or in business at all).

Recognizing that software was an essential ingredient for their customers' enjoyment of the hardware, the computer makers almost uniformly included a programming language with the computer. The idea— presumptuous in retrospect— was that the customer would "roll his own" software. That meant, of course, that learning to program the computer was virtually a prerequisite to making the machine do something other than play the handful of games that began to appear on software shelves.

## ONCE UPON A BASIC TIME

The programming language that went with most of these machines was called BASIC, an acronym for Beginner's All-purpose Symbolic Instruction Code— a mouthful, to be sure. Compared to many other programming languages available at the time, BASIC was easy to learn. But that's not to say that it was a snap to begin writing useful applications. For many people, it was a struggle. Even the idea of having to learn a programming language to use a computer was enough to scare masses away from computers. Today, many noncomputing people still equate *using* a computer with *programming* a computer. You, of course, have proven them wrong already, by using a prewritten application like HyperCard to store and retrieve names and phone numbers.

Anyway, this tradition of including a programming language with a computer extends all the way up to the IBM Personal Computer, released to the world in late 1981. When you buy a PC and the traditional operating system software, PC-DOS, you get the BASIC language on the operating system disk (a reduced version is even in a chip on the PC's circuit board). Many of the PC's first generation of business software was written in the BASIC supplied with the computer.

Then came the Macintosh in early 1984. Among the many traditions this machine broke was the one about including a programming language with the computer. A major principle guiding the machine's design was that no one should have to "get his hands dirty" to use a computer effectively. Instead, the computer came packaged with real productivity software for doing word processing (MacWrite) and graphics (MacPaint). At the time of release, the Macintosh had only two other software packages available, the Multiplan spreadsheet and, you guessed it, BASIC. The BASIC, however, didn't really let even experienced BASIC programmers reach into the Macintosh's bag of tricks (called the Toolbox) for doing pull-down menus, standard file dialog boxes, and the like. The user community had to wait for commercial programs to be delivered— a waiting game that lasted longer than early Macintosh buyers care to recall.

Today, the wait for quality commercial programs is long over. The catalog of Macintosh software is quite extensive, ranging from easy-to-learn starter programs, like Microsoft Works, to heavy-duty offerings in desktop publishing and three-dimensional engineering graphics. In fact, devoted Macintosh users consider the software offerings for the Macintosh family to be superior to those in the MS-DOS world. While I'll leave the resolution of that contention to the pages of computer magazines, one thing is definite: The consistency of the Macintosh user interface has allowed the user community to focus more on what a software product does rather than on how to use it.

## THE MACINTOSH AND GREAT EXPECTATIONS

As a result, Macintosh owners have a generally higher expectation of what a software program should do for them. The challenge that software developers have, then, is to make software that is almost infinitely flexible, to accommodate the whims and desires of each user. This largely flies in the face of software development of yore, in which the program designer imposed a way of doing things that the user was forced to accept. By and large, Macintosh owners won't stand for that.

At the same time, more Macintoshes are getting into the hands of people who have very special information-handling needs for the machines—needs that may appeal to too small a group to attract commercial programmers. There are plenty of general-purpose databases and spreadsheets out there. But what if your company or department desperately needs training software customized for company policies and procedures? Or what if you want to design a computerized, fully cross-referenced catalog of your company's product line for telephone salespeople to use as a reference?

Prior to HyperCard, the answers to those questions would entail the hiring of experienced Macintosh programmers who could design custom applications from scratch. As any Macintosh programmer will tell you, writing a Macintosh application is not as easy as writing programs for computers like the IBM PC. More forethought and care must go into the program design to meet the user-friendly expectations of Macintosh users.

With HyperCard, however, many custom information-handling needs can be met by designing HyperCard stacks. To give authors additional flexibility and power in stack design, HyperCard includes the HyperTalk language, with which you can automate a number of HyperCard processes for yourself and others.

In one way, the inclusion of HyperCard with every Macintosh revives the tradition of supplying a custom development tool with the computer. But in the tradition of Macintosh's "clean hands" philosophy,

HyperCard and its HyperTalk language are substantially easier to master than other customizing environments, like BASIC, despite the overall complexity of designing for the Macintosh.

## PREPROCESSING

The feature of HyperCard and HyperTalk that makes authoring for the Macintosh so much easier is that a great deal of the concerns that sidetrack professional programmers have already been covered for you. A good example is the concept of the screen button. In a traditional programming environment, much planning goes into the inclusion of a button on the screen and its corresponding action when someone clicks on it. While a programmer would have to painstakingly determine the screen coordinates for a button on the screen, a HyperCard author simply drags a selected button on the screen and adjusts its size with the cursor. The thought of the button's coordinates needn't ever cross the author's mind— although HyperCard is working diligently behind the scenes recording screen locations and many other properties of the button. In a sense, HyperCard is your partner: It preprocesses all the gobbledygook out of sight.

*A Word to Experienced Macintosh Programmers:* Even the event loop is preprocessed for you in HyperTalk. HyperCard does all the trapping for keyboard and mouse events for you, including routing to the correct button handler when a mouse event occurs inside a button's rectangle. Most of what you program in HyperTalk are button and other object-handler routines.

As you may have deduced, it is difficult to discuss HyperTalk separately from HyperCard. They are intricately intertwined. While you can use HyperCard and even create a HyperCard stack without writing a word of HyperTalk, you can't work with HyperTalk without HyperCard. HyperTalk is not a stand-alone language like BASIC, Pascal, or C. It is the language solely of HyperCard, operating on HyperCard objects and on the information they contain.

Unlike a stand-alone language, you don't use HyperTalk to create stand-alone programs. HyperCard stacks are like tapes that run on the HyperCard player. HyperTalk gives you the power to customize a stack— give the stack more information-handling power than it can acquire on its own. In other words, you can use HyperCard without HyperTalk to link and search for information; if you want to manipulate the information in any way— to bring it to life, as it were— HyperTalk is there to follow your bidding.

The language was painstakingly designed to be easy to learn and use. The goal was to put powerful authoring tools into the nontechnical hands of those who need custom applications that no commercial developer would dream of. The HyperCard environment puts programming into the hands of specialists in areas other than computers—a huge universe that can benefit from Macintosh computing.

## *HyperTalk, the Language*

HyperTalk is, indeed, a language, albeit a written one. Like any language, it has a vocabulary and rules of syntax.

For HyperCard users in English-speaking countries, the HyperTalk vocabulary is all English, with full English words. There is none of the GOSUB kind of pseudo-English, as in BASIC. Commands are complete English sentences. If you'd tell a friend, "Go next door," then you can tell HyperCard, "Go to the next card."

HyperTalk's syntax rules are perhaps the most flexible you'll find in any programming language. If you've ever done programming before, you'll recall how picky computer languages normally are regarding the crossing of every t and dotting of every i. Typing an extra space between two words in a statement may mean a one-way ticket to Error Message Purgatory. HyperTalk is not only completely forgiving of things like extra spaces, but it anticipates multiple ways you may have for expressing a command. For instance, if it is awkward for you to say "Go to card 1," you can say "Go to first card." Both commands deliver the first card of the current stack to the screen.

You enter HyperTalk commands in two possible places. One is in the Message Box, the other is in a script.

Message Box commands, as you saw in chapter 1, can prove helpful at times when you wish to navigate within HyperCard from the keyboard. The Go command is perhaps the most frequent command you'll give in the Message Box. When you type a command in the Message Box and press Return or Enter, HyperCard carries out the command immediately. You may issue only one command at a time from the Message Box. Incidentally, the Message Box need not be showing for you to type a command into it. But, for this "blind typing" to work, you must check the Blind Typing box in the Home Stack's Preferences card.

Script commands, on the other hand, are carried out at a later time, such as when you click on a screen button. Script commands may be as short as one line (the actual command part, that is) but are frequently listed with other commands to carry out a series of actions without any intervention from the user. You saw an example of this feature in chapter 17, when examining the button that links the To Do stack to the Datebook stack. When you click on that button, HyperCard carries out the list of commands in that script.

## *What You Can Do with HyperTalk*

Trying to characterize the kinds of things you can do with HyperTalk inside HyperCard is like trying to characterize the kinds of things you can do with a deluxe Swiss Army knife. HyperTalk is so open-ended, authors will be finding new things for HyperTalk to do for a long time to come.

Still, we can help you visualize some of the tasks you can set your first scripts to carry out, at least in terms of the objects you've already learned about. One type of task that we've already hinted at in an earlier chapter is the ability to create a link between stacks that is more "intelligent" than the hard link between two cards. For instance, you can write a script that looks at the text you've selected in a field in one stack and then searches a second stack for the occurrence of that selected text.

Scripts can also perform a variety of information-lookup tasks. For example, let's say you create a stack of time sheet cards to record the hours spent on client projects. Elsewhere in the stack is a special card (something like a Setup or Preferences card) that has a field in which you enter the usual hourly rate you bill your clients for time. You fill out a regular time sheet card whenever you spend billable time working on a client's project. If you wish to have HyperCard calculate and display the billing amount for each card, you could write a script that looks up your hourly rate, displays it on the time sheet card, and multiplies the elapsed time by the hourly rate (Figure 18–1).

Other powers of scripts include the ability to post information into fields in another card without bringing the other card into view. A script can perform any HyperCard menu command, including Macintosh painting. You can instruct HyperCard in a script to run another application, like a communications or word processing program: When you quit the external program, you return to HyperCard viewing the very same card as when you left HyperCard. Scripts can also prompt the user for information by way of a dialog box.

More advanced script powers let HyperCard test for certain conditions and make simple decisions based on the results of the test. For example, in an interactive training stack, you may end each lesson with a quiz in which the user must type in one-word answers to questions. You can write a script to examine the content of an answer. If it is the correct answer, the script may proceed to the next lesson; if the student types in a common wrong answer you anticipated, the script can branch to a special card to help the student make the differentiation between the right answer and the common error; and if the student types in a completely wrong answer, the script starts the lesson over.

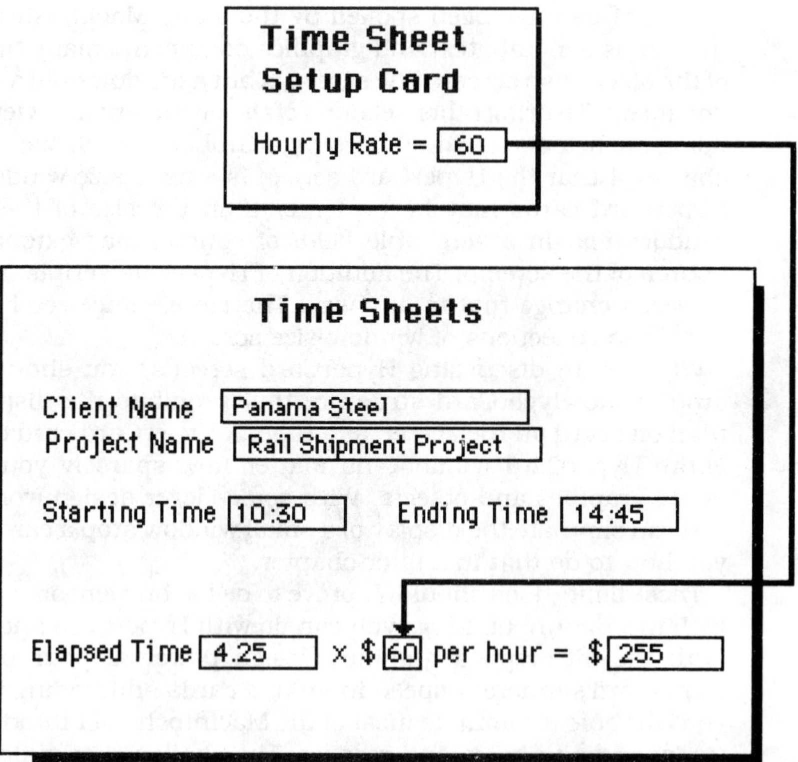


*Figure 18-1. A HyperTalk script can retrieve data from other cards and perform calculations combining retrieved and current card information.*

Finally, scripts have the ability to retrieve information about various conditions in the computer, such as the date and time, location of the mouse, and whether certain modifier keys (Shift, Option, Command) were held down when the mouse button was pressed. Combining these functions with HyperTalk's commands offers a multitude of possibilities for creating stacks and cards of real value to browsers.

## *What HyperTalk Cannot Do*

It is actually easier to quantify those things that you can't do with HyperTalk and HyperCard. There are some limitations you should be aware of before you begin dreaming of stacks. The two major ones are: 1) you are limited in your manipulations of the size of the HyperCard window; and 2) you can view only one card at a time.

Most of us have been spoiled by the many Macintosh applications that let us generate text and graphics documents many times the size of the Macintosh screen. The screen is but a window onto a much larger document. To bring other sections of the document into view, we scroll, using such tools as scroll bars or a Grabber hand. We explained in chapter 4 that the HyperCard screen is a fixed-size window and that HyperCard cards may be no larger than the size of the HyperCard window (text in a scrollable field, of course, may extend below the bottom of the screen). The addition of HyperTalk scripts in our stacks does not change that in any way. Therefore, conceive of your stacks simply as collections of window-size screens.

While we're discussing HyperCard screens, you should also plan around the HyperCard structure that prohibits the display of more than one card on the screen at a time. A HyperCard card occupies the entire HyperCard window, no matter how sparsely you design the card's graphics and objects. With some clever design work, however, you can simulate the display of a small window atop a card. We'll show you how to do that in a later chapter.

These limitations shouldn't prove to be too burdensome, particularly with the amount of things you can do with HyperCard and HyperTalk. With the bit-mapped graphics design power at your bidding, and HyperCard's inherent speed in linking cards and finding information, you'll be able to simulate most of the Macintosh user interface features you've come to know and respect. The challenge of building familiar looks with the tools of HyperTalk is half the fun.

## *HyperTalk Modularity*

Writing HyperTalk scripts is different from traditional computer programming in many ways, but the most obvious difference is in modularity. The program listing in languages like BASIC, Pascal, or C can be printed out and studied almost like a word processing document. To get the computer to follow the instructions in the program, the user "runs" the program. As the program runs, the computer follows the instructions in the designated sequence (the precise sequencing varies with the language). The program is self-contained. It has a beginning and an end.

Programming in HyperTalk is very different. There is really no such thing as a HyperTalk "program" that controls the activity in a stack from beginning to end. Instead, HyperCard objects (stacks, backgrounds, cards, fields, and buttons) contain short scripts, which HyperCard follows whenever events occur that affect those objects. For example, you may want HyperCard to retrieve information from a stack's

Preferences card each time you create a new card in that stack. Or you may wish HyperCard to place the current time and date in a field when you click on a button. The instructions for each of these actions should be placed in short scripts attached to the appropriate objects. Therefore, when you create a new card, HyperCard looks into a background or stack script for instructions to follow whenever a new card is created in that background and stack. Similarly, when you click a button, HyperCard looks into the button's script to find out what to do each time you click that button. A script comes to life only when called upon by HyperCard.

You need write scripts only for the actions you want the stack to respond to. If you don't want anything special to happen when a new card is created, don't write a script that responds to the creation of a new card. HyperCard will simply create a new, blank card and wait for your next keyboard or mouse action.

A script is entered, inspected, and edited in a special dialog box called the Script Editor, which is accessible for every kind of HyperCard object: buttons, fields, cards, backgrounds, and stacks. Each object has its own script (or no script). Therefore, if you have card domain buttons that are supposed to behave differently on each of forty cards, you can write forty different scripts, one for each button. Knowing which object to attach a script to requires some thought and awareness of the HyperCard concept of *hierarchy*, which we'll cover in chapter 19.

The value of HyperTalk scripts being so modular and spread out among so many objects in a stack is twofold. First, it makes it easier to test each script module while you design the interaction of various objects in a stack. Second, you can add features at a later time without having to rewrite or modify an entire program, as in a traditional computer program. Often, added features require little more than modifying a single script or adding a script segment to an object. All in all, it's a sensible system that makes learning HyperTalk far easier than other languages.

## Using the Script Editor

The HyperTalk Script Editor is a self-contained environment for working with HyperTalk scripts. It features a large box in which you type and edit the text that comprises HyperTalk scripts. Although the Edit menu is not available while you use the Script Editor, you can still use Cut, Copy, and Paste commands via their keyboard equivalents Command-X, Command-C, and Command-V, respectively. You select text for cutting and copying, just as you do in any Macintosh text-editing environment. The content of the Clipboard stays active when you leave the Script Editor, so you can copy and paste scripts from one object to another.

While you are in the Script Editor, you may use the keyboard arrow keys to move the cursor one space in the direction of the arrow. It is often more convenient to shift the cursor a few spaces with the keyboard than to use the mouse.

A HyperTalk command line can be any length, including longer than the width of the Script Editor window. Since a command line ends with a carriage return (a press of the Return key), you don't want to press Return until you have finished the entire command line. If you wish to break a long command line in the middle, however, you can type Option-Return to place a "soft" carriage return in the line. The Script Editor places a special symbol (¬) to indicate the soft return, and the text on the next line is automatically indented to match the first line. Use soft returns to break up long lines where you want them broken, to improve script readability for later editing.

To search for a word in a script, click the Find button in the Script Editor dialog box, or type Command-F. A smaller dialog box appears, requesting that you type the word or string to find. When you press the Return key, HyperCard finds the first occurrence of that string after the location of the flashing text insertion pointer. Type Command-G to find the next occurrence. You may also select a chunk of text in the script window and copy it into the Script Editor's find string by typing Command-H. This action also finds the next occurrence of that string. Continue pressing Command-H or Command-G to keep finding additional matches.

You may print a script from the Script Editor by clicking the Print button or typing Command-P. If you select a portion of the script first, only that portion will print. The printout contains a page header listing the current date and time, plus the name of the object whose script you are printing (for example, script of card ID 2379 = "Setup Card").

If you have been editing a script and decide you'd rather return to the original version, click the Cancel button. If you click the OK button or press the Enter key, HyperCard accepts the current script as it stands and automatically saves it to disk.

## *Structure of a Script*

By now you've probably seen enough scripts to get some notion about the way a HyperTalk script is structured. Remember, when we say "script" we mean just a short series of instructions that HyperCard carries out as the result of some kind of action.

The way you let HyperCard know that it should carry out instructions upon a particular action is to virtually say, "Hey, HyperCard, when you encounter action A, carry out the following instructions." HyperCard dutifully monitors every action that takes place on the HyperCard screen and in the Macintosh system. For every action it encounters, it looks for a script starting with the name of that action. If it doesn't find any such script, it ignores the action and waits for the next one. This search for a matching script takes only a tiny fraction of a second, so there is no speed penalty when HyperCard finds no scripts for its many actions. If HyperCard does find a script, it follows the instructions entered there by an author. When the script ends, HyperCard returns to its vigilant monitoring of actions. The task of the author, then, is to let HyperCard know on which actions to detour into an instruction list.

The mechanism for catching HyperCard actions is to begin a script with the word "on," followed by the name of the action (we'll see what the standard actions are in the next chapter). You've already seen that to alert HyperCard to go to a different card at the click of a HyperCard button, the button's script begins as follows:

```
on mouseUp
```

That tells HyperCard to follow instructions on succeeding lines of the script whenever the user releases the mouse button with the Browse tool atop the button.

A script needs an ending, too, because an object may have more than one set of script instructions etched to it. For instance, an object may have two different scripts to be carried out as the result of both a press and a release of the mouse button. The two scripts would start "on mouseDown" and "on mouseUp," respectively. To keep the instructions in these two scripts separated from each other, each script ends with the word "end" and the name of the action that started the script in the first place. Therefore, the last line of a script that begins "on mouseUp" would read:

```
end mouseUp
```

Now when HyperCard begins carrying out the instructions in the "on mouseUp" script, it will know when to stop. Without the "end" marker, HyperCard would try to continue on to the next script, carrying out instructions it should not be doing.

To sum up, each script must begin with an "on" statement and finish with an "end" statement, as follows:

```
on [action]
        instruction 1
        instruction 2
        .
        .
        .
end [action]
```

The "on" and "end" statements in a HyperTalk script are always at the left margin of the script. Instructions between those two points are indented. Fortunately, you won't have to worry about the formatting of HyperTalks scripts. As you type lines of script into the Script Editor and press Return at the end of a line, HyperCard automatically formats the script for you. You may also press the Tab key at any time to adjust the formatting. As your scripts become larger and more complex (with multiple levels of indentation), the Script Editor's automatic formatting will help you know when you closed all the potential loose ends of such a script.

## *Pieces of a HyperTalk Script*

So far, we've been talking about "actions" as the triggers of scripts. We've been using that term as a matter of convenience, since it is fairly easy to visualize a HyperCard action as being the result of a physical action, like pressing and releasing the mouse button. There are more accurate terms to describe these actions and the other elements of a HyperTalk script. We'll introduce you to them in this section. It's important that you grasp their meanings and feel comfortable with the terms. The remaining chapters assume a familiarity with these terms.

### OBJECTS

We've had quite a number of dealings with the five basic kinds of items in HyperCard: the button, the field, the card, the background, and the stack. To HyperCard, each of these items is known as an *object.* HyperCard objects are the familiar "things" that you work with, either as a browser or author. You may not be able to physically touch a HyperCard object, but each kind of object has a certain three-dimensionality to it that lets your mind grasp it.

To help you visualize the relationships among the five HyperCard objects, we'll present an extended metaphor. First we'll set the scene of the metaphor and, later, apply HyperCard objects to the various objects in the metaphor.

Imagine a large, multilevel building designed as a hotel. Each of the building's levels consists of a long corridor with doors leading to many rooms. The rooms on a given level are identical in shape, color, furnishings, and furniture arrangement. All rooms on one level, for instance, may have beds for one person per room. A different level has rooms designed for two people per room. While all the rooms were designed to be identical, occasionally one room will have an added feature, like an extra light switch on the wall or a folding bed tucked away in the closet so that an extra person can sleep there. But by and large, the rooms are the same. The only thing that differentiates one room from the next on the same floor is its room number and the person who sleeps in the bed(s). Once the hotel is built, all the action takes place in the rooms, notably who's sleeping in the beds on any night and what happens when switches are pressed.

The analogues to HyperCard objects can be summed up as follows:

| | |
|---|---|
| Hotel Building | Stack |
| Floor | Background |
| Standard Bed | Background Field |
| Standard Switch | Background Button |
| Room | Card |
| Extra Bed | Card Field |
| Extra Switch | Card Button |
| Room Occupant | Information |

Now let's examine these relationships in more detail.

A HyperCard stack is an all-encompassing object. That is, the stack consists of many pieces (other objects), just as the hotel building consists of various building blocks like floors, rooms, and beds. A stack, of course, is much more easily modified than a concrete building. You can add backgrounds, cards, and other objects to it at any time. The main point is, however, that if you wish to find a piece of information, you must know the stack in which it resides. In the hotel metaphor, if you were looking for an overnight guest to your town, it wouldn't help to know only his room number or name. You must know which hotel he's in before you can start looking up a number or name. There may be twenty hotels in town with a room number 201. But there's only one hotel with your friend in its room number 201. And what distinguishes one hotel from others— at least in the sense of narrowing the search for your friend— is not its contents or constituent pieces, but its name and address.

In our hotel, we said that each floor was designed according to a plan that calls for identical rooms for one floor. The plan for a floor is very much like a HyperCard background. The background domain is shared by every card in the stack, just like the room design for a given floor is shared by every room. The color scheme, carpet pattern, room layout, and furnishings are determined by the floor plan. In a HyperCard stack, a background typically sets the scene for a group of cards, complete with forms design, background patterns, arrangement of elements on the screen, and so on. If your stack requires a different arrangement of elements for a second group of cards, you add a background, just as the hotel might add a floor of differently designed rooms to accommodate families in addition to their usual business travelers.

When the hotel designer planned the rooms, he established the location of the furnishings and electrical wiring. In the design, every room on a floor has a bed in the exact same location. What the plan does not account for, of course, is who will be sleeping in each bed each night. That's no concern of the plans, anyway. All the designer is concerned about is the size, location, and firmness of the bed that goes in each room. The beds can be likened to HyperCard background fields. Properties of background fields are established in the grand design of the group of cards: A field in that background will have the same size, location, and other properties on all cards, as decided in its background specifications.

In the electrical department, the designer specifies that wall switches are installed in the same place in each room. That way, maids and frequent guests will know where to reach for lights in any room on the floor. Think of the light switches as background buttons. They're in the same place on every card sharing the same background, and the action is the same when you press the same button on every card sharing the background.

Perhaps the best way to sum up the background objects in the hotel metaphor is to say that the designer designs a room only insofar as the room will serve as a model for identical rooms. He doesn't design room 411 specifically, but rather the model for all rooms on the fourth floor. (In truth, a hotel designer is not so ruthlessly cookie-cutter-oriented, but bear with us for a while longer.)

Now we tighten our focus and look at an individual room: the card object in HyperCard. Just as a hotel room exists for the purpose of housing a guest, so does a HyperCard card exist for the purpose of giving information a place to rest. All empty rooms on a floor look alike. All empty cards in a one-background stack look alike. You see the buttons and fields, but there is nothing distinguishing one empty card from another except for its card ID. That's where HyperCard has one up on the hotel. The hotel manager is stuck with unsold rooms when no one checks into them on some nights. He can't delete the room to cut down on his financial overhead. But a HyperCard stack doesn't need empty cards at all. In fact, you may add and delete cards as information "checks in" and "checks out."

Textual information, as we've seen throughout this book, is stored only in text fields. In our hotel scenario, you would say that a guest is identified not only by the room number he's in, but also by the bed he's sleeping in. Remember that the floor plan determines the properties of the bed, but the bed is only useful when someone is sleeping in it. The same is true for a background field. It is always on the card, but the card isn't productive unless information is in the field. When there are several fields in the card, each is differentiated from the other by an identification number, like beds in a hotel room may be known as "Bed 1" and "Bed 2." Every room on that floor has a Bed 1 and Bed 2, but John Doe is sleeping in Bed 2 of only one room; Sally Roe is sleeping in Bed 2 of another room on the floor.

It turns out that there is the possibility that not all rooms on a floor are the same, just as all cards of a background need not be completely identical. One room, for instance, may have a folding bed in the closet. This was certainly not in the floor plan and is specific only to the one room. In HyperCard parlance, this would be equivalent to a card field: a field you add to the card domain of one card only. Therefore, if the room with the folding bed can house one additional guest for the night, so can your card with the extra field contain one more piece of information. No other card in the stack will be aware of this extra field.

Similarly, if the hotel experiments with a bathroom fan in one room and adds a switch to the wall plate, that extra switch is not in the original floor plan. It is analogous to the card button: one that carries out an action only from the card in which it is placed. You don't see it on other cards, any more than guests in other rooms would see a fan switch on their wall plates.

We hope you're still with us on this extensive metaphor. The purpose of it all was to demonstrate that HyperCard objects are entities unto themselves yet have complex interrelationships with other objects. Moreover, as we'll see much more in the next chapter, there is a very specific *hierarchy* of objects. We must make sure that you appreciate the difference between object relationships and the layering principles detailed in previous chapters. The two subjects are quite separate from each other. Layering is predominantly concerned with the physical appearance of cards on the screen. The object hierarchy operates almost entirely behind the scenes and becomes important to the HyperCard author as he peeks behind the HyperTalk curtain.

## MESSAGES

We'll begin this section with the following statement: HyperTalk is built around a system of sending messages to objects. We don't expect that statement to mean too much right now, but when we repeat it at the end of this section, it will make incredible sense. We just wanted to show you where you're headed before you set out.

In the real world of interacting with people, it's quite natural to send messages to another human being. Sometimes messages are written as notes or formal letters. Other messages may be sent electronically, like electronic mail. And still others may be transmitted without exchanging a single word. A menacing glare can be a potent message, as was a thumbs down signal in a Roman amphitheater. A message, therefore, may be a command to do something ("Do this") or simply a statement of fact ("It is now 3 P.M.").

HyperCard is constantly generating statement-of-fact messages behind the scenes. Even when you're not touching the mouse or keyboard and HyperCard seems to be taking a nap, the program is generating messages. For example, when nothing appears to be happening on the screen, HyperCard is generating a message that says "idle," meaning that nothing else is going on and it is idling, like a car in neutral. When you press the mouse button, HyperCard yells, "mouseDown." When you release the mouse button, the message is "mouseUp."

These messages are not general broadcasts to the world. They are addressed to specific recipients, each of whom is a HyperCard object. Exactly which object is the addressee depends on factors such as the nature of the message and how it was sent. We'll look more closely at "who gets what" in the next chapter.

As you'll recall, a HyperTalk script is attached to a particular object, like a button or a card. The script's underlying purpose is to intercept a HyperCard message. When the script identifies a message addressed to its object and its own script name, it directs HyperCard to follow instructions in the script. A script that reacts to a message is officially called a *message handler.* When the script intercepts a message, it handles the message accordingly. Technically speaking, a *script* may contain one or more message handlers; the script, therefore, is everything you see in the Script Editor window.

Let's visualize the mechanism that generates messages and what happens when a script intercepts one (this is simplified for our first excursion behind the script scenes—more detailed explanations will follow in the next chapter). In Figure 18–2, HyperCard is merrily sending idle messages while nothing is happening on the screen. Suddenly, at the press of the mouse button, HyperCard sends a mouseDown message to the button that is under the Browse tool at that instant. Quickly searching the button object's script for a mouseDown message handler, it finds none and resumes sending its idle message many times a second.

In Figure 18–3, the string of idle messages is interrupted first by a mouseDown message, then by a mouseUp message, which corresponds to the release of the mouse button pressed just an instant ago. This time, when HyperCard searches the button's script for a mouseUp message handler, it finds one. Before HyperCard can resume sending

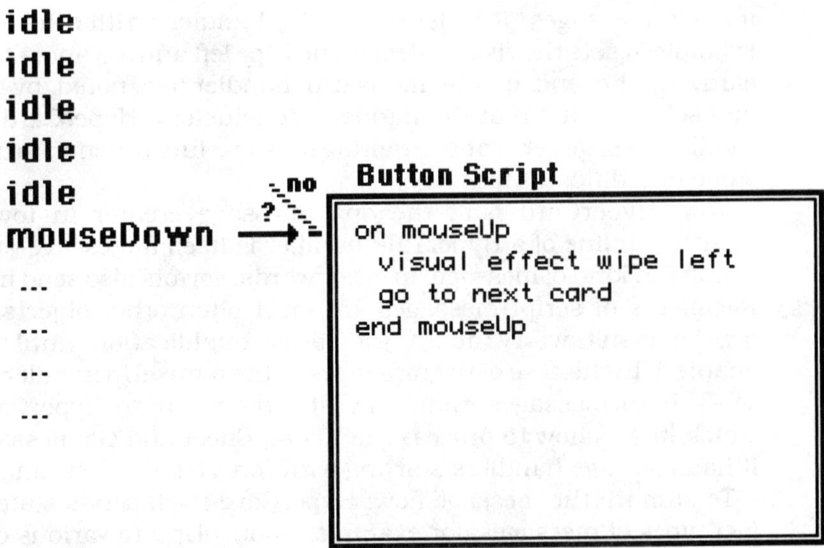


*Figure 18-2. HyperCard continually sends idle system messages until a keyboard or mouse action, such as pressing the mouse button. It sends a mouseDown message to the button clicked on by the user. HyperCard searches the script for a message handler for that message.*

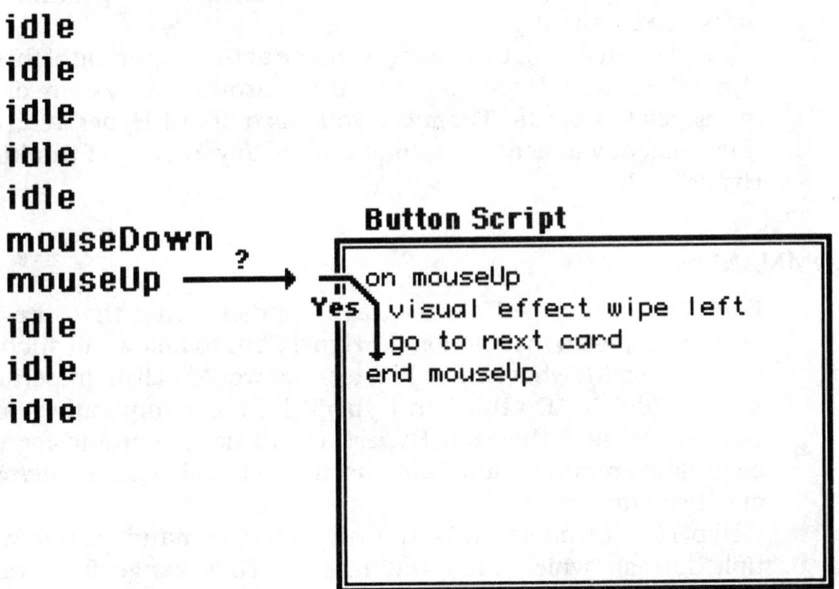


*Figure 18-3. When HyperCard finds a matching message handler, it carries out the script within that handler before returning to the stream of system messages.*

its own messages, it must follow the handler written for it. In this example, it sets the visual effect to the wipe left and advances to the next card. At the end of the mouseUp handler (so noted by the "end mouseUp" notation at the hander's conclusion), HyperCard resumes its idle message generation, waiting for some future action to trigger the same or a different message.

Now, HyperCard isn't the only message creator in town. Each instruction line of a HyperTalk handler is itself a message—usually a command kind of message. In other words, scripts also send messages. Recipients of script messages are most often other objects, but not always (don't worry about the latter qualification until the next chapter). In the case of the messages in the mouseUp handler in Figure 18–3, both messages eventually find their way to HyperCard itself, which knows how to process the Visual Effect and Go messages, as if it had message handlers starting with "on Visual Effect" and "on Go."

To sum up the message flow: HyperCard itself sends statement-of-fact types of messages (for example, "mouseUp") to various objects in a stack. Scripts send command-like messages to other objects and to HyperCard itself, the latter for carrying out built-in commands. You can also send an immediate message yourself by typing it into the Message Box. You'll learn later that you can instruct a script to impersonate HyperCard by sending statement-of-fact messages to other objects—a powerful feature that advanced HyperTalk programmers use frequently.

Now we can repeat the assertion made at the beginning of this section: HyperCard and HyperTalk are built around a system of sending messages to objects. The more you learn about HyperTalk, the more this concept will become second nature to your way of thinking about HyperCard.

## COMMANDS

Each line of a HyperTalk message handler, other than the "on" and "end" lines, is an instruction for HyperCard to follow. All such instructions start with what an English teacher would call an imperative verb, like the "do" in "Do this." In HyperTalk, these imperatives are called *commands*, and they tell HyperCard to do something for us. Most commands require additional information (called *parameters*) to carry out the command.

HyperCard understands around forty commands (some with multiple forms), which are built into it. They range from navigation commands to arithmetic to information manipulation commands and others. We'll examine each command in detail, starting in chapter 21.

Since you can send a command message to HyperCard directly from the Message Box, that's a good place to experiment with commands. Let's try some.

Our first experiment will be to issue a command that brings into view the card following the one you're looking at. We'll use the Go command along with parameters that let HyperCard know where it should go. Since HyperCard understands the phrase "next card" as a legitimate place to "go," that will finish the command.

1. Open any HyperCard stack, making sure the Browse tool is selected.
2. If the Message Box is not visible, press Command-M or choose Message from the Go menu.
3. Type *go to next card* into the Message Box and press Return or Enter.

HyperCard dutifully obeys your command message and brings the succeeding card into view. Since the message stays in the Message Box, you can press Return or Enter a second time to advance one more card through the stack.

HyperCard is pretty smart, because it knows that when you issue the Go command and an adjective like "next" or "previous," you can only be referring to cards. While you can Go to a different stack, there is no real next or previous stack. Only next and previous cards. Therefore, if you type only *go to next* into the Message Box, HyperCard knows you meant *go to next card.* Try it.

What happens if you issue a command that HyperCard doesn't know? In return, it presents a small dialog box telling you that it doesn't understand the particular command (Figure 18-4). Try typing *Flub next* into the Message Box and pressing Return or Enter. HyperCard won't understand the command Flub.

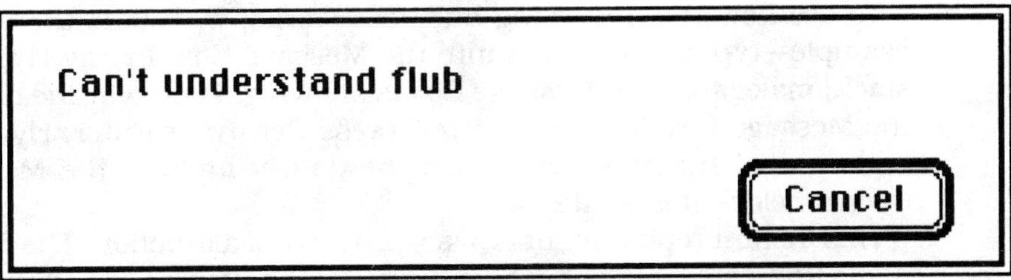


*Figure 18-4. When HyperCard doesn't find a handler for a message, it tells you it can't understand that message.*

A command, then, is the first word of a message, whether the message is in the Message Box or in a script. A more advanced feature of HyperTalk, as you'll learn in the next chapter, is that you are not limited to the command vocabulary of HyperCard. The language is extensible, which means you can add commands to HyperCard as you see fit. As complicated as this may sound, it is no more complex than writing a script whose "on" word is the name of the command you're creating.

## FUNCTIONS

There are times in a HyperTalk script when you need some information about the condition of the Macintosh system. For example if your stack is supposed to place today's date into a field of a new card, you need a way to fetch the Macintosh clock's date. Or if you wish to have two different actions result from the click of the same screen button, you may want the button's script to carry out different commands when the Option key is pressed along with the mouse button. You need a way to "read" the Macintosh keyboard to see if the Option key was pressed concurrently with the mouse button. In both cases, you summon HyperCard *functions*.

It's easy to mistakenly conceive of a function and a command as being identical when you experiment with functions in the Message Box. You can type a function name into the Message Box and press Return, just like a command. The most visible difference between a command and a function, however, is that a function always comes back with some kind of answer or reading from the depths of the computer. Programmers often refer to this handing back of information by saying that a function "returns" or "gives" an answer. Therefore, the HyperCard *the time* function *returns* the time from the system clock. Although we're not trying to turn you into a computer hacker, the "returns" designation works well within HyperCard, so we'll use it frequently. After all, you send a function to HyperCard, and it returns an answer to you.

To see how this returning business works, we'll take the simplest example— typing a function into the Message Box. In any HyperCard stack, make sure the Message Box is showing. Then type *the date* into the Message Box. The instant you press Return or Enter, HyperCard replaces the function name with the date it finds in the Macintosh internal clock (Figure 18-5).

This instant replacement is a key property of a function. The function name (*the date*, in the above example) can be used as the equivalent of the value returned by that function. If we had a script whose duty was to place today's date into a field on a card, the message the script would send to HyperCard would be *put the date into field 1.* When HyperCard encounters the function in the message, it automatically supplies the

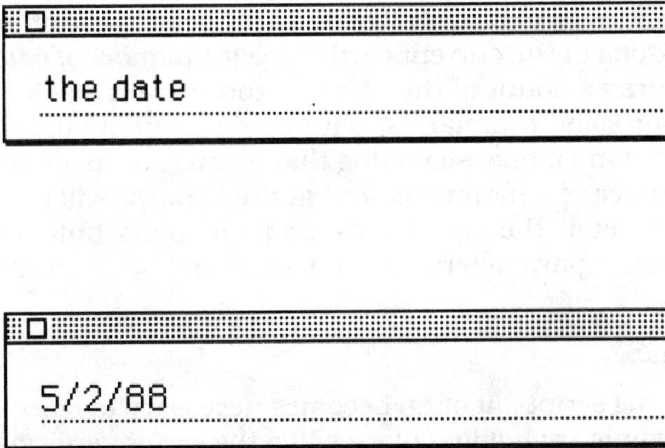


*Figure 18-5. Functions return a calculated value in place of the function name.*

current Macintosh clock's date for the function itself when it follows the instruction. The result, therefore, is that the actual Macintosh clock time is put into field 1, not the words "the date." (If you wanted to put the actual word into the field, the message should read *put "the date" into field 1*, the quote marks indicating a text string as opposed to a function.)

As a rule, then, you place a HyperCard function in a message where you wish to insert a reading from inside the Macintosh, like polling the clock or special keys on the keyboard. There are a few other types of functions, which we'll examine in full detail in a later chapter.

## PARAMETERS

You've already been introduced to the idea of parameters— modifying words or numbers following a command or function, and separated from the command by at least one space. The parameters you saw in the Go command acted like adverbs to HyperTalk command verbs specifying where to go. One command that drives home the idea of parameters quickly is the *beep* command. The beep command accepts a number as a parameter to instruct HyperCard how many times to sound the Macintosh beeper. In the Message Box type *beep 2*. When you press Return or Enter, the machine beeps twice. Now type *beep 5* and press Return or Enter. The machine beeps five times. The number is a parameter (also called an argument).

Functions can also have parameters. For example, *the number* function can reveal a great deal of information about the number of buttons, fields, cards, or characters, depending on the parameter after the function name. If you type *the number of background buttons* into the Message Box, HyperCard returns a count of the background buttons in the current card. Type *the number of cards*, and HyperCard returns a count of the cards in the current stack.

For some commands, parameters are optional. Beep, for instance, can stand alone, signifying that a single beep should result; but add a number as a parameter and multiple beeps will result. In the chapters that detail the commands and functions built into HyperCard, all possible parameters will be spelled out.

## VARIABLES

In long scripts, it often becomes necessary to place text or numbers in a temporary holding place while the script performs another action. If you've ever assembled a toy model or kit, you may recall a phrase like, "Set this subassembly aside for use later." That is often the case in a HyperTalk script (or any computer program, for that matter). These temporary containers are called *variables*.

You can experiment with variables from the Message Box, although most of your variable work as a HyperCard author will be in HyperTalk scripts. In the Message Box type *put "hello" into greeting*. This command places the text "hello" into a variable container called "greeting." You didn't have to do any preparation to use the variable name. By simply telling HyperCard to put something into a container with a name HyperCard didn't recognize as an existing object, HyperCard automatically created the variable with that name.

Once you've placed something into a variable, the variable name can be used to stand in for its content in a command line. Therefore, if you type *greeting* into the Message Box, HyperCard understands you to mean that you want the content of the variable called "greeting." It places *hello* into the Message Box in return. Even though the variable showed you its content in the Message Box, the variable still contains the information stored in it. Prove it by typing *greeting* into the Message Box again. For this kind of variable (that is, one generated in the Message Box), the variable will be active as long as you don't quit HyperCard. When you quit HyperCard, the variable is erased.

In the meantime, however, you can freely change the contents of the variable. If you now type *put "good-bye" into greeting*, the original contents are covered by the new phrase. Type *greeting* into the Message Box to show that the variable now contains the phrase *good-bye*.

Unlike the shenanigans of many computer programming languages, you can use most variables in a HyperTalk script without warning HyperCard that you're going to use them. Nor do you have to declare that a variable will be used for a number or text (HyperCard treats every character as text, although it knows by certain arithmetic commands to convert text digits into numbers for math manipulations). Not only that, but you can give any name you wish to a variable when you store something in it— as long as the name is one word. This gives you the flexibility of assigning names to variables that mean something to you while you're writing the script. Let's look at an example.

Suppose you're performing a string of calculations, such as adding the contents of three fields to achieve a total. The total number will eventually go into the fourth field on the card. The addition is performed as the result of clicking on a button labeled "Add." The script that performs the addition, then, would be attached to the Add button. To accomplish the addition in HyperCard, the HyperTalk script will fetch the first number, store it in a variable, and then add each of the second and third numbers to the variable. Once the addition is completed, the contents of the variable will be placed into the fourth field, where the total should go. The script is shown below:

```
on mouseUp
    put field "first number" into holder
    add field "second number" to holder
    add field "third number" to holder
    put holder into field "total"
end mouseUp
```

In the first message, HyperCard retrieves the content of the field named "first number" and places it into a variable called "holder." Therefore, if you had typed a 10 into the first field on the card, the variable holder would contain the number 10 after the first message of the script.

The second message performs some arithmetic. It fetches the content of the second field and adds that to whatever is in the variable "holder." We noted earlier that the numbers in fields and variables are actually stored as text. The Add command performs some lightning-fast conversions to change the field and variable contents to numbers for the math. Then it stores the result in the variable as text digits. If the second field on the card had a 20 in it, the variable holder would have the number 30 in it after the second message.

The third message is like the second, but it fetches the number from the third field and adds it to the variable. If the third field had a 25 in it, the variable holder would be 55 after the third message. Notice that holder's content varies with each message— hence its designation as a variable.

Once the arithmetic is finished after the third message, the handler can now place the content of the variable into the fourth field on the card, named "total." To do this, the handler message simply places the variable— remember, HyperCard interprets the variable's name as meaning the content of the variable— into the field on the card. By the end of the handler, HyperCard has placed the 55 into the total field.

An interesting property of regular variables like holder, above, is that they exist in memory only during the running of the handler that mentions them. In other words, the minute the handler finishes, HyperCard has no recollection of any variable named "holder." Therefore, if you ran the handler and then typed "holder" into the Message Box, HyperCard would say it doesn't understand holder: It finds no variable, command, or function with that name. The upside to this is that you can reuse variable names in every handler without fear of HyperCard accidentally using the content of a variable activated earlier. You might develop a habit of using the same variable names in handlers when the variables perform similar jobs in different handlers. For instance, we frequently use variable designations *temp1, temp2,* and so on in all complex handlers inside a stack to designate temporary holding places. The variable temp1 in one button's handler does not get mixed up with temp1 in another button's handler. In programming terms, these variables are said to be *local variables,* because their existence in HyperCard's eyes is limited to the handler in which they are mentioned: They are local, or private, to a single handler.

A second kind of variable, called a *global variable,* transcends the boundaries of a single handler. The kind of variable you create in the Message Box is a global variable. It will maintain its contents during and after the execution of any handler. As long as you don't quit HyperCard, a global variable remembers its content.

The global variable is the one exception about declaring your intention for a variable inside a handler. Since a HyperTalk handler will automatically make any undeclared variable a private variable, you must include a message in your handler that you intend a variable to be a global variable. Such a declaration for a variable named "PhoneNumber" would read *global PhoneNumber* in a HyperTalk handler. The only time you need to declare a global variable is if you intend the *content* of a variable to be used by more than one handler. In other words, a handler may put a phone number into a variable, and you want that number to stay with that variable after the initial handler ends. Later, you'd be able to retrieve that phone number very quickly from the global variable rather than from the card containing the number in the first place.

## *The "It" Local Variable*

HyperCard has one special local variable. This variable has a name already assigned to it: It. A few HyperTalk commands use the It variable in a handler as a repository for information that comes back as the result of the command. The Get command, in particular, always puts something into It. For instance, the command *get the date* is identical to *put the date into it.* Beginning with the next line of the handler, you may use the contents of It just like any local variable.

It's a good idea not to let important information stay in It for long inside a handler, because another Get command (also Ask, Answer, or Convert commands) will automatically re-use It and overwrite its previous contents. If your handler will need the contents of It later on, then put It into another local variable.

## *Other Terms*

In learning about HyperTalk commands, functions, and script structures, you'll encounter a few other terms that should be introduced at this stage. They'll be used in later chapters that describe the detailed workings of commands and functions.

### SOURCE, DESTINATION, AND CONTAINERS

Several HyperTalk messages move information around from one field to another or between a field and a variable. The two locations are sometimes referred to as the *source* and the *destination.* The source, obviously, is the location of the text before anything happens to it; the destination is the receiver of the text.

Another term you may see in this context is *container.* A variable, a field, or a text selection inside a field is a container of information.

### BOOLEAN

We'll run into the idea of a boolean expression a few chapters from now. A Boolean is named after the nineteenth-century mathematician George Boole, who devised an arithmetic system based on the logic of true and false properties.

In HyperTalk, certain functions produce Boolean results, literally returning the words "true" and "false." For example, type *10<5* into the Message Box and press Return. HyperCard returns "false" because ten is not less than five. A HyperTalk script will use these Boolean results to make limited decisions about what part of the script to process next. For instance, if the Option key is pressed when a button is clicked, the script proceeds down one path; if the Option key is not pressed, the script proceeds down another path. We'll see more about how Booleans work in a later chapter.

## Foreign Language HyperTalk

Generally speaking, a computer language is regarded as a stand-alone language, just like English, French, or Hindi. Learning a programming language, then, is like learning a foreign tongue. Japanese BASIC programmers use the same GOSUB and INPUT commands as Canadian BASIC programmers. In one sense, the commonality of the language makes sharing across cultures easy. But learning can be much more difficult when the person's native language is not the English on which the programming language is based.

HyperTalk was designed around a natural-sounding English language by its American designers. But they didn't stop there. Non-U.S. versions of HyperCard will eventually contain translation modules that convert English HyperTalk into the user's native tongue and vice versa. HyperTalk scripts are always stored on disk in English. The user in a non-English-speaking country selects his native language in the Home Stack Preferences card to inspect scripts in his language. Conversely, when he types HyperTalk scripts into the Script Editor in his own language, HyperCard translates the text into English before saving it to disk.

The implications of this system are profound. First, it will make it much easier for anyone in Apple's localized countries to learn HyperTalk. Secondly, someone will be able to write a script in Spanish, send the disk to a colleague in Germany, and let that colleague inspect the script in German. All the while, HyperCard is operating behind the scenes in English.

This chapter has been an introduction to the underlying concepts and terms involved with planning and writing HyperTalk scripts. We must devote extra time, however, to the underlying structure of the HyperCard message system. That's what happens in the next chapter, in which we solve the mysteries of HyperCard's hierarchical system.

# CHAPTER 19

# Messages, Hierarchy, and Inheritance

THE TITLE OF THIS CHAPTER MAY SEND YOU RUNNING FOR COVER, BUT DON'T BE discouraged by all the heavy-handed terminology. By necessity, we're inching up the ladder of complexity within HyperTalk. That you have stayed with us so far indicates that you are already way ahead of HyperCard users who have never ventured into the realm of HyperTalk.

This chapter will be a turning point in your full understanding about how HyperTalk works inside your HyperCard applications. Once the concepts here have sunk into your mind—and they will without much difficulty—your imagination will start reeling with possibilities for HyperCard stacks.

## *Messages, Again*

We'll begin our discussion with a quick refresher about messages, which we covered in detail in the last chapter.

Recall that HyperCard sends system messages to a stack's objects. These messages are almost entirely about the current condition of the Macintosh or HyperCard system at that moment. Therefore, when you press the mouse button, HyperCard sends a "mouseDown" message to the object under the Browse tool at that instant. If the tool is atop a button, HyperCard sends "mouseDown" to that button; if there is no button or text field under the tool, HyperCard sends "mouseDown" to the current card.

The object, in turn, may contain a message handler that waits for the mouseDown message. The script begins "on mouseDown," meaning, essentially, whenever HyperCard sends the message "mouseDown", follow the next instructions until the end of the handler.

It turns out that the instructions within an object's script are also messages. Figuring out which object is to be the recipient of such messages is the subject of this chapter. Messages aren't sent out into thin air. Every message must have a recipient, even if the recipient doesn't intercept the message but passes it along to another. For most messages—those that contain built-in HyperCard commands and functions—you won't have to worry about the explicit recipient, because HyperCard gets those messages automatically. For other types of messages, however, you have to be aware of who is sending them and who is listening for them.

(It's often more convenient to talk about a message sender and receiver as a "who" instead of a "what," because objects seem to come to life in the context of sending and receiving messages. Therefore, while objects are inanimate, intangible things inside HyperCard, we will frequently refer to them as if they were living creatures.)

All the while you are in HyperCard, messages are being sent all over the place. Even when nothing is happening on the screen, HyperCard is sending the idle system message; when you open a stack, HyperCard sends the "openStack" message; when you press the Tab key to advance the text cursor from one field to another, HyperCard sends "closeField" to one field and "openField" to the second field. To paraphrase a 1950's rock and roll music hit, "There's a whole lot of messagin' goin' on."

## Hierarchy

When HyperCard sends a message to an object, that message may fall on deaf ears, so to speak. For example, if HyperCard sends a "mouseUp" message to a particular button because you released the mouse button with the Browse tool atop that button, the button must contain an "on mouseUp" message handler, or it will never react to that specific message. Even if the button has a script that begins "on mouseDown," it won't intercept the mouseUp message that HyperCard sends. What happens to the mouseUp message?

Well, it doesn't just disappear right away. Instead, the message goes one rung up HyperCard's *hierarchy* of objects. If the object in that next level has an "on mouseUp" message handler, HyperCard will follow the instructions in that script. If there is no such script, the message goes yet one more level up the hierarchy. It's an electronic way of passing the buck.

## REAL-LIFE HIERARCHIES

Buck-passing happens to be a good way to visualize what's going on here. Imagine you shop in a large department store where your primary contact is with sales clerks behind the counter. Above the clerks in the store's management structure are the department manager, store manager, merchandise buyer, and so on up to the president.

Now suppose that you'd like to recommend that the store carry a line of clothing that you like. If you talk to a clerk, he or she might say something like, "That's not my job. Go see my boss." The department manager might be sympathetic to your request, but says, "The store manager is the one who determines which items we carry in the store." When you make the same request of the store manager, he might say, "Well, that line is not on the list of items I can bring in to the store. It's the merchandise buyer who makes that decision." Finally, after a discussion with the buyer, your recommendation is acted upon, because the buyer has the authority to make that decision. Your message about carrying a line of clothing had to work its way up the store's hierarchy until it reached a level of personnel who knew how to act on the message.

If your message had been a request for a merchandise exchange, the message would have been acted upon by the sales clerk at the first level. In that case, the clerk had been trained to handle that message without having to pass it on to upper levels of the hierarchy.

## THE HYPERCARD HIERARCHY

Just like the job levels in a store, HyperCard has a number of levels, each of which corresponds to an object type. When an object receives a message, it will act on it if it has been trained to act on it– if it has a message handler named for that action (for example, "on mouseUp"). If the object has no such script, the message goes to the object one level higher.

Fortunately, there aren't too many levels in the HyperCard hierarchy to remember. Moreover, the hierarchy for message handling greatly resembles the visual hierarchy you have already dealt with in creating the sample stack in chapter 17. The hierarchy is illustrated in Figure 19–1.

To see how messages work their way up the hierarchy, let's follow the travels of several messages at various stages of a real stack's development.

The scene is a simple clip art stack. When the stack is complete, each card will contain a bit-mapped graphic in the card graphics layer. The background features a photo album look, a background text field, and

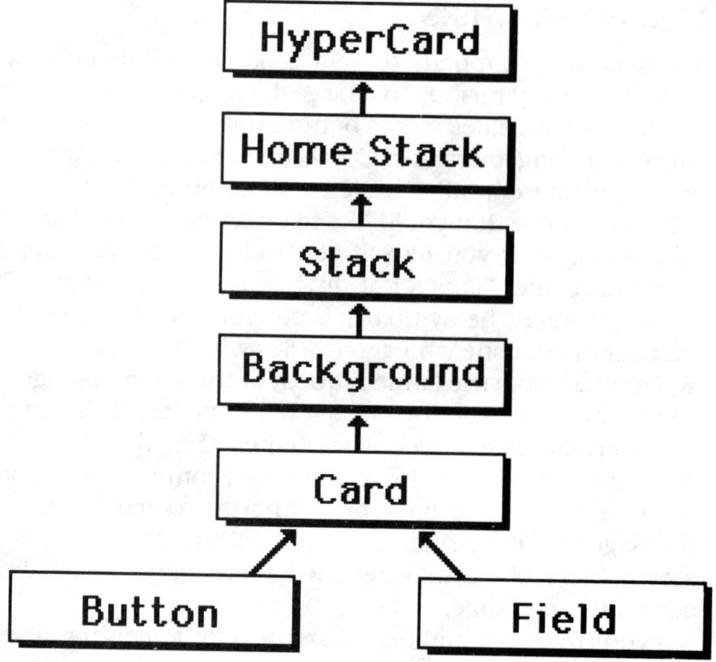


*Figure 19-1. The HyperCard object hierarchy*

two background text buttons, labeled "Home" and "Index" (Figure 19-2). The Home button will take you to the Home card; the Index button takes you to the first card in the current stack, which contains an index to the clip art in the stack (much like the Stack Ideas and Art Ideas stacks on the HyperCard ideas disk). Additionally, the design goal is to allow the user to progress to the next card in the stack by simply clicking the mouse with the cursor anywhere on the card except on the buttons.

Now follow what happens to the mouseUp message as we build the stack and assign message handlers in stages.

In Stage One, we don't have the buttons in the stack yet. We've just defined the new stack and placed a few pieces of clip art into it to see how it looks. If we click the mouse anywhere on the card, HyperCard sends a mouseUp message to the card. So far, however, we haven't defined a mouseUp script for the card, so the message continues up the hierarchy. According to the hierarchy map in Figure 19-1, that means that the background will be the next object to receive the mouseUp message (quicker than the blink of an eye). No mouseUp scripts have been defined for the background or stack objects. Nor is there any built-

*Figure 19-2. To demonstrate how the hierarchy works, we'll use this stack with two buttons as an example.*

in mouseUp script in HyperCard. Therefore, at this stage, the mouseUp message passes right up through the hierarchy untouched. If it makes it all the way to HyperCard without a match, the message disappears (Figure 19-3).

At Stage Two of our stack development, we insert the script that causes the mouse click to advance from the current card to the next. Our two most obvious choices for locating this script are either in the background or the stack. Deciding where a script like this goes is part of the skill you will develop as you learn more about HyperTalk in this chapter and others. For now, we'll put the script in the background object. The script reads:

```
on mouseUp
    go to next card
end mouseUp
```

With this script in place, when we click the mouse with the cursor anywhere on the screen (except in the menubar), HyperCard sends a mouseUp message to the card, just as before. But this time, as the

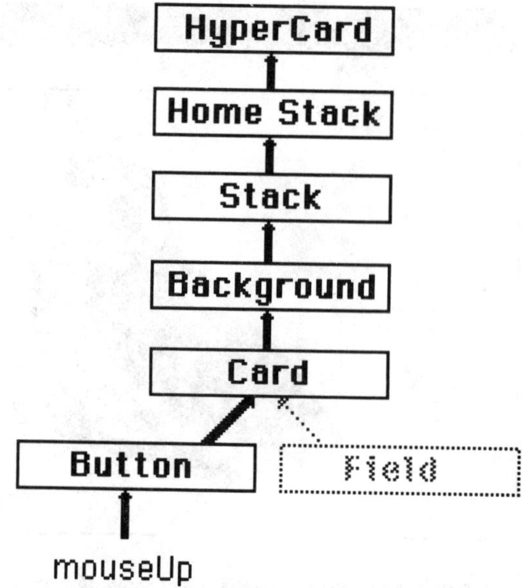


*Figure 19-3. If a system message does not encounter a matching message handler at any stop along the hierarchy, the message passes out of the system and disappears.*

message works its way up the hierarchy, it encounters a match in the background object (Figure 19-4). The mouseUp script in the background object has, in a sense, *trapped* the message on its climb through the object hierarchy.

Interestingly, when the script traps the mouseUp message, it sends a message of its own, the "go to next card" message. That message starts its own trip up the hierarchy, starting at the same level in which it started, the background. Since the "go" message is a common HyperCard command, existing in the HyperCard object, this message will find its way to the HyperCard object (Figure 19-5). It is possible to write a script in an intermediate object, like the stack, that would do something different to the "go" message than what HyperCard does. But you should avoid getting in the way of HyperCard commands and functions, at least until you've gained more experience with HyperTalk.

## ADDING BUTTON SCRIPTS

Stage Three calls for the addition of the two background buttons. When we choose New Button from the Objects menu, HyperCard puts a text button on the screen, which we can modify, as we've already seen. We'll

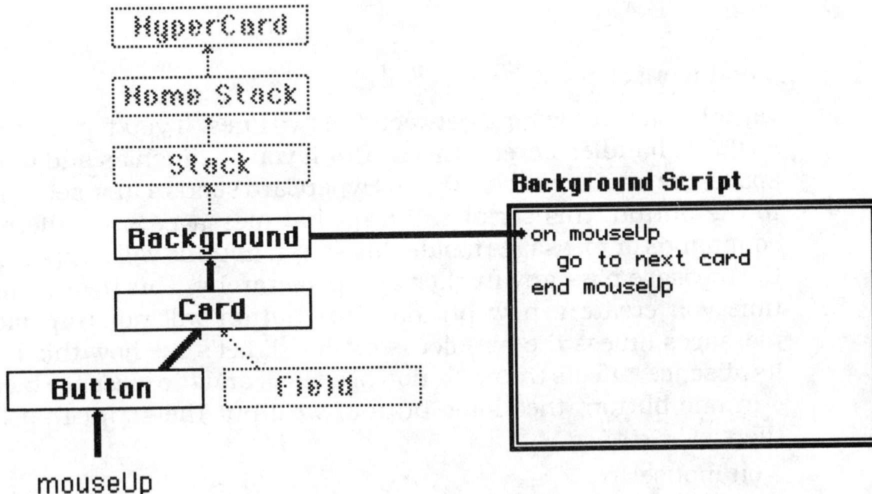


*Figure 19-4. Without any button scripts, the mouseUp message will work its way to the background script, which contains a mouseUp message handler.*

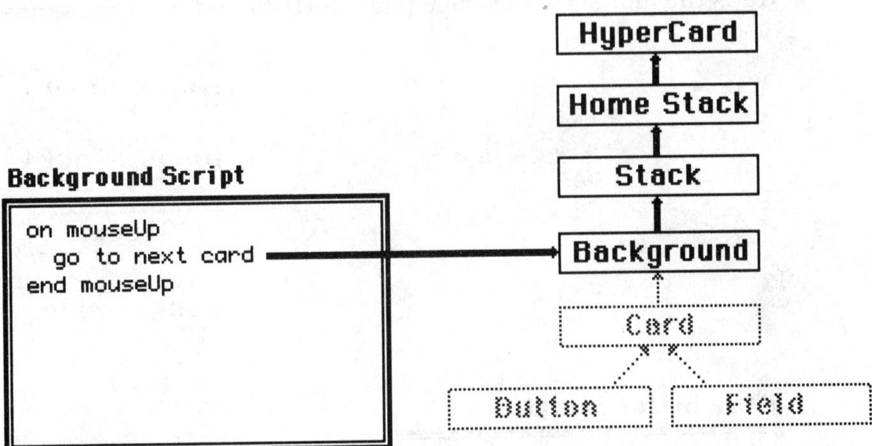


*Figure 19-5. The background script message handler sends a message of its own, the go message, which starts at the same level in the hierarchy and works its way to the HyperCard object, which understands this message.*

stick with the text button style for our experiment here, but we'll name one "Home" and a second one "Index."

When you ask HyperCard to create a new button, HyperCard starts the button script for you. For, if you open the button script dialog box of a new button, you'll see the following script:

```
on mouseUp

end mouseUp
```

with the cursor flashing between the two lines. If you type nothing, it's as if this handler weren't there. But if you so much as add or delete a space, the handler sticks. When HyperCard sends a mouseUp message to the button, this script will trap that message. Since there are no commands or messages inside this script, nothing will happen. Nor will the message pass any further up the hierarchy. This means that each time you create a new button, that button will not trap mouseUp messages unless the handler is modified. Let's see how this trap–and its absence–affects the operation of a stack and the message hierarchy.

In one button, the Home button, we'll put the script that belongs there:

```
on mouseUp
    go Home
end mouseUp
```

When we click the Browse tool atop this button, the button's script traps the mouseUp message (Figure 19–6) and, in turn, sends the "go

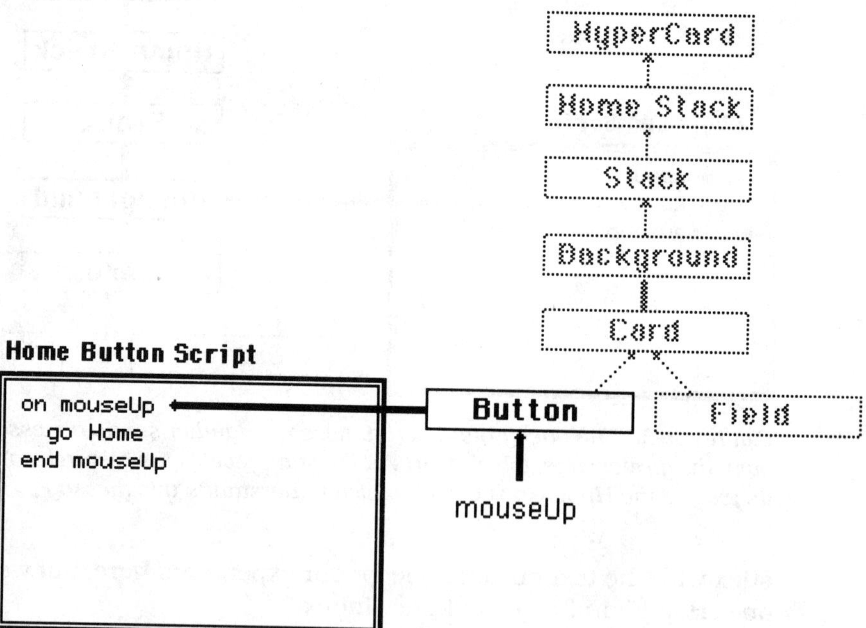


*Figure 19–6. A mouseUp message handler in the Home button's script traps the mouseUp message low in the hierarchy.*

Home" message on its way up the hierarchy to the HyperCard object (Figure 19-7).

In the Index button, if we temporarily remove its starting script, leaving a completely blank script dialog box, the button will not trap the mouseUp message HyperCard sends when we click this button. Instead, the mouseUp message continues up the hierarchy, until it encounters the mouseUp script in the background object. At this level, the message is trapped, and HyperCard ultimately advances the view to the next card—hardly the desired result from clicking on an Index button (Figures 19-4 and 19-5).

To achieve the desired result, we need to trap the mouseUp message at the Index button level. Therefore, we'll add the script,

```
on mouseUp
    go to first card
end mouseUp
```

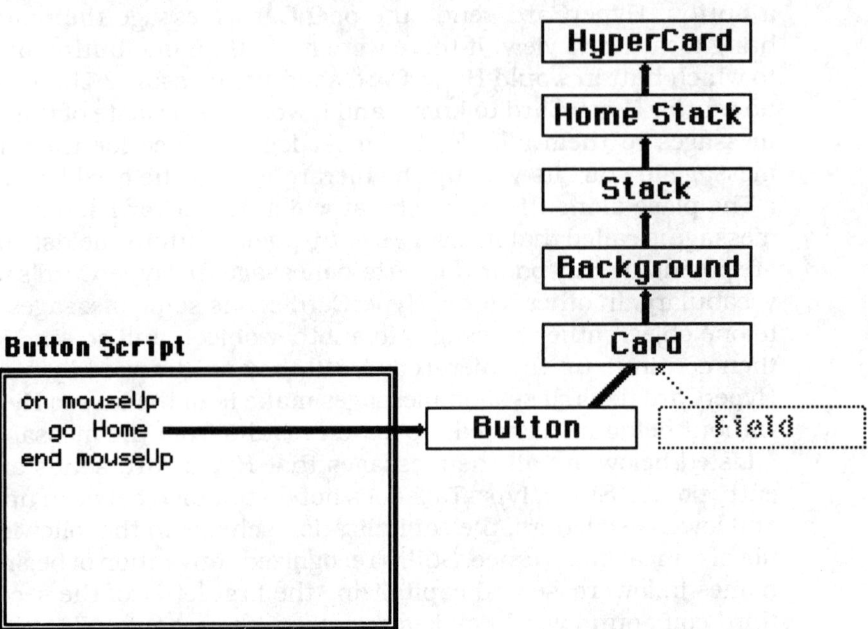


*Figure 19-7. The Home button's script sends a go message, which starts at its own level and works its way up to the HyperCard object, since no other script along the way trapped for go.*

to the Index button object. With this script in place, the message path looks like that in Figures 19-8 and 19-9.

Notice one important concept. The two button scripts, although trapping for the same message, are entirely separate entities as far as HyperCard is concerned. In other words, when you click on the Home button, the mouseUp message goes only to that button (at first). No other object at the same hierarchy level— buttons, here— ever sees that message. All scripts and properties of an object are private to that object, shared by no other object on the same level.

## *Message Entry Points*

By now you may be wondering how HyperCard knows where to send messages, such as mouseDown and openCard. Not every HyperCard message starts at the button or field level in the object hierarchy. For example, it wouldn't make any sense to send an openCard message to a button. HyperCard sends the openCard message the instant you bring a card into view. If there were more than one button on a card, to which button would HyperCard send the message? There would be no way for HyperCard to know, and it would be a waste of time to send messages to them all. No, the most logical place for the openCard message to start its way up the hierarchy is at the card level.

The place along the hierarchy at which HyperCard sends a system message is called that message's *entry point*. Buttons, fields, and cards are potential entry points for certain messages in HyperCard's message vocabulary. In other words, HyperCard sends some messages initially to one object, other messages to another object, and so on. Messages then continue up the hierarchy until they are trapped by a script or HyperCard itself. If system messages make it all the way to HyperCard without being intercepted, no action results from the message.

Listed below are all the messages that HyperCard sends and their entry points. Since HyperTalk does not distinguish between uppercase and lowercase letters, the capitalization scheme in the following list is not of critical importance. Still, a recognized convention of beginning all names in lowercase and capitalizing the first letter of the second and third compound words makes scripts quite readable. We urge you to follow this convention.

We'll examine the nature of the messages in the next section, but for now, see if you can make out a kind of pattern in the messages and their initial destinations along the hierarchy.

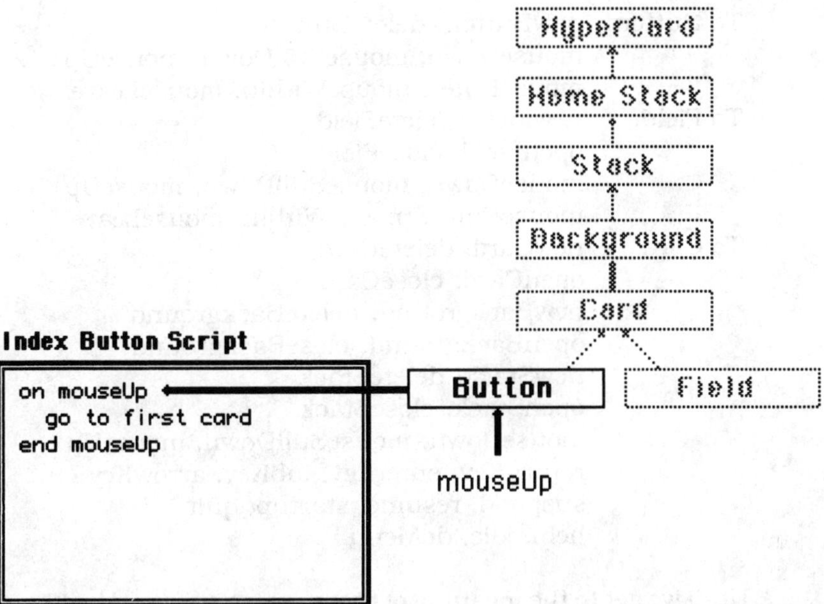


*Figure 19-8. The Index button's script traps for the mouseUp message when the user clicks on the Index button.*

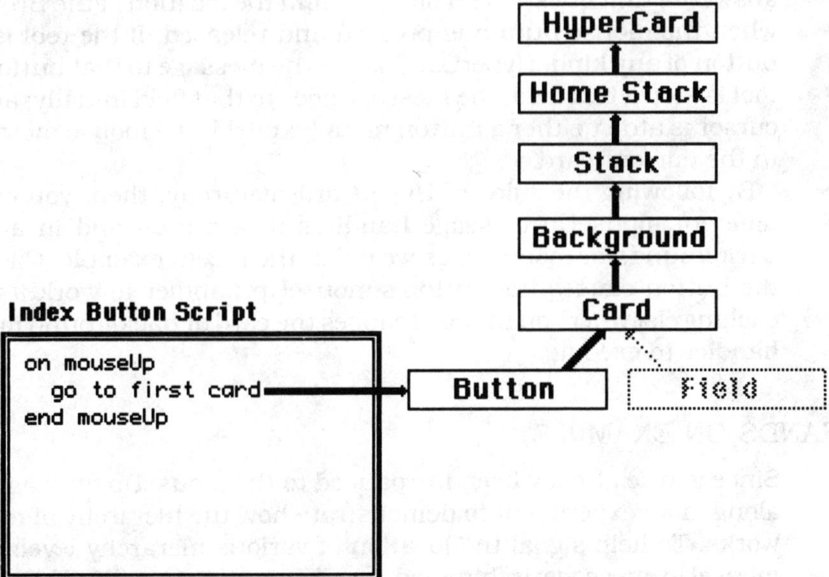


*Figure 19-9. The Index button's script sends a go message (although with different parameters than the Home button's go message), which wends its way up the hierarchy to the HyperCard object.*

| | |
|---|---|
| To Button: | newButton, deleteButton<br>mouseDown, mouseStillDown, mouseUp<br>mouseEnter, mouseWithin, mouseLeave |
| To Field: | newField, deleteField<br>openField, closeField<br>mouseDown, mouseStillDown, mouseUp<br>mouseEnter, mouseWithin, mouseLeave |
| To Card: | newCard, deleteCard<br>openCard, closeCard<br>newBackground, deleteBackground<br>openBackground, closeBackground<br>newStack, deleteStack<br>openStack, closeStack<br>mouseDown, mouseStillDown, mouseUp<br>returnKey, enterKey, tabKey, arrowKey<br>suspend, resume, startup, quit<br>help, idle, doMenu |

Until we get to the meaning of these messages, we should explain one point about the above listing. You may be wondering how HyperCard can send the same messages (mouseDown, mouseStillDown, and mouseUp) to three different objects as "initial" destinations. The answer to that question revolves around the location of the Browse tool when the mouse button is pressed and released. If the tool is atop a button of any kind, HyperCard sends the message to that button; if the tool is atop a text field, the message goes to that field initially; and if the cursor is atop neither a button nor a text field, the mouse messages go to the current card.

By following the rules of HyperCard hierarchy, then, you can have different mouseUp message handlers in a button and in a card or background, for instance, as we did in the recent example. Clicking on the button causes the button's mouseUp handler to work its magic; clicking elsewhere on the card causes the card or background mouseUp handler to execute.

## A HANDS-ON EXAMPLE

Since you've already been introduced to the mouseUp message, follow along in an experiment to demonstrate how the hierarchy of messages works. To help signal the location of various hierarchy levels when a mouseUp message is handled, you'll use the HyperTalk Beep command. This will give you an audio clue as to what's going on inside the HyperTalk scripts. Your first group of tasks includes setting up the visual environment of the experiment.

1. From the Home Stack, pull down the File menu and choose New Stack.
2. At the dialog box, type in a stack name, such as “Beeper” and press Return.
   The new stack looks like an empty Home card.
3. Select the Field tool in the Tools palette.
   The outline of the background text field appears.
4. Double-click on the field to bring up its Field Info dialog box; select shadow style; select Locked Text; and click OK.
5. Resize the field similar to the field shown in Figure 19-10.
6. Hold down the Option key and drag (peel off) a clone of the field, leaving it just below the original.
7. Double-click on the second field to bring up its Field Info dialog box; turn off the Locked Text setting; and click OK.
8. Choose New Button from the Objects menu.
9. Double-click on the button to bring up the Button Info dialog box, type “One Beep” into the button name box, and click OK.
10. Hold down the Option key and drag a clone of the first button, positioning it on the screen so that it overlaps the original button, as shown in Figure 19-11.

*Figure 19-10. Adjust the sample field as shown.*

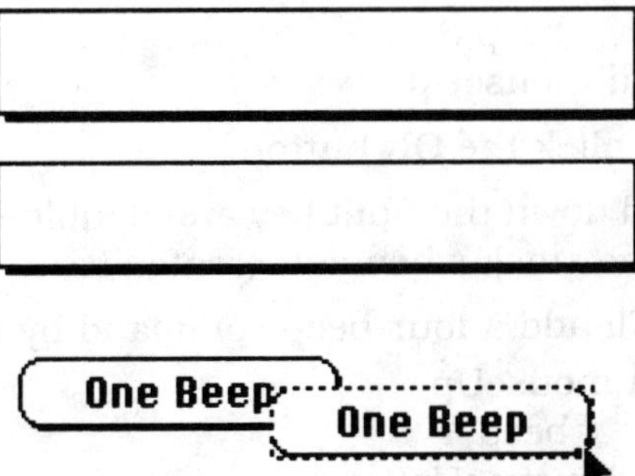


*Figure 19-11. Position the two buttons so that one overlaps the other slightly.*

11. Double-click on the second button to view the Button Info dialog box, and type the name "Two Beeps" into the name box. Click OK.

You're now ready to begin adding some mouseUp message handlers to each of five objects: two buttons, two fields, and the background.

1. With the Button tool selected (it may still be selected from the previous steps), double-click on the One Beep button.
2. In the Button Info dialog box, click on the Script button.

   A more efficient way to get to the Script Editor is to double-click on the button with the Button tool while holding down the Shift key.
3. In the blank line between the message handler start and finish (which HyperCard automatically puts in the script for you), type the following line

   ```
   beep 1
   ```

   and click the OK button.
4. Hold down the Shift key and double-click on the Two Beeps button.
5. In the script's blank line, type

   ```
   beep 2
   ```

   and click the OK button.
6. Now select the Field tool, hold down the Shift key, and double-click on the second drop-shadow field you created earlier.
7. Since fields are not often the recipient of mouseUp messages, the mouseUp handler is not pretyped for you. You'll have to type the entire script into the script dialog box. Type

   ```
   on mouseUp
         beep 3
   end mouseUp
   ```

   and click the OK button.
8. Hold down the Shift key and double-click on the field that was in the stack when you created it.
9. You'll add a four-beep command by typing

   ```
   on mouseUp
         beep 4
   end mouseUp
   ```

   and clicking the OK button.

10. Hold down the Shift key and choose Background Info... from the Objects menu.

    As with the other Shift key Script Editor shortcuts, this one bypasses the Background Info dialog box, which you don't need to examine for this experiment.

11. Type a five-beep command handler by typing

    ```
    on mouseUp
          beep 5
    end mouseUp
    ```

    after the existing handler and click the OK button.

12. Select the Browse tool.

You're now ready to try out your beepers. Click on the two buttons first, noting that HyperCard sends the mouseUp message to the button that "sees" the Browse tool when you click the mouse button. Since the One Beep button is partially obscured by the other, it can't see the tool when you click on the Two Beeps button area that overlaps the first button.

Now try clicking on the drop shadow field you created. "Ah," you'll say, "there's something wrong with my script." Actually, there's nothing wrong with the script (provided you followed the directions above). What happens, however, is that whenever the Browse tool is in the region of an unlocked text field, the tool turns to an I-Beam text cursor. This kind of cursor has a different purpose from the Browse tool. A click of this cursor means, "Put the flashing text insertion pointer on the same line I'm clicking." When the cursor is a text cursor, HyperCard does not send any mouse messages. Please make a mental note of that.

To hear the three beeps you placed in this field's script, select the Field tool, double-click on the field, and check the Lock Text box in the Field Info dialog box. When you click OK and return to the Browse tool, you can now click in the field, and you'll hear the script's three beeps.

Click in the field that was originally in the stack when you created it. This field has four beeps in its script. The field is also locked, so HyperCard sends it a mouse message.

Finally, click anywhere on the card where there are no buttons or fields. With no other objects in its way, HyperCard sends the mouseUp message initially to the card, as described earlier. But since you placed the mouseUp message in the background, the message has to go up one level before executing the command to sound five beeps.

One last part of the experiment will further demonstrate the ways messages wend their way up the hierarchy. You'll be adding one script to the stack level and removing one of the button scripts.

1. Hold down the Shift key and choose Stack Info... from the Objects menu.

   This brings you to the Script Editor for the Beeper stack you've been working in. The handlers in the Script Editor came from the Home Stack when you created this stack.

2. Type the following script at the bottom of the Editor

```
on mouseUp
    beep 10
end mouseUp
```

   and click the OK button.

3. Select the Button tool, hold down the Shift key, and double-click on the One Beep button.

4. Select the entire script with the text cursor, and press the Backspace key to remove the script.

Can you predict what will happen when you click on the One Beep button? Work it out in your mind. When you click on the One Beep button, HyperCard will send a mouseUp message to that button. Since you just removed the mouseUp message handler from that button's script, the message will work its way up the hierarchy, searching for a matching handler. It won't find one until it reaches the background, which has a five-beep script in it (Figure 19–12).

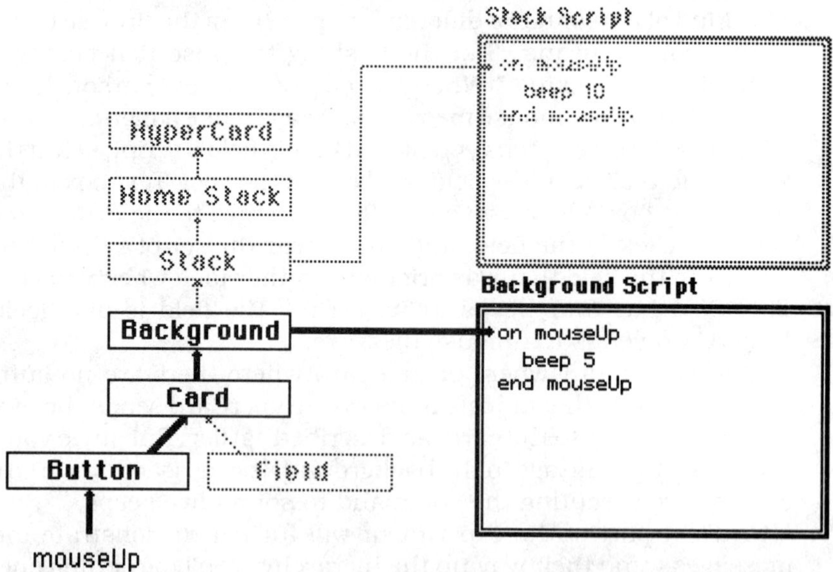


*Figure 19–12. With the mouseUp handler removed from the One Beep button's script, the message goes all the way to the background, which has a mouseUp handler to trap the message.*

So what happened to the stack script and its ten beeps? Well, since all mouseUp messages start their journeys at the button, field, or card levels, any untrapped mouseUp message (like the one sent to the One Beep button) will be trapped for sure in the background script in this sample stack. No matter what you click on, the mouseUp message will never pass higher up the ladder than the background level.

HyperTalk offers two ways of modifying the path that a message takes, but we won't go into too much detail about them at this time. One way lets an object "pass" a message through its own level and continue up the hierarchy. Another method is to write a message that sends a message to an object. For example, you can type into the Message Box a message that sends the mouseUp message to the Beeper stack. Try it now. Type

```
send "mouseUp" to this stack
```

into the Message Box. When you press Return, you'll be assaulted by a beep barrage. What you have done is sent a system message to start at an object other than its normal starting place. As you'll see in later chapters, this feature is a valuable tool in any HyperCard author's arsenal.

## *System Messages*

The messages HyperCard sends to objects—as differentiated from messages sent by scripts—concern the state of the Macintosh system at any given instant. These messages, therefore, are called system messages. While such messages are most frequently mouse-related, they may also reveal what's going on with certain keys of the keyboard and actions that HyperCard is itself taking, such as creating new objects or deleting objects.

We can now examine each of the HyperCard system messages. We'll look at what goes on to generate them and why they go initially to the objects they do.

### MOUSEDOWN, MOUSESTILLDOWN, AND MOUSEUP

What you probably consider to be one action—clicking the mouse button—HyperCard sees as three distinct actions: pressing the mouse button, holding the button down, and releasing the button. Each one of those actions triggers a HyperCard message.

The instant you press the mouse button, HyperCard sends a mouseDown message to the appropriate object, which may be a button, field, or card, depending on the object that "sees" the Browse tool when you press the button. You would trap for a mouseDown message when you wish to carry out some script when the mouse button is pressed, but before the button is released.

All the while the mouse button is held down, HyperCard sends a steady stream of mouseStillDown messages to the current object. The messages come at a pace of many times each second. We can't demonstrate the exact speed of these mouseStillDown messages, but we can show you how to watch the process in action.

1. Create a new button with the following script:
```
on mouseStillDown
    add 1 to the Message Box
end mouseStillDown
```
2. Before clicking on the button, show the Message Box (type Command-M) and type a zero into it.
3. Press and hold the mouse button with the Browse tool atop the new button.

   Each time HyperCard sends the mouseStillDown message, the button's script traps it and increments the content of the Message Box by one.

While the increase of the value in the Message Box might seem fast, it is really much slower than the frequency of the mouseStillDown messages coming from HyperCard. Each time HyperCard sends the message, the script must take extra time carrying out the script's commands and displaying the new value on the screen. When it doesn't have to update the screen, HyperCard sends messages many times faster than what you see.

Use the above button and script to observe one additional property of the mouseStillDown message. HyperCard sends the mouseStill-Down message to the same object that received the mouseDown message when you pressed the mouse button. Therefore, if you hold down the mouse button and drag the Browse tool outside the button, the button will keep getting the mouseStillDown messages, and the value in the Message Box will keep increasing. Conversely, if you press the mouse button outside the button, hold down the mouse button, and drag the Browse tool into the screen button, HyperCard keeps sending the mouseStillDown message to the card, not the button. The value in the Message Box won't budge, even when you drag the tool into the button's region. Therefore, keep in mind that the mouseDown and mouseStillDown messages from a single press of the mouse button *go to the same object.*

At the release of the mouse button, HyperCard sends the mouseUp message to the current object, provided the Browse tool is atop the same object it was at the time HyperCard sent the mouseDown message. On the first pass, this may sound a bit confusing, but as you'll see in a moment, the special behavior properties of the mouseDown message follow exactly the way the mouse behaves in a regular Macintosh application. To demonstrate, we'll look at how items in a typical dialog box respond to the mouse.

1. Choose Page Setup from the File menu.

   You'll see the Page Setup dialog box.

2. Place the arrow cursor atop one of the radio buttons that is not selected (Figure 19-13), but don't press the mouse button just yet.

3. Now press and hold the mouse button without moving the cursor on the screen. Do not release the mouse button yet.

   Notice that the inside lining of the radio button has darkened a bit. This is visual feedback that you are about to select this button (Figure 19-14).

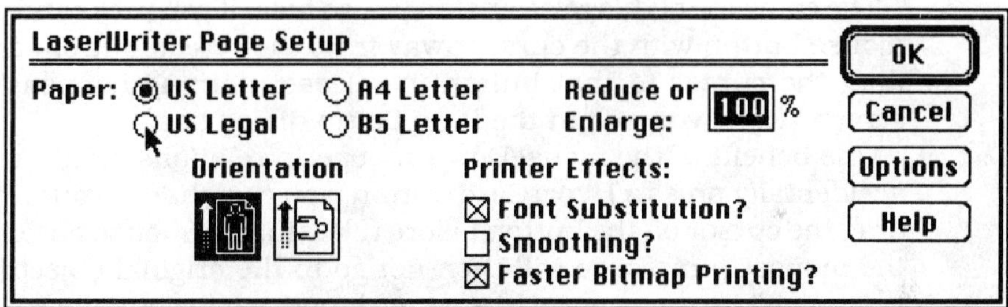


*Figure 19-13. Place the cursor atop one of the radio buttons, but don't press it yet.*

*Figure 19-14. When you press the mouse button and hold it down, the button highlights somewhat, providing visual feedback that you are about to select this button.*

4. While still holding down the mouse button, drag the cursor away from the button toward the bottom of the screen.

   The instant the cursor leaves the region of the button, its inside lining unhighlights, showing you that it will not be selected when you release the mouse button.

5. Now release the mouse button.

   Nothing changed on the screen, because the mouseUp action took place off the button in which the mouseDown action occurred.

Let's stop for a moment and analyze what happened here in HyperCard terms. If this were a HyperCard card, you'd say that HyperCard sent a mouseDown message when you pressed the mouse button atop the screen button. As long as you continued to keep the mouse button depressed, HyperCard was sending mouseStillDown messages to the screen button, even when you dragged the cursor away from the button. But when you released the mouse button, HyperCard didn't send a mouseUp message, because the mouseUp action occurred somewhere other than in the object of the mouseDown action.

The converse of this relationship is also true. If you press and hold the mouse button with the cursor away from the screen button, and then drag the cursor to that button to release, nothing happens on the screen. Try it yourself in the Page Setup dialog box.

One benefit of the mouseDown-mouseUp relationship is that if you accidentally press a HyperCard button, you can change your mind and drag the cursor off the button before releasing the mouse button. Since the mouseUp message will then not go to the original object (in fact, there won't be any mouseUp message), nothing in your stack changes.

All of this is explanation for the reason behind most mouse-based scripts in HyperTalk being mouseUp message handlers, as opposed to mouseDown handlers, as you might expect at first glance. Anytime you write a script that is to be in response to a traditional click of the mouse button, put that script inside a mouseUp message handler. That's precisely the behavior found in mainstream Macintosh buttons.

## MOUSEENTER, MOUSEWITHIN, AND MOUSELEAVE

Three other mouse-based messages are directly related to the position of the cursor on the screen with respect to objects like buttons and fields. HyperCard sends these messages to buttons and fields whenever the cursor enters the object's screen region, while the cursor is in that region, and when the cursor exits the object's screen region, respectively. At no time is the mouse button pressed when HyperCard sends these messages. These are excellent examples of the kinds of messages HyperCard sends when you believe not much is going on.

If you wish to see how these messages work, especially in relation to the mouse button messages described above, place the following handlers into a button script:

```
on mouseStillDown
    add 1 to the Message Box
end mouseStillDown

on mouseEnter
    beep 1
end mouseEnter

on mouseWithin
    add 10 to the Message Box
end mouseWithin

on mouseLeave
    beep 2
end mouseLeave
```

With this set of handlers, HyperCard will do the following: When you move the cursor inside the screen button, HyperCard will beep once; while the cursor is inside the button, the value of the number in the Message Box will increase in increments of ten; when you press and hold down the mouse button while the cursor is inside the screen button, the Message Box value will increment only by one, since the mouseStillDown message will be sent to the button instead of the mouseWithin message; when you release the mouse button with the cursor still inside the screen button, the Message Box value will return to incrementing by ten; and when you move the cursor outside the screen button area, HyperCard will beep twice. To gain further experience with the operation of all mouse-related messages, experiment with the above scripts by dragging the cursor in and out of the button with the mouse button pressed.

It is unlikely that you'd put handlers for mouseEnter, mouseWithin, or mouseLeave messages in objects other than fields and buttons, since the cursor can't really "leave" or "enter" a card or background, both of which take up the entire screen. Still, these mouse messages go up the hierarchy just like any untrapped message.

## NEW AND DELETE OBJECT MESSAGES

Each kind of HyperCard object, from button and field through stack, can be created and deleted by various means. As you'll come to appreciate the more you work with HyperTalk and HyperCard, there will be times when you will want to trap for the creation or deletion of an object. For example, when the user of the stack creates a new telephone log card, the stack will trap for the newCard message and insert the current date and time into fields on the new card. Or you may wish to warn a user that when they delete a button in a stack they should make special modifications elsewhere.

Each time a new button, field, or card is created or deleted, HyperCard sends a relevant message of that event initially to the same level as the object that was created or deleted. On creating and deleting backgrounds or stacks, the corresponding messages are sent to the current card. Therefore, when you choose New Card from the Edit menu, HyperCard sends a newCard message to that new card. In the case of a new object created with a menu selection (for example, New Card, New Field, etc.), the object won't have any scripts in it to trap for the newCard message, so the handler for that message should go into a higher level, such as the background or stack. But if you clone a field or button (holding down the Option key and dragging a copy from the original), the object can already have a newField or newButton message handler in it to respond to HyperCard's messages.

## OPEN AND CLOSE OBJECTS

Every object *except* the button opens and closes. When you click on any text field to insert or edit text, you open that field. If you modify the contents of a field and then either select another field or click the mouse outside of the field, you close that first field. Each time you navigate to a new card, you open that card. Proceeding to the next card in the stack closes the first card and opens the next one. A background opens when you arrive at a new background from a different one. A stack opens when you go to that stack; a stack closes when you go to a different stack.

It's not so much that the objects actually open and close as it is HyperCard sending messages like openStack and closeField on those occasions. These are system messages, like the others we've been discussing so far, because HyperCard sends these messages after reacting to what is occurring inside HyperCard.

Open and close messages are relatively common in HyperTalk scripts. For example, if you design a stack that has cards describing cities around the world, you will want HyperCard to calculate the current time in the city when you open the card. To accomplish that, you'd need a script that traps for the openCard message. In another common use, a HyperCard stack should restore certain settings when it closes. For instance, if your stack turns off the menubar when it opens (in response to an openStack message), it should show the menus when it closes (in response to a closeStack message) so that the user has menus available when going to another stack.

## RETURNKEY, ENTERKEY, AND TABKEY

HyperCard monitors whether the user presses the Return, Enter, and Tab keys outside of text fields, and sends corresponding messages. As with mouse-related messages, the keyboard messages are not sent when you are editing text in a text field. Recall that in field text editing, the Return key advances the text pointer to the next line in the field; the Enter key closes the field by removing the text pointer from whatever field it is in; and the Tab key advances the text pointer to the next field on the card. Therefore, these keys won't affect HyperTalk scripts from their text field activities.

How you decide to trap returnKey, enterKey, and tabKey messages will vary markedly from one stack to another. One potentially helpful application is to avoid possible confusion between the Find and Message capabilities of the Message Box. If you instead create a stack button that prompts the user (inside a separate dialog box) for a search string, you can create scripts that let the user continue searching for that string by pressing the Return key, just as if the search string were in a Find Box.

Being able to trap for these three keys will prove a flexible feature when you start developing your own stacks.

## ARROWKEY

Each time you press one of the arrow keys on the keyboard, HyperCard sends an arrowKey message plus the name of the key as a parameter, as in *arrowKey left* or *arrowKey down*. The advantage to trapping for these keyboard actions is that you can intercept or modify these actions when you don't want the standard actions to apply (see chapter 2 for details on standard arrow key actions).

A good example is in a multiple-background stack. If you wish to keep the browser in a single background while he presses the left and right arrow keys, you would include a message handler in the background or stack that traps for the arrowKey message. If the parameter sent along with the message is "left," then have the script go to the next card only in the current background. That means that when the browser is at the first card of the background and presses the left arrow key, the script wraps the progression through cards around to the last card of the background. You would include a similar trap for the "right" parameter.

## DOMENU

HyperCard gives its programmers complete control over the way a browser accomplishes tasks through menus. Each time a menu command or its Command-key equivalent is invoked, HyperCard sends a doMenu message, with the menu item as a parameter, as in *doMenu Find...* or *doMenu Home.* The parameter is spelled exactly as it appears in the menu, complete with three dots (an ellipsis) if they're in the menu.

By trapping for menu commands, you can do things like disable specific menu items for the sake of information or stack protection. Or you may wish to enhance certain menu commands, like flip to a "good-bye" card when the user chooses Home from the Go menu. If you recall the arrowKey trap to keep browsers in the same background, you would do the same kind of trapping for the Next and Previous menu items in the Go menu.

You must be aware, however, that when you trap for doMenu, every menu selection gets trapped at the same time, even though you want to trap for only one or two items. To let other menu selections work their way up to HyperCard for execution, you'll have to *pass* the message along the hierarchy. Here's a typical script that traps for the Home menu command.

```
on doMenu item
    if item is "Home"
    then put "Thanks for browsing" into Message Box
    pass doMenu
end doMenu
```

We'll be covering the if-then-else and pass constructions later, but this should keep you out of trouble if you rush to experiment now.

By the way, if you discover that you entered a doMenu message handler into a card or background script without the pass command, you won't be able to open the Script Editor for that object. To get out of this jam, type one of the following command lines into the Message Box (even if you have to type blindly into a hidden Message Box).

```
set script of this card to empty
```

or

```
set script of this background to empty
```

Unfortunately, if there were other message handlers in the object's script, they'll be erased with these commands. Therefore, experiment with doMenu in object scripts that have no other message handlers in them.

## IDLE

Several times we have demonstrated that HyperCard sends the idle message when nothing apparently seems to be going on in a stack. Interestingly, when HyperCard sends a mouseWithin message, it alternates between the mouseWithin and idle messages. This occurs so quickly that it may appear as though HyperCard is sending both messages simultaneously. Let's examine this in slow motion so you can witness what's going on behind the scenes.

To demonstrate this, you'll be putting an idle message handler in a card script and a mouseWithin handler in a button script. Each handler will perform a different arithmetic operation on a value in the Message Box. The idle handler will increment the value by 10; the mouseWithin handler will increment the value by 1. Before you begin, make sure the Message Box is either empty or has a zero in it.

1. If you still have one of the sample buttons from an earlier experiment, open its script dialog box.

   If not, create a new button and click on the Script button in the Button Info dialog box.

2. If the button has other scripts in it, delete them all so that nothing will interfere with your experiment.

3. Type the following script into the button's script dialog box:

   ```
   on mouseWithin
           add 1 to message
           wait 20
   end mouseWithin
   ```

   and click the OK button.

4. Hold down the Shift key and choose Card Info... from the Objects menu to reach the card's script dialog box.

5. Make sure there is no other "on idle" message handler in the script.

   If there is, delete it.

6. Carefully type the following script into the card's script dialog box:

   ```
   on idle
           add 10 to message
           wait 20
   end idle
   ```

   and click the OK button.

The addition of the "wait 20" commands will slow things down enough so you can see how the idle and mouseWithin messages work with each other. When you close the card's script dialog box, the value in the Message Box should be slowly incrementing by 10. Move the Browse tool into the button containing the mouseWithin script you just entered and watch what happens in the Message Box. The value increments by 10, then 1, then 10, and then 1 again. The instant you remove the Browse tool from the button, the increment returns to the idle's 10 only.

If you press the mouse button, HyperCard stops sending the idle or mouseWithin messages, because it is busy sending the mouseDown and mouseStillDown messages to whatever object the Browse tool is atop at the moment, whether it be the card or button.

Idle handlers can be useful for effects such as displaying an elapsed timer on a card, in which the current time is continually being placed into a text field. The Home card has just such a message handler in its script.

## STARTUP, SUSPEND, RESUME, AND QUIT

Four system messages let you trap for your movement into and out of HyperCard. HyperCard sends a startUp message to the first card of the stack that HyperCard opens at the beginning of a session. If you double-click on the HyperCard icon from the Macintosh desktop, HyperCard will automatically start up with the Home stack. But you can also start with a different stack if you double-click on the icon of a HyperCard stack on the Desktop. In that case, HyperCard sends the startUp message to the first card of that stack. StartUp message handlers, however, are more often placed in the stack script, since it is more natural to think about the stack starting up than the card.

The quit message functions similarly to the startUp message, except HyperCard sends it when it receives the Quit command from the File menu (or a press of Command-Q or a script message that performs the Quit operation). A good application of the quit message would be to trap for it and display a good-bye card directed at the user.

Both the suspend and resume messages revolve around HyperCard's ability to run (launch, or open) other Macintosh applications from within HyperCard. When you open another application, HyperCard sends the suspend message. When you quit the external application, you automatically come back to HyperCard at the exact spot from which you launched. HyperCard sends the resume message, meaning you are resuming your HyperCard session.

It's important to recognize that a resume message is entirely different from a startUp message. Therefore, if your Home stack script features special instructions upon start-up, such as showing the Message Box at a particular location, then the same instructions should be in the resume script so that the same settings will be in effect when you come back from running an external application. If you inspect the HyperCard Home Stack script, you'll see that HyperCard goes through identical setup procedures (in a long message handler called getHomeInfo) both on startUp and resume.

That concludes the list of HyperCard system messages and their workings within the hierarchy. There aren't that many, yet they carry the bulk of what your stacks will be working with. You'll also be able to create your own HyperTalk messages and message handlers, which we'll get to in a later chapter.

## *Where to Place Message Handlers*

Since HyperCard system messages can go in so many different levels of the hierarchy, you may be concerned about choosing the "correct" location for various message handlers. Of course, handlers for field- or button-specific functions belong in those objects. But you may often be faced with the choice of putting a message handler in the stack or background object. Moreover, as a stack design evolves, you want to know that your script work won't be in vain.

As a general rule, place your scripts as low in the hierarchy as you deem feasible. For instance, a newCard message handler is best placed in the background rather than in the card, even if your stack design seems to call for only one background. By placing the script in the background, you leave yourself open to adding new functionality to the stack in the form of another background design for a second group of cards (perhaps a help section) with its own newCard message handler.

Later, when you learn to make your own HyperTalk messages and message handlers, you'll begin to load up your Home stack with all kinds of useful scripts that simplify your stack creation or navigation around your HyperCard world. The reason these handlers will go into your Home stack is because you'll want access to them from any stack or card you use. When the handler is in the Home stack, you know for certain that the message will find its handler. If the handler is in a different stack, you'll have access to it only from within that stack.

A stack with a single background would place most of its handlers in the background. A stack with only one card would have most of its handlers in the card, including handlers like openStack and closeStack.

The bottom line, then, is to think through the intended scope of each message handler before assigning it to an object's script. Do your best to visualize all the possibilities of where you'll be in your HyperCard world when you want that handler to come to life. Start visualizing with the handler in the Home stack. Then try it one level lower, in the stack object, and see if it "works" there. Keep inching down the hierarchy until you find that the handler will no longer be accessible from every possible circumstance. Then place the handler in the object one rung above that. Study the card, background, and stack scripts in the HyperCard Home Stack to see how handlers are assigned to various hierarchy levels.

## External Resources

One of the exciting design features of HyperCard is that it is open-ended to the extent that experienced Macintosh programmers can literally write their own extensions to HyperCard's powers. If HyperCard doesn't contain a command or feature that you want, you can add it in Pascal, C, or assembly languge, provided you have the know-how for such explorations. The additional programming you'd add would be turned into a chunk of computer code called a resource.

Resources can be added to a HyperCard stack using a resource mover utility program. The resource code bears the name of a command you would put in a HyperTalk script or type into the Message Box. When HyperCard sends the message with that command in it, the message works its way up the hierarchy.

When it reaches the stack level, the message first seeks a match in the stack script. If there is no match there, it looks for a match in an external resource, if one is attached to the file. It follows the same procedure at the Home Stack level, as well. If there is still no match, then HyperCard shows the alert box that it can't understand that command.

Many third-party HyperCard developers are taking advantage of this resource extensibility of HyperCard to build in many features you can't get from HyperCard alone. You will find these HyperCard resources circulating among user groups and electronic bulletin boards. They may even intrigue you enough to pursue learning one of the development languages for the Macintosh so that you can write your own resources. This feature makes HyperCard the kind of software "engine" you can't really outgrow.

## *Inheritance*

In all our discussions about the HyperCard hierarchy and the passing of messages, we've been taking the perspective of the message—watching the message start at one object level and claw its way up the ladder. More traditional approaches to the object orientation of the HyperTalk language might look at this hierarchical system from the opposite direction, that is, how objects lower in the hierarchy bear resemblances to certain properties of objects higher up the ladder. Let's take as an example the relationship between two HyperCard objects, the stack and the background.

If we start off with a stack, we know its properties. From there we can define an object, called a background, which has some of the properties of a stack (its ability to pass messages, for instance) but also some unique properties of its own, such as its graphics layer. In a more formal object-oriented language, we'd say that the background inherits the properties of the stack and then adds some properties of its own.

A favorite way for writers to explain inheritance is to use some profession, like accountants or physicians, as a metaphor. For example, all doctors have a basic core of medical training, which they pick up during their medical school years. As each doctor progresses through schooling and residency, he or she picks up a specialty. Despite the specialty, the doctor inherits all the basic medical knowledge by virtue of going through medical school.

Now, this is grossly oversimplified, compared to the structure of a full object-oriented language, like SmallTalk or MacApp (an object-oriented Pascal language available to professional Macintosh programmers). But the point is that these languages start with a core of objects from which the programmer creates derivative objects (descendants, as it were), which inherit some or all properties of their ancestors and add some of their own. HyperCard, on the other hand, has already predefined the derivative objects from the HyperCard "object." Those are the now-familiar Home, stack, background, card, field, and button. Since these objects are already defined, we can take a simpler view of how the HyperTalk object-oriented system works. We can watch a message be sent to one object and passed up the hierarchy until it finds a match (or disappears without a match). This viewpoint is so much easier to visualize that we can leave further discussions of inheritance to the textbooks.

## CHAPTER 20

# Introduction to HyperTalk Commands

THE BULK OF THE MESSAGES YOU WRITE IN YOUR HYPERTALK SCRIPTS START WITH HyperTalk commands—those operations, like Go, built into HyperCard. In most cases, your scripts elsewhere in the stack won't trap for these command words, because you'll want HyperCard to carry them out unaltered.

HyperTalk command words comprise a large portion of the vocabulary of the HyperTalk language. The commands also make your stacks come to life, performing tasks that affect the information stored in cards and that affect how you or another browser interacts with the stack application. It is therefore essential that you understand the meaning of each word in the command and function vocabulary (functions are covered in chapters 28–32). You may not use every command word in your stacks, but the more you know about the capabilities of the language, the easier it becomes to dream of HyperCard applications. In fact, chances are that many of the capabilities of HyperTalk commands and functions will give you ideas for stacks and information management tasks you'd like your Macintosh to perform for you.

In the next seven chapters, we'll examine each command word, explaining what it does, how it might be used in a stack, and anything you should watch out for when using it. Each command's explanation will be a stand-alone section, so you can use this part of the book later as a reference guide to a particular command you wish to place in a stack of your own design. To make it easier to learn the commands and find them later, we've divided the words into groups of related commands, within each group, from the simple to the complex..

Before we jump into the commands, however, we must explain conventions we use to list the parameters of each command.

## *Notation Conventions*

Virtually every HyperTalk command requires additional words following it. Usually, the words, known as *parameters*, describe what the command should be working on. For example, in the command "Go next card," the words "next card" define where HyperCard should "go" as the result of the command. Depending on the nature of the command, parameters may be text, numbers, or a combination of the two. Moreover, some commands have more than one parameter.

### COMMAND PARAMETERS

To designate a parameter in the following listings, we'll use the same notation convention you'll find in the HyperCard on-line help system. All parameters are enclosed inside less than and greater than symbols (< and >). Please note: This notation is for the convenience of the listings only; none of the enclosing symbols or brackets actually appears in a HyperTalk script.

The word used to describe the parameter tries to detail the nature of the parameter that HyperCard expects to find after each command. For example, the "next card" parameter is called a destination, since it specifies a location to which HyperCard should "go." Therefore, the command notation would be

go <destination>

This means that any valid destination may be substituted for "next card" in a Go command (we'll see what constitutes a valid destination in a moment).

Some commands also have parameters that you don't always need, depending on the circumstances. If you don't fill in this parameter, HyperCard usually assumes some default or previous setting. For example, the Play command has an optional parameter, which specifies the tempo at which some musical notes should be played. If you don't supply the tempo parameter, HyperCard assumes you mean the tempo that is currently in effect. Notation for this type of parameter consists of square brackets enclosing the name of the parameter, as follows

play <voice> [tempo <tempo>] <notes>

Notice that there is a word inside the square brackets but outside the optional parameter's symbols, the word "tempo." What this means is that if you specify the tempo parameter, you must also precede it with the word "tempo." Therefore, an actual two-parameter command line in a script would look like

play "Harpsichord" tempo 120 "c d e f g a b c"

You'll see apparently free-standing words in the command notations quite often, as in

multiply <destination> by <source>

which mean that you must have two parameters (neither one is optional, since there are no square brackets), and they must be separated by the word "by."

## OPTIONAL COMMAND WORDS

HyperTalk tries to emulate the English language as much as possible so that newcomers to programming will feel comfortable issuing commands they recognize. At the same time, a more experienced HyperTalk user may prefer to issue commands in shorter forms. To accommodate the newcomer, HyperTalk accepts additional words in several commands that make it easier to understand the meaning of the command. The Go command is a good example.

A more natural-sounding Go command would be "go to," as in "Go to card ID 300." HyperTalk will accept either form, although it considers the "to" as optional. The notation that shows you which command words are optional are square brackets. Therefore, the notation of the Go command now reads

go [to] <destination>

You can use the "to" if you wish, but it is not mandatory.

Several HyperTalk commands accept more than one word as parameters or parameter separators. For example, the Put command lets you put a source before, into, or after a destination. HyperTalk accepts any one of the three prepositions as a valid parameter separator. In the following chapters' listings, the command notation that shows your choice of alternatives is a vertical bar between the choices, as in

before | into | after

resulting in a final notation of

put <source> before | into | after <destination>

for the Put command. In all the command explanations in the following chapters, we'll provide several examples of what real command lines look like, so don't be too frightened by the apparent complexity of this notation. With a little practice, it will become second nature to you.

## *Containers*

Many HyperTalk commands perform operations on information. But for this to occur, the information must be located someplace that a script can access by name or number. These places are called *containers*, and they take many forms in HyperCard.

Among the most recognizable containers are text fields and variables. Now add to that list the special It variable, the Message Box, and any text selected in a field, which automatically becomes a container called "selection." All these containers hold information that can change as the result of a HyperTalk command acting on that container.

All containers store the information in text form, even when the text is all numbers. If the HyperTalk command expects a number in the containers it deals with, HyperCard will internally turn the text numbers into values for the command to work on. Even if some arithmetic is performed on the value of numbers in a container and a new number is placed back in the container, it goes back into the container in the same text form. This eliminates the nasty prerequisite in most information storage programs (databases) of predefining a field as either a numeric or text field. In HyperCard, the same container may be called upon to hold what seems to be a numeric value at one time, and a text string at another, or a date at yet another time.

A comforting feature about containers is that whatever you can do to information in one kind of container, say a field, you can do to any other kind of container, say It. You can treat all containers the same, as far as manipulating their information is concerned. But you must respect their distinctive properties.

### FIELDS

All fields hold information for a single card, whether the field is in the background or card layer. Therefore, when you refer to a field in a HyperTalk script, you will usually refer to the field by its domain (background or card), by the field name or number, and by the name or number of the card in which the field is located (unless it is the current card). The form would be "card field ID 203 of card 'Jane'" in a script. If you don't specify a domain for a field, HyperCard assumes that you mean a background field. But if the field you're referring to is a card field, you must specify the card domain as part of its notation.

One special property of fields that no other containers have is that a field retains its contents even if you quit HyperCard. The information stored in a field is written to the disk before you close a card.

Information stored in all other containers is *volatile*, meaning that it disappears at various times, as noted below.

## LOCAL VARIABLES

You may recall our discussion about local variables in chapter 18. A local variable is assigned a name when you place information into it. From there, you can perform any HyperTalk operation on the information that you would with any other container, provided you perform the operation within the same handler that created the variable in the first place. A simple script involving a variable would look like this:

```
on mouseUp
    put 10 into hat          -- creates a variable named "hat" and
                             -- stores 10 into it
    add 20 to hat            -- adds 20 to the value stored in "hat"
    put hat into Message     -- places a duplicate of the
                             -- contents of "hat" (which is now 30)
                             -- into the Message Box
end mouseUp
```

The instant that this script ends, the variable "hat" is no longer remembered, nor is its content. Therefore, you use local variables as temporary holding places while a handler is running.

You don't really see variables, like you do fields and the Message Box. When you store information in a variable, you have to trust that HyperCard will keep the information intact (it does). You can store as much information in a variable as you can in a field, including multiple lines of text.

## IT

The special local variable, It, is not remembered after the end of the handler it is used in.

As you'll learn shortly, It is the recipient of much information available about objects. For example, you can issue a HyperTalk command that gets the screen coordinates of a particular button. HyperCard places that information into It, where you can retrieve the data and do whatever you planned for that information. You also have complete access to It, just as with any variable, but you should be aware when HyperTalk's other commands might overwrite whatever is in that variable. For that reason, use the It variable only when you know for certain that no other HyperTalk operation will change its contents between the time you store something there and need to retrieve it.

### GLOBAL VARIABLES

As a container, a global variable is identical to a local variable, with one exception. The content of a global variable is not forgotten when a handler using it ends. Therefore, you can use a global variable to hold information between scripts, even if the scripts are in objects of different stacks. HyperCard keeps global variables alive, independent of the stacks you open and close. Once you quit HyperCard, however, the global variable and its content are erased.

Creating a global variable is a slightly different process than creating a local variable. In chapter 24, you'll meet a HyperTalk command that both gives a global variable life and lets HyperCard know that you're going to use a previously created global variable in a script.

### THE MESSAGE BOX

Perhaps the most "physical" container in HyperCard is the Message Box. Designed as a window, you can drag it around the screen, taking its contents wherever it goes.

The Message Box differs from other containers in one important respect. It holds only one line of text. Even if you try to put a multiple-lined chunk of text into the Message Box, only the first line is stored there.

The content of the Message Box is erased when you quit HyperCard.

### SELECTION

Whenever you click and drag across text in a card or background field, that selected text becomes a container called Selection— like a container (selection) in a container (field). Scripts may then treat its contents like any container, including putting it into another container, performing arithmetic with it, or even replacing it with the contents of a different container.

Programming scripts to work with selection is more convenient for the user than making him Command-drag over text to pick it up before searching or dialing.

## *Container Components*

Since a container may hold many words and lines of text, your scripts need a way of accessing individual pieces of that text. For example, if a three-line field in a card has three telephone numbers in it, you may wish a button script to dial only the number in the first line. The script needs to extract the first line from the entire field.

Information in a container consists of four different components: items, characters, words, and lines.

## ITEMS

An item is any string of text between commas. For example, if a field named "Friend" has "Joe Jones, 1212 Main Street, Brooklyn, Iowa, 50040" in it, there are five separate items in that container. If you then want a script to put only some items into another card, you could single out the name as

```
item 1 of field "Friend"
```

HyperCard interprets this line as meaning "Joe Jones" in this case, without the following comma. In fact you can try this using the Message Box and the Address stack supplied with HyperCard. Open that stack and create a new card, which you'll use as a testing ground. Next, type some information into the first field of the card (where the name and address usually go), complete with commas between several words. Into the Message Box now type

```
item 1 of field 1
```

HyperCard immediately interprets and replaces your phrase with the content of the first item in that field. Try the phrase again with different item numbers. Notice that when you specify an item as a component in some operation, the comma is not carried along with the information. You get the pure information without the comma separators.

## CHARACTERS, WORDS, AND LINES

HyperCard also gives you access to individual characters, words, and lines of a container. Starting from the beginning of the text string in the field, count the number of the character, word, or line you wish to extract or change. Then refer to the component by its name, *character* (or *char*), *word*, or *line*, plus the number.

You may also refer to a range of components by name and number, as in *word 1 to 5 of field "Address."* By extracting a range of components at one time, you will speed numerous text manipulation tasks in HyperTalk.

In its attempt to be more English-like, HyperTalk provides an alternative way to refer to the first ten, the last, the middle, and random components in a container. Instead of referring to *word 1* in a script, for example, you can also write *first word.* HyperTalk provides the following *ordinal* numbers and references:

| | |
|---|---|
| first | eighth |
| second | ninth |
| third | tenth |
| fourth | last |
| fifth | any |
| sixth | mid |
| seventh | middle |

The "any" reference will give you a random component of the container, as in *any word of field ID 109,* while "mid" and "middle" give you the middle component, even of a multiple line field.

## CONCATENATING COMPONENTS

As you begin extracting components from containers in your scripts, you will occasionally find it necessary to join components together in a second container. For example, if you wish a newCard script to place the current hour in a new card's Time field, you could call upon HyperCard's *the time* function, which returns the 12-hour time in a form like 4:10 PM. But since you don't want the minutes to appear in the Time field, then you'll need to build the contents of that field from components. You would want to join the hour and the AM/PM designation together. Joining text like this is called concatenating (kon-kat'-en-a-ting) text.

In HyperTalk, the mechanism that concatenates two pieces of text is the ampersand symbol: &. When this symbol appears between two pieces of text, the pieces are immediately considered one piece. Watch how this works, using the Message Box and the Address stack you used a moment ago.

1. Clear the text in the new card you just created.
2. Type the word "hello" into the first line of the name field.
3. Now type the following statement into the Message Box:

```
char 5 of field 1 & char 1 of field 1
```

Granted it's a long way to go to get HyperCard to say "oh" in the Message Box, but this exercise demonstrates how the ampersand works to concatenate text.

Notice, however, that there are no spaces between the components joined by the ampersand. That's fine when you're joining characters into a word, but you will need spaces when joining words together. To add a space while concatenating components, type two ampersands together, as in

word 1 of field "Names" && word 3 of field "Names"

If you need even more spaces, you can place strings of spaces amid the components being joined, such as

word 1 of field ID 908 & "     " & word 5 of field ID 908

## COMPONENTS OF COMPONENTS—CHUNKS

So far, we've been looking at how you refer to single components inside a container. But you can also specify a component in relation to other components inside that container. If the first line of a field contains two four-letter words separated by a space, you could refer to the beginning letter of the second word as being either the sixth character (four characters of the first word plus one space character) or the first character of the second word (char 1 of word 2).

You can freely "nest" these component expressions—*chunk expressions*, they're called—as you see fit. You specify chunk expressions from the narrowest to the broadest chunks, as in "char 2 of word 3 of item 1 of line 6 of field 10."

We can now move onto the actual commands in the HyperTalk language. We'll cover them in logical families to help you better learn the commands in context.

# CHAPTER 21

# Navigation Commands

Among the most common HyperTalk commands you'll use in your scripts are navigation commands— those that take the user from one card or stack to another. Also in this group is the Find command, which lets you add much perceived power to button scripts, since a click of such a button will not only go to another card or stack but will locate desired information for the user. All the other commands in this group affect the way the user wends his way through your stacks and HyperCard in general.

## Go

[to] <destination>

**Purpose:** Takes the browser from one card to another card, or from one stack to another stack.

**When to Use It:** A simple shift from one stack to the first card of another stack uses this command, specifying only the name of the stack as a parameter. You can be more specific in your motion to another stack by specifying a particular card in the second stack, if you like. This command also links any two cards together, whether they be in the same stack or different stacks.

While a browser has menu commands and arrow keys available for moving to the next and previous cards, many stacks also have left- and right-facing arrow buttons that perform the same functions as the menu commands— going to the previous and next cards. Any button that links two cards must employ the Go command to make that link happen. In fact, HyperCard itself generates Go commands when you use the Link To... option in the Button Info dialog box. The vast majority of button scripts will contain a Go command.

**PARAMETERS:** The <destination> parameter accepts all possible ways of referring to a card and/or stack in HyperTalk. If the destination is a specific card, the parameter must contain the word "card" somewhere (with exceptions noted below). If you refer to a card by its name, number, or ID number, the form for the parameter would be

```
card "Index 1"
card 24
card ID 4A58
```

All of these identifying names and numbers tacked onto the word "card" can also be inside containers, like fields or variables. For example, if the text "Index 1" were in a variable named "Tom," you could issue the Go command in the following manner:

```
go card Tom
```

Another card destination type is any ordinal number, optionally followed by the word "card," as in

```
go third card
go any card     -- goes to a random card in the stack
go last         -- the word "card" is optional with an ordinal
```

Additional card destinations you can use with or without the word "card" are found in the HyperCard Go menu:

Back
Recent
Previous (and Prev)
Next
Home
Help

If the destination is in another stack, the stack name must be part of the destination parameter, and the stack name should be enclosed in quotes (although it's not mandatory). The word "stack" is optional. For HyperCard to find the stack by itself, the stack must be in a path listed in the Stacks card in the Home Stack. Otherwise, the standard file dialog box will ask you to find the stack file and open it. Optionally, you can spell out the stack's entire file path as part of the stack designator parameter to the Go command. When you specify a stack name as a destination, HyperCard opens the stack and leaves you at the first card of the stack.

**EXAMPLES:**

```
go to card "Index 2" -- a card named "Index 2" in current stack
go "Address"          -- go to first card of a stack named "Address"
go to card ID 431 of stack "Invoices"
go to card "summary" of Invoices
go to background 2          -- the fifth card of the current stack
go any card of stack "Dice" -- a gambler's random call
```

**YOU TRY IT:** From the Home stack, type Command-M to show the Message Box and type in the following series of Go commands. If the Message Box disappears along the way, bring it back into view with Command-M. Watch what happens after you press Return with each command.

```
go "Datebook"
go next
go to card ID 51275 of stack "Help"
go back
put "Datebook" into variable
go second card of variable
go home
```

## find

[char[acter]s | word] <source> [in <field>]

**PURPOSE:** Searches the current stack (or just one field in the current stack) for the occurrence of a text string.

**WHEN TO USE IT:** Use the Find command to search for the occurrence of text in a stack. This is the same Find command that appears in the Message Box when you choose Find from the Go menu. When a script issues the Find command, HyperCard remembers the text the script is searching for. If you then choose Find from the Go menu (or type Command-F), the search text will already be inserted in the Find string.

A Find command is not like the Message Box type of search in one respect. When the Find command performs the first search and comes up with a match other than the one you wanted (for example, a different "John" in your name card file), you can't simply press the Return key right away to keep searching for other occurrences of the text string. Pressing Return becomes a natural reaction to browsing through a stack, to be sure. If you wish to continue browsing for the string in the scripted Find command, choose Find from the Go menu and then press Return (or Enter). You won't have to retype the find string, because HyperCard automatically inserts the last text it was asked to find.

If your overall goal is to find text in a card from a different stack, then make it a two-step process. In the first step, use the Go command to get to the desired stack. In the second step, use the Find command.

**Parameters:** You can instruct HyperCard to search for a match of the text either as a whole word or just as characters within a word. When you don't specify one or the other (as happens in the Message Box), HyperCard assumes you want to search for whole words only. This is the most likely type of search you'll want your stacks to perform. But if you wish to search for characters inside words (like "our" inside "source"), then specify either *chars* or *characters* after the command.

The <source> parameter is a common parameter type, standing for any kind of container, like the contents of a field or variable. Therefore, you can type in a specific text string for the Find command to look for if you wish, like

```
find "Harry"
```

but string-specific searches are usually more appropriate for Message Box searches, in which you type the text to search. In scripts, you will more often use a container as the source of search text.

There will also be times when it is appropriate to search for the results of a function, particularly date and time functions. For example, if you have a daily appointment book that has each day's date listed in a field in the format returned by the date function, you can use that function as the source of the search string, as in

```
find the date
```

But since searches are done on the text makeup of the date function, the format of the dates in the card fields must be identical to that of the function used to search for the card (see chapter 30 on time and date functions).

It is sometimes helpful to narrow the search to a single background field with the <field> parameter. Two benefits shine brightly for narrowing the search. The first is that the Find command will not stop on a match in a field you're not interested in. Second, the searching will take less time, because HyperCard will find fewer possible matches when it performs its searching wonders.

A field parameter, which must be separated from the source parameter by "in," requires the word "field" and some identifier to single out which field you wish. The three ways of identifying a field—name, number, and ID number—apply here, so you can say,

```
find "Harry" in field "Name"
```

You may also use ordinal field numbers if you prefer, such as

```
find "Harry" in second field
```

**Examples:**

find field 1 in field 2
find variable1 -- concatenate text into a variable to find
find "312-" in field "Area Codes"

**You Try It:** Go to the Address stack, show the Message Box, and type in the following commands. After typing each command, press the Return key a few times to see how many matches HyperCard finds.

find chars "a"
find word "a"
find "Ron" in field 1
find chars "Ron" in field 1
find "John" in field 2
find "555" in field 2
find chars "22"
find chars "22" in field 2

## push pop

**push** [ this | recent ] card
**pop** card [ into <container> ]

**Purpose:** Push temporarily marks a card for instant retrieval with the Pop command.

**When to Use It:** We can use the old library card catalog metaphor to explain the concept of pushing a card. Imagine that you've found a card to which you want to refer after checking out some other cards. In the library, you might place a slip of yellow paper or other flag that will be easy to find, even if you wander off into other card drawers. When you wish to see that card again, you look for that flag.

In HyperCard, pushing a card is the same as tagging the one card. When you push a card, you can then wander about any HyperCard stacks and cards as you please. To see that marked card, you simply issue the command *Pop card.* HyperCard presents the marked card before your eyes.

Pushing a card frequently makes sense when you are constructing elaborate HyperCard environments for yourself or others, particularly those that branch all over the place. By pushing a card before branching and then offering a button with a script to pop the card, you help the user navigate through the environment, by providing a consistent and convenient method of instantaneously returning to some landmark.

The instant you pop the card, HyperCard removes the marker.

This push and pop terminology didn't originate from a library environment but from a programming concept commonly modeled after a spring-loaded stack of cafeteria trays. When you push a tray onto an existing stack of trays, the one you most recently pushed will be the first one to be pulled off— popped— by the next person in line. As you pop a card, HyperCard displays that card and removes it from the internal pile. It is critical to remember that pushed cards operate in a last-in, first-out environment. Unless your scripts exert unusual control over the browser's navigation through a stack, it's best to push cards no deeper than the topmost level.

Another design consideration is whether the burden of pushing a card belongs to a card prior to linking or to a card after linking. This decision depends on the stack and link structure.

If your links are set up so that the only way to get to card B is from card A, then you can safely place a Push card command in card A's button script that links the two cards. But if the stack is such that several cards link to card B, it will be more efficient to place the command

```
push recent card
```

into the openCard script of card B. Then, no matter what card you were viewing prior to reaching card B, that card will be pushed onto the pile, ready for popping when you're done with card B.

**PARAMETERS:** The Push command requires a parameter only if the card to be pushed was the card prior to the current card. If so, then specify the *recent* parameter. If you don't specify which card to push, HyperCard assumes you mean the current ("this") card.

The Pop command has an optional parameter that lets you pop a card without actually going to that card. You can pop a card into a container. Two things happen when you do this. First, the card comes off the pile without showing it on the screen. Second, the popped card's ID and stack location go into the container you specified.

Let's say you push two cards onto the pile and want to go back to them not in the reverse order (which plain Pop card would do), but in their original order. One way to handle this would be to pop the top card into a global variable, pop the next card to actually go to it, and later go to the card whose ID is stored in the global variable.

**EXAMPLES:**

```
push card
push recent card
pop card
pop card into it
```

**You Try It:** Since there isn't a lot to experiment with in the way of different forms for this command, let's try pushing and popping some. Type the following commands into the Message Box from the Home card:

```
go card 10 of "Address"
push card
go card 3
pop card
pop card      --this takes you back to the Home card
go card 100 of "Help"
push card
go next
push card
go first
pop card into firstOut
pop card
go card firstOut
```

# help

**Purpose:** Brings the user to the HyperCard help system.

**When to Use It:** It's unlikely you'd use this command in a script unless you plan to trap for the help message to bring the user to a stack-specific help system of your own design. HyperCard help is available from the menu (in the Go menu) and a keyboard equivalent (Command-?), so unless you turn off the menus in your application, you can leave access to the HyperCard help system to the menu.

**Parameters:** This command has no parameters.

**Example:**

```
help
```

**You Try It:** Even though the HyperCard help system is available via the menus, you can also access it at any time by typing *help* into the Message Box. Try it now.

# CHAPTER 22

# Action Commands

THE ACTION COMMAND CATEGORY CONTAINS SOME OF THE MOST POWERFUL COMmands in the HyperTalk language. The most important of these is the Put command, which you'll use constantly to move information around among fields, variables, and other containers. Other commands let you do things such as making menu selections from a script, dialing the telephone, launching other Macintosh applications, sorting information stored in fields, and even controlling a videodisc player.

## put

<source> [ into | after | before <container> ]

**PURPOSE:** Moves new information into a container or moves information from one container into another container.

**WHEN TO USE IT:** You'll use the Put command more often than any other command in your HyperCard scripts. This is the command you use to retrieve information from fields for manipulation; it's also the command you use to shift the manipulated information back into fields for display and permanent storage. In the interim, you'll be "putting" information into local and global variables, the Message Box, the selection, and It.

Despite this command's simple syntax, it is capable of rather remarkable information manipulation itself. It allows you not only to insert information anywhere inside a container (for example, between the second and third words of the fourth line) but also to replace one container component with new information without having to disassemble a container's content and reconstruct it.

A typical application of the Put command would be to put the contents of a field into a local variable. Then other HyperTalk commands either perform various operations with the variable or append additional information to the variable. Finally, the information from the variable is put into a field in a different card. This is but one of myriad ways to use the Put command in a script.

**Parameters:** If you do not specify a container parameter, the Put command places the text of the source parameter into the Message Box.

Both the source and container parameters can be containers. That includes any or all components of a container, like the "fifth word of the second line of field ID 40716." Additionally, the source parameter can be any text string or any arithmetic expression. Strings must, of course, be surrounded by quotation marks. Arithmetic expressions are those expressions that would resolve to a number if they were typed into the Message Box.

When you put an all-numeric text string into a container, HyperCard still stores the information as a text string. If, later, you perform an arithmetic operation on the container, HyperCard will try to resolve the contents as a number, so you don't have to worry about whether a digit is looked upon as text or a numeric value. While it is always stored as text, HyperCard will view it as text or number, as the situation warrants. Consequently, the following two commands accomplish the same result:

```
put 10 into field 2
put "10" into field 2
```

Either way, you can later perform arithmetic on field 2.

If you wish to add more than one word from one container to another container, you may do so with the help of ampersand (&) concatenation. For example, you could take the second and third words of two fields and place them into a variable called "box" with this command

```
put word 2 of field 1 && word 3 of field 4 into box
```

with the double ampersand assuring the inclusion of a space character between the two words when they reach the variable, box.

Your choice of preposition (into, before, after) turns out to be a powerful choice. Let's examine what happens with each one.

The *into* choice can best be characterized as the preposition that signals the replacement of the destination container's content by the source's content. Therefore, if your command puts "hello" into a field, then no matter what was originally in that field (or any container), it will be entirely overwritten by the new "hello." You can narrow the original text that is being replaced by the Put into command if you are more specific in naming the destination. An example will help demonstrate this. Say that field 1 contains the following text,

To goof is human

To replace the word "goof" with the word "err," you'd issue the following command:

put "err" into word 2 of field 1

This method of replacing text works with only one container component at a time, but one container component can be a range of components. For example, if the original text in field 1 was

To goof up is human

you could replace "goof up" with "err" by one command

put "err" into word 2 to 3 of field 1

In summary, then, use Put into to replace text in a container.

Also be aware that you initialize a new local variable in a script by putting information into it. In other words, if you say

put "My name is Bill" into greeting

you both create a new local variable, called "greeting," and put the text string into it in one step. Typing this line in the Message Box creates a global variable called "greeting".

One other feature of the *into* preposition has to do with multiple-lined fields. If you wish to place an item into an empty line in a field several lines below the last item, you can simply specify the line number in the destination parameter. HyperCard will automatically place the requisite number of return characters between the last entry and the line of the new information.

With the *before* preposition, you can insert the <source> parameter into an existing container without harming the container's original contents. If the destination container is specified as simply a field or variable, the new information is inserted at the very front of the text in that container. Therefore, still using our "to err is human" field above, we can say

put "Alex Pope says, '" before field 1

which results in field 1 reading

Alex Pope says, 'to err is human

Notice that we place all separating spaces and single quote mark in the text string we're adding to the field. By placing as much of this extra stuff into one text string, we obviate the need to go back and insert spaces, a process that slows the execution of the script.

You can use the "before" preposition and a more detailed destination specification to insert information before a character, word, line, or item in a container. For example, we can now say

put ", the writer, " before word 3 of field 1

to turn field 1 into

Alex Pope, the writer, says, 'to err is human

making sure we add the required spaces to fill out the sentence.

The *after* preposition works just like the *before* preposition, except that it tacks information onto the destination container or component. If we say

put ", to forgive Divine.'" after field 1

the field will read

Alex Pope, the writer, says, 'to err is human, to forgive Divine.'

Similarly, you can put information after any component in a container, such as after the second character or the third item.

An intriguingly powerful ability of the Put command is to post information to containers in cards other than the one you're looking at. The destination card must be in the same stack as the current card, but you don't have to go to it before putting the information there.

The Put command, together with its three preposition possibilities and the degree of specificity offered by naming container components, provides you with enormous flexibility in retrieving and modifying text in any kind of HyperCard container.

**Examples:**

```
put "Howdy, Jerry" into field "Greeting"
put field 2 into temp  -- temp is a local variable
put word 3 of field 4 && word 6 of field 4 into temp
put temp into temp 2
put word 1 of temp 2 into word 1 of field 3
put firstName & empty before field "Last Name"
put empty & field "ZIP" after field "State"
put "555-0700" into line 8 of field 3
put the time into field "Time"
```

**You Try It:** Putting information into fields, variables, and other containers is a lot of fun to experiment with by way of the Message Box. Make a blank card in the Address stack so that you have two fields to play with. Then type the following commands into the Message Box:

```
put "Bill" into field 1
put "Atkinson" into field 2
put "William" into field 1
put "Bill " before field 2              -- note the extra space
put field 2 into field 1
put the long date into field 2
put "1966" into item 3 of field 2
put word 1 of field 1 into temp         -- a global variable
temp
put "Mr. " before temp
temp
put temp into word 1 of field 1
put item 3 of field 2 into temp2
add 20 to temp2
put temp2 into item 3 of field 2
```

By all means, continue playing with this great HyperTalk command.

## get <expression>

**Purpose:** Places the contents or value of an expression into It.

**When to Use It:** This version of the Get command is a shortcut to the Put command when the destination container is It. In other words, *get field 1* is identical to *put field 1 into It.* Neither method is better than the other, except the Get command takes up fewer characters in the script, something good programmers try to achieve.

**Examples:**

```
get the long date
get item 4 of field "Settings"
```

**You Try It:** Use a blank card in the Address stack for this experiment. Type the following messages into the Message Box.

```
put "text from field 1" into field 1
put empty into it
it
get field 1
it
get the long time
it
```

## **delete** <component>

**Purpose:** To remove text from a field of the current card or other container.

**When to Use:** The Delete command is not at all like the Cut menu command but more like the Clear menu command, which erases an item without putting it into the Clipboard. This command gives your script the power to pick single components of any container (characters, words, items, lines) for deletion. Importantly, when you delete a line of a container, the entire text, plus its carriage return character, is deleted with it. All text lines below the original line then move up one. Deleting words or characters does not take care of the carriage return.

Remember that this command does not delete an object, just text inside a container.

**Parameters:** Any valid component name may be used as a parameter for the Delete command. The component must include the name of the container, such as a field or variable name.

**Examples:**

```
delete word 3 of field "Currency"
delete item 2 of it
delete line 5 of field 6
delete char 3 of word 4 of line 5 of field 1
```

**You Try It:** Go the the Address stack, create a blank card, and fill fields 1 and 2 with text of your choosing. Then type the following messages into the Message Box:

```
delete word 1 of field 1
delete line 1 of field 1
get rect of field 1
it      -- the rectangular coordinates of field 2
delete item 4 of it
it
delete item 3 of it
it
click at it
delete line 1 of field 2
```

## **doMenu** <menu item>

**Purpose:** Chooses a menu item while a script is running.

**When to Use:** Even if you turn off the menus for your application, you can build access to menu items into object scripts with the DoMenu command. This includes, incidentally, apple menu items if you wish to call up a desk accessory. For example, if you build some music into an application, you can include a setup card that reminds the user to adjust the volume on the Macintosh Control Panel and provide a screen button that brings up the Control Panel, in case the user doesn't remember how to get at it.

It's hard to predict which menu items you'll call most often from your scripts, but our best guess would be the New Card and Delete Card items in the Edit menu. An incoming telephone logbook, for instance, might create a new card whenever the user opens that stack, since the main purpose of going to that stack is to make a new entry. The DoMenu command, then, would be part of the openStack message handler.

**Parameters:** The DoMenu command must have a valid menu item as a parameter. The text of the menu item parameter must be exactly as the item appears in the menu. This means that if a menu item has an ellipsis (three dots) following it, the text of the parameter must also have the ellipsis. Spaces between words in the menu item must be preserved. And finally, the text must be either in quotation marks or come from a container (which stores text as valid text strings that all commands recognize).

There are some instances of DoMenu possibilities that would seem redundant. Most of the items on the Go menu can be just as easily carried out by a regular Go command in a script.

You'll have to watch out when specifying items in the Paint menu (which appears only when you are using a painting tool). Most items there require that a graphics area be selected first. If your script didn't previously select a region, HyperCard won't let you issue that menu command. That also goes for menu items that require selecting buttons or fields using their respective tools.

Also watch out for the Cut, Copy, Paste, and Clear menu commands: The precise wording of these items changes depending on the material you're working with. For example, if you choose the Button tool and click on a button (either manually or within a script), the Cut, Copy, and Clear items all have the word "Button" appended to them, as in Copy

Button. This word must be part of the DoMenu command parameters. Similarly, the Paste menu item changes to reflect the type of material in the Clipboard ready for pasting. It may be a Button, Field, Text, Picture, or Card.

**Examples:**

```
doMenu "New Card"
doMenu "Print Stack..."
doMenu "Print Card"
```

**You Try It:** Although the power of the DoMenu command really makes sense only from within a script, you can still have fun with it from the Message Box, even if the operations you'll perform as experiments will be more efficiently carried out via the menus. Type the following commands into the Message Box from any card in the Address stack.

```
doMenu "Last"              -- go to last card in stack
doMenu "New Card"
doMenu "First"             -- go to first card
doMenu "Background"        -- turn on Background editing mode
doMenu "Background"        -- turn it off
doMenu "Last"              -- go to newest card
doMenu "Delete Card"
```

This should leave you with the same stack you started with before the experiment.

## wait

[for] <time quantity> ticks | seconds
until <boolean>
while <boolean>

**Purpose:** Pauses execution of a script for a set time or until certain conditions are met.

**When to Use It:** There are two times in particular when you'll need to summon the help of the Wait command that is tied to specific times. One is when a script carries out commands so fast that you need to slow things down between some or all steps. The other is when you wish to set up a self-running stack that flips through cards and stacks at a predetermined pace that someone can read without using the mouse or touching the keyboard.

Delaying execution of fast-paced HyperTalk commands happens often during the creation and debugging of HyperTalk scripts. In chapter 19, for example, we were running a demonstration of how HyperCard mingles idle and mouseWithin messages. In order to show you how the two messages worked with each other, we had each message perform some math and display the result in the Message Box. We had to slow the performance of these math problems with Wait commands. Even after you've debugged a HyperTalk script, if you find that users have problems with parts of the stack because certain operations take place too quickly for them to digest, you will probably have to insert some Wait commands to slow things down.

Another application of the Wait command is during the opening seconds of a stack. If you wish to display a brief title card that acknowledges the stack's author and contains a copyright notice, you can set up an openStack message handler that shows that opening card for a specified period of time and then moves onto the functional part of the stack. The delay is carried out with the Wait command. So as not to stand in the way of an impatient user, that openStack message handler may also have a method of intercepting the waiting by a click of the mouse button, thus shortening the delay.

Waiting until or while certain conditions are met can be particularly useful if you want the execution of a message handler to be interrupted by the browser. For example, a handler might hold up at the Wait command if the mouse button is held down (wait while the mouse is down). The instant the mouse button is released, the handler continues on.

**PARAMETERS:** The Wait command lets you specify the delay in one of two time units: ticks and seconds. Ticks are the number of Macintosh clock cycles passed along to the system. These come roughly sixty times a second, but the exact quantity varies with the Macintosh model you have and the amount of disk activity taking place during the running of the script containing the Wait command. Seconds are more accurate. At least you know there are always sixty seconds to a minute, regardless of how many ticks there may be. If you specify no time unit, however, HyperCard assumes you mean the much shorter ticks unit.

To specify the quantity of seconds or ticks, you can type in a number or any arithmetic expression (that is, any container or text string that evaluates to a number). Most of the time, however, your Wait command will contain a straight number, as in *wait 10*.

If you are more comfortable writing *Wait for* a certain amount of time, feel free to do so. HyperCard ignores the *for*, but it more closely resembles English.

Parameters for the Wait Until and Wait While forms are Boolean (true or false) expressions. Generally speaking, these will be the result of mouse and keyboard functions that return true or false. See chapter 31 for further information about these kinds of functions.

**Examples:**

wait for 5 seconds
wait 20
wait 90 ticks
wait for field "delay" seconds
wait until the shiftKey is up

**You Try It:** It's pointless to type a Wait command into the Message Box, unless it's merely for demonstration. Wait commands really belong only inside scripts. But we can show you how effectively the Wait command puts the Macintosh to sleep for the duration of the wait time. Go to the Address stack and place the Browse tool atop any one of the fields in such a way that the tool turns into the I-Beam cursor— but don't click the mouse button. Now type the following message into the Message Box

wait 20 seconds

Immediately move the cursor to the menubar. Notice that the cursor stays in the I-Beam, and you can't pull down a menu. When the twenty seconds are up, the Macintosh wakes up from its nap, and the cursor changes to the familiar arrow in the menubar.

Now try the same demonstration, but with the ticks unit. Notice how quickly control of the Macintosh returns to you when you use ticks quantities under 100. Try other ticks and seconds quantities.

## dial <phone number> [with [modem] <modem parameters>]

**Purpose:** Dials a telephone number through either a modem or an audio device capable of sending Macintosh tones over the telephone line.

**When to Use:** HyperCard's Address stack comes equipped with a script that allows your Macintosh to dial a telephone number typed into a card. If you develop stacks for yourself that include phone numbers of any kind, you will want to have a button handy that will dial a number directly from that card, rather than having to shift to another HyperCard stack to do the dialing.

There are many ways to implement the Dial command in a stack design. For instance, you can program the Dial command to dial a number that the browser picks up from a text field or selects in a field. Or if a phone number is restricted to a particular field or line in a field, the Dial command can point directly to that spot and dial the number without the user having to pick up the text.

To utilize the intelligent dialing features built into HyperCard, you will have to program the dialing script to first go to the Phone stack, which comes with HyperCard. This stack selects the dialing method best suited to your equipment situation (direct tone dialing from the Macintosh, tone dialing via modem, or pulse dialing via modem), and provides assistance in filtering out your local area code from listed phone numbers. The stack will also add dialing prefixes for local and long distance calls, if needed for your phone system.

If you decide to skip the Phone stack in your dialing script, you have complete control over the dialing method, but you lose the "intelligence" of the stack. If you are dialing through a modem, you can issue as detailed a set of modem instructions as you desire. This, of course, depends on how well acquainted you are with modem commands detailed in your modem manual.

Before a browser can utilize a script including a Dial command, he must have his Macintosh connected to the phone line either by way of a modem or the audio connector box offered by Borland International.

**Parameters:** Every Dial command must have a telephone number as a parameter, even if you use the HyperCard Phone stack. The phone number must be a text string enclosed by quotation marks, unless it is in a container (in which case, HyperCard sees the container's content as a text string anyway). If you type a Dial command into the Message Box or as part of a script using the actual telephone number in the script, the number must be between quotation marks. Otherwise, HyperCard will see the number as a subtraction arithmetic expression (for example, 555-3443 becomes 555 minus 3443). Therefore, always include the quotation marks, as in

```
dial "555-3443"
```

in either the Message Box or in a script.

More often, however, your Dial commands in scripts will look to containers for the phone numbers, especially fields, variables, and the Message Box. If the user is instructed to "pick up" the text of a telephone number from a field, the phone number automatically goes into the Message Box. Your script, then, would say,

```
dial Message Box
```

to dial the number there. Similarly, you can instruct your user to select the phone number with the I-Beam cursor. This action places the text in a container called Selection, and the script would say: *dial selection.* Since the number is in a valid container, HyperCard considers it a valid text string for the Dial command.

When you specify the Dial command with just the phone number as the only parameter (in any stack other than the Phone stack), HyperCard generates the dialing tones for each digit internally. To have a modem dial the number for you, you need to add parameters about the modem. By saying *dial <phone number> with modem*, you instruct HyperCard to send the phone number and the following modem parameters to the modem via the Macintosh serial port, rather than generate the tones internally.

Modem parameters vary with the type of modem you use, but the vast majority of modems connected to personal computers these days are compatible with a command language popularized by modems from Hayes-Microcomputer Products Company. Such modems are said to be "Hayes compatible," because they respond to the same software commands that Hayes brand modems do.

A modem needs a few instructions from the computer before it can dial a number. Those instructions are frequently called AT commands, because the instructions always start with the letters AT, which alert the modem that some further instructions are on the way. Subsequent instructions tell the modem to dial the next digits it receives with rotary pulses (like a rotary dial phone) or tones (like on most pushbutton phones). The command that gets a modem to dial with tones is "AT DT."

You may send a string of instructions about how the modem should behave during and after dialing some digits after a single AT command. For instance, on the Hayes 2400 baud modem, you can soften the loudness of the modem's internal speaker by sending the L0 (that's L plus a zero). The complete command would then be "AT L0 DT."

Another bank of modem instructions lets you adjust internal modem settings called *registers*. While these are largely fine the way they are when you turn on the modem, one register in Hayes compatible modems, called S7, should be adjusted to facilitate using the modem strictly as a dialer for voice calls. This register controls how long the modem stays on the line after it dials the number. Normally, it sticks around for up to thirty seconds, depending on your modem brand. For HyperCard dialing, however, it is helpful to set this register to one second. You can do that by adding the command S7=1. What this means to the user is that he must pick up the phone within one second of the modem finishing dialing (of course, he can pick it up before or during modem dialing, as well).

Modems aren't picky about the order in which these commands arrive, nor whether any spaces come between them, as long as the AT command comes first. Therefore, one useful set of modem parameters you can send to a Hayes-type 2400 baud modem would be "ATS7=1L0DT." If your modem does not have a volume control command (the Hayes 1200 baud modems do not, for instance), you can shorten the command to "ATS7=1DT." Consult your modem manual for other commands and register settings you may wish to make with a HyperCard Dial command.

**Examples:**

```
dial "(212) 555-9099"
dial "555-1526" with modem "ATS7=1DT"
dial line 1 of field "Phones" with modem "ATDT"
dial empty with modem "ATH"        -- force hang up
```

**You Try It:** So you don't accidentally dial long distance numbers or annoy your fellow townspeople, use your own telephone number for the following command experiments. You'll only get a busy signal. If you don't have a modem, the modem experiment (the last one) won't work. Type these commands into the Message Box in any stack but the HyperCard Phone stack.

```
dial "555-1212" -- you'll hear tones from your Mac speaker
put "555-1212" into temp
dial temp
dial temp with modem "ATS7=1DT"
```

## send <message> to <target>

**Purpose:** Sends a message (usually a system message) to specific objects not in the regular hierarchy of the current script.

**When to Use It:** The Send command is one of those that grows on you as you learn more about HyperTalk and how to apply it to your applications design. It turns out that there are times in the design of a HyperCard stack when you wish to initiate an action that is already defined in an object. For instance, let's say you have a button on a card that creates a new card in the current stack and background when you click it. You may discover that every time you come to this stack from one particular stack, you always click that button to create a new card; when you come from other stacks, you don't usually want to create a new card, because you'd rather browse for existing information. What you want, then, is for the script that brings you from that one stack to click that new card button for you. That's exactly what the Send command can do.

In this case, the script would start with a command to go to the second stack; then comes a message that instructs HyperCard to send a mouseUp message to that new card button. As far as that button is concerned, it appears as if HyperCard has sent a mouseUp message because of a clicking of the mouse button. Instead, it's more like a "paper" command, just as some communities have "paper streets" that exist on the maps but not on the ground.

In other words, the Send command lets you "play HyperCard" by sending system messages to any object you like, regardless of the location along the hierarchy of the script that sends the message.

Another way to look at the Send command is that it lets you set up what some computer users know as *macros*, in which the script takes over for human physical action.

**PARAMETERS:** Any valid HyperTalk message will suffice for the <message> parameter. Most of the time, you'll want to send system messages to objects (mouseUp is perhaps the most popular). The message must also be a text string, which means it must either be inside quotation marks or be stored in a HyperCard container.

The <target> parameter is the name of any valid HyperCard object: button, field, card, background, stack, Home, or HyperCard. You may refer to an object by name, number, or id, and you must be specific about its location in the stack.

**EXAMPLES:**

```
send "mouseUp" to button "New Card"
send "resume" to stack "Home"
send "mouseEnter" to field ID 5231
send "doMenu Quit" to HyperCard
```

**YOU TRY IT:** There's little need to issue the Send command from the Message Box, but you can use it here to see it in action. You'll be sending some mouseUp messages to several buttons around the stacks supplied with HyperCard. From the Home card, type the following messages into the Message Box:

```
send "mouseUp" to bkgnd button "Next"    -- to next card
send "mouseUp" to bkgnd button "Prev"    -- to previous card
send "mouseUp" to bkgnd button ID 3      -- to Address
send "mouseUp" to bkgnd button "Return"
```

## do <source>

**PURPOSE:** Carries out HyperTalk commands located in the first line of a container.

**WHEN TO USE:** Because HyperTalk scripts are strictly lines of text, HyperCard can also build the equivalent of a script inside a container, like a variable or field, for later execution.

As an example, you may guide a user through a setup card at the beginning of a HyperCard application. Depending on various choices the user makes on these cards (by clicking screen buttons), the scripts inside these buttons build a HyperTalk message in a container like a global variable or a field in the first card. When the user is finished making the various choices, he can click on a button labeled "OK" or "Do It" or something similar. The script for that button contains a Do command pointing to the text in the container holding the command line. HyperCard sends the message just as if it was in an object script.

**PARAMETERS:** The instructions for the Do command must be in a single line of a container, most likely a field or variable. You may use all possible field names and numbers to identify a field that holds the instructions.

**EXAMPLES:**

```
do field ID 6706
do second line of third field of card "Preferences"
do field "Do It" of card ID 3001
do format  -- format is a global variable
```

**YOU DO IT:** You cannot issue the Do command from the Message Box. Instead, create a card button on a blank Address stack card. Place the script *do field 1* into the button's mouseUp handler. Then type each of the following commands into the first line of the top field and click the button.

```
put 100 into field 2
multiply field 2 by 50
divide field 2 by pi
beep 3
go card "Stacks" of "Home"
```

Experiment with other commands in lines of field 1 and click the button.

## choose <tool name> tool

**PURPOSE:** Selects any tool in the Tools palette.

**WHEN TO USE IT:** The Choose command becomes very important when your scripts need to access painting or object tools for the browser. The commands are the electronic equivalent of clicking on a tool in the Tools palette.

When you design one or more Choose commands into a script, be sure you return the active tool to the Browse tool before ending the script. It's not a nice thing to leave a potentially inexperienced stack user in a tool other than the Browse tool, because he may be hopelessly lost and unable to click buttons.

You'll also use the Choose command when your script creates or selects a field or button (with the doMenu command). Creating a new field or button automatically changes the tool to the Field or Button tool. The script should choose the Browse tool before returning control to the user. If you find that one of your scripts or someone else's script leaves you dangling in a tool other than the Browse too, type Command-Tab to choose the Browse Tool from the keyboard.

**Parameters:** For the Choose Tool command, you must enter the correct name of the desired tool into the <tool name> parameter. Following the order of the tools on the Tools palette, here are the official names of each tool

| | | |
|---|---|---|
| browse | button | field |
| select | lasso | pencil |
| brush | eraser | line |
| spray [can] | rect[angle] | round rect[angle] |
| bucket | oval | curve |
| text | reg[ular] polygon | polygon |

Always be sure to include the word "tool" at the end of this command.

**Examples:**

```
choose oval tool
choose browse tool
choose field 3 tool -- field 3 contains tool name
```

**You Try It:** To demonstrate the Choose command, tear off the Tools palette from the menubar and watch various tools become selected as you type the following messages into the Message Box:

```
choose button tool
choose field tool
choose bucket tool
choose lasso
choose lasso tool
choose rect tool
choose rectangle tool
choose text tool
choose browse tool
```

## click

at <location> [ with <modifier key>]

**Purpose:** Performs an electronic equivalent of clicking the mouse at a specific coordinate location on the screen.

**When to Use:** Whenever you wish to automate a process that normally involves clicking the mouse button with the cursor at a specific spot on the screen, the click command is the one to use. Because HyperTalk lets you select any of the tools in the Tools palette from a script, you can do so before issuing the click command. Therefore, you might develop a script that chooses the Button tool, clicks on a button to select it, and then copies the button for later pasting in another card or stack.

**Parameters:** You must specify a screen coordinate location as a parameter to the click command. A coordinate point is represented by a horizontal and vertical measure (in pixels) separated by a comma, in the form h,v. To click the cursor at the point 100 pixels across and 175 pixels down, the command would be:

```
click at 100,175
```

Because many functions and properties return locations in this h,v format, you will be able to use the results of such items directly in the click command (see chapters 27 and 31).

You may also specify a modifier key (Shift, Command, or Option) be "held down" during the click to accomplish the same enhancement you get when you click manually. Just add the *with* parameter and one of these three possibilities: ShiftKey, CommandKey, or OptionKey. You can even specify multiple modifier keys, as long as you separate them with commas, as in

```
click at 100,100 with CommandKey,OptionKey
```

**Examples:**

```
click at 10,100
click at it          -- when It holds a valid location
```

**You Try It:** Go to the Address stack and type the following messages into the Message Box:

```
get location of field 1
it             -- a valid location at the center of the field.
click at it    -- the cursor flashes at the left margin
get location of background button 1  --  the left arrow
click at it    -- just as if you had clicked it yourself
click at it
```

## drag

from <location> to <location> [with <modifier key>]

**Purpose:** Performs the electronic equivalent of dragging the mouse across the screen.

**When to Use:** As you've experimented with various tools in the Tools palette and their authoring powers, you've surely come to realize that much of the stack object and graphics creation processes revolve around clicking and dragging various tools across the screen. It turns out that anything you can do manually you can also do via a script, including painting graphics. You can literally select painting tools and tell them where to draw lines, circles, rectangles, and so on.

Among the ready applications for this power is graphing bar and pie chart from numbers stored in a card's text fields. With the help of a little math, you can establish graph scales or divisions in a pie chart, then select the appropriate painting tools and instruct them to drag their magic across the screen.

You may also specify that a modifier key (Shift, Command, or Option) be "held down" during the drag to accomplish the same enhancement you get when you drag manually. Just add the *with* parameter and one of these three possibilities: ShiftKey, CommandKey, or OptionKey. You can even specify multiple modifier keys, as long as you separate them with commas, as in

```
drag from 100,100 to 312,320 with OptionKey,ShiftKey
```

**Examples:**

```
drag from 100,100 to 250,300
drag from temp1 to temp2
```

**You Try It:** In the following experiment, you'll be creating a pie chart piece by piece. To see how the commands influence the various palettes, tear off both the Tools and Patterns palettes, and place them off to the side of the screen. Create a new card in the Address stack, which you'll use as a backdrop for the chart. Then type the following messages into the Message Box:

```
choose oval tool
set linesize to 2
set centered to true
drag from 340,135 to 420,215
set centered to false
choose line tool
drag from 340,135 to 340,55
drag from 340,135 to 410,175
drag from 340,135 to 265,115
choose bucket tool
set pattern to 14
click at 375,95
set pattern to 22
```

```
set pattern to 13
click at 305,95
choose browse tool
```

## type <source>

**Purpose:** Performs the electronic equivalent of typing text into a field or selection.

**When to Use:** The Type command operates differently than the Put command when it comes to placing text inside a field. The Put command places the text there in one quick lump, while Type does so one character at a time, as if a fast typist was entering the text. If you use this command to enter actual text characters into a field, it may make for an interesting self-running demonstration, because the user could see characters being entered one at a time.

A more likely application of this command is to have a script type a Tab character at the opening of a card. By doing so, the script places the flashing text insertion pointer in the first field of the card, ready for the browser to enter information. Moreover, because the script typed a Tab character, any text that might be in that field will be selected, similar to the way many database program forms behave.

The Type command is also the one you use to generate graphics text under script command. For example, you could prompt the user for his name (or retrieve it from the UserName global property set in the Home Stack Preferences card), choose the paint text tool, click at the head of a card background, and imbed the person's name into the background graphics layer of a stack. The browser never need know about painting tools to make that happen.

**Examples:**

```
type "This is a demonstration of typing."
type userName
type "c" with CommandKey              -- "Copy" command
```

**You Try It:** Because the Type command usually follows a Click command, you won't be able to experiment with the Type command from the Message Box. The instant you issue the Click command in a text field, the next character you type (the Type command) will go into the field. Therefore, go to the Address stack, create a blank card, and create a new card button. Enter the following script into the button and then watch what happens.

```
on mouseUp
        choose browse tool
        get loc of field 2
        click at it
        type "Some demo, huh?" & return & "You said it."
        get loc of field 1
        choose text tool
        click at it
        type "This is painted text."
        choose browse tool
end mouseUp
```

**sort** [ ascending | descending ]
[ text | numeric | international | datetime ] by <container>

**Purpose:** Sorts the cards in a stack according to a very specific container component (for example, last word in the first line of first field).

**When to Use It:** HyperCard's very fast searching ability often obviates the need to sort a large stack. But if you believe users of a stack you're designing will likely want to browse through the cards one at a time, you may wish to provide a button that sorts the cards according to rules you establish for the stack.

Rules will be different for each stack, because not every stack is constructed with the same methodology of key words. For example, a sales catalog, in which each card lists the details about a particular item, might best have the cards sorted by part number— a numeric sort on an entire part number field in the card. A name and address stack, on the other hand, may be best sorted alphabetically by the last word of the first line of the name field; for mailings, you may wish to sort by the last word of the address field: the zip code.

In your stack design, you can establish the rule or two that you believe most users will want. If they are knowledgeable enough, they can also type a Sort command into the Message Box to follow some other rule.

**Parameters:** The only required parameter is the container by which the sort should take place. This must be a valid field designator, referred by field name, number, or ID number. If no other parameters are specified, HyperCard automatically selects the text ascending order on the container.

An important parameter to watch for is the one that chooses from text, numeric, and international sorting orders. The text choice sorts according to the ASCII value of the text in the sort field. In case you've never heard of ASCII (pronounced, "ASS-key"), it is a standard code recognized by most personal computers for each character of the keyboard (plus some others you can't get to from the keyboard). The ASCII numbers assigned to the characters are completely independent of their actual position in the alphabet or in the digits zero through nine. The important thing to remember about ASCII sorting is that it is best used for sorting text, because it does not sort numbers according to the actual value of the numbers (an ASCII sort puts the text "144" lower than the text "21" because 144 starts with a 1, while 21 starts with a 2, which has a higher ASCII value). Therefore, if the field on which you wish to sort cards in a stack is predominantly text, use the text (ASCII) sorting parameter.

One sorting trick is worth noting. If your stack features an opening card that you'd like to be sure is always in the front of the stack, leave the sort field empty. For example, in the Address stack, on which you generally sort on the last name in the first line of the name field, you can leave the first line of the field blank (just a return character). When HyperCard sorts ascending by text (ASCII), the return character comes out about as low in the ASCII rankings as you can get, guaranteeing that card's place at the head of the stack.

The *number* parameter sorts cards based on the correct numeric value of numbers in the sort field. A field with 200 in it will be lower than a field with 1200, as you would expect. If the sorting encounters text in a field, HyperCard will place the text at the beginning of the stack (in ascending sort order) but will not perform any sorting on the text cards.

Sorting with the *international* parameter primarily affects the way characters known as *ligatures* are treated during a sort. In languages that contain ligatures (like æ and œ), sorting must be treated differently than strict ASCII order. For English sorting, the *text* parameter is preferred. Use international sorting if the data in text fields contains ligatures and umlauted characters.

If you intend to sort cards in a stack by a background field containing dates, use the *dateTime* parameter. As long as the dates or times in the field are in one of the many valid date and time formats, the Sort command will make the proper conversions and evaluations while sorting the cards, but without disturbing the format stored on the cards. Dates may even be in different formats on different cards. As long as the formats are valid, (see the Convert command in chapter 23), the *dateTime* sort parameter will handle them properly.

Most of your stack sorts will be ascending, so you don't have to specify a directional parameter. But you always have the descending parameter available if you need it for those stacks better served by a sort in this direction.

**Examples:**

```
sort by field "Department"
sort by first word of field "Client"
sort descending numeric by field "Amount Due"
sort by last word of first line of field "Name"
sort numeric by last word of field "Address"
```

**You Try It:** You're most likely to have the largest stack of accumulated information in your Address stack, so use that one in your sorting experiments. Go to that stack and type the following messages in the Message Box. After each message, flip through the stack a minute to see how the sorting command affected the data in your stack.

```
sort by last word of first line of field 1      -- same as the Sort
                                                 -- button
sort by last word of field 1
sort descending by last word of field 1
sort by first word of field 2
sort numeric by first word of field 2
sort by last word of first line of field 1      -- return to a
                                                 -- usable order
```

## open [<document> with] <application>

**Purpose:** Launches any Macintosh application or document. This is different from the *open file* command.

**When to Use It:** Early in this book, we mentioned that HyperCard can become the center of your Macintosh World. The HyperTalk command that facilitates building this world is the Open command. This command will find its way most likely into button scripts. The buttons will be labeled or be styled with icons of the document or application involved. Whenever you wish to branch to an external Macintosh document or application from a HyperCard stack, this is the command that gets you there.

When HyperCard executes this command, HyperCard sends a suspend system message to the current card. It then clears itself from memory entirely, as if quitting. In the process, however, it alerts the Macintosh System File in your System Folder that when you're done with the external application, the System should hand control back to HyperCard by restarting HyperCard. When HyperCard restarts, it sends the resume message to the current card— the card from which you suspended HyperCard previously.

Deciding how you wish to make HyperCard the center of your Macintosh World is not an easy task, because HyperCard gives you extraordinary flexibility in design. Various philosophies will likely arise from HyperCard's launching abilities. For example, you might wish to place all your Open command buttons in a special stack containing references to your frequently used documents and applications. Or you may wish to distribute the buttons throughout your stacks—like a button leading to a relational database file from a HyperCard customer list stack. Anything is possible.

You will also make decisions about how much you wish to hide the name of the application when your buttons refer to documents. Do you want to concern yourself with knowing both the document and the application that created it? Or is it enough just to know the document name and organize your documents by document type rather than by the application that created them?

**Parameters:** If you wish the Open command to launch just an application (that is, no document with it), then you need to specify only the application's file name. This might prove tricky at first, depending on the applications you intend to open. The text of the application name in the Open command parameter must be identical to the application's actual file name that you see in the Finder. While capitalization is not important, special characters, such as the trademark symbol that appears in some file names, must be in the parameter text. The same goes for the proper number of spaces and other notations, such as version number (for example, "v 1.1").

If the application's file name contains special characters, like the trademark character, you have two options. One is to rename the application file in the Finder. This almost never has any negative effect on the running of the application. The other option is to recreate the special charcters in the Open command's <application> parameter. The trademark character is, indeed, available from the keyboard. Hold down the Option key and type the 2 character from the top row of the keyboard. Other common symbols are as follows:

| | | |
|---|---|---|
| Registered Trademark | ® | Option-R |
| Copyright | © | Option-G |
| Bullet | • | Option-8 |

You can always look for other symbols by opening the KeyCaps desk accessory. With the miniature keyboard on the screen, press the Option key and then the Option and Shift keys together to see all the characters available in most Macintosh fonts. If the character appears in an application's file name in the Finder, you will be able to recreate it in the text of the Open command parameter.

Spaces between characters in an applications' desktop file name are sometimes not easy to discern. If single spaces between words or elements of a name don't work in your Open command's parameters, study the actual file name carefully, looking for extra spaces (including a possible extra space before the start of the file name— sometimes a pesky problem that's hard to find unless you know to look for it). You can always select the text of the actual name in the Finder and copy it into the clipboard. Then go into your HyperTalk script and paste the text into the appropriate location in the command line. That should take care of strange characters and spaces.

Document parameters must also be text (that is, enclosed in quotes or from a container, such as a field). As with the application file name, the document parameter must be identical to the actual file name in the Finder. It seems that errant leading spaces crop up more readily in file names that you create, so be on the watch for them if your script has difficulty finding a document. When specifying a document, you must also specify the application that originally created the document, separating the two parameters with the word "with." Although you may be setting up a HyperCard "front end" to your documents to disguise the applications that control your documents, you'll have to make the connection once, as you create the script that opens the document. After that, you can forget which application was used to create a document or template.

It's also important to keep in mind that when you put a new document or application into an Open command script, the Home Stack's Documents and Applications cards must contain the paths to the files. If the files you specify in a script are in new folders, be sure to add paths to those folders in the Look for Documents In... and Look for Applications In... Preferences cards. Of course, if you specify the complete pathname in the command's parameters, you won't have to worry about the contents of the Preferences card, because HyperCard will automatically read the pathname from the script.

**EXAMPLES:**

```
open "MacPaint"
open "Hard Disk:Applications:Excel"
open "No.10 Envelope" with "MacWrite"
open field "Title" with "Word 3.0"
open line 4 of field 2 with "More™"
```

**YOU TRY IT:** Without knowing which applications and document names you have stored on your disk(s), we can't show you precisely how to experiment with the Open command. All we can say is to use the above your own from the Message Box. You can do this while viewing any card in any stack. Remember to use quotation marks around the text of each parameter. Quit each application to return to the card from which you left HyperCard.

## open printing [ with dialog ]
## print [ all | <number> cards ] | [ this <card> ]
## close printing

**Purpose:** Set up a print job that queues individual cards for printing as if a single stack.

**When to Use:** There will be many times in your stack design when you will want to offer your users the opportunity to print selected cards within a stack or across multiple stacks. While you can easily print each card, one per page with the doMenu "Print Card" command, your user loses the many printing effects available in the Print Stack dialog box, such as multiple cards per page, split page printing, and so on. The Open Printing, Print, and Close Printing commands let you send specific cards to the printing queue so they print as if they were all in a single stack.

**Parameters:** When the Open Printing command executes, there is a pause for a few seconds while HyperCard's printing system gets set to accept a list of cards to print. If the Open Printing command specifies the *with dialog* parameter, then the Print Stack dialog appears, allowing the user to specify the way the cards should be printed out and whether there should be a header printed on each page.

The script then queues cards to print by either going to the desired cards and issuing the *Print this card* command, or printing a set number of contiguous cards, or printing individual cards denoted by their ID numbers and stack locations. If the user selected half-size cards in the Print Stack dialog box, HyperCard will begin printing as soon as eight cards have been selected for printing.

At the end of the print job, your script should send the Close Printing command. If, for example, you have selected printing eight cards per page and only five have been selected, Close Printing will tell HyperCard to print the page as currently assembled. Close Printing also makes sure HyperCard closes down the printing system correctly.

**Examples:**

```
open printing with dialog
print 12 cards
```

```
print this card
print card ID 4988
close printing
```

**You Try It:** From the Message Box, you'll still be able to experiment with these commands. In fact, you'll see one particularly beneficial aspect of them from the knowledgeable HyperTalk programmer's standpoint. Once you open the printing job, control of HyperCard returns to you, so you can navigate through your stacks as if nothing was in the way. When you reach a card you wish to print, simply type *print this card* into the Message Box. HyperCard places that card in the queue. Let's try it now. When the dialog box comes up, select half-size cards.

```
open printing with dialog
go Home
print this card
go previous
print this card
go to stack "Help"
print 3 cards
close printing
```

# CHAPTER 23

# Arithmetic Commands

WHILE MATH IS OFTEN A PROGRAMMING ROADBLOCK FOR NONTECHNICAL FOLKS, BASIC arithmetic shouldn't be. The commands in this chapter are simple arithmetic—operations your scripts perform on numbers stored in containers.

**add** <source> to <container>

**PURPOSE:** Adds one number (or number in a container) to another number already in a container.

**WHEN TO USE IT:** Any time you need to sum two numbers, use the Add command. Note that the result of the addition operation is put into the destination container: You are adding one number *to* the second. Therefore, if you add the number in field 1 to the number in field 2 (*add field 1 to field 2*), nothing will change in field 1, but field 2's content will become the sum of the two numbers. The original value in field 2 will no longer be stored or retrievable. If your script needs that original value later, you should put that value into a local variable before performing the Add command.

The Add command is a completely separate kind of addition than what you have available by typing in an addition formula into the Message Box (chapter 1). If you were to include a script line such as *10 + 50*, HyperCard would not know where to put the result of the addition. That's why the Add command exists: so that you can not only add two numbers but hold onto the result for display in a field or for further arithmetic.

**Parameters:** Both the <source> and <container> parameters may be containers of any type. The most common containers you'll use with the Add command are variables and fields.

Additionally, the <source> parameter may be any arithmetic expression, such as a number or a math formula that evaluates to a number (for example, *4 * 5 / (field "cost" + 11)* or functions like *the seconds*). One way to test whether a formula evaluates to a number is to type it into the Message Box (if the formula refers to fields, make sure typical data is typed into the fields of the current card). If you type in the formula, press Return, and see a number, then you're all set to include the formula wherever an arithmetic expression is allowed, as in the <source> parameter of the Add command.

**Examples:**

```
add field "Item 1" to field "Total"
add field ID 19084 to temp -- temp is a local variable
add field 1 + 100 to field 6
add temp to field "Sum"
add 1 to counter           -- counter is a local variable
add temp1 to temp3         -- summing two local variables
```

**You Try It:** Use fields of a blank Address stack card to work with the following experiment. Start out by placing the values 10 and 20 into the name and phone number fields, respectively. Then type these commands into the Message Box:

```
put 0 into var       -- initializes global variable "var"
add field 1 to var
var                  -- var now has a 10 stored in it
add field 2 to var
var                  -- var is now 30
add var to field 2
add field 1 to field 2
add 100 to var
var                  -- var is now 130
add var to field 1
```

## **subtract** <source> from <container>

**Purpose:** Subtracts one number (or number in a container) from another number already in a container.

**When to Use It:** Any time you need to subtract two numbers, use the Subtract command. Note that the result of the subtraction operation is put into a container– you are subtracting one number *from* the second. Therefore, if you subtract the number in field 1 from the number in field 2 (*subtract field 1 from field 2*), nothing will change in field 1, but field 2's content will become the difference of the two numbers. The original value in field 2 will no longer be stored or retrievable. If your script needs that original value later, you should put that value into a local variable before performing the Subtract command.

The Subtract command is a completely separate kind of operation than what you have available by typing in a subtraction formula into the Message Box (chapter 1). If you were to include a script line such as *100 - 50*, HyperCard would not know where to put the result of the subtraction. That's why the Subtract command exists: so that you can not only subtract two numbers but hold onto the result for display in a field or for further arithmetic.

**Parameters:** Both the <source> and <container> parameters may be containers of any type. The most common containers you'll use with the Subtract command are variables and fields.

Additionally, the <source> parameter may be any arithmetic expression, such as a number or a math formula that evaluates to a number (for example, *4 * 5 / (field "cost" + 11)* or functions like *the seconds*). One way to test whether a formula evaluates to a number is to type it into the Message Box (if the formula refers to fields, make sure typical data is typed into the fields of the current card). If you type in the formula, press Return, and see a number, then you're all set to include the formula wherever an arithmetic expression is allowed, as in the <source> parameter of the Subtract command.

**Examples:**

```
subtract field "Discount" from field "Subtotal"
subtract field ID 2080 from temp  -- a local variable
subtract field 1 + 100 from field 6
subtract temp from field "Days To Go"
subtract 1 from counter           --counter is a local variable
subtract temp1 from temp3         --two local variables
```

**You Try It:** Use fields of a blank Address stack card to work with the following experiment. Start out by placing the values 500 and 100 into the name and phone number fields, respectively. Then type these commands into the Message Box:

```
put 25 into var              -- initializes global variable "var"
subtract var from field 2
var                          -- var still has a 25 stored in it
```

```
subtract field 1 from var
var                              -- var is now -475
subtract var from var
var                              -- var is now zero
subtract field 2 from field 1
subtract var from field 1
```

## multiply <container> by <source>

**Purpose:** Multiplies one number already in a container by another number (or another number in a container).

**When to Use It:** Any time you need to multiply two numbers, use the Multiply command. Note that the result of the multiplication operation is put into the destination container—you are multiplying one number *by* the second. Therefore, if you multiply the number in field 1 by the number in field 2 (*multiply field 1 by field 2*), nothing will change in field 2, but field 1's content will become the product of the two numbers. The original value in field 1 will no longer be stored or retrievable. If your script needs that original value later, you should put that value into a local variable before performing the Multiply command.

The Multiply command is a completely separate kind of multiplication than what you have available by typing in a formula into the Message Box (chapter 1). If you were to include a script line such as *10 * 50*, HyperCard would not know where to put the result. That's why the Multiply command exists: so that you can not only multiply two numbers, but hold onto the result for display in a field or for further arithmetic.

**Parameters:** Both the <container> and <source> parameters may be containers of any type. The most common containers you'll use with the Multiply command are variables and fields. Notice that the order of destination and source parameters is the opposite of the Add command. The destination parameter (that is, where the result lands) is the first parameter.

The <source> parameter may be any arithmetic expression, such as a number or a math formula that evaluates to a number (for example, *4 * 5 / (field "cost" + 11)* or functions like *the seconds*). One way to test whether a formula evaluates to a number is to type it into the Message Box (if the formula refers to fields, make sure typical data is typed into the fields of the current card). If you type in the formula, press Return, and see a number, then you're all set to include the formula wherever an arithmetic expression is allowed, as in the <source> parameter of the Multiply command.

**Examples:**

```
multiply field "Subtotal" by field "Sales Tax Rate"
multiply field ID 500 by temp        -- temp is a local variable
multiply field 6 by field 1 + 100
multiply temp by field "Sum"
multiply temp1 by temp3              -- two local variables
```

**You Try It:** Use fields of a blank Address stack card to work with the following experiment. Start out by placing the values 25 and 100 into the name and phone number fields, respectively. Then type these commands into the Message Box:

```
put 5 into var               -- initializes global variable "var"
multiply field 1 by var
var                          -- var still has 5 stored in it
multiply var by field 2
var                          -- var is now 500
multiply var by 0
var                          --  var is now zero
multiply field 2 by field 1
```

## divide <container> by <source>

**Purpose:** Divides one number already in a container by another number (or another number in a container).

**When to Use It:** Any time you need to divide two numbers, use the Divide command. Note that the result of the division operation is put into the destination container: You are dividing one number *by* the second. Therefore, if you divide the number in field 1 by the number in field 2 (*divide field 1 by field 2*), nothing will change in field 2, but field 1's content will become the quotient of the two numbers. The original value in field 1 will no longer be stored or retrievable. If your script needs that original value later, you should put that value into a local variable before performing the Divide command.

The Divide command is a completely separate kind of division than what you have available by typing in a formula into the Message Box (chapter 1). If you were to include a script line such as *10/50*, HyperCard would not know where to put the result. That's why the divide command exists: so that you can not only divide two numbers but hold onto the result for display in a field or for further arithmetic.

**Parameters:** Both the <container> and <source> parameters may be containers of any type. The most common containers you'll use with the Divide command are variables and fields. Notice that the order of destination and source parameters is the opposite of the Subtract command. The destination parameter (that is, where the result lands) is the first parameter.

The <source> parameter may be any arithmetic expression, such as a number or a math formula that evaluates to a number (for example, *4 * 5 / (field "cost" + 11)* or functions like *the seconds*). One way to test whether a formula evaluates to a number is to type it into the Message Box (if the formula refers to fields, make sure typical data is typed into the fields of the current card). If you type in the formula, press Return, and see a number, then you're all set to include the formula wherever an arithmetic expression is allowed, as in the <source> parameter of the Divide command.

**EXAMPLES:**

```
divide field "Average" by field "Total Number"
divide field ID 9007 by temp          -- temp is a local variable
divide field 3 by field 2 * 100
divide temp by field "Subtotal"
divide temp1 by temp3                 -- two local variables
```

**YOU TRY IT:** Use fields of a blank Address stack card to work with the following experiment. Start out by placing the values 5 and 1000 into the name and phone number fields, respectively. Then type these commands into the Message Box:

```
put 10 into var        -- initializes global variable "var"
divide field 1 by var
var                    -- var still has 10 stored in it
divide field 2 by var
divide var by 0
var                    -- var is infinity—you can't divide by zero
divide field 2 by field 1
```

## convert <container> to <format>

**PURPOSE:** Converts date and time to formats for calculation and display.

**WHEN TO USE IT:** Used primarily in conjunction with date and time functions (chapter 30), the Convert command is a gateway to time and date arithmetic, like finding the days between two dates, time zone conversions, and so on. HyperCard offers seven different formats for displaying or storing time and date information. All dates, however, must be since January 1, 1904.

Notice that the conversion takes place in the container. If you have a date in a field and convert it to seconds for some calculations, the field contents will change from the traditional date to an enormous number of seconds. Therefore, perform conversions in variables inside scripts.

**PARAMETERS:** The first parameter, <container>, is any valid HyperCard container. Typically you'll work with conversions behind the scenes in variables rather than out in the open in fields.

HyperCard's date and time formats in the U.S. version are as follows:

| Format Name | Example |
|---|---|
| seconds | 2631100380 |
| long date | Tuesday, November 17, 1987 |
| short date | 11/17/87 |
| abbreviated date | Tue, Nov 17, 1987 |
| long time | 1:16:03 PM or 13:16:03 |
| short time | 1:16 PM or 13:16 |
| dateItems | 1987,11,17,13,16,3,3 |

The seconds format is the total number of seconds the date and time you're converting represents since 12:00:00 A.M. on January 1, 1904. That's the time the Macintosh clock uses as a base reference point. While conversion to the short date always shows slashes between month, day, and year items, you may enter a date with hyphens as separators, as in 11-17-87. The Convert command recognizes this as a valid short date. The abbreviated date format may be referred to in three ways: *abbreviated date*, *abbrev date*, and *abbr date*. Any one of those three format names is valid. Long and short times show AM and PM when you select the 12-hour setting in your Control Panel. Otherwise, all times are shown in 24-hour time (sometimes called "military time").

The dateItems format is one you'll use frequently in date and time arithmetic. The items are, from left to right, the year, month, day, hour, minute, second, and day of the week (Sunday = 1). You may add to any item, even if the result seems unusual (for example, the 35th day). Upon conversion to another format, the proper date and time are computed. You may not, however, subtract from items when the result is negative (or zero for the date items). If you need to subtract dates and times from each other, it is best to convert everything to seconds before subtracting; you can then reconvert to a more recognizable format.

# CHAPTER 24

# Object Manipulation Commands

HyperCard lets the author access and change a lot of information about certain objects, particularly buttons and fields. The commands that make this happen are in this group of object manipulation commands. We've also added commands that affect HyperCard global variables. While they are technically not HyperCard objects (you cannot send messages to them), you tend to think of them as entities. For the sake of the command organization, we'll temporarily cover them with our object umbrella.

**hide** menubar | <window> | <button or field>

**Purpose:** Hides screen objects from view.

**When to Use:** If the stack you are designing is best served by occupying the entire HyperCard window, you may wish to have the stack hide the menubar in the openStack message handler. That's where you'd put the Hide Menubar command.

Hiding the menu bar is a design decision that should not be taken lightly. By removing the menubar, you assume the burden of providing all navigation buttons for the user. Menu commands like those in the Go menu (including Home) will be gone once the menus are hidden. Additionally, if the stack is one that calls for the user to generate or delete cards, you'll have to provide a way for the user to issue those commands as well. The same goes for printing and using the Edit menu's text editing choices.

Fortunately, even though the menus are hidden, an experienced user may access those menu commands that have keyboard equivalents (for example, Command-V for Paste). But if you are designing a stack for others, you should not assume that the user will be so knowledgeable as to remember the Command-key equivalents for even the simplest menu item. You'll need explicit buttons or other instructions on the screen to make up for the missing menus.

Still, in a heavily graphics-oriented stack, particularly one that is for viewing only, it may be very desirable to remove the menus. For the uninitiated computer user, even short menus may make the stack appear more complicated than it is.

Additionally, if you hide the menubar with an openStack message handler, it should be your responsibility to show the menubar with a corresponding closeStack message handler. See the Show command, below, for details on bringing the menubar back into view.

You may also use the Hide command to make windows (the message, tool, and pattern windows) and objects like fields and buttons disappear from the screen. A common application is to hide a shadow text field that contains some instructions or explanatory text. When the user clicks on a button for help, for instance, the field appears on the screen at a predetermined location (see the Show command). Then the user can click on the field (provided you created it as a locked text field). A script in the field's mouseUp message handler then hides the field.

Another application might be to keep a secondary set of buttons hidden from view until the user needs them. Then, when he presses on a button that says "More," the user is presented with additional buttons. To have all these buttons visible on the card all the time might make the card look too complicated. By placing these less-frequently-used buttons on a secondary palette of buttons, the user can more easily focus on the application. When the user clicks on one of the secondary buttons, not only does the button carry out its appointed task, but it also hides all the secondary buttons so that they're out of the way.

Showing and hiding the Message Box is another useful capability. You'll frequently design stacks that have no place for a Message Box. When such a stack opens, you'll want to place a Hide Message command in the openStack message handler, just in case the preceding stack didn't hide the Message Box upon closing.

**PARAMETERS:** When the Hide command is directed at the menubar, simply add "menubar" as a one-word parameter.

To hide buttons and fields, refer to the objects by name, number, or ID number. Card fields and background buttons must also include their respective domain names. Remember that these target references can also come from containers, especially variables. In chapter 37, we'll show you how to use a repeat loop construction that hides a series of buttons quickly, addressing each button's name with a variable.

As for hiding the Message Box, you can use four different names for it: *message window, message box, message,* or *msg.* Hiding the tools or patterns windows, however, requires their full names: *tool window* and *pattern window.*

**Examples:**

```
hide button ID 302
hide field "Extra"
hide message
hide button counter -- counter is a local variable
hide menubar
hide tool window
```

**You Try It:** You can't really try hiding objects without also showing them— otherwise you may forget the objects are there, and you'll be lost. Therefore, in the following list of messages to type into the Message Box, there will be a corresponding Show command to restore the objects to their original, visible status. Experiment with these messages in the Address stack.

```
hide menubar
show menubar -- you can also type Command-Spacebar
hide bkgnd button 1
hide field 1
hide bkgnd button 2
show tool window
show pattern window
hide pattern window
hide tool window
show field 1
show bkgnd button 2
show bkgnd button 1
```

**show** menubar | <window> | < button or field> [ at <location> ]
**show** [ <number> | all ] cards

**Purpose:** Shows menus, buttons, fields, and windows at a desired location on the screen. Show Cards displays a set number of cards in the current stack.

**When to Use It:** Since menus, buttons, and fields are created as visible entities on the screen, there is little need to use the Show command for these items unless they have been hidden by a previous Hide command. As far as windows go, you'll find yourself hiding and showing the Message Box in various stacks you design, while the tool and pattern windows will rarely be controlled by stacks.

Since you never know how someone else's stack will leave the Message Box when it closes, you should plan to write an openStack message handler that shows or hides the Message Box as your stack design requires. There will be no damage or errors if your openStack handler includes a *show message* command and the Message Box is already visible. It is good practice, moreover, to include a closeStack message handler that hides the Message Box for the next stack.

The Show Cards command is a different kind of Show command, because it deals strictly with cards that can't ever be hidden. When you show all cards, HyperCard begins flipping rapidly through the stack, flashing each card before your eyes for a quick browse. A click of the Browse tool stops the parade. The "speeding cards" icon button in the Address stack has a *show all cards* command in its script. You may also specify a specific number of cards, beginning with the card after the current card.

**Parameters:** When the Show command is directed at the menubar, simply add "menubar" as a one-word parameter.

To show buttons, fields, or windows, substitute the item's name as a parameter. Buttons and fields can be referred to by name, number, or ID number. Card fields and background buttons must also include their respective domain names. Remember that these target references can also come from containers, especially variables. In chapter 37, we'll show you how to use a repeat loop construction that shows a series of buttons quickly, addressing each button's name with a variable.

As for showing the Message Box, you can use four different names for it: *message window, message box, message,* or *msg.* Showing the tools or patterns windows, however, requires their full names: *tool window* and *pattern window.*

Additional parameters to the Show command let you establish the location on the screen of an object you wish to become visible. Locations refer to the horizontal and vertical screen coordinates. The point you establish as being the location of the object depends on the kind of object it is. Coordinates for fields and buttons are for the center of the object; for windows, the point corresponds to the upper left corner of the window's content region— the area just below the window's grey title bar. Therefore, if you wish to show the Message Box near the top of the screen instead of the bottom, you could show the Message Box at coordinates 25,50. As with all numeric parameters in HyperTalk, the two numbers must be separated by a comma.

While HyperCard won't let you manually drag an object beyond the screen's edge, the Show At command lets you specify coordinates well beyond the 511, 341 endpoint of the screen (including negative coordinates). Exercise care in setting location coordinates.

Be careful in showing objects when you're not sure how they'll look on the screen. Objects will be cut off at the window's edge if you place them too close. The Message Box is a good example of why you need careful placement. If you show it at a horizontal coordinate in excess of 50, you start to lose the right edge of the box.

Here's a trick to help you determine the coordinates to assign to an object. Visualize where on the screen you want the object's centerpoint (buttons and fields) or top left corner (windows) to be and place the tip of the Browse tool's index finger at that location. Type *the mouseloc* into the Message Box. HyperCard will return the screen coordinates of that spot on the screen. Experiment with the Message Box first, by hiding and showing the object that will eventually be controlled by a script. Keep notes of which coordinates look the best. Then include those coordinates as parameters to the Show command in your script.

**Examples:**

```
show menubar
show message
show msg at 30,200
show button ID 4676
show button george -- george is a local variable
show field 3 at 100,120
```

**You Try It:** We refer you to the You Try It section of the Hide command, above, for some examples of the Show command. What you can experiment with here, however, is the way you can specify a location of a shown object. From the Address stack, type the following messages into the Message Box.

```
get location of bkgnd button 2
hide bkgnd button 2
show bkgnd button 2 at 256,171
show bkgnd button 2 at it
show message at 0,0
show message at 300,50
show message at 25,300
```

**get** <property> [ of <target> ]
**set** <property> [ of <target> ] to <new setting>

**PURPOSE:** Get retrieves object properties; Set assigns new settings to object properties.

**WHEN TO USE IT:** Because Get and Set are so complementary, we'll discuss these commands together. While they work in opposite directions, their treatment of parameters is nearly identical. The only difference is that the Set command has one additional parameter.

When the Get command retrieves an object property, the result of the retrieval automatically goes into the local variable It. You may then work with the information as you would information from any container: Put it into a field, perform math on numeric information, modify the text, and so on.

Both of these commands allow the HyperCard author to incorporate scripts into stacks that retrieve and modify the properties of certain global variables, stacks, backgrounds, cards, fields, and buttons, without forcing the user to get into the object dialog boxes. For example, you could establish a setup card at the beginning of a stack that prompts the user for the way he would like certain text buttons to read or which kind of icon (from a selection on the card) he'd like his Home button to have. The script would first use the Get command to retrieve the current settings to display on the setup card. Then, by simply typing in a name or clicking on selections, the user will have his preferences inserted into the stack with the help of the Set command script you've carefully laid out for him behind the scenes. Virtually every property you can set in object dialog boxes, plus several important global, window, and painting properties, can be retrieved and modified with the Get and Set commands. Properties are discussed in detail in chapter 28

**PARAMETERS:** All Get commands need to know the name of the property you wish to retreive and, when necessary, the object that has the property. When the property is a global or painting property, the target name is not needed. Otherwise, the target is one of five possible HyperCard objects or the name of a window (windows are not technically HyperCard objects). You may refer to these objects by name, number, or id number. Be sure you specify the type of object, as in

button ID 46403

Each of the five HyperCard objects has different properties that you can plug in as parameters to the Get command. They are listed briefly in Table 24-1, and discussed in detail in chapter 28.

| Property Name | Global | Window | Stack | Bkgnd | Card | Field | Button | Painting |
|---|---|---|---|---|---|---|---|---|
| autoHilite | | | | | | | • | |
| blindTyping | • | | | | | | | |
| brush | | | | | | | | • |
| centered | | | | | | | | • |
| cursor | • | | | | | | | |
| dragSpeed | • | | | | | | | |
| editBgknd | • | | | | | | | |
| filled | | | | | | | | • |
| grid | | | | | | | | • |
| hilite | | | | | | | • | |
| icon | | | | | | | • | |
| language | • | | | | | | | |
| lineSize | | | | | | | | • |
| location | | • | | | • | • | • | |
| lockScreen | • | | | | | | | |
| lockText | | | | | | • | | |
| multiple | | | | | | | | • |
| multiSpace | | | | | | | | • |
| name | | | • | • | • | • | • | |
| numberFormat | • | | | | | | | |
| pattern | | | | | | | | • |
| polySides | | | | | | | | • |
| powerKeys | • | | | | | | | |
| rectangle | | • | | | | • | • | |
| script | | | • | • | • | • | • | |
| scroll | | | | | | • | | |
| showLines | | | | | | • | | |
| showName | | | | | | | • | |
| style | | | | | | • | • | |
| textAlign | | | | | | • | • | • |
| textFont | | | | | | • | • | • |
| textHeight | | | | | | • | • | • |
| textSize | | | | | | • | • | • |
| textStyle | | | | | | • | • | • |
| userLevel | • | | | | | | | |
| visible | | • | | | | • | • | |
| wideMargins | | | | | | • | | |

*Table 24-1.*

Property parameters to the Set command are the same as for the Get command. The additional parameter is the new setting you wish to apply to the object. If the parameter is a text string, such as the object's name or button style, place the parameter in quotation marks, as in

```
set name of field ID 104 to "Phone Number"
```

A number of object properties have very specific requirements about what settings they'll accept. For example, the textStyle property of a field will accept only the styles listed in the Field Info dialog box. The setting must be spelled properly in the Set command's parameter. If HyperCard doesn't find a match for the setting, you'll get a message advising that HyperCard doesn't understand the arguments (that is, parameters) to your Set command.

**EXAMPLES:**

```
get userLevel
get location of button var -- var is a local variable
get textFont of field "Name"
set lineSize to 2
set textFont of field "Name" to "Times"
set textSize of field "Name" to 18
set name of button 5 to "Cancel"
```

**YOU TRY IT:** These two commands are fun to explore because you can see immediate results on the screen from your Message Box messages. Create a blank card in the Address stack and create one new button, leaving its settings to the ones supplied by HyperCard. Choose the Browse tool and put a line or two of text into each of the text fields on the card. Then type in the following messages.

```
get location of button "New Button"
it                  -- see the coordinates of the button
put 50 into item 1 of it
set location of button "New Button" to it
set name of button "New Button" to "Mac Forever"
get name of button "Mac Forever"
it                  -- see the button name
set hilite of it to true
get textFont of field 1
put it into temp
get textSize of field 1
put "-" & it after temp
temp                -- see the font and font size in a familiar format
get style of field 1
it
```

```
set style of field 1 to shadow
set style of field 1 to it
```

Feel free to continue your experimentation with get and set.

## global <variable list>

**Purpose:** Initializes a HyperTalk global variable; alerts HyperTalk that you will be using an existing global variable in a script.

**When to Use It:** A global variable, as you'll recall, is a container that will hold information after a message handler ends. You initialize a global variable differently than a local variable. When you put a number or text string into a local variable, you've initialized it. But with a global variable, you must use the Global command to get things going.

Once you initialize the global variable (some experienced programmers might also call this "declaring" the variable), you can put information into it or manipulate information inside it like any container.

Later, if you wish to use a global variable's information in a different message handler, you'll use the Global command again to let HyperTalk know that you will be using that particular global variable in the current message handler. The only rule about placing the Global command in a handler is that it be in a line above the command that uses the variable. It is better form, however, to declare all global variables at the top of a handler so you can see at a glance which globals are used throughout the handler.

You should use global variables sparingly, because once you assign a variable name to it, you won't be able to use that name as a local variable without the possibility of getting mixed up. Most of what you need variable containers for can be handled by local variables.

**Parameters:** The only parameter for the global command is any name or comma-separated list of names you wish to assign to variables. Do not put quotation marks around a variable name. A variable name, however, must be one word. That means you cannot have spaces between parts of the variable name, but you can use techniques like capitalizing each component word or using an underline character to fill in for the space.

**Examples:**

```
global hank
global stereo1,stereo2,stereo3,mono
global BookNumber
global areaCode
```

**You Try It:** All variables you initialize from the Message Box are global variables, because there is no message handler that a variable can be "local to." Therefore, to see how you use the Global command in typical scripts, create a new button in any stack of your choice. Enter the following lines of text into the script dialog box:

```
on mouseDown
    global howMany
    put 2 into howMany
end mouseDown

on mouseUp
    beep howMany
end mouseUp
```

When you try clicking on this button, you'll get an error message telling you that the parameter to beep (in the mouseUp handler) is invalid. That's because the global variable howMany was not redeclared in the mouseUp message handler.

Now open up the button's script dialog box and modify the mouseUp message handler to look like this:

```
on mouseUp
    global howMany
    beep howMany
end mouseUp
```

When you click on the button this time, you'll hear two beeps, because the global variable carried over successfully to the mouseUp message handler, thanks to the redeclaration of the variable howMany.

## edit script of <target>

**Purpose:** Opens Script Editor window for a given object.

**When to Use:** It is unlikely that you'll openly invite nontechnical browsers to dig into your scripts, so access to the Script Editor via a script won't find its way into many applications. But it does become useful when a HyperTalk programmer develops utility types of scripts that aid in the programming task. One such utility might search all object scripts in a stack for a particular command or word. If the script finds a match, the Edit Script command will open up the Script Editor for that object, bypassing all the object selection and double-clicking that is otherwise necessary.

If your stacks are destined to be used by nonprogramming types, make other provisions for user-modified scripts. The Set command allows you to write scripts that modify any object script without opening the Script Editor. If you can design a less-frightening interface to the script than the Script Editor, do so. Let a script make the actual changes in the object scripts.

**Parameters:** The only parameter to the Edit Script command is the name of the object whose Script Editor you wish to open. You may refer to the object by its name, ID, or number, just as in referring to objects with other HyperTalk commands.

**Examples:**

```
edit script of background button ID 4
edit script of background "Country Maps"
edit script of card field 1
edit script of stack "Address"
```

**You Try It:** From the Home Card, type the following messages into the Message Box:

```
edit script of this stack
edit script of background field 1
edit script of background button "Next"
```

# CHAPTER 25

# Screen Manipulation Commands

HYPERCARD GIVES YOU COMMANDS TO INFLUENCE THE VISUAL EFFECT OF SHIFTING from one card or one stack to another. You also have commands that present dialog boxes on the screen, which prompt the user for information.

**visual** [effect] <effect name> [<speed>] [ to black | white | gray | inverse ]

**PURPOSE:** Controls the built-in visual effect for the next switch to another card.

**WHEN TO USE IT:** For a visual effect to impact the switch to the next card, you must specify the effect some time prior to the next card switch but within the same handler. It may be in the script line just above the Go command or anyplace earlier in the script, as long as there is no intervening Go command (or Find command whose search will show a different card). Internally, HyperCard remembers the last Visual Effect command that was sent and holds that effect in safekeeping for the next time HyperCard goes to another card. But at the end of the handler (that is, at "idle" time), the visual effect is forgotten.

To keep your visual effects connected to the desired card switch, it is perhaps best to place the Visual Effect command immediately preceding the Go or Find command that calls up the next card. This will also help you find a Visual Effect command that needs editing, since it will be close to the card shift command in question.

**Parameters:** The word "effect" is optional in the command, but you may find it helpful in long scripts to have the longer version, because it makes it easier to find the command line with "visual effect" in it. Effect names must be the correct name from the following list:

| | | | |
|---|---|---|---|
| zoom open \| in | zoom close \| out | | |
| iris open | iris close | | |
| barn door open | barn door close | | |
| wipe right | wipe left | wipe up | wipe down |
| scroll right | scroll left | scroll up | scroll down |
| dissolve | checkboard | venetian blinds | |

**Visual Effect Techniques:** Be aware that the zoom open and zoom close visual effects start or end their zooming on the point of the Browse tool's location when the mouse button is released. Therefore, if you have a zoom open visual effect assigned to a button at the lower left corner of the screen, the zooming look will emanate from that corner when you release the mouse button. Similarly, a zoom close effect would zoom *to* that spot. If that's the desired effect, use it.

If the stacks you create are on-screen metaphors for real-world card files or forms files, be on the lookout for visual effects that emulate the flipping through of the cards when browsing to next and previous cards. Wipes are often good choices for this effect.

For a link that takes the viewer to a perceived lower, more microscopic level, consider the iris open visual effect. The iris opens from the center of the screen. When the link action is to a perceived higher level, use the opposite, iris close.

This brings up an important design point. You will help your browser get a better feeling for navigation through the stack if you choose complementary visual effects when the link branches to a card with a different look. For example, you might consider a barn door open effect when the browser clicks on a Help button in your stack to get to a help card. When the browser has finished the help card, he can press a "return" button to resume navigation through the primary stack. The return link should use the barn door close visual effect, the opposite of the one that brought the browser to the help card. The open and close variations of the effects help the browser perceive a distinct difference between the help system and the main part of your stack— like opening a reference book and then closing it when finished. These are useful psychological aids to help the browser successfully navigate your stack.

Another parameter, which controls the apparent speed of the visual effect, is optional. Possible choices are:

very slow
slow
fast

If you don't specify a speed parameter, HyperCard assumes you want normal speed.

Effects may also include an intermediate black or white screen between cards with the optional *to black* or *to gray* or *to inverse to white* parameters. These options open many more visual effects opportunities, such as replicating the wipe action of a slide projector. A button script for this action would be

```
on mouseUp
        visual effect wipe left fast to black
        visual effect wipe right fast
        go to next card
end mouseUp
```

**Examples:**

```
visual effect barn door right
visual dissolve to black
visual effect wipe up slowly
visual effect iris open very slowly
```

**You Try It:** You can perform the experiments here in any stack, but there's no guarantee that each of the effects will carry their full impact. That often depends largely on the graphics and text field content of the card designs you're switching between. The point here will be for you to watch closely how various effects look. Making the proper choice for your own stacks will be a matter of trial and error. Since visual effects are purged during idle time, you won't be able to experiment with them from the Message Box. Go to the Address stack and create a new card. Into a card script handler starting "on effectShow" type each of the visual effects commands separated by a *go next card* command line. Type *effectShow* into the Message Box, and watch the parade of visual effects on the stack.

## answer <question> [with <reply> [or <reply> [or <reply>] ] ]

**Purpose:** Prompts the user to make a choice from one, two, or three text buttons inside a small dialog box.

**When to Use It:** Whenever you need to ask the user to choose between two or three possibilities or just alert the user to something, the Answer command produces just the right dialog box (Figure 25–1). You can ask the user any question you want, as long as the question fits inside the width of the dialog box. You may specify up to three replies as parameters to the command. Each reply appears as a text button inside the dialog box, and the rightmost one is pre-highlighted for acceptance with a press of Return or Enter.

Typical applications include warnings, in which there might be a single button with "OK" in it. Better yet, the script that produces this kind of dialog box should offer both an "OK" and a "Cancel" button so that the user can back out of a button action taken inadvertently.

When the user clicks on a button, the text of the reply is put into the local variable It. From there, your script can make further decisions based on the content of that container (decision-making is explained in detail in chapter 37). The user may also exit the answer dialog without sending any reply to It by typing Command-Period.

**PARAMETERS:** The Answer command must have at least the <question> parameter supplied by the author. Text for the question should be placed into the command enclosed in quotation marks. The text may also come from a container, like a field or variable, in case your script will be tailoring the question based on the content of a field in the card. The question should be less than about forty characters to fit inside the dialog box. Chicago-12 is the only font allowed for the questions and replies inside the dialog box.

When phrasing the question, try to take the point of view of the stack's user. If the user will likely be an inexperienced computer or HyperCard user, avoid Macintosh or HyperCard jargon at all cost. If the dialog box is a warning, explain the consequences of proceeding.

If you don't include at least one <reply> parameter, HyperCard automatically inserts one that says "OK." HyperCard starts filling reply buttons in the dialog box from the right edge of the box. An answer command with two <reply> parameters will display the two buttons at the center and at the right of the box.

You don't have a lot of room for reply text, since the width of the reply buttons in the dialog box is fixed, and the text font is a rather robust Chicago-12. Therefore, be brief with your replies. Try to hold them to one word or two very short words.

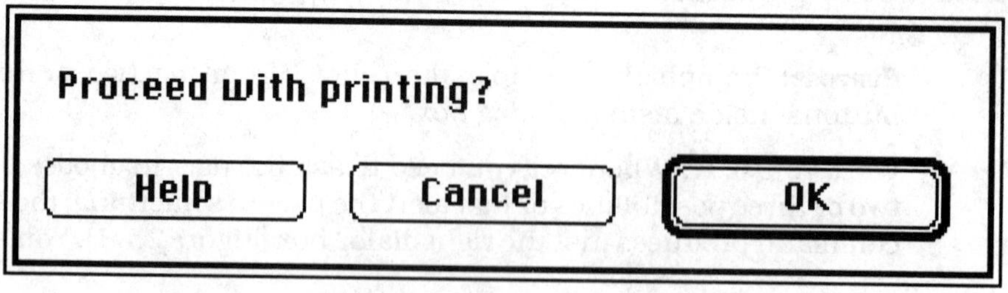

*Figure 25-1. The answer dialog box*

**Examples:**

```
answer "Pausing until you're ready..."
answer "Go ahead and erase card?" with "OK" or "Cancel"
answer "Who's your favorite?" with "Larry" or "Moe" or "Curly"
```

**You Try It:** If you've been looking for the power to produce dialog boxes on the screen, this is the experiment for you. You have full access to the Answer command from the Message Box. From any stack, type the following messages into the Message Box:

```
answer "What program are you using?" with "HyperCard"
it      -- contains the reply
answer "Proceed to blow up neighbor's PC?" with "OK" or "Cancel"
it      -- contains the reply you chose
answer "Take a break from this book?"with "Yes" or "No" or "Help"
it      -- contains the reply you chose
```

## ask <question> [with <reply>]
## ask password <question> [with <reply>]

**Purpose:** Prompt the user to type a text response.

**When to Use It:** The Ask command differs from the Answer command in that the ask dialog box produces a text field in which the user may type an answer, instead of having to choose only one of the options presented with the Answer command (Figure 25-2). Incorporate the Ask command into a script when you need additional information from your user. Often, the ask dialog makes a more controllable substitute for Message Box finding.

When the user types in the reply and presses Return or clicks the box's OK button, the text of the reply is automatically put into the It container. You may then retrieve the text, manipulate it, and insert it into other containers (fields and variables most likely) at your discretion.

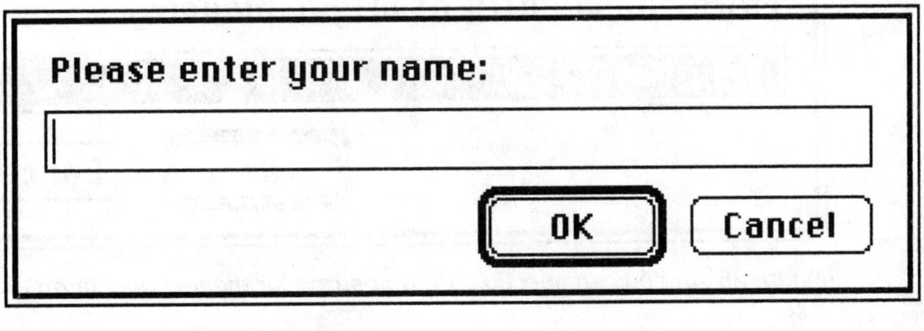

*Figure 25-2. The ask dialog box*

The Ask Password variation goes one step further. Instead of returning the text of the reply to It, HyperCard returns an encrypted integer representing the reply typed into the ask dialog. This feature allows an author to build password protection into a stack separate from his own Protect Stack system. At setup time, the stack should ask the browse to type a name or password, whose encrypted integer gets stored in a field someplace in the stack. Then, when someone tries to use the stack, he or she must know the password, whose encrypted integer is compared with the stored integer. Even if someone could "break into" the stack, the password would not be there—only its encrypted representation.

**PARAMETERS:** The Ask command must have at least the <question> parameter supplied by the author. Text for the question should be placed into the command enclosed in quotation marks. The text may also come from a container, like a field or variable, in case your script will be tailoring the question based on the content of a field in the card. The question should be less than about forty characters to fit inside the dialog box. Chicago-12 is the only font allowed for the questions and replies inside the dialog box.

When phrasing the question, try to take the point of view of the stack's user. If the user will likely be an inexperienced computer or HyperCard user, avoid Macintosh or HyperCard jargon at all cost.

If you don't specify a <reply> parameter to the Ask command, HyperCard presents an empty text box inside the dialog box. You may, however, present in that field a default reply, which the user may accept or type over. The default reply is automatically selected for the user when the box appears (Figure 25-3). You may use any container as the source of the text for the reply parameter. If the input your stack needs must be in a particular format (like a date), you can place a sample of the format as the default reply to show the user how to type the information.

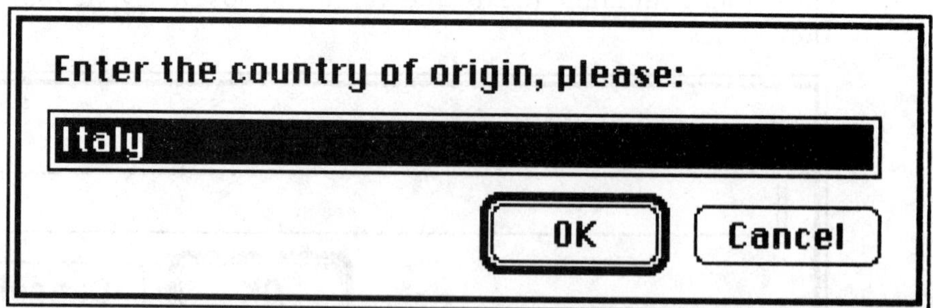


*Figure 25-3. You can specify a default string for the text field in an ask dialog box.*

**Examples:**

```
ask "What's cookin' tonight?"
ask "Search for..."
ask "Enter hourly rate:" with "25"
ask "Enter your name:" with field "Name" in card "Setup"
ask "Enter your birthdate:" with "3/15/55"
```

**You Try It:** As with the Answer dialog box, you may play to your heart's content with the Ask dialog box from the Message Box. For starters, type the following messages in the Message Box in any stack:

```
ask "Name your favorite music performer:"
it      -- contains the name you typed in
ask "Enter your desired salary..." with "$100,000"
it      -- contains either $100,000 or another number you typed in
ask Password "What's your name?"
it      -- contains the encrypted integer of your reply.
```

# CHAPTER 26

# Sound Commands

HYPERCARD IS CAPABLE OF PRODUCING TWO KINDS OF SOUNDS, INCLUDING ONE YOU'VE probably heard plenty of: the Macintosh beep. The other is an entirely open-ended system that allows you to play back electronically recorded sounds from the real world. That includes real voices, sound effects, and music.

## beep [<number of beeps>]

**PURPOSE:** Emits the Macintosh system beep through the computer's speaker or audio port.

**WHEN TO USE IT:** As you've seen in dozens of examples throughout this book, the Beep command is often helpful in exploring the workings of scripts and commands. When placed in strategic locations throughout a message handler, this command provides an aural clue about what's going on inside a handler as it runs.

The beep tone is a fixed one and cannot be played at any other pitch or length. You can control the number of beeps, however. Still, the Beep command is not the one to use if you wish your HyperCard stacks to play a tune at a particular juncture in its operation (see the Play command).

Outside of programming and script debugging, the Beep command can be quite functional in a HyperCard application when you wish to call attention to something, like an Answer dialog box. Sometimes you have to alert the user that he must take some action. A beep serves well as that alarm.

**Parameters:** The sole parameter to the Beep command influences the number of times the Macintosh beeps. You may use a plain number, any arithmetic expression (that is, any formula that evaluates to a number), or a container that holds a number. If you leave off the parameter, HyperCard beeps once.

If you specify multiple beeps and find they occur too close together for your liking, you can artificially slow down the beep effect. One way would be to issue single Beep commands with Wait commands interleaved. If the number of beeps is fairly large, however, you may want to place this beep-and-wait combination in a repeat looping construction (detailed in chapter 35).

**Examples:**

```
beep
beep 3
beep field "beeps"
beep beeper -- beeper is a local variable
```

**You Try It:** You may already have beeped enough, but if you'd like to hear a few more, type the following messages into the Message Box from any stack:

```
beep
beep 1
beep 5
put 2 into beeper
beep beeper
```

## play

<voice> [tempo <speed>] [ <notes> ] [# | b] [octave] [duration]

**Purpose:** Plays prerecorded sounds as musical notes at varying tempi, pitches, and lengths.

**When to Use It:** Built into HyperCard is a rather extensive single-voice music generator controlled by the Play command. What it does, actually, is extract the waveform from a prerecorded sound and allows you to play it through the Macintosh speaker or audio port at any tempo and note pitch you wish. In order to use this feature to the fullest, it helps to know something about musical notation, because the parameters are largely based on standard musical terminology.

Recording the actual sounds requires an external device called a digitizer. This box has a microphone and other audio input connectors. The unit records short segments of any sound— including real voices— as electronic signals, similar to the way digital audio on the compact disc works. These sounds need to be converted into a Macintosh resource file and added to a HyperCard stack file using a resource mover utility program.

In addition to playing back the direct sound as it was recorded, HyperCard can play back any sound with a wide variation in speed and pitch. If you string together many notes in a Play command, you can literally have your HyperCard application play a single voice of music for the user at key places in your stack. HyperCard comes equipped with the following sounds already installed as resources on the Home stack:

Harpsichord
Boing
Silence
Dialing Tones

**Parameters:** The Play command has what may look to be a complicated set of parameters. Not all of them are necessary, although they are if you intend to make music with digitized sounds.

The only required parameter is the name of the voice the Play command should use. The name must be in quotation marks and must match the spelling of the resource name containing the waveform.

Tempo is optional. If none is specified, HyperCard uses the last one set (or a medium value of 200). It's difficult to attribute a tempo value to the more traditional way of measuring tempo, beats per minute. You may wish to assign the tempo as the last parameter you insert into the Play command. Get the notes down first, then work on adjusting the tempo.

Calling for notes is as simple as using the familiar letters (a, b, c, d, e, f, and g) of the scale. Notes may be natural (no accidental parameter), sharp (#), or flat (b). If you don't specify any octave for the first note in a Play command, HyperCard plays in the middle octave (around middle C), which has an octave value of 4. Once you set an octave value in the command, it remains in effect for subsequent notes in the same command line or until you specifically change it. An octave value runs from c through the next higher b. Figure 26–1 shows how the middle three octaves break out according to HyperCard octave values.

Notes are also assigned note numbers, with 60 being middle C. Each number up or down represents one-half step. If you use note numbers, you needn't bother with octave and accidental parameters.

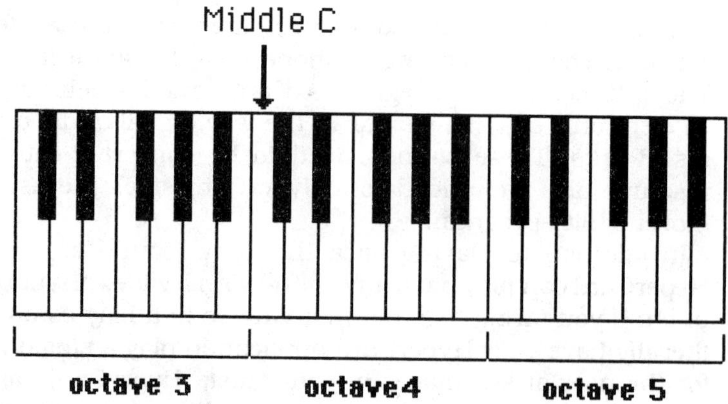


*Figure 26-1. The middle three octaves of the Play command are the ones with the best audio quality on the Macintosh Plus speaker.*

Note duration may range from a whole note to a 32nd note. The notation for the duration parameter is as follows:

| | |
|---|---|
| w | whole note |
| h | half note |
| q | quarter note |
| e | eighth note |
| s | sixteenth note |
| t | thirty-second note |

You may extend the duration of a note by one-half its value by typing a period after the note value, as in a dotted eighth note (e.). To turn a note into a triplet at the current tempo and note value, add a 3 to the note duration.

To play a continuous musical melody, string all the notes of the melody together after a single Play command. A quarter note scale from middle c to one octave above middle c (c') would look like this:

```
play "boing" tempo 200 "cq d e f g a b c5"
```

Notice that once an octave and note value are set, they remain in effect throughout the rest of the Play command, unless either of those values changes for a note. Treat each note as a single entity, no matter how many parameters it requires. For example, an eighth note f-sharp an octave below the middle octave would be f#3e.

If the sound recorded by the digitizer is self-contained, like a sound effect or a person's voice you'd like to play at the original pitch and speed, then simply issue the Play command with the name of the sound. No other parameters are necessary.

**Examples:**

play "boing"
play "breakingGlass"
play "harpsichord" tempo 120 "ce e g c5 e g4 c5 e"

**You Try It:** We could go on all day providing you with ditties to type into the Message Box, but we'll give you only a couple. If you're musically inclined, you will know how to apply your own music to the Play command and work up a single-voice symphony. Experimenting with the Play command in the Message Box is also the way you should develop Play commands that will eventually go into stacks. By typing the command there, you can immediately hear it and make any changes to iron out the clinkers. Then copy the finished command and paste it into your script.

So have fun, and type the following messages into field 1 of an empty Address stack card without pressing Return until you've typed the entire command. Then create a new card button with the mouseUp handler that reads *do field 1* and click the button to make these commands work.

play "harpsichord" tempo 180 "a es eq es f# g# a b c#5q a4s
aq g#3s a b aq ew"
play "Boing" tempo 240 "c#4e d# f f# a#t g#e g g# f f# g# a# b
d#5t c#5e c c5# bb4e. be d5t d#e g#4 bb4t be f
gt g#e c# et fe f# at a#e c# et f#e a3# c4t c#e f#3w"

CHAPTER 27

# File Manipulation Commands

ALTHOUGH HYPERCARD IS A POWERFUL ENVIRONMENT UNTO ITSELF, IT DOES NOT operate in a vacuum. You can import information from other applications and export HyperCard information to other documents. These abilities are carried out by the file manipulation commands. So is the ability to print any Macintosh document (for which you have the application on disk) from within HyperCard.

## open file <file name>
## close file <file name>

**PURPOSE:** Prepares the pathway between HyperCard and the external disk file for subsequent reading or writing; closes the pathway when it is no longer needed.

**WHEN TO USE IT:** The Open File and Close File commands are used only when you import or export text. Before you can read or write textual information outside HyperCard, you must tell HyperCard that it should open the file. This gives HyperCard an opportunity to create the file on the disk (if it isn't there to begin with) or find it on the disk (if it is). Without this preconditioning, HyperCard won't be able to send text from a stack's fields to a disk file, nor will it be able to read text from an external file and "type" it into a card's fields.

Experienced programmers will recognize these commands, because virtually every computer's operating system software requires that a file be specifically "opened" before anything can be read from it or written to it. Similarly, once all the manipulation is done, the file must be "closed" to prevent any accidental writing to it. Therefore, be sure that all Open File commands have corresponding Close File commands in the script.

**Parameters:** The only parameter for Open File and Close File is the name of the file. The name must appear in quotation marks. If you don't specify a path name to the file, HyperCard looks only at the root (topmost) level of the current disk. You may detail a different path as part of the file name parameter.

As with any text parameter, the file name parameter may be straight text, or text from a container. Therefore, you can build a file name inside a container before calling the Open File command, if, for example, you wish to append the date to the file name you're going to write to.

**Examples:**

```
open file "Expenses"
open file ":Membership:Roster:Labels"
open file newFile -- newFile is a local variable
```

**You Try It:** Since these two commands don't appear to do anything when you call them, there is little point in experimenting with them from the Message Box. To prove that the commands access the disk drive, you can try the following messages in the Message Box from any stack:

```
open file "Open Test"
close file "Open Test"
```

## read

from file <file name> until <delimiter character> |
for <number of bytes>

**Purpose:** Imports text data from an external file into fields in the card.

**When to Use It:** Importing text from external files is particularly useful if you have database or spreadsheet information you'd like to convert to HyperCard. This is not a simple operation if the information consists of many fields per card. We explain more about this ability of HyperCard in Appendix A.

A good place to start learning about the Read From File command is the following Import Text button. The script in this button is a basic skeleton of the kind of script you use to retrieve data from an outside file and put it into a stack's cards. The script reads as follows:

```
on mouseUp
	ask "Which file do you wish to import?" with "Transfer Text"
	if it is empty then exit mouseUp
	put it into fileName
	open file fileName
	go to last card
	repeat forever
		doMenu "New Card"

		read from file fileName until return
		if it is empty then
			go to first card
			close file fileName
			exit mouseUp
		else put tab into last char of it
		repeat with x= 1 to the number of fields
			put char 1 to offset (tab,it) of it into field x
			delete last char of field x
			delete char 1 to offset (tab,it) of it
		end repeat
	end repeat
end mouseUp
```

The basic construction reads a full record (up to the return character) into memory at once. When there are no more records to import, the handler ends. In the meantime, external data from each field is placed into its own card field (minus the tab character) and deleted from memory (field by field) with each journey through the loop.

**Parameters:** The <file name> parameter must appear in quotation marks. If you don't specify a path name to the file, HyperCard looks through only to the root (topmost) level of the current disk for the file name. You may also detail a different path as part of the file name parameter. Importantly, the file must have been opened with the Open File command earlier in the script for this command to work.

As with any text parameter, the file name parameter may be straight text or text from a container.

When reading from a file, this command needs to know when to pause gathering information so that it doesn't overload a card or field. The command may read until it encounters a particular character or a fixed number of characters (1 byte = 1 character).

A <delimiter character> is a special character in a file that sets apart individual items. The most common delimiter character used to separate field information in database and spreadsheet files is the Tab character. The character used to separate one group of information from another group (in HyperCard terms, one card from another card) is the Return character. In other words, these characters are stored in the file along with the textual information. By specifying what the delimiter characters are in the file, the Read From File command will know when to stop filling information into a field and to proceed to the next field on the card. Then your script can check for the delimiter character that means all the fields have been filled and it's time to make a new card.

Study the skeleton script, above, and follow the logic of its execution.

**Examples:**

```
read from file "Sales Data" until tab
read from file temp until return -- temp is local variable
read from file "My File" for 40
```

**You Try It:** Combine experiments on the Read command with experiments on its counterpart, Write, below.

## write <source> to file <file name>

**Purpose:** Exports text data from a HyperCard card to a Macintosh text file.

**When to Use It:** Exporting text to external files is particularly useful if you wish to convert HyperCard information to data usable in external database or spreadsheet programs. This is not a simple operation if the information consists of many fields per card. We explain more about this ability of HyperCard in Appendix A.

A good place to start learning about the Write To File command is the following Export Text button script. The script in this button is a basic skeleton of the kind of script you use to send data to an outside file. The script reads as follows:

```
on mouseUp
    put the short name of this stack && " text" into fileName
    ask "Export text to what file?" with fileName
    if it is empty then exit mouseUp
    put it into fileName
    open file fileName
    go to first card
    repeat for the number of cards
    put empty into tempRecord
        repeat with x=1 to the number of fields
            put field x & tab after tempRecord
        end repeat
        put return into last char of tempRecord
```

```
            write tempRecord to file fileName
            go to next card
        end repeat
        close file fileName
    end mouseUp
```

The basic construction requires the script to store individual HyperCard fields in a local variable, inserting a tab character at the end of each field. When all the fields in the card are stored, the script adds a return character, writes the contents to the file, and goes to the next card in the stack to repeat the process (the repeat structures will be explained in chapter 37).

You can use the basic script for a great deal of the exporting tasks you'll need in HyperCard. If you need further help in customizing the script for special purposes, consult Appendix A.

**PARAMETERS:** The <source> parameter is the name or number of a field. HyperCard must know which field's information is to be exported for each card.

The <file name> parameter must appear in quotation marks. If you don't specify a path name to the file, HyperCard places the file in the root directory of your disk. You may also detail a different path as part of the file name parameter. Importantly, the file must have been opened with the Open File command earlier in the script for this command to work.

As with any text parameter, the file name parameter may be straight text or text from a container.

Unlike the Read command, the Write command does not include delimiter characters to outgoing text. Your script must write these, as indicated in the sample script.

**EXAMPLES:**

```
write to file "Mailing Labels"
write to file temp -- temp is a local variable
```

**YOU TRY IT:** The best way to try the Write and Read commands would be to use the button scripts provided above. That will give you an idea of the way a script can repeat the procedure.

In the meantime, here's a simple way to write out one field from an address card and then import it back into another card. Before you begin, be sure you have no existing disk file called "New File." If you do, this experiment will erase it. Type the following messages into the Message Box from a filled-in card in the Address stack:

```
open file "New File"
write field 1 to file "New File"
write tab to file "New File"
```

```
close file "New File"
doMenu "New Card"
open file "New File"
read from file "New File" until tab
put it into field 2
close file "New File"
```

## print <file name> with <application>

**Purpose:** Prints a file generated by another Macintosh application.

**When to Use:** The Print command gives you the opportunity to recreate from within HyperCard the same Print command available in the Finder. That command lets you select a document and print it directly from the Finder, without having to open the document first.

When you issue this Print command from a HyperTalk script, HyperCard launches the application and loads the document for printing. When it is finished printing, the application automatically quits, and you come back to the place in HyperCard from which you generated the Print command.

**Parameters:** Two parameters are required for the Print command. The first is the name of the document file you wish to print. The file name must be in quotation marks or be in a container. HyperCard looks to the Documents card in the Home Stack for the possible pathnames for documents to search for the file. You may also specify a full pathname as the file name parameter.

The second parameter is the name of the application program that created the document you wish to print. Application names must be in quotation marks or in containers. HyperCard looks to the Applications card in the Home Stack for the possible pathnames for applications, or you may specify a full pathname for the application parameter.

It's important to remember that the application name parameter must match the precise name given the application in the Finder. That means all special characters, like the trademark symbol, must be in the parameter. Such special characters are available from the keyboard, usually in Option-key combinations. Some of the most popular ones are:

| | | |
|---|---|---|
| Registered Trademark | ® | Option-R |
| Copyright | © | Option-G |
| Trademark | ™ | Option-2 |
| Bullet | • | Option-8 |

**Examples:**

```
print "3/12 Letter" with "Word 3.0"
print temp with "Excel" -- temp is a local variable
print "Report" with  "Works"
```

**You Try It:** Since there's no way for us to know the documents and applications you have on your disk, you'll have to experiment with this command on your own. Just be sure you include the quotation marks around your document and application names, and watch out for special symbols (and version numbers) in the actual names of application programs.

This concludes the tour of the HyperTalk command set. In the next chapter, we look at the many properties that you can inspect and set through HyperTalk.

# CHAPTER 28

# HyperCard Properties

IN CHAPTER 24, WE INTRODUCED THE CONCEPT OF PROPERTIES, WHICH CAN BE retrieved and set by the Get and Set commands, respectively. Now you'll see precisely what these properties are all about and how useful they can be when you try to automate processes for nonprogramming HyperCard browsers. Virtually every setting you can make in an object dialog box or in the HyperCard Preferences card can be set from a HyperTalk script.

The importance of being able to "get" a property is that you can read what it currently is from within a script. If the setting is different from what you want it to be (something the script can determine with an *if-then-else* control structure), the script can make the desired setting. You should also endeavor to reset properties to their original settings after you've modified them for the purposes of a single message handler.

When you use the Get command to retrieve a property, HyperCard places the current reading into It. From there, your handler may make whatever decisions or conversions are necessary inside that variable.

HyperCard properties fall into eight natural classes, although some classes have many more properties than others. We'll follow this classification system, working our way from the most "global" to the narrowest property settings, those having to do with fields and buttons.

HyperCard lets you be terse or more English-like in your syntax when referring to properties that have parameters following them. On the terse side, you can say things like *get loc of Message*; but it may be more natural to say *get the location of the Message Box.* In other words, you may put *the* in front of a property name, and in front of any reference to the Message Box.

If the property has no parameters, then *the* is required before the name of the property, except in Get and Set command lines. It's a good idea to get in the habit of using *the* with such properties, because their behavior is very similar to functions, as you'll see in a later chapter.

## *Global Properties*

In the global properties categories are those that can have a major effect on the operation of a stack or how the user interacts with a stack. You might think of these properties as properties of the HyperCard object in the hierarchy of objects. The settings in the Home Stack's Preferences card set global properties.

### **blindTyping** <true or false>

**PURPOSE:** Controls the ability to type into a hidden Message Box.

**WHEN TO USE IT:** When you check the Blind Typing checkbox in the Preferences card, the blindTyping property is set to true, meaning that you can type into the Message Box even if it is not showing on the screen. Beginners should probably keep this property set to false, because it may be disconcerting to type and not get any visual feedback that the Message Box is actually accepting the text. But more experienced HyperCard users may prefer to be able to type blindly to enter quick commands without having to show the Message Box.

When typing blind, however, you had better be an accurate typist. Since you can't see any mistakes you make, all you'll get is a beep and an alert box from HyperCard if you make a slip of the digit. Fortunately, because whatever you type into a hidden Message Box stays in the box, you can see it by typing Command-M or choosing Message from the Go menu.

**EXAMPLES:**

```
get the blindTyping
set the blindTyping to false
```

**YOU TRY IT:** Use a blank Address stack card for this experiment. Make the Message Box visible, and type the following messages into it:

```
get the blindTyping
set the blindTyping to true
```

```
hide msg
put "howdy" into field 1
show msg
set the blindTyping to false
hide msg
uh oh
(Command-M)
set the blindTyping to it
```

## **cursor** <ID number or name>

**Purpose:** Controls which preset cursor displays on the screen during a script.

**When to Use It:** You may change the shape of the cursor during the execution of a script by setting the cursor property to an existing cursor. The Macintosh system has four predefined cursors that you can call up by their internal ID numbers. They are shown in Figure 28-1.

Perhaps the most important one to note is the watch cursor. If you have designed an extensive script that causes the user to have to wait more than about one second, it would be a good idea to set the cursor to 4 prior to undertaking the rest of the lengthy script. Macintosh users are accustomed to waiting relatively patiently when the watch cursor is on the screen. If any other cursor is showing while a script is silently churning away, the user may feel that the program has "hung up" or is unnecessarily slow in its execution. Surprisingly, the watch cursor eliminates many of those negative feelings.

The cursor property always reverts to HyperCard's normal cursor settings when a script ends, that is, when HyperCard starts sending idle messages. This property is settable only. The Get command does not work with the cursor property.

**Examples:**

```
set the cursor to 1
set the cursor to 4
```

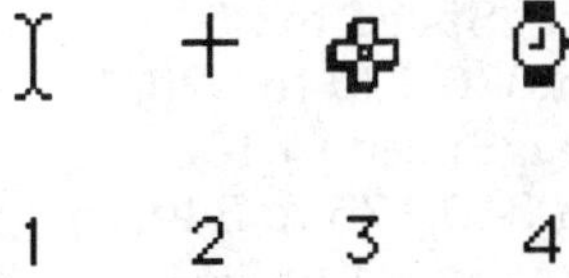


*Figure 28-1. The four cursors installed in the Macintosh System and their ID numbers.*

**You Try It:** Because the cursor property returns to its regular HyperCard setting at idle time, it will be difficult but not impossible to see the four cursors available to you from the Macintosh system while typing a Set cursor command into the Message Box. The trick is to type the message and hold down the Return key while the cursor quickly flashes between the Browse tool and the selected cursor. Try it now with the four cursor settings.

## dragSpeed <number>

**Purpose:** Controls the speed, in pixels per second, at which the Drag command operates.

**When to Use It:** If your script uses the Drag command, principally to draw shapes on the screen with any of the painting tools, you can control the speed at which the drawing occurs with the dragSpeed property. If you set the number to zero, the tool will drag at the fastest speed your Macintosh is capable of. Other settings, however, control the number of pixels per second at which the tool will traverse the screen.

In certain instructional stacks, you may want to slow down dragging so the user can see exactly how a drawing is made. A comfortable speed to watch drawing is at around 150. At idle time, the dragSpeed property returns to zero.

**Examples:**

```
get the dragSpeed
set the dragSpeed to 185
```

**You Try It:** Since the dragSpeed property returns to zero at idle time, you'll have to place a script in a button to see how various settings affect the drag speed of a painting tool. Go to a blank card in the Address stack and create a new button. Enter the following script into the button, and watch what happens when you click that button.

```
on mouseUp
    choose line tool
    set the lineSize to 2
    set the dragSpeed to 25
    drag from 320,175 to 320,75
    set the dragSpeed to 100
    drag from 340,175 to 340,75
    set the dragSpeed to 200
    drag from 360,175 to 360,75
```

```
        set the dragSpeed to 0
        drag from 380,175 to 380,75
        choose browse tool
    end mouseUp
```

## editBkgnd <true or false>

**Purpose:** Controls the edit domain.

**When to Use It:** If your scripts perform any actions in a background—painting pictures, pasting buttons or fields—use the editBkgnd property to go to and from the background domain. Setting this property to true places you in the background editing mode, complete with hash marks on the menubar.

As in the nonscripted world of HyperCard, if your script chooses the Browse tool, the editBkgnd property is set to false and the background editing mode is cancelled.

**Examples:**

```
get the editBkgnd
set the editBkgnd to true
```

**You Try It:** Type the following messages into the Message Box in any stack:

```
get the editBkgnd
it
set the editBkgnd to true
choose pencil tool
choose button tool
choose browse tool
```

## language <language name>

**Purpose:** Controls which language translator is in use.

**When to Use It:** Editions of HyperCard that have language translators built in can take advantage of this global property, which is also set in the Preferences card of the Home Stack. This property controls the way the Script Editor translates the English scripts stored on disk to the user's native language. There is likely little need to change the language property anyplace other than in the Preferences card. Still, you may wish to find out which language the user has his HyperCard set to in case your scripts address the user in multiple languages.

**Examples:**

get the language
set the language to German

**You Try It:** If your edition of HyperCard does not have any language translators in it, you won't be able to try this property, other than to get the alert box that tells you no translator is installed for that language. You can try it anyway. Type the following messages into the Message Box in any stack:

get the language
it
set the language to Japanese
set the language to it

## lockScreen <true or false>

**Purpose:** Controls screen updating during script execution.

**When to Use It:** Some message handlers need to go to various cards on their way to retrieve information or find a specific card in another stack. All the screen activity associated with such motions may be distracting to the user. If you prefer to hide all the commotion from sight, you can set the lockScreen property to true, prior to shifting around the stacks. This action essentially freezes and disconnects the screen from HyperCard. In the meantime, HyperCard can go ahead and perform any activity it would do normally, including putting information into fields, cutting and pasting buttons, and drawing graphics in the background. HyperCard also records each card the script attends to in its card history (although not in Recent), even though you don't see the cards pass before your eyes.

By locking the screen, you also help speed execution of a script that would otherwise be drawing many cards on the screen each time a new card appeared. You might still wish to set the cursor property to 4, so that the watch cursor indicates something is happening, when there is no action on the screen.

Even though the screen is locked, Message Box showing and hiding is still active. That means, however, that if the Message Box is hidden in the middle of a locked screen script, the Macintosh won't fill in the blank space underneath the box. Therefore, carefully orchestrate the showing and hiding of the Message Box to take place when the screen is not locked.

The lockScreen property reverts to false at idle time, so you needn't set the property to false at the end of a script. You may, however, wish to lock the screen during only part of a lengthy script. In that case, set lockScreen to false when you're ready for the user to see some action and the script still has more to do.

**Examples:**

```
get the lockScreen
set the lockScreen to true
```

**You Try It:** Because the lockScreen property returns to falseat idle time, you won't be able to test it from the Message Box. Go to the Address stack and create a card button on a blank card with the following script. Then click on the button and watch what happens and what doesn't happen.

```
on mouseUp
        set the cursor to 4
        set the lockScreen to true
        go next
        go next
        go "Home"
        go card "Stacks"
end mouseUp
```

## numberFormat <format string>

**Purpose:** Controls the format of the displayed result of a math calculation.

**When to Use It:** Scripts often perform calculations on numbers. Currency or metric conversions, for instance, often require that highly disparate magnitudes of values be multiplied or divided. When such calculations are performed, their accuracy is heavily influenced by the number of digits to the right of the decimal point to which the calculations are carried out. The greater the number of digits, the higher the accuracy. In math circles, this type of accuracy is called *precision.*

Unlike a spreadsheet program, HyperCard stores numbers in its fields as straight text. If a number is stored as 3.96, that's all that HyperCard knows about the number, even if it was the result of a much more precise calculation that had several digits further to the right of the decimal. When the number was stored in the HyperCard field with two decimal digits, any further precision was lost.

The numberFormat property establishes the precision (that is, the number of digits to the right of the decimal point) to which the result of any calculations in a script will be displayed or stored in a container.

After the script, at idle time, the numberFormat returns to the default setting of six digits to the right of the decimal.

The parameter to the numberFormat property is a string with a sample of what the format should be, using three special characters: the zero, the decimal, and the crosshatch. When you specify a zero in a location on either side of the decimal point, you tell HyperCard to display a zero in that location if no other number fills it. For example, the format "0.00" is the one you would use for displaying dollars and cents, because you always want the one cent column to have a digit there. A calculated result of 7.6 would display as 7.60.

Use the crosshatch character when you are not concerned about displaying zeros but want displayed precision to a certain number of digits to the right of the decimal. Therefore, the format "0.######" displays the result with up to six digits to the right of the decimal and always shows a zero in the ones column of a result.

Since the format change takes effect only after the next arithmetic operation, the script may have to perform a "dummy" operation, like adding a zero, to apply the format to the number. If the new format is shorter than the previous one, HyperCard rounds the digits cut off by the new format.

**Examples:**

```
get the numberFormat
set the numberFormat to "0.00"
set the numberFormat to "0.############"
set the numberFormat to "00.00"
```

**You Try It:** The numberFormat property returns to the default setting at idle time, so you'll have to experiment with the help of a button script in a blank card of the Address stack. Enter the following script in a card button:

```
on mouseUp
    set the numberFormat to "0.00"
    put 1/8 into line 1 of field 1
    set the numberFormat to "0.000"
    put 1/8 into line 2 of field 1
    set the numberFormat to "0.00"
    put "$" && 1/8 into line 3 of field 1
end mouseUp
```

## powerKeys <true or false>

**Purpose:** Controls Power Keys setting.

**When to Use It:** Power Keys are the keyboard shortcuts available when you use the Painting tools. The powerKeys global property is the one that turns them on for you when you set the Preference card to do so. It is unlikely you'll need to adjust this setting in a script, but the stack script in the HyperCard Home stack sets it each time you start HyperCard.

**Examples:**

```
get the powerKeys
set the powerKeys to true
```

**You Try It:** You may send a *set powerKeys to false* message from the Message Box if you like, just to verify that this property does work. Then choose a painting tool, select a graphic element, and try one of the Paint menu items normally controlled by a Power Key. It won't work from the keyboard. We suggest you keep Power Keys turned on to help speed your painting work.

## userLevel <1 to 5>

**Purpose:** Controls the User Level for an entire HyperCard session.

**When to Use It:** The five possible settings correspond to the levels listed in the Home Stack's Preferences card:

| | |
|---|---|
| 1 | Browsing |
| 2 | Typing |
| 3 | Painting |
| 4 | Authoring |
| 5 | Scripting |

As you recall, each of these levels provides a fixed amount of access to modifying information in a stack or the stack itself. If you are distributing a stack whose access you wish to restrict, your openStack script would set the userLevel property to the one that is most appropriate for that stack.

If you do change the userLevel in a stack, it is your responsibility to get the previous userLevel (or fetch it from the Preferences card) and restore the property to its original setting upon closing the stack. You might want to get the property at the open, place the numbered setting in a global variable, and use that variable to restore the setting in a closeStack script.

**Examples:**

```
get the userLevel
```

```
set the userLevel to 2
set the userLevel to priorLevel -- a global variable
```

**You Try It:** Type the following messages into the Message Box and check the menubar and menus after each to see how the setting changed the user access to the system.

```
get the userLevel
it
set the userLevel to 1
set the userLevel to 2
choose pencil tool            -- not at this level!
set the userLevel to 3
choose pencil tool            -- OK now
choose browse tool
set the userLevel to it       -- restore level
```

## *Window Properties*

HyperCard has three windows whose properties you may read and, in some cases, change from a script. The windows are known as the *Message Window* (and its variants: *Message Box, Message*, or just *Msg*), *Tool Window*, and *Pattern Window*. You may get the location of the center of a window, the coordinates of the rectangle comprising a window, and the current visibility of a window.

# loc[ation]

**Purpose:** Controls the top left corner point of a window.

**When to Use It:** You may get and set the location of any window on the screen, using the coordinate system of the Macintosh screen. When you get the location of a window, HyperCard returns (into It) the coordinates of the top left corner of the window's content region (just below the grey title bar). To place the window somewhere else on the screen, simply set the location to a different set of coordinates. Coordinate parameters, which list the horizontal measure first, must be separated by a comma.

Setting the location of a window does not influence its visibility. Therefore, you may set the location of a window, like the Message Box, without showing it first on the screen.

**Examples:**

```
get the location of Tool Window
```

```
set the loc of Pattern Window to 200,70
set the loc of Msg to 25,310
```

**You Try It:** Type the following messages into the Message Box in any stack:

```
get the loc of msg
it
show tool window
get the loc of tool window
it
subtract 25 from item 1 of it
set the loc of tool window to it
hide tool window
```

## rect[angle]

**Purpose:** Reveals the top left and bottom right coordinates of a window.

**When to Use It:** The rect property cannot be set, because the sizes of the three windows are fixed within HyperCard. You can, however, get their screen coordinates if it is important for you to make sure they don't overlap each other or some graphical element on your screen when the windows appear.

The rectangle coordinates returned by the *get rect* command (the coordinates go into It), are in the form *left,top,right,bottom*— four numbers separated by commas. You are free to perform calculations on any item in the coordinates. For example, if you determine that the bottom right corner of a window will overlap a special graphics area on a card by 15 pixels in the horizontal plane, then you can subtract 15 from the first item in It, delete the last two items, and set the location of the window to It.

**Examples:**

```
get the rect of Message Box
get the rect of Tool Window
```

**You Try It:** Since this is a read-only parameter, the following experiment lets you find the current coordinates of the three windows. Type these messages into the Message Box in any stack:

```
get the rect of Message
it
get the rect of Tool Window
it
get the rect of Pattern Window
it
```

## visible <true or false>

**Purpose:** Controls the visibility of a window.

**When to Use It:** The visible property is more likely to be used with the Get command than the Set command, because it is quicker to type the shorter Hide and Show commands into a script. In practice, it will be more efficient for your script to simply hide or show a window regardless of its current visibility state. To test for whether a window's visible property is true or false will be a waste of HyperTalk's time. There is no penalty for hiding a window that is already hidden.

**Examples:**

```
get the visible of msg
set the visible of tool window to true
```

**You Try It:** Although it's a lot more typing than the Hide and Show commands, type the following visible property messages into the Message Box in any stack:

```
get the visible of msg
it
set the visible of tool window to true
set the visible of tool window to false
set the visible of msg to false
set the visible of msg to true -- how good is your blind typing?
```

# *Painting Properties*

When your scripts invoke the painting tools to draw graphics on cards, you will probably need access to various painting properties. These are the settings largely contained in the Options menu, which applies to all tools, and in the font dialog box, which applies to the text tool only. Virtually everything you can set manually can also be set from a script, giving your scripts the ability to work as fully as a human operator could.

## brush <brush number 1 to 32>

**Purpose:** Controls the brush shape for the Paintbrush tool.

**When to Use It:** Prior to dragging the brush from one point to another, you may wish to choose a brush shape other than the default round dot.

Setting this property to one of the thirty-two possible brush shapes is the same as clicking on one of the shapes in the brush shape dialog box.

In that dialog box are graphic representations of all brush shapes in a twelve-by-eight table. Each brush shape has a number assigned to it from 1 to 32. The numbering starts at the top left corner and works its way down the first column. The brush shape at the top of the second column from the left is number 5. Unless you change the brush shape, the default setting is shape number 8. Use the Set command to set the brush property to the desired shape.

**Examples:**

```
get the brush
set the brush to 12
set the brush to 8
```

**You Try It:** To see the effect setting the brush property has, you can leave the cursor anyplace on a card and type the following messages into the Message Box. Watch the cursor change with each command.

```
choose brush tool
set the brush to 1
set the brush to 32
set the brush to 9
set the brush to 8
choose browse tool
```

## centered <true or false>
## filled <true or false>

**Purpose:** Controls the Options menu settings Draw Centered and Draw Filled.

**When to Use It:** Both the Draw Centered and Draw Filled commands apply to drawing shapes with the Rectangle, Round Rectangle, and Oval tools. Draw Filled also applies to the Curve, Regular Polygon, and Irregular Polygon tools. If your scripts are about to invoke any of these tools for drawing, consider whether you want the drawing to be from a centerpoint or filled with a pattern. Bear in mind that setting the filled property to true causes HyperCard to paint with the currently selected pattern. If you prefer a different pattern, then adjust the pattern property (see below).

**Examples:**

```
get the centered
set the centered to true
get the filled
set the filled to false
```

**You Try It:** The simplest way to watch these properties react to the Get and Set commands is to select any paint tool and pull down the Options menu after each command to see how the check-mark settings in the menu are affected. When the property is set to true, the item is checked in the menu, even though it was turned on by command rather than by menu selection. Type the following messages into the Message Box and inspect the Options menu after each command.

```
choose rect tool
get the centered
it
set the centered to true
get the centered
it
set the filled to true
```

## grid <true or false>

**Purpose:** Controls the painting Grid.

**When to Use It:** Turning on the Grid from a script may make sense if you're not sure that the coordinates you assign to the drag commands are completely accurate. With the Grid in force, the shapes will be drawn to the nearest 8-pixel square, assuring that shapes will be aligned to the invisible grid.

When a script turns on the Grid, the Grid item in the Options menu is checked, just as if you had turned it on with a menu selection.

**Examples:**

```
get the grid
set the grid to false
```

**You Try It:** Pull down the Options menu after typing each of the following lines into the Message Box. Watch the check mark next to the Grid menu item.

```
choose pencil tool
set the grid to true
set the grid to false
```

```
set the grid to true
choose browse tool
```

## lineSize <line thicknesses 1, 2, 3, 4, 6, or 8 pixels>

**Purpose:** Controls the thickness of lines painted by various tools.

**When to Use It:** Prior to dragging any tool that leaves a line (except the single-pixeled Pencil), consider adjusting the lineSize property. This is the same as selecting from the line size dialog box. If you don't adjust the lineSize property, the default setting is one pixel line thickness.

**Examples:**

```
get the lineSize
set the lineSize to 3
```

**You Try It:** Because the cross-hair cursor for all tools that draw with lines of varying thicknesses adjusts itself to the thickness of the lineSize property, you may watch the cursor get fat and thin with the typing of the Message Box messages below.

```
choose rect tool
set the lineSize to 2
set the lineSize to 3
set the lineSize to 8
get the lineSize
it
set the lineSize to 1
choose browse tool
```

## multiple <true or false>
## multiSpace <1 to 9>

**Purpose:** Controls the Draw Multiple menu option and the number of pixels between multiple images.

**When to Use It:** By setting the multiple property to true, you turn on the Draw Multiple item in the Options menu. This setting applies to drawing shapes with tools like the Rectangle, Round Rectangle, Oval, and Regular Polygon tools. A script may also adjust the spacing between multiple drawings by setting the multiSpace property to a number from 1 to 9. The number represents the number of pixels between each of the multiple shapes left in the wake of the tool.

**Examples:**

```
get the multiple
set the multiple to true
set the multiSpace to 5
```

**You Try It:** Create a new card in the Address stack in which you can experiment with drawing multiple shapes. After each set multiSpace command below, drag the chosen paint tool to see the effects.

```
choose round rect
set the multiple to true
set the multiSpace to 1
set the multiSpace to 4
set the multiSpace to 8
choose browse tool
```

## pattern <pattern number 1 to 40>

**Purpose:** Controls the currently selected pattern.

**When to Use It:** Filling areas with patterns and drawing filled patterns are both possible from scripts. Before you can do either, however, you must set the desired pattern by way of the pattern property.

Each of HyperCard's forty patterns has an identifying number based on its location in the Patterns palette. This palette displays samples of the patterns in four columns of ten patterns. Numbering starts with 1 at the upper left corner and works its way down the leftmost column. The pattern at the top of the second column from the left is pattern number 11.

To fill an existing enclosed region from a script, first set the pattern. Then choose the bucket tool and issue the *click at* command, specifying a pixel coordinate someplace inside the enclosed region.

**Examples:**

```
get the pattern
set the pattern to 12
```

**You Try It:** Type the following messages into the Message Box in any stack, and watch the pattern palette change with each setting of the pattern property.

```
set the visible of pattern window to true
get the pattern
it
set the pattern to 1
set the pattern to 25
```

```
set the pattern to 40
hide pattern window
```

## polySides <number of polygon sides greater than two >

**Purpose:** Controls the number of sides drawn by the Polygon tool.

**When to Use It:** The Regular Polygon tool lets the HyperCard author select from a palette of six standard polygons with 3, 4, 5, 6, 8, and infinite sides. Whatever number of sides is selected is stored in the polySides painting property. The minimum number of sides allowed is 3. You can set polySides to 12 to make a dodecagon. The problem with polygons with too many sides, however, is that the resolution of the Macintosh screen limits your ability to distinguish sides. After about fifteen sides, the objects look like circles.

Just as you set the number of polygon sides before dragging a regular polygon tool, so too do you set the polySides property in a script before the Drag command.

**Examples:**

```
get the polySides
set the polySides to 8
```

**You Try It:** Type the following messages into the Message Box. After each Set polySides command, drag a polygon on a blank card to see how the number of sides looks.

```
choose reg polygon tool
get the polySides
it
set the polysides to 2          -- 3 is the minimum
set the polysides to 12
set the polysides to 20
set the polysides to 5
choose browse tool
```

## textAlign <left | right | center>
## textFont <font name>
## textHeight <leading>
## textSize <font size>
## textStyle < bold | italic | underline | outline | shadow | condense | extend | plain>

**Purpose:** Controls font attributes of text painted with the Text tool.

**When to Use:** These five properties all represent settings in the font dialog box you can adjust when typing text with the painting Text tool. This gives you full control over the way painted text appears when a script types it into a card or background graphics layer.

Parameters to each of the properties should be self-explanatory in the list above, since the terms should be familiar to you by this point. When you set the textSize property, HyperCard automatically sets the textHeight (leading) property to approximately one-third again as large. If the default leading is acceptable, you won't have to adjust the textHeight property. The textStyle property may have any number of the parameters listed as possible styles. Simply list them as comma-separated parameters to the textStyle property.

**Examples:**

```
get the textHeight
set the textFont to New York
set the textSize to 14
set the textHeight to 16
set the textAlign to center
set the textStyle to condense, underline
```

**You Try It:** Type the following messages into the Message Box in a blank card of any stack. After a Set message, type a few words of paint text to see the results of the new setting. To type the next command, click the text insertion cursor inside the Message Box and press the Clear key to remove the previous message.

```
choose text tool
get the textFont
it
set the textFont to Chicago
set the textAlign to right
set the textStyle to underline, extend
set the textFont to Geneva
set the textSize to 9
set the textStyle to plain
choose browse tool
```

## *Stack, Background, and Card Properties*

There are only two properties that you can inspect or adjust for stacks, backgrounds, or cards. The properties are the object's name and script.

## **name** of <object>

**Purpose:** Controls the name of the object.

**When to Use It:** You may read or change the name of any stack, background, or card object by summoning the name property for that object. In the case of retrieving the name of the current object, simply specify which object you want, as in *get the name of this background.* Following the convention of the Get command, HyperCard places the response in the It variable.

When an object has a name assigned to it (all stacks automatically have names), the response includes the type of object and the object's name, the latter enclosed in quotation marks. Therefore, getting the name of the Home stack would leave

stack "Home"

in It. If an object does not have a name assigned to it, HyperCard leaves the type of object and its ID number in It.

You may obtain a shortened or longer name for the object by specifying *short* or *long* before the name property, as in *short name of bkgnd button ID 12.* The short name gives only the object's name. The Home Stack's short name, for instance, is simply Home, without any quotation marks around it. The long name, on the other hand, gives you the position of the stack, background, or card in the HyperCard universe. A named card in a named background would return a long name property like this:

card "Set Up Card" of stack "HD-20:HyperCard Stacks:My Stack"

All named objects may have their name changed from a script by setting the name property to a new name. This also goes for stack files.

**Examples:**

```
get the name of this card
set the short name of background to "Forms 1"
get the long name of stack
```

**You Try It:** Type the following messages into the Message Box while at the Home Card:

```
name of this stack
short name of stack
long name of stack
get the name of this background
it
set the name of background to "Home Background"
name of background
```

name of prev card
name of card 5

## script of <object>

**Purpose:** Controls scripts from within a script.

**When to Use It:** A remarkable feature about HyperTalk and the HyperCard structure is that scripts are self-modifiable. That means that scripts may open other scripts and make changes to them. A HyperCard author, therefore, may make some requests of the user the first time the user opens the stack and insert those preferences into scripts. The stack will be fully customized for the preferences of that user. A well-crafted HyperTalk script might even be designed so that it learns its user's habits and adjusts its scripts accordingly. The potential for self-modifying scripts is enormous.

Using the Get and Set commands with the script properties of stacks, backgrounds, and cards (as well as buttons and fields, below), one script can reach into another script and put any kind of text into that script. The procedure would be to first put the script from the object into a variable. Make all necessary adjustments to the script, and then set the object's script to the contents of the variable.

**Examples:**

get the script of this stack
set the script of card to empty

**You Try It:** To experiment with getting and setting a script, first create a new card in the Address stack. Then open its Script Editor and enter the following script:

```
on mouseUp
    beep 2
end mouseUp
```

Close the Script Editor and click once anywhere on the card (except in a text field). HyperCard should beep twice. Now type the following messages into the Message Box:

get the script of card
it -- you can see only the first line, but all three lines are in It.
set the script of this card to empty

Now click on the card. Since you emptied the script, the beep instructions are no longer there. Type the next line into the Message Box:

set the script of card to it

This restores the script to the beep script. Click once on the card to see for sure.

## *Field Properties*

Every field you create has fifteen properties that can be adjusted from a script. These properties will be familiar to you as the settings in the Field dialog box and the Font dialog box you can reach from it.

### loc[ation]

**Purpose:** Controls the center point coordinates of a field.

**When to Use It:** Unlike the location property of windows, the field *loc* property monitors the centerpoint of the field. By returning this location, you can make a script click in the center of the object with the Field tool to select the field. Then you can copy or cut the field into the Clipboard for later pasting on a different card or in a different stack.

You have to be careful, however, when getting the location of the field to click the Browse tool as a means of setting the text insertion pointer flashing in a particular field for the user. If the field is a multiple-line field, the Click command will end up placing the text insertion pointer in a line other than the first line. In fact, that action will place return characters in every line above the insertion pointer (see the *rect* property for a way around this).

**Examples:**

```
get the location of field ID 4312
set loc of field 1 to 32,145
```

**You Try It:** Go to the Address stack and create a new card field on any card in the stack with the New Field menu command. Adjust its attributes to be a rectangle style and check the Show Lines box. Choose the Browse tool, and enter some text into the field. You'll use this field for other experiments about field properties below. Now type the following messages into the Message Box:

```
get loc of card field 1
it
add 50 to item 1 of it
set the loc of card field 1 to it
click at it
```

## lockText <true of false>
## showLines <true or false>
## wideMargins <true of false>

**Purpose:** Controls the features of a field.

**When to Use It:** Authors of stacks whose contents are intended for reading only may wish to lock the fields after the text is typed into those fields. The HyperCard Help stacks, for instance, have locked fields, because it would not be particularly helpful for a user to change—intentionally or accidentally—the contents of the help cards.

If your stacks consist of many fields, you, as stack author, may hasten the locking and unlocking of all possible fields in the stack by writing a script that finds each background and card field, and changes the setting of the lockText property for every field. Remember that when you lock a field, the Browse tool, when atop the field, remains as the hand, and the field can respond to mouse-related system messages.

The showLines and wideMargins properties are also available for setting from scripts. It is more likely that authors will modify these settings in the course of their stack development than in scripts the user will ever use, except when user scripts create new fields.

**Examples:**

```
get lockText of card field 4
set showLines of field "Text 1" to false
set wideMargins of field 3 to true
```

**You Try It:** Using the sample card field from the last experiment, place the Browse tool atop the field and watch it change as you type the following messages into the Message Box. Also watch other attributes of the field and text inside the field change with the commands.

```
set lockText of card field 1 to true
set lockText of card field 1 to false
set showLines of card field 1 to false
set wideMargins of card field 1 to true
```

## name

**Purpose:** Controls the name of the field.

**When to Use It:** You may read or change the name of any field by summoning the *name* property for that field. Simply specify which field you want by field number or ID, as in *name of field 4*. If the field is a card domain field, the domain name must be part of the field name (for example, *card field "Names").* Following the convention of the Get command, HyperCard places the response in the It variable.

When a field has a name assigned to it, the response includes the type of object and the object's name, the latter enclosed in quotation marks. Therefore, getting the name of a field called "Address" would leave

field "Address"

in It. If a field does not have a name assigned to it, HyperCard leaves "field" and its ID number in It.

You may obtain a shortened or longer name for a field by specifying *short* or *long* before the name property, as in *get short name of field ID 12.* The short name gives only the object's name. The short name of the above example field, for instance, is simply Home, without quotation marks. The long name, on the other hand, gives you the position of the field in the HyperCard universe. A named field in a named background would return a long name property like this:

bkgnd field "Address" of background "Rolo" of stack
"HD-20:HyperCard Stacks:Addresses"

A named field may have its name changed from a script by setting the *name* property to a new name.

**EXAMPLES:**

```
get name of field 1
set name of card field ID 20 to "Special"
put the name of field ID 9887 into field 2
```

**YOU TRY IT:** Type the following messages into the Message Box while in the Address stack.

```
name of field 1
name of field 3
set name of field 3 to "Say What?"
name of field 3
set name field 3 to "Date"
```

## rect[angle]

**PURPOSE:** Controls the size and location of a field.

**WHEN TO USE IT:** Because every field maintains information about the coordinates of its upper left and bottom right corners, you can retrieve those properties or set them in a script. Notice that because the coordinates are those of the Macintosh screen, you can both resize and move a field by one setting of the rect property.

When you get the rect property, HyperCard places four coordinate numbers into It. They represent the horizontal and vertical measures of the top left corner and the same for the bottom right corner. Each number is separated from others by a comma. When you set coordinates for the *rect* property, the coordinates must be in this comma-separated format.

Get the rect property of a multiple-lined field to find the location of the top left corner for clicking the text pointer at the top of the field. The experiment below shows you how to manipulate the property information in a variable to make the Click command work the way you expect.

**Examples:**

```
get rect of field "Entry"
set rect of field ID 53819 to 34,150,134,250
```

**You Try It:** Use the card field from the previous experiments, and type the following messages into the Message Box:

```
put the rect of card field 1 into myRect
delete item 4 of myRect
delete item 3 of myRect
click at myRect
set the rect of card field 1 to 20,20,100,300
```

## script

**Purpose:** Controls a field script from within a script.

**When to Use It:** Using the Get and Set commands with the *script* properties of fields, a script can reach into a field script and put any kind of text into that script. The procedure would be similar to that outlined for modifying stack, background, or card scripts, above.

**Examples:**

```
get the script of field ID 43387
set script of field "Record Number" to empty
set the script of this background to the script of this stack
```

**You Try It:** To experiment with getting and setting a script, go to the Home Stack and type the following messages into the Message Box:

```
put "on mouseUp" & return into scriptMaker
put "go next" & return after scriptMaker
put "end mouseUp" after scriptMaker
set the script of field 1 to scriptMaker
set the lockText of field 1 to true
```

Click on the card's title field. That field now has a script in it that instructs HyperCard to advance to the next card in the stack each time you click on the field. And that was done completely without opening the Script Editor to that field. Open the Script Editor to see the results of your handiwork.

## scroll <pixels>

**Purpose:** Controls the number of pixels a scrolling field has scrolled from the top of the text.

**When to Use It:** Each time a card with a scrolling field in it appears on the screen, its natural tendency is to display its text starting with the first line. That may not be the desired effect for your card and stack design. By setting the scroll property of a scrolling field, you can automatically advance the text further down the block.

The parameter to the Scroll property is the number of pixels from the very top of the text. If the position of scrolled text is to be saved for each card for the next time it comes into view, retrieve the current Scroll amount and store the value in a hidden field in the course of a closeCard message handler. In an openCard handler should be a corresponding Set command to restore the previous scrolled location.

**Examples:**

```
put the scroll of field "Description" into field "placeHolder"
set the scroll of field "Description" to 3 * the textHeight¬
        of field "Description"
```

**You Try It:** Go to the Address stack card with the sample field you made at the start of the field properties section of this book. Enter several lines of text into the card field such that the text runs below the bottom of the field. Then type the following messages into the Message Box.

```
set the rect of card field 1 to 100,100,250,200
set the style of card field 1 to scrolling
put the scroll of card field 1 into message
set scroll of card field 1 to 20
set scroll of card field 1 to 120
```

## style < transparent | opaque | rectangle | shadow | scrolling>

**Purpose:** Controls the field style.

**When to Use It:** Just as you manually adjust the style of a field in the Field Info dialog box, so can a script make the style adjustment by setting the style property. Parameters to the style property are the same style names that you find in the dialog box. Scripts that generate new fields for a user would be likely candidates for setting this property. The new field procedure might start with a doMenu "New Field" command, which brings up the default, transparent style. If the new field is supposed to be a rectangle field, the style of that new button would be set to "rectangle."

**EXAMPLES:**

get style of field 3
set style of card field ID 4 to shadow
set style of field "ZIP" to transparent

**YOU TRY IT:** Use the card field from previous experiments in the Address stack, and watch the changes to the field after you type each of the following messages into the Message Box.

put the style of card field 1 into priorSetting
set style of card field 1 to shadow
set style of card field 1 to scrolling
set style of card field 1 to priorSetting

**textAlign** <left | right | center>
**textFont** <font name>
**textHeight** <leading>
**textSize** <font size>
**textStyle** < bold | italic | underline | outline | shadow | condense | extend | plain>

**PURPOSE:** Controls font attributes of a field.

**WHEN TO USE:** These five properties represent settings in the font dialog box you normally see by clicking the Font button in a Field Info dialog box. These properties give you full control over the way text appears in a field of your choice.

Parameters to each of the properties should be self-explanatory in the list above, since the terms should be familiar to you by this point. When you set the textSize property, HyperCard automatically sets the textHeight (leading) property to approximately one-third again as large. If the default leading is acceptable, you won't have to adjust the textHeight property. The textStyle property may have any number of the parameters listed as possible styles. Simply list them as comma-separated parameters to the textStyle property.

**Examples:**

get textHeight of field ID 9808
set textFont of field "Day 1" to Chicago
set textSize of card field 2 to 10
set textHeight of field ID 1212 to 12
set textAlign of field ID 1212 to right
set textStyle of field ID 1212 to outline

**You Try It:** Use the card field from the previous experiments and type the following messages in the Message Box.

get textFont of card field 1
it
set textFont of card field 1 to New York
set textAlign of card field 1 to center
set textStyle of card field 1 to bold
set textFont of card field 1 to Geneva
set textSize of card field 1 to 9
set textStyle of card field 1 to extend, underline

## visible <true or false>

**Purpose:** Controls the visibility of a field.

**When to Use It:** The visible property is more likely to be used with the Get command than the Set command, because you can hide and show fields with the shorter Hide and Show commands. In practice, it will be more efficient for your script to simply hide or show a field regardless of its current visibility state. To test for whether a field's visible property is true or false would be a waste of HyperTalk's time. There is no penalty for hiding a field that is already hidden.

**Examples:**

get visible of field ID 12
set visible of field "Help" to true

**You Try It:** Although it's a lot more typing than the Hide and Show commands, type the following visible property messages into the Message Box in the stack and card you used for the other experiments in this section. When you're finished with the experiment, delete the card field.

visible of card field 1
set visible of card field 1 to false

```
visible of card field 1
show card field 1
```

## *Button Properties*

Most properties of buttons are like those of fields, except for the special items that buttons, alone, have, such as their check-box settings. You can also make changes to button text properties, which you cannot make from the Button Info dialog box.

### **autoHilite** <true or false>
### **showName** <true or false>

**Purpose:** Controls the highlight and name features of a button.

**When to Use It:** If your scripts create new buttons for the user, you'll want to make adjustments just as you would from the Button Info dialog box. The Auto Hilite and Show Name settings are check-box settings in the Button Info dialog box. By setting these properties to true, the script does the same as checking these items.

**Examples:**

```
get autoHilite of button ID 43
set showName of background button 1 to true
```

**You Try It:** For all experiments in this section, create a card button in any card of any stack you like. Use the New Button menu option to create the button, and leave the default settings the way they are. Now type the following messages into the Message Box.

```
put the showName of button "New Button" into msg
set showName of button "New Button" to false
set autoHilite of button "New Button" to true
                        -- click on the button now
set showName of button "New Button" to true
```

### **hilite** <true or false>

**Purpose:** Controls highlighting of a button.

**When to Use It:** You'll get and set hilite property of a button most often when you're in the check box and radio button styles. As noted in the discussions about these button styles, the responsibility of making one of a series of radio buttons the highlighted button lies with a script that responds to the mouseUp system message. The script must change all other radio buttons in the cluster to false highlighting, while setting the button just clicked to true highlighting. When a radio button is highlighted, it has a black dot in its center; when a check box is highlighted, it has an X in its box.

You may wish to highlight other button styles, depending on the function of the button and stack design. For example, if a card features a row of buttons, each of which links to a stack with a special function, you may want that stack's button to be highlighted when you are in that particular stack. The extra visual feedback reinforces in the user's mind which of the special function stacks he is in.

**Examples:**

get hilite of bkgnd button 1
set hilite of button "Choice 1" to true

**You Try It:** Choose the button tool and double-click on the new button used in the previous experiment. Change the style to the radio button style and return to the Browse tool. Now type the following messages into the Message Box to see how the hilite settings influence this style of button.

set hilite of button "New Button" to true
set hilite of button "New Button" to false

## icon <icon number or name>

**Purpose:** Controls which icon art is attached to a button.

**When to Use It:** When a script creates a new button, it can assign an icon graphic to the button and turn the button into an icon button all at once by setting up the icon property with a valid icon number or name. Just as in the Button Info dialog box the entry of an icon number both assigns the art and makes the button an icon button, so too does the icon property influence a button from a script. An icon setting of zero removes icon art from the button and terminates the button's designation as an icon button.

If your script is changing a button to an icon button, chances are that the button will also have to be resized to accommodate the art. The default new button size is usually not tall enough to show the entire icon graphic.

**Examples:**

get icon of button ID 40

```
set icon of bkgnd button "Help" to 25002
set icon of bkgnd button "Help" to "Med Help"
```

**You Try It:** Since the new button you've been experimenting with will not be tall enough to accept icon art, select the button with the Button tool and adjust it so that it is approximately one inch square. Also open the button's dialog box to change the style to round rectangle. Then select the Browse tool and type the following messages into the Message Box.

```
put the icon of button "New Button" into message
set style of button "New Button" to round rect
set icon of button "New Button" to 1000
set icon of button "New Button" to 14953
set icon of button "New Button" to "Mac"
set icon of button "New Button" to 18814
```

## loc[ation]

**Purpose:** Controls the centerpoint coordinates of a button.

**When to Use It:** Like the location property of fields, the button *loc* property monitors the centerpoint of a button. By returning this location, you can make a script click in the center of the object with the Button tool to select the button. Then you can copy or cut the button into the Clipboard for later pasting on a different card or in a different stack.

**Examples:**

```
get the loc of button "Cancel"
set loc of field 1 to 200,150
```

**You Try It:** Type the following mouseUp handler into the Script Editor of the card button from previous button property experiments. Then click the button and watch what happens.

```
get loc of button "New Button"
add 30 to item 1 of it
set loc of button "New Button" to it
choose Button tool
click at it
doMenu "Copy Button"
go next card
doMenu "Paste Button"
go prev
choose Browse tool
```

# name

**Purpose:** Controls the name of the button.

**When to Use It:** You may read or change the name of any button by summoning the *name* property for that button. Simply specify which button you want by button number or ID, as in *name of button ID 300.* If the button is a background domain button, the domain name must be part of the field name (for example, *bkgnd button "OK").* Following the convention of the Get command, HyperCard places the response in the It variable.

When a button has a name assigned to it, the response includes the type of object and the object's name, the latter enclosed in quotation marks. Therefore, getting the name of a button called "Print Cards" would leave

button "Print Cards"

in It. If a button does not have a name assigned to it, HyperCard leaves "button" and its ID number in It.

You may obtain a shortened or longer name for the object by specifying *short* or *long* before the name property, as in *get short name of bkgnd button ID 12.* The short name gives only the object's name. The short name of the above example, for instance, is simply Print Cards, without any quotation marks around it. The long name, on the other hand, gives you the position of the button in the HyperCard universe. A named button in a named background would return a long name property like this:

bkgnd button "Help" of background "Help Form" of stack
"HD-20:HyperCard Stacks:Help"

A named button may have its name changed from a script by setting the name property to a new name.

**Examples:**

```
get the name of button 3
set name of bkgnd button to "Excel"
get name of button ID 12123
```

**You Try It:** Use the card button from previous experiments in this section and type the following messages into the Message Box.

```
set name of button "New Button" to empty
get name of card button 1
it
set name of it to "Change"
```

# rect[angle]

**Purpose:** Controls the size and location of a button.

**When to Use It:** Because every button stores information about the coordinates of its upper left and bottom right corners, you can retrieve those properties or set them in a script. Notice that because the coordinates are those of the Macintosh screen, you can both resize and move a button by one setting of the rect property.

When you get the rect property, HyperCard places four coordinate numbers into It. They represent the horizontal and vertical measures of the top left corner and the same for the bottom right corner. Each number is separated from others by a comma. When you set coordinates for the rect property, the coordinates must be in this comma-separated format.

**Examples:**

```
get the rect of background button "Accept"
set rect of button ID 802 to 15,300,65,330
```

**You Try It:** Use the card button from the previous experiments, and type the following messages into the Message Box:

```
get rect of button 1
subtract 10 from item 1 of it
add 10 to  item 3 of it
set rect of button 1 to it
```

# script

**Purpose:** Controls a button script from within a script.

**When to Use It:** Using the Get and Set commands with the script properties of buttons, a script can reach into a button script and put any kind of text into that script. The procedure would be similar to that outlined for modifying field scripts, above.

**Examples:**

```
get script of button id 23
set the script of button "Cancel" to empty
```

**You Try It:** Use the previous card button, and type the following messages into the Message Box:

```
set script of button 1 to empty
put "on mouseUp"  & return & "beep 3" & return &
      "end mouseUp" into scriptHolder
set script of button 1 to scriptHolder
```

Click on the button. It should beep three times. Open the Script Editor to see the results of your handiwork.

## style

< transparent | opaque | rectangle | shadow | roundRect | checkBox | radioButton >

**Purpose:** Controls the button style.

**When to Use It:** Just as you manually adjust the style of a button in the Button Info dialog box, so can a script make the style adjustment by setting the *style* property. Parameters to the *style* property are the same style names that you find in the dialog box. Scripts that generate new buttons for a user would be likely candidates for setting this property. The new button procedure might start with a doMenu "New Button" command, which brings up the default, round rectangle style. If the new button is supposed to be a radio button, the style of that new button would be set to "radio button."

**Examples:**

```
get style of button ID 50989
set the style of bkgnd button 4 to transparent
set style of button "OK" to roundRect
```

**You Try It:** Use the card button from previous experiments and watch the changes to the button after you type each of the following messages into the Message Box.

```
get the style of card button 1
it
set style of button 1 to checkBox
set style of button 1 to radioButton
set the style of button 1 to it
```

**textAlign** <left | right | center>
**textFont** <font name>
**textHeight** <leading>
**textSize** <font size>
**textStyle** < bold | italic | underline | outline | shadow | condense | extend | plain>

**Purpose:** Controls font attributes of a button's name.

**When to Use It:** Although the Button Info dialog box gives you no choice to change the font attributes of a button, you can modify them at will with these five text properties. The settings are the same as you normally find in a font dialog box.

Parameters to each of the properties should be self-explanatory in the list above, since the terms should be familiar to you by this point. When you set the textSize property, HyperCard automatically sets the textHeight property to approximately one-third again as large. Since button names can be only one line, however, the textHeight property is not used. The textStyle property may have any number of the parameters listed as possible styles. Simply list them as comma-separated parameters to the textStyle property.

**Examples:**

```
set textFont of button ID 3 to Chicago
set textSize of button "OK" to 10
set textAlign of bkgnd button 3 to right
set textStyle of button "Help" to italic, extend
```

**You Try It:** Use the card button from the previous experiments and type the following messages in the Message Box.

```
set icon of button 1 to zero
put the textFont of button 1 into message
set textFont of button 1 to Geneva
set textAlign of button 1 to right
set textStyle of button 1 to outline, extend
set textFont of button 1 to New York
set textSize of button 1 to 9
set textStyle of button 1 to italic
```

## **visible** <true or false>

**Purpose:** Controls the visibility of a button.

**When to Use It:** The visible property is more likely to be used with the Get command than the Set command, because you can hide and show buttons with the shorter Hide and Show commands. In practice, it will be more efficient for your script to simply hide or show a button regardless of its current visibility state. To test for whether a button's visible property is true or false would be a waste of HyperTalk's time. There is no penalty for hiding a button that is already hidden.

**Examples:**

```
get visible of background button 2
set visible of bkgnd button "Itinerary" to true
```

**You Try It:** Although it's a lot more typing than the Hide and Show commands, type the following visible property messages into the Message Box in the stack and button you used for the other experiments in this section. When you're finished with the experiment, delete the card button.

```
visible of button 1
set visible of button 1 to false
visible of button 1
show button 1
```

From properties, we now move onto HyperTalk's built-in functions.

# CHAPTER 29

# Introduction to HyperTalk Functions

IN OUR DISCUSSIONS DIRECTED AT HYPERTALK AUTHORS SO FAR, THE TWO MAJOR AREAS we've been looking at are objects and commands. Commands are the first words in HyperTalk script lines. HyperTalk also contains many words in its vocabulary that let you retrieve information about internal system workings, like the clock and the location of the cursor on the screen, plus information about text in containers. At the same time, HyperTalk lets you perform many math operations, which end up coming in very handy, even if you tend to shy away from math. Finally, HyperTalk provides a number of predefined constants—plain words that stand in for important values your scripts need from time to time. The next six chapters focus on all these items—elements that make up the balance of what most scripts require. About the only other knowledge you'll need to get rolling on HyperTalk scripts is information on how HyperTalk makes decisions in your scripts. We cover that in chapter 37.

For now, we'll demonstrate all the other parts of HyperTalk that fill out your scripts. We'll divide the discussion into three broad categories: functions, operators, and constants. The format we'll use is the same as for commands and properties in the last several chapters, so you'll have a chance to experiment with each item when we explain it.

## Functions

The first point we must make about functions is how they differ from commands. At first glance, they may appear to be quite similar, since you can type commands and functions into the Message Box and have something happen in either case. But in actuality, commands and functions are very different, both in the way HyperCard treats them and the way you incorporate them into your scripts.

By and large, commands are orders directed at something. Whether you type a command into the Message Box or put it into a script, a command tells HyperCard to carry out some action. It may be putting some information into a field or locking the screen. When you issue a command, it affects or changes the state of some entity—a container, an object, a tool, a menu item, the screen, the system. The key word, then, is *action.*

A function, on the other hand, does not provoke action. Instead, it retrieves the current status of an entity and tells you what that status is. Nothing about that entity changes as the result of peeking at it with the function, although it may change later or on its own. For example, several HyperTalk functions look at the internal Macintosh clock to tell you things like today's date or the current time (according to the settings of the internal clock). The function only tells you what those settings are at the instant it looks at the clock. The clock, of course, continues to tick away at its steady pace. If you want an update on the clock's status, you use the function again.

The answer that a function produces for you is called its *result.* Another common way to express how a function operates is to say that a function *returns* a certain kind of value, like the date or the location of the cursor on the screen. Understanding how a function returns its result is of fundamental importance.

## Using Functions in Scripts

The name of a function essentially acts as a substitute in a script line for the type of information it returns. For instance, if you wish to design a stack that automatically places the current time into a card's field on the creation of a new card, the newCard message handler would look like this:

```
on NewCard
  put the date into field "Date"
end NewCard
```

Let's examine what happens in the command line. The Put command, as you'll recall, requires two parameters: a source and a destination container. The destination parameter you'll readily recognize as being a field, named "Date." According to HyperTalk syntax for this command, the source parameter must be either a text string, an arithmetic expression, or the content of any container.

The convenient property about the date function is that it returns a text string (in the form 3/4/88). A function's underlying mechanism lets us substitute the function name (*the date*) in the command line where we'd normally type in a text string. As HyperCard encounters the function name in the script, it practically says to itself, "OK, this is a function, so let's use its returned result as the parameter here."

Whenever a command parameter calls for a text string, you can substitute a function. All HyperTalk functions return text strings (although many results are entirely numbers). We repeat: All HyperTalk functions return text strings that can be used as text parameters for HyperTalk commands. All you do is plug in the function where the parameter belongs.

HyperCard functions may be written in a script (or typed into the Message Box) in a couple ways, according to some simple rules based on the *arguments* following the function name.

An argument is like a parameter, and usually consists of a piece of information the function needs to calculate. If a function is calculating the sine of 50, for example, the number 50 is an argument to the sine function; if a function calculates the average of five numbers, then the average function is said to have five arguments.

If a function requires one argument or no arguments, then the form may be either of two ways: 1) the function name preceded by the word "the"; or 2) the function name followed by the argument in parentheses. In the case of the latter, if there are no arguments, then you type a left and right parenthesis without any spaces or characters between them. Here are examples of valid functions

```
the sin of 50
sin (50)
the date
date()
```

When a function expects two or more arguments (or a variable number of arguments), then you may use only the parenthesis style, with arguments inside the parenthesis separated by commas. Here's what some of these functions look like

```
max (10,30,40)
average (3,6,12,9,8)
```

In our discussions of functions in the next several chapters, we'll show the function name in the "the" style wherever possible. This form is more natural sounding in a script and is thus more true to the spirit of HyperTalk.

In scripts, functions must not be surrounded by quotation marks. If they are, they are viewed as a text string consisting of the function name. Therefore, if you were to issue the following command,

```
put "the date" into field "Date"
```

HyperTalk would put the words *the date* into the field. Just plug in function names as if they were a regular part of the HyperTalk language—because they are.

You can test the type of information that virtually any function returns by typing the function into the Message Box. Since the function substitutes for some internal Macintosh or HyperCard value, you simply type the function name (and the prefix "the" or with parentheses around its arguments), and HyperCard instantly shows you its result.

To show you all the HyperTalk functions, we provide the following reference chapters. We've divided the functions into five subject areas: time and date functions; keyboard and mouse functions; text functions; math functions; and miscellaneous functions (including user-definable functions). We strongly suggest you work your way through every function, even if you won't necessarily use them all right away. The more you are aware of the powers available to you, the more likely you are to think of ways to use them. In later chapters, we'll apply most of these functions to real-world HyperCard applications.

# CHAPTER 30

# Time and Date Functions

IF YOU PLAN TO USE HYPERCARD TO HELP ORGANIZE YOUR TIME, THE HYPERTALK TIME and date functions will become some of your most valuable programming aids. You'll have access to the internal Macintosh clock and a few different formats for this information. Typically, you'll also call upon the Convert command to perform additional time and date arithmetic.

## the date
## the abbreviated | abbrev | abbr date
## the long date

**RETURNS:** The current date, as maintained by the internal Macintosh clock.

**WHEN TO USE IT:** Many stacks in a business environment will need some form of date stamping, often upon creation of a new card or when information is updated on an existing card. Any one of the three date function formats should prove workable.

The shortest of the three formats is the function, *the date*, which presents the date in a format like 8/6/87. One level higher in completeness is *the abbr date*, which has a format like Thurs, Aug 6, 1987. At the high end is *the long date* function, which spells out everything, as in Thursday, August 6, 1987.

The long date is the function to use if you need only the current day of the week or month in textual form. Rather than build long scripts that painstakingly convert the numbers of the day of the week into each day's text, simply extract the desired component from the long date's results. For example, if you need only the day of the week, use the long date function as a parameter to the command, as in

```
put first item of the long date into field "Day of the Week"
```

Similarly, for the month, extract only the first word of the second item of the long date, as in

```
put first word of item 2 of the long date into field "Month"
```

These two methodologies will prove to operate much faster than any other approach.

Treat the results of these functions as straight text. You won't be able to perform any date arithmetic with these functions directly. Use the Convert command and its seconds or dateItems formats to perform date calculations.

**EXAMPLES:**

```
put the long date into field "Date"
put the abbrev date into it
open file the date
```

**YOU TRY IT:** Type the following functions and messages into the Message Box from any stack:

```
the date
the abbr date
the long date
first word of the long date
item 2 to 3 of the long date
```

# the time
# the long time

**RETURNS:** The current time as determined by the Macintosh clock

**WHEN TO USE IT:** Both time functions will probably get a lot of use if the kinds of stacks you design involve managing time during the day. Time-stamping the creation of a new card in a stack is a popular application.

Your choice of function depends on the format you prefer. The *time* function presents time in the format 3:03 P.M. if you've selected 12-hour time in the Control Panel, 15:03 if you've selected 24-hour time. If you want the seconds to appear in the results, use the *long time* function, which returns in the formats 3:03:15 P.M. in 12-hour time or 15:03:15 in 24-hour time.

Treat the results of these functions as straight text. You won't be able to perform any time arithmetic with these functions directly. Instead, convert the results of these functions to seconds or dateItems for calculation.

**Examples:**

```
put the long time into field "Start Time"
ask "Starting Time?" with the time
```

**You Try It:** Type the following functions and messages into the Message Box from any stack:

```
the time
the long time
put "Experiment started at " & the long time
```

# the seconds
# the secs

**Returns:** Total number of seconds since 0:00:00, January 1, 1904.

**When to Use It:** Use the seconds function when you need an accurate counting of seconds within a HyperCard application. The internal Macintosh clock uses January 1, 1904 as the starting point of its time- and date-keeping. As a result, the number of seconds returned by this function is enormous— in the billions.

Since the measure is from a constant starting point, you can compare the total elapsed time in seconds between any two points in the life of a HyperCard application, even when the computer is turned off between sessions.

**Examples:**

```
put the seconds into field "Hidden"
subtract the secs from elapsedSecs
                -- elapsedSecs is a local variable
```

**You Try It:** Type the following functions and messages into the Message Box from any stack:

```
the seconds
put the secs into temp
temp
the secs - temp
the seconds / (365.25*24*60*60) -- how many years since 1904
```

# the ticks

**Returns:** The number of 1/60th seconds since the last system start-up.

**When to Use It:** All the while the Macintosh is running, it keeps track not only of the ongoing time according to the clock, but also the number of tick intervals (1 tick = 1/60 of a second) since the machine was last turned on. In other words, each time you turn on your Macintosh, the system starts counting ticks from zero. When you turn off the machine, the tick counter stops, and the number of ticks is erased.

In practice, the Macintosh sometimes misses a heartbeat as far as the tick counter goes. This may occur during disk drive access or during the flow of information through the serial ports. Therefore, the tick counter should not be deemed a reliable time counter over the length of a typical Macintosh work session. If you need accurate timings for long periods, use the other functions that take readings from the internal clock.

The most practical application of the ticks function is to trap for a user's double-click. Since HyperCard itself does not have a double-click detector (that is, it sends only single mouseDown and mouseUp messages), you can build a script that checks for how closely two mouseDown or mouseUp messages were sent by HyperCard. If the messages were sent very closely together— such as within twenty ticks of each other— the user issued a double-click. A sample script is shown below (although it uses some decision-making that will be covered in chapter 37):

```
on mouseDown
      global clicktick                 -- declare global variable
      put clicktick into temp          -- retrieve previous click time
      put the ticks into clicktick     -- put new click time in
                                       -- global variable
      if (clicktick - temp) < 20 then beep 2 -- subtract and
                                             -- beep twice if close
end mouseDown
```

In the above script, we use a global variable, *clicktick*, to store the tick count of the most recent mouseDown message after the mouseDown message handler has ended. At the next mouseDown message, the script retrieves the previously stored tick count and places it into a local variable, temp. The last line of the script compares the two times by simple subtraction. If the two mouseDown messages occurred within nineteen ticks of each other (that is, less than twenty), then, in this simple example, the script issues the Beep command.

Place this script in a button and try it for yourself. See how far apart the two clicks of the mouse button need to be before the script no longer considers it a double click. Increase the number if you want more distant clicks to be accepted as double-clicks. Note that since you are actually programming the double-click mechanism here, the Control Panel setting for the double-click distance does not affect what's going on here. That affects only other applications and the desktop.

**EXAMPLES:**

```
put the ticks into counter   -- counter is a local variable
divide field 3 by the ticks
```

**YOU TRY IT:** Type the following functions and messages into the Message Box from any stack:

```
the ticks
put the ticks into howMany
howMany
the ticks - howMany
the ticks - howMany          -- see how quickly they tick!
```

CHAPTER 31

# Keyboard and Mouse Functions

A SECOND IMPORTANT GROUP OF FUNCTIONS LETS YOUR SCRIPTS OBTAIN INFORMATION about the current status of the screen cursor and modifier keys (Shift, Option, and Command) on the keyboard. As with many of the functions, these functions end up being used as decision aids for a HyperTalk script. Although we haven't delved into decision-making yet, you'll get a gentle introduction to the basic concepts in this chapter as you see how decisions in scripts are based on the condition of keyboard modifier keys or the location of the cursor.

## the mouseH
## the mouseV
## the mouseLoc

**RETURNS:** Coordinate locations of the hot spot of the screen cursor

**WHEN TO USE IT:** The need for summoning the screen coordinates of the cursor may not seem obvious at first. But in many advanced HyperTalk programming situations, a well-crafted script can perform wonders with one button that might otherwise require dozens.

For example, if a card features a list of To Do items, you might wish to add a column next to the items so you can check off each item when completed. One method to allow the user to check off an item with the mouse would be to put individual buttons over each check box. That, however, could add twenty or more buttons to the card. As an alternative, you could create one large button over all the check boxes. Then use the script to retrieve the coordinates of the Browse tool when the user clicks the mouse (on mouseUp). Depending on the vertical coordinate along the column, the script could fill in the appropriate line with a check mark character. One button, one script. We'll show you how to do this when we modify the To Do stack started in chapter 17.

Another application might call for the card to show a button or field when the user glides the cursor atop a specific spot or area on the screen. In this case, the card's script (or background script, more likely) would have an Idle message handler that continually reads the mouse location with the mouseLoc function. When the coordinates match those of the secret spot, the script shows the field or button.

A HyperTalk author with the Pascal, C, or Assembly language experience could also design a different cursor style as a HyperCard resource. Whenever the user drags the cursor into the designated area, the cursor changes from the Browse tool to the new cursor. Commercial applications do it all the time.

So, you see, there are several opportunities to use the mouse location functions. The three you have available let you obtain the vertical (the mouseV), horizontal (the mouseH), and both coordinates (the mouseLoc). When you request a single coordinate, the function returns just the one number. When requesting both coordinates, the mouseLoc function returns coordinates in the proper HyperTalk format for multiple parameters—separated by commas—with the horizontal coordinate first.

We mentioned above that the coordinate returned by the functions is where the cursor's hot spot is. One of the design parameters of any cursor (C, Pascal, and Assembly language programmers get involved with this, not HyperTalk programmers) is the pixel that represents the action point of the cursor. For example, when the arrow cursor is in the menubar, the hot spot is the very tip of the arrow. That is the pixel that must be in the menu title for you to pull down the menu. In the Browse tool, the hot spot is the very point of the index finger (see Figure 31-1). That's where you should point to find the location of a screen object with the mouseLoc function.

**Examples:**

```
show button ID 200 at the mouseLoc
if the mouseV > 120 and the mouseV < 140 then¬
        put "OK" into line 3 of field 2
show message at the mouseV + 25,the mouseH + 25
```

**You Try It:** Type the following messages into the Message Box from any stack. Move the mouse around and try the same messages to get a feel for the coordinate system of the HyperCard screen.

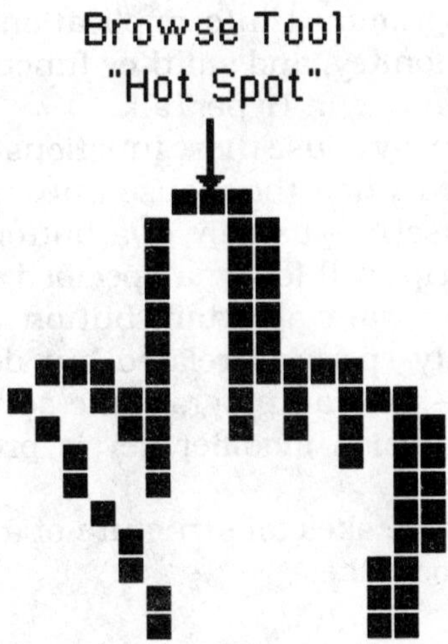


*Figure 31-1. The browse tool's "hot spot" is the reference point for HyperCard's mouse and mouseLoc functions.*

```
the mouseV
the mouseH
the mouseLoc
put the mouseLoc into temp
show message at temp
add 50 to item 1 of temp
add 100 to item 2 of temp
show message at temp
```

## the commandKey
## the optionKey
## the shiftKey

**Returns:** Up or Down, depending on the state of the key at the time the function runs

**When to Use It:** The Command, Option, and Shift keys are called *modifier keys* in Macintosh programming parlance. They get this name because, according to Apple's Macintosh User Interface Guidelines, you can modify an operation by holding down one of these keys while pressing any other key or the mouse button. We've seen how the Shift key modifies the letters of the alphabet to capitals. Most of us have also experienced how the Command key alters the behavior of most keyboard keys when we wish to perform one of the keyboard menu shortcuts programmed into applications like HyperCard. The commandKey, optionKey, and shiftKey functions give you the same power when programming in HyperTalk.

The primary way to use these functions is to test whether any of these keys is pressed when the mouse button is pressed (mouseDown) or released (mouseUp)—usually in a button script. Generally speaking, the button script will follow a specified path if none of these keys is pressed. If you want a certain button to perform double, triple, or quadruple duty—perform related but decidedly different operations when clicked—you can program the script to follow a different path, depending on which modifier key is pressed along with the mouse button.

Here's what the skeletal structure of a quadruple-purpose button's script would look like:

```
on mouseUp
    if commandKey is down then
        carry out the command-key version of this button
        exit mouseUp
    if optionKey is down then
        carry out the option-key version of this button
        exit mouseUp
    if shiftKey is down then
        carry out the shift-key version of this button
        exit mouseUp
    otherwise carry out the plain version of this button
end mouseUp
```

You don't have to set traps for each of the modifier keys in such a script. If you have only one alternate, say for the Option key, you would only test for the Option key. Even if the Command or Shift keys were held down, the script would *fall through* to the plain version of the button, because the script ignores the condition of the other two keys.

You can also trap for the simultaneous pressing of two modifier keys. A script to do that for both the Shift and Command keys would look like this (you can try it in a button script):

```
on mouseUp
    if the shiftKey is down and the commandKey is down
    then beep 4
    else beep 1
end mouseUp
```

If you hold down both modifier keys and click on the button, the script will beep four times. With only one or no modifier keys held down, you'll get only one beep.

All three functions return the text responses "up" or "down," which can be put into containers. This is good to know, because in a long button script, you should place the test for a modifier key at the start of the script. If the test is later in the script, the user may remove his finger from the modifier key before the script gets to the modifier key function. For the function to return a "down" result, the modifier key must be down when the function acts. Therefore, consider testing for the modifier key(s) first and placing the results of the test in a local variable that can be used later in the script, such as:

```
on mouseUp
    put the optionKey into keyState
    -- keyState is the local variable
            .
            .
            .
    if keyState is down then¬
            carry out the option key modified version
            exit mouseUp
    end if
    carry out the regular version
end mouseUp
```

As you design your stacks and lay out the buttons on the cards, always look for possibilities of ganging up functions on fewer screen buttons. Too many buttons can make the screen look cluttered and confusing to the user. At the same time, however, make sure that the functions you apply to the same screen button are logically connected. For example, an unmodified click of a button may create a new card in a stack; a shift-click of the same button may delete the current card. And then, if there is a pattern to the modifier keys' actions to your buttons, maintain consistency throughout your environment. For instance, if you set an option-modified button in one stack to mean that the stack branches to a different background and searches text right away, then keep that system going throughout the environment you establish for your users.

**EXAMPLES:**

```
if the shiftKey is down then doMenu "Delete Card"
put the commandKey into command -- local variable
if the optionKey is down then update
            -- "update" is a message handler
```

**YOU TRY IT:** Most of what we've been showing you about the modifier keys require incorporating the functions into decision-making scripts (see chapter 37). From the Message Box, however, you can see the effect of pressing the modifier keys on the functions. Type each of the messages below into the Message Box in any stack. Do each message twice. The first time, don't hold down the designated modifier key when pressing the Return key; the second time, keep the key pressed when you also press the Return key. You'll see that the modifier key must be down while the function runs for the function to return the "down" result.

```
the optionKey
the shiftKey
put optionKey into temp
temp
```

## the mouse
## the mouseClick

**Returns:** Up or Down for the mouse; true or false for the mouseClick.

**When to Use It:** We'll talk about these two functions together, because they both relate to actions the user takes with the mouse button. In some cases, the two functions are interchangeable (although the construction of the decision-making HyperTalk code differs slightly), but there is a distinct difference between the two.

The mouse function should be used when an indication of the current state of the mouse button is required. If the mouse button is down at the instant HyperTalk executes the function, the function returns the text word "down." If the mouse button is up, the function returns the word "up." A fun example of this function is to write the following card script:

```
on mouseDown
        repeat while the mouse is down
                show message at the mouseloc
        end repeat
end mouseDown
```

This script starts when you press the mouse button on the card (not in a text field, however). As long as you keep the mouse button pressed, HyperCard draws the Message Box wherever the cursor is on the screen. The repeat construction (explained in chapter 37) keeps requesting the mouse function and executes the next line, provided the mouse function returns "down" as the result.

The mouseClick function returns either "true" or "false." One of the best ways to use this function is trap for the click of the mouse button. In other words, a script might keep repeating itself until the user clicks the mouse button. You can try this by setting up the following message handler in a card or background script:

```
on beeper
    repeat until the mouseClick
        beep
        wait 5
    end repeat
end beeper
```

Then type *beeper* into the Message Box. This starts the script going. It will continue to repeat the beep and wait loop until the mouseClick function returns a true. A press of the mouse button will make that happen, thus ending the repeat and the message handler.

Notice that the mouseClick function returns a true upon pressing the mouse button. It doesn't wait for the mouse button to be released.

**EXAMPLES:**

See above.

**YOU TRY IT:** Be sure to try the examples shown above. They demonstrate the dynamics of these two functions. Unfortunately, you can't experiment with these two functions from the Message Box except with the mouse button released. As long as the mouse button is down, you won't be able to send the message in the Message Box. Still, type the two functions into the Message Box to see how HyperCard responds with the mouse up.

```
the mouse
the mouseClick
```

## the clickLoc

**RETURNS:** The screen coordinates of the last mouse click (at the cursor's hot spot), regardless of current cursor position

**WHEN TO USE IT:** Because it is so easy to move the cursor on the screen, even accidentally after clicking the mouse, it's nice to know that HyperCard keeps track of the location of the last time you clicked. Especially if you need to use the mouse coordinates in an extended mouseUp message handler, the cursor may have long moved from the original point by the time the script gets to the coordinate call (making the mouseLoc function useless). While you could save the mouseLoc coordinates at the beginning of the script, the clickLoc function saves you from that step.

As a rule, then, whenever you need to retrieve the screen location of a mouse click within a script, use clickLoc instead of mouseLoc. The fast mousers in your user constituency will appreciate it.

Like the mouseLoc, the clickLoc returns screen coordinates separated by commas. The horizontal coordinate comes first.

**EXAMPLES:**

```
if first item of the clickLoc < 30 then beep
show field "Help" at clickLoc
```

**YOU TRY IT:** One easy way to try this function is to click the mouse at the upper left corner of the screen and type *the clickLoc* into the Message Box. You should get the coordinates 0,0. Then move the mouse around the screen without clicking the mouse button and type the clickLoc again into the Message Box. The location stays the same. Click the mouse button with the cursor somewhere near the middle-left edge of the screen. Then type the following messages into the Message Box from any stack.

```
put item 1 of the clickLoc into x
put item 2 of the clickLoc into y
add 300 to x
add 20 to y
show message at the clickLoc
show message at x,y
```

# CHAPTER 32

# Text Functions

HYPERTALK INCLUDES TWO TYPES OF TEXT FUNCTIONS. ONE TYPE LETS YOU LEARN about the characteristic of text inside a container. The other type accommodates conversion between ASCII values and characters. This latter type is offered as a convenience to experienced programmers. Fortunately, even for them there is little need to get "down and dirty" into ASCII code, since HyperTalk has simpler ways of handling the most-used control characters.

All of these text functions have arguments attached to them. Therefore, for this section, we include a discussion about arguments for each function.

## the length of <container>

**RETURNS:** The number of text characters in a container

**WHEN TO USE IT:** Whenever your script needs to know the total number of characters in a variable, text field, or other container, use the length function. It counts the total number of characters (that is, including invisible return characters) in a container.

The length function may be used to establish an endpoint for text analysis. You can also use it to validate the length of an entry into a small text field. For example, if you set up narrow text fields on a card form, you might want to limit the number of characters that a user can enter into the boxes. While the actual number that will fit varies with the proportion of skinny-to-thick letters (most Macintosh fonts are proportionally spaced), you could select an average length that will fit comfortably in the box. Your script would be a handler triggered by the closeField message. In that message handler would be a section like the following:

```
if the length of field "Name" > 25 then
    beep
    put "The name must be fewer than 25 characters"
end if
```

As with most other functions, you can place the results of the length function into a variable or other container and use it for further calculations in the script.

**ARGUMENTS:** The sole argument of the length function is the name of the container whose text it is to measure. Remember that a container may be any text field, local or global variable, the Message Box, the special local variable, It, or a selection. You can also substitute an actual text string as the argument, but that wouldn't seem to make much sense in a HyperTalk script: If you already know the text, you certainly know its length and don't need a HyperTalk script to figure it for you.

**EXAMPLES:**

```
put the length of field 3 into howLong -- a local variable
if the length of title > 50 then beep  -- title is a local variable
put the length of field 2 / 6 && "words" into message
```

**YOU TRY IT:** For this experiment, it will help if you have access to a card with different-length text strings. You can use the Address stack, create a blank card, and type one long string into field 1, a shorter one into field 2. Then type the following messages into the Message Box:

```
the length of field 1
the length of field 2
put the length of field 1 into temp
put "Field 1 has " & temp / 6 & " words in it." into message
```

## offset (<expression>, <expression> )

**RETURNS:** The starting position of a text string within another text string.

**WHEN TO USE IT:** Because the information that HyperCard stores in its fields and in its object names is so dominated by text (despite HyperCard's heavily graphical environment), it is important to have the flexibility to perform a full array of analyses on the text. One of those analytical tools is the offset function.

With this function, you can compare any piece of text (which may be a text string or the contents of a container) against the entire content of a container. The function returns a number corresponding to the number of the character at which the test string starts. Let's see how this works.

If field 1 of a card contains the text "Crime and Punishment," you can try a couple of offset functions on it to see what it comes up with. If you were to type into the Message Box

```
offset ("Crime", field 1)
```

the result comes back as 1, because "crime" starts at the first character of field 1. If you then type

```
offset ("and", field 1)
```

the result comes back 7, because "and" starts at the seventh character of the field's text. You can also test for the occurrence of single letters. Therefore, if you type

```
offset ("i", field 1)
```

the result is 3. The function stops at the first occurrence, so it won't find the second letter "i" in "punishment."

Chances are that you will use the offset function in the same script with one or more other text functions in your analyses. For example, if you wish your script to capitalize a word in a container, you would first find the starting location of that word with the offset function. Then you'd work with the characters one at a time and change from lower case to upper case with the charToNum and numToChar functions (below). You'd have to put the capital letter into the lower case letter in the container, so the offset function would help in giving you the starting character number.

**Arguments:** Both arguments to the Offset function may be straight text, but the more likely scenario will be for both to be containers. The first expression will probably be in a local variable, and the second expression will be either in a field or another local variable. If you use a plain text string as either or both arguments, be sure each string is in quotation marks.

**Examples:**

```
put offset (field 5, field 1) into temp -- local variable
put offset ("Boston", field "Cities") into it
```

**You Try It:** The Offset function is not one you're likely to use from the Message Box, but you can experiment with it just the same. By following the messages below, you'll put a text string into a variable and then perform some offset functions about it. Type the following messages into the Message Box from any stack.

```
put "When in the course of human events..." into it
it
offset ("course", it)
put word 6 to 7 of it into temp
temp
offset (temp, it)
offset ("events", it)
offset ("events", temp)
```

## the number [of] <components> in <container>

**Returns:** The number of components in a specified container

**When to Use It:** When performing analyses on text in a container, you usually need the maximum number of components before you can set up a repeating script structure (see chapter 37). Once you have the maximum number of words, for example, the repeating structure can begin looking at word 1, continue with word 2, and so on, until the word count equals that of the total number of words in the container. Then the repeating structure can stop.

Another application occurs frequently in multiple-lined fields. If your script needs to add a new item to a list in a field, it cannot predict how many items will already be in the list when it makes its addition. The script can use the number of lines function to find out how many lines are occupied with text. Then the script can put the new text in the maximum number of lines plus one. Here's how such a script would look:

```
on mouseUp
      answer "Any additions to the list?"
      put number of lines in field "List" into counter
      add 1 to counter
      put it into line counter of field "List"
end mouseUp
```

You'll discover that once you can retrieve the total number of text components in a container, you can gain quick access to specific parts of the text.

(See chapter 34 for another version of *the number* function.)

**Arguments:** Any valid component name works in the first argument. This includes *chars*, *words*, *lines*, and *items*.

For the second argument, any valid container name is accepted. Most of the time this argument will be a field (identifiable by field name, number, or ID number) or a local variable.

**Examples:**

```
put the number of lines of field 12 into fieldLines -- local variable
put the number of items of it into howMany          -- local variable
put the number of chars of first word of field 1 into it
```

**You Try It:** Artificial though it may be, you'll use the Message Box to experiment with the number function. Create a new card in the Address stack and type any kind of information into the first field, including text on many lines, and some series items separated by commas. Now type the following messages into the Message Box.

```
the number of lines of field 1
the number of chars of field 1
the number of words of field 1
the number of items of field 1
put the number of words of field 1 into theWords
      -- "theWords" is a one-word local variable
put the number of chars of field 1 into theChars
put "Field 1's average word is " & theChars / theWords
     & " characters long." into message
```

## the charToNum of <character>
## the numToChar of <ASCII value>

**Returns:** The charToNum returns the ASCII value; the numToChar returns the actual character

**When to Use It:** These two functions are direct opposites of each other. The charToNum function converts a keyboard character into its ASCII value; the numToChar function converts an ASCII value into a character as it appears on the screen when typed from the keyboard.

Both functions have ready application when it becomes necessary to work with characters that you cannot normally access from the keyboard– primarily control codes at the bottom end of the ASCII value table. Most of these codes are for use with printers and telecommunications devices, although several of them find their way into standard files, such as the Tab and Return characters. Fortunately, for the common control codes, HyperCard provides constants in the form of plain words that we can plug in for those characters (see discussion about constants later in chapter 36).

One special character you might be interested in is the apple character that appears at the top of the desk accessories menu. This character is not available from the keyboard in any fashion, but it is

ASCII character 20 in the Chicago font. Therefore, if you wanted to use this character in a text field set for the Chicago font, you'd have to send a message like this:

```
put numToChar of 20 into field 2
```

Another application for these two functions is converting uppercase to lowercase letters and vice versa. Since an uppercase letter and its lowercase counterpart have different ASCII values (separated by a value of exactly 32 across the entire alphabet), you can make conversions quite simple in a script. Here's an example of how a script would convert lowercase text in a field to all uppercase:

```
on convert                                  -- message handler name
    repeat with x = 1 to the length of field 2
                                            -- repeat for each character
        put the charToNum of char x of field 2 into temp
                                            -- get ASCII value
        if temp >= 97 and temp <=122  then
                                            -- if it's in lowercase range
            put temp - 32 into temp
                                            --  put it in uppercase range
            put the numToChar of temp into char x of field 2
                                            -- replace lower with upper
        end if
    end repeat
end convert
```

In this case, the two functions were used in tandem: once to convert the character to the ASCII value for the arithmetic; the second time to convert the result back into the character for the text string. Try this on a blank Address card. Place this script in the card's script, and type a mixture of uppercase and lowercase letters into the second field. Then type *convert* into the Message Box. Watch as each lowercase letter is turned into its uppercase equivalent.

**ARGUMENTS:** The argument for the charToNum function is any character you can type from the keyboard or any nonkeyboard character that was put into a container via the numToChar function at an earlier time. When the character is not one you can type from the keyboard, it usually appears as a small rectangle. Because this argument can be any keyboard character you can use alternate characters, like the ones available by pressing the Option and Shift-Option keys. Choose Key Caps from the apple desk accessory menu and press the Option key to see some of the alternate characters.

For the numToChar function, the argument is any ASCII value from 0 to 255. If you specify a number above 255, HyperCard automatically subtracts 255 (or multiples of 255) so you have only one set of characters, the first 256 available largely from the keyboard.

**EXAMPLES:**

```
put the numToChar of 27 before field 3
put the charToNum of "æ" into temp
```

**YOU TRY IT:** The sample script above is a good experiment to try yourself. You may also do some conversions via the Message Box to help you get the feel of these two functions. Type the following messages into the Message Box from any stack.

```
the numToChar of 167
the charToNum of "a"
the charToNum of "b"
the charToNum of "B"
put the charToNum of "A" into temp
add 32 to temp
put the numToChar of temp into message
```

# CHAPTER 33

# Math Functions

AS YOU'VE SEEN, YOU CAN GO PRETTY FAR WITH HYPERTALK WITHOUT EVER GETTING into advanced math. In fact, you may not ever need the functions in this chapter. But for more experienced programmers or those who are comfortable with things like logarithms and compound interest, HyperTalk has many built-in functions to aid in those calculations.

A few of the math functions require the full treatment that we give to functions in other chapters. A majority, however, are self-explanatory, and we'll treat them in a way that will help those familiar with the functions to use them quickly. We'll start with the more in-depth functions first.

## the random of <upper bound>

**RETURNS:** Random number between 1 and upper bound

**WHEN TO USE IT:** While business applications are not necessarily a likely target for a random number generator, many kinds of entertainment and education applications are. HyperTalk lets you request a random number between 1 and any number up to 32767.

In an educational application, the random number may be used in interactive math quizzes, so that not every problem is the same when the same user comes to the application repeatedly. In an entertainment program, the random number generator can mix up the pattern of the game to keep it fresh.

You don't have to use the random function when you wish the user to advance to a random card in a stack. For that task, the *go to any card* message is the desired route.

**Examples:**

```
put the random of 12 into field "Dice"
if the random of 31 is 11 then¬
        put "This is your lucky day" into message
if the minute is the random of 60 then beep
```

**You Try It:** First try typing *the random of 100* into the Message Box several times to get an idea of how random the random number generator really is. Then type the following handler into a new card script in the Address stack. Then type *dice* into the Message Box.

```
on dice
        repeat until the mouseClick
                put "The roll is: "& the random of 6 && the random of 6
        end repeat
end dice
```

## **the value** of <container or expression>

**Returns:** The calculated value of the arithmetic expression in a container

**When to Use It:** Information is stored in a container strictly as text information. That includes individual numbers and numbers linked together by operator signs like plus, minus, and so on. Therefore, if a container holds the text, 4 * 5, HyperCard sees it as a string of five characters: a 4, a space, an asterisk, a space, and a 5. There are times, however, when you need to know the calculated value of an expression like that when it is stored in a container.

When a HyperTalk command calls for a container parameter, you usually plug in the name of the desired container, like *field 1* or *field ID 890*. Doing so is the same as writing the text of that container into the parameter. But if the parameter calls for a number, which happens to be the result of an arithmetic expression stored in a container, then use the value function to calculate that expression. Here's an example.

On a card that resembles a scaled-down spreadsheet, there are twelve fields set up in a grid, as illustrated in Figure 33-1. Each field is named with its cell designation, like A1, B2, and so on. Near the bottom of the card is a place for you to type in the formula that will ultimately calculate the desired result of the numbers you type into various cells. So, you might type

```
field "A1" + field "A2" + field "A3"
```

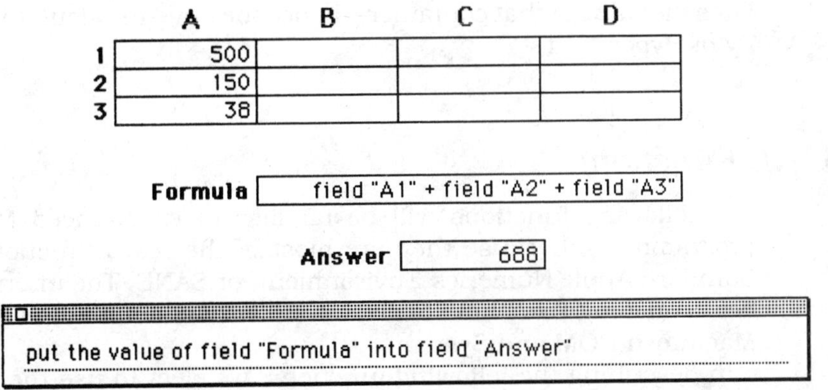


*Figure 33-1. The text in the "formulas" field needs to be evaluated to get the result. Use the value function.*

into the formula field. That container now holds the text of the formula, but does not perform any of the arithmetic implied in the string. For that, you would have another cell, named "Answer," into which the value of the formula field goes when you click the Calculate button. That button's script would be:

```
on mouseUp
    put the value of field "Formula" into field "Answer"
end mouseUp
```

The value function performs whatever calculations are in the container specified in its argument and returns that answer. That answer, of course, becomes text again when it is placed into the destination container.

**Arguments:** The sole argument for the value function must be a valid arithmetic expression, whether it is entered directly into the argument (for example, the value of "12 / 5") or comes from a container. If there is text in the expression that cannot be resolved into a number (remember, a text string could represent a local or global variable holding a number), then an error message will result.

**Example:**

```
put the value of field "Formula" into it
```

**You Try It:** The best way to experiment with the value function is to place arithmetic expressions in a card's field and type *the value of field x* into the Message Box, where x is the number of the field. Notice that the Message Box is a special container in this regard, because if you type an arithmetic expression into it, HyperCard automatically calculates the value of that container— hence the built-in calculator capability of HyperCard.

## *SANE Functions*

The following functions will be familiar to experienced Macintosh programmers, because they are most of the math functions in the Standard Apple Numerics Environment, or SANE. The internal-number crunching that these functions perform is actually built into the Macintosh ROM and System.

In describing the following functions, we elect to use the alternate format for designating functions— the function name and parentheses. Those HyperTalk programmers who are familiar with the purpose of these functions should feel comfortable with the format. Just the same, you may use the *the* function style for all functions that take fewer than two arguments, as in *the cos of 40.*

### abs (number)

**RETURNS:** The absolute value of the number parameter

**EXAMPLE:**

abs (-23) returns 23

### annuity (periodic rate, number of periods)

**RETURNS:** The present value of one payment unit. Internally, this function performs the following calculations:

$$\text{annuity}(r,n) = \frac{1 - (1 + r)^{(-n)}}{r}$$

To calculate the present value for the actual payments of an annuity, multiply the result of the annuity function times the amount of a single periodic payment.

**EXAMPLE:**

annuity (0.1,12) returns 6.8137

**atan** (angle in radians)

**Returns:** The arctangent of an angle

**Example:**
atan (25) returns 1.5308

**average** (number list)

**Returns:** The average of the numbers presented in a comma-separated list

**Example:**
average (10,20,30) returns 20

**compound** (periodic rate, number of periods)

**Returns:** The future value of a periodic payment unit. Internally, this function performs the following calculation:

$$\text{compound}(r,n) = (1 + r)^n$$

To calculate the future value of an actual investment, multiply the results of the compound function by the periodic payment.

**Example:**
compound (0.1,12) returns 3.1384

**cos** (angle in radians)

**Returns:** The cosine of an angle

**Example:**
cos (50) returns 0.965

**exp** (number)

**Returns:** The natural (base-e) exponential

**Example:**
exp(4) returns 54.5982

## exp1 (number)

**Returns:** The natural exponential minus 1

**Example:**

exp1(4) returns 53.5982

## exp2 (number)

**Returns:** The base-2 exponential

**Example:**

exp2(5) returns 32

## ln (number)

**Returns:** The natural (base-e) logarithm of the number

**Example:**

ln(4) returns 1.3863

## ln1 (number)

**Returns:** The natural log of 1 plus the number, as in ln(1+x)

**Example:**

ln1(4) returns 1.6094

## max (number list)

**Returns:** The highest value in a comma-separated list of numbers

**Example:**

max(20,50,30,49) returns 50

## min (number list)

**Returns:** The lowest value in a comma-separated list of numbers

**Example:**

min(20,50,30,49) returns 20

## round (number)

**RETURNS:** The nearest whole number

**EXAMPLE:**

round(12.5) returns 12, while round(12.51) returns 13.

## sin (angle in radians)

**RETURNS:** The sine of the angle

**EXAMPLE:**

sin(75) returns -.3878

## sqrt (number)

**RETURNS:** The square root of the number

**EXAMPLE:**

sqrt(144) returns 12

## tan (angle in radians)

**RETURNS:** The tangent of the angle

**EXAMPLE:**

tan(33) returns -75.313

## trunc (number)

**RETURNS:** The next lowest whole number of a number

**EXAMPLE:**

trunc(4.825) returns 4

If you try these math functions and insert invalid numeric arguments, the function may return the error message "NaN," which means the result is "Not a Number."

CHAPTER 34

# Miscellaneous Functions

IN THIS CATCH-ALL CATEGORY ARE FUNCTIONS THAT PROVIDE INFORMATION ABOUT objects and messages. Most of these will be of interest to more advanced HyperTalk programmers, but you should be aware of what these functions are. You never know when a function's capability will spark an idea for a stack or operation in a stack. We also explore the powerful HyperTalk feature known as user-definable functions.

## the number of cards | buttons | fields

**RETURNS:** The number of cards in the current stack; the number of buttons or fields in the current card.

**WHEN TO USE IT:** A common application that uses the total number of objects is when you need to set up a repeat loop to adjust each item in the stack or card. The total number of objects is used as the maximum number of times the repeated procedure should be done.

For example, let's say you wish to store information in one card that draws information from field 1 of every card in a small stack. The task of the script would be to retrieve the text from each card's field 1. For the script to know how many times to do this, it uses the number of cards function to obtain a count of the cards. The script would look something like this:

```
on accumulate
    repeat with x = 1 to the number of cards
        put field 1 of card x after field "Summary"
    end repeat
end accumulate
```

As you'll learn more in chapter 37, the repeat construction shown above initializes the local variable, x, and assigns the value of 1 to it at the outset. In the next line of the script, HyperTalk recognizes the variable as a valid card number (the straight card number, not its ID). The next time through the repeat construction, the local variable, x, is automatically incremented by 1 to a value of 2, and the Put command works on card 2. This repetition continues until x equals the value returned by the number of cards function. After that, the repeat cycle ends, and so does the handler in this case.

Use the number of buttons and the number of fields functions carefully. If you don't specify a domain, the fields count will be background fields; the buttons count will be card buttons. To get the number of fields on a card, the function must read *the number of card fields*. Background buttons are counted by *the number of bkgnd buttons* (*bkgnd* and *background* are synonymous throughout HyperCard). If you want a grand total of both background and card layer objects, you'll have to perform that arithmetic in the script, as follows:

```
the number of background buttons + the number of card buttons
```

**EXAMPLES:**

```
put the number of background buttons into temp
set name of card field id 20 to "Field " & the number of fields
if the number of cards > 100 then beep
```

**YOU TRY IT:** Use the Home card for this experiment, because it contains both background and card objects. Show the Message Box and type the following messages into it.

```
the number of cards
the number of fields
the number of card fields
the number of background fields
the number of buttons
the number of card buttons
the number of background buttons
```

## the result

**Returns:** Indications that a Find or Go command failed

**When to Use It:** HyperTalk provides a bit of what is commonly called error-trapping when a script attempts to find a string or go to a particular card and is unable to do so. Failure to find a match causes the function to return *not found* or *invalid date*, depending on the nature of the find string. Failure to find a card specified in a Go command causes the result function to return *no such card*. If the failure to accomplish the command affects the way your message handler proceeds, insert *the result* function immediately after a Find or Go command.

As part of an if-then-else construction (chapter 37), *the result* function will let your handler take whatever action is necessary to make the handler run smoothly after a command failure. As part of a Find command, *the result* function might be used like this:

```
on mouseUp
        find message
        if the result is not empty then
                ask "Sorry, I couldn't find that." with "OK"
                exit mouseUp
        end if
        ...
end mouseUp
```

The best way to handle *the result* function is to simply test for the presence of any string that the function might return. Since the function returns an empty string on a successful Find or Go, you can test whether *the result* is empty. If not, the message handler can branch to an error-handling script elsewhere, as in:

```
if the result is not empty then doError
```

Here, the error-handling message handler is called *doError*.

**Examples:**

See above.

**You Try It:** Go to the Home Stack and type the following messages into the Message Box.

the result

```
find the seconds
the result
go card 20  -- cancel the alert box
the result
go card 2
the result
```

## the sound

**Returns:** Done if no play command is active; the name of the sound resource playing.

**When to Use It:** Whenever your script issues the Play command (see chapter 26), you can think of it as instantaneously sending all the note parameters to a separate section of the Macintosh to be carried out. That means that as the music is playing, the script continues to move on to the next line. If you want the script to halt while the music plays, your script should find out when the music is completed before proceeding. The sound function helps with that task.

Used primarily in conjunction with "repeat" decision constructions (see chapter 37), the sound function returns the name of the Play command's voice parameter while the music is still playing. Once the music finishes, the function returns "done." A typical script construction would look like this:

```
on mouseUp
      play <parameters for long music>
      repeat while the sound is not "done"
      end repeat
      .        -- further commands
      .
      .
end mouseUp
```

Notice that the repeat section performs no other commands. It simply loops in circles between the repeat and end repeat lines until the sound function returns "done." Then the script breaks out of the loop and continues to carry out further commands.

One reason you'd want to hold up further execution during a Play command's music is that some disk drives may interfere with the tonal quality of the Play command's sound. A command after the Play command in the script may access the disk drive. A floppy disk or the original Apple HD-20 hard disk will cause momentary garbling of the sound when accessed during play. A SCSI hard disk should not interfere with the sound. But if you don't know what kind of hardware the users of your stack may be using, play it safe by trapping for the sound function after a play command.

**Examples:**

See Above.

**You Try It:** If you type the sound into the Message Box, it will return "done" as long as no music is playing. To see the function return a voice name, go to the Play command's help card in the HyperCard Help stack (card ID 85099). Show the Message Box and drag it so you'll have access to the sample sound buttons on the card. Before clicking a button, type *the sound* into the Message Box. Now click a button and press Return to test the function. The name of the voice will appear in the Message Box.

## the target

**Returns:** The ID number of the object receiving the last message sent up the HyperCard hierarchy

**When to Use It:** Since this function lets you discover who the original target of the current message is, your script could use this information to send a different message.

For example, you might set up a card in your Home Stack with several icon buttons representing stacks you've designed. If you name the buttons with the stack names, you only need one message handler—in the card object—to link those buttons to their respective stacks. The card handler would read:

```
on mouseUp
        get short name of the target
        go it
end mouseUp
```

The first command puts the button's short name—the same as the desired stack name—into it, because the button became the target when you clicked it. Then the Go command uses the button's name as its parameter.

You can keep adding new stacks' buttons to this card without ever writing another linking script between a new button and its stack.

**Examples:**

```
send "mouseUp" to the target
get the name of the target
```

**You Try It:** If you try typing *the target* into the Message Box, it will always return the current card's ID number, because that's where the

Message Box sends all its messages. To see a different result from this function, create a new button in a stack and enter the following script into it:

```
on mouseUp
    put the target into message
end mouseUp
```

When you click on the button, the button ID will appear in the Message Box.

## the param of <parameter number>
## the paramcount
## the params

**RETURNS:** The text of parameter specified by <parameter number>; the number of parameters; and the complete list of parameters to the current message, respectively.

**WHEN TO USE IT:** These three functions can contribute a substantial amount of power to your scripts, because they allow you to retrieve parameters that you send with your scripts. This requires a bit of explanation.

Most of the message handlers described so far in this book have been those that trap for system messages that HyperCard sends to various objects in the hierarchy— things like mouseUp, openCard, and so on. But there is an entirely different class of messages: messages that your scripts send to other message handlers that carry out tasks you design. Experienced programmers call these other message handlers *subroutines*.

Let's say that you have designed a card with five fields in it. Let's also say that you want all text in each field to be all uppercase. In case the user forgets to type in uppercase, you plan to include a script in each field that will convert lowercase letters to uppercase letters automatically when the user advances to the next field (that is, on closeField). As we saw in our explanation of the charToNum and the numToChar functions, the conversion routine takes several lines of HyperTalk instructions. While you could write the complete conversion routine in each field's script, there is a shortcut: Put the conversion routine in a stack or background script, and let the field scripts branch to the single conversion routine whenever they need it.

Such a background script might trap for the message *toUpper*. Its message handler, then, would begin with *on toUpper* and finish up with *end toUpper*, as shown below:

```
on toUpper
    repeat with x = 1 to the length of field 3
        get the charToNum of char x of field 3
        if it >= 97 and it <=122  then
            subtract 32 from it
            put the numToChar of it into char x of field 3
        end if
    end repeat
end toUpper
```

Since the field script is located in an object very low in the hierarchy, its toUpper message would first go to its own object and then work its way up the hierarchy until the background message handler, on toUpper, traps it. When the conversion is completed, the original script in the field object continues on.

But there is a special problem with this kind of subroutine. The toUpper message handler needs to know which field it should convert. You solve that by sending a field number, ID, or name as a parameter along with the convert message, as in *toUpper 3* for converting field 3. Inside the toUpper message handler, then, you can retrieve the parameter with the help of one of these three functions and insert the number in the appropriate parts of the convert script, as shown below:

```
on toUpper
    put the param of 1 into whichField
    repeat with x = 1 to the length of field whichField
        get the charToNum of char x of field whichField
        if it >= 97 and it <=122  then
            subtract 32 from it
            put the numToChar of it into char x of field ¬
                  whichField
        end if
    end repeat
end toUpper
```

In the script for field number 3, then, would be the following message handler:

```
on closeField
    toUpper 3
end closeField
```

The number 3 will be used by the toUpper message handler as the number of the field to convert to uppercase.

These three functions, then, give your scripts access to parameters that are sent along with messages. Here's how they differ.

The param function lets you extract a known parameter from the list. In the above example, only one parameter was sent along with the message, but that's not always the case. For example, if you send parameters specifying the location of an object on the screen, there will be two parameters in the message, separated by commas, (such as, (50,75)). By specifying a parameter number in the function's parameter (in the <parameter number>), your script can pick out a single parameter and act on it, if necessary. The param of 0 is the message name; the param of 1 is the first parameter of the message; and so on.

If your script needs the entire message, complete with parameters, then the params function (notice the "s" on params) returns the entire message. By putting the complete message into a container, like a variable, you can then dissect the parts as needed.

Lastly, to help in extracting multiple parameters from a series of many parameters, you can use the paramcount function to determine the total number of parameters in the message. As with most other functions that return the total number of something, the paramcount function will most often find itself at home as a counter within a repeat construction (see chapter 37).

**EXAMPLES:**

```
put the params into fullMessage -- a local variable
show message at the param of 1,the param of 2
add 100 to item the paramcount -1 of fullMessage
```

**YOU TRY IT:** Working with these functions from the Message Box won't be too helpful in your understanding of these functions. It's more important that you try the toUpper message handler shown above and understand its workings.

Since menu commands send some parameters, you can try a short card script that displays the results of each parameter function in a field on a blank Address stack card. Type the following script into a blank card's Script Editor. Then choose menu items like Message, Find..., or desk accessories, which don't move you from the card. Compare the values of each function type.

```
on doMenu
        put empty into field 1
        put "The paramCount function returns "¬
        & the paramCount into line 1 of field 1
        put "The params function returns "¬
        & the params into line 2 of field 1
        repeat with i = 0 to the paramCount
                put "Param " & i & " is "¬
                & param(i) into line i+3 of field 1
```

```
        end repeat
        pass doMenu
end doMenu
```

## *User-Defined Functions*

You aren't restricted to HyperCard's built-in functions. You may create your own to perform any frequently used calculations in your work. User-defined functions, just like HyperTalk functions, return values and may be used like any HyperTalk function in your message handlers.

To define a function, you type it into an object script in the following form:

```
function <function name>   [ parameter ]
        <command>
        <command>
        return <value>
end <function name>
```

Here's a sample function you might find useful in your stacks:

```
function dayOfWeek date
        get date
        convert it to long date
        return item 1 of it
end dayOfWeek
```

To use this function, type *dayOfWeek("11/12/87")* into the Message Box. You could also say *put dayOfWeek(the date) into field 1*, just like any valid function. Note that user-defined functions must be called with the parenthesis form, not the "the" form.

Here is another function you can use to calculate factorials of numbers (for example, factorial 5 = 5 * 4 * 3 * 2 * 1):

```
function factorial n
        if n <= 2 then return n
        else return n * factorial (n-1)
end factorial
```

This example serves double duty, because it demonstrates not only a function definition's basic structure, but also a doubling back on itself (*recursion*) by calling itself.

If you create or discover functions that might apply to many stacks, you'll be best off to place the scripts for those functions in your Home Stack. Since function calls follow the same hierarchy through the

HyperCard system that messages do, you'll want the functions to be in a place accessible to all stacks.

As you develop functions that other people might find useful, don't keep them a secret. Spread them around through user groups. There will surely grow large libraries of public domain HyperCard functions we can all use and learn from.

CHAPTER 35

# Mathematic Operators

IF THERE IS ONE PART OF COMPUTER PROGRAMMING THAT USUALLY FRIGHTENS newcomers, it's math. We hope, however, that you've seen how much you can accomplish without getting deeply into mathematics. In fact, most HyperTalk programming requires little more than a basic working knowledge of arithmetic. In this section, we explain each of the operators you use in HyperTalk scripts to perform math and mathematical comparisons (for example, whether one value is greater than another).

These operators behave very much like functions. They return values, either the result of the actual math performed or a true/false determination. Like a function, the result may then be placed into a container. You'll see many examples of what we mean in the following operator descriptions.

## + (plus)

**RETURNS:** The sum of two numeric values

**WHEN TO USE** It: The plus operator lets you sum two numbers together in an arithmetic expression. You can add two straight numbers, any container that evaluates to a number, any function that returns a number, or any combinations thereof.

**Examples:**

```
put item 3 of the long date + 2 into field "Future"
show message at param 1 + 25,param 2 + 25
put field 1 + field 2 + field 3 + field 4 into field "Total"
```

**You Try It:** Type the following messages into the Message Box from any stack:

```
put 10 into temp1
put 500 into temp2
temp1 + 1
temp1          -- the container doesn't change
put temp1 + 1 into temp1
temp1          --  now it changes
temp1 + temp2
add temp1 to temp2
temp1
temp2
add temp1 + temp1 to temp2
temp2
```

## -            (minus)

**Returns:** The difference between two numeric values

**When to Use It:** The minus operator lets you subtract two numbers in an arithmetic expression. You can subtract two straight numbers, any container that evaluates to a number, any function that returns a number, or any combinations thereof.

**Examples:**

```
put item 3 of the long date - 1 into field "Last Year"
put "almost" after the number of words -1 in field id 0770
```

**You Try It:** Type the following messages into the Message Box in any stack:

```
put 500 into big
put 5 into small
big - small
small - big
subtract small from big
big
```

```
small
add small - 5 to big
big
small - 5
```

## * (multiply)

**Returns:** The product of two numeric values

**When to Use It:** The multiply operator (the asterisk character, Shift-8) lets you multiply two numbers together in an arithmetic expression. You can multiply two straight numbers, any container that evaluates to a number, any function that returns a number, or any combinations thereof.

**Examples:**

```
put field "Monthly Rate" * 12 into field "Annual Rate"
put 2 * 2 * 2 into field "Two Cubed"
```

**You Try It:** Type the following messages into the Message Box in any stack:

```
put 10 into x
put 5 into y
x * y
put x * y into it
it
add y + y to y
y
multiply x by y
x
y
```

## / (divide)

**Returns:** The quotient of two numeric values

**When to Use It:** The divide operator lets you divide two numbers in an arithmetic expression. You can divide two straight numbers, any container that evaluates to a number, any function that returns a number, or any combinations thereof.

**Examples:**

```
put field "Total Year" / 365 into field "Per Day"
put x / y into z  --  three local variables
```

**You Try It:** Type the following messages into the Message Box in any stack:

```
put 100 into big
put 5 into small
big / small
small / big
put big / small into it
it
put small & " is 1/" & big / small & "th of " & big
```

## =

## is

(equals)

## <>

## ≠

## is not

(is not equal)

**Returns:** True or False, based on an arithmetic comparison of two expressions or containers

**When to Use It:** The equals and is operators may be used interchangeably. When comparing two expressions or containers placed on either side of the operator, HyperCard evaluates whether the two items have the same value. If so, the operator returns true. If not, the operator returns false.

The other three operators, also interchangeable with each other, test for whether the items on either side are not equal. If they evaluate to different numbers, the operator returns true. If the items are the same, then the operator returns false. To type the first of these operators, type the less than symbol (<) followed immediately by the greater than symbol (>) without any space in between. For the second "does not equal" symbol, a common math symbol, hold down the Option key and press the equals key. The "not equals" character appears in most fonts, but not all. Even if the symbol doesn't appear, the character's number is duly logged, so you don't have to see it to use it. The symbol does appear, fortunately, in the font used for HyperTalk scripts, so feel free to use it there.

**EXAMPLES:**

```
if field 1 = field 2 then¬
        ask "Should both fields be the same?" with "Yes" or "No"
if x ≠ 0 then put 0 into x
repeat while the hour is 9
if field "Year" <> the year then beep 2
```

**YOU TRY IT:** Type the following messages into the Message Box from any stack:

```
put 100 into temp1
put 100 into temp2
put 99 into temp3
temp1 = temp2
temp1 is temp2
temp1 <> temp2
temp1 ≠ temp2
```

| | |
|---|---|
| **<** | (less than) |
| **<=** | (less than or equal to) |
| **≤** | (less than or equal to) |
| **>** | (greater than) |
| **>=** | (greater than or equal to) |
| **≥** | (greater than or equal to) |

**RETURNS:** True or False, based on an arithmetic comparison of two expressions, containers, functions, or any combinations thereof.

**WHEN TO USE IT:** These four operators let you test for greater precision of a comparison than just whether two numbers are or are not equal to each other. They let you test for a value being in a range, like whether a number is less than 10 or greater than 100.

The addition of the equal sign helps you in the definition of the limit of the range. This is especially helpful when the limit is defined by a function, whose value you never know beforehand. If you want to know if a variable is less than or equal to the current minute (as derived from a dateItems conversion), you can do that. If the current minute should not be in the limit, then use the simple less than operator. (To define both an upper and lower limit to a range, see the *and* operator).

To type the special single character symbols for less than, greater than, or equal to, type Option-Comma and Option-Period, respectively. These symbols may be more familiar to you from your math training.

Almost every application of these operators will be in repeat and decision making constructions, as detailed in Chapter 37.

**Examples:**

```
if field 3 < 0 then put 0 into field 3
repeat while item 5 of field "Time" <= 5
if item 3 of the long date > 2000 then¬
      put "Reset your clock" into message
```

**You Try It:** Type the following messages into the Message Box in any stack:

```
put 100 into temp1
put 100 into temp2
put 50 into temp3
temp1 <= temp2
temp2 <= temp1
temp3 >= temp1
temp3 <= temp1
temp1 + temp3 >= temp1 * 2
```

## div (divide and truncate)
## mod (modulo)

**Returns:** Div returns the whole number of times one number is divisible by a second; Mod returns the remainder left after dividing one number by a second.

**When to Use It:** These two functions come in much handier than you might think at first (that is, unless you're a seasoned programmer and already appreciate their importance). When you divide one number by another, there is a good chance that the result will not be a whole number, but usually a number and a decimal, like 5 / 2 = 2.5. But in the way we learned division in the second grade, the problem resolves to an answer of 2 with a remainder of 1 (see Figure 35–1). These div and mod functions let you isolate the whole number and the remainder of a division problem.

If we take a new problem and apply each of the functions to it, you'll see the distinction between the two. The problem is that we are reviewing a project schedule that extends over a fixed number of days, 98. We also know that the project schedule started counting on a Sunday sometime back. What we want to know first is how many weeks

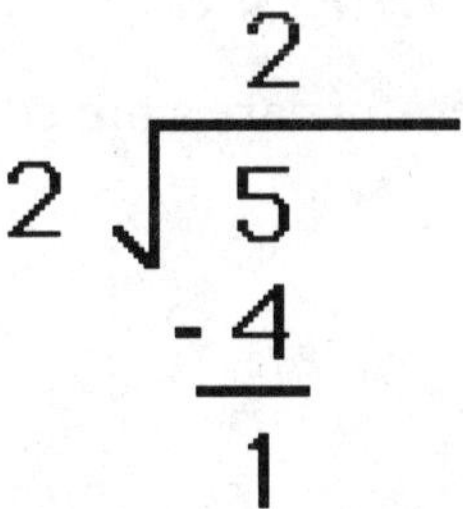

*Figure 35-1. Division the way we learned it in grade school.*

the 98 days account for. For that answer, we use the div operator. Solving for 100 div 7, the answer comes to 14. In one operator, we both divide 100 by 7 and strip away the decimal part of the answer, since we're only interested in knowing the total number of weeks. Of course, this response tells us only the number of full, seven-day weeks. We don't know if there were any extra days into the eighth week. That's what the mod operator finds for us.

By solving for 100 mod 7, the answer comes to 2. If we had simply divided 100 by 7, the answer would have been 14.2857 weeks. How many days is 0.2857 weeks? The mod operator tells us that it is exactly 2. So the project took 14 weeks and 2 days. Not only that, since we know the project started on a Sunday (day 1 of the first week), the project ended on a Monday (day 2 of the 15th week).

**EXAMPLES:**

```
put "$" & (amt div 1) & "." & (amt*100 mod 100) into money
if it mod 2 is zero then put "Even" into field 2
```

**YOU TRY IT:** Type the following messages into the Message Box in any stack:

```
put 100 into temp1
put 103 into temp2
temp1 div 5
temp2 div 5
temp1 mod 5
temp2 mod 5
temp2 div 5 & " with a remainder of " & temp2 mod 5
50 div -10
50 mod -10
```

## *Miscellaneous Operators*

The remaining operators are a mixed bag of logical, text, and command operators.

### and
### or
### not

**Returns:** And and Or return True or False depending on the logical relationship between two comparison expressions; Not returns the opposite of the logical result of a comparison expression.

**When to Use It:** All three of these expressions are used primarily in repeat and decision-making constructions (see chapter 37). They are sometimes called Boolean operators, because they're based on Boolean algebra, a math system founded by George Boole in the nineteenth century.

The And operator lets you establish two comparison criteria, both of which must be true for the operator to return true. If one of the comparisons is false, then the operator returns false. In other words, condition A must be true *and* condition B must be true for the whole statement to be true.

You have a few important ways to apply this tool. For example, you can specify a range of numbers within which a comparison figure must be before a certain procedure is carried out. If you want the script to beep when a number in a field is between 10 and 20, the conditional test would look like this:

```
if field 1 >= 10 and field 1 <= 20 then beep
```

Notice that on either side of the And operator is a complete comparison statement, including the field number and the math range. Both sides must be complete statements, as shown. You cannot use *if field 1 >= 10 and <= 20 then beep.* The script doesn't remember the field 1 part for the second comparison.

If you change the direction of the less than and greater than signs in the above conditional construction, you can test for a number that is outside the range of 10 to 20, as follows:

```
if field 1 < 10 and field 1 > 20 then beep
```

indicating that the number is out of the desired range.

You may also test for two completely different conditions, both of which must be met for the operator to return a true. For instance, you may insist that one field have a number greater than 100 while a second field has specific text in it. Such a test would look like this

if field 1 > 100 and field 2 is "Pounds" then...

In other words, any two comparisons may be used on either side of an And operator. The key is that both must evaluate to true if the And operator is to return a true.

The Or operator is similar to the And operator, but only one of the two comparison expressions must be true for the Or operator to return true. Therefore, the expression

3 < 100 or 5 = 20

returns true, because the first comparison, that 3 is less than 100, is true. Even though 5 = 20 on its own returns false, the Or operator returns a true because at least one of the two comparisons is met. If both are met, the Or operator still returns a true. If neither comparison returns true, the Or operator returns false.

The Not operator works with only one comparison and turns its result into the opposite. Therefore, if the comparison

20 > 10

returns true on its own, the comparison preceded by the Not operator, as in

not (20 > 10)

returns false. In other words, the Not operator returns what the following expression is NOT. If it's not true, then it must be false, and vice versa.

You'll see these expressions frequently in Chapter 37 where we demonstrate the conditional constructions.

**Examples:**

```
if field 1 is true or field 2 is true then put true into answer
repeat while theHour > 10¬
      and theHour < 11 -- theHour is a local variable
```

**You Try It:** Type the following messages into the Message Box in any stack:

```
put 1 into temp1
put 100 into temp2
temp1 > 0 and temp2 > 0
temp1 < 0 and temp2 > 0
temp1 < 0 or temp2 > 0
temp1 < 0 or temp2 > 100
temp1 = 1
not (temp1 = 1)
```

**&** (concatenate)
**&&** (concatenate and space)

**Returns:** The combined text string from two individual text strings

**When to Use It:** The concatenate operators are demonstrated frequently in chapters about HyperTalk commands. Generally speaking, the concatenate operators link two text strings together into one string. This is used primarily as a way of combining text components from diverse sources before putting the result into a container, like a field or variable.

A practical application of concatenation revolves around a system of naming cards in a stack in such a way that you can assemble the card name from various components before going to the card. At one stage of development of Bantam Electronic Publishing's Business Class™, for instance, cards with country maps contained a row of buttons linking to information cards about that country. The button scripts assembled the name of the information card from two sources: the first item of a hidden text file containing one or more country names, and a text string in the button script representing the type of card, such as Currency or Air Travel (Figure 35-2).

When the user clicked on the Currency button in the France card, the button script assembled the information card's name by concatenating the country name, France, and a three letter code for the Currency card, "Cur." The script looks something like this:

```
on mouseUp
        put item 1 of field "Country Name" & "Cur" into goName
        go to card goName in stack "Currency"
end mouseUp
```

Over in the Currency stack, France's card was named "FranceCur," and HyperCard zipped to that card as quickly as it could.

Since the Concatenate command, by itself, abuts two pieces of text without any spaces, HyperTalk includes a shortcut to adding a space between the pieces: the double ampersand operator. This operator works just like the regular concatenate operator but also inserts a space between the pieces.

You can also link more than one concatenation together in a script line as well as a mixture of single and double ampersands. It's not uncommon to see constructions like

```
field 1 && field 2 & field 3
```

in a script.

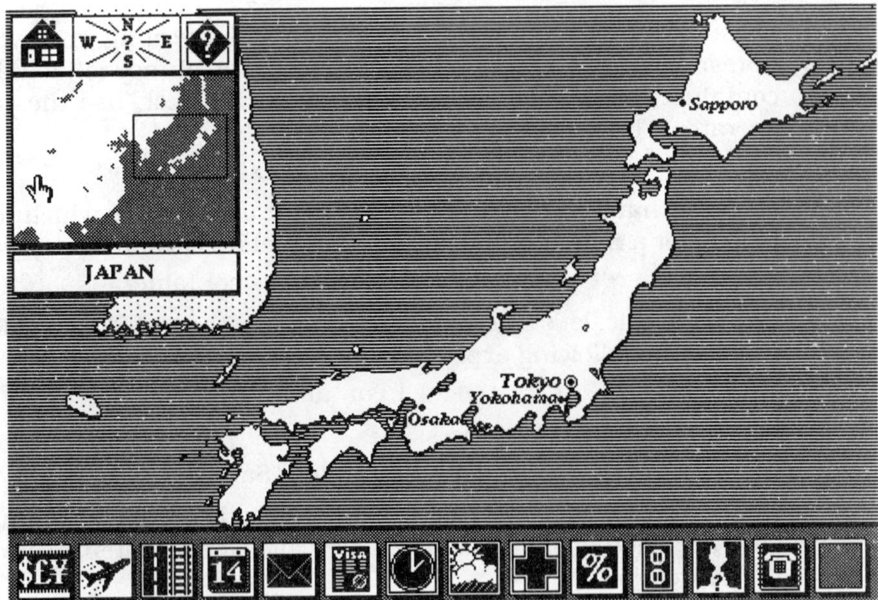


*Figure 35-2. In Activision's Business Class™ stackware for HyperCard, the button scripts linking country maps to information cards for currency, air travel, and other data, at one time used the concatenate feature of HyperTalk.*

**Examples:**

```
put item 1 of the long date && item 2 of the long date
open file the date & the time
```

**You Try It:** Type the following messages into the Message Box in any stack:

```
put "Howdy" into temp1
put "Doody" into temp2
put temp1 & temp2 into message
put temp1 && temp2 into message
put "It's the " & temp1 && temp2 & " Show!"
```

## contains
## is in

**Returns:** True or false, depending on whether one text string is in another.

**When to Use It:** You'll find times in your script-writing when you want to test whether a certain character, word, or phrase is included in a container like a field or variable. For such a test, use the contains operator. The syntax is as follows:

<container> contains <text to look for>

meaning that the first parameter holds the text through which you wish to look for a match of the second parameter. The alternate syntax is

<text to look for> is in <container>

For example, let's say that field 1 contains the text, "Larry, Moe, and Curly." The following expression,

field 1 contains "Moe"

returns true. But the expression

field 1 contains "Sarah"

returns false. The operator performs strictly a text-matching task, ignoring whether the parameters are valid words or items. Therefore, the expression

field 1 contains "r"

returns true, although this fact doesn't tell you a lot, since there are three instances of the letter r in the container.

**Examples:**

```
if field "date" contains the long date then...
repeat while temp contains the time
if field "checkmark" contains "√" then go card id 1655
```

**You Try It:** Type the following messages into the Message Box in any stack:

```
put "Four score and seven years ago..." into speech
speech contains "four"
speech contains "4"
speech contains " "          -- a space between quotes
speech contains "r s"        -- r, space, s
"four score" is in speech
```

(comment)

**Returns:** Nothing. HyperTalk skips the script line.

**When to Use It:** While it's true that HyperTalk scripts are in more of a natural language than most programming languages, it is still an excellent idea to place comments in your scripts to help you find sections or long scripts or remind you later of the technique used to carry out a particular operation. When you type two hyphens in a script line (even as the first characters of the line), HyperTalk skips over the words following them on the line. This is where you can place your comments about the script.

If your stacks are going to be used and customized by other people, then be as helpful as you can by providing many clues in your scripts regarding techniques and philosophies about your stack and script-design decisions. You might even include instructions in the script for ways of customizing certain parts of it.

**EXAMPLES:**

```
put 1 into x  --  x is local variable, used for counter.
              --  this section calculates the metric conversion...
```

**YOU TRY IT:** Typing comments into the Message Box is a waste of time, since nothing happens. We have been using comments so liberally throughout this book that they should be rather familiar to you by now.

## *Precedence*

While we've covered all the HyperTalk operators, there is one aspect about them that is not obvious. If more than one operator or more than one type of operator is located in a single script line, HyperTalk obeys strict rules as to which operators are evaluated first— and it doesn't go from left to right. The rules are based a lot on algebra (don't run away!) and can be summarized here.

HyperTalk performs operations in this order:

1) Operators within parentheses are performed before those outside parentheses.
2) minus sign (for a negative number) and boolean not
3) ^ (to the power)
4) * / div mod
5) + -
6) & && (concatenate)
7) > < <= >= ≤ ≥ contains is in
8) = <> ≠
9) and
10) or

What this all means is that HyperTalk picks apart a line of script and calculates each operator in accordance with the priorities listed above. No script line will contain all these operators, but HyperTalk still adheres to the list.

The importance of understanding *precedence*, as it is called, can be demonstrated in a simple comparison of two formats for the same arithmetic expression:

a) 4 * 5 + 10

b) 4 * (5 + 10)

Because of HyperTalk's rules of precedence, expression a) would evaluate to 30. Expression b) evaluates to 60. That's quite a difference for the addition of a couple parentheses, but those parentheses can help you direct HyperTalk to interpret your intention (which was, in this case, to add 5 to 10 before multiplying the result by 4).

A lot of HyperTalk's precedence rules are almost automatic. For example, the way you've learned about the And and Or operators, you pretty much expect the other arithmetic operators to have been completed before the anding and oring is performed. That's exactly how the rules are already set. The important thing to remember is that when you assemble complex arithmetic expressions (including those using containers as numbers), you should run a simple test with small values like 1 and 0 to be sure the expression is evaluating correctly. If they're not, you may need to add a set of parentheses or two to force HyperTalk into following your lead on how to evaluate the expression.

CHAPTER 36

# Constants

HYPERTALK SIMPLIFIES THE ENTRY OF CERTAIN VALUES THAT ARE NORMALLY DIFFICULT to get to from the keyboard, like the values for the Return or Tab characters and an empty string. These characters are given plain language words that substitute for the longer, more cumbersome ways of expressing them. For instance, inserting a tab character between field entries in a Write To File command would normally require knowing the ASCII value of the Tab character and performing a numToChar conversion. Instead, HyperTalk gives you a constant, called Tab, which you use in the script as if it were a standard text character.

In this section, we examine each of the constants HyperTalk provides its programmers. Some constants—like true, false, up, and down—HyperCard uses to convey information at the return of a function or operator.

## true
## false
## up
## down

**WHEN TO USE IT:** If you've studied HyperTalk functions and operators, you've seen that HyperCard uses these four constants frequently. True and False are often the result of comparison operators, while Up and

Down represent the condition of various keyboard keys and the mouse button at the time a function executes.

But HyperCard doesn't have a monopoly on these functions. You are free to use them as you see fit. In fact, programmers commonly apply the True and False constants to set variables so that they behave as markers for where they've been. For example at the beginning of a long script, the programmer may set a variable to true (*put true into marker*). If the script includes a decision point (see chapter 37) and the execution proceeds down one path, the script in that path may set the variable to false. Later in the script, where execution continues regardless of intervening paths, the script can test the variable. If the variable returns false, the script knows one path has been taken and can then act accordingly. This methodology is often called setting flags, because the variable, by its true or false setting, flags the script as to which route the script has followed.

Also, as you'll see in chapter 37, any variable set to true or false can substitute for a longer comparison operation that also returns true or false. Therefore, instead of saying *if marker is true then beep*, you can simply say *if marker then beep*. The variable "marker" by iself returns its content, which could be true or false. That meets the requirement of the conditional construction.

**EXAMPLES:**

```
if the Optionkey is down then go card id 100
repeat while marker
if the ShiftKey is down and the sound is done then go Home
```

**YOU TRY IT:** The right way to experiment with these constants is in the context of if-then structures. Since you cannot execute if-then structures from the Message Box, place the following handler in a new button script in a blank card of the Address stack. Then click the button while holding down one or more modifier keys.

```
on mouseUp
        put "The Option Key is " & the optionKey into line 1 of field 1
        put "The Command Key is "¬
        & the commandKey into line 2 of field 1
        put "The Shift Key is " & the shiftKey into line 3 of field 1
        if the optionKey is down or the commandKey is down¬
        or the shiftKey is down
```

```
    then put "Modifier(s) in effect." into line 4 of field 1
    else put empty into line 4 of field 1
end mouseUp
```

## empty

**When to Use It:** The Empty constant is the same as the null text string (that is, two quotation marks with nothing in between, ""). Not only is it easier to put an empty constant in a container to clear it, but it is also more natural-sounding in a script to test for whether a container is empty than to bother with the null string.

**Examples:**

```
put empty into field 1
if field "Name" is empty then ask "Enter Name:"
```

**You Try It:** Type the following messages into the Message Box while viewing a blank card in the "Address" stack:

```
put "hello" into field 1
put empty into char 2 of field 1
put "everybody" into line 2 of field 1
put empty into line 1 of field 1
```

## quote

**When to Use It:** If you've ever tried to place a quotation mark in a field or variable, you probably were frustrated, because HyperCard sees a quote mark as the beginning or end of a text string. You couldn't place a quotation mark inside two quotation marks. That's why HyperCard has a quote constant. It substitutes for a quotation mark in a text string when that string should contain the quotation mark.

**Example:**

```
put "Say " & quote & "Hello" & quote & " to everybody."
put "Coordinates: " & field 3 & quote && field 4 & """
```

**You Try It:** Type the following messages into the Message Box in any stack:

```
put "He said, "My name is Joe." "into message   -- not allowed
put "He said, " & quote & "My name is Joe." & quote into message
```

## return
## space
## tab

**When to Use It:** These three constants substitute for keyboard characters. Return and Tab are used most often in the Write to file command. In typical scripts built around the Write to file command you must insert field and card (record) delimiters. This assures that the external Macintosh application can read the information from the text file created by HyperCard.

If information in a text field needs additional spaces between items, a script can use the Put command and the space constant to insert a space where necessary. The alternative would be to put a text string consisting of quotation marks surrounding one or more spaces. The difficulty with that construction is that it becomes very difficult later to determine exactly how many spaces are between the quote marks. With the space constant, you can tell exactly how many are there, because there is one constant per space.

**Examples:**

```
put space & space & space after word 1 of field 3
read from file "Database" until tab
write return to file "Expense Report"
```

**You Try It:** Use a blank card in the Address stack for these experiments. Type the following messages into the Message Box:

```
put "Three blind mice. See how they run." into field 1
put space & space after word 1 of field 1
put return after word 1 of field 1
put return before word 2 of field 1
put return before word 3 of field 1
```

## formfeed
## linefeed

**When to Use It:** The formfeed and linefeed constants are control characters usually used for printers (although some communications services respond to the linefeed character). These two characters are not available from the keyboard, so HyperCard provides a way to send them primarily to text files you create with the Write command.

A linefeed character (ASCII value 10) differs from return. On telecommunications terminals (and also on the old teletype machines), a return character sends the print cursor (or printhead) to the left edge of the screen (or page) without advancing to the next line. To advance the cursor (or paper) to the next line, the Linefeed character command is required. Today, most printers automatically insert a Linefeed command when they receive a return command (this ability is one of the settings of the small DIP switches inside dot-matrix and letter-quality printers— laser printers don't need to bother). If you find that the text files you write from HyperCard cause the printer to print text all on the same line without advancing the paper, either change the printer's switch setting or include a linefeed character along with the return character in the printing script.

Formfeed is another character (ASCII value 12) that causes the paper to advance to what the printer considers to be the top of the next page. The need for this constant will be rare, but it is here if you need it.

**EXAMPLES:**

```
write return & linefeed to file "Print File"
write formfeed to file "Pages and Pages"
```

**YOU TRY IT:** Since you cannot see these characters on your HyperCard screen, there is little need to experiment with them here. To prove these constants are legitimate ASCII characters, however, type the following messages into the Message Box:

```
the charToNum of lineFeed
the charToNum of formFeed
```

This concludes our discussions about functions, operators, and constants. There is one more fundamental subject area you should know about before we get into some sample HyperTalk applications: control structures. That's the subject of the next chapter.

CHAPTER 37

# HyperTalk Control Structures

MUCH OF WHAT WE, AS HUMANS, DO EVERY DAY CAN BE DESCRIBED IN TERMS OF WHAT HyperCard calls *control structures*. The two basic structures involve 1) making simple decisions and 2) repeating actions with slight variations.

In the course of a day, you make many decisions, most of them unconsciously. For intance, if the television set is too loud, then you turn the volume down. If it is getting dark, then you turn on a light. If it is a nice, warm day and if you have a free moment, then you'll step outside for a breath of fresh air. You may make thousands of these if-then decisions per day. HyperCard, too, can make if-then decisions.

A number of daily tasks are repetitive actions. Again, you probably don't recognize such tasks as being repetitive. But, even while you're reading this book, you're performing a repetitive task: reading one word or phrase at a time, then advancing your eye to the next word or phrase. You continue repeating this action until you finish the book or stop reading because you're tired or have something else to do. The same can be said for paying bills from a checkbook. The basic action, writing a check, is repeated until all the bills are paid or your checkbook balance is zero. Some details of each step in the repetition are different, like the payee and the amount, but the basic action is still repeated. HyperCard allows you to program similar kinds of repeated actions, allowing for slight modifications at each step.

The HyperTalk syntax provides several construction options for if-then and repeat control structures. Each has a specific purpose that affects the flow of logic through a HyperTalk script. We'll discuss each one in detail, following a format similar to what you saw for commands and functions earlier.

Rather than offer separate experiments for you to try, we'll show you real-life examples in each discussion, which you can place in button or card scripts to try yourself. These constructions generally involve multiple-line scripts, so the Message Box approach is out of the question. All examples will be presented in such a fashion that you can write them into card scripts attached to blank cards in the Address stack. Each sample script will be a complete message handler with its own name. To try the script after typing it into the card's Script Editor, type the name of the message handler into the Message Box (for example, if the message handler starts with *on fourTimes*, then type *fourTimes* into the Message Box). HyperCard, as you'll recall, sends the message from the Message Box to the current card.

## *If-Then Decision*

All HyperTalk if-then constructions have one important characteristic in common. Each one begins by testing whether a certain condition is true. By that we mean that whatever expression is under test, it must evaluate to either a true or false. If the result is true, HyperTalk progresses down the special path set aside for it whenever the expression returns true. If the result is false, HyperTalk ignores the special path and zips to the next regular line in the script. This process is pictured in Figure 37–1.

If you think back to the last chapters, which covered functions, operators, and constants, you'll recall that a few functions and many operators return either a true or false. Any one of those expressions may be used in the test part of an if-then construction. You'll commonly test for things like: whether a container is equal to (or less than or greater than) a certain value; whether a container is empty; whether a container holds a specific text string; whether two containers are equal (or less than or greater than) each other. You may also test directly for the true or false setting of properties, like whether a button is highlighted.

All if-then constructions, therefore, begin with the word "if," followed by the true/false expression and the word "then." Here are some examples of this prefix:

```
if x < 3 then...
if item 3 of the long date > 1989 then...
if field 3 <> field 1 of card id 7067 then...
if field "Name" is empty then...
```

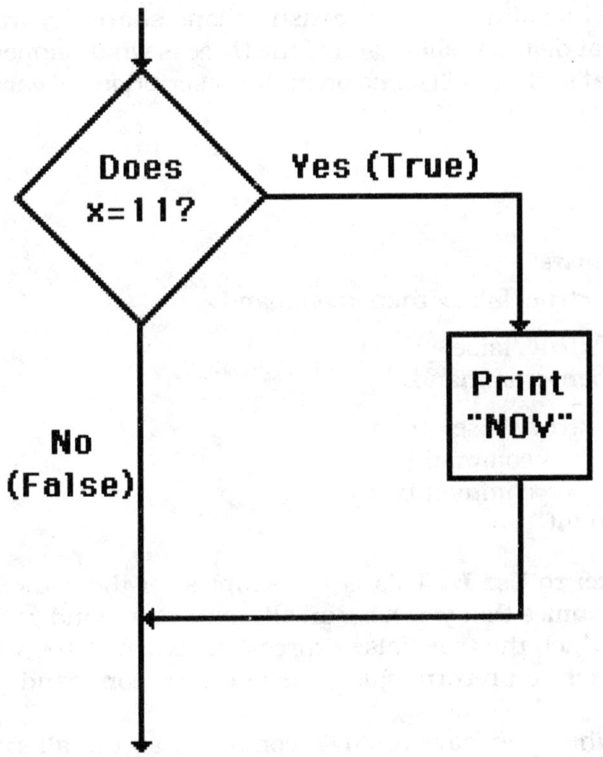


*Figure 37-1. The result of a decision is either true or false. A script can perform different or extra steps based on the results of a decision.*

With the help of the And and Or boolean operators, you can set more than one expression for the true/false test. For example, if you want HyperTalk to execute some special instructions only if the current year is between 1980 and 1990 (inclusive), you could first put item 3 of the long date function into It. Then set up the following prefix to an if-then construction:

if it ≥ 1980 and it ≤ 1990 then...

Following the rules of the And operator, the expression will return a true only if the year is 1980, 1981,...,1990. You can use the Or operator to allow execution of the special code only if the month function returns 1980 or 1990 in the following prefix:

if it is 1980 or it is 1990 then...

Using the Not operator, you can test for all conditions except one. All years other than the one specified will divert to the command(s) following the "then" part of the construction:

if it is not 1984 then...

While all the if-then constructions share the true/false structure, what distinguishes each of the three is what happens after the "then." That's what we'll focus on in the descriptions of each if-then construction.

## if...then

**Formats:**

```
if <true/false> then <command>

if <true/false>
then <command>

if <true/false> then
      <command>
      <command>
end if
```

**When to Use It:** This is the simplest of the if-then constructions. It presumes that you have an alternate command path set for instances in which the true/false expression returns true. When the true/false expression returns false, the alternate command path is not carried out.

When you have a single command as the alternate path, use the simple, one-line if...then format. When the one line command is a long one, it may be more convenient to use the second format. When multiple commands apply to the alternate path, use the third format. The HyperTalk Script Editor automatically indents commands beneath the *if* statement. But also notice that multiple command lines require an *end if* marker to let HyperCard know that it has reached the end of the *if* commands.

A <command> is any HyperTalk command that you would normally put at the beginning of a script line. Use this construction whenever your script needs to make some kind of simple adjustment whenever a certain condition is true.

**Examples:**

```
on insert
      if field 1 is empty then put the long date into field 1
      get item 3 of field 1
      if it < 1988 then put "Your clock may be off"
end insert

on openCard
      if field 1 is empty then
```

```
            put the long date into field 1
            put the time into line 2 of field 1
      end if
      ask "Is the current time " & line 2 of field 1¬
            & " correct?" with "OK" or "No"
      if it is "No"
      then put "Please adjust time in Control Panel."
end openCard
```

## if...then...else

**FORMATS:**

```
if <true/false> then <command> else <command>

if  <true/false> then <command>
else <command>

if <true/false> then
      <command>
      <command>
else <command>

if <true/false> then <command>
else
      <command>
      <command>
end if

if <true/false> then
      <command>
      <command>
else
      <command>
      <command>
end if
```

**WHEN TO USE IT:** Use the if-then-else construction when you have two possible side paths for HyperTalk after a decision, one path for true, one for false. When the expression returns true, HyperTalk pursues the first path (the one after the "then"); when the expression returns false, HyperTalk pursues the second path (the one after the "else"). Figure 37-2 illustrates this execution path.

You can use this construction even if you have only one command for each condition or different numbers of commands for each. Since the true/false expression will return one of those two possibilities, the

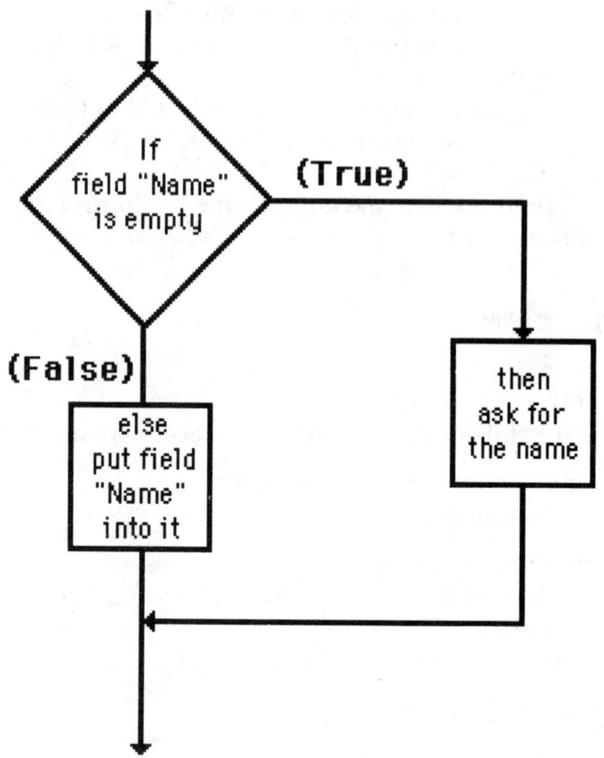


*Figure 37–2. An if...then...else construction lets your script perform two distinct operations based on the results of a decision.*

script will execute one of the two banks of commands before proceeding through the script.

Only when the *else* part of the construction contains multiple command lines do you need the *end if* marker, as in the last two formats, above.

**EXAMPLE:**

```
on quiz
        put empty into message
        ask "What is another name for Britain?"
        if it is "England" or it is "United Kingdom"¬
        or it is "U.K." then put "Correct" into message
        else
                beep
                answer "Sorry. Try again?"
        end if
end quiz
```

## *Nesting If-Then Decisions*

You may place an if-then construction within another if-then construction— a format called nesting. It's not uncommon to require nested if-then constructions, because the world is not black-and-white (or true-and-false). Even when something tests to be true, it may still undergo further scrutiny to help narrow the decision process.

The best way to observe this is to watch it in action inside a real script. The following message handler presents a dialog box requesting whether you wish to know how many days are in the current month. It then reads the current month from the Macintosh clock and makes further determinations before presenting the reply in another dialog box.

```
on hathMonth
        answer "Do you wish to know how many days in this month?"¬
        with "Yes" or "No"
        if it is "Yes" then
                get the date
                convert it to dateItems
                put item 1 of it into year
                put item 2 of it into month
                if month is 4 or month is 6 or month is 9¬
                or month is 11
                then put 30 into howMany
                else put 31 into howMany
                if month is 2 then
                        if year mod 4 = 0
                        then put 29 into howMany
                        else put 28 into howMany
                end if
                answer "This month has " & howMany & " days in it."
        else answer "Just thought we'd ask"
end hathMonth
```

This may seem to be an extreme case, but it does demonstrate that you can nest if-then constructions quite deeply, mixing single and multiple command line constructions as needed. And, despite what seems to be many lines of code, HyperCard goes through its paces rather quickly. Try the message handler above to see for yourself. Place it in a card script and type *hathMonth* into the Message Box.

## *Repeat Constructions*

HyperTalk offers four different repeating control structures from which to choose: repeat for, repeat until, repeat while, and repeat with. While their uses are quite different, they share two common characteristics.

The first characteristic is that in the same line as the repeat command you will be providing information that controls when the repetition is to end. Sometimes the repetition ends after a specific number of times; at other times, the repetition ends only upon a certain condition being met, a condition that changes each time through the repetition. Repetitions like these are sometimes called loops, because the execution of the instructions runs in circles until it can break out of the cycle.

The second characteristic has to do with the ending of the repeat construction within the script. The command End Repeat must be entered on its own line at the close of the repeat grouping. This is like a marker to HyperTalk so that it knows how far down the script to go before looping back to the beginning of the repeat construction.

Now we can look at each repeat construction in detail.

# repeat for

**FORMAT:**

```
repeat [for] <number of times> [times]
    <command>
    <command>
end repeat
```

**WHEN TO USE IT:** This repeat construction repeats the indented commands a fixed number of times. The <number of times> parameter may be a plain number, an arithmetic expression, or a container (provided the container evaluates to a number).

**EXAMPLES:**

```
on addCards
    ask "How many new cards do you want?"
    repeat for it
        doMenu "New Card"
        put "This is a new card" into field 1
    end repeat
end addCards

on showTime
    put "Hooray for HyperCard!"
```

```
        repeat 10 times
            put space before msg
        end repeat
        repeat  20 times
            put space before word 3 of msg
            beep 1
        end repeat
        repeat 20 times
            put empty into char 21 of msg
        end repeat
        repeat 10 times
            put empty into char 1 of msg
        end repeat
    end showTime
```

## repeat until

**Format:**

```
repeat until <true/false>
    <command>
    <command>
end repeat
```

**When to Use It:** In the Repeat Until structure, the indented commands are executed until the true/false expression returns a true. In other words, if the expression returns a true the first time, none of the indented commands are executed. But if the expression is false, the loop starts and continues until the expression returns a true.

Obviously, the commands inside a Repeat Until construction must have some effect on the factors in the true/false expression. If nothing about that expression changes, the loop will drone on endlessly. In fact you will have caused what is known as an endless, or infinite, loop. The only way to break out of an infinite loop is to hold down the Command key and press the period key. That key combination halts a HyperTalk message handler in its tracks.

A common application for Repeat Until is to keep a loop going while waiting for a mouse click. There doesn't have to be a command between the *repeat* and *end* repeat parts of the construction. If you include no command lines between the start and end of a repeat, the repeat loop keeps cycling very tightly until the true/false expression returns true.

As an aid to debugging Repeat Until loops, you can place a command that puts the value of the changeable variable into the Message Box.

That way, you can keep an eye on what's happening to your true/false expression as the repeat construction cycles round and round.

**EXAMPLES:**

```
on jumpWeeks
        repeat until the mouseClick
                get number of this card
                go card (it + 7)
                wait 1 second
        end repeat
end jumpWeeks
```

## repeat while

**FORMAT:**

```
repeat while <true/false>
        <command>
        <command>
end repeat
```

**WHEN TO USE IT:** The Repeat While construction is essentially the opposite of the Repeat Until construction. In this case, the indented commands are carried out as long as the true/false expression remains true. If it is false to begin with, HyperTalk will skip right past it.

As with Repeat Until, your indented commands must have some effect on the items being compared or measured in the true/false expression. If these factors never change, then your script will be in an infinite loop.

Use the Message Box debugging aid with Repeat While, too. Place a command among the indented commands that isolates the changeable value and put the results into the Message Box. You'll then be able to watch the value change each time the loop makes a cycle. If the loop works too fast for you to watch closely, then insert *wait 1 second* as another command inside the loop.

**EXAMPLES:**

```
on tunes
        put the random of 60 into note
        if note < 40 then put 40 into note
        if note mod 2 is not zero then add 1 to note
        repeat while note ≤ 82
                put note
                play "Harpsichord" temp 700 note
```

```
        add 2 to note
    end repeat
end tunes
```

## repeat with

**Format:**

```
repeat with <variable> = <low number> to <high number>
    <command>
    <command>
end repeat

repeat with <variable> = <high number> down to <low number>
    <command>
    <command>
end repeat
```

**When to Use It:** While the Repeat With construction may seem like the most complicated of the four, it is perhaps the most commonly used. With this construction, you can both initialize a variable and set bounds for it. Each time through the loop, the value of the variable is increased or decreased by one. The loop continues cycling until the value of the variable equals that of the second number.

This is so valuable because you can use the variable within the indented commands to perform actions on any numbered group of objects or components. Therefore, if you initialize a variable "a" and give it the bounds 1 through 5, each time through the loop you can issue a command like *put the date into field "Date" of card a.* The first time through the loop, the date goes into card 1; the second time through, the date goes into card 2; and so on.

Parameters for either boundary number may be a plain number, an arithmetic expression, a function, or a container. Therefore, if you wish to perform an operation on every field in a card, the repeat construction would start out like this:

```
repeat with x = 1 to the number of fields
```

Then, within the indented commands, the instructions calling for a field designator would look like this:

```
put empty into field x
```

The beauty of this repeat construction is that you can condense an awful lot of HyperTalk code into just a few lines by repeating the same code over and over, but incrementing (or decrementing) the object or container designator each time. Whenever you notice that a script repeats the same commands to similar kinds of objects, you probably have a candidate for condensation with the Repeat With construction.

**Example:**

```
on makeCards
        ask "Please enter the starting date:" with the date
        convert it to seconds
        put it into start
        ask "Please enter the ending date:"
        convert it to seconds
        put it into finish
        put finish - start into howLong
        divide howLong by 24*60*60
        repeat with count = 1 to howLong
                doMenu "New Card"
                put "Day " & count into field "Which Day"
                put start into field "Date"
                convert field "Date" to long date
                add (24*60*60) to start
        end repeat
end makeCards
```

## *Modifying Repeat Execution Order*

Normally, within a repeat construction the commands are executed in the order in which they appear. That's as it should be. But there may be times when you might not want the cycle to include some commands. In other words, you'd like the cycle to skip the remaining commands and start over at the top of the cycle, incrementing the counter, if it's the Repeat With construction. HyperTalk has a command that does that: Next Repeat.

You can also exit a repeat construction in the middle of it, if a condition you're looking for is met before execution reaches the bottom and starts over. The command that takes care of that is Exit Repeat.

# next repeat

**When to Use It:** You can set up any valid conditional test (if-then) within the indented commands of a repeat construction, in such a way that a test returning true executes the Next Repeat command. A skeletal repeat script set up this way would look like this:

```
repeat until <true/false expression>
    <command 1>
    <command 2>
    if <true/false expression> then next repeat
    <command 3>
end repeat
```

HyperTalk would start following the repeat commands as usual. If the conditional test after command 2 proves true, the next repeat command tells HyperTalk to loop back to the top of the repeat and start over. If the repeat construction had been the Repeat For or Repeat With, the counter would have increased by one.

The Next Repeat command is used to trap a special case in a repeat loop and prevent further commands within the repeat to be executed. A practical application for this construction is within a repeat with loop in which you want the counting variable (that is, the "x" in *repeat with x = 1 to 100*) to increment by numbers other than 1. If, for instance, you want to use the counting variable only when it is even, you could place an if-then statement at the very beginning of the repeat loop that tests whether the counter mod 2 is not zero. If it's not (meaning the counting variable is an odd number), then do a next repeat without performing any other commands in the loop. Experienced BASIC programmers will recognize this method as an equivalent to the REPEAT...STEP construction.

**Example:**

```
on plan
    repeat with count = 1 to 14
        if count mod 7 is 0 then
            put "No scheduled work on Sundays" ¬
                into line count of field 2
            next repeat
        end if
        put "Day " & count into line count of field 2
    end repeat
end plan
```

## exit repeat
## exit if
## exit <handler name>

**When to Use It:** You may also test for a condition within a repeat loop that is different from the one the repeat is looking for. For example, the repeat may be waiting for a mouse click all the while some math is going on within the indented commands. If you want to exit the repeat without a mouse click when the math reaches a certain value, you'd test for that value and issue the Exit Repeat command. The skeletal construction looks like this:

```
repeat until the mouseClick
    <command 1> -- does things to the contents of field 3
    <command 2>
    if field 3 > 100 then exit repeat
    <command 3>
end repeat
```

In this case, the loop will stop before a mouse click if the content of field 3 grows to over 100. This is assuming, of course, that the commands in this loop have some effect over field 3 during the execution of the loop.

It also turns out that the Exit command is rather universal, covering if-then constructions and message handlers in general. Within a message handler situation, the Exit If command comes in quite handy when the script needs to perform special actions only when the if-then condition is true. All the rest of the commands in the message become superfluous, so you can break out of the entire handler. This speeds execution, because HyperCard doesn't have to evaluate other if-then decisions later in the handler. When the handler exits, then it's all through.

**EXAMPLES:**

```
on mouseUp
    -- monthly interval between calendar cards
    if field "interval" is "monthly" then
            go next card
            exit mouseUp
    end if
    if field "interval" is "yearly" then
            get number of this card
            add 12 to it
            go card it
    else  put "Sorry, cannot find the interval— go to Setup Card."
end mouseUp
```

## **pass** <message>

**WHEN TO USE IT:** Occasionally, you will want to trap a HyperCard system message or other kind of message whose primary handler is way up the

HyperCard hierarchy. If you'd like to add some extra feature to the handler or trap the message when it has a particular parameter (like a menu item name), issue the special command, and then send the message on its way up the hierarchy, as if it had never been trapped. You send it on its way with the Pass command.

The one parameter to the Pass command is the name of the message that you originally trapped for. For example, if you have a button script that traps for mouseUp and there is a background script also for mouseUp, your button script would trap the mouseUp message first. After it has done its thing, it may then pass the mouseUp message to the next level up the hierarchy. When the background mouseUp message handler gets the mouseUp message, it will not know that the message had been intercepted anywhere along the path.

Trapping for menu items is a popular application for the Pass command. Since the doMenu system message comes with a parameter consisting of the name of the menu item, you can perform operations in a handler for one or more menu items. But you must also pass the message to HyperCard so it can respond to other menu items. If you don't pass doMenu, the system message would be forever trapped in the handler— one method, by the way, of protecting read-only stacks from saboteurs.

**EXAMPLES:**

```
on doMenu whichItem
    if whichItem is "Help"
    then go card "Custom Help"
    else pass doMenu
end doMenu
```

This concludes the discussion about HyperCard's control structures. In the following chapters, we'll be applying the concepts learned in the preceding chapters. Together, we'll build some practical HyperCard applications, while you learn more about the commands, properties, functions, operators, constants, and control structures in action.

# PART FOUR

# APPLYING HYPERCARD AND HYPERTALK

CHAPTER 38

# Introduction to Applications

EACH OF THE NEXT SIX CHAPTERS CONTAINS DETAILED SPECIFICATIONS FOR HYPERCARD applications you can use as they are or adapt for many other purposes. The intent of these examples is to demonstrate HyperTalk techniques and strategies in real working environments.

The applications cover a wide range of complexity, from a simple "brute force" stack (simple to implement, although an experienced HyperTalk hand would be able to accomplish the same stack functions with fewer cards) to a stack whose scripts run a couple of pages of Script Editor printout.

For each stack, we start with an overview of how the stack operates, so that you can appreciate its functions and the interaction among cards, buttons, and fields. Then we let the stack itself do most of the talking. We extracted the object scripts and properties directly from the stack and reproduced them here. When additional comment is necessary, we help explain HyperTalk constructions that may be new to you or that are representative of techniques you should strive for. In all cases, the scripts are examples of HyperTalk programming style and practice as envisioned by the language's creators.

Wherever possible, we tried to use the graphic elements supplied on HyperCard's ideas disk. These stacks are supposed to represent stacks that anyone— including those with less than spectacular painting tool mastery— can recreate. Those ideas disks are valuable resources you should use regularly in your stack design.

The only way to become proficient in HyperTalk is to use it on real stacks. Start by recreating the stacks in the following chapters. Then modify them to suit your particular applications. Always be on the lookout for techniques that might apply to the things you want to do with HyperCard.

As you build a HyperCard stack, do it in stages, testing each message handler as you go. When you get alert messages indicating that HyperCard can't do something or doesn't understand a particular construction, click on the alert box's Script button to zoom in on the problem. Make the necessary repair and test the handler again. Keep at it until you've worked out all the kinks. Then move on to the next handler.

Another useful technique when designing your own scripts from scratch is to get the functionality of the script working, even if the code is not especially elegant or compact. Once the handler is doing what it should, go back to it and look for ways of making it more efficient and simpler, or perhaps for ways that it can be shared by other objects when placed at a higher level. You'll see some examples in the next chapters in which there are no button scripts in a stack (at least for the main action buttons). The handlers that perform the action are in the background or stack object, taking their cues from the name of the button clicked by the user (*the target*, in HyperTalk functions parlance). One script ends up performing the tasks of a dozen.

But don't worry if you cannot seem to make your scripts as tightly woven as the examples we show here. The fact that you can make a stack do what you want it to do is a significant accomplishment— and very much in the spirit of HyperCard.

## *A Useful Utility Script*

Each time you create a new HyperCard stack, it is helpful to have a Home Stack button created so you can go to that stack easily. That way, you won't have to try to find the stack with the Open Stack... method. Here's a suggestion.

In your Home Stack, make a new card immediately after the Home card. Name it "My Stacks," both in the card name property (using the Card Info... dialog box) and in the title field at the top of the card. If that field is locked, double-click the field with the Field tool, and change the Locked Text setting to off.

Then add the following handler to your Home Stack script. Use it by typing *makeButton* into the Message Box while in the new stack you're making. The handler makes a button of whatever stack you're in and places it in this My Stacks card of the Home Stack. It leaves the Button tool selected so you can drag the button to an empty spot on the card. The next time you wish to go that new stack, simply click that button.

Here's the handler:

```
on makeButton
      put the short name of this stack into stackName
      go card "My Stacks" of "Home"
      set lockScreen to true
      doMenu "New Button"
      set rect of button "New Button" to 200,100,280,160
      set icon of button "New Button" to 1000
      set showName of button "New Button" to true
      set style of button "New Button" to transparent
      set name of button "New Button" to stackName
      put "on mouseUp" into newScript
      put "go to" && stackName¬
      into line 2 of newScript
      put "end mouseUp" into line 3 of newScript
      set script of button stackName to newScript
      put "Now drag the button "&¬
      "to the desired location...and type Command-Tab"
end makeButton
```

Enjoy!

# CHAPTER 39

# A Corporate Directory

WHEN A COMPANY STARTS SPREADING ITS PEOPLE ACROSS SEVERAL BUILDINGS AND shifts people around offices regularly, it becomes important that both employees and guests find their way to offices quickly. The corporate directory stack is an application that can be recreated quite simply, and without too much artistry.

## *Overview*

The stack environment shown here consists of a single stack with three backgrounds (although in practice, it would contain many more). If the company has thousands of people, you might prefer to divide the environment into two or three stack files.

The first background consists of a Staff Directory card (Figure 39-1), which contains information about each person employed by the company. Items in the card are filled in as individual text fields. Most of the buttons and their actions should be familiar to you by now. The arrow buttons take you to the previous and next cards in the stack. The Home button takes you to the Home Stack. The Sort button presents an answer dialog box with options for sorting by name or department. We'll get to the Print button in a moment. Next to the Extension field is a telephone button, a click of which causes the stack to dial the extension listed in the field. In that button's script is also a second possibility. In case the extension is actually an outside phone number

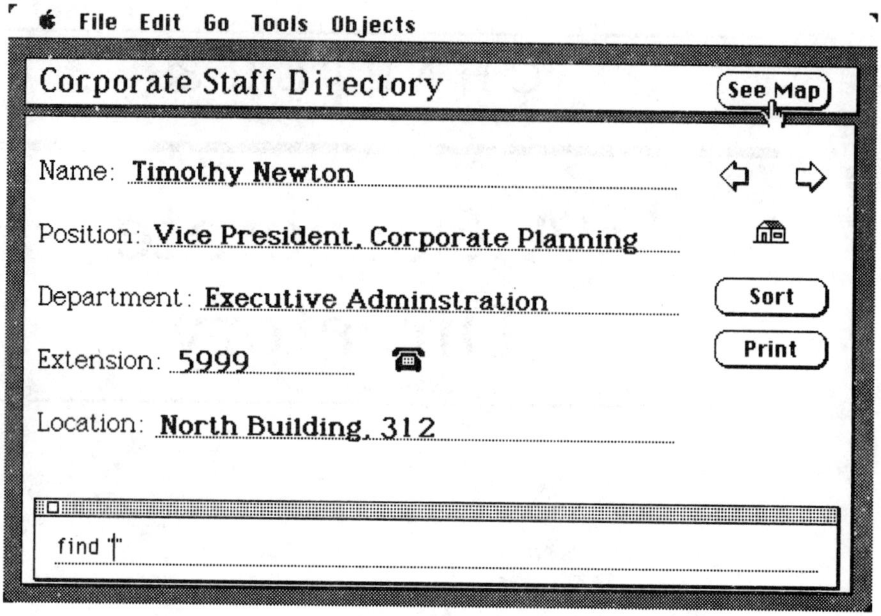

Figure 39-1.

(that is, is longer than four digits), the button dials a 9 and the number in the field (presuming the stack is being used on a corporate phone system).

The See Map button links the Directory card to cards in the next background. In this second background are a few cards containing maps of the entire corporate grounds (Figure 39-2). Each card highlights the building in which the person in the Directory card is located. Therefore, there are only as many cards in this background as there are buildings to highlight. Each card's name is the name of the building, so the handler in the See Map button (on the Directory card) goes to the card whose name is the first item of the Location field in the Directory card.

In the campus map background is a button called Zoom In. This button takes the second item of the Directory card's location field, the office number, and searches for that number in a text field in the third background (Figure 39-3). In this third background is a floor plan of one wing of one building. Each card has a card field with the number of a different office, and that office's cubicle is filled with a pattern. Note that the pattern and the field are in the card layer, while the rest of what you see is in the background layer.

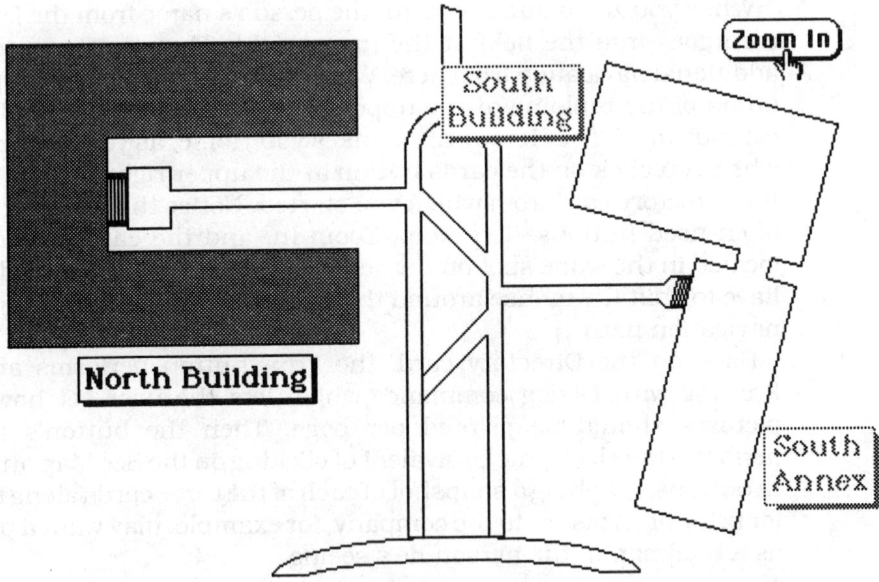


*Figure 39-2.*

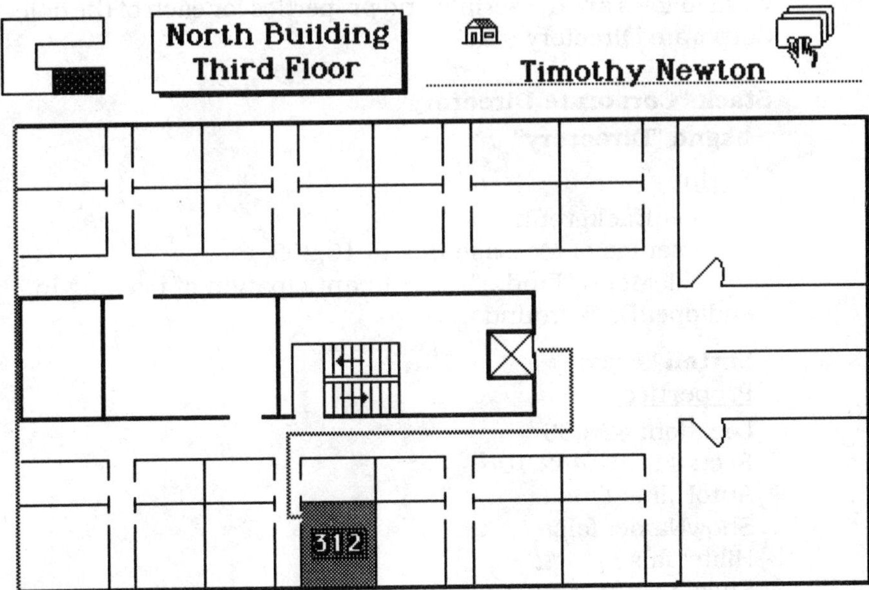


*Figure 39-3.*

When you zoom into this card, the person's name from the Directory card goes into the field at the upper right. Three buttons offer you additional navigation from here. When you click on the small representation of the building at the upper left, you go back one card, to the campus map. The Home button takes you Home, as you'd expect. And when you click on the cards button at the upper right, you go back to the Directory card from which you started. Notice that the three most-often-used buttons— See Map, Zoom In, and the cards button— are located in the same spot on the screen. That way the browser does not have to shift the mouse around the screen to follow the most common navigation path.

Back on the Directory card, the Print button performs an Open Printing with Dialog command, which lets the user set how many pictures should be printed per page. Then the button's handler performs the electronic equivalent of clicking on the See Map and Zoom In buttons, grabbing a snapshot of each of the three cards along the way for printing. A visitor to the company, for example, may want a printout as a roadmap to the person he's seeing.

## *Scripts and Properties*

What follows are the scripts and properties for each of the objects in the Corporate Directory stack.

**Stack "Corporate Directory"**

**bkgnd "Directory"**

Script

```
on openBackground
      set loc of Message Box to 19,293
      doMenu "Find..."      -- in anticipation of needing to Find
end openBackground
```

**button "Prev"**

Properties

Location: 428,93
Rect: 414,81,442,106
AutoHilite: true
ShowName: false
Hilite: false
Style: transparent
Icon: 1014
Visible: true

Script

```
on mouseUp
        visual effect wipe left
        go to prev card of this background
        -- keeps browsing within Directory cards
end mouseUp
```

**button "Next"**

Properties

Location: 473,93
Rect: 459,81,487,106
AutoHilite: true
ShowName: false
Hilite: false
Style: transparent
Icon: 1013
Visible: true

Script

```
on mouseUp
        visual effect wipe right
        go to next card of this background
end mouseUp
```

**button "Home"**

Properties

Location: 451,127
Rect: 433,113,469,142
AutoHilite: true
ShowName: false
Hilite: false
Style: transparent
Icon: 20689
Visible: true

Script

```
on mouseUp
        go home
end mouseUp
```

**button "See Map"**

Properties

Location: 451,45
Rect: 418,34,485,56
AutoHilite: true
ShowName: true

Hilite: false
Style: roundRect
Icon: 0
Visible: true
<u>Script</u>

```
on mouseUp
    global name,location     -- used by other buttons and cards
    push this card           -- need this to return later
    put field "Name" into name
    put field "Location" into location
    go to card item 1 of location
    -- the name of the Campus Map card
end mouseUp
```

**button "Sort"**
<u>Properties</u>
Location: 451,163
Rect: 418,152,485,174
AutoHilite: true
ShowName: true
Hilite: false
Style: roundRect
Icon: 0
Visible: true
<u>Script</u>

```
on mouseUp
    answer "How would you like to sort this directory?"¬
    with "By Name" or "By Dept." or "Cancel"
    if it is "By Name" then sort by last name of field "Name"
    else if it is "By Dept" then sort by field "Department"
end mouseUp
```

**button "Dial"**
<u>Properties</u>
Location: 238,201
Rect: 224,190,252,213
AutoHilite: false
ShowName: false
Hilite: false
Style: transparent
Icon: 10610
Visible: true

Script

```
on mouseUp
    put msg into temp      -- save Msg for later
    put "Now Dialing " & field "Name" & "..." into msg
    if the length of field "Extension" ≤ 4 then
    dial field "Extension"
    else dial "9" & field "Extension"
    -- dialing an outside number
    put temp into msg      -- restore original Msg contents
end mouseUp
```

**button "Print"**

Properties

Location: 451,193
Rect: 418,182,485,204
AutoHilite: true
ShowName: true
Hilite: false
Style: roundRect
Icon: 0
Visible: true

Script

```
on mouseUp
    open printing with dialog
    print this card
    send mouseUp to bkgnd button "See Map"
    print this card
    send mouseUp to bkgnd button "Zoom In"
    print this card
    close printing
    send mouseUp to button "ReturnToDirectory"
end mouseUp
```

**Comment:** By sending mouseUp to each of the buttons mentioned in the script, the handler is doing the same as the user clicking the buttons. Going to each card, the handler then puts the printed version of the card into the printing queue. At Close Printing, the queue is flushed out, and the last page of printing is sent to the printer.

**field "Name"**

Properties

Location: 233,95
Rect: 70,85,397,105

LockText: false
ShowLines: true
WideMargins: false
Style: transparent
Text Align: left
Text Font: New York
Text Height: 18
Text Size: 14
Text Style: bold
Visible: true

**field "Position"**

Properties

Location: 240,131
Rect: 83,121,398,141
(all other properties same as "Name")

**field "Department"**

Properties

Location: 256,167
Rect: 114,157,398,177
(all other properties same as "Name")

**field "Extension"**

Properties

Location: 153,203
Rect: 97,193,209,213
(all other properties same as "Name")

**field "Location"**

Properties

Location: 242,240
Rect: 88,230,397,250
(all other properties same as "Name")

**bkgnd "Campus Map"**

Script

```
on openBackground
     hide message
end openBackground

on mouseUp
     -- clicking on the card brings you back to Directory
     pop card
end mouseUp
```

**button "Zoom In"**

<u>Properties</u>

Location: 450,49
Rect: 418,38,483,60
AutoHilite: true
ShowName: true
Hilite: false
Style: roundRect
Icon: 0
Visible: true

<u>Script</u>

```
on mouseUp
    global location
    push this card          -- pushed atop Directory card
    visual effect iris open
    find item 2 of location
end mouseUp
```

**bkgnd "Detail-North West"**

<u>Script</u>

```
on openCard
    global name
    put name into field "Name"
    -- reminds browser who he's looking for
end openCard
```

**button "ReturnToMap"**

<u>Properties</u>

Location: 53,51
Rect: 25,30,82,73
AutoHilite: false
ShowName: false
Hilite: false
Style: transparent
Icon: 0
Visible: true

<u>Script</u>

```
on mouseUp
    pop card             -- go back to Campus Map card
end mouseUp
```

**button "ReturnToDirectory"**

<u>Properties</u>

Location: 454,40
Rect: 437,28,472,53
AutoHilite: true
ShowName: false
Hilite: false
Style: transparent
Icon: 17481
Visible: true

<u>Script</u>

```
on mouseUp
        pop card into it        -- nothing happens to display
        pop card                -- now pop Directory card
end mouseUp
```

**button "Home"**

<u>Properties</u>

Location: 282,43
Rect: 266,30,298,57
AutoHilite: true
ShowName: false
Hilite: false
Style: transparent
Icon: 20689
Visible: true

<u>Script</u>

```
on mouseUp
        go home
end mouseUp
```

**field "Name"**

<u>Properties</u>

Location: 368,63
Rect: 250,53,486,74
LockText: false
ShowLines: true
WideMargins: false
Style: transparent
Text Align: center
Text Font: New York
Text Height: 18
Text Size: 14
Text Style: bold
Visible: true

**field "Office"** -- the field containing the office number

<u>Properties</u>

Location: 203,307
Rect: 184,297,223,317
LockText: false
ShowLines: false
WideMargins: false
Style: transparent
Text Align: center
Text Font: Chicago
Text Height: 16
Text Size: 12
Text Style: shadow,condense
Visible: true

## *Further Ideas*

There are many ways to streamline this stack. First, in locating the detail floorplan for a particular office, you could do away with the Office field and assign office numbers as card names. The hazard with this, however, is that a card name is easier to work with when it is letters (or starts with letters) instead of all numbers. When it's all numbers, the Go Card X command will go to a card number instead of to a card whose name is that number. But if the card name is preceded with a word, like "cubicle," the script can still use the location global variable to help track that card. Before doing the Go command, precede item 2 of the location variable with the word "cubicle." Then go to that card name. Going to a card name is inherently faster than finding a text string.

To reduce the floorplan card count substantially, you could design the card so that each office has its own opaque background button, sized to match the boundaries of each office. Each button would have a name linked to its office number. When the Zoom In button activates the floorplan card, that card's script sets the hilite property of the desired office's button to true, turning it black. Perform a five-time repeat loop that sets the hilite property to true and false alternately, making the office location flash on the screen several times.

One more point. If you were to break out this environment into multiple stacks, two stacks should be sufficient, one with the actual directory, one with all the maps. Be sure that any Go commands pointing to cards in the other stack have the stack name as a parameter to the command.

CHAPTER 40

# A Telephone Logbook

MANY EXECUTIVES AND SELF-EMPLOYED PROFESSIONALS NEED TO RECORD THEIR outgoing telephone calls— the date and time, the person called, the phone number called, the content of the call, and to what account or project the time and phone call charges should be billed. What we'll show you here is the beginning of what could become an elaborate system. It ties directly into the Address stack supplied with HyperCard.

## *Overview*

Whenever you are in the Address stack (Figure 40–1) and dial a call, a modified dial button script not only dials the number as it always did but also goes to a different stack of telephone logbook pages (Figure 40–2) and generates a new card. When a new card is made, four items in the card are automatically filled in for you: the current date, the time, the name of the person appearing in the Address stack card you just dialed, and the phone number just dialed.

You may also generate a new card while in the Telephone Log stack by choosing New Card from the Edit menu. When you do this, the date and time are placed into the card. Because the card doesn't know whom you're calling, you'll have to type in the name and phone number.

At any time while you are in the Log stack, you may check the person's Address stack card by clicking on the cards button in the upper right. That button's script goes to the Address stack and performs a search

*Figure 40-1.*

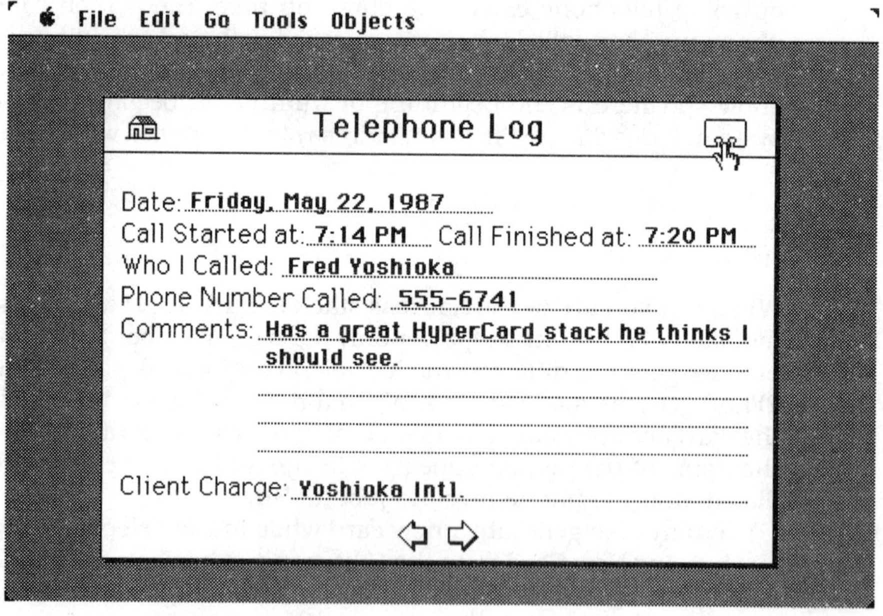


*Figure 40-2.*

on the name in the Log card. If no match is found, you are given the choice to make a new Address stack card for this person or not. If you choose yes, a new Address card is made, placing the person's name in the Name spot and the phone number into the Phone Number field on the Address card.

When you are finished with a call, you may click anywhere on a transparent button that lies atop the field labeled Call Finished at. This action places the current time into the adjacent field. If there is already an ending time in that field, a click of that button won't accidentally overwrite the time.

In practice, a professional person would perform a Message Box Find command on a project or client name when it comes time for billing. Also, if you are looking at a telephone bill and don't recognize a number, search for that number to find the outgoing phone call that generated the call.

## Scripts and Properties

We start with the dial button script in the Address stack, as revised for use with the Log stack. No other changes were made to the button or the rest of the Address stack. From there we move onto the scripts and properties of the Log stack. Refer to Figure 40-2 to get your bearings when we describe fields and buttons.

**stack "Address"**

**button "Dial"**

Script

```
on mouseUp
    if first char of selection is in "(0123456789" then
            get selection
    else if first char of msg is in "(0123456789" then
            get msg
    else get first line of field "Phone Number"
    if it is not empty then
            put it into phoneNumber
            put first line of field¬
            "Name and Address" into phoneName
            phone phoneNumber,phoneName
    end if
end mouseUp
```

```
on phone phoneNumber,phoneName
        visual effect zoom open
        go to "Phone"
        dial phoneNumber
        set lockScreen to true
        go to last card of "Telephone Log"
        doMenu "New Card"
        put phoneName into field "Person"
        put phoneNumber into field "Number"
        set lockScreen to false
end phone
```

**Comment:** This script is divided into two handlers for ease of readability and maintainability. Each handler performs a distinctly different task. The mouseUp handler determines whether the number is in a selection (as selected with the Text tool), the Message Box (as picked up by the Browse tool), or just the first line of the Phone Number field. The handler is selective about using the selection or Message Box text. It only takes on the text if it starts with a number or a left parenthesis. If the text starts with anything else, it cannot possibly be a telephone number. Only when there is a number in It does the handler place the number and name into their respective variables (phoneNumber and phoneName). These variables are then passed as parameters to the phone handler, which performs the dialing action and then some. We could also have used global variables for the number and name, but since this information isn't needed beyond the phone handler, it's a bit "cleaner" to pass them as parameters.

The phone handler accepts the parameters, assigning them to the same names as they had in the mouseUp handler (this is not necessary but sure makes it easier to keep track of the contents). Then we go to the Phone stack, dial the number (using the special settings in that stack), and lock the screen for the next bit of manipulation.

In one command, we go to the last card of the Telephone Log stack to keep the new card in chronological order. When the new card is created, the Telephone Log stack's own newCard handler performs some things (you'll see in a moment). Then the name and number are posted to the new log page. Setting lockScreen to false is optional, because it automatically reverts to false at idle time.

**stack "Telephone Log"**

**bkgnd "Log Sheet"**

Script

```
on newCard
        -- happens after doMenu "New Card" in
        -- phone handler of Address stack
```

```
    put the long date into field "Date"
    put the time into field "Start"
end newCard

on openStack
    hide msg
end openStack
```

**button "Prev"**

Properties

Location: 241,302
Rect: 228,290,255,315
AutoHilite: false
ShowName: false
Hilite: false
Style: transparent
Icon: 1014
Visible: true

Script

```
on mouseUp
    visual effect scroll left
    go to prev card
end mouseUp
```

**button "Next"**

Properties

Location: 270,302
Rect: 257,290,284,315
AutoHilite: false
ShowName: false
Hilite: false
Style: transparent
Icon: 1013
Visible: true

Script

```
on mouseUp
    visual effect scroll right
    go to next card
end mouseUp
```

**button "To Home"**

Properties

Location: 81,73
Rect: 68,62,95,84
AutoHilite: true

ShowName: false
Hilite: false
Style: transparent
Icon: 20689
Visible: true

Script

```
on mouseUp
     visual effect iris close
     go home
end mouseUp
```

**button "To Address"**

Properties

Location: 423,71
Rect: 408,60,439,82
AutoHilite: true
ShowName: false
Hilite: false
Style: transparent
Icon: 3430
Visible: true

Script

```
on mouseUp
     put field "Person" into personCalled
     put field "Number" into numberCalled
     get long id of this card
     put it into saveCard  -- in case we need to come back
     set lockScreen to true
     go to stack "Address"
     find personCalled
     if the result is "not found" then  -- only if no card found
          answer "No card found. Add one?"¬
          with "Yes" or "No" or "Cancel"
          if it is "Cancel" then go to saveCard  -- glad we saved it
          else if it is "Yes" then
               go to last card
               doMenu "New Card"  -- new Address card
               put personCalled into field 1
               put numberCalled into field 2
          end if
     end if
end mouseUp
```

**button "Finished"**

<u>Properties</u>

Location: 312,132
Rect: 255,124,369,141
AutoHilite: false
ShowName: false
Hilite: false
Style: transparent -- sits atop label "Call Finished At"
Icon: 0
Visible: true

<u>Script</u>

```
on mouseUp
	if field "End" is empty then put the time into field "End"
end mouseUp
```

**field "Date"**

<u>Properties</u>

Location: 182,114
Rect: 104,104,261,124
LockText: false
ShowLines: true
WideMargins: false
Style: transparent
Text Align: left
Text Font: Geneva
Text Height: 16
Text Size: 12
Text Style: bold
Visible: true

**field "Start"**

<u>Properties</u>

Location: 215,133
Rect: 177,123,253,143
(all other properties same as "Date")

**field "End"**

<u>Properties</u>

Location: 406,132
Rect: 370,122,442,142
(all other properties same as "Date")

**field "Person"**
Properties
Location: 273,151
Rect: 162,141,384,161
(all other properties same as "Date")

**field "Number"**
Properties
Location: 305,169
Rect: 227,159,384,179
(all other properties same as "Date")

**field "Comments"**
Properties
Location: 294,222
Rect: 149,177,439,268
(all other properties same as "Date")

**field "Charge To"**
Properties
Location: 304,278
Rect: 169,268,439,288
(all other properties same as "Date")

## *Further Ideas*

As you use this stack, you'll find many things you can add that will make its application more carefree. For instance, you'll quickly discover that you leave many notes in the Comments field about getting a busy signal or no answer. You might want to add buttons that automatically place those notes into the Comments field with the click of the mouse button.

Another button you can add is one that redials the number in the current card. The handler for this will generate a new card and carry over the name and number items into the new card's fields. You can always add buttons that link to other stacks you need while on the phone, like your calendar or appointment book.

If you have other stacks that dial phone numbers, consider modifying those dial scripts to come to the Telephone Log stack and make a new card. Eventually, you can build a highly integrated empire of telephone-related stacks.

# CHAPTER 41

# A Time Sheet

MANY PROFESSIONAL PEOPLE MUST MAINTAIN RECORDS OF TIME SPENT WITH CLIENTS OR on particular projects. These time sheets are then tabulated for billing purposes. When the professionals are part of a firm, an office manager or controller is usually responsible for distributing and collecting time sheets. By maintaining time sheets in a HyperCard stack, the sheets can be distributed electronically (either on disk or via a local area network). Moreover, the stack can be designed to encourage submission of time sheets at the end of each billing period. When they're not turned in on time, the stack won't let the user enter any new sheets.

## *Overview*

The Time Sheets stack consists of two backgrounds. While the basic artwork for each background is the same (the "Spiral Page" card ID 62720 from the "Stack Ideas" stack), one background has no fields on it, while the other does.

In the example of the cover card background in Figure 41-1, the artwork for the law firm name, field labels, and hourglass is all in the card graphics layer. The four fields are card fields. Information in this card would be filled out by the person responsible for distributing and tabulating the time sheets for the firm.

The cover card shows for a couple of seconds whenever the stack opens, as a quick reminder of the period covered by the stack. Then the

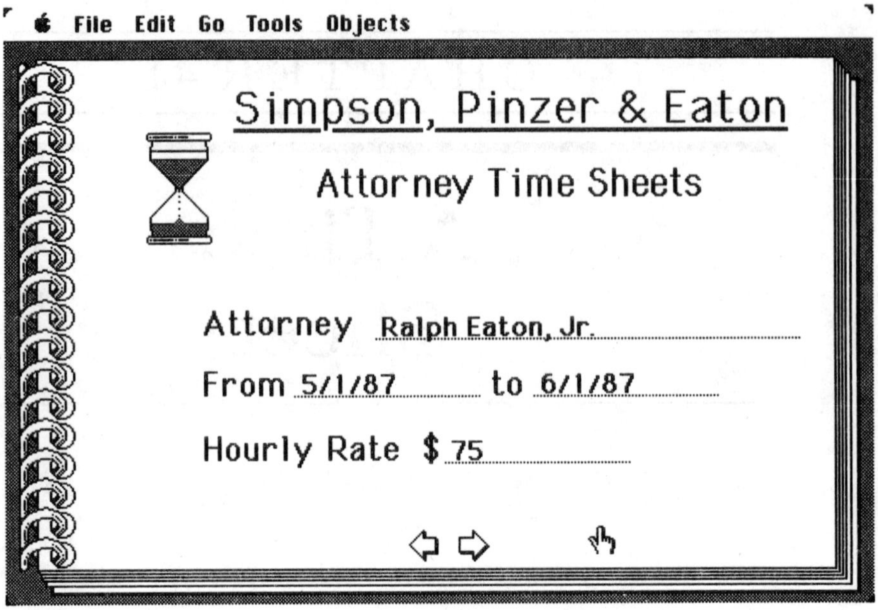

*Figure 41-1.*

stack moves to the last card in the stack, from which any new card is generated (by the New Card menu command).

If the current date is after the ending date of the period, the stack won't let the user create a new card. A dialog box advises what to do. Upon creation of a new card within a valid time period, the current date and time are placed in their respective fields (Figure 41–2). The hourly rate is retrieved from the cover card and placed in the appropriate field.

The total billing amount is calculated after any of three actions: 1) pressing the "End" button; 2) changing the hourly rate on a card; or 3) adjusting the end time field. The End button places the current time into the End field and starts computation based on the elapsed time between the start and end times. The script that performs the calculation has been designed in such a way that billing increments are by quarter-hour. Elapsed time display will always be displayed in quarter hour fractions of one hour.

Sorting, as carried out by the handler in the Sort button script, arranges the cards in the stack by client name. Because cards are created in chronological order (always after the last card), then sorting by client will place each client's time sheets in chronological order for easy tabulation into an invoice.

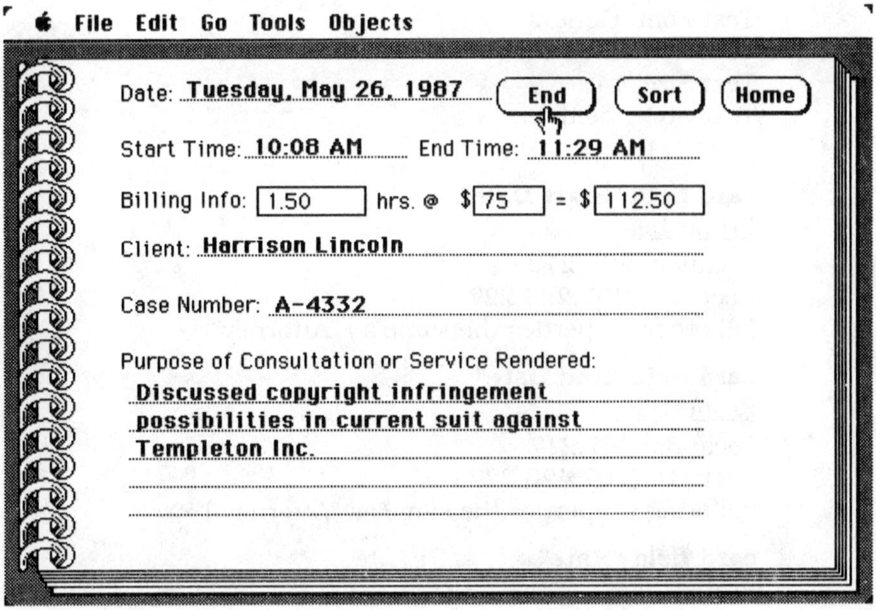

*Figure 41-2.*

## *Scripts and Properties*

Here are the objects and their scripts for the Time Sheet stack.

**stack "Time Sheet"**

<u>Script</u>

```
on openStack
      go to last card
end openStack
```

**bkgnd "Cover Card"**

**card field "Attorney"**

<u>Properties</u>

Location: 344,184
Rect: 218,174,470,194
LockText: false
ShowLines: true
WideMargins: false
Style: transparent
Text Align: left

Text Font: Geneva
Text Height: 18
Text Size: 14
Text Style: bold
Visible: true

**card field "Start Date"**

Properties

Location: 227,217
Rect: 171,207,283,227
(all other properties the same as "Attorney")

**card field "End Date"**

Properties

Location: 367,217
Rect: 311,207,423,227
(all other properties the same as "Attorney")

**card field "Rate"**

Properties

Location: 314,255
Rect: 258,245,370,265
(all other properties the same as "Attorney")

**bkgnd "Sheets"**

Script

```
on doMenu item
    if item is not "New Card" then pass doMenu
    get card field "End Date" of card "Settings"
    convert it to seconds
    if it >= the seconds then pass doMenu
    else answer¬
    "The period is over. Submit this file to Off. Mgr."
end doMenu
```

**Comment:** Most HyperTalk time comparisons are done in seconds. Seconds are absolute measures of time and make a good common ground for performing time and date arithmetic. If the end date of the period is greater than or equal to the current seconds reading from the Macintosh clock, the doMenu "New Card" command is passed up to HyperCard, so that it can make that new card. If it is now after the end date of the period, making a new card is out of the question.

```
on newCard
    put the long date into field "Date"
    put the time into field "Start Time"
```

```
        put card field "Rate" of card "Settings" into field "Hourly"
end newCard

on computeBill
        put field "Start Time" into startTime
        convert startTime to seconds
        put field "End Time" into endTime
        convert endTime to seconds

        put (endTime - startTime)/(60*15) into quarterHours
        put quarterHours - trunc(quarterHours) into fracQuarter
        put trunc(quarterHours) into quarterCount
        if fracQuarter is not zero then add 1 to quarterCount

        put quarterCount/4 into hours
        set numberFormat to "0.00"
        put quarterCount/4 into field "Total Time"
        put hours * field "Hourly" into field "Total Bill"
end computeBill
```

**Comment:** The computeBill handler is spaced into three readable groups, each of which performs a distinctly different kind of operation in this handler. In the first group, the field information is retrieved and placed into variables for manipulation later in the handler. Notice that both times are converted into seconds. The numberFormat property is adjusted to allow for greater precision in calculating time in the following commands.

Group two uses the start and ending time (in seconds) to calculate the number of quarter hours to be counted for billing purposes. Remember that the design calls for a fraction of a quarter hour to be billed as a complete quarter hour. The first line determines the raw number of quarter hours, which may have a fraction as part of it (for example, 5.34 quarter hours). The second line obtains that fractional amount (for example, 5.34 minus trunc(5.34) = 0.34). The whole number of quarter hours goes into the variable quarterCount in line 3 (for example, 5). Then line 4 checks whether the fractional quarter is zero. If it is, the quarter count is not adjusted upward (as in 5 hours and no fractions, which should be billed only as 5 hours). If the fraction is anything but zero, an additional quarter hour is tacked onto the total time to be billed.

In the third group occurs the calculation of the information that goes into the fields. First comes the calculation of the number of hours (with the numberFormat adjusted to two places to the right of the decimal) and then the total billing amount.

**button "End"**

<u>Properties</u>

Location: 319,52
Rect: 290,41,348,63
AutoHilite: true
ShowName: true
Hilite: false
Style: roundRect
Icon: 0
Visible: true

<u>Script</u>

```
on mouseUp
    if field "End Time" is empty then
        put the time into field "End Time"
        computeBill
    end if
end mouseUp
```

**button "Sort"**

<u>Properties</u>

Location: 385,52
Rect: 359,41,412,63
AutoHilite: true
ShowName: true
Hilite: false
Style: roundRect
Icon: 0
Visible: true

<u>Script</u>

```
on mouseUp
    sort by field "Client"
end mouseUp
```

**button "Home"**

<u>Properties</u>

Location: 448,52
Rect: 422,41,475,63
AutoHilite: true
ShowName: true
Hilite: false
Style: roundRect
Icon: 0
Visible: true

Script

```
on mouseUp
	go home
end mouseUp
```

**button "Prev"**

Properties

Location: 247,308
Rect: 234,296,261,321
AutoHilite: false
ShowName: false
Hilite: false
Style: transparent
Icon: 1014
Visible: true

Script

```
on mouseUp
	go to prev card
end mouseUp
```

**button "Next"**

Properties

Location: 276,308
Rect: 263,296,290,321
AutoHilite: false
ShowName: false
Hilite: false
Style: transparent
Icon: 1013
Visible: true

Script

```
on mouseUp
	go to next card
end mouseUp
```

**field "Date"**

Properties

Location: 196,49
Rect: 103,39,289,59
LockText: false
ShowLines: true
WideMargins: false
Style: transparent
Text Align: left

Text Font: Geneva
Text Height: 16
Text Size: 12
Text Style: bold
Visible: true

**field "Start Time"**
Properties
Location: 190,82
Rect: 141,72,239,92
(all other properties the same as "Date")

**field "End Time"**
Properties
Location: 359,83
Rect: 307,73,411,93
(all other properties the same as "Date")
Script

```
on closeField
	computeBill
end closeField
```

**field "Client"**
Properties
Location: 262,138
Rect: 112,128,412,148
(all other properties the same as "Date")

**field "Case Number"**
Properties
Location: 283,172
Rect: 154,162,413,182
(all other properties the same as "Date")

**field "Purpose"**
Properties
Location: 242,252
Rect: 73,212,412,293
(all other properties the same as "Date")

**field "Total Time"**
Properties
Location: 181,111
Rect: 149,103,213,120
LockText: false
ShowLines: false

WideMargins: false
Style: rectangle
Text Align: left
Text Font: Geneva
Text Height: 16
Text Size: 12
Text Style: plain
Visible: true

**field "Hourly"**

Properties

Location: 297,111
Rect: 276,103,318,120
(all other properties the same as "Total Time")

Script

```
on closeField
    computeBill
end closeField
```

**field "Total Bill"**

Properties

Location: 379,111
Rect: 347,103,412,120
(all other properties the same as "Total Time")

## *Further Ideas*

You can make the Sheets form behave even more like a relational database, if you like, by linking it to a stack containing client names and other data. By typing in the client's number, the Time Sheets stack could reach into the Client stack and fetch information like client name, address, and quoted hourly rate.

This stack also cries for many reporting possibilities using the Write to File command. This part of the stack would be used by the person who assembles the bills, but essentially a reporting script could write selected fields to a text file from all time sheets for a given client. The file could be incorporated into a spreadsheet program or word processor for generation of an invoice.

CHAPTER 42

# A New and Improved To Do List

IN THIS CHAPTER, WE'LL ENHANCE THE TO DO LIST STACK FIRST SHOWN IN CHAPTER 17. If you make the changes as indicated in this chapter, you'll have not just a rolling seven-day To Do stack, but a stack with a card for every day of the year. As a bonus, we throw in a script that makes cards for as many days as there are between a starting and an ending date you specify.

## *Overview*

To make the changes to the old stack, start with a new stack cloned from the original one. The new stack will ultimately look like the card shown in Figure 42–1. Use New Stack from the File menu to accomplish this, making sure you select the Copy Current Background button in the standard file dialog. Next erase the day buttons at the top. Following the properties and specifications listed below, add fields and buttons to the background, as shown in the button and field exposures in Figures 42–2 and 42–3. Don't worry about the highlighting of the D, W, or M buttons. The scripts will take card of that.

A new feature added to this version is the ability to check off each item in a line. A narrow transparent text field is placed to the left of each items column. A transparent button is placed atop that field. When you click on the button at a particular line, a script places a check mark in the field directly below it. For one button to handle the entire column

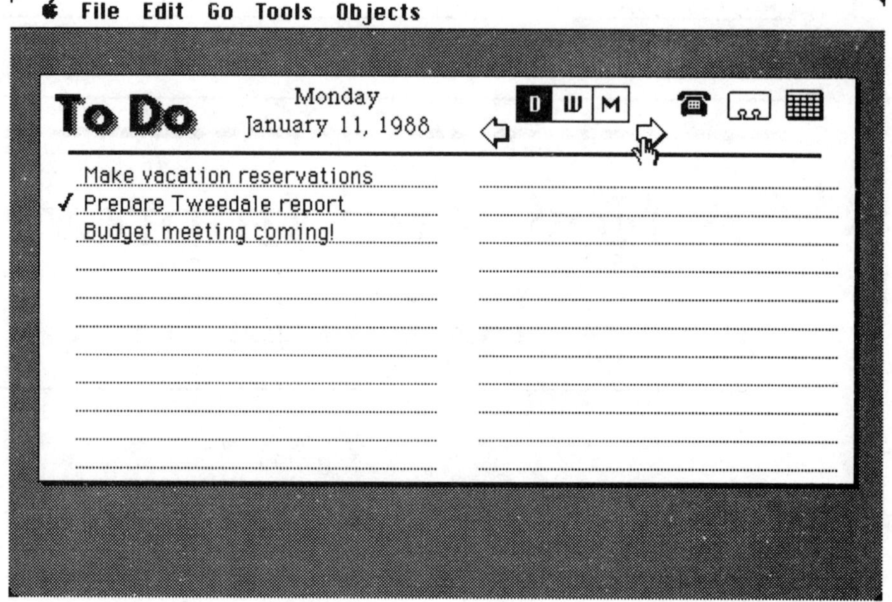


*Figure 42-1.*

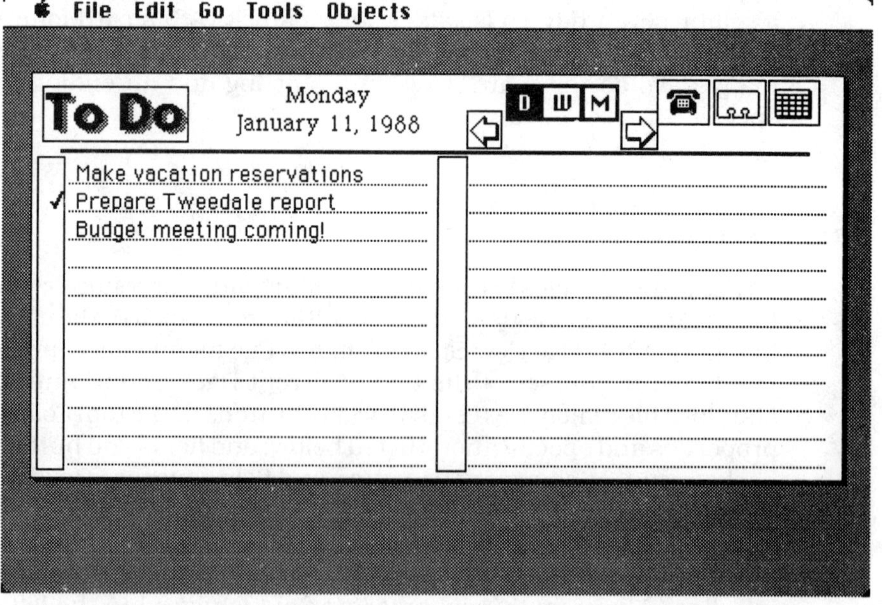


*Figure 42-2.*

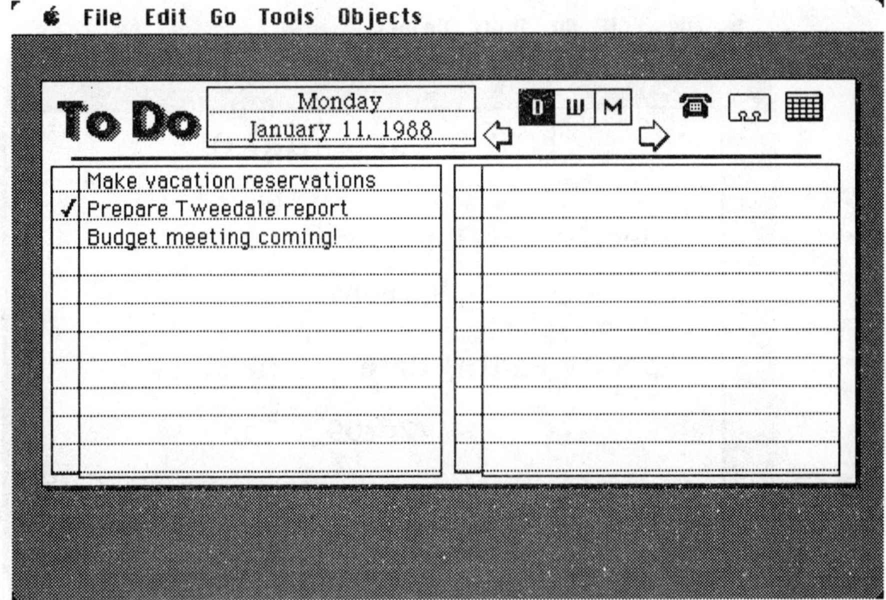


*Figure 42-3.*

requires a little math to measure the coordinates of a mouseclick, but it's not too difficult to understand.

The only tricky part of this stack is a hidden field called Interval. It is a background field (although it could also be a card field), whose content remembers which interval (Day, Week, or Month) you used the last time you worked with the stack. Upon opening the stack, the openStack handler retrieves the interval and places that information into a global variable (also called interval), which the left and right buttons use to skip ahead or back in the stack at the desired interval.

To create a hidden field, create it as you normally would. It may be of any size you like. Be sure you set its properties, especially its name. Then type hide field "Interval" into the Message Box. You won't be able to see it, but your scripts will be able to find it, put information into it, and retrieve from it as well.

A second background of this stack environment is a stack maker (Figure 42-4). The openStack script is set up in such a way that if you have not made a supply of To Do cards with real dates in them, you come to the To Do Maker card. Here you specify the starting and ending dates of the sequence of cards you want generated. Upon pressing the OK button, a script takes over, making the cards you requested, plugging in the complete date as it goes. You will watch as each card is created and dated.

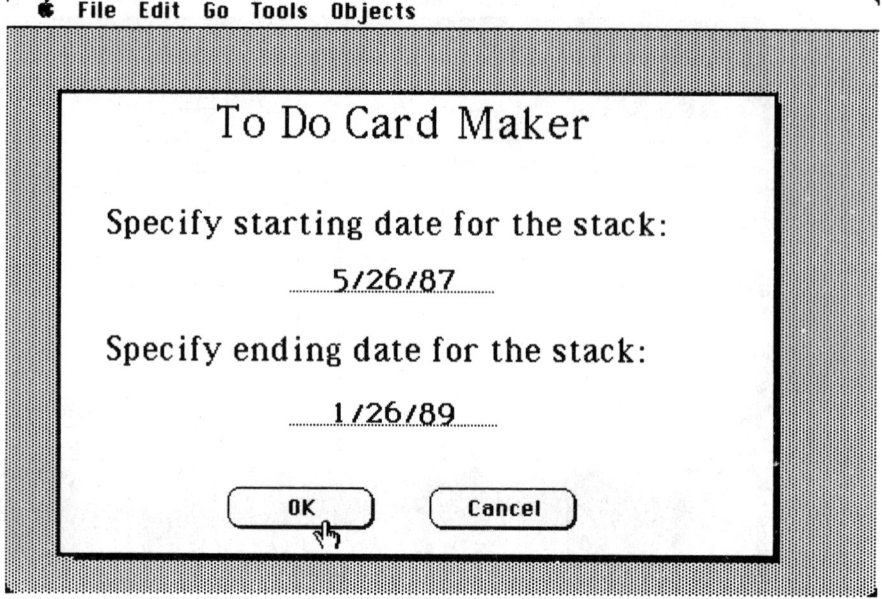


*Figure 42-4.*

Once the stack is filled out with dated cards, the stack automatically goes to the current day's To Do card whenever you open the stack.

Pay special attention to the handlers in the To Do Form background script. Surprisingly, all script action for this stack (other than the stack-making stuff, which you do only once in a blue moon) is contained in the background script. That means that even all the button activity on a card is handled by the background script. This is starting to get a bit advanced, but you should see how it is done. The result is a remarkably compact application.

## Scripts and Properties

Because the To Do Form background is actually the first background in the stack, its scripts and its objects will be listed first. The To Do Maker background and its objects are listed later in this section.

**stack "My To Do 2.0"**

Script

```
on openStack
        global interval
```

```
        put field "Interval" of card 1 into interval
        -- from the hidden field
        if the number of cards < 3
        then go to card "Setup"
        else
                get word 2 to 4 of the long date
                find it   -- find today's card
        end if
end openStack

on closeStack
        global interval
        put interval into field "Interval" of card 1
        -- save our interval
end closeStack
```

**bkgnd "To Do Form"**

Script

```
on mouseUp
        --  all mouse activity in the stack is performed
        --  by this handler
        global interval

        get short name of the target
        if it contains "checkOff" then
                do it
                exit mouseUp
        end if

        if "interval" is not in it then pass mouseUp

        set hilite of bkgnd button "D Interval" to it = "D Interval"
        set hilite of bkgnd button "W Interval" to it = "W Interval"
        set hilite of bkgnd button "M Interval" to it = "M Interval"

        put first word of it into interval
end mouseUp
```

**Comment:** After reinitializing the global variable, this handler first sees if the object that received the last mouseUp message has the name CheckOff in it. As you'll see below, the buttons atop the check off fields are named CheckOff 1 and CheckOff 2. Notice that the next handler in this script is called CheckOff with a parameter looking for a column number. It turns out that the name of a CheckOff button can be used as the message that triggers the following handler. Since the short name of the target button contains the name of the object/handler, the It variable contains the appropriate command. By doing It, the script above is saying the same as CheckOff 1.

The next command group in the above handler is looking for a target name that contains the word interval. If the target doesn't contain that word, the mouseUp message is passed up the hierarchy (where it will not find any other handlers). The three buttons that set the D, W, and M interval are called D Interval, W Interval, and M Interval, respectively. When you click the D Interval button, for instance, this mouseUp handler processes it all the way to the set hilite commands. These commands adjust the hilite properties of the three buttons. When the button pressed is D Interval, the it = D Interval expression in the first set hilite line returns true. That turns on the highlighting for that button. The other two buttons are automatically set to false, because the short name (in It) is not D Interval.

Finally, the first word of the name (that is, the letter) goes into the global variable, interval. This variable is used later, in the skip handler.

```
on checkOff colNum
    put (item 2 of the clickloc - 76) div 16 into lineNum
    if line lineNum of bkgnd field ("OK" & colNum) is empty
    then put "√" into line lineNum of bkgnd field ("OK" & colNum)
    else put empty into line lineNum of¬
    background field ("OK" & colNum)
end checkOff
```

**Comment:** The first line of this handler calculates the line number of the underlying field that should get the check mark. It takes the second item of the coordinates returned by the clickloc function, subtracts 76 from it, and divides it by 16. The 76 represents the number of pixels from the top of the screen that line zero (that is, the line above the first line of the field) would be. The 16 is the line height of the text field. Each line is 16 pixels tall. When you click at the location atop the first line of the underlying field, a 1 is put into the lineNum variable. If it's empty, the handler places the check mark (the character you get by pressing Option-v) into the corresponding line number of the "OK" field in the current column. If the line is not empty (meaning a check mark is already there), the mark is removed.

```
on skip direction
    global interval
    if interval is "D" or interval is "W" then
        get number of this card
        if interval is "D"
        then add direction to it
```

```
                else add direction * 7 to it
                go card it
        else
                get line 2 of field "Date"
                convert it to dateItems
                put (item 2 of it + direction) mod 13 into item 2 of it
                if item 2 of it = 0 then
                        put (13 + direction) mod 13 into item 2 of it
                        add direction to item 1 of it
                end if
                convert it to long date
                find (word 2 to 4 of it)
        end if
end skip
```

**Comment:** This handler performs the skipping back and ahead through the cards, depending on which interval you have selected. The direction parameter, passed by the left and right arrow buttons, is either a -1 (back) or 1 (forward). When the interval variable is D, the direction is added to the number of the current card, and the handler issues a Go command to that card number; when interval is W, the direction times 7 (days in a week) is added to the current card number, and the Go command sends you to the previous or next week, depending on the direction.

Because the number of days in a month varies, you cannot simply add or subtract 30 days to the card and go there. You must invoke help from the date arithmetic facilities of HyperTalk. Starting with the date in the current card (it can work with the date parts in line 2 of the Date field), all necessary conversions are made, including accounting for the changeovers between years (when item 2 of dateItems is zero). Converting the new date back to the long date format, the handler then applies the Find command to locate the card matching words 2 to 4 of the long date.

**button "D Interval"**

Properties

Location: 307,61
Rect: 298,52,317,71
AutoHilite: false
ShowName: false
Hilite: false
Style: transparent
Icon: 0
Visible: true

**button "W Interval"**

<u>Properties</u>

Location: 329,61
Rect: 318,52,341,71
(all other properties the same as "D Interval")

**button "M Interval"**

<u>Properties</u>

Location: 352,61
Rect: 342,52,362,71
(all other properties the same as "D Interval")

**button "To Calendar"**

<u>Properties</u>

Location: 465,61
Rect: 450,48,481,74
AutoHilite: false
ShowName: false
Hilite: false
Style: transparent
Icon: 15972
Visible: true

<u>Script</u>

```
on mouseUp   -- from the original button in "Stack Ideas"
    get "Jan 1, 1987"
    convert it to seconds
    put 1 + (the seconds - it) div (60*60*24) into dayOfYear
    put 1 + (dayOfYear + 2) div 7 into whichWeek
    visual effect zoom open
    go to card (whichWeek + 2) of "Datebook"
end mouseUp
```

**button "To Name/Address"**

<u>Properties</u>

Location: 433,61
Rect: 418,48,449,74
AutoHilite: false
ShowName: false
Hilite: false
Style: transparent
Icon: 3430
Visible: true

<u>Script</u>

```
on mouseUp
    get the selection
    if it is empty then get Msg
    go to stack "Address"
    find it
end mouseUp
```

**button "Dial"**

<u>Properties</u>

Location: 400,61
Rect: 385,48,416,74
AutoHilite: false
ShowName: false
Hilite: false
Style: transparent
Icon: 10610
Visible: true

<u>Script</u>

```
on mouseUp
    visual effect zoom open
    get selection
    if it is empty then get msg
    go to "Phone"
    dial it
    go to "Telephone Log"
end mouseUp
```

**button "CheckOff 1"** -- no script needed

<u>Properties</u>

Location: 29,182
Rect: 21,93,38,272
AutoHilite: false
ShowName: false
Hilite: false
Style: transparent
Icon: 0
Visible: true

**button "CheckOff 2"**

<u>Properties</u>

Location: 266,182
Rect: 257,92,275,272

(all other properties same as "CheckOff 1")

**button "Skip Back"**

Properties

Location: 375,77
Rect: 364,66,386,88
AutoHilite: true
ShowName: false
Hilite: false
Style: transparent
Icon: 1013
Visible: true

Script

```
on mouseUp
	skip -1
end mouseUp
```

**button "Skip Ahead"**

Properties

Location: 284,77
Rect: 274,66,295,88
AutoHilite: true
ShowName: false
Hilite: false
Style: transparent
Icon: 1014
Visible: true

Script

```
on mouseUp
	skip 1
end mouseUp
```

**button "To Today's Card"**

-- located atop "To Do" at upper left of card

Properties

Location: 65,69
Rect: 31,53,99,85
AutoHilite: false
ShowName: false
Hilite: false
Style: transparent
Icon: 0
Visible: true

Script

```
on mouseUp
        get word 2 to 4 of the long date
        find it
end mouseUp
```

**field "Left Column Items"**

Properties

Location: 145,183
Rect: 39,94,252,272
LockText: false
ShowLines: true
WideMargins: false
Style: transparent
Text Align: left
Text Font: Geneva
Text Height: 16
Text Size: 12
Text Style: plain
Visible: true

**field "Right Column Items"**

Properties

Location: 380,183
Rect: 275,94,486,272
(all other properties same as "Left Column Items")

**field "OK1"**

-- where the check marks go next to left column

Properties

Location: 31,182
Rect: 23,94,40,270
LockText: false
ShowLines: false
WideMargins: false
Style: transparent
Text Align: left
Text Font: Geneva
Text Height: 16
Text Size: 12
Text Style: bold
Visible: true

**field "OK2"**
-- where the check marks go next to right column
<u>Properties</u>
Location: 267,182
Rect: 259,94,276,270
(all other properties same as "OK2")

**field "Date"**
<u>Properties</u>
Location: 181,66
Rect: 102,49,260,84 -- set as two lines
LockText: false
ShowLines: false
WideMargins: false
Style: transparent
Text Align: center
Text Font: New York
Text Height: 16
Text Size: 12
Text Style: plain
Visible: true

**field "Interval"**
<u>Properties</u>
Location: 405,33
Rect: 376,24,435,43
LockText: false
ShowLines: false
WideMargins: false
Style: transparent
Text Align: left
Text Font: Geneva
Text Height: 16
Text Size: 12
Text Style: plain
Visible: false -- the hidden field

**bkgnd "To Do Maker"**

**button "OK"** -- the button that starts the stack-making
<u>Properties</u>
Location: 175,293
Rect: 132,281,218,305
AutoHilite: false
ShowName: true

Hilite: false
Style: roundRect
Icon: 0
Visible: true
<u>Script</u>

```
on mouseUp
      buildStack  -- do the buildStack handler below
      hide msg
      openstack  -- act as if opening stack (find today)
end mouseUp

on buildStack
      put 24*60*60 into dayLength

      put field "Start Date" into startSeconds
      convert startSeconds to seconds
      put field "Ending Date" into endingSeconds
      convert endingSeconds to seconds

      put (endingSeconds - startSeconds) div
      dayLength into dayCount
      put "In the process of making " & dayCount &¬
      " To Do cards."

      go to first card
      put startSeconds into currSeconds
      repeat dayCount times
            doMenu "New Card"
            put currSeconds into currDate
            convert currDate to long date
            put item 1 of currDate into line 1 of field "Date"
            put word 2 to 4 of currDate into line 2 of field "Date"
            add dayLength to currSeconds
      end repeat
end buildStack
```

**Comment:** This handler begins by adjusting the math precision to six digits to the right of the decimal for date arithmetic and putting the number of seconds per day into the variable dayLength (this value will be used a few times in this handler, so the variable name is easier to use than all the numbers). In the second group, the start and end dates are retrieved from the To Do Maker card and converted into seconds.

Group three's commands first calculate the number of days between the start and end dates. Then it places a message into the Message Box to let you know how many cards the script will make.

In group four, the real action happens. First the starting time is placed into a variable called currSeconds, which will be used as the time counter through the repeat loop that makes the cards. The loop gets repeated for the number of days. Inside the loop, a new card is made, and the number of current seconds is converted into the long date by way of another variable, currDate (this prevents reconverting back to seconds for the next loop). The first word of the long date (the day of the week) goes into line 1 of the Date field in the card. Then the remainder of the long date goes into line 2. Finally, currSeconds is increased by the number of seconds in a day to bump it one day for the next loop.

**button "Cancel"**

<u>Properties</u>

Location: 293,293
Rect: 250,281,336,305
AutoHilite: false
ShowName: true
Hilite: false
Style: roundRect
Icon: 0
Visible: true

<u>Script</u>

```
on mouseUp
	go home
end mouseUp
```

**field "Start Date"**

<u>Properties</u>

Location: 228,162
Rect: 167,153,289,172
LockText: false
ShowLines: true
WideMargins: false
Style: transparent
Text Align: center
Text Font: New York
Text Height: 18
Text Size: 14
Text Style: bold
Visible: true

**field "Ending Date"**

<u>Properties</u>

Location: 228,238
Rect: 166,229,291,248
(all other properties the same as "Start Date")

**card "Setup"**

Script

```
on openCard
    put the short date into field "Start Date"
end openCard
```

**Comment:** We placed this script here to place today's date into the Start Date field in an easy-to-enter format (the short date). By providing a sample of the date, the script helps prompt the user for a valid date format that the buildStack handler will understand.

## *Further Ideas*

If you plan to keep a To Do file open for more than a couple of years, you may wish to add a Y button to the card and a yearly interval routine to the script. Another handler could sort the items in the lists according to a priority number you assign to each item.

Another useful enhancement is a button that carries over unfinished (that is, unchecked) items to the next day's card. When you do this, however, be sure you take into account the fact that you may have already entered items into tomorrow's card. The items carried over should not overwrite previously entered items.

# CHAPTER 43

# A Conversion Calculator

MANY BUSINESSES HAVE NEED FOR MATH CONVERSIONS BETWEEN UNITS. ASIDE FROM the common metric conversions, professionals may need temperature, currency, or other unit conversions, like typesetting points to inches or vice versa.

In this chapter, we present the basis for a calculator that may be customized for whatever unit conversions you need in your work. The sample here deals with linear metric conversions, but the principles apply to any conversion.

## *Overview*

The calculator, equipped with a linear unit overlay, is shown in Figure 43-1. Looks can be deceiving in this stack, because what appear to be buttons with the names of units are actually locked text fields. Each field has two lines of information in it, although the fields have been sized to allow only the first line of the information to show through to us. On line one is the name of the unit; on line two is a conversion factor, which we'll get to in a moment. The round rectangles around the unit names are drawn in the card graphics layer with the round rectangle tool.

The big upward-pointing arrows are in the card graphics layer, filled with opaque white. In the background domain behind each arrow is an

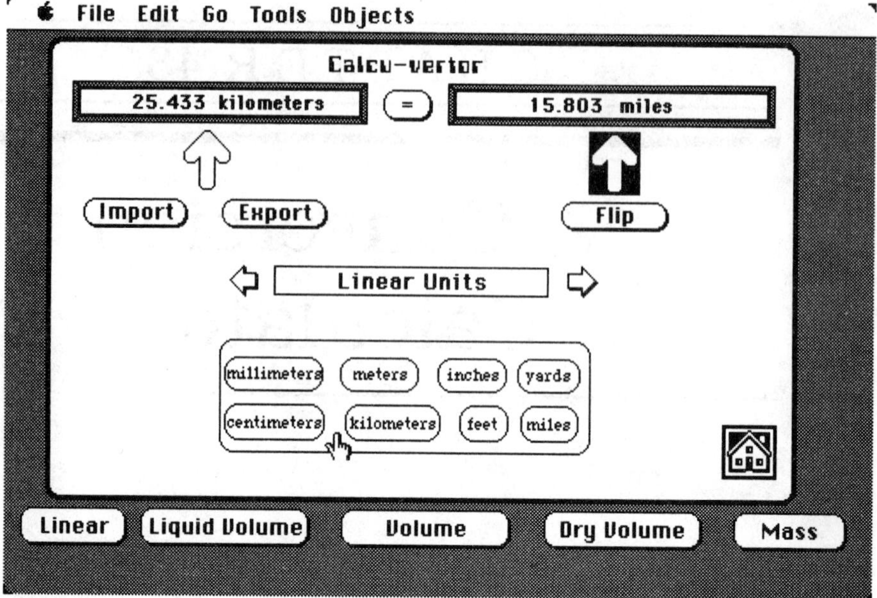


*Figure 43-1.*

opaque rectangular button. When the button's hilite property is set to true, the area under the arrow turns black.

The calculator works like this. First you type a number into the left-hand numbers field. When the big arrow points to the left side, whatever units "button" you click, that unit appears in the left side of the conversion equation. To put a different unit into the right side— the side whose units you're solving for— click on the right-hand arrow and on the desired units "button" below. At a change of the units in either window, or on the entry of a new number into the left side of the equation or a press of the equals button between the two sides causes the calculator to compute the solution. The solution goes into the right-hand numbers field. Figure 43-2 shows where the fields are located in this background.

During calculation, the handler that performs the actual computation performs two conversions. The first converts the left-hand number and units to an intermediate unit— the inch, in this case. All conversions in this linear measure calculator revolve around the common unit of the inch. Next, the handler converts the inch value into the unit appearing in the right-hand units field. All conversion factors are relative to the inch. Therefore, the conversion factor associated with the feet unit is 12; the factor associated with the centimeter is .3937008. In other words, there are 12 inches to the foot and .3937008 inches to

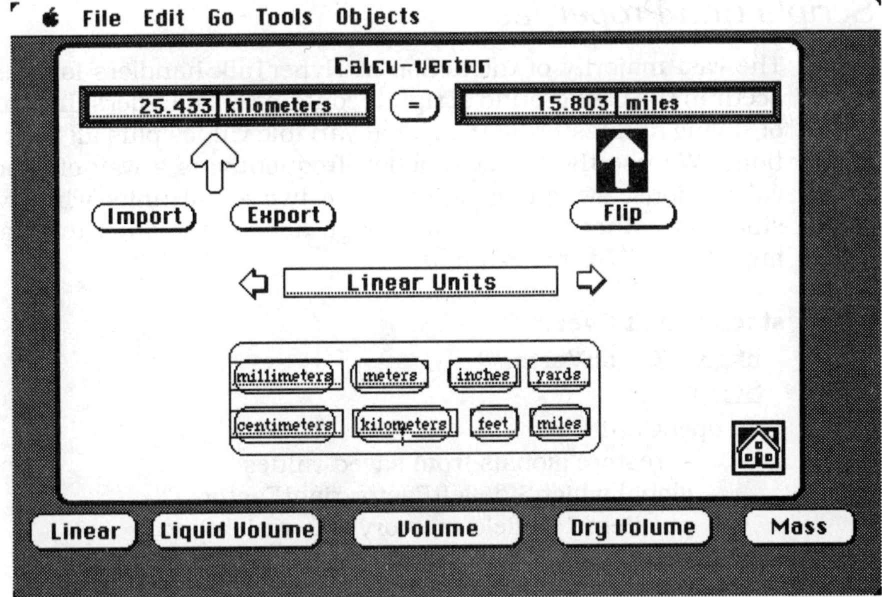


*Figure 43-2.*

the centimeter. If you plan to make other conversion calculator templates, find an intermediate unit for your conversion calculations.

Each card shares a background field named Memory. Into this field go the last settings of the left and right conversion factors for the card, plus the side that the arrow is pointing to each time the card closes. On opening the card, the three items are placed into global variables (leftFactor, rightFactor, and whichSide), which are used in other handlers in the stack.

Three buttons on the calculator allow you to manipulate the input or output numbers. Import copies a number from the Message Box and puts it into the left-hand number field. Export copies the number from the right-hand number field and puts it into the Message Box. You can use the Message Box as a holding place if you need numbers from other stacks converted. Carry over the input number in the Message Box and click the Input button. After calculation, click the Export button and return to your other stack, where you can copy and paste the result into the stack. The Flip button copies the output number and unit to the left-hand side. Therefore, if you make a calculation and wish to further convert the answer, click the Flip button to shift the answer to the left-hand side. Then click another units "button" below for another calculation.

## *Scripts and Properties*

The vast majority of the action in HyperTalk handlers for this stack occur in the background script. It contains six handlers that take care of saving and restoring the global variable values plus all the calculations. We use the target function frequently as a way of processing calculations, switching units in the two small units windows, and shifting to other templates (although none of the other templates are implemented in this example).

**stack "Book Cvert"**

**bkgnd "CalcuVertor"**

Script

```
on openCard
    -- restore globals from saved values
    global whichSide,leftFactor,rightFactor
    put item 1 of field memory into whichSide
    put item 2 of field memory into leftFactor
    put item 3 of field memory into rightFactor
end openCard

on closeCard
    -- save globals for next time
    global whichSide,leftFactor,rightFactor
    put whichSide into item 1 of field memory
    put leftFactor into item 2 of field memory
    put rightFactor into item 3 of field memory
end closeCard

on closeField
    calculate
    -- whenever you enter a new number and press Enter
end closeField

on mouseUp
    if the target contains "field" then
    -- one of the units "buttons"
        do "get line 1 of " & the target
        put it into name
        do "get line 2 of " & the target
        put it into factor
        changeUnits name,factor
        calculate
    else if the target contains "button" then
    -- buttons to other templates
```

```
                get short name of the target
                go to card it
                if the result is not empty
                then answer it & " is not yet implemented"
        end if
end mouseUp

on changeUnits name,factor
        global whichSide,leftFactor,rightFactor
        if whichSide is "left" then
                put name into field "Input Units"
                put factor into leftFactor
        else
                put name into field "Output Units"
                put factor into rightFactor
        end if
end changeUnits

on calculate
        global leftFactor,rightFactor
        put leftFactor / rightFactor into scale
        set numberFormat to "0.000"
        put scale * field "Input Number" into field "Output Number"
end calculate
```

**button "="**

Properties

Location: 237,61
Rect: 223,52,252,70
AutoHilite: false
ShowName: true
Hilite: false
Style: roundRect
Icon: 0
Visible: true

Script

```
on mouseUp
        calculate
end mouseUp
```

**button "Import"**

Properties

Location: 78,123
Rect: 47,115,109,132
AutoHilite: false
ShowName: true

Hilite: false
Style: roundRect
Icon: 0
Visible: true
<u>Script</u>

```
on mouseUp
    put message into field "Input Number"
    calculate
end mouseUp
```

**button "Export"**
<u>Properties</u>

Location: 160,123
Rect: 129,115,191,132
AutoHilite: false
ShowName: true
Hilite: false
Style: roundRect
Icon: 0
Visible: true
<u>Script</u>

```
on mouseUp
    put field "Output Number" into message
end mouseUp
```

**button "Flip"**
<u>Properties</u>

Location: 317,123
Rect: 286,115,348,132
AutoHilite: false
ShowName: true
Hilite: false
Style: roundRect
Icon: 0
Visible: true
<u>Script</u>

```
on mouseUp
    global rightFactor,leftFactor
    put field "Output Number" into field "Input Number"
    put field "Output Units" into field "Input Units"
    put rightFactor into leftFactor
end mouseUp
```

**button "Prev"**

<u>Properties</u>

Location: 142,160
Rect: 132,150,153,171
AutoHilite: true
ShowName: false
Hilite: false
Style: transparent
Icon: 1014
Visible: true

<u>Script</u>

```
on mouseUp
    go to prev card    -- to another template if one is available
end mouseUp
```

**button "Next"**

<u>Properties</u>

Location: 342,161
Rect: 331,151,353,172
AutoHilite: true
ShowName: false
Hilite: false
Style: transparent
Icon: 1013
Visible: true

<u>Script</u>

```
on mouseUp
    go to next card
end mouseUp
```

**button "Left"**
-- behind the big upward pointing arrow on the left

<u>Properties</u>

Location: 120,93
Rect: 105,75,135,111
AutoHilite: false
ShowName: false
Hilite: false
Style: opaque
Icon: 4167
Visible: true

<u>Script</u>

```
on mouseUp
    global whichSide
```

```
        put "left" into whichSide
        set hilite of bkgnd button "Left" to true
        set hilite of bkgnd button "Right" to false
end mouseUp
```

**button "Right"**

Properties

Location: 359,93
Rect: 344,75,374,111
(all other properties same as "Left")

Script

```
on mouseUp
        global whichSide
        put "right" into whichSide
        set hilite of bkgnd button "Right" to true
        set hilite of bkgnd button "Left" to false
end mouseUp
```

**button "Linear"**

Properties

Location: 44,303
Rect: 10,293,78,314
AutoHilite: false
ShowName: true
Hilite: false
Style: roundRect
Icon: 0
Visible: true

**button "Mass"**

Properties

Location: 463,307
Rect: 430,296,497,318
(all other properties same as "Linear")

**button "Liquid Volume"**

Properties

Location: 136,303
Rect: 86,292,186,314
(all other properties same as "Linear")

**button "Volume"**

Properties

Location: 250,304
Rect: 200,293,300,315
(all other properties same as "Linear")

**button "Dry Volume"**

Properties

Location: 360,304
Rect: 314,293,407,315
(all other properties same as "Linear")

**button "Home"**

Properties

Location: 439,258
Rect: 421,241,457,275
(all other properties same as "Linear")

Script

```
on mouseUp
    visual effect checkerboard
    go home
end mouseUp
```

**field "Input Number"**

Properties

Location: 83,61
Rect: 45,52,122,70
LockText: false
ShowLines: false
WideMargins: false
Style: transparent
Text Align: right
Text Font: Geneva
Text Height: 13
Text Size: 10
Text Style: bold
Visible: true

**field "Input Units"**

Properties

Location: 167,60
Rect: 122,51,212,69
(all other properties same as "Input Number")

**field "Output Number"**

Properties

Location: 311,60
Rect: 266,53,356,68
(all other properties same as "Input Number")

**field "Output Units"**
<u>Properties</u>
Location: 402,60
Rect: 356,52,449,68
(all other properties same as "Input Number")

**field "Template"**
-- displays the name of the calculator template
<u>Properties</u>
Location: 240,161
Rect: 160,153,321,170
LockText: true
ShowLines: false
WideMargins: false
Style: rectangle
Text Align: center
Text Font: Geneva
Text Height: 16
Text Size: 12
Text Style: bold
Visible: true

**field id 57**
-- the first of 8 fields holding units and factors
<u>Properties</u>
Location: 199,76
Rect: 188,68,211,85
LockText: false
ShowLines: false
WideMargins: false
Style: transparent
Text Align: left
Text Font: Geneva
Text Height: 16
Text Size: 12
Text Style: plain
Visible: false

**field id 58**
<u>Properties</u>
Location: 439,77
Rect: 428,69,451,86
(all other properties the same as field id 57)

**field id 69**
Properties
Location: 162,214
Rect: 130,206,195,223
(all other properties the same as field id 57)

**field id 70**
Properties
Location: 224,216
Rect: 204,208,245,224
(all other properties the same as field id 57)

**field id 71**
Properties
Location: 277,215
Rect: 257,207,297,223
(all other properties the same as field id 57)

**field id 72**
Properties
Location: 321,215
Rect: 303,207,340,223
(all other properties the same as field id 57)

**field id 73**
Properties
Location: 163,242
Rect: 131,234,196,250
(all other properties the same as field id 57)

**field id 74**
Properties
Location: 236,242
Rect: 206,234,266,250
(all other properties the same as field id 57)

**field id 75**
Properties
Location: 287,241
Rect: 273,233,301,249
(all other properties the same as field id 57)

**field id 76**
Properties
Location: 321,241
Rect: 304,233,339,249
(all other properties the same as field id 57)

**field "Memory"**
Properties
Location: 346,271
Rect: 240,263,452,280
LockText: false
ShowLines: false
WideMargins: false
Style: rectangle
Text Align: left
Text Font: Geneva
Text Height: 16
Text Size: 12
Text Style: plain
Visible: false -- this is a hidden field

## *Further Ideas*

The most apparent enhancement is adding templates with other kinds of conversions. The buttons below the calculator indicate some of the calculation templates you might wish to try if they apply to your work. Just make a new card and enter both the unit names and the conversion factors into lines 1 and 2, respectively, of each unit button you want in the calculator.

Another possibility is adding an on-screen version of a numeric keypad. You could then enter numbers into the left-hand side of the calculator by simply clicking on the number buttons in the keypad. That would be an improvement over selecting the field with the mouse and then typing, as you must do with the design above.

# CHAPTER 44

# A Visual Outliner

EVER SINCE OUTLINING PROGRAMS REACHED THE PERSONAL COMPUTER, THEY HAVE found applications in many disciplines. Some people keep expense records on them, others plan projects, and others find additional ways of organizing nested information. In this chapter, we present our most ambitious stack of the book— a visual outliner. The principles in this stack can be applied to many ways of organizing information that depend on subordinate information. The example we'll show will be based around a project planning situation.

## *Overview*

The stack, as presented here, is actually a stack that makes another stack. The starting stack has three backgrounds: Stack Maker, Overview, and Detail.

The Stack Maker background (Figure 44-1) has one card that requests three information items: the name of the project you need the outliner for, the starting date, and the ending date. Taking this information, a handler first copies the Detail card template into the Clipboard. Then it goes to the Overview card, from which it generates a new stack file with that card's background.

Action then hands off to a newStack handler that is passed along with the Overview card in the new stack. This handler pastes the Detail card

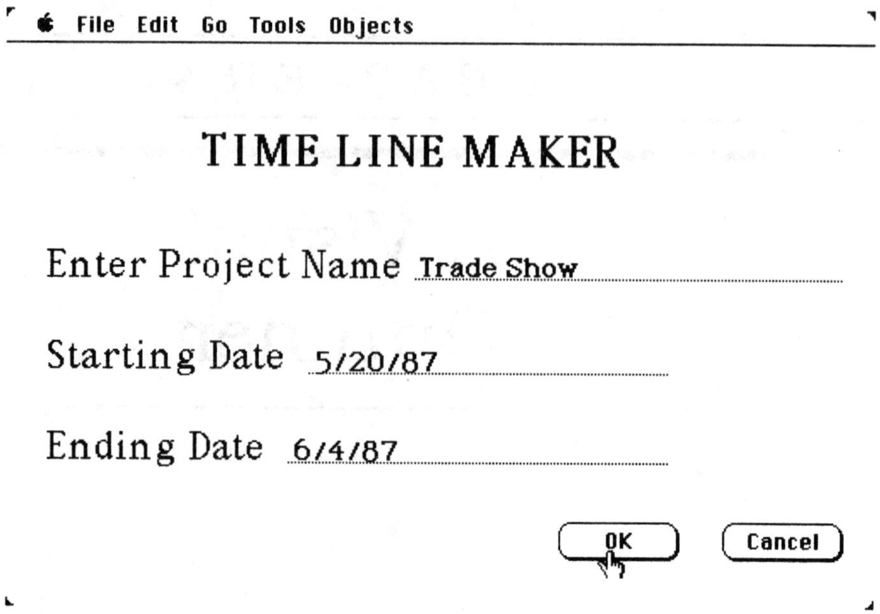

*Figure 44-1.*

from the clipboard. Recall that when this occurs, HyperCard automatically creates a new background in the current stack with that card.

Back on the Overview card, the newStack handler fills in as much information as it can. The Overview card (Figure 44–2) gives a five-day glance of a project. Each column has headings displaying the day number of the project, the day of the week, and the date (in short-date format). The newStack handler's main responsibility is to fill in the top part of the card and these headers for as many days as there are in the total project. If the project lasts more than five days, a new Overview card is generated and filled in (with "Day 6," "Day 7," etc.). This procedure carries on as long as there are days in the project.

In the daily columns of the Overview card, you can type in short, one-line tag names for tasks that need to be completed or performed on that day. When some text is in a line of the column, you may click on the adjacent button. That's where the stack-level mouseUp and page-long toDetail handler (also a stack script) take over.

Like the CheckOff buttons in the To Do List application, the buttons that ultimately make the connection between the task item in the list and its detail card are tall buttons encompassing several background art buttons (the small drop shadow squares). The seven HyperCard button locations are shown in Figure 44–3. Coordinates of the mouse location are used to establish which line the click was intended for.

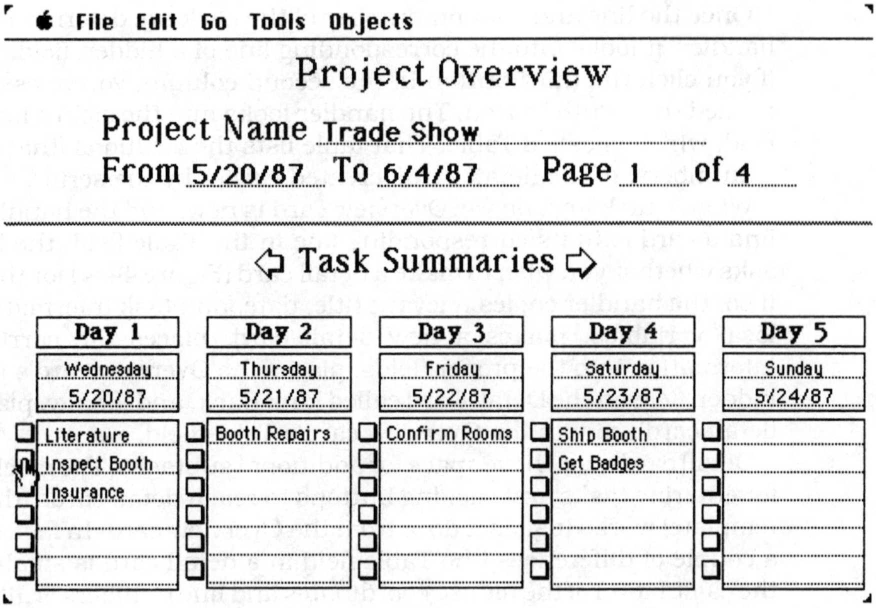

File Edit Go Tools Objects

Project Overview

Project Name Trade Show

From 5/20/87 To 6/4/87 Page 1 of 4

Task Summaries

| Day 1 | Day 2 | Day 3 | Day 4 | Day 5 |
|---|---|---|---|---|
| Wednesday 5/20/87 | Thursday 5/21/87 | Friday 5/22/87 | Saturday 5/23/87 | Sunday 5/24/87 |
| Literature | Booth Repairs | Confirm Rooms | Ship Booth | |
| Inspect Booth | | | Get Badges | |
| Insurance | | | | |

*Figure 44-2.*

File Edit Go Tools Objects

Project Overview

Project Name Trade Show

From 5/20/87 To 6/4/87 Page 1 of 4

Task Summaries

| Day 1 | Day 2 | Day 3 | Day 4 | Day 5 |
|---|---|---|---|---|
| Wednesday 5/20/87 | Thursday 5/21/87 | Friday 5/22/87 | Saturday 5/23/87 | Sunday 5/24/87 |
| Literature | Booth Repairs | Confirm Rooms | Ship Booth | |
| Inspect Booth | | | Get Badges | |
| Insurance | | | | |

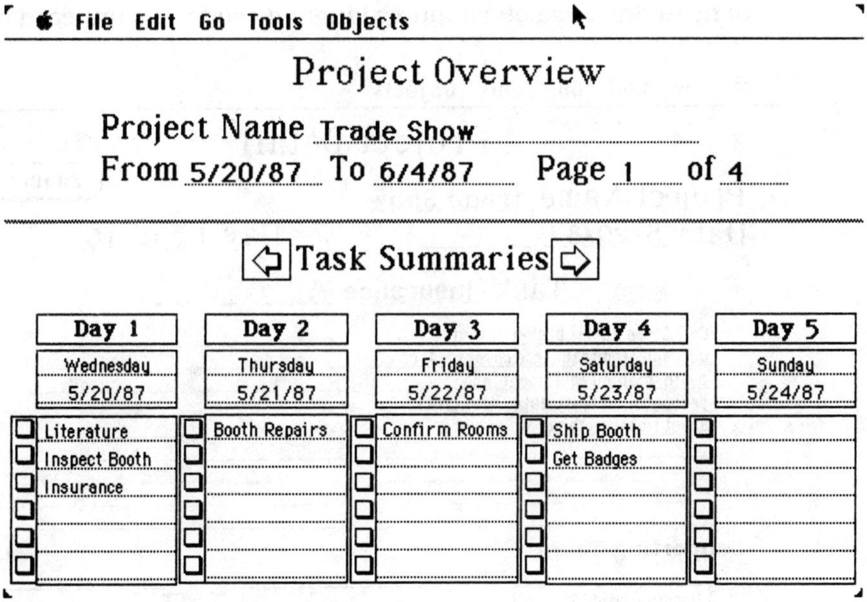

*Figure 44-3.*

Once the line and column number of the click are determined in the handler, it looks into the corresponding line of a hidden field. That is, if you click the third button in the second column, you've essentially clicked the eighth button. The handler looks into the eighth line of the field, which is called Table. That table lists the locations (that is, card ID numbers) of the detail cards created earlier by the script.

When a task item on the Overview card is new, and the handler can't find a card ID in its corresponding line in the Table field, the handler asks whether you wish to make a detail card (Figure 44–4) for this item. If so, the handler copies relevant title, date, and task information into local variables, makes a new detail card, places the carried-over information into the proper fields, places the Overview card's ID into a hidden field on the Detail Card called Link Back, and, finally, places the detail card's ID into the Overview card's Table field.

Detail cards, too, have space for additional subtasks. The mechanism for entering tasks and clicking buttons to reach detail cards (the same template) works just as it does from the Overview card. In fact, despite a couple of differences (the Table field in a detail card is smaller, and the calculation of the mouse coordinates and line numbers is different), Detail cards use the same toDetail stack script as Overview cards do.

If it seems that there's a lot going on in this stack, well, there is. But imagine writing a visual outlining program in which the outlining part is done in one page of computer language code. It's unheard of.

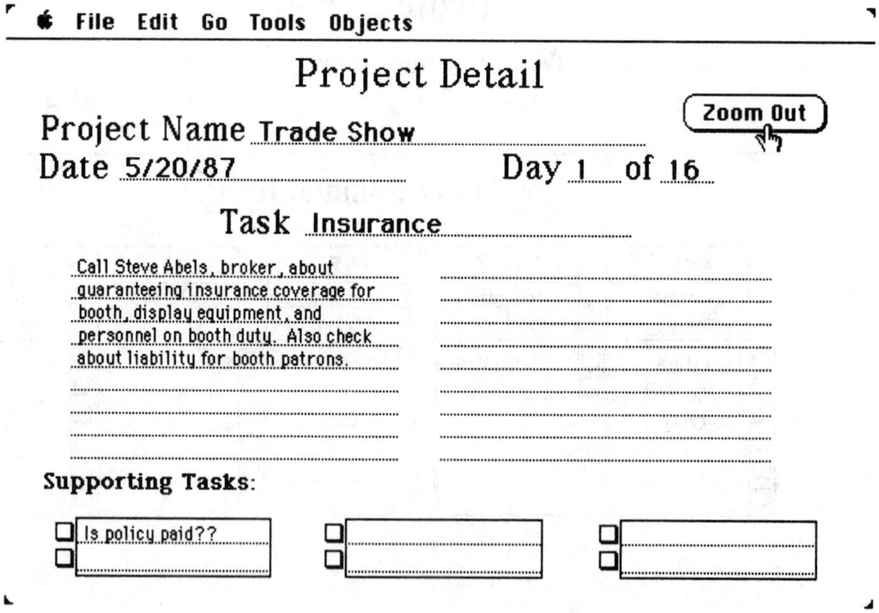

File Edit Go Tools Objects

Project Detail

Project Name Trade Show

Zoom Out

Date 5/20/87 Day 1 of 16

Task Insurance

Call Steve Abels, broker, about guaranteeing insurance coverage for booth, display equipment, and personnel on booth duty. Also check about liability for booth patrons.

**Supporting Tasks:**

Is policy paid??

*Figure 44–4.*

## Scripts and Properties

Now we get into the scripts that perform all these miracles. Remember that the stack-making aspect of this application is quite separate from the outlining part. Once the new outliner stack is made, the stack-making part remains back on the original stack.

**stack "Visual Outliner"**

Script

```
on mouseUp
    if the target contains "button" then
        get short name of the target
        put word 2 of it into colNum
        toDetail colNum
    end if
end mouseUp
```

**Comment:** This stack script is the one that intercepts the mouseUp messages sent when you click on the buttons next to the columns of tasks. Those buttons have no scripts whatsoever, so their mouseUp messages head up the hierarchy, until they reach this handler in the stack script. The buttons are named Column 0, Column 1, and so on. This handler passes the number part of the name as a parameter to the toDetail handler, below. That's the only information toDetail needs from the button. It figures out all the rest (such as which background it's in).

```
on toDetail colNum
    global totalDays

    put "Column" & colNum + 1 into columnName
    get rect of the target
    put 1 + (item 2 of the clickLoc - item 2 of it) div¬
    16 into lineNum
    put line lineNum of field columnName into detailName
    if detailName is empty then exit toDetail

    get short name of bkgnd
    put it into bkgndName
    if it is "Overview" then put 7 into colSize else¬
    put 3 into colSize

    put line lineNum + colNum * colSize of field "Table"¬
    into detailCard
    if detailCard is not empty then
        visual effect iris open
```

```
            go to detailCard
            exit toDetail
    end if

    answer "Do you want a detail card for this item?"¬
    with "Yes" or "No"
    if it is "No" then exit toDetail

    get short name of this card
    put it into linkBack
    put field "Project Name" into projectName
    put line lineNum of field columnName into taskName
    if bkgndName is "Overview" then
            put line 2 of field ("Date" & colNum + 1) into date
            put word 2 of field ("Day Number " & colNum + 1)¬
            into dayNumber
    else
            put field "Date" into date
            put field "Day Number" into dayNumber
    end if

    if lineNum is 1
    then go to card "Detail Template"
    else go to line (lineNum + colNum * colSize) - 1 of field Table
    doMenu "New Card"

    put projectName into field "Project Name"
    put date into field "Date"
    put dayNumber into field "Day Number"
    put taskName into field "Task Name"
    put totalDays into field "Days Total"
    put linkBack into field "LinkBack"

    get name of this card
    put it into detailCard

    set lockScreen to true
    go to linkBack
    put detailCard into line lineNum + colNum * colSize¬
    of field "Table"
    go to detailCard

end toDetail
```

**COMMENT:** This is the monster handler that makes the connections between levels of detail. After reinitializing the global variable, the first group of commands first establishes the line number of the click location (figuring it out from coordinates of the clickloc relative to the rectangle property of the button last clicked—the target). Then it fetches the task item in the designated line number of the column. If there is no item in the task field, the handler exits.

In the next three-line group, the handler determines which kind of card the button was clicked in. If it is an Overview card, the colSize variable is set to 7; otherwise it is set to 3. This variable is used as a factor to calculate the line number of the hidden Table field where the linked card IDS are stored.

That's exactly what happens in the third group of commands. The handler retrieves the contents of the designated line in the Table field. If there's something there, the handler opens that card and leaves the handler. If there's nothing there, the handler continues. You're asked whether you want to create a detail card for the item. If so, you continue still further.

This next group picks up information from the current card that needs to be carried over to the detail card. Each item goes into its own distinctively named variable for later placement into fields of the new card. The date and day number are in different forms on the Overview and Detail cards, so the handler accommodates those differences.

In the four-line group that follows, the handler looks to see if the task is at the head of a column. If it is, it makes the new card from the template card. But if there are other tasks in the column, it goes to the detail card of the last item in the column before making a new card. This assures that detail cards for the same day are kept together in the card order. You'll be able to press the left and right arrow keyboard keys to view tasks on the same day.

Next comes the placement of all those variables into their fields on the new card. Field LinkBack is hidden, but it now contains the ID of the card that lists the current card as a subtask. The Link Back button uses this field to find its way back to the next higher level.

The final tasks entail grabbing the current card's ID number, locking the screen, and inserting it into the appropriate line of the Table field of the linked card. The handler even uses the detailCard variable as a means of returning to the detail card where you can continue working with it from the keyboard.

```
on newStack
    global totalDays,project,start,ending

    set lockScreen to true
    doMenu "Paste Card"
```

```
        go to first card
        set lockScreen to false

        put start into currSeconds
        put 24*60*60 into dayLength
        put ending into endDate
        convert endDate to short date

        repeat with whichDay = 0 to totalDays - 1
            if whichDay mod 5 is 0 then
                if whichDay > 0 then doMenu "New Card"
                put project into field "Project Name"
                get currSeconds
                convert it to short date
                put it into field "Start Date"
                put endDate into field "End Date"
                put (totalDays div 5) + 1 into ¬
                field "Total Pages"
                put (whichDay div 5) + 1 into field "This Page"
            end if

            put "Day Number " & (whichDay mod 5) + 1¬
            into fieldName
            put "Day " & whichDay + 1 into field fieldName

            put "Date" & (whichDay mod 5) + 1 into fieldName
            get currSeconds
            convert it to long date
            put item 1 of it into line 1 of field fieldName
            convert it to short date
            put it into line 2 of field fieldName

            add dayLength to currSeconds
        end repeat
    end newStack
```

**Comment:** This is the second part of the stack-making procedure. It picks up just as the new stack has been made from the Overview card. The Detail card is in the Clipboard. Thus the handler's first task is to paste the Detail card and return to the Overview card, where the rest of the action takes place.

In the second large group of commands, a few preliminary date conversions and variables are set to facilitate later calculations.

The lengthy repeat construction is what places the day numbers, days of the week, and short dates into the tops of the columns. It also checks, at the top, for whether it's time for a new card. When it is, it fills in lots of information from the global variables, as well as calculating the number of total pages and the current page. The currSeconds is the major date-controlling factor throughout this repeat loop. It increments at the end in preparation for the next time through.

The balance of this handler makes necessary date conversions and field insertions, adjusting the names of field destinations each time through the loop (for example, put into field Day 1; put into field Day 2). Despite all the conversions and variable-naming that goes on here, this handler works remarkably fast. Also, it only works once for each new stack you create. You can delete this handler from the stack script of the new stack, because you won't need it again. The next time you need a new stack, you'll create it from the stack-maker edition of this stack.

**bkgnd "Stack Maker"**

**button "OK"**

Properties

Location: 362,304
Rect: 327,293,398,315
AutoHilite: true
ShowName: true
Hilite: false
Style: roundRect
Icon: 0
Visible: true

Script

```
on mouseUp
	global totalDays,project,start,ending

	put field "Project Name" into project
	put field "Start Date" into start
	put field "End Date" into ending

	if project is empty or start is empty or¬
	ending is empty then
		answer "All three fields must be filled out." with "OK"
		exit mouseUp
	end if

	convert start to seconds
	convert ending to seconds
	put 1 + (ending - start) div (24*60*60) into totalDays
```

```
        if totalDays  < 1 then
                answer "How can you end before you start?"¬
                with "Just Kidding"
                exit mouseUp
        end if

        go to card "Overview Template"
        set lockScreen to true
        go to card "Detail Template"
        doMenu "Copy Card"
        go to card "Overview Template"
        set lockScreen to false
        doMenu "New Stack..."
end mouseUp
```

**COMMENT:** This is the first part of the stack-making procedure. Its first tasks include grabbing the information from the card's fields and placing them into global variables for use later on. The handler also tests for whether all three information items have been filled out. It won't let you continue if any item is empty.

Next it calculates the number of total days of the project. Notice that by subtracting the start date's seconds from the end date's seconds, you actually miss one of the days of the project. Because the number of days is inclusive, we add 1 to the calculation of total days. We also throw in a little test to make sure the person has entered start and end dates in the correct sequence.

Finally, the handler prepares for making the new stack. It goes to the Overview card, locks the screen, goes to the Detail card, where it copies it into the Clipboard, and returns to the Overview card for making the new stack. Notice that this zigzag approach lets us carry two card backgrounds from one stack to a new one. This is a lot faster than doing one transfer at a time.

**button "Cancel"**

Properties

Location: 458,304
Rect: 423,293,494,315
AutoHilite: true
ShowName: true
Hilite: false
Style: roundRect
Icon: 0

Script

```
on mouseUp
        go Home
end mouseUp
```

**field "Project Name"**
<u>Properties</u>
Location: 367,150
Rect: 240,138,494,162
LockText: false
ShowLines: true
WideMargins: false
Style: transparent
Text Align: left
Text Font: New York
Text Height: 18
Text Size: 14
Text Style: bold
Visible: true

**field "Start Date"**
<u>Properties</u>
Location: 285,202
Rect: 178,192,392,213
(all other properties same as "Project Name")

**field "End Date"**
<u>Properties</u>
Location: 279,254
Rect: 166,243,393,265
(all other properties same as "Project Name")

**bkgnd "Overview"**

**button "Column 0"**
<u>Properties</u>
Location: 12,285
Rect: 4,237,20,334
AutoHilite: false
ShowName: false
Hilite: false
Style: transparent
Icon: 0
Visible: true

**button "Column 1"**
<u>Properties</u>
Location: 113,285
Rect: 105,237,121,334
(all other properties same as "Column 0")

**button "Column 2"**
<u>Properties</u>
Location: 214,285
Rect: 206,237,222,334
(all other properties same as "Column 0")

**button "Column 3"**
<u>Properties</u>
Location: 315,285
Rect: 307,237,323,334
(all other properties same as "Column 0")

**button "Column 4"**
<u>Properties</u>
Location: 416,285
Rect: 408,237,424,334
(all other properties same as "Column 0")

**button "Prev"**
<u>Properties</u>
Location: 156,147
Rect: 142,135,171,159
AutoHilite: true
ShowName: false
Hilite: false
Style: transparent
Icon: 1014
Visible: true
<u>Script</u>

```
on mouseUp
	go to prev card of this bkgnd
end mouseUp
```

**button "Next"**
<u>Properties</u>
Location: 339,147
Rect: 325,135,354,159
(all other properties same as "Prev")
<u>Script</u>

```
on mouseUp
	go to next card of this bkgnd
end mouseUp
```

**field "Project Name"**
<u>Properties</u>
Location: 298,73
Rect: 182,63,415,83
LockText: false
ShowLines: true
WideMargins: false
Style: transparent
Text Align: left
Text Font: Geneva
Text Height: 18
Text Size: 14
Text Style: bold
Visible: true

**field "Start Date"**
<u>Properties</u>
Location: 148,97
Rect: 106,87,190,107
(all other properties same as "Project Name")

**field "End Date"**
<u>Properties</u>
Location: 261,97
Rect: 218,87,305,107
(all other properties same as "Project Name")

**field "This Page"**
<u>Properties</u>
Location: 382,97
Rect: 361,87,404,107
(all other properties same as "Project Name")

**field "Total Pages"**
<u>Properties</u>
Location: 446,97
Rect: 425,87,468,107
(all other properties same as "Project Name")

**field "Day Number 1"**
<u>Properties</u>
Location: 61,187
Rect: 19,178,104,196

LockText: false
ShowLines: false
WideMargins: false
Style: rectangle
Text Align: center
Text Font: New York
Text Height: 16
Text Size: 12
Text Style: bold
Visible: true

**field "Day Number 2"**
Properties
Location: 162,187
Rect: 120,178,205,196
(all other properties same as "Day Number 1")

**field "Day Number 3"**
Properties
Location: 263,187
Rect: 221,178,306,196
(all other properties same as "Day Number 1")

**field "Day Number 4"**
Properties
Location: 364,187
Rect: 322,178,407,196
(all other properties same as "Day Number 1")

**field "Day Number 5"**
Properties
Location: 465,187
Rect: 423,178,508,196
(all other properties same as "Day Number 1")

**field "Date1"**
Properties
Location: 61,216
Rect: 19,199,104,233
LockText: false
ShowLines: true
WideMargins: false
Style: rectangle
Text Align: center

Text Font: Geneva
Text Height: 16
Text Size: 10
Text Style: plain
Visible: true

**field "Date2"**
<u>Properties</u>
Location: 162,216
Rect: 120,199,205,233
(all other properties same as "Date1")

**field "Date3"**
<u>Properties</u>
Location: 263,216
Rect: 221,199,306,233
(all other properties same as "Date1")

**field "Date4"**
<u>Properties</u>
Location: 364,216
Rect: 322,199,407,233
(all other properties same as "Date1")

**field "Date5"**
<u>Properties</u>
Location: 465,216
Rect: 423,199,508,233
(all other properties same as "Date1")

**field "Column1"**
<u>Properties</u>
Location: 61,286
Rect: 19,237,104,335
LockText: false
ShowLines: true
WideMargins: false
Style: rectangle
Text Align: left
Text Font: Geneva
Text Height: 16
Text Size: 10
Text Style: plain
Visible: true

**field "Column2"**
<u>Properties</u>
Location: 162,285
Rect: 120,236,205,334
(all properties same as "Column1")

**field "Column3"**
<u>Properties</u>
Location: 263,285
Rect: 221,236,306,334
(all properties same as "Column1")

**field "Column4"**
<u>Properties</u>
Location: 364,286
Rect: 322,237,407,335
(all properties same as "Column1")

**field "Column5"**
<u>Properties</u>
Location: 465,286
Rect: 423,237,508,335
(all properties same as "Column1")

**field "Table"**
<u>Properties</u>
Location: 437,43
Rect: 408,33,467,54
LockText: false
ShowLines: false
WideMargins: false
Style: transparent
Text Align: left
Text Font: Geneva
Text Height: 16
Text Size: 12
Text Style: plain
Visible: false -- the hidden field with all the card ids in it

**bkgnd "Detail"**

**button "Column 0"**
<u>Properties</u>
Location: 35,308
Rect: 25,290,45,327
AutoHilite: false

ShowName: false
Hilite: false
Style: transparent
Icon: 0
Visible: true

**button "Column 1"**
Properties
Location: 193,308
Rect: 183,290,203,327
(all other properties same as "Column 0")

**button "Column 2"**
Properties
Location: 354,308
Rect: 344,290,364,327
(all other properties same as "Column 0")

**button "Zoom Out"**
Properties
**Location: 441,60**
Rect: 399,49,484,71
AutoHilite: false
ShowName: true
Hilite: false
Style: roundRect
Icon: 0
Visible: true
Script

```
on mouseUp
    visual effect iris close
    go to field "LinkBack"
end mouseUp
```

**field "Project Name"**
Properties
Location: 261,72
Rect: 145,62,378,82
LockText: false
ShowLines: true
WideMargins: false
Style: transparent
Text Align: left
Text Font: Geneva
Text Height: 18

Text Size: 14
Text Style: bold
Visible: true

**field "Date"**
Properties
Location: 152,93
Rect: 66,83,238,103
(all other properties same as "Project Name")

**field "Day Number"**
Properties
Location: 347,93
Rect: 330,83,364,103
(all other properties same as "Project Name")

**field "Days Total"**
Properties
Location: 401,93
Rect: 384,83,418,103
(all other properties same as "Project Name")

**field "Task Name"**
Properties
Location: 273,124
Rect: 176,114,371,134
(all other properties same as "Project Name")

**field id 7** -- left-hand notes field
Properties
Location: 136,202
Rect: 39,142,234,262
LockText: false
ShowLines: true
WideMargins: false
Style: transparent
Text Align: left
Text Font: Geneva
Text Height: 13
Text Size: 10
Text Style: plain
Visible: true

**field id 8** -- right-hand notes field
<u>Properties</u>
Location: 354,202
Rect: 257,142,452,262
(all other properties same as field id 7)

**field "Column1"**
<u>Properties</u>
Location: 101,309
Rect: 43,292,159,326
LockText: false
ShowLines: true
WideMargins: false
Style: rectangle
Text Align: left
Text Font: Geneva
Text Height: 16
Text Size: 10
Text Style: plain
Visible: true

**field "Column2"**
<u>Properties</u>
Location: 260,309
Rect: 202,292,318,326
(all other properties same as "Column1")

**field "Column3"**
<u>Properties</u>
Location: 421,309
Rect: 363,292,479,326
(all other properties same as "Column1")

**field "LinkBack"**
<u>Properties</u>
Location: 458,57
Rect: 425,47,492,67
LockText: false
ShowLines: false
WideMargins: false
Style: transparent

Text Align: left
Text Font: Geneva
Text Height: 16
Text Size: 12
Text Style: plain
Visible: false
-- hidden field with id of card next up the outline

**field "Table"**
Properties
Location: 471,88
Rect: 437,79,505,98
LockText: false
ShowLines: false
WideMargins: false
Style: transparent
Text Align: left
Text Font: Geneva
Text Height: 16
Text Size: 12
Text Style: plain
Visible: false
-- hidden, just like Table field in Overview

## *Further Ideas*

Your imagination can run wild with this stack when it comes to adding features. A helpful addition would be some way of denoting in the Overview level when an item has subtasks attached to it, just like the text-oriented outliner programs do.

Also, you'd like to know when tasks are completed. A check-off system would be nice, provided it worked intelligently. By that we mean that if you check off a detail task, its item is automatically marked on the Overview card. You should go one step further, however. If a Detail card has subtasks attached to it, you shouldn't let the Detail card be checked off until all its subtasks are checked off in their Detail cards— and so on down the hierarchy.

Here's another suggestion. How about trapping for the Copy and Paste menu items so that if you move a task item from one day to the next, its detail card's ID moves to the corresponding Table field line as well. That, too, would be the way traditional text-based outliners operate.

## *A Final Note*

If you have worked your way through this book one page at a time, you are to be congratulated for having the desire and patience to learn HyperCard inside out. We hope that in the spirit of HyperCard's creator, Bill Atkinson, you will share your experiences with others. Most importantly, we hope HyperCard unlocks your imagination to create new uses for the Macintosh in areas we haven't yet dreamed.

# PART FIVE

# HYPERCARD 1.1 AND 1.2

# CHAPTER 45

# Making the (Up)Grade

WHETHER YOU USE HYPERCARD AS A "PLAYBACK MACHINE" FOR OTHER PEOPLES' stacks or as a development system for software you design, you owe it to yourself to upgrade to the latest version of HyperCard as soon as possible. In fact, each day that goes by after the release of a new version increases the need for you to keep up. Here's why.

## *The Importance of Upgrades*

First, significant upgrades, like HyperCard version 1.2 (and any related maintenance releases, such as 1.2.1) give the developers of stacks that you run new powers not before possible. Stacks created with 1.2 will probably have features that work only on your copy of HyperCard 1.2. Running such stacks on HyperCard versions earlier than 1.2 may give you problems– if they work at all. If the stack designer did his homework, the stack will actually prevent you from using it on a HyperCard version less than 1.2. A dialog box will come up to advise you that you need HyperCard 1.2 or later to use the stack.

Second, many of the new features built into HyperCard 1.2, particularly in the HyperTalk programming language, will let you add features and user interface friendliness to stacks that you build. You will likely find new, efficient ways of performing previously cumbersome processes. The new HyperTalk commands, functions, properties, and system messages may even give you new ideas for stacks and features.

A third reason for keeping pace with upgrades is probably obvious to anyone with even limited experience with personal computer software. Each new release of HyperCard repairs potentially hazardous bugs, some of which may even accidentally and unexpectedly corrupt a stack you've spent a long time building. Each generation is "cleaner" than the previous one.

Improved performance, too, is always high on the agenda for producing a new release of HyperCard. Sometimes the improvement is in the HyperTalk part of things, other times in the HyperCard part, such as searching speed. Bill Atkinson and the father of HyperTalk, Dan Winkler, expend a great deal of effort to improve the execution speed of various parts of HyperCard. Many of those improvements show up in version 1.2.

## *Update Chronology*

Notice about HyperCard updates does not reach every Macintosh owner. This also holds true for System and Finder updates. Apple leaves it up to Macintosh users to learn about the availability of upgrades from dealers, user groups, and computer journals. As a result, a large number of Macintosh owners haven't been aware of the upgrades issued by Apple since HyperCard first shipped in August of 1987. The following chronology should bring you up to speed.

### HYPERCARD 1.0.1

The first version was numbered 1.0.1. It was supposed to be 1.0, but testing of 1.0 immediately before shrink-wrapped boxes left the Apple factory uncovered a couple problems that had to be repaired. No copies of version 1.0 were ever officially released to retail stores.

### HYPERCARD 1.1

HyperCard version 1.1 was officially released in February of 1988. Only two new visible features were added: the ability to undo a Delete Card action and the textArrows property. Text importing and export buttons, which had inadvertently been left out of the Button Ideas stack of the first release, were included. There were also many bug fixes. Perhaps the fix that was most visible to serious stack developers was that HyperCard behaved much better with stacks consisting of many thousands of cards. For users overseas, substantial work went into making HyperCard work with System files in countries other than the United States. The vagaries of date and time presentations in other

HyperCard v 1.1
Update Notes

HyperCard version 1.1 contains a few changes and some new features that you need to know about.

- Enhancements to stacks
- Minimum memory settings
- Text arrows
- User Guide updates
- Import and export buttons
- Updating the Home stack

Minimum Memory Setting

HyperCard won't run properly under MultiFinder if you set Application Memory Size in its Get Info box to less than 750K: Paint tools won't work properly, and you won't be able to paste graphics. Other less predictable consequences might also occur.

You can set Application Memory Size to higher than 750K (1 Megabyte is suggested for best performance, assuming you have enough memory); you just can't set it lower.

*Figure 45-1 a and b . Two cards from the HyperCard version 1.1 Update Notes stack.*

## Text Arrows

HyperCard's new Text Arrows option lets you use the arrow keys when you edit text fields or the Message box. When you click any user level button except Browsing on the User Preferences card, a check box labeled Text Arrows appears. With Text Arrows checked, the Left Arrow and Right Arrow keys move the insertion point to the left and right over text in a field or in the message box; the Up Arrow and Down Arrow keys move up and down through lines in a field.

To move to the previous or next card, or to go back and forward through cards you've seen, hold down the Option key as you press the appropriate arrow key. (With Text Arrows unchecked, you don't need to hold down the Option key.)

For details on the User Preference card, see pages 22 and 50 of the HyperCard User's Guide. For more information on the actions of arrow keys with Text Arrows unchecked, see pages 116 -120.

## User Guide Mistakes *

On page 29 under "Some Paint Tool Tips," the first sentence reads "To select a Paint tool, just drag to the one you want on the Paint menu. . . ." It should read ". . . to the one you want on the Tools menu. . . ."

On Page 113 under "Delete Card," the last sentence says that you can't cut the last card in a stack. Actually you can cut the last card; but you can't delete the only card.

On Page 121, the section labeled "Searching in a Specific Field" implies that you can limit searching to a specific card field. Actually, you can limit searching to a specific background field, but not to a specific card field.

* The Author is abashed.

*Figure 45-1 c and d. Two cards from the HyperCard version 1.1 Update Notes stack.*

countries had to be addressed for HyperCard to be widely accepted around the world.

The release came on an update diskette complete with three of HyperCard's original stacks updated where necessary. Another stack outlined the changes. Figure 45-1a to 45-1d shows several cards from this 10-card stack. Among the most important items of this stack was an update button that added a checkbox to the User Preferences card of the Home stack and made slight modifications to two handlers in the Home stack scripts. These changes are detailed later in this chapter.

## HYPERCARD 1.2, 1.2.1 AND 1.2.2

Even before a large number of HyperCard users had heard about version 1.1, Apple released version 1.2 in May, 1988. First shipments were packaged in the shrink-wrapped HyperCard box, with the official upgrade not available through Apple dealers and user groups until June 15. Fortunately, the wait was worth it, because some bugs appeared in 1.2. By the time the official update came out, version 1.2.1 was in place.

If you are a HyperCard user in the United States, you won't hear much about version 1.2.2. It is released only outside the U.S., because it contains small repairs to the localization facilities of HyperCard—how it works with System files for other countries. There are no feature differences between 1.2.1 and 1.2.2.

Since there is no functional difference among 1.2, 1.2.1 and 1.2.2, these releases will be generically referred to as 1.2 throughout the remainder of this book.

The primary reason for coming out with HyperCard 1.2 was to make HyperCard work on read-only storage media, notably Apple's CD-ROM (Compact Disc–Read Only Memory) player. A CD-ROM disc can hold up to 550 megabytes of information for browsing, but the user cannot store information on the disc. Prior to HyperCard 1.2, HyperCard always wrote information to the disk while you or a HyperTalk script made changes to a field's contents, an object or a picture in a stack. Trying to open a stack on a locked floppy disk, for instance, prompted HyperCard to tell you that the disk was locked. The stack would not open. Since HyperCard "sees" a CD-ROM as just another disk, the software must open a stack on that disk—even though the disk is forever locked.

While they were at it, Bill Atkinson and Dan Winkler made a number of additions to the rest of HyperCard. Those new features are detailed in subsequent chapters.

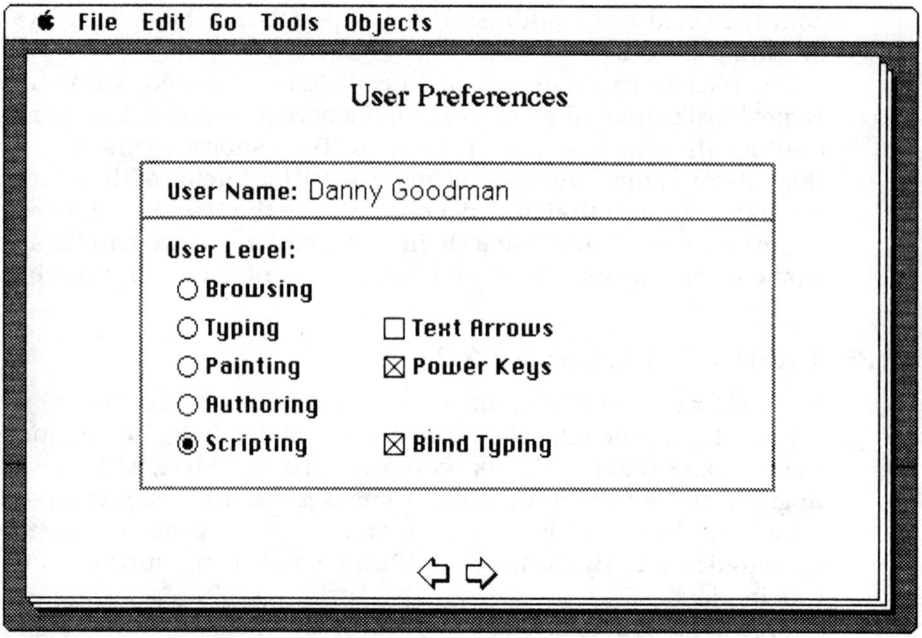

File Edit Go Tools Objects

User Preferences

User Name: Danny Goodman

User Level:

- Browsing
- Typing ☐ Text Arrows
- Painting ☒ Power Keys
- Authoring
- Scripting ☒ Blind Typing

*Figure 45-2. The Text Arrows button is added to the Home Stack's User Preferences card.*

## *How to Upgrade*

To make your HyperCard environment completely state-of-the-art requires three steps on your part. First, replace whatever version of HyperCard you're using with version 1.2 (or later). Second, you must be sure the User Preferences card of your Home stack has the latest button configuration and script. Third, you should compact your stacks with HyperCard 1.2. Let's look at these items in detail.

### COPYING THE HYPERCARD APPLICATION

If you're using HyperCard on a floppy disk based system, then you need to change the HyperCard startup disk you've been using to start your Macintosh. On a fresh disk, copy every file from your everyday HyperCard startup disk, except for HyperCard itself. Then copy HyperCard 1.2 to that new disk. Label the disk so that you can recognize it readily as your HyperCard 1.2 startup disk.

On a hard disk system, drag your old HyperCard program file to the Trash. Then copy the HyperCard 1.2 file to the hard disk in the same folder as your original HyperCard file. If the HyperCard 1.2 file is labeled with the version number, you can change it to read, simply, "HyperCard." Remember that you can always check the Get Info dialog box on the HyperCard file from the Finder to see which version you are using. The About HyperCard dialog, available from within HyperCard, also reveals the exact version number you're using.

## UPDATING THE HOME STACK

As noted above, the changes to the Home stack were instituted in the version 1.1 release. Many HyperCard owners did not get that release, or at least not the stack that made the changes to the Home stack for you (it's also in the 1.2 Update stack). If that's your case, then follow the directions in this section to bring your Home stack up to date.

Your goal is to make the User Preferences card in your Home stack look like the one in Figure 45-2. The addition of the Text Arrows button is the only visible change. To do that:

1. Make sure your are *not* in background editing mode.
2. Set the User Level setting to Scripting.
3. Choose New Button from the Objects menu.
4. Double-click on the new button to bring up the Button Info dialog box.
5. Name the button *Text Arrows*.
6. Check the checkbox style button.
7. Check the Auto-Hilite button.
8. Click the Script button to bring up the Script Editor.
9. Type the following script:

   ```
   on mouseUp
       set textArrows to the hilite of me
   end mouseUp
   ```

10. Close the Script Editor by clicking the OK button.
11. Choose the Browse tool.
12. To make the button the proper size and place it where it belongs type the following line into the Message Box:

    ```
    set rect of last button to 211,166,314,187
    ```

That takes care of the button. Next, we modify the Home stack script.

1. From the User Preferences card, choose Stack Info from the Objects menu.
2. In the Stack Info dialog box, click the Script button.

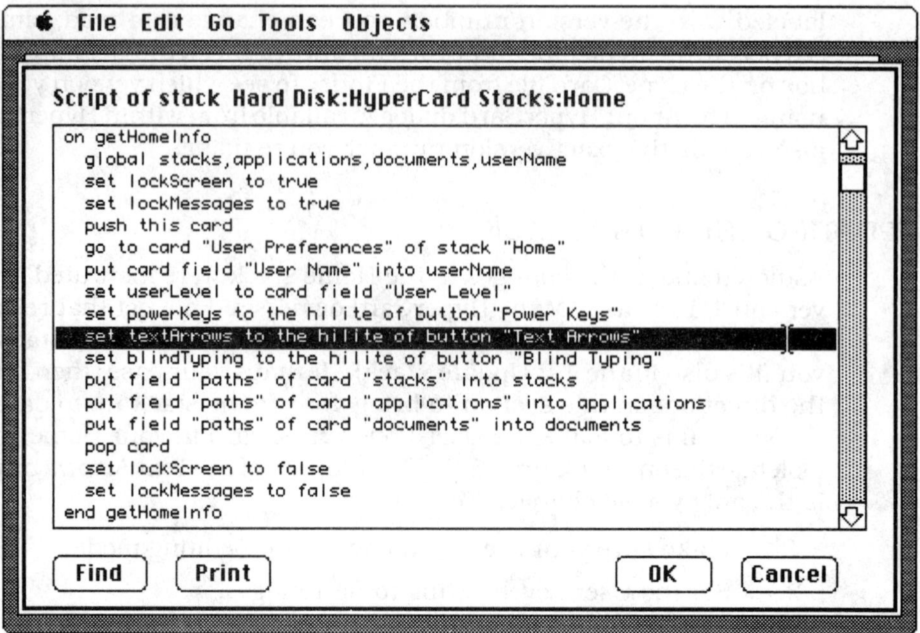


*Figure 45-3. Insert the highlighted text line into the stack script of the Home stack.*

3. Scroll through the stack script until you locate the "on get-HomeInfo" handler. If you haven't modified your stack script, this will be immediately visible.
4. In that handler, locate the two adjacent lines that set the powerKeys and blindTyping properties.
5. Between these two lines, insert the following line:

   set textArrows to the hilite of button "Text Arrows"

   Figure 45-3 highlights the new line in the designated location. This is the location specified by the script that did the updating automatically in the HyperCard 1.1 release.
6. Click the OK button to leave the stack Script Editor.

The last step is to update the card script of the User Preferences card.

1. Choose Card Info from the Objects menu.
2. In the Card Info dialog box, click the Script button.
3. Find the "on setUserLevel whatLevel" handler in the script. If you have not modified this card script, it should be immediately visible.

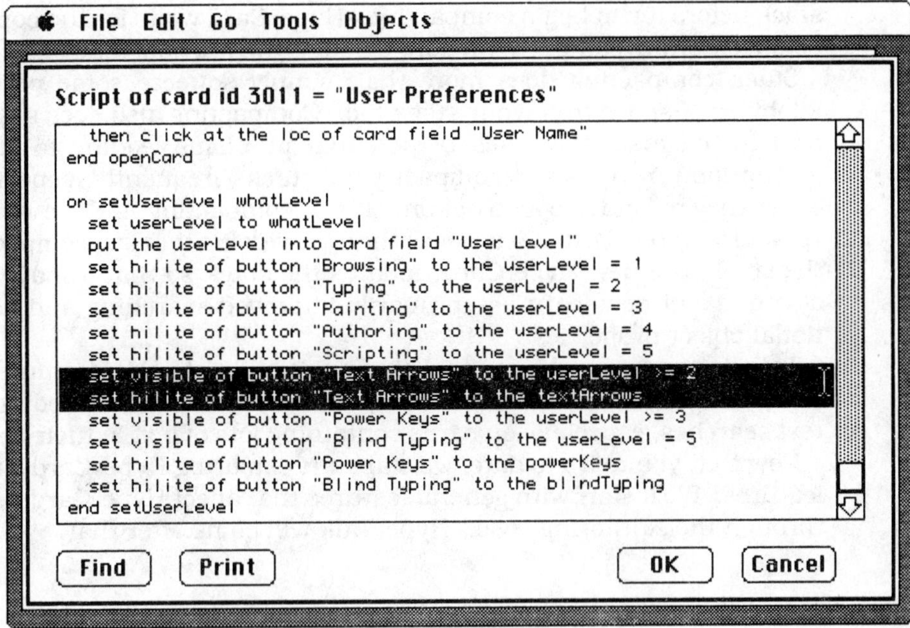

File Edit Go Tools Objects
Script of card id 3011 = "User Preferences"
then click at the loc of card field "User Name"
end openCard
on setUserLevel whatLevel
set userLevel to whatLevel
put the userLevel into card field "User Level"
set hilite of button "Browsing" to the userLevel = 1
set hilite of button "Typing" to the userLevel = 2
set hilite of button "Painting" to the userLevel = 3
set hilite of button "Authoring" to the userLevel = 4
set hilite of button "Scripting" to the userLevel = 5
set visible of button "Text Arrows" to the userLevel >= 2
set hilite of button "Text Arrows" to the textArrows
set visible of button "Power Keys" to the userLevel >= 3
set visible of button "Blind Typing" to the userLevel = 5
set hilite of button "Power Keys" to the powerKeys
set hilite of button "Blind Typing" to the blindTyping
end setUserLevel
Find
Print
OK
Cancel


*Figure 1-4. Insert the two highlighted lines into the card script of the Home Stack's User Preferences card.*

4. Locate the script line that sets the hilite of the "Scripting" button.
5. After this line, insert the following two lines:

   set visible of button "Text Arrows" to the userLevel >= 2
   set hilite of button "Text Arrows" to the textArrows

Figure 45-4 highlights the new lines in the script.

6. Click the OK button to leave the card Script Editor.
7. Choose Compact Stack from the File menu.

Your Home stack is now up to HyperCard 1.2 standards.

## COMPACTING STACKS

As you may have noticed in your HyperCard wanderings, compacting a stack writes a new copy of your stack onto disk, deleting the old one. If you ever tried to compact a stack on a floppy disk and received the error message that there wasn't sufficient room to compact, the reason was that HyperCard needs space on the disk for a copy of the current stack before it can begin compacting. HyperCard waits for the copy to be successfully compacted before deleting the previous one.

Stack compacting does more than simply squeeze some padded kilobytes of space from your stack file. Compacting also does a great deal to "cleanse" the stack of potential problems leading to stack corruption. You should compact your stacks frequently, especially while they're under construction. If the compacting is done with a version of HyperCard that is newer than the version that last compacted the stack, the new HyperCard updates the stack so that it may take advantage of new features— primarily improved searching and additional object properties.

To bring your stacks up to 1.2 compatibility, Apple recommends compacting your stack twice. The second pass will aid in speeding up text searches, especially on cards containing lots of text in their fields.

Now that you're up to date, we can start exploring HyperCard's new features. We'll start with general features that affect HyperCard users through the Authoring level. HyperTalk will come after that.

# CHAPTER 46

# New HyperCard Features

EVEN IF YOU'RE NOT A HYPERTALK PROGRAMMER, HYPERCARD 1.2 OFFERS A number of features that you'll find helpful in authoring stacks. I make the distinction between authoring and scripting levels, because I don't want you to get the impression that all improvements have been made only for the benefit of experienced "HyperHackers."

Some of the finest stacks I've seen— including the winner of a European stack design contest in early 1988— have been written with little more than Go commands and visual effects. So, while it's easy to be intimidated by stack experts who spend more time in HyperTalk programming than in careful stack organization, you don't have to be "stackhead" to create an excellent stack.

Improvements have been made on a number of fronts, so the discussion in this chapter may seem to jump around a bit.

## *TextArrows Property*

Since we just finished installing a button in the Home stack that switches the textArrows property on and off, let's examine this feature. As noted earlier, this property was actually added to HyperCard in version 1.1.

Prior to version 1.1, the only way you could adjust the position the flashing text pointer from character to character in a text field was to click with the mouse. There were no keyboard actions that could, for example, move the cursor back a couple characters so you could insert a word you missed. You'd have to reach for the mouse and position the cursor where you wanted it. If you pressed the right arrow key on the keyboard, you went to the next card in the stack (unless it was programmed otherwise).

That went against the grain of many users who were accustomed to a bit of cursor navigation via the keyboard in word processing and other text entry programs. To accommodate such keyboard control, the TextArrows property lets you control the text insertion pointer inside a field, provided the pointer was there to begin with— either by tabbing to the field or clicking the mouse inside the field to open it (HyperTalk considers the positioning of the pointer inside a field ready for typing as opening the field). Left and right arrow keys move the pointer left and right, respectively; up and down arrow keys move the pointer to the previous or next lines of text in the same field, respectively.

With textArrows engaged, you can still use the keyboard arrow keys to navigate through a stack by holding down the Option key along with the desired arrow key. You must use this keyboard combination for navigation, even when no field is open.

TextArrows is a two-edged sword for HyperCard pioneers who cut their teeth on version 1.0.1. For instance, I'm so used to navigating through a stack via the keyboard that having textArrows engaged would be frustrating, because I'd have to scramble for the Option key to do my navigating. If I were to encounter a stack that took it upon itself to change the textArrows property to true, I'd have to dive into the scripts immediately and change that.

Since the textArrows setting is made in the User Preferences card, I think it best to leave that choice up to the user of your stack. If the user is comfortable with using the Option and arrow keys to navigate in return for the privilege of having text field navigation, then let the User Preferences card rule, as it does automatically upon starting HyperCard. In other words, don't adjust this property with a script in your stack.

## *HyperCard and MultiFinder*

With so many HyperCard stacks being of the "information-on-tap" variety, it is an attractive proposition to run HyperCard along with one or more applications in MultiFinder. If you have two or more megabytes of RAM in your Macintosh, then this is a reasonable request.

The first release of MultiFinder coincided with the first release of HyperCard. At that time there was precious little experience running

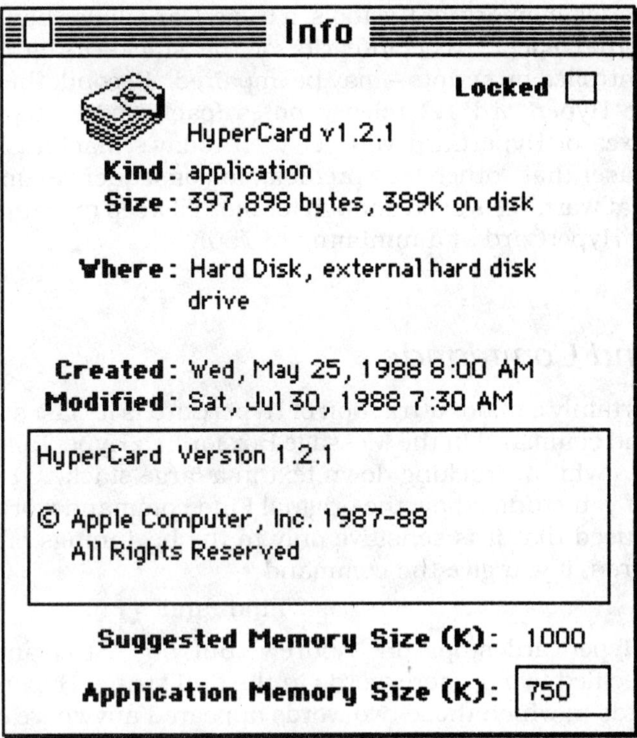


*Figure 46-1. You may adjust the Application Memory Size for HyperCard to 750K when running in MultiFinder, and still have access to the Painting tools.*

both environments together, other than enough to know that HyperCard could co-exist with MultiFinder.

To have access to all HyperCard tools, HyperCard must have at least 750K of RAM available to it. If it has a little more RAM, the better it works. In fact, the Application Memory Size of HyperCard out of the box is set to 1 megabyte— the amount of RAM it really likes, provided your machine has that much to devote to HyperCard. But if you're running on a machine with less than 2.5 megabytes of RAM and expect to load a couple heavy duty applications (like Microsoft Word, Excel, or a graphics program), then you may need to adjust the Application Memory Size down to 750K (Figure 46-1).

It is possible to crank down the Application Memory Size to less than 700K, if you don't need the painting tools. This is a dangerous maneuver, however, for two reasons. First, there are many stacks out there that use the Paint tools in the course of using the stack, even though you don't realize the Paint tools are being chosen. If there isn't enough memory for the tools, a HyperCard dialog box message appears to that effect. The integrity of the stack– its graphic information controlled by scripts– may be impaired. Second, there is a warning in the HyperCard 1.2 release notes (packaged in the shrink-wrapped boxes of HyperCard you get with today's Macintosh hardware purchase) that "other less predictable consequences might also occur." That warning is good enough for me. I'll keep my MultiFinder partition for HyperCard at a minimum of 750K.

## *New Find Commands*

Certainly a major attraction of HyperCard is its fast search ability. The Find command in the Message Box (or in a HyperTalk script) proves to be a whiz at tracking down text in a large stack.

If you studied how the original Find command works, you may have noticed that it is sensitive only to the beginnings of words. In other words, if you give the command

Find "and"

HyperCard stops on "Andrew" but not "Streisand." Also, if you specified two or more words in the find string, HyperCard stopped on cards in which those two words appeared anywhere on the card, even in different fields. For instance, the command

Find "George Washington"

stops not only on the card of the first U.S. president, but also on a card in the same stack containing the name "George Smith" and his address in "Washington, D.C."

The Find command has been expanded in HyperCard 1.2 to allow fast searches for characters within a word and for occurrences of multiple words appearing only next to each other. Here are the details.

### FIND STRING

The new Find String command works like the existing Find Chars command, except that under one condition it uses HyperCard's fast search.

If you wish to find a match for characters inside a single word, then you can use Find String or Find Chars interchangeably. In other words, the two commands

Find chars "ard"
Find string "ard"

would locate those characters in the word "HyperCard" at the same leisurely pace.

To make HyperCard's fast search ability kick in, you can add a space and at least the first three characters of the next word in the string. Therefore, the command

Find string "ard Han"

would use HyperCard's fast search to locate that string in the two-word combination, "HyperCard Handbook."

There is no keyboard shortcut to get the Find String command to appear in the Message Box. You can choose Find from the Go menu and manually insert the "string" part of the command, or just type the entire command. Be sure the search string is inside quotes, as shown in the examples above.

## FIND WHOLE

When you want to search a stack for whole words or the occurrence of two contiguous words— like finding only George Washington's card— then use the new Find Whole command. Unlike the plain Find command, Find Whole is sensitive to both word beginnings and endings. In other words, HyperCard considers the start of the search string as the beginning of a word and the end of the search string as the end of a word. Here are some examples.

The command

Find Whole "Steve"

would find only occurrences of people entered as "Steve," but not "Steven." Find Whole believes the final "e" of the search string must be at the end of a word for a match to be valid. Conversely, the command

Find Whole "Steven"

would not stop on "Steve" in your cards, because HyperCard would locate only complete words that start with "S," end with "n," and have "teve" in between.

In one sense, Find Whole helps you narrow your searches, but it makes you be more accurate in defining your search string than with the plain Find command.

A search string in a Find Whole command may also contain a space, thereby letting you search for occurrences of two or more words that appear together. Remember, they must be whole words. The command

Find Whole "Eddie Mur"

would not find "Eddie Murphy," because HyperCard seeks a string whose word beginning is "E," whose word ending is "r," and whose insides are "ddie Mu."

The good news about this command, however, is that all words in the search string must be contiguous on the card for HyperCard to find it. Therefore, the command

Find Whole "Turk Murphy"

won't stop on a card with Eddie Murphy's name on Turk Street, which the plain Find command would.

HyperCard offers a keyboard shortcut to get the Find Whole command into the Message Box (Figure 46-2). From the keyboard, you can type Command-Shift-F, which is simply a shifted version of the Command-F that brings up the plain Find command. Also, if you hold down the Shift key while choosing Find from the Go menu, the Message Box will also have the Find Whole command ready for you.

## *Auto Tab*

One common frustration among early HyperCard stack designers and users was the problem caused by pressing the Return key when the text pointer was on the last line of a field (Figure 46-3). Unlike the action in field-intensive programs like databases, HyperCard's Return key caused the text pointer to advance to the next line of the field, even if that line was not visible to the user. The pointer just seemed to disappear. The user had to know that only the Tab key advanced the pointer to the next field in the field order. And, because a HyperTalk programmer may have set up some action to take place upon closing the field (e.g., calculating a new total based on the figure just entered into a field), there had to be all kinds of warnings in the help screens

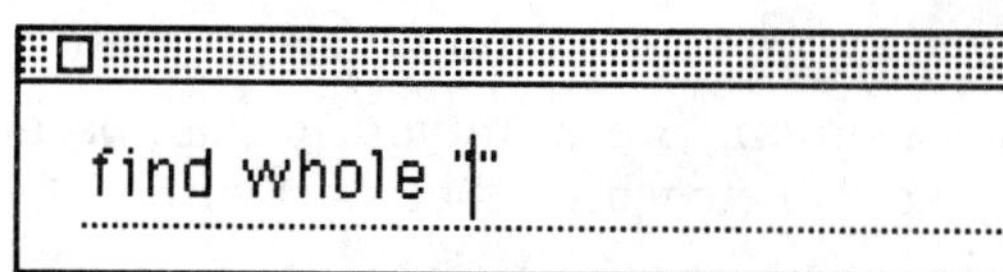


*Figure 46-2. Shift-Command-F writes the Find Whole command to the Message Box for you.*

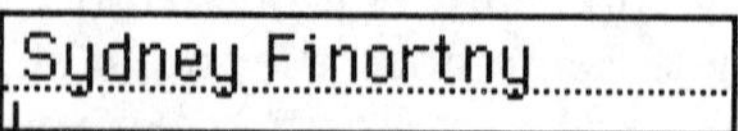


*Figure 46-3. Without AutoTab turned on, a press of the Return key at the end of a field causes the insertion pointer to advance to the next line, which may be out of view.*

and manual to press either the Tab or Enter keys, both of which officially closed the field.

HyperCard 1.2 adds a new property for fields that puts an end to that problem– provided the property is set for each field with HyperCard 1.2. That property is called Auto Tab, and it appears in the Field Info dialog box at the end of a list of other properties (Figure 46-4).

With Auto Tab turned on for a field, the user may enter information into a field. When the pointer is at the last visible line of any *non-scrolling* field, a press of the Return key advances the pointer to the next field in tabbing order. The important point is that the text pointer must be in the last visible line of the field. The field may still hold more characters than may fit within the visible area on the screen, but if you press the Return key with the pointer in the last visible line or below, the pointer will behave just as if you had pressed the Tab key. Therefore, if you type into a field, and the text wraps to the second line (in which case you won't see the text you're typing or the pointer), you may press Return to advance the pointer to the next field. The text you type below the visible line is stored safely in the field, but you won't be able to see it.

By restricting this Return key behavior to the last visible line of a field– defined as any line with more than one-half its text height visible

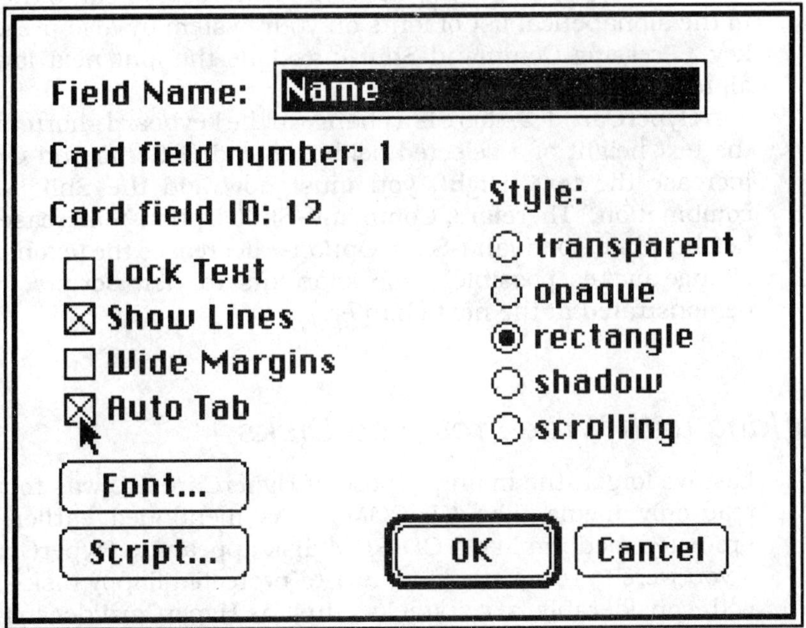


*Figure 46-4. The Auto Tab checkbox lets you engage the AutoTab property for any field.*

in the rectangle of the field—you may still press the Return key elsewhere in a multiple-lined field to create new lines, paragraphs, or empty lines. Moreover, because scrolling fields are often the repositories of indeterminant lengths of text, Auto Tab does not work in scrolling fields.

Turning on Auto Tab is very good practice for all one-line fields. Anyone used to working with a database will expect the Return key to advance the cursor to the next field. For multiple-lined fields, your decision to turn on Auto Tab will depend largely on the kind of information users are likely to enter into those fields. If you offer a five-line field, but most users will be entering a single line of information, the extra return characters entered into the field to force the cursor to the end of the field will be stored along with the text. That may not be desired if you perform some operations later on that text, such as exporting it.

## Keyboard Shortcut Change

HyperCard lets you adjust the text font and text height of a *selected* field from the keyboard. For instance, by holding down the Command and Shift keys, you can set the text font of a selected field to the next font in the alphabetical list of fonts on your system by also pressing the > key. Pressing Command-Shift-< assigns the font next lower in the alphabetical list.

In HyperCard 1.2, there is a change in the keyboard shortcut to adjust the text height of a selected field. Instead of Command-Option-> to increase the text height, you must now add the Shift key to the combination. Therefore, Command-Shift-Option-> increases the text height, while Command-Shift-Option-< decreases the text height. This change makes possible some shortcuts to view scripts, as will be demonstrated in the next chapter.

## Working with Write Protected Disks

Lest we forget, the main purpose of HyperCard 1.2 was to work with read-only media, like CD-ROMs. As mentioned earlier, a write-protected medium like a CD-ROM disk appears to HyperCard just as if you were to run a stack on a write-protected floppy disk—of course with considerably larger stacks. Just as HyperCard doesn't balk at a read-only CD-ROM, it no longer refuses to open a stack on a write-protected floppy disk or a stack on a hard disk that has been locked from the Finder.

*Figure 46-5. Whenever a stack is locked, the padlock icon appears to the right of the last menu title.*

Protect Stack:
Can't modify stack
Can't delete stack
Private Access
Set Password
Limit user level to:
Browsing
Typing
Painting
Authoring
Scripting
OK
Cancel

*Figure 46-6. The Protect Stack dialog box is where you manually lock a stack.*

You'll be able to recognize a write-protected stack immediately by looking in the menubar. A small padlock icon appears to the right of the last menu in the menubar (Figure 46-5). When you see that icon, you won't be able to add new cards to the stack or delete cards. Depending on how the stack was designed, you may be able to enter text into a field of one card, but that text won't be stored in the stack. In fact, the instant you go to another card in the stack, the text you typed will disappear.

There are so many fine points about working with write-protected stacks, that I've reserved Chapter 53 for an in-depth discussion of the subject. For now, however, just be aware that when the padlock appears in the menubar, changes you make to a card's fields or graphics won't be saved.

Also, you can artificially protect a stack from within HyperCard, even if the stack resides on a read-write medium, like a hard disk. The Protect Stack dialog (choose Protect Stack from the File menu) now offers a choice called "Can't modify stack," as shown in Figure 46-6. If you check this box, users can't accidentally create or delete objects such as cards, buttons, and fields. Nor will they be able to accidentally delete the stack. Stacks that are to be put out in open areas for many people to use should be protected in this manner.

The rest we'll save for Chapter 53. In the meantime, let's start looking at the new HyperTalk features in HyperCard 1.2.

# CHAPTER 47

# New HyperTalk Features

BEFORE DIVING HEADLONG INTO THE INDIVIDUAL COMMANDS, FUNCTIONS, AND PROPERTIES of HyperCard 1.2, we should spend some time with more global concerns for HyperTalk writers. Many of the improvements are tailored to making HyperTalk writing more convenient. Among the topics we'll cover here are a series of new object abbreviations, two new system messages, several new keyboard shortcuts to speed access to object scripts, enhancements to the way you can lock and unlock screens with visual effects, and a batch of odds and ends all stack developers should know about.

## *Abbreviations and Synonyms*

While most HyperTalk authors are familiar with the *bkgnd* abbreviation for the word *background*, HyperCard 1.2 comes with a large selection of even shorter abbreviations to speed script writing. One set offers shortcuts to referring to objects. These are:

| Abbreviation | Meaning |
|---|---|
| cd | card |
| cds | cards |
| bg | background |
| bgs | backgrounds |

| | |
|---|---|
| fld | field |
| flds | fields |
| btn | button |
| btns | buttons |

Use the singular of these abbreviations when referring to a single item, as in

```
go to cd "Preferences"
get the name of this bg
get fld "Name"
set hilite of btn "OK" to true
```

Use the plural forms of these abbreviations when referring to all objects of that type, as in

```
repeat with x = 1 to the number of cds
get the number of bg flds
```

While I'm not sure this system adds to the readability of scripts for HyperTalk newcomers trying to learn the language, these frequently used abbreviations are helpful for script writers. You are free to mix abbreviations with their full spellings, even in the same command line. Therefore, the command

```
get the number of background flds
```

works without a hitch.

You will welcome another group of new words if you've ever written scripts that involve time conversions. You may have found it awkward to refer to a singular second or tick in the plural. There were only seconds, secs, and ticks. Even one unit of those had to be addressed in the plural, as in

```
wait 1 seconds
```

Three new synonyms now allow correct English when specifying singular intervals:

second

sec

tick

These three are indeed true synonyms with their plural forms. They'll work even if the number specifying them is greater than one (e.g., 4 second). Use them interchangeably, or whichever way sounds best to you.

Another abbreviation allows you to refer to a picture with the shortcut:

pict

Since, as you'll learn in the next chapter, you can now hide and show the card or background picture, you might want to refer to the picture by its abbreviation, as in

```
show card pict
hide bg pict
```

One last synonym involves the painting tools. Recall that visual effects let you modify each effect by adding one of the four possible "color" adjectives: black, white, gray, and inverse. It seems that enough stack developers out there prefer to spell the color *gray* as *grey*. Therefore, you can use the two words interchangeably, as in

```
visual effect dissolve to gray
visual effect dissolve to grey
```

Webster's Dictionary and most spelling checkers won't mind either.

## *Two Old System Messages*

Now that more Macintosh users are typing on Macintosh SE and Macintosh II keyboards, two existing system messages, *controlKey* and *functionKey*, can play a more prominent role in stack design. The controlKey message is sent whenever the Control key is pressed in concert with another key. The functionKey message is for the Extended Keyboard, which includes a row of 15 function keys along the top. Pressing one of these keys sends the functionKey message. Both system messages are sent initially to the current card.

Both messages are sent with parameters. In the case of the controlKey message, the parameter is the ASCII code number for the character whose key is pressed along with the Control key. For example, if you type Control-a, the system message sent is

```
controlKey 97
```

because 97 is the ASCII value of a lowercase letter "a." Therefore, your handlers that trap for this message must also look for the character number. Here's a handler that lets you open up the stack, background, and card info dialog boxes by typing Control-s, -b, and -c, respectively:

```
on controlKey whichKey
    if whichKey is 98                -- "b"
    then doMenu "Bkgnd Info..."
    else if whichKey is 99           -- "c"
    then doMenu "Card Info..."
    else if whichKey is 115          -- "s"
    then doMenu "Stack Info..."
```

```
    pass controlKey
  end controlKey
```

The keyboard on the Macintosh Plus does not have a Control key nor any key that equates it in HyperCard's eyes. Assign processes to this system message that are optional, unless you know that all users of your stack will be using the new keyboards for the Mac SE and Mac II.

The functionKey message also sends a parameter along: the number of the function key, from 1 to 15. Here's a handler that lets function keys take the place of some HyperCard menu items:

```
on functionKey whichKey
   if whichKey < 6 then pass functionKey
   else if whichKey is 6 then doMenu "Delete Card"
   else if whichKey is 7 then doMenu "Compact Stack"
end functionKey
```

Remember, too, that function keys are available only on the Apple Extended Keyboard, which is not the most common keyboard. But if you use that keyboard, you can certainly program the function keys to do some utility work for your stack development.

## New System Messages

Two new system messages allow you to trap for the press of the Return and Enter keys whenever the text pointer is in a field or text in a field is selected. These messages are called *returnInField* and *enterInField*. For example, if you are typing text in a field and press the Return key, HyperCard sends a returnInField message to that field.

By being able to trap for these two messages, you can program very specific actions depending on which of these keys the user presses. In chapter 8, you'll see an example of how these two messages help a columnar arrangement of fields behave much like a group of Excel spreadsheet cells. A press of the Return key advances the cursor to the next cell, while a press of the Enter key officially "enters" the text into the cell, closing the field.

Importantly, with these two system messages, you can actually prevent a field from closing when these keys are pressed. Or, you can prevent these keys from doing anything. Let's look at some simple examples.

First, if you include a handler for either of these system messages, the normal action of these keys will not be known by HyperCard. For example, in the following field handler,

```
on returnInField
end returnInField
```

nothing whatsoever occurs in the stack when the Return key is pressed, even if the user is in a field whose Auto Tab property is set to true. Pressing the Return key sends the returnInField message. But by trapping it with this handler, that Return key press never makes its way up the hierarchy to HyperCard— the Auto Tab never gets the instruction to advance the text pointer. And so, with this two-line handler in a field, the user could press the Return key forever and never get any results from it. That also means that return characters don't make it into the field either. This is one way, I suppose, to make sure users type only one HyperCard line of text in a field (recall that a "line" is any string of text up to a return character, even if the text wraps to multiple lines in a field).

Second, if you want the Return or Enter key presses to go all the way to HyperCard after you've performed some other actions in the keys' handlers, you can pass the key's message at the end of the handler. Let's say that you have a long scrolling field into which the user enters names for a seminar registration. As you enter each name, you'd like to have HyperCard check it against the names you've already entered, making sure you don't enter duplicates. A handler to take care of that would look like this:

```
on returnInField
    get me                      -- the contents of the current field
    delete last line of it      -- remove the line just entered
    if last line of me is in it then
        answer "This is a duplicate."
        select last line of me -- selects line for retyping
    else pass returnInField  -- advance pointer to next line
end returnInField
```

This handler first puts a copy of the entire contents of the field into the It local variable and removes the last line— the one just entered— from the variable. In the if-then construction, the line just entered is compared against the copy of the field in the It variable. If the name is already in the variable, an answer dialog box alerts the user that the name is a duplicate. The line just entered is selected (this is a HyperCard 1.2 command, detailed in Chapter 49), making it easy to type a new name to replace the duplicate. But if the name is not a duplicate, the returnInField message passes up the HyperCard object hierarchy. When the message reaches HyperCard, it is interpreted as an unmodified press of the returnKey. In a scrolling field, that means that a return character is placed at the location of the text pointer.

In a non-scrolling field, whose Auto Tab property is set to true, if the returnInField message is unimpeded (i.e., there is no returnInField handler or the message is passed, as above), HyperCard then sends a

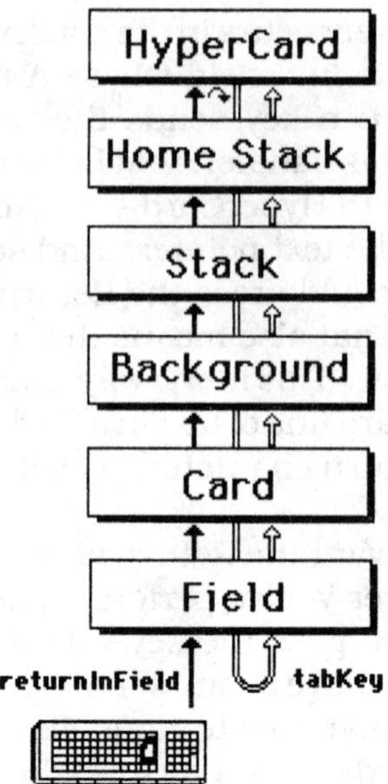


*Figure 47-1. The ReturnInField message, when it reaches HyperCard, triggers a TabKey message, which starts through the hierarchy again from the original field.*

tabKey message to the field when the text pointer is in the last visible line of the field. Let's follow this again. Let's say we have a single line field whose Auto Tab property is turned on. We know from earlier discussions that pressing the Return key in this field (when the text pointer is in the last visible line) will advance the pointer to the next field in tabbing sequence. But what is going on at the system message level is that first HyperCard sends a returnInField message to the field in response to the press of the Return key. If that returnInField message makes it all the way up the hierarchy to HyperCard, then HyperCard sends a tabKey message to that field. If the tabKey message makes its way up the hierarchy, then the pointer advances to the next field (Figure 47-1).

From a user interface standpoint, there are no formal guidelines as to what kind of action should occur with the press of the Return key versus the Enter key. Without such a guideline, things might get confusing for users of many stacks whose authors have different ideas about these keys' use. I believe, however, that it is a natural expectation that the Return key should advance the pointer to the next field in a sequence. You might then use the Enter key for some special operation that is unique to your stack, or, if there is nothing special required, let the enterInKey message pass to HyperCard to close fields.

## *Keyboard Shortcuts*

HyperCard 1.2 gives HyperTalk programmers much quicker access to object tools and object scripts, all with keyboard commands (or some with keyboard-and-mouse combinations). If you've done a lot of HyperTalk programming with previous versions, it may take awhile for some of these shortcuts to sink in so they come naturally. But once they do, your productivity as a programmer definitely increases. To help put the new shortcuts in perspective, I'll also list the shortcuts that were around from Day 1.0.1.

### CHOOSING TOOLS

You've always been able to return to the Browse tool from any other tool by typing Command-Tab. In fact, when you're perhaps the most distant from the Browse tool— using a Painting tool in the background editing mode under FatBits— Command-Tab brought you out of background editing mode and FatBits, as well as choosing the Browse tool.

New for HyperCard 1.2 are Command-Tab combinations that let you choose the Button and Field tools without having to show or choose the Tools tear-off palette. By holding down the Command key and pressing the Tab key twice quickly (inside about one-half second) you choose the Button tool. The Command key and three quick presses of the Tab key chooses the Field tool. Here's a summary table of these shortcuts:

| | |
|---|---|
| Command-Tab | Browse tool |
| Command-Tab-Tab | Button tool |
| Command-Tab-Tab-Tab | Field tool |

No matter which of these tools you're in, if you type the shortcut for another tool, you'll get there. You can go from the Button tool to Field tool, for instance, by typing Command-Tab-Tab-Tab, or from the Field tool to Button tool by typing Command-Tab-Tab.

## *Peeking at Objects*

A common practice for experienced HyperCard users when viewing a new stack is to immediately press the Command and Option keys to see where the buttons are. This is called *peeking* at buttons. The outline rectangles of all visible (i.e., not hidden) buttons appear on the screen as long as you keep those keys pressed.

You may now also peek at fields. When you hold down the Shift key in combination with the Command and Option keys, you see outlines of buttons and fields. You cannot isolate peeking of fields without also peeking at buttons. If a card has many button and field objects on it, you can get an idea of where only the fields are by holding down the Command and Option keys, and then pressing and releasing the Shift key. When the Shift key is down, you see field outlines; releasing the key causes the field outlines to disappear.

Peeking only lets you see where these objects are. You must still select a button or field with its respective tool to resize or move it, or double click on it to see its info dialog box.

## *Peeking at Scripts*

Prior to HyperCard 1.2, gaining access to an object's script was a tedious process at best, even with some of the shortcuts built in from the beginning. For instance, you could go to a stack script by holding down the Shift key while choosing Stack Info from the Objects menu. The same was true for background and card scripts. To get to a button or field script, however, you had to first choose the object's tool, and then Shift-double-click on the object whose script you wished to see. While all of these shortcuts were far better than going to the script by way of the object's info dialog box, there was enough inconsistency to make it difficult for many users to remember the shortcuts.

Now there is a new system of shortcuts that is much more consistent across the board. Apple calls this feature "peeking at scripts," but I see it simply as faster shortcuts to the scripts.

The foundation of this system is the combination of Command and Option keys, the same pair that lets you peek at the locations of buttons. When you hold down these keys, you can click on any button and immediately open up the Script Editor for that button— even when in the Browse tool (but not in the Field tool). To close the Script Editor, you can Command-Option-click (the I-beam cursor becomes the watch while the Command and Option keys are held down). You may also close the Script Editor by clicking the Cancel or OK buttons or by pressing the Enter key (the method I prefer). If you've made a change to the script and close the Script Editor by Command-Option-clicking, a dialog box asks whether you wish to save the changes you made (Figure 47-2).

To open the Script Editor for a field, you hold down the Command, Option and Shift keys to peek at all field locations, then click on the desired field. Command-Option-click (or Command-Option-Shift-click) closes the Script Editor.

There are even shortcuts to the scripts of cards, backgrounds and stacks. By holding down the Command and Option keys and then typing "c" for card, "b" for background or "s" for stack, you go immediately to those objects' scripts. Command-Option-click or Command-Option-any-key closes the Script Editor. These are wonderful time savers, and since all script shortcuts operate around the Command-Option key combo, they're much easier to remember.

When the Button tool is selected, you are restricted from peeking at field scripts, although you can still zip to card, background and stack scripts. When the Field tool is selected, you cannot zip to button scripts, but you can to all other objects.

To summarize, here is a helpful table:

| | |
|---|---|
| **From all object tools:** | |
| Command-Option-c | card script |
| Command-Option-b | bkgnd script |
| Command-Option-s | stack script |
| **From the Browse tool:** | |
| Command-Option-click (on a button) | button script |
| Shift-Command-Option-click (on a field) | field script |
| **From the Button tool:** | |
| Command-Option-click (on a button) | button script |
| **From the Field tool:** | |
| Shift-Command-Option-click (on a field) | field script |

If these shortcuts are new to you, I suggest working them into your stack development work flow gradually. Try to recognize when you are using less efficient methods and remind yourself of the shortcuts. Eventually, the shortcuts will become second nature, but you'll wish there were also shortcuts to getting to the info dialog boxes from the Browse tool. So far, there aren't.

*Figure 47-2. If you make a change to a script and close the Script Editor with the Command-Option-any-key shortcut, you'll be prompted to save or discard changes to the script.*

## *Testing for the HyperCard Version*

Because there are new features in HyperCard that require version 1.2 or later, it is critical that stacks employing those features know for certain that the user has 1.2 running. With each increase in HyperCard's functionality, it becomes even more important that your stacks use the Version function to make sure your users are up to speed with their HyperCard version.

The Version function has been around since the first release of HyperCard, but until the significant changes of 1.2, testing for the version was a moot point: a stack designed with 1.1 would work with 1.0.1 without any conflicts or missing commands.

If you are designing a stack for general consumption, you have to ask yourself whether the 1.2-specific features you're building into the stack are essential. If not, you can branch your scripts around those parts that require 1.2 whenever the user has versions less than 1.2.

This will work mostly for less critical parts of scripts, like visual effects. Since you can now unlock a locked screen in concert with a visual effect with 1.2, you can test for the HyperCard version before making that call. Such a test would look like this:

```
if the version < 1.2 then set lockScreen to false
else unlock screen with wipe left
```

Since versions prior to 1.2 would choke on the Unlock Screen command, you can't let HyperCard 1.0 or 1.1 see that statement. You can be assured, however, that even if the user later upgrades to a future release of HyperCard whose number is greater than 1.2, all previous commands will work. Bill Atkinson insists on that.

The more deeply you involve yourself with HyperCard 1.2's commands and functions, however, the less likely you'll be able to program your way around them. You'll add features that cannot be recreated in earlier versions and are essential to the stack's functionality. In such cases you should test for the version at the opening of the stack (i.e., in an openStack handler). If the version is less than 1.2, alert the user that he needs to upgrade his HyperCard, and then return the user to Home. Such a handler would look like this:

```
on openStack
    if the version < 1.2 then
        answer "Sorry, you need HyperCard 1.2 for this stack."
        go Home
    end if
end openStack
```

HyperCard 1.2 also now lets you test for the version of a stack. One value of this is to make sure your stack will keep pace with HyperCard's development. If the version of your stack is less than the version of HyperCard the user is running, then you can instruct HyperCard to compact the stack under the new HyperCard version. Chances are that your stack will take advantage of whatever performance improvements come with future HyperCard versions when compacted. This function is described fully in chapter 50.

## Locking and Unlocking Screens

You may lock and unlock screens by setting the lockScreen property to true or false. This has been true since HyperCard 1.0.1. In fact, in the course of a long handler, you are free to set the lockScreen property to true or false as often as you like. For example, you may want the user to see the current screen of a complex handler occasionally, but shield the user from some other operations which might only confuse the situation.

If you set lockScreen to true and then set it to false later, however, you can not take advantage of visual effects. Even if you set a visual effect and go to another card, setting lockScreen to false cancels the visual effect.

A new pair of commands let you take advantage of visual effects when unlocking the screen. The commands are

lock screen
unlock screen [with <visual effect>]

Actually, *lockScreen* and set *lockScreen* to true are interchangeable. You may use either one, no matter how you decide to unlock the screen.

The difference comes in unlocking the screen. If you use *unlock screen* instead of *set lockScreen* to false, you can also specify a single visual effect as a parameter. In Chapter 49, we give more details about these two commands, but they're important enough to single out here, because they may affect the way you design your stacks and links.

Some important changes were also implemented that affect what happens when the screen is locked by a handler. Several previously distracting screen items no longer reveal the "secret" that your handler is working feverishly behind the scenes. Here's what you can count on when you lock the screen:

- The HyperCard window title bar (visible when running HyperCard on large monitors) remains unchanged, even when a handler goes to other stacks. If the final destination is a different stack, the title bar changes when the handler unlocks the screen or the screen unlocks automatically at the end of the handler (at idle time).

- The menubar doesn't change, even if your handler chooses Painting tools.
- The tool and pattern tear-off palettes (if visible) don't change even when different tools and patterns are chosen.
- The cursor doesn't change to reflect changes in tools. You still have control over the cursor choice in a script after locking the screen.

These improvements make complex handlers more "transparent" to the user, as well as improving performance of tasks that involve changing tools and stacks.

## *Target and Me*

Before HyperCard 1.2, the words *target* and *me* referred strictly to objects, rather than their contents (in the case of fields). For example, the following handler

```
on closeField
   put the target
end closeField
```

puts the name of the field, not the contents of that field, into the Message Box. If you wanted to obtain the contents of the field by referring to the target, then you'd have to get the value of the target.

The reason you'd even bother with the target nomenclature doesn't become evident until you place a single closeField handler in a background to take care of the closing of several fields on the card. Instead of having the identical closeField handler in each field, a single handler in the background will trap all closeField messages initially sent to each field. You may then obtain the name of the field (via the target function) to identify which one closed. For example,

```
on closeField
   get the target
   if it contains "Amount" then recalc
end closeField
```

only recalculates (recalc is a custom handler elsewhere in the card, background or stack) when a field whose name contains the word "Amount" closes—is the initial target of the closeField message.

All this still holds true for HyperCard 1.2, but you may now have more direct access to the contents of the field, both retrieving its contents or putting something in it. The syntax is the word Target without the leading *the*. Target is a container. You can put its contents into another container, such as a field or variable. You can also put any text into that container.

But like the Target function, Target refers to the contents of the object that first received the system message. For instance, in a background closeField handler like this one:

```
on closeField
    put target into temp
    ...
end closeField
```

the text that goes into that local variable, temp, is the text from the field just closed. Working in the other direction, let's say you have a column of fields, each named "Amount" plus the number of the cell, as in "Amount 1," "Amount 2," and so on. If you wanted to make sure that all number entries are adjusted to dollars and cents, a single closeField handler in the card or background could take care of it all. Here it is:

```
on closeField
    get the target              -- the NAME of the target field
    if "Amount" is in it then -- do only for "Amount" fields
        set numberFormat to "0.00"
            add zero to target  -- the CONTENTS of the target field
      end if
      pass closeField
end closeField
```

Notice how you can treat Target just like a container, in this case the field that just closed. Adding zero to the contents of the field with numberFormat set to "0.00" formats the number in that field to two places to the right of the decimal.

Another word in the HyperTalk vocabulary gains similar powers: Me. Previously, you could use Me in an object's own handler to derive properties of the object, as in:

```
on mouseUp
    set the hilite of me to not the hilite of me
end mouseUp
```

This handler toggles the hilite property of a button with each click of that button. The handler, however, must be in the object's own script. Since Me refers to the object in which the handler appears, placing the above handler anywhere but in a button script would be meaningless.

For fields, however, you may now use Me as a container that holds the contents of the field. For example, if a user is supposed to enter a date into a field on a card, you may want to make sure all dates are stored in that field in a particular date format. To guarantee that, and then to lock that field, you might use the following handler:

```
on closeField
    convert me to long date          -- the CONTENTS
    set the lockText of me to true  -- the OBJECT
end closeField
```

In this case, Me (without the "of") refers to the contents of the field—the very field in which this handler is located. You can still refer to the object to get or set properties of that object, but the syntax is

set the <property> OF me to <setting>.

In the last closeField handler, you could have also used Target instead of Me in both cases. In an object's own handler, Target and Me are interchangeable. Generally, I use the Target syntax in handlers that might intercept messages from several related objects, while using Me in an object's own handlers. Reading aloud a script of an object in which there are references to itself or its contents makes more sense with Me than with the Target syntax. Wherever possible, I prefer scripts that make sense reading them aloud.

## *Other Improvements*

This last section is a grab bag of improvements that HyperCard programmers should know about. Two of them are performance improvements when navigating through a stack via HyperTalk.

HyperCard 1.2 is faster than its predecessors when you specify going to a particular card ID number. You may now also safely specify going to the first, last, next or any card of a particular background name and expect fast performance. Also sped up is the transition time switching in and out of the Painting tools.

On the subject of fields, since HyperCard 1.2 lets you select text in fields from HyperTalk, you should be aware of the case in which text is selected in a locked field. This could happen in a field in which the mouse selects a line of text for further action. Unlike text selections in unlocked fields, these are impervious to erasure by typing fresh text from the keyboard. If the field is locked, the selected text in a locked field is deselected when you press a key, and the typed text goes into the Message Box. If text is selected in the locked field and you choose Paste Text from the Edit menu, the selection is unchanged.

And speaking of the selection— the container holding the contents of selected text— it may now hold 30,000 characters, like any container.

One last field-related point has to do with clicking the text cursor below the last line of text in a field. Unlike most text editors you're probably familiar with, HyperCard automatically places extra carriage return characters between the last line of text and the line at which you click the cursor. With HyperCard 1.2, however, holding the Shift key down when clicking the I-beam cursor below text in a field will cause the flashing text insertion pointer to rest after the last character in the field. If the field is empty, the text insertion pointer stays at the top left corner of the field.

Behavior is slightly different, however, if there is text in the field and you click the mouse above the last line of the field with the Shift key down. This action selects all text between the last character of the field and the click location.

Here are the last odds and ends of enhancements:

- Using HyperCard with MultiFinder is now better controlled when your HyperCard script opens another application. If that application is already open under MultiFinder, HyperCard simply switches to the application, rather than alerting you that the application is already open.
- If the HyperCard message "Can't understand end of line" drove you crazy, that was because the Message Box was empty and you pressed either the Return or Enter keys. HyperCard was receiving only an end-of-line characters as a message, and nothing more. In HyperCard 1.2, HyperCard no longer complains when the Message Box is empty or there are only spaces in the box.
- When the Painting tools are selected, the File menu lets you access the New Stack, Open Stack, and Save a Copy menu items in addition to the Import Paint, Export Paint, and Quit HyperCard items.

## *Bug Fixes in HyperCard 1.2*

In addition to the new features, there are several bugs from previous versions that have been fixed in 1.2. Many of the repairs are not readily apparent to most users. Those that are worth noting are:

- When you delete a card, HyperCard does not send a closeCard message to the deleted card before it disappears, nor does it send an openCard message to the card that appears as a result of the deletion.
- A text selection in one field (locked or unlocked) is preserved intact when you click on a locked field elsewhere on the card. As before, a text selection is not preserved when you click on the

card (i.e., not on a field or button) or on a button whose Autohilite property is set to true.

- Previously, if a transparent part of a picture image overlapped a text field, that field would not print in a laser font on a LaserWriter. Instead, the text printed at the same resolution as bit-mapped text. That is no longer the case with HyperCard 1.2. An unobstructed text field prints with laser fonts on a LaserWriter.
- Problems with skipped pages and oddly wrapped data in mailing labels from HyperCard's Print Report selection has been reportedly repaired for the ImageWriter and LaserWriter.
- Tabbing to a field containing text selects the entire content of the field, up to the field's limit of 30,000 characters.
- The stack size, as reported in the Stack Info dialog box now accurately displays the size of the entire file, including resource fork.
- When creating a new stack and the Copy Current Background option is not checked, the new stack does not automatically receive the resources of the original stack. In other words, the new stack is completely bare.
- XCMD and XFCN authors may now create global HyperTalk variables by sending the setGlobal command from their XCMD code.

## XCMD Enhancements

This section is for those HyperTalk stack authors who also write external commands and functions (XCMDs and XFCNs). If these terms are unfamiliar to you, consult chapter 54.

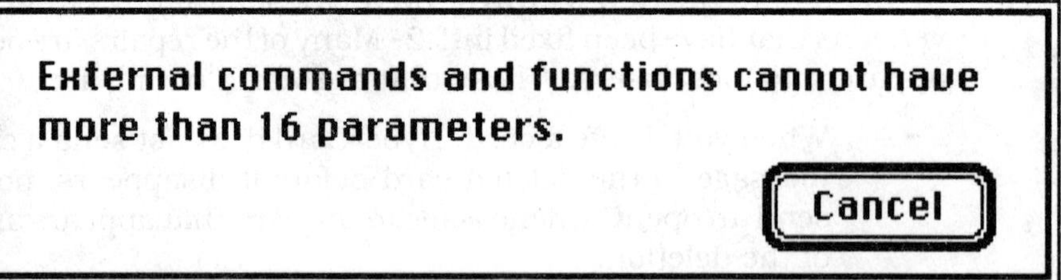


*Figure 47-3. This message appears if you try to send too many parameters to an XCMD or XFCN.*

HyperCard 1.2 offers several changes that make communications between HyperCard and XCMDs more robust. For instance, if you try calling an XCMD with more than 16 parameters (16 is the limit), you will receive a dialog box message to that effect (Figure 47-3). In the XCMD parameter block, outArgs[1] will be NIL if it is not a valid handle. Your XCMD does not have to check for a result of xresFail to determine if the handle is valid.

Also new is that XCMD-related errors do not present error messages to the user. It is up to the XCMD author to check for a result of xresFail after callbacks to HyperCard and handle any errors within the XCMD. Even after an error occurs, XCMDs will now continue to make additional callbacks to HyperCard without interruption.

As you can see, a lot of work went into many parts of HyperCard for the 1.2 release. But there's still much more.

CHAPTER 48

# HyperTalk Expressions

BEFORE WE GET TO THE HYPERTALK COMMANDS UPDATE, LET'S LOOK INTO A TERM THAT you will see more and more often when book and magazine article authors refer to parameters of HyperTalk commands and functions: *expression.*

## *Everyday Expressions*

We use expressions in our daily language without thinking twice. For example, if we say "I'm going to watch television," the last word, "television" is understood to be the device that plucks moving pictures and sound out of the ether. We use the word "television" as an expression to stand in for the meaning of perhaps a more formal or complete definition of that device. By common use, "television" has become a standard expression for that device, and we understand what that word means when we hear it.

Quite often, we use other expressions to refer to that television. Consider the following:

I'm going to watch *TV.*
I'm going to watch *`1tube.*
I'm going to watch *the idiot box.*

All three of those sentences end with different expressions (or symbols, or representations) for the same thing. That is, when we hear those three expressions, we instantly convert them in our minds to whatever definition or perception of television we have stored in there. The point is, however, that "television," "TV," "the tube," and "the idiot box," are all *valid expressions* for that picture-and-sound device.

If you're walking toward your TV set as if to turn it on, and then say

I'm going to watch the telephone,

anyone in the room who sees and hears that combination will say, "What?" That's because their expectation was for you to produce some expression for the TV set. Instead, you said "the telephone," which is not a valid expression for that picture-and-sound device. Therefore, while the sentence "I'm going to watch the telephone" is good and proper English, it doesn't make any sense in the context of your heading toward the one-eyed monster (another valid expression). What was expected was a valid television expression. "Boob tube" is a valid television expression, "tree" is not.

## Expressions in HyperTalk

HyperTalk commands and functions often expect expressions of certain kinds. The type of expression depends on the command. For instance, look at the variations of the Go command:

go to <card expression>
go to <bkgnd expression>
go to <card expression> of <bkgnd expression>
go to <stack expression>
go to <card expression> of <stack expression>
go to <bkgnd expression> of <stack expression>
go to <card expression> of <bkgnd expression> of <stack expression>

A card expression is a description that can be interpreted as a card. Some literal card expressions are:

first card
card 25
card id 5039
card "Preferences"

Because a card can be summoned by its number (in order of cards in the stack), its unique ID number, or its name, there are many valid expressions for cards. But notice that all have one element in common: the word "card." That word lets HyperCard distinguish this from other types of expressions. When the word "card" is in the expression, then HyperCard will accept a number, ID number (along with the word "id"), or name. Similarly, when the expression contains the words "card id," HyperCard expects the next "word" to be a valid ID number. By valid, I don't necessarily mean an ID number of a real card, but a number that HyperCard would accept as an ID number worth looking for. In other words, if you give the command

```
go to card id "Preferences"
```

HyperCard will reply in an dialog box that it doesn't understand the arguments to the Go command. That's the same as the other person in your TV room saying, "What?" "Card id 'Preferences'" is an invalid card expression.

## *Evaluating Expressions*

Now, HyperCard is also smart enough to know that you may offer it valid expressions in other forms. In the following repeat loop,

```
repeat with x = 1 to 10
    go to card x
end repeat
```

the value of x will be different each time through the loop. But each time through the loop, the combination of "card" and the value of x comprise a valid card expression. In other words, when HyperCard sees a variable or container as part of an expression, it tries to evaluate the variable or container to see if it holds a piece of the puzzle making up a valid expression. In the repeat loop above, HyperCard evaluates the "x" variable each time through the loop, substituting its value for the variable, and then piecing it together with the rest of the arguments. The first time through the loop, it understands "card x" to be "card 1," a valid card expression.

You've seen HyperCard evaluate expressions many times before if you've ever typed some arithmetic into the Message Box or typed the name of a global variable into the Message Box to see its contents. When you type

```
4 * 5
```

into the Message Box and press Return, HyperCard automatically tries to evaluate what's there. In this case, it comes up with 20.

As for evaluating a variable, the Message Box is the place for that as well. When you start up HyperCard, part of its start up routine is to fetch the path names in the Stacks, Documents, and Applications cards of the Home stack. Those path names are maintained in separate global variables all the time you're in HyperCard. If you type the global variable "stacks" into the Message Box, you'll see the first line of that variable's contents (the Message Box is capable of displaying only one line at a time). What's going on is that HyperCard tries to evaluate that word, stacks. Doing so produces its contents, or at least as much as can be viewed there.

An even more bizarre-looking extension of these principles involves storing a list of card IDs in a field. Each card ID is stored on its own line in the field (let's call it a field named "linkList"), and refers to a card that is linked in some way to the current card. When you click on one button, it is supposed to zip you to the card whose ID is located in the first line of that field; a second button zips you to the card referred to in the second line; and so on. The contents of the field would look like this:

```
card id 4039
card id 1029
card id 1492
```

The script for the button that takes you to the first linked card would be

```
on mouseUp
   go to line 1 of field "linkList"
end mouseUp
```

At first glance, it looks quite strange to try to go to a line of a field. But HyperTalk is tolerant of strange behavior. It first tries to evaluate the "line 1 of field 'linkList'" expression. In a blinding flash, it discovers that the expression evaluates to "card id 4039," a valid card expression. Therefore, the Go command in the mouseUp handler is valid, and HyperCard tries to take you to card id 4039.

Just because you give HyperCard a valid expression doesn't mean that it will be successful in carrying out the command. For instance, if there were no card with the id 4039 in the stack, HyperCard would first accept the command as valid (i.e., there are no errors in the syntax) and do its best to carry out the command, but you'd receive a "No such card" message in return.

## *Expression Types*

HyperTalk's commands and functions expect many different kinds of expressions. How they're defined (e.g., *card expression*) tells you what kind of arguments they must be. A background expression must evaluate to something that consists of the word "background" (or synonym) and a number, ID number, or name. A stack expression must evaluate to something that consists of a stack name (the word "stack" is optional, because if HyperTalk encounters a name alone in an argument, it assumes "stack"). A numeric expression must evaluate to a number, while a string expression evaluates to any text.

A Boolean expression is either "true" or "false." Therefore you might see syntax for an if-then construction like this:

if <Boolean expression> then <statement>

which means that the expression must evaluate to "true" or "false." Comparison operations (e.g., $5 \geq 3$) evaluate to "true" or "false," so they are the most common types of expressions used in if-then constructions.

## ANY OLD EXPRESSION

The Get command will accept any expression. If you say

get 5

HyperCard places 5 into It. In cases in which a command would require a number as an argument, the argument would have to be a numeric expression (if the number had to be an integer, the argument would have to be an integer expression). But since Get takes anything you give it and places that "stuff" in It, the syntax for that command is

get <expression>

Some expressions will accept other kinds of expressions as valid. A case in point is the container expression. A container, you'll recall, is any variable, field, selection, Target, Me, or the Message Box. Therefore, a container expression might also be a valid field expression or variable expression. For instance, the Put command has this syntax:

put <expression> into <container expression>

That means you can put virtually anything (a number, a text string, a field's contents) into any container. Thus, the statement

put "Bill" into field "Name"

has valid expression and container expression arguments. But notice that the container expression, field "Name," is also a valid field expression. In other words, a container expression is a broad category that encompasses several different kinds of expressions.

## CHUNK EXPRESSIONS

One of those expressions under the container heading is the *chunk expression*. As noted in the *Handbook*, a chunk is a specific section of text in a field. It may be a character, word, item, or line inside a field, or a range of characters, words, items, or lines inside a field.

If you say

put "Minnesota" into line 3 of field "Address"

HyperCard puts that state name into a specific location in the field. "Line 3" is a chunk expression, indicating the precise spot within the "Address" field. You may be much more specific, of course. Here are some examples of chunk expressions for field "Address"

word 3 of field "Address"
word 3 of line 2 of field "Address"
last word of line 1 of field "Address"
character 10 of word 3 of line 2 of field "Address"
item 1 of line 3 of field "Address"

To specify a range of characters, words, lines, or items within a field, you first specify the type of chunk you're singling out, and then the numbers of the beginning and ending chunk, separated by the word "to." Here are some examples:

char 1 to 5 of field "Address"
item 3 to 10 of line 3 of field "Address"
word 2 to 3 of line 2 of field "Address"
line 1 to 5 of field "Address"

Notice that you don't repeat the type of chunk for the second number. Also, the syntax won't allow you to mix chunk types when specifying a range. "Char 1 to word 3 of field 'Address'" is not valid. Nor is "word 3 to last" valid, because chunk expressions expect integer numbers specifying the ranges. But, following HyperTalk's efforts to evaluate things, if you assign an integer to a variable, you may use that variable as one of the range values in a chunk. Thus, the syntax for a chunk expression is

char | word | line | item <integer expression>
[to <integer expression>]

with the latter integer expression optional unless you're specifying a range.

Getting back to container expressions, you may use chunk expressions within container expressions. Therefore, while a container expression may be a field expression, that field expression may be modified by a preceding chunk expression, as in

put "hello" into line 4 of field "Greeting"

HyperTalk evaluates "line 4 of field 'Greeting'" as a valid container. And so, the combination of the chunk and field expressions comprise a valid container expression.

Here is a list of common expressions in HyperTalk syntax, plus one or more examples of each:

| <u>Expression Type</u> | *<u>Example</u>* |
|---|---|
| window | card window<br>tool window |
| stack | "Home"<br>stack "Home" |
| background | background 3<br>background "Help" |
| card | card id 5023<br>any card |
| button | card button "OK"<br>button id 42<br>bkgnd button 3 |
| field | card field "Date"<br>bkgnd field 1<br>field id 52 |
| chunk | word 5<br>item 3 to 6<br>line 1 to 5<br>last word of line 1<br>char 1 of word 2 of item 3 of line 4 |
| string | "Hello"<br>field 1 (which contains "Hello") |
| numeric | 10<br>x (variable with the value of 4.04)<br>pi |
| integer | 10<br>x (variable with the value of 4) |
| date | "12/25/88"<br>the long date (HyperCard function)<br>field "Date" (which contains "Sun, Dec 25, 1988") |
| container | x (variable with any value in it)<br>field "Name"<br>it<br>msg (the Message Box)<br>the selection (HyperCard function)<br>line 3 of field "Name"<br>userName (global variable) |

## *Expression Notation*

In the HyperTalk command descriptions in the next few chapters and in the revised HyperTalk Reference in Appendix B, expression names are used in argument designations whenever the argument is general enough to encompass a wide range of arguments. For example, the Ask command syntax is truly:

ask <string expression> [with <string expression>]

But when you're searching for a command and how to use it, the entry will make more sense if the purpose of the string expressions is more concrete, as in

ask <question> [with <reply>]

This entry is more likely to jog your memory about the makeup of arguments to the command.

Other entries, however, are so generic in their argument specifications, that the expression name is most appropriate, as in

select <button expression>

because any valid button expression works here.

## *"Do" and Expressions*

Most of the time, HyperTalk makes a single pass on an expression to evaluate it before passing the entire statement to HyperCard. There are instances, however, in which the expression is actually two evaluations distant from its most reduced form.

For example, one of the new HyperTalk functions, the FoundChunk, returns a chunk expression defining the characters contained within the rectangle following a successful Find command. But if you try to put some text "into the foundChunk," HyperTalk claims not to understand the arguments specifying the destination container of the Put command. What's happening is that HyperTalk evaluates the FoundChunk function on its one-and-only pass through the Put statement line. The result of that evaluation— a chunk expression— is not reduced enough for HyperCard to accept it as a valid container. It must be evaluated once more before putting it together with the Put command.

To force a preliminary evaluation of the expression in this case, you can assemble the Put command after the Do keyword, like this:

```
do "put hello into" && the foundChunk
```

With the FoundChunk function outside of quote marks, HyperTalk will evaluate it to a chunk expression while concatenating the expression to the Put command. Now the Put command has a valid container argument—a real chunk expression—which can be evaluated to its base value for HyperCard to carry through. Thus, when you are told over and over that an argument is not acceptable, even though you think it should be, look at the possible need to doubly evaluate the expression with the help of this Do keyword construction.

# CHAPTER 49

# HyperTalk Commands Update

THIS CHAPTER FEATURES ALL THE COMMANDS THAT ARE NEW TO HYPERTALK FOR HyperCard 1.2, as well as two commands that are not be explained fully in the *Handbook*. Let's start with the two commands that have been in HyperCard since the beginning, followed by several new commands.

## exit to HyperCard

**PURPOSE:** Stops all HyperTalk handler execution.

**WHEN TO USE IT:** This command is a variation on the Exit command that you frequently use in if-then and repeat constructions. In the case of an if-then construction, you may wish to stop the handler from going any further if a certain condition is met. For instance, if you wish to exit the handler if a reply to an Ask dialog box is empty, the construction would be like this:

```
on mouseUp
    ask "Export text to what file?"
    if it is empty
    then exit mouseUp   -- exit the handler now!
    else
        [statements to export the data]
    end if
end mouseUp
```

But what happens when one handler calls another handler? If you exit the second handler in the way just shown, then execution returns to the first handler. Let's say there is one main handler that calls three custom handlers, each of which is a distinct module of a long, involved process:

```
on mouseUp
    doFirst
    doSecond
    doThird
end mouseUp

on doFirst
    ask "Export text to what file?'
    if it is empty
        then exit doFirst
        else ...
    end if
end doFirst
```

If the Ask dialog box of the doFirst handler is not filled in, then execution halts in that handler, but the original mouseUp handler is still in force. Execution continues to the doSecond handler. That may be fine if that's how you want your handlers to work. But if the cancellation of the Ask dialog should stop the entire sequence, you must change the Exit doFirst statement to Exit to HyperCard to this:

```
on doFirst
    ask "Export text to what file?'
    if it is empty
        then exit to HyperCard  -- quits the whole shebang
        else ...
    end if
end doFirst
```

The instant you exit to HyperCard, any pending handlers cease to be. You're back at an idle state.

This command would be employed only in control structures—if-then-else and repeat constructions. Anywhere you might use an Exit <handler> statement, you could use Exit to HyperCard. You can also use this command as a debugging tool, since you can plug this command anywhere inside a handler (even outside a control structure) to stop the handler's execution and check the status of your variables, fields, and so on.

**Parameters:** There are no parameters to this command, although technically, "to HyperCard" is an argument to the plain Exit command.

**Examples:** See above.

**You Try It:** To prove to yourself that this command works as advertised, set up these two simple handlers in a card script of a blank Address stack card:

```
on mouseUp
    doBranch
    put "I made it back."
end mouseUp

on doBranch
    answer "Should I go back?" with "No" or "OK"
    if it is "No" then exit to HyperCard
end doBranch
```

Click anywhere on the card other than on a field or button. When you click the OK button, execution returns to the mouseUp handler, otherwise, execution stops with the Exit to HyperCard statement.

## reset paint

**Purpose:** To return all Paint properties to their original states (i.e., their states when you start up HyperCard).

**When to Use It:** If your scripts have been accessing the painting tools and changing the settings of any of the 14 properties, you may wish to reset all the properties in one command so that the default values are ready again for your next time at the tools, either from a script or manually. This command takes care of all 14 in an instant.

The default settings of the painting properties are:

| Property | Default Setting |
|---|---|
| brush | 8 (small circle) |
| centered | false |
| filled | false |
| grid | false |
| lineSize | 1 (single pixel thickness) |
| multiple | false |
| multiSpace | 1 |
| pattern | 12 (black) |
| polySides | 4 (square) |
| textAlign | left |
| textFont | Geneva |
| textHeight | 16 |
| textSize | 12 |
| textStyle | plain |

Generally speaking, it is good practice to reset the painting properties after adjusting them in a script.

**Parameters:** There are no parameters to this command.

**Examples:** Since this is a simple statement with no parameters, an example is hardly necessary.

**You Try It:** In any stack tear off the Tools and Patterns palettes. Select some pattern other than black. Then pull down the Options menu and turn on Grid, Draw Filled, Draw Centered, and Draw Multiple. The shape tools in the Tools palette will be shaded to show you that Draw Filled is turned on. Double click on the Line tool to bring up the Line Size dialog. Choose the rightmost, fattest line thickness. When that dialog closes, you'll see that the line tool cursor is now the same thickness as the line size selected.

Show the Message Box and, after clicking the cursor in the Message Box, type

Reset Paint

but don't press Return quite yet. Make sure you can see the line tool cursor. Then press the Return key while watching the screen closely. In a flash, the pattern returns to black, the line thickness to 1, and the filled shapes return to their original, empty selves. A check of other settings will reveal that they, too, are back to normal.

## select <button expression> | <field expression> | me | target

**Purpose:** To select a button or field from within a HyperTalk script.

**When to Use It:** While properties of buttons and fields may be retrieved or set with the Browse tool in force, there are some actions that simply require that the object be selected. For instance, if you wish to delete a button by hand, you must click the desired button with the Button tool to select it and then choose Cut Button or Clear Button from the Edit menu or press the Delete key.

This version of the Select command allows you to perform the same action within a HyperTalk script as choosing the Field or Button tool, and then clicking the desired object to select it ready for deleting, copying, or dragging. After the command is given, the object's tool remains selected in the Tool palette, even if the palette is not showing.

When copying the object, bear in mind that the exact wording of the Copy choice in the Edit menu depends on which type of object is currently selected. If you select a field, the menu item is Copy Field. Any DoMenu command must be identical in wording to the current state of the menu. Therefore, the corresponding menu command would be

```
doMenu "Copy Field"
```

With the field in the clipboard, you will then have to be specific in the wording of the DoMenu Paste command as well (doMenu "Paste Field"). An alternate, which obviates the need to be specific about copying and pasting objects, is to give the command

```
type "c" with commandKey
```

or

```
type "v" with commandKey
```

which are the HyperTalk equivalents for the keyboard shortcuts for copying and pasting.

**PARAMETERS:** Any field or button expression may be used as arguments to the Select command. If you are deleting a series of objects, you may do so in a Repeat With loop, as in

```
on getRidOfFields
    repeat with x = the number of bkgnd fields down to 1
        select bkgnd field x
        doMenu "Clear Field"
    end repeat
end getRidOfFields
```

Note that the counting variable inside the repeat loop works backwards. If you counted from 1 to the number of fields, you would miss every other field: after deleting field 1, field 2 becomes field 1, yet the x counting variable would be 2 the second time through the loop.

In a field or button object's own script, a handler may select the object (either a field or button) with the

```
select me
```

statement. This may seem a bit inconsistent with the concept that "me" by itself usually refers to the contents (of a field object). But, unless told specifically otherwise (see next version of the Select command), HyperCard expects a field or button object as a parameter, and will do everything possible to derive such information from the argument. Select Me only works when the object is a button or field.

Select Target is also another way to select a field or button, provided that object has been the recipient of the message whose handler contains the Select Target statement. Thus, a card or background handler might look like this:

```
on closeField
    if the shiftKey is down then
```

```
            select target       -- or "select the target"
            doMenu "Copy Field"
        end if
    on closeField.
```

Provided no field trapped the closeField handler earlier in the hierarchy, this handler would select the field originally receiving the closeField target.

**Examples:**

```
select field "Name"
select card field 1
select field id 29
select bkgnd button id 5
select card button "OK"
```

**You Try It:** Go to the Address stack, and tear off the Tools palette. Type the following lines into the Message Box one at a time, and watch what happens to the Tools palette and to the objects in the card.

```
choose browse tool  -- make sure we're at the top
select field 1
select field 3
select bkgnd button "Return"
select bkgnd button 4
```

## select

[ before | after ] text of <field expression>
[ before | after ] <chunk expression> of <field expression>
empty

**Purpose:** To select text inside a field from within a HyperTalk script.

**When to Use It:** While the other version of the Select command selected objects with their respective object tools, this version concerns itself with the text inside a field. From a HyperTalk script, you may select text within any field (or the Message Box, as it turns out).

This is a powerful command for use with HyperTalk-created lists that you can select with the mouse. In fact, this application is so valuable, that it will be described in detail in chapter 8, along with a companion group of functions that reveal information about selected text in a field.

Another application, however, might be in a handler that tests for the data input in a field. If the input is not of the right type or in the desired range (as tested by your HyperTalk script), the text in the field is selected so that the user may immediately type in a new entry. Such a handler would look like this:

```
on closeField
    if the length of me is not 4 then
        answer "Four digits are required."
        select the text of me
    end if
end closeField
```

This command also allows you to place the text insertion pointer anywhere you wish within a field from a HyperTalk handler. A popular request is to place the text pointer at the end of a field, no matter how much text (if any) is in the field— this positions the pointer so that the user just begins typing to append text to the field. The version,

```
select after the text of field "Entry"
```

does just that. You may place the insertion pointer not only before and after the entire text, but anywhere inside a chunk expression, such as

```
select after word 3 of line 2 of field "Entry"
```

This places the insertion pointer immediately after the last character of the designated word. To place the pointer immediately in front of the first character of the next word, the command would be

```
select before word 4 of line 2 of field "Entry"
```

Chunk expressions, you'll recall, may also indicate a range of characters, words, lines, or items. Selecting a range of text by HyperTalk is the same as dragging the text cursor across those characters, words, lines, or items. Thus,

```
select line 2 to 3 of field "Address"
```

leaves the first line and any line from 4 onward untouched. Only the second and third lines are selected.

Once text is selected, you may type manually or from HyperTalk (with the Type command) to replace that selected text. Using the Type command is recommended only when you wish the user to see the equivalent of someone typing character by character (albeit speedily). To replace the selected text most quickly, use the Put command and the Selection function (see chapter 50).

You may de-select any selected text by using the Select Empty command. This command also removes the flashing text insertion pointer from a field. If the content of a field has changed since the insertion pointer went into that field, Select Empty closes the field (i.e., sends a closeField message to the field).

**PARAMETERS:** Any field expression is a valid argument. Notice that if you don't specify a chunk expression, you must include the phrase "text of" to signify to HyperCard that you mean the Select Text variety of the

Select command. Ignoring the phrase will cause HyperCard to select the field with the Field tool, not the field's contents. If you specify a chunk expression, however, HyperCard is smart enough to recognize that you mean text—that's the only thing a chunk expression can mean.

The "before" or "after" modifiers are optional, and depend on where you wish to place the text insertion pointer relative to other text—either text of the complete field or a chunk of a field.

**Examples:**

select text of field "Name"
select after text of field id 20
select before word 3 of line 2 of field 1
select item 4 of field "List"
select word 1 to 3 of field "Information"
select line 3 of the target
select after text of me

**You Try It:** Go to a fresh Address stack card. Enter five lines of information into the first field (put a comma somewhere within the five lines). Then type the following commands into the Message Box. Between each command, deselect the selection by clicking on the background picture, someplace outside the field. If you type a command and accidentally delete the text in the field, immediately choose Undo from the Edit menu (or type Command-Z).

select field 1 -- selects the field
select text of field 1
select item 1 of field 1
select word 10 of field 1
select word 1 to 5 of field 1
select after field 1 -- invalid argument
select after first word of field 1
select before second word of field 1
select text of msg

## hide

card | background picture
picture of <card expression> | <background expression>

## show

card | background picture
picture of <card expression> | <background expression>

**Purpose:** To hide or show picture layers.

**When to Use It:** In addition to hiding and showing fields, buttons, and windows, you may also hide and show the picture layers of either the card or background domain.

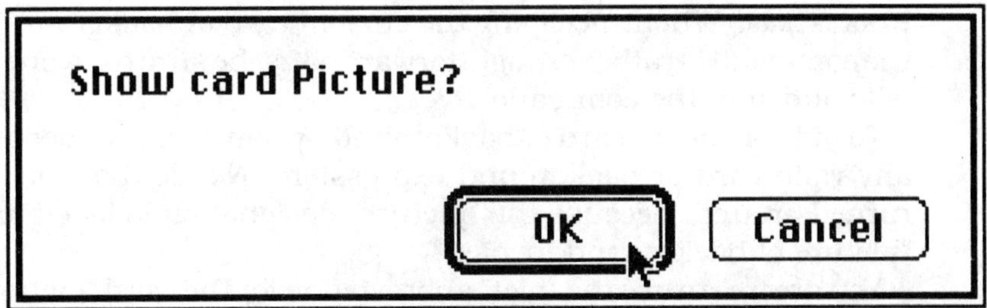


*Figure 49-1. Trying to edit a hidden picture layer brings up this message.*

The difference between the two versions of each command is centered around whether the picture is in the current card/background or some other card/background. Therefore, you may hide (or show) the current card picture, the current background picture, the card picture of some other card in the same stack, or the background picture of another background in the same stack. You may not hide or show the picture in a different stack without first going to that stack.

If you hide a picture and then attempt to draw with one of the painting tools in that picture's domain, you will be prompted with a dialog that asks whether you wish to show that picture first (Figure 49-1). In other words, you may not edit a picture unless it is visible.

Some interesting visual techniques are possible with the hiding and showing of pictures. For instance, you may flash one picture atop another all on one card. In concert with Lock Screen, Unlock Screen, and visual effects, you can give the impression that a card graphic is dissolving on and off. Here's how such a handler might look:

```
on openCard
    repeat 3 times
        lock screen
        hide card picture
        unlock screen with dissolve
        wait 2 seconds
        lock screen
        show card picture
        unlock screen with dissolve
        wait 2 seconds
    end repeat
end openCard
```

If the card picture includes a drop shadow on its objects, the flashing picture can appear to overlay the background picture with a three-dimensional look to it.

**Parameters:** When specifying the current card or background picture, the command is rather straightforward. Just be sure the word "picture" is included in the command.

To hide or show a card or background by name (or number or ID), use any valid card or background expression. Notice that the syntax is turned around, because the "picture" designation is listed first, as in "picture of background Invoice."

You are free to use the "pict" abbreviation for the word "picture" in any of these commands.

**Examples:**

show card picture
hide bg pict
show picture of first card
show picture of bkgnd "Entries"
hide picture of card "Introduction"

**You Try It:** Create a new card in the Address stack and draw some lines or shapes in the card picture layer. Then type the following commands into the Message Box, and observe the results.

hide card picture
show card picture
hide bg picture
show bg picture
hide bkgd picture of card "File Card"
show bg pict

When you have finished, you may delete the card or erase the card picture with the Eraser tool.

## lock screen
## unlock screen [with <visual effect> [<speed>] [to <color>]]

**Purpose:** To lock and unlock a screen, especially when visual effects are desired when unlocking the screen.

**When to Use It:** These commands are alternate ways of setting the lockScreen property. The value of this version, however, is that you may unlock a screen in concert with a visual effect– something you cannot do when you "set the lockScreen to false." In fact, the "Set" version ignores all pending visual effects, and they are all flushed from the queue after the handler ends, even if they were not used.

The syntax of these command versions seems more natural than setting a property, so eventually the property version may fall into disuse. Just the same, the Lock Screen and Unlock Screen commands do adjust the global property, lockScreen, whose setting (true or false) you may retrieve, like any property.

The lockScreen property resets to false at idle time (i.e., when no other system messages are being sent or handlers are running). Therefore, it is not necessary to unlock the screen at the end of a handler. Use Unlock Screen when you wish the screen activity to resume within a handler or if, at the end of a handler for instance, you wish to produce some visual effect on the screen. For example, if you have a button in one stack that goes to a daily appointment stack and finds the card for today, the script would look like this:

```
on mouseUp
    lock screen
    go to stack "Appointments"
    find the long date in field "Date"
    unlock screen with iris open
end mouseUp
```

If you didn't lock the screen in this stack transfer, the user would see the first card of the Appointments stack while the handler looked for the date. If the handler didn't have the Unlock Screen command, but let the screen unlock itself at idle time, there would have been no visual effect— nor is there a way to set a visual effect for that kind of screen unlocking.

You may lock and unlock the screen as often as you like inside a handler.

The optional <color> parameter may be any of the following: black, white, gray, grey and inverse. Another valid <color> parameter is *card*, but this is the same as specifying no color parameter.

Note to Macintosh II owners with color monitors: For visual effects to be visible on color monitors, you must adjust the Monitors Control Panel Device to Black & White and 2 colors. A handy public domain fKey, called *Switcharoo*, lets you change between color and monochrome with a couple key presses.

**Parameters:** Lock Screen accepts no parameters. Unlock Screen, on the other hand, may accept any valid visual effect (along with the word "with"). That includes effects modified by slow, fast, and so on. Unlock Screen works with only one visual effect at a time. You may not combine multiple visual effects when unlocking the screen, even though you can do that with the regular Visual Effect command.

**Examples:** Since these are rather simple statements, examples other than the sample script, above, are not necessary.

**You Try It:** Because the lockScreen property switches to false at idle time, you won't see any effects of locking or unlocking the screen from the Message Box. Instead, create a card button in the Address stack, and attach the following handler:

```
on mouseUp
    push card
    lock screen
    go Home          -- you won't see the Home Card
    go to prev card
    unlock screen with barn door open
    lock screen
    find "Hyper"     -- must be somewhere in this stack!
    unlock screen with zoom open
    lock screen
    pop card
    unlock screen with dissolve
end mouseUp
```

**find** whole <string expression>
**find** string <string expression>

**Purpose:** Performs special variations of HyperCard's Find command to find whole words or strings.

**When to Use It:** These variations of the Find command let you specify that HyperCard match only whole words or a specific string of characters.

Find Whole is sensitive to word beginnings and endings. HyperCard considers the string expression you pass as an argument to be whole words. The command

find whole "and"

does not stop on the text "Andrew," because the search string, "and," is considered to be an entire word. The search will stop only on the whole word, "and."

This also applies to multiple words in the search string. Find Whole sees two or more words as one unit. The matching string in a stack field must begin and end with the same characters as the search string, regardless of how many words are in the search string. This contrasts from the plain Find command, which sees multiple words as independent, searchable units.

Find String is the same as the Find Chars variation, but with one important difference. If the search string has a space in it, and that space is followed by at least three characters of another word, HyperCard employs its fast searching techniques to find a match for the string. As with Find Chars, Find String will seek matches of characters inside a word. Thus, the command

find string "script"

will stop on the word "nondescript," while Find, Find Word, or Find Whole would not stop here. And, because the search string does not have a space and three characters of the next word, the search speed will not be as fast as HyperCard's fastest search abilities.

**Parameters:** Technically speaking, "whole" and "string" are arguments to the Find command. An additional argument, the search string, must be any valid string expression. This includes, of course, text retrieved from a variable or field. While HyperCard can accept a single word string expression without quote marks around it, multiple words require quote marks around them. It is good practice to put quote marks around every search string (i.e., just literal strings, not the names of containers holding strings).

**Examples:**

```
find whole "Bill Atkinson"
find whole it                 -- It contains a string
find string "tosh"            -- same as find chars "tosh"
find string "tosh comp"       -- turns on high-speed search
```

**You Try It:** Since the contents of each person's Address stack is different from the rest, you're on your own to test out these two commands, searching for a whole word, multiple words, and strings. In particular, try using Find Whole on only partial words to see how it fails such searches. For both these Find variations, it is just as important to know how they work as how they don't work.

# CHAPTER 50

# HyperTalk Functions Update

SOME OF THE MOST POWERFUL ADDITIONS TO HYPERCARD 1.2 ARE AMONG THE functions. A few of them offer new features, while several of them provide shortcuts to retrieving coordinates of objects. We'll start, however, with three functions, the HeapSpace, the StackSpace and the DiskSpace, which have been around since the beginning.

## the heapSpace
## the stackSpace

**RETURNS:** The size, in bytes, of Macintosh memory locations called the applications heap and the stack.

**WHEN TO USE IT:** These functions tell you something about what's going inside the memory ranges of your Macintosh while HyperCard is running. The heap is generally used to store active portions of the application program, temporary data, the clipboard, copies of handlers while they're running and copies of XCMDs while they're running. When you select a Painting tool, the Paint buffers load. The stack (not related to HyperCard stacks in any way) is another memory zone, traditionally used by programs to store pending instructions and other very low-level items rarely noticed by the program's users. Both memory zones are constantly changing, so you may not receive the same values with two successive readings of these functions.

Of these two functions, the HeapSpace is usually the more useful when debugging scripts. On a 1-megabyte RAM Macintosh, the HeapSpace function typed into the Message Box can tell you approximately how much contiguous space there is in the heap zone of memory. Occasionally, running an XCMD (or having an XCMD end in an error) or moving resources around leaves insufficient heap space for opening the Painting tools, especially if the user has a memory-hungry desk accessory, like the TOPS local area network. In rare, severe cases, there won't be sufficient heap space to perform the simplest HyperTalk commands. In practice, you'll probably be able to open Painting tools with less memory, because 88K of the tools' buffers don't need a contiguous heap zone. The real hazard, however, is when the HeapSpace nears 32,000. HyperCard will balk at continuing with so little space. Your scripts may check for the HeapSpace prior to opening the Painting tools and deny access if the function returns a value less than 120,000. When the heap zone gets too small to perform needed operations, the best way to recover the space is to quit HyperCard and restart from the Finder.

**EXAMPLES:**

```
put the heapSpace
if the heapSpace < 50000 then exit to HyperCard
```

**YOU TRY IT:** To see how the Painting tools gobble up heap space, type *the heapSpace* into the Message box with the Browse tool selected. On a 1-megabyte machine, the resulting value could be over 300000 or much less if you have a lot of desk accessories and INITs running. Then choose a painting tool, and see the difference in the heap value.

## the diskSpace

**RETURNS:** The amount of free disk space (in bytes) on the current volume.

**WHEN TO USE IT:** Your scripts need to be aware of available disk space in only a few instances, such as just before opening a text file for importing or exporting data, prior to sorting, and prior to compacting the stack. In other words, if an operation is going to take up space on the disk, you may wish to check the DiskSpace function first. If the returned number of bytes is smaller than your operation requires (e.g., approximately twice the Size of the stack for sorting or compacting) then you can alert the user that this operation cannot be performed on the current disk, and then bypass the operation in the script. Employing a strategy for disk management is needed much more for stacks operating on floppy disks than on a hard disk.

**Examples:**

```
get the diskSpace
if the diskSpace > size of this stack * 2
then doMenu "Compact Stack"
```

**You Try It:** Simply type *the diskSpace* into the Message Box to see the current amount of free space on the current disk.

## the clickH
## the clickV

**Returns:** The horizontal and vertical number of pixels, respectively, from the top left corner of the screen of the last click location.

**When to Use It:** While the ClickLoc function allows you to obtain the complete point coordinate of the last click location, these functions let you retrieve just the horizontal or vertical coordinate if that's all you need for some computation. For example, in a locked field, you can calculate which line of a field has been clicked by extracting the ClickV location, and calculating it in relation to the top coordinate of the field and the TextHeight of the field. Here is a field mouseUp handler that displays the clicked line number of a non-scrolling field in the Message Box:

```
on mouseUp
    put the clickV - top of me into clickOffset
    put 1 + clickOffset div textHeight of me into lineNumber
    put lineNumber
end mouseUp
```

This generic handler can be placed in any field's script, because it gets its coordinates from the field itself ("me").

For this kind of operation, it is best to use the click-related functions than the mouse-related functions. In a slow moving handler (or on a slow moving Macintosh Plus), the user may move the mouse from the click location before the handler tries to get the coordinates of the click. The mouse coordinates may be in error by the time they are retrieved, while the click coordinates stay fixed until the next click.

**Examples:**

```
get the clickV
if the clickH > 300 then answer "Too far right."
```

**You Try It:** Click the mouse with the cursor anywhere on the screen and then type these messages into the Message Box

```
the clickLoc
the clickH
the clickV
```

Then click in other places and see how these functions return various coordinates.

## the selectedText
## the selectedChunk
## the selectedLine
## the selectedField

**Returns:** The actual text, the chunk expression, the line number, and the name of the field of whatever text is selected in a field.

**When to Use Them:** Text may be selected in one of two ways: a) manually by holding down the mouse button and dragging the text cursor across text in a field; or b) by a HyperTalk script that selects text with the Select command. Whichever way text is selected, you may want a script (probably in a button) to do something with that text. For instance, you may want to bring the contents of that selected text into a variable. Or you may want to know where in the field that text is located so you can replace it or determine if the selection is the one your handler expects it to be.

The SelectedText function returns the same information—the contents of the selection—as the Selection function does. The difference is that the Selection is also recognized as a container, allowing you to put text into it. The SelectedText is strictly a function. Neither form is preferred over the other, but the SelectedText version may be easier to remember since it now has three related functions.

The other three forms of this function return not the text, but rather information about where the text is located. The SelectedChunk function returns an expression in the form

char <number> to <number> of card | background field <number>

In other words, it gives you the chunk expression equivalent of the selected text, plus the field number. Notice that the field is designated by its number (not its ID number). While it is often hazardous to refer to one field (out of many) by its number rather than something more permanent like its ID number or name, this is not a big issue in this instance. Since you use this function inside a handler, it's not likely that the handler will change the field order between the time you use this function and have to do something to text in that field. The field number should be good, as long as your handler does not delete the field or otherwise adjust the field order.

HyperCard considers a flashing text insertion pointer as a selection—one of zero length. To depict a zero-length selection as a chunk expression requires a bit of a twist. The expression is in the form *char b to char a of a field*, where *char b* is the character immediately after the pointer and *char a* is before the pointer. Thus, if the pointer is between the "r" and "C" of "HyperCard" in a one word field, the SelectedChunk function would return

char 6 to 5 of field 1

The SelectedLine function returns the line number and field number in the form

line <number> of card | background field <number>

You are free to extract the line number from the expression that this function returns, and with that, perform some actions on the selected line of a field. Chapter 52 demonstrates some techniques along this line.

The SelectedField function returns the number of the field holding the selected text. The form is

card | background field <number>

Again, the field is referred to by its number, not is ID number.

Which one of the location-based functions you use depends on how much information you need to derive from the selection. Use the function for the unique information it provides. While you can derive the field number from all three, if that is the only information you need, then use the simplest form, SelectedField.

**EXAMPLES:**

```
get the selectedText
put the selectedChunk into where
put word 2 of the selectedLine into lineNumber
get the selectedField
```

**YOU TRY IT:** Because you cannot manually select text in an unlocked field and then type into the Message Box, create a card button on a fresh card in the Address stack. We'll use the Name field as an output area, while using the Phone field as the place for selecting text. Here's the script for the button:

```
on mouseUp
    put the selectedText into line 1 of output
    put the selectedChunk into line 2 of output
    put the selectedLine into line 3 of output
    put the selectedField into line 4 of output
    put output into field 1
end mouseUp
```

Type three lines of text into the Phone field. Be sure to type carriage returns between the lines to guarantee that there are three HyperCard lines in the field.

Finally, use the mouse to select various parts of the text in the Phone field and then click the mouse button. Watch for the results in the first field, and study how each function reacts to the text selection.

## the foundText
## the foundChunk
## the foundLine
## the foundField

**Returns:** The actual text, the chunk expression, the line number, and the name of the field of whatever text is inside the outline box as a result of a Find command.

**When to Use Them:** Whenever you issue a Find command in a script, these functions let you derive the text or the location of the found text in the field—the text inside the rectangle outline after a successful search. Being able to derive the location of found text allows the programming in HyperTalk of search-and-replace scripts. Such a script is described in detail in Chapter 52.

The extent of the text encircled by the Find command is largely dependent upon the variation of that command you issue. For instance, if you use the plain Find command, specifying two words as the search string, HyperCard encircles only the first word it finds on a card. Whatever is in the box is the foundText, and its location is returned by the other functions. The text and location of the second word is not readily available. In contrast, if you perform a Find Whole on two words, both complete words are encircled in the box. Details about both words are available through these functions.

The FoundText function returns the contents of the text inside the box. If you say

Find "and"

in your script, HyperCard would stop on a card whose field contains the name "Andrew." In fact, the way the Find command works, the entire word would be encircled in the box (Find Chars or Find String would limit the box to the "and" characters). Thus, the FoundText after this Find command would return the entire name, "Andrew."

The other three forms of this function return not the text, but rather information about where the text is located. The FoundChunk function returns an expression in the form

char <number> to <number> of card | background

field <number>

In other words, it gives you the chunk expression equivalent of the found text, plus the field number. Notice that the field is designated by its number (not its ID number).

The FoundLine function returns the line number and field number in the form

line <number> of card | background field <number>

You are free to extract the line number from the expression that this function returns, and perform some actions on that line of the field. Let's say we have a membership roster stack that lets the user enter searches for partial names— the user isn't sure if someone's name on the roster is "Andy" or "Andrew." Rather than browse through cards of possible matches, the script gathers a list of matches for display in a field on a different card. The script, via an Ask dialog, prompts the user for a string to search. If the user types "And," HyperCard can locate the line of each match for the first name. Knowing the line of the matching string, the entire line may be copied into a local variable. That local variable accumulates a list of all possible matches. When all matches are found, the script goes to a special card with a scrolling field in it. There, the contents of the local variable are shown, with an on-screen list of all possible matches.

The FoundField function returns the number of the field holding the found text. The form is

card | background field <number>

Again, the field is referred to by its number, not its ID number.

Which one of the location-based functions you use depends on how much information you need to derive from the found text. Use the function for the unique information it provides. While you can derive the field number from all three, if that is the only information you need, then use the simplest form, FoundField.

If a Find command fails to locate a match in the stack, then any of these four functions will return empty. In any case, these functions must be used after Find commands in scripts. They do not work with Find commands issued from the Message Box.

**Examples:**

```
put the foundText
put the foundChunk into where
put word 2 of the foundLine into lineNumber
```

**You Try It:** Since these functions require that a Find command be executed in a handler before the functions are called, experiment with these functions in a card button in the Address stack. Here is a button script that will let you experiment with three different types of Find commands:

```
on mouseUp
    ask "Find what string?"
    if it is empty then exit mouseUp
    else put quote & it & quote into searchString
    answer "What kind of 'Find'?" with "String" or "Whole" ¬
        or "Plain"
    if it is "Plain" then put empty into searchType
    else put it into searchType
    do "find" && searchType && searchString
    put the foundChunk   -- try other 'found' functions here
end mouseUp
```

This handler places the results of the FoundChunk function into the Message Box after each find. This function is perhaps the most revealing about how Find works and what characters are considered "found." For further experiments, substitute other functions for the FoundChunk to see how they report the text or location of found text in a field.

## the number of cards of <background expression>

**Returns:** The number of cards of a particular background of the current stack.

**When to Use It:** This function is a HyperCard 1.2 extension of the Number of Cards function that has been in the HyperTalk vocabulary since its release. When stacks grow to include more than one background, it is sometimes helpful—especially in repeat loops—to know how many cards there are in a background. Usually, the concern is for the current background, but it could be for any background in a stack.

To obtain the number of cards in the current background, you can use the construction

```
the number of cards of this bkgnd
```

rather than citing the background's number, ID, or name. If the handler that needs to know the number of cards in a background is in the stack script, it may be prudent to refer to the background by its number, ID, or name. That way, you're always guaranteed that the handler is referring to the correct background.

If you fail to limit the function to a background, the function returns the number of cards in the entire stack. Also, you cannot obtain the number of cards of a background in a different stack without first going to that stack.

**Examples:**

```
the number of cards of this background
the number of cards of bg "Name & Address"
```

**You Try It:** The best experiments can be conducted in stacks with multiple backgrounds, like the Datebook stack that comes with HyperCard. It has three backgrounds, named To Do, Weekly, and Six Monthly. Go to that stack, and type the following statements into the Message Box.

```
the number of cards    -- of the stack
the number of cards of this bkgnd
the number of cards of bg "To Do"
the number of cards of bg "Weekly"
the number of cards of bg "Six Monthly"
```

## the version [of HyperCard]
## the long version [of HyperCard]
## the version of <stack expression>

**Returns:** Version information about HyperCard or a stack.

**When to Use It:** If your stacks are created with HyperCard version 1.2 and take advantage of any commands, functions, or properties new to that version, then your stack should test for whether the user is running HyperCard 1.2. If the user tries to run your 1.2-specific stack on version 1.1 or 1.0.1, error messages will crop up, because those versions of HyperCard won't understand the new words you're using in your scripts.

The best way to test for the version of HyperCard is to do so in the openStack handler. Such a handler would look like this:

```
on openStack
   if the version of HyperCard < 1.2 then
      answer "Sorry, HyperCard 1.2 or later is required."
      go Home
   end if
end openStack
```

The Version function returns what you could call the "version family number" of the user's HyperCard application. In other words, all incarnations of HyperCard 1.2—the buggy 1.2, the official release

1.2.1, and the international 1.2.2– all respond with plain "1.2." That makes the value a legitimate number, which may be compared numerically against some value, like the version you're working with.

The Long Version returns an 8-digit number that comes from the vers resource attached to HyperCard. For HyperCard 1.2, that value is

01208000

which indicates version 1.2 and a file format number 8– the same format that has been used for HyperCard since its initial release (earlier numbers were used during development). The rest of the digits are reserved for later use. At the moment, there is little reason to call the Long Version function.

You may also determine the version of a stack. The function returns a five-item result that reveals information about:

- the version of HyperCard used to create the stack
- the version of HyperCard that last compacted the stack
- the oldest version of HyperCard used to modify the stack since its last compaction
- the version of HyperCard that last modified the stack
- the time and date, in seconds, of the most recent stack modification.

Each of the first four items– HyperCard versions– are in the same 8-digit format as the Long Version of HyperCard function value. If the version referred to is earlier than 1.2, the value will be 00000000.

If a stack had been created with version 1.0.1 and had been recently compacted with HyperCard 1.2, the Version of the stack function would return a value like this:

00000000,01208000,01208000,01208000,2667909870

The last item will be as many digits as required for the number of seconds, as read from the Macintosh internal clock. This value may be converted to other time formats if you desire.

By checking the version of HyperCard last used to compact the stack, you can make sure your stacks remain up to date by having them compact the stack under versions higher than the last compaction. It is likely, however, that if a major upgrade to HyperCard requires compaction before running the stack (e.g., to an updated file format), then HyperCard will probably trap for this and alert you about impending compacting. But for intermediate upgrades, a test on your own will keep the stack functioning with the kind of performance provided by whatever new version of HyperCard comes around.

**Examples:**

the version
the long version
the version of HyperCard
the version of this stack
the version of stack "Projects"

**You Try It:** From any stack, type the following commands into the Message Box.

the version
the version of HyperCard
the long version
the version of this stack
the version of stack "Address"

## the screenRect

**Returns:** The coordinates (left, top, right, bottom) of the rectangle of the screen containing HyperCard's menubar.

**When to Use It:** With the proliferation of so many different screen sizes attached to Macintoshes, you never know how large a screen will be using your stacks. Generally, this doesn't make a difference in an interactive way, because you should create your stacks to run on all sizes of monitors (stack authors should read Chapter 2, " Designing for all Macintosh Models" in my book, *Danny Goodman's HyperCard Developer's Guide*, for a complete discussion of this important subject).

One case in which the size of the screen might be of value to your stack is in the placement of the Message Box. The default location of the Message Box is near the bottom of the HyperCard window. This allows Macintosh Plus and Macintosh SE style computers to display the Message Box atop the card, all within the 512 by 342 pixel screen. But if you'd prefer that users who are blessed with larger monitors have the Message Box below the HyperCard window, then use the ScreenRect function to determine upon opening the stack how large the monitor is.

On a Macintosh Plus and Macintosh SE, the ScreenRect function for the internal monitor returns the value

0,0,512,342

meaning that the screen begins at coordinate 0,0 for the top left corner, and ends at coordinate 512,342 for the bottom right corner (actually in the order of right, bottom). In virtually every case, the top left coordinate will be 0,0. What will distinguish a larger, external monitor from the internal Macintosh monitor will be either of the right or bottom coordinates. If you test the last coordinate, and find that it is greater than 342, then the user has a larger monitor.

Except for the portable Dynamac screen, which is 600 by 400 pixels, the next larger size monitor will be 640 by 480, the size of the Apple RGB and Monochrome monitors for the Macintosh II. It should be a safe bet that if you adjust the location of the Message Box based on a screen size greater than 512 by 342, the location will work for all screens your stack will encounter. Such a handler would look like this:

```
on openStack
   get last item of the screenRect
   if it > 342 then set loc of msg to 20,355
end openStack
```

If your stack launches to another application, be sure your Resume handler also performs this test. Otherwise, the Message Box will go back to its default location when the user returns from the external application.

**EXAMPLES:**

```
get the screenRect
get item 3 to 4 of the screenRect
```

**YOU TRY IT:** Unless you have access to more than one size monitor, you'll be limited to trying this function on your single screen. Type the function into the Message Box and you'll see the coordinates of your monitor's opposite corners.

CHAPTER 51

# HyperTalk Properties & Operator Update

HyperCard 1.2 adds 13 new properties (eight of which are related) and one operator. The bulk of these new features reduce the amount of HyperTalk arithmetic required to obtain information about button, field, and window objects, while another important group controls aspects of working with read-only disk media. Other properties give you more control over the cursor, picture visibility, and using the Return key to "tab" to fields. We'll start, however, with descriptions of four properties from HyperCard 1.0.1—LockMessages, LockRecent, Size, and FreeSize.

## lockMessages

**Returns:** True or false, depending on whether system messages are allowed to be sent while a handler executes.

**When to Use It:** While this global property is often confused with controlling the Message Box, it actually concerns itself with system messages. Frequently, when a handler retrieves information from another card or stack, it may be thrown off the track because an openCard, closeCard, openBackground, closeBackground, openStack, or closeStack handler has gotten in the way. For instance, let's say a stack's openStack handler automatically takes you to the last card of the stack. If another stack needs to fetch data from a named card in the stack, the openStack handler will leave you at the last card of the stack, rather than at the named card. Further action may be impossible if the two cards don't have the same field names. In any case, the correct data won't be where you expect it.

To obviate this hazard, your handler should set the LockMessages property to true before leaving the current card. Not only will this halt HyperCard's sending of system messages while the handler runs, but it also will probably speed up handler execution. Without those system messages and handlers running, only the current handler takes up clock time. This will also prevent the Message Box from flashing on and off if one or more of the system message handlers in the transaction normally shows or hides the Message Box. Locking the screen, on the other hand, does not prevent a Message Box from appearing if a handler shows it. Only the LockMessages property can prevent the Message Box from appearing mid-stream.

The LockMessages property returns to false at idle time, although you may set this property as often as necessary while a handler is running.

**Examples:**

```
set lockMessages to true
set lockMessages to false
```

**You Try It:** Since this property reverts to false at idle time, you'll need to test this inside a button. The Address stack normally shows the Message Box when it opens. In another stack, create a temporary card button with the following handler in it:

```
on mouseUp
    set lockMessages to true
    go to stack "Address"
    go back
end mouseUp
```

Try this button with the LockMessages setting and without. Then substitute the LockScreen property for the LockMessages property. Notice how locking the screen lets the Message Box flash on and off, even though you don't see the Address stack.

## lockRecent

**Returns:** True or false, depending on whether the cards are being written to the Recent dialog box.

**When to Use It:** This global property differs from LockScreen or LockMessages in that the only action it inhibits is whether a card will be recorded in the Recent dialog box as being a card visited in the course of going to a card. HyperCard normally writes to the Recent buffer any card you see on the screen. Thus, when you lock the screen, no cards that appear on the screen while the screen is locked are stored in Recent. The LockRecent property, however, lets you keep the screen unlocked, but prevents the visit to the card from being stored in Recent.

The LockRecent property returns to false at idle time.

**Examples:**

```
set LockRecent to true
set LockRecent to false
```

**You Try It:** Since this property reverts to false at idle time, you'll need to test this inside a button. From any stack, create a temporary card button and insert the following handler, substituting the name of a stack that you haven't gone to in the current HyperCard session.

```
on mouseUp
    set lockRecent to true
    go to stack "Your Stack"
    go back
end mouseUp
```

Click the button. Notice first that you can see the second stack when it opens. Upon your return to the first card, check the Recent dialog box. The miniature picture of that other stack's card will not be present.

## size of <stack expression>
## freeSize of <stack expression>

**Returns:** The HyperCard's stack size on the disk (in bytes) and the amount of free space in the stack file, respectively.

**When to Use It:** These two properties are the same numbers that appear in the Stack Info dialog box as Size of Stack and Free in Stack. Size is the total size of the data and resource forks, while freeSize indicates the amount of disk space that can be recovered with compacting the stack. Unlocked stacks tend to grow larger than the exact amount of disk space required for the file, primarily for the sake of improved disk performance. But when a stack changes radically, such as after deleting objects or modifying object properties, the amount of free space in the stack file may grow quite large in proportion to the stack size.

While it is good practice to compact frequently changing stacks from time to time, you can also program the stack to compact itself upon closing when the FreeSize function returns a value that is excessive, like 25 percent of the stack size. After compaction (i.e., the next time the stack opens), performance will probably improve somewhat. Here is one way to carry out this idea:

```
on closeStack
   if freeSize of this stack ≥ size of this stack / 4 then
      put "Compacting stack..."
      doMenu "Compact Stack"
      put empty
      hide msg
   end if
end closeStack
```

This tidies up the stack whenever it closes and the FreeSize gets too big. These properties are read-only—you may not set them.

**EXAMPLES:**

```
put freeSize of this stack
put freeSize of this stack / size of this stack into bloatFactor
get size of stack "Address"
```

**YOU TRY IT:** You can try these properties from the Message Box. Look into the sizes of the current stack or any stack of your choosing. Compare the values with the reports in the Stack Info dialog box.

**left** of <button expression> | <field expression> | <window expression>

**top** of <button expression> | <field expression> | <window expression>

**right** of <button expression> | <field expression> | <window expression>

**bottom** of <button expression> | <field expression> | <window expression>

**topLeft** of <button expression> | <field expression> | <window expression>

**bottomRight** of <button expression> | <field expression> | <window expression>

**botRight** of <button expression> | <field expression> | <window expression>

**width** of <button expression> | <field expression> | <window expression>

**height** of <button expression> | <field expression> | <window expression>

**RETURNS:** The coordinate or calculated dimension of a button, field, or window.

**When to Use It:** While the Rect property allows you to derive and set the coordinates of the top left and bottom right corners of an object's rectangular area (in item form, as in 45,100,250,300), extracting one coordinate takes extra programming. Similarly, finding the width or height of an object in pixels requires programming some calculations on those coordinates. The properties in this section provide shortcuts to obtaining or setting whatever elements of coordinates you need.

Changing any coordinate property (left, top, right, bottom, topLeft, bottomRight, botRight) does not affect the size of the object. In other words, if the Rect of a button is 100,100,200,200, and you change the topLeft to coordinate 0,0, then the bottomRight coordinate will also change to follow the topLeft. In this example, the new rect of the button would be 0,0,100,100. The size of the button didn't change, just its location on the screen.

Adjusting the width or height of a button or field is possible by setting the width and height properties of those objects. All adjustments are performed from the center of the object. Therefore, if you double the width of a button, its center point (its Loc) stays the same, but both sides extend in equal direction. Similarly, shrinking an object brings its sides closer to the unchanging center point.

Of all these properties, the only ones that will complain if you try to set these for windows are the width and height properties. Since the tool, pattern, message and card windows are all of a fixed size, their width and height properties may only be retrieved, but not altered.

While you may set the arguments to these properties to negative numbers or to numbers greater than the number of pixels on your screen, be careful not to move a window out of view. You may not find it again until you restart HyperCard. While there may be valid reasons to positioning an object off the screen, it is usually better to hide an object you don't wish to see.

**Examples:**

```
get topLeft of field "Name"
set width of bkgnd button "OK" to 100
set height of bg btn 2 to 2 * height of bg btn 2
set bottomRight of msg window to 512,342
```

**You Try It:** On a fresh card in the Address stack, create a new card button. Also, show the tool palette. Then, type the following messages into the Message Box.

```
put topLeft of card button 1 into field 1
put bottomRight of card button 1 into line 2 of field 1
put rect of card button 1 into line 3 of field 1
set height of cd btn 1 to 3 * height of cd btn 1
```

```
set width of cd btn 1 to height of cd btn 1
set topLeft of cd btn 1 to 50,50
topLeft of tool window
set topLeft of tool window to 256,171
get topLeft of card window  -- original spot
set topLeft of card window to 100,100 -- wild on Plus or SE
set topLeft of card window to it  -- restore location
```

**cursor** none | watch | busy | hand | arrow | iBeam | cross | plus

**When to Use It:** This is no different from the Cursor property described in the *Handbook*, except that HyperCard now gives the author access to seven system cursors by name, plus the ability to turn off the cursor altogether during execution of a handler. As before, the cursor changes back to the browse tool (or button or field tool, if either is the current tool) at idle time.

The complete set of cursors (other than "none") now looks like that shown in Figure 51-1.

By setting the cursor to None, the cursor disappears while a handler is running. This is desirable when the other actions in the handler affect the screen (as in showing or hiding a picture). In these cases, the cursor may flicker and be distracting to the visual effect you're trying to achieve. Turning off the cursor eliminates this distraction.

You may recreate the effect of the spinning beachball cursor, which HyperCard does during stack sorting and finding. By setting the cursor to Busy, the cursor changes to the beachball. Each time the cursor is set to busy in the same handler, the beachball "rotates" one-eighth of a turn. Therefore, to achieve the effect of a spinning beachball, your handler must set the cursor to Busy several times. As a result, this effect is best achieved inside repeat loop constructions, which advances the beachball one-eighth turn each time through the loop. In long handlers without a repeat loop, the spinning beachball effect will be achieved only by liberal sprinkling of the *set cursor to busy* statement throughout.

*Figure 51-1. Seven cursor styles are available by setting the cursor to one of these names.*

**Examples:**

```
set cursor to none
set cursor to busy
set cursor to iBeam
```

**You Try It:** Because the cursor reverts to the current tool at idle time, you'll have to experiment with this property in a handler. Create a card button in any stack, and enter the following script into the button.

```
on mouseUp
    put "watch,busy,hand,arrow,iBeam,cross,plus,none" ¬
      into cursorList
    repeat with x = 1 to the number of items of cursorList
      put "This is the" && item x of cursorList && "cursor."
      set cursor to item x of cursorList
      wait 5 seconds -- time to see it
    end repeat
    put "Now spinning..."
    repeat 100
      set cursor to busy
    end repeat
    put empty
end mouseUp
```

Click on the button, and bring the cursor into the Message Box so you can read the type of cursor and see it at the same time. You'll also see how quickly the Busy cursor spins, even if you are using a Macintosh Plus.

## cantDelete

of <card expression> | <background expression> | <stack expression>

**Returns:** True or false, depending on the Can't Delete checkbox associated with the specified object.

**When to Use It:** This property allows you to perform from HyperTalk the same action as checking or unchecking the Can't Delete checkbox of a card, background (in their respective info dialog boxes), or stack (in the Protect Stack dialog). This property for any given object is either True (locked) or False (delete-able).

Any handler that creates a new stack or background should probably set the CantDelete property to true for that new object, unless it is a transient object. Cards need be protected only when the deletion of a particular card would be catastrophic, as in a single card containing scripts that perform special calculations.

A handler may turn off CantDelete if it is safe to free up an object for deletion either by the handler or the user. Change this property only in controlled situations— in which deletion of objects is either under control of the handler or the user will be prevented from accidental deletion of a crucial stack, background, or card. Any protected object presents a dialog box alerting the user to the fact that he or she can't delete the protected object.

**Examples:**

```
get cantDelete of this stack
set cantDelete of card 2 to true
set cantDelete of this bkgnd to false
```

**You Try It:** In the Address stack, set the CantModify property of the stack, background and any card. Then check the Protect Stack, Background Info, and Card Info dialog boxes to see the results in the Can't Delete checkbox settings. Try setting the CantDelete property of another, distant card in the same stack. Then go to that card and inspect the setting of the Can't Delete box of the Card Info dialog box.

## **cantModify** of <stack expression>

**Returns:** True if the stack is locked, otherwise false.

**When to Use It:** This property governs whether a particular stack may be changed by the user— including whether the stack may be deleted or compacted. When the CantModify property is set to true, the stack is locked. You can recognize a locked stack in a couple ways. First, the HyperCard menubar acquires a small padlock icon to the right of the rightmost menu title. Second, if you pull down the File menu, the Delete Stack and Compact Stack items are dimmed, indicating they are not available. The same is true for most of the Edit menu. Third, if you choose Protect Stack in the File menu, the Protect Stack dialog box indicates that the stack may not be modified.

When you set cantModify to true, cantDelete is also set to true. Conversely, when you set cantModify to false, cantDelete is also set to false, with one exception: If CantDelete is set to true *before* the CantModify property is adjusted, CantDelete is not affected when CantModify is set to false.

This property is cognizant of the condition of the stack. Therefore, if the stack resides on a locked disk (including CD-ROM) or is locked on an AppleShare network file server, then you may not set the CantModify property. In other words, the condition of the file outside of the control of HyperCard determines whether the property may be set.

Even when CantModify is set to true, a HyperTalk script may put text into fields, create fields and buttons, set field and button scripts, and draw pictures with the Painting tools. All changes you make with this property set to true are canceled the instant you close the card. Therefore, if you frequently rest HyperCard at a card that displays the current time (like the Home Card), you can reduce the wear and tear on your hard disk by setting CantModify to true when this card opens. The HyperTalk script will dutifully update the time, but the change won't be written to the disk each minute. And since it isn't important for the proper time to be in that field when you're not in the card, it's okay to discard changes when leaving the card.

**Examples:**

```
get cantModify of this stack
set cantModify of stack "Address" to true
```

**You Try It:** In any stack, type the two following lines into the Message Box, one at a time.

```
set cantModify of this stack to true
set cantModify of this stack to false
```

After each setting, notice the condition of the padlock icon in the HyperCard menubar. Also pull down the File menu to check the condition of the Protect Stack dialog box. Compare the states of the File and Edit menu items under both settings

## userModify

**When to Use It:** If a stack's cantModify property is set to true (either automatically because it's on a locked disk or manually by setting the property), a user will be prevented from making any changes to the stack. Even attempting to type a character in an unlocked field will result in an alert message that you cannot modify the stack. The UserModify property is a global property (i.e., it doesn't belong to any particular object), which allows the user to type into fields, move or resize buttons and fields, and edit pictures with the Painting tools.

Any changes made to a card whose CantModify and UserModify properties are set to true are discarded the instant the user closes the current card. Thus, if you wish to maintain a data entry card in its original, pristine form for each person who comes to it, you would set these properties to true. It is up to your handlers, however, to manipulate the information entered by each user before the card closes. Perhaps that means posting information in other (unlocked) cards or stacks; perhaps you need to gather the information in global variables, which will survive the close of the card.

When the CantModify and UserModify properties are set to true, HyperCard does not write manual or HyperTalk script-based field entries to the disk, as it normally does.

The UserModify property comes into play only when the stack is locked. If the stack is not locked, the UserModify property is ignored. In other words, when a stack is unlocked, setting the UserModify property to false has no effect.

**EXAMPLES:**

```
set userModify to true
set userModify to cantModify of this stack
```

**YOU TRY IT:** The best way to see the difference this property makes is to go to a stack and lock it via the Protect Stack dialog. Do that in the Address stack, checking the Can't Modify checkbox of that dialog. The padlock icon should appear in the menubar. Try to type or edit an entry in a field. At the first character, you receive the alert that you cannot modify the stack. Now, type the following message into the Message Box

```
set userModify to true
```

and try to edit the field again. The field accepts your entry. Go to the next card and come back. Your previous entry or edit will have disappeared.

## autoTab of <field expression>

**WHEN TO USE IT:** The AutoTab property corresponds to the Auto Tab setting in a Field Info dialog box. Because this property is primarily a concern of the person creating a stack, the property will rarely be changed in the course of running a completed stack. This is one property that should remain consistent for any given field while a user is entering information into a card.

Still, it is possible you'll need access to this property in a HyperTalk script. For instance, if you have created a series of fields in a new background and discovered that you forgot to set the Auto Tab checkbox in the fields, you can write a quick handler that sets the property for every field in the card. That handler would be

```
on fixIt
    repeat with x = 1 to the number of bkgnd fields
        set autoTab of bkgnd field x to true
    end repeat
end fixIt
```

This changes the AutoTab properties to all fields in the blink of an eye.

**Examples:**

get autoTab of field "Name"
set autoTab of field 3 to true

**You Try It:** From any card in the Address stack, type the following message into the Message Box

set autoTab of field 1 to true

Bring up the Field Info dialog box for that field to see the checkbox setting. Close the dialog and type the following into the Message Box

set autoTab of field 1 to false

Reopen the dialog to see that the checkbox is now unchecked.

## showPict of <card expression> | <background expression>

**When to Use It:** While you can show and hide pictures in both the card and background domains by the Hide and Show commands, you may also set the showPict property of a card or background. The setting is either true or false. The availability of the property also lets you check for the condition of the picture at any given moment

One reason to use this method of hiding and showing a picture is to reduce the length of a handler that toggles the picture on and off. For example, using the Hide and Show commands, the long way would be to use a combination of the ShowPict property and the commands, as in

```
on mouseUp
    if showPict of this card is true
    then hide card picture
    else show card picture
end mouseUp
```

This entire process may be sped up considerably by using the Boolean nature of the property— setting the property to the opposite of what it currently is, as in

```
on mouseUp
    set showPict of this card to not showPict of this card
end mouseUp
```

Therefore, if the current condition is true, the opposite of it is false (i.e., not true). You can set the property to what it currently is not.

**Examples:**

get showPict of this card
set showPict of bkgnd 2 to true
set showPict of card "Calculator" to false

**You Try It:** Use a blank card in the Address stack to draw some card-domain picture with the Painting tools. Then type the following messages into the Message Box:

set showPict of this bkgnd to false
set showPict of this bkgnd to true
set showPict of this card to false
set showPict of this card to not showPict of this card

With the last message in the Message Box, press Return several times, and notice how the card picture toggles on and off with each sending of this message.

## within

**Returns:** True or False depending on whether a specified coordinate point is inside the boundary specified by a set of rectangular coordinates. This is a HyperTalk operator.

**When to Use It:** Perhaps the most common use of this operator is to test for whether the cursor is in a particular area on the screen, including atop a button or field rectangle. The syntax for using this operator is as follows:

<point expression> is [not] within <rectangle expression>

A point expression is any expression that offers two coordinate numbers separated by a comma, such as

100,150
topLeft of field 1
bottomRight of bkgnd button "OK"

Similarly, a rectangle expression is any expression that offers four coordinate numbers separated by commas, such as

100,150,300,300
rect of field 1
rect of bkgnd button "OK"

Don't, however, use this operator when a mouseWithin handler is possible.

**Examples:**

the mouseLoc is in rect of bkgnd button "OK"
topLeft of field 3 is not in "200,200,300,300"

**You Try It:** Position the cursor atop the Name & Address field of any card in the Address stack. Then type the following messages into the Message Box.

```
the mouseLoc is within rect of field 1
the mouseLoc is within rect of field 2
the mouseLoc is within rect of card window
```

# CHAPTER 52

# New HyperTalk Features at Work

In this chapter, we'll focus on applying several of the HyperTalk commands and functions that have been added to HyperCard 1.2. We'll build two stacks. The first, another style of address card, is used to demonstrate a search-and-replace handler that you can use in any stack that has text fields in it. The second stack demonstrates two useful techniques: creating efficient spreadsheet-like series of fields and scrolling multiple fields. All of these techniques can be adapted to a wide variety of specific applications you develop with HyperCard.

## *Search-and-Replace*

HyperCard's built-in searching capabilities should be second nature to you by now. But while you can find text information quickly, HyperCard offers no built-in method of replacing found text with some replacement string.

With the new functions in HyperCard 1.2 that allow you to derive the location of found text in a card, it is now possible to program a button to perform a search and replace function, using HyperCard's fast Find command to locate the text in the first place. By working with this quick search, a HyperTalk-based search-and-replace application works faster than many word processing programs, like the Microsoft Word 3.0 series.

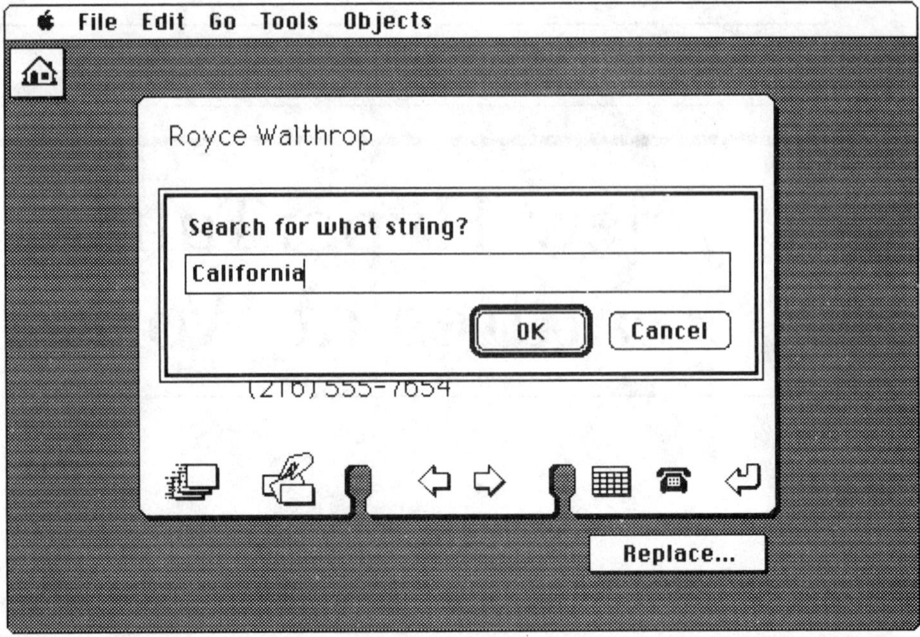


*Figure 52-1. The address card used for the example stack was taken from the Stack Ideas stack that comes with HyperCard. Here is the first Answer dialog of the Search and Replace script.*

Figure 52-1 shows the card we'll use for this stack. The stack was created anew from an address card format in HyperCard's Stack Ideas stack. I've added the Replace button at the lower right corner. No other changes need to be made to the stack, because all search and replace actions are handled by the script of that button.

Here's the script:

```
on mouseUp
    put 0 into counter

    ask "Search for what string?"
    if it is empty then exit mouseUp
    else put it into findString

    ask "Replace "" & findString & "" with what?"
    if it is empty then exit mouseUp
    else put it into replaceString

    if findString = replaceString then exit mouseUp

    repeat forever
        set cursor to busy
```

```
        find whole findString
        if the result is not empty
        then exit repeat
        else do "put replaceString into " & the foundChunk
        add 1 to counter
    end repeat
    if counter is zero
    then answer "No occurrences were found."
    else answer "Replacement of" && counter && ¬
      "occurrences complete."
  end mouseUp
```

At the start of the handler, a local variable, called counter, is initialized to a value of zero. This variable has numbers added to it later. For that to happen, some numeric value must already be in that variable.

Next an Ask dialog box prompts the user to type in the text to search for. If the user types nothing or clicks the dialog's Cancel button, the handler ends. Otherwise, the text that the user types in goes into another local variable, called findString.

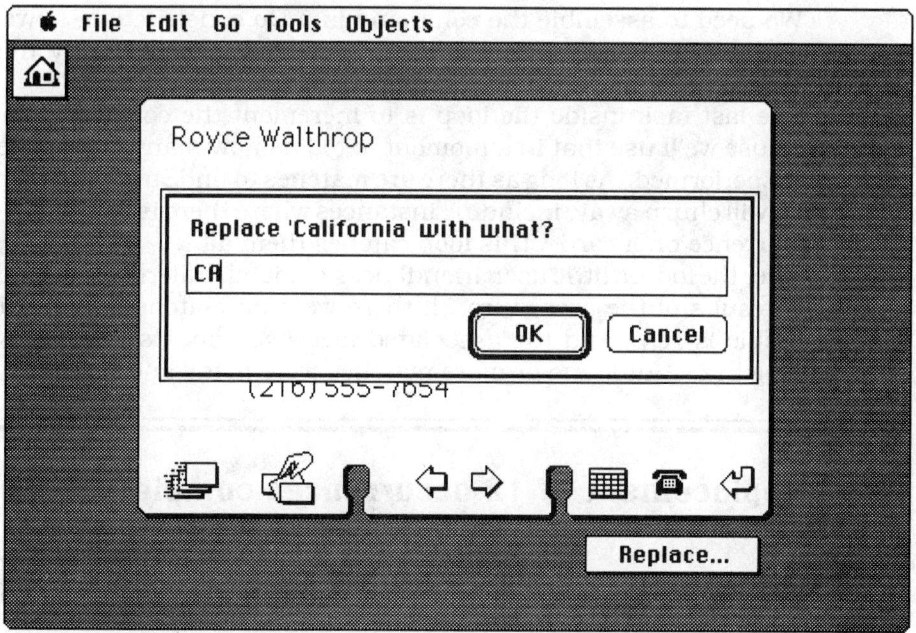


*Figure 52-2. The second Answer dialog box displays the search string in its prompt as a friendly reminder.*

A second Ask dialog box prompts for the replacement string. Notice that the text of findString is included in the prompt for the replacement string (Figure 52-2). This is in lieu of the ability to display two Ask dialog boxes at the same time (or a dual entry dialog box) in HyperTalk. The text typed in by the user goes into a local variable called replaceString. If the user types the same text for both strings, the handler exits. Otherwise we'd end up with the infinite loop below.

The main action of the handler is inside the repeat loop. It uses a Repeat Forever construction, because a conditional if-then construction nested inside tests for when the loop should exit, as we'll see in a moment. At the top of the repeat loop is a statement that sets the cursor to busy. Each time through the repeat loop— each time it seeks a match for findString— the beachball cursor rotates one-eighth of a turn.

Assuming that the user will most typically replace one whole word with another, the handler uses the Find Whole command to locate matches to findString. When a search fails— meaning that there are no matches or no more matches to be found— the repeat ends, thus breaking out of the "forever" loop. But when a match is located, the FoundChunk function is called into action to give us the chunk expression of the found text. Armed with that knowledge, we can put the replacement string into that chunk.

We need to assemble the command in a Do construction, however. See the last section of Chapter 48 for a discussion on why this is necessary.

The last task inside the loop is to increment the counter variable, because we'll use that in a moment to tell us how many replacements were performed. As long as there are matches to findString, this repeat loop will churn away, including instances where there is more than one occurrence on a card. This loop catches them all.

After the loop, a little user-friendliness is added to alert the user about the results of the procedure. If there were no matches, the counter variable is zero, and the associated message appears in an Answer dialog box. But if one or more matches were made and replaced, the

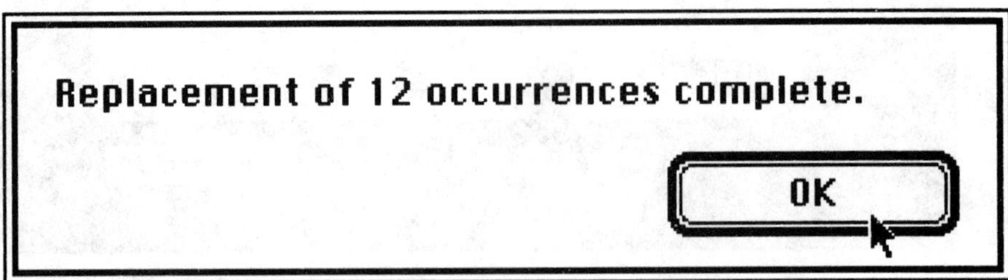


*Figure 52-3. After all replacements are made, an Answer dialog box confirms how many were found.*

number of replacements is made a part of the second Answer dialog box (Figure 52-3).

As with any HyperCard button, if you create this button in one stack, you may copy and paste it into another stack. It will be ready to use without any adjustments required for the HyperTalk code.

## *An Efficient Spreadsheet*

Our next application uses the new commands and functions that let us determine where the text insertion pointer is located on a card and where we'd like that cursor to be next– all under control of HyperTalk.

The card design we'll be working with for the rest of the chapter is shown in Figure 52-4. It is a type of spreadsheet that could be used to track labor expenditures (or any kind of expenditure) for a project and client. As you enter information into each line, you have the choice of charging time by the hour (according to an hourly rate) or charging a flat fee for the service. When you enter any number in the Hrs, $/Hr., or Flat $ columns, the total is automatically calculated along each line and down the column to provide a grand total. The fields are set up to

File Edit Go Tools Objects

**Labor Logbook**

**Project Number** 249
**Project Name** Environmental Manual
**Client Name** Devour Industries

| Date | Description | Hrs. | $/Hr. | Flat $ | Total |
|---|---|---|---|---|---|
| 7/5/88 | Phone consult | 0.50 | 35 | | 17.50 |
| 7/11/88 | On-site meeting | 4.50 | 35 | | 157.50 |
| 7/12/88 | Phone consult | 1.25 | 35 | | 43.75 |
| 7/13/88 | Photography Subcontract | | | 250.00 | 250.00 |

**Total** 468.75

*Figure 52-4. The Labor Logbook is an example of a columnar layout using very few fields, in concert with some of HyperCard 1.2's new functions and commands.*

scroll so that you can put more information on a card than would normally fit there.

## *Multiple Scrolling Fields*

I have seen a few elaborate methods of scrolling multiple fields in unison in HyperTalk. Some of those methods are very good. Except for slow response speed, inherent in the internal HyperTalk calculations that make the effect possible, the scroll bar really seems to control two or more fields in unison, as if they were columns in a spreadsheet.

Most of the systems I've seen, however, have been designed for read-only stacks— stacks that come with information that you browse through. It's much easier to control multiple scrolling columns in such a situation, because you can freely use Idle handlers to do a lot of the maintenance of keeping every column in alignment. But as experienced HyperTalk programmers will tell you, Idle handlers wreak havoc with stacks that invite the user to enter information. Typically, actions in Idle handlers (updating the screen or putting information into another field) tend to grab the text insertion pointer from the user, causing all kinds of confusion.

One other question you must ask yourself about incorporating an elaborate scrolling scheme is whether the many kilobytes of scripts just for the scrolling effect carry their own weight. In other words, in the interest in keeping scripts to a minimum, is the feature of a 100 percent Macintosh-compatible scroll bar as important as other parts of the background and stack scripts? Before you answer, bear in mind that the performance hit that such a scheme takes by running in HyperTalk will make them seem very slow compared to "real" scroll bars. For my money, when dealing with an information management style of stack— one that handles information I enter into it— the only time I'd use a scrolling field is if the information is frequently stored there, but rarely browsed. For information that is to be frequently browsed, I believe the information should be divided among see-it-all-at-a-glance cards (see also my comments on the subject in Chapter 6 of my *HyperCard Developer's Guide*). Therefore, for the example in this chapter, I choose to use a less elaborate, but still functional method of scrolling multiple fields in unison.

### ASSEMBLING THE FIELDS

Creating fields that can be scrolled in unison takes a small bit of planning. When you look at the columnar fields in Figure 52-4, you see only one scrolling field, the Total field. Actually, each field is a scrolling

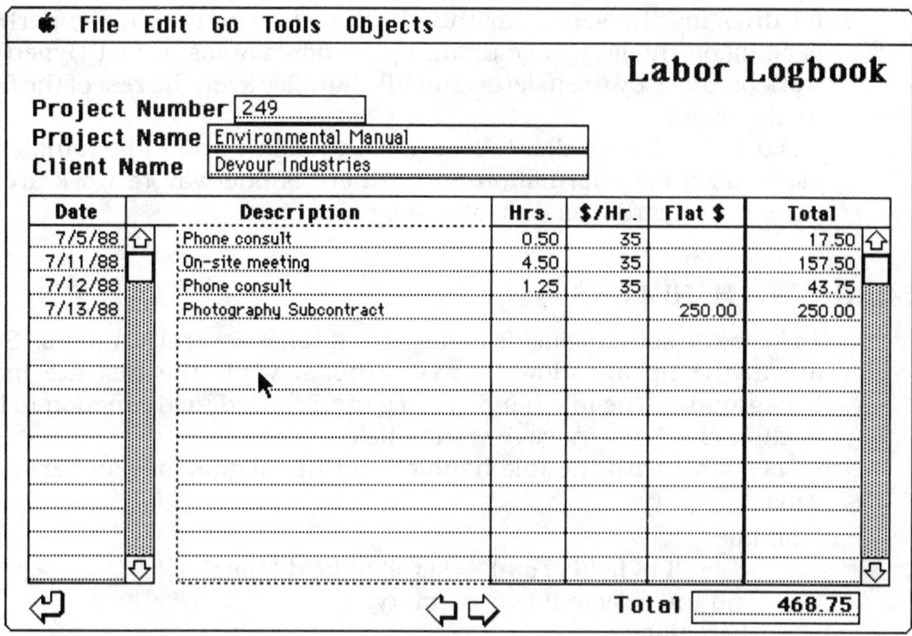


*Figure 52-5. Sliding away one of the fields reveals that all are scrolling fields, with the field to the right overlapping the scroll bar of the one to the left.*

field. It's just that they are layered atop one another in such a way that you cannot see the scroll bars of the other fields. Therefore, the Date field was created first. When the Description field was created, it was one layer closer to the user, and therefore could cover up any part of the Date field. Figure 52-5 shows the Description field shifted a little so you can see the Date field's scroll bar beneath it. Similarly, all other fields were created in turn, and positioned atop the scroll bars of the fields to their left. When the edges are exactly atop each other, the graphic effect is of a single line divider. For the Total field, however, the right edge of the active text area of the Flat Fee field and the left edge of the Total field were lain side-by-side, creating the impression of a double thickness line between the two fields.

Titles across the top of each column are in the picture layer, as are the lines surrounding them. All fields with numbers in them are right-aligned so that figures line up in columns as you would expect. The Description column, on the other hand, is left aligned for the text.

The scroll setting of the Total field drives the scroll settings of the other fields in the group. Two transparent buttons are located on top of the up and down arrows of the scroll bar. We'll see how they work later. As for dragging the scroll bar thumb (the white square in the bar) and clicking on the grey page up and page down areas, we let HyperCard work on those by itself, letting an Idle handler keep the rest of the fields in alignment.

Did I say Idle handler? Yes. Even though I avoid Idle handlers in cards used for information entry, there is one way to work around potential hazards, as we'll also see soon.

## SCROLLING HANDLERS

To keep the scrolling fields in alignment takes several handlers. Some are in the up and down arrow buttons, while the rest are in the background. The Idle handler uses the SelectedField function to hold itself in check when we're editing fields.

Let's start with the Idle handler and the alignment handler that it calls:

```
on idle
    if scroll of field "Total" ≠ scroll of field "Date"¬
    and the selectedField is empty
    then align
    pass idle
end idle

on align
    lock screen
    get scroll of field "Total"
    set scroll of field "Date" to it
    set scroll of field "Description" to it
    set scroll of field "Hours" to it
    set scroll of field "Rate" to it
    set scroll of field "Flat" to it
end  align
```

In the Idle handler, the scroll properties of the Total and Date fields are compared. These fields are chosen because they are the ones most likely to be out of alignment with each other after entering data into the fields. Another condition is whether the selectedField function returns anything. If it does (i.e., it is not empty) then it means that the text insertion pointer is inside a field someplace on the card. You don't want the alignment handler to operate while you're entering text. Therefore, only if the fields are out of alignment *and* no field is being edited, then execution branches to the Align handler.

In the Align handler, all fields are set to the scroll of the Total field. Notice two things. First, the screen is locked before setting the scrolls. If it were not, you would see a kind of stair-stepped adjustment to each field in turn. It would also take almost four times as long, because the screen would have to update for each field's adjustment. Second, the adjustments are done in turn by field name, rather than in a repeat loop. Even if the field numbers or ID numbers were in sequence, the execution of a repeat loop of this many items takes longer than hard-coding the repetitive commands. Normally, this amount of repetition is a signal of a bloated script— one that could be shortened by a repeat loop. But since this scrolling operation must be done as quickly as possible, performance should overrule script style. Choosing this non-repeat loop method came only after testing the comparable speed of a repeat loop method (see Chapter 22, HyperTalk Script Style and Practice, in *Danny Goodman's HyperCard Developer's Guide* for further discussion on testing execution speeds).

The other part of the scroll control is located in the scripts of buttons on top of the scroll bar arrows. Here's the script for the up arrow button:

```
on mouseUp
end mouseUp

on mouseDown
    mouseStillDown
end mouseDown

on mouseStillDown
    lock screen
    get scroll of field "Total" - textHeight of field "Total"
    if it < 0 then get 0
    set scroll of field "Date" to it
    set scroll of field "Description" to it
    set scroll of field "Hours" to it
    set scroll of field "Rate" to it
    set scroll of field "Flat" to it
    set scroll of field "Total" to it
    unlock screen
end mouseStillDown
```

The action for scrolling via the arrow button is handled in a mouseStillDown handler, because you want to be able to click and hold on the button to continuously scroll— just like in a "real" scroll bar. MouseUp system messages are trapped, in case some other mouseUp handler in the background is used for other purposes. This button's mouseUp message will never get there. And, to speed up the initial process of scrolling, the mouseDown message— the first one to reach the button when clicking it— sends a mouseStillDown message to get the scrolling started. Even a quick click triggers the scroll field.

In the MouseStillDown handler, the screen is first locked to help speed the screen updating. Next, the current scroll setting of the Total field is decreased by the height of one line of the field. Recall that the scroll property is recorded not by the number of lines, but by the number of pixels. Therefore, the textHeight property of the field reveals the number of pixels of a single line of text. Using the property as the measure also assures that if someone changes the font or leading of the fields, this handler will work.

After getting the new setting for the scroll property, an if-then construction tests for whether the value is less than zero, which it would be if the starting scroll value was less than the textHeight of the field. Since the scroll property of a field cannot be set to anything less than zero, all negative values are set to zero. The Get 0 command is a faster way of saying Put 0 into it.

With the new scroll setting ready to go, all fields' scroll properties are set to that value. The screen is unlocked in the handler so that the user doesn't have to wait for idle time to naturally unlock the screen.

The down arrow script looks like this:

```
on mouseUp
end mouseUp

on mouseDown
   mouseStillDown
end mouseDown

on mouseStillDown
   if the number of lines of field "Date" < 16
   then exit mouseStillDown
   lock screen
   get scroll of field "Total" + textHeight of field "Total"
   set scroll of field "Date" to it
   set scroll of field "Description" to it
   set scroll of field "Hours" to it
   set scroll of field "Rate" to it
   set scroll of field "Flat" to it
   set scroll of field "Total" to it
   unlock screen
end mouseStillDown
```

Only two items are different in this script from the corresponding up arrow button script. First, there is a test at the beginning of the mouseStillDown handler as to whether the number of lines of information in the Date field is less than 16. Since there are 15 visible lines of the fields, you shouldn't let the field scroll until they're all filled. Incidentally, for universality, the 16 value could also be calculated by dividing the height of the field by its textHeight.

The other difference is that the scroll of the field is incremented by one line each time the handler executes fully. This means, however, that you can scroll beyond the last data line of a field. But that's not a problem if you wish to scroll up past the bottom line and leave many unfilled lines for new data entry. That's very much like the way you'd scroll a spreadsheet anyway.

With the above combination of handlers, when you scroll with the up and down arrow buttons in the Total field's scroll bars, all fields scroll in unison. When you click in the page up and page down areas of the scroll bar, or drag the thumb, the Total field advances instantly, with a momentary delay before the other fields catch up. While the delay is noticeable (especially on slower Macintoshes), it shouldn't be objectionable given the simplicity of the code that makes this work.

## *Field Bugs*

You should be aware of two bugs related to text fields. One applies to all field styles, one only to scrolling fields.

First, you may have noticed that word wrapping in fields is quirky when the last character before the right margin is a quote mark or a parenthesis. The text editing routines that HyperCard uses (from the Macintosh ROM) is responsible for this erratic behavior. If you are locking text in a field for read-only purposes, proofread the text carefully. When a lone quote or left parenthesis is hanging at the right margin, insert a carriage return to force a line break before the character.

Second, a scrolling field sometimes gets out of alignment with itself. Deleting some lines from the field may cause the scroll bar thumb to be all the way up, but you still can't see the beginning of text in the field. The Scroll property even returns zero. To clear up the mess, go to another card and come back. All will be cleaned up upon your return.

## *Turning Lines into Spreadsheet Cells*

The other technique we'll demonstrate in this Labor Log card is how you can use the SelectedLine function and Select command together to recreate in HyperCard columnar fields the feeling of navigating through a spreadsheet. Without these new HyperTalk features, the process was cumbersome and the overall performance of the card much slower.

Figure 52-6 illustrates the original version of an Estimated Materials worksheet that was part of Focal Point, a commercial stack I developed (marketed under the Activision/MEDIAGENIC brand name). Each cell of this worksheet was actually its own field. Eighteen rows by five

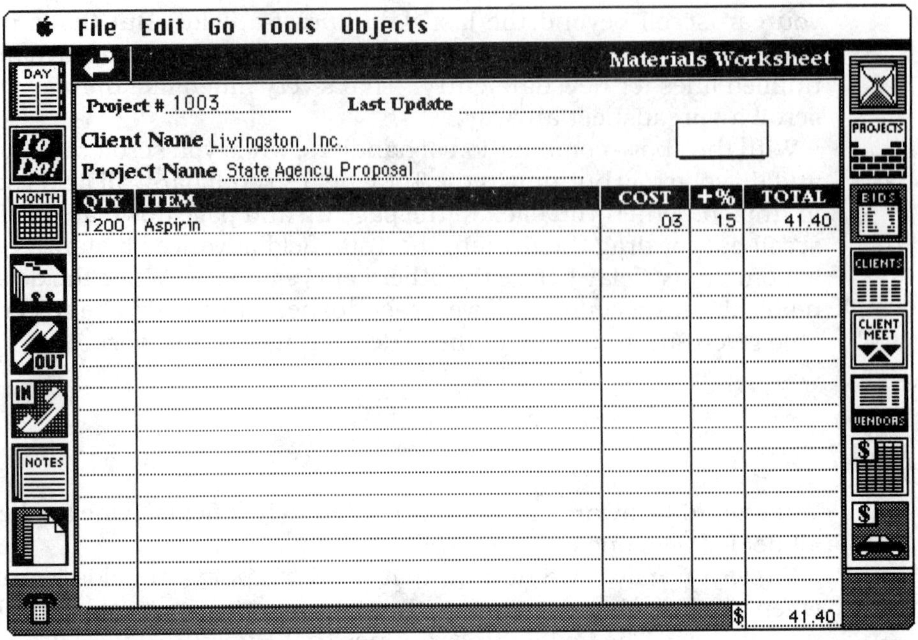

*Figure 52-6. The Materials Worksheet card from Focal Point required one field for each cell—90 in all.*

columns—a total of 90 fields. Anyone who has tried to work with a HyperCard design with this many fields can tell you that everything slows down, even going from one card to the next. Not only that, but because each cell was its own field, there was no chance to extend the data on the card. You have 18 rows, and that's it.

Using techniques discussed in this chapter, the same card in Focal Point II, shown in Figure 52-7, has the same five columns, but the number of fields comprising that part of the card has been cut from 90 to just 5. Not only that, they are scrolling fields, so the amount of information the card can accommodate is substantially increased.

The handlers in this section will allow you to advance the cursor from a given line in one cell to the same line in an adjacent column or to an adjacent line in the same column. In other words, you'll be treating each line of a field as if it were a distinct cell in a spreadsheet.

How you program the actions of the Tab, Return and Enter keys in a spreadsheet equivalent depends largely on what you think the users of the HyperCard spreadsheet will expect. For instance, they may expect the Tab key to advance the cursor to the right, a Shift-Tab to advance the cursor to the left. The Return key should perhaps advance the

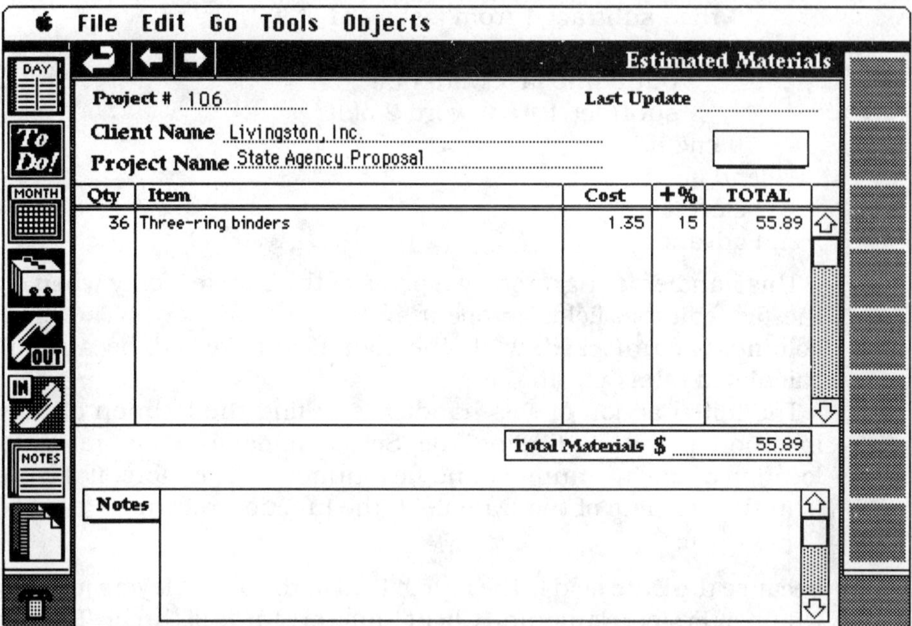


*Figure 52-7. The same card function in Focal Point II, which requires HyperCard 1.2, has the same number of columns, but with five scrolling fields, allowing many more entries and improved performance.*

cursor to the next "row" or to the next "column." You may have to experiment for the setting that works best for your users. The nature of the data entry will also influence your decision, especially if typical entries go predominantly across the spreadsheet or down the spreadsheet.

Almost all the action connected with this technique is in a single background handler. Here it is:

```
on advance
    get the selectedLine
    if the shiftKey is not down then
        if last word of it ≠ 8
        then add 1 to last word of it
        else
            put 4 into last word of it
            add 1 to word 2 of it
        end if
    else
    if last word of it ≠ 4
```

```
        then subtract 1 from last word of it
        else
            put 8 into last word of it
            subtract 1 from word 2 of it
        end if
    end if
    select it
end advance
```

This handler is triggered by a press of the Tab key (only when one of the five editable fields is open) and the Return key. The first five columns are unlocked, while the Total field is locked, because it has calculated totals put into it.

The initial action of this handler is to find the location of the text insertion pointer. Calling the SelectedLine function returns the location of the line number and field number. Therefore, if the cursor is in the first line of the Date field, the function returns

line 1 of field 4

because the Date field is the fourth field in the object layers (the Project Number, Project Name, and Client Name are the first three). To advance the cursor to the same line of the next field, we must increment only the field number (assuming the unlocked fields making up our columns are in numerical sequence from left to right). In other words, by adding 1 to the field number (last word of the returned value of the SelectedLine function), and then selecting that newly specified line with the Select command, we'd advance the cursor to the next "cell." If there is text on that line when it's selected, then the text of the entire line is selected; if there is no text, then the text pointer just flashes ready for entry of text.

The Advance handler does this incrementing and (with the Shift key down) decrementing of the field number. When the selected field is at the end of a line, then some additional corrections are made to put the pointer in the right spot. For example, when the pointer is at the rightmost cell of the first row— line 1 of field 8— the next press of the Tab key must get it to line 2 of field 4. Thus, the formula for advancing to the next line is to add 1 to the line number and change the field number to the leftmost field, field 4. When the Shift key is down, and the motion is reversed, then the line number is decreased by 1, and the field number is bumped up to the rightmost field number, 8.

If you follow the logic of the Advance handler, you'll see that it first determines where the pointer is. Then as long as the Shift key is up, the handler checks to see if the current field is the rightmost field, field 8. If it's not, then the handler just increments the field number; if so, then it makes the adjustments to change the field number to 4 and increment the line number. With the Shift key down, the operations are reversed, with appropriate values adjusted. In either case, the expression that denotes the line and field to be selected is maintained in It. That's what the Select command, at the end of the handler, uses as an argument.

One way this Advance handler is triggered is when the user presses the Tab key while the text pointer is in a field. Here's the background handler that takes care of that:

```
on tabKey
    if "field" is in the target
    then advance
    else
        get number of lines of field "Date"
        select line it + 1 of field "Date"
    end if
end tabKey
```

As long as the word "field" is in the name of the target, then the Advance handler activates. If not— meaning that the user is pressing the Tab key as if to begin entering information— this tabKey handler selects the next empty line at the bottom of the Date field. Thus, with a press of the Tab key, the user can immediately begin entering a new line of information into this spreadsheet, instead of having to carefully position the cursor or tab through several lines of cells.

A press of the Return key can have the same effect as a press of the Tab key from within a field with the aid of the following background handler:

```
on returnInField
    advance
end returnInField
```

Advancing the text pointer horizontally with the Return key may speed up data entry for those who expect the pointer to automatically advance to the next field of entry. If you'd rather the text pointer go to the next line of the same field, you can write a separate handler that does that in response to the returnInField system message.

## *Adding it All Up*

One other feature mentioned about this card is that as you enter a figure into the Hrs., $/Hr., and Flat $ fields, the amounts are automatically calculated for you. Each of these fields has the following handler in it:

```
on closeField
    lineTotal
    pass closeField
end closeField
```

The LineTotal handler which it calls looks like this:

```
on lineTotal
    set numberFormat to "0.00"
    put 0 into running
    repeat with x = 1 to the number of lines of field "Date"
        set cursor to busy
        put line x of field "Hours" * line x of field "Rate" ¬
        + line x of field "Flat" into line x of theTotals
        add line x of field "Total" to running
    end repeat
    put theTotals into field "Total"
    put running into field "Total Labor"
end lineTotal
```

It calculates the totals line-by-line, placing those totals both in the proper line of a local variable (theTotals), and in a running total local variable. At the end of the repeat loop, the local variables are placed into their respective fields. Because repeated "putting" of text into fields is more time consuming in HyperTalk than putting text into variables, the individual line totals are temporarily stored in a local variable (theTotals) and then put into the Total column in one sweep.

The examples in this chapter should give you a number of ideas of how to apply several HyperTalk features that have been added to version 1.2. From here we go to a discussion of more 1.2-specific applications: using HyperCard with locked media and on local area networks.

# CHAPTER 53

# Using HyperCard on Locked Media and Networks

THE PRIMARY REASON FOR THE RELEASE OF HYPERCARD 1.2 WAS SO THAT IT COULD work with stacks stored on Compact Disc–Read Only Memory—CD-ROM. As you are probably aware, unless otherwise instructed, a stack on a read-write medium, like an unlocked floppy disk or a hard disk, has information saved to it very frequently. Putting text into a field causes HyperCard to write automatically all changes to the disk. Planting or erasing pixels with any Painting tool causes those changes to be saved to the disk when you return to the Browse tool. In other words, there is a lot of disk writing occurring in a typical session with a HyperCard stack.

For HyperCard to work with CD-ROM, it must treat the stack as if it were completely locked. No changes can be written to the disk, because the CD-ROM player is incapable of writing information to its disks. While stacks destined for CD-ROM distribution must be designed around the way HyperCard treats locked media, this situation also opens up opportunities to use stacks on other locked media, such as a locked floppy disk, to avoid accidentally modifying a stack. It also allows HyperCard to operate on a network such that more than one HyperCard user can access a stack (albeit with restrictions outlined below).

## *What Exactly is CD-ROM?*

The terminology for CD-ROM is frequently thrown about, yet it is a new technology with which not everyone is familiar. If that's your case, then a definition is in order.

Let's start by briefly describing how a floppy or hard disk works—something you're probably more comfortable with. The surface of these kinds of disks contains microscopic magnetic particles. It is the orientation of these magnetic particles on the disk surface that determines what information is stored on the disk. The disk drive head reads and converts the organization of particles into electrical signals, which are further converted into the characters and pictures we see. When storing information on the disk, the drive head generates a magnetic field to change the pattern of those microscopic particles to reflect the new data that is to be stored on the surface.

Magnetic media, as these type of disks are called, must be treated with care. Other magnetic objects, like the ringers in standard telephones, can make a disk unreadable if the magnetic field disturbs the layout of the particles on the disk. Also, the surface is very sensitive to dust, dirt, and oils from the touch of our skin. That's why the spring clip over the 3-1/2" floppy disk prevents the disk surface from being exposed.

The latest technologies are using different methods of storing information on a disk. Instead of the medium being magnetic, it is optical. Information is stored on the disk as a layout of microscopic holes (called pits) etched into the surface at time of duplication. A finely focused, low power laser beam in the disk player bounces light off the pitted surface of a spinning disk. The pattern of reflections is converted to electrical signals, which are then converted into characters and graphics we eventually see on the screen. CD-ROM players for the Macintosh are currently in the $1000-1200 range, but their cost will drop gradually over the next few years.

Among the advantages of optical media over magnetic media are vastly improved information density and improved durability of the disk. CD-ROM disks are the same size as the Compact Disc audio platters: about 4.7 inches in diameter (in fact, most CD-ROM players also have a headphone jack on their front panels so that you can listen to audio discs when not using the player for its information ability). On that small disk is space to store roughly 550 megabytes of data—the equivalent of 687 double-sided Macintosh floppy disks. Its silvery surface is coated with a durable lacquer that lets finger smudges or dust be wiped from the surface without a big production. And because there is no chance of the surface being touched by any drive head, the disk is impervious to physical damage by the disk player.

CD-ROM has one disadvantage over hard disks (other than its read-only status, of course). Access speed to this vast amount of information is slower than today's typical hard disks. As the technology continues to improve, this will become less of an issue.

## *CD-ROM and HyperCard*

HyperCard is a driving force for the adoption of CD-ROM as a common medium for information distribution. HyperCard stacks that contain megabytes of graphics and sound practically require a large-scale medium for their distribution. Such collections often become unwieldy for distribution on 800K floppy disks, or they must be unnaturally subdivided to fit on diskettes.

A significant advantage to putting a huge HyperCard information base on CD-ROM is that you can maintain an enormous single stack—probably with many backgrounds—instead of dividing the collection into multiple stacks. Given the comparatively slow access speed of a CD-ROM player, performance will be much better in one large stack than in a collection of linked stacks.

HyperCard treats the CD-ROM player just like another disk device attached to your Macintosh. This one just appears to be locked. Consequently, you may wish to combine a stack on magnetic media with a huge collection of read-only stack data on CD-ROM. The stacks on magnetic disks will allow the user to enter and store his or her own information, such as preferences. These preferences may then influence the way the user is allowed to browse through the CD-ROM based stack. Another possibility is to use the CD-ROM stack(s) as instructional material, and use magnetic media stacks for quizzes or simply as the repository for the scores to quizzes presented on the CD-ROM stack.

Just because a stack is locked doesn't mean that you cannot save anything that is entered into a card. First of all, however, the global property, UserModify, must be set to true for the user to be able to type into fields or otherwise make changes to a card. Those changes are discarded the instant he or she navigates to another card. But before that happens (e.g., in the closeCard handler), you can grab information typed into fields and store it safely in global variables. Those variables will remain intact until you quit HyperCard. Therefore, you may accumulate information typed into fields of a locked stack, and then put the data safely into cards in a read-write stack on a floppy or hard disk.

## *Getting a Stack onto CD-ROM*

The process of turning a stack from your hard disk into a CD-ROM stack requires making a master disk and then pressing copies of that master. All these procedures are performed by disk pressing services springing up in several cities across the country.

Usually, these plants request the stack be delivered to them on a hard disk or in the form of a tape made from tape back-up recorders. There are different formats of tape, so if you are making the recording yourself, you should make sure that the format of tape backup machine you have will be acceptable by the pressing plant.

Costs for creating the master disk and subsequent impressions continue to decline, as competition and plant capacity increase. The 3M Corporation (Building 223-5S-01, 3M Center, St. Paul, MN 55144, 612/736-3274), for example, offers a new customer package that includes making a master disk and 25 pressings for $1500. The process takes 5 to 10 days upon receipt of your material. For mass production of disks, prices are in the $3 per disk range (varies with quantity).

Because a stack on a CD-ROM cannot be repaired or erased if a bug is found, it is critical that your stacks be tested extensively before making the master disk. If a bug is discovered after making the master disk, there is no discount for re-doing the master.

Until more CD-ROM players are attached to Macintoshes or Macintosh local area networks, there will be a limited market for CD-ROM based HyperCard applications. I believe that the high cost of the players will keep CD-ROM applications as shared resources on networks, where the heavy hardware investment can quickly pay off. The day of one-machine, one-CD-ROM is a long way off. The advent of affordable, erasable optical media in a few years may be a better approach. In any case, the advent of low-cost, high density storage media is welcome, given the amount of information that stack authors are seeking to put into HyperCard stacks.

## *HyperCard on a Network*

Opening up HyperCard to run with read-only media also opened up the possibility of multi-user access to HyperCard stacks. This is not without some important limits, but HyperCard has ways of working around those limits if you don't mind getting into some new HyperTalk features.

On networks such as AppleShare and TOPS, HyperCard sees file servers or other user's published volumes just as another disk drive attached to the Macintosh. If you have a button in a stack on your own disk that is linked to a stack on a file server, the pathname for that server stack will be stored in your Home stack's pathname card for stacks, just as it would be if it were on your own hard disk. Access speed is throttled by the speed of your network and how many users are on the network at the same time. Also, interbridges between network zones also tend to slow down access. But if you've been working on a network for other productivity software, you are probably already accustomed to the delays.

The most efficient way to use HyperCard on a network is for each user to have a copy of HyperCard on his or her own hard disk attached to the desktop machine. Stacks used only by an individual should also be "local" to that person's Macintosh disk. There's no advantage to putting such a stack on the file server, since no one else needs access to that stack. Shared stacks, on the other hand, should be on the file server or, in the case of a TOPS network, on a published volume. TOPS users will have to mount the published volume using the TOPS desk accessory. The shared volume must be "visible" to your own Macintosh's System.

The one limitation you should be aware of is that while more than one user on a network may access a stack, only the first person in the stack has writing privileges to the stack, regardless of how open the file is specified by the file server software (as in the case of AppleShare). Moreover, if the first person opening the stack leaves the stack, no other user currently using that stack will gain write privileges. The write privilege is set when a user opens a stack. That privilege is in effect until the user leaves the stack. Re-opening the stack a second time, that user may be the only person accessing the file, thus gaining write privileges.

## SCRIPTING FOR A SHARED STACK

If a HyperCard application running on a network involves the writing of data into a shared stack, you must be aware of what happens internally when a script tries to write to a stack that is already open. It is very possible that the writing to a field will go without any error indication appearing at the "sender's" end. Yet the information was not truly stored in the recipient's stack.

Before writing information to a shared stack, your script should check the CantModify property of the stack. If CantModify is true, then you should forget trying to write the data to the stack. If CantModify returns false, then it means that you have the sole writing privileges to the stack while you're in that stack. Feel free to create new cards, and put data into the fields. As long as the stack is not otherwise locked (i.e., manually locked by the network administrator or someone else) your

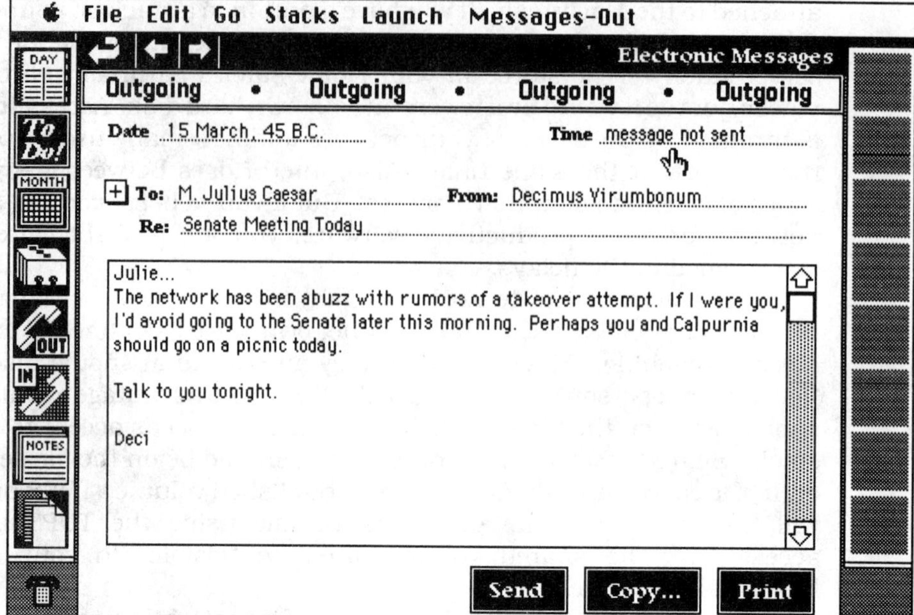


*Figure 53-1. The Electronic Messages stack in Focal Point II sends messages to others on the network. If the recipient's stack is busy, an reminder is left in the outgoing card, and the operation is stored in a queue for later transmission.*

changes will be saved to the stack automatically, just like in any read-write stack.

Some server software setups (e.g., when every user is a Guest on AppleShare) may even prevent opening the stack if someone else is already there. The server software dialog box will interrupt your script. An XFCN (see next chapter) that first tests for whether the file is already open is the best way to discover whether you'll be granted access to the stack.

## QUEUEING

This brings up an important feature that you need to build into a stack that writes to shared stacks. If the writing of information to that stack is of critical value, then the originating stack will have to record in some fashion the fact that an attempt was made to write to the shared stack but the attempt failed. A queuing mechanism will have to be instituted that records unsent information, and gives you the chance to retry later. That means, of course, that this queue should be stored in a field where it will be safe from exits from HyperCard. When you come back to the stack, you should be reminded of unfinished business.

Such a queuing mechanism is built into the Message and Task Manager (delegating system) stacks of Focal Point II. For instance, when sending a message to another user on the network, a failed attempt displays a note to that effect on the sender's copy of the message (Figure 53-1). Meanwhile, the address of the card is stored in a field in another stack (the Startup stack) as a network queue. Each time you start Focal Point II, it goes through this Startup stack. If the network queue has something in it, the user is reminded of unsent messages, and offers a chance to send them. Similarly upon entering either the Message or Task Manager stacks, the network queue field in the Startup stack is checked for pending transmissions.

While this limitation to shared use of a stack causes more complex HyperTalk scripting, it nonetheless offers substantial information handling power. Most shared stacks, however, will probably be of the read-only variety anyway. They will be information resources that everyone on the network may use. The stack will probably be locked to all users, so the limited writing privileges will be of no concern. Nor will any special HyperTalk scripting or queuing be required for browsing through such a shared stack.

If you develop what I call information publishing stacks— those that come full of information for users to browse through—you should be aware that such a stack might be used on a network. Interactive cards, which invite users to type data into fields for calculations or other processes, should set the userModify property to true, even if the original design of the stack calls for it to be used on read-write media. If you set the UserModify property to true on such cards, they'll be immediately usable on networks in which some users may not be granted writing privileges because they're not the first ones to open the stack. Also, since you cannot count on information typed into a field to survive viewing of the current card, critical data that affects other cards (things like conversion factors, the user's name, and so on) should be stored in global variables. That will keep the information available to even a completely locked card (i.e., one in which the userModify property has not been set to true). Since scripts work on fields of locked cards without complaint, the globals will work fine (but changes to fields, graphics, and objects will not be saved).

Today you may believe that a local area network is beyond your need-to-know. I felt that way only a couple years ago. Today, I have two Macintoshes, one IBM AT clone, and a LaserWriter on a TOPS network in my one-person office. Even the most esoteric technologies tend to trickle down into the mainstream sooner or later.

# CHAPTER 54

# Introduction to External Resources

HYPERCARD IS LIKE THE BASE MODEL OF AN AUTOMOBILE. AS IT COMES FROM THE factory, it does its job well, and comes with enough features built-in to make it quite useable without modification. But you can also add accessories that give HyperCard features that are important to you. Just as you may add a ski rack to your car because you're a skier, so too in HyperCard you can add sounds or icons because they'll help you make HyperCard the special purpose tool you need.

Five types of accessories are possible with HyperCard. Four of them will probably be familiar to you just from your exposure to HyperCard and other Macintosh applications: fonts, cursors, icons, and sounds. The fifth kind comes in two flavors, called external commands (XCMDs) and external functions (XFCNs). Usually lumped together under the heading of XCMDs, these accessories are capable of extending the power of the basic HyperCard beyond what's built inside. To use the auto metaphor, they can turn the base model auto into a family station wagon, a racy sports car, a limousine, or a recreational vehicle. In other words, XCMDs build on the foundation of HyperCard and let it do special purpose things not offered in the base model.

## *Resources—the Building Blocks*

The internal facility that lets you add these accessories is called the *resource*—the clever invention of the original Macintosh design team.

Its first purpose was to simplify the programming and internationalization of Macintosh applications. Certain visible attributes of a program, such as menu bars and dialog boxes, are maintained as elements separate from the main program code. Thus, a simple modification to a menu item or the size of a dialog box could be made quickly by modifying the resource, instead of digging into hundreds of pages of code and recompiling the entire program (a process that, in the early days, could take one-half hour). A resource could be modified with a separate program, called a Resource Editor. One such program, ResEdit, is still a popular tool among Macintosh programmers and the curious.

A Macintosh file may consist of two files, called a data fork and a resource fork. Even when both forks are present in a file, the Macintosh File System presents them to our eyes as a single unit.

The data fork generally contains information that we enter into a document. Typically, a word processing document file consists of a data fork only, without a resource fork at all. The characters we type in and the formatting specifications we choose are saved in the file as data.

The resource fork of a file generally consists of items other than user-entered data. A Macintosh application program, for example, contains nothing but resources, including the code for the program. This code is rarely editable, because it has been compiled into machine code from a higher level programming language, such as Pascal, C, or Assembler.

HyperCard stack files represent instances in which a file may contain both a data fork and a resource fork. The data fork consists of the text in the fields, the pictures, and the specifications of every object in the stack. But we can also add resources that let us employ special fonts, change the cursor, introduce new icon art for buttons, play new sounds, and extend the vocabulary of HyperTalk. If you've used the Font/DA Mover utility, which lets you install desk accessories and fonts into your System File, then you've already had experience shifting resources around. Fonts are resources in your System.

It is safe to visualize resources as kinds of objects (not HyperCard objects) that you can attach to stacks as you need them. There is even a useful utility that helps in that task: ResCopy.

## About ResCopy

Soon after HyperCard's release, Steve Maller of Apple Computer, Inc. got the insightful notion that users would want to shift resources in and out of stacks quickly. At that time the only viable tool was the ResEdit programmer's tool. He came up with a system of moving resources

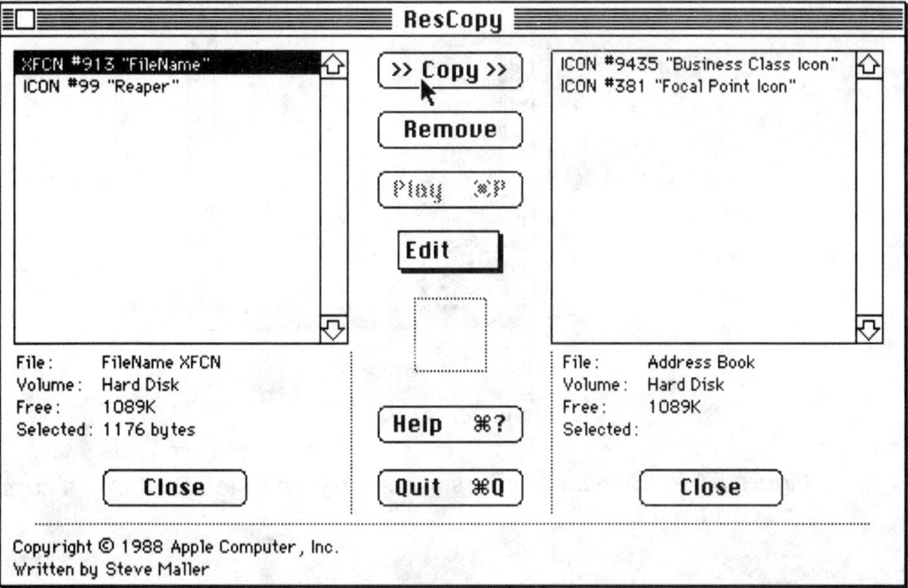


*Figure 54-1. ResCopy, written by Steve Maller for Apple Computer, provides a familiar interface to copying resources from stack to stack.*

around stacks with the same kind of user interface as the Font/DA Mover. That tool, called ResCopy (for Resource Copy) is now published by Apple Computer, and is available in prototype form from many user groups.

ResCopy is, itself, a resource— one of those XCMDs. This fact allows you to work with ResCopy while in a HyperCard stack. Figure 54-1 shows what ResCopy looks like when you start it. In the left window is a list of all resources in the current stack. Notice that each resource has a four-character leading identifier. This is the resource type name. There are a couple dozen standard resource names. The ones we'll be concerned with here are

| | |
|---|---|
| FONT | font |
| CURS | cursor |
| ICON | icon |
| snd_ | sound |
| XCMD | external command |
| XFCN | external function |

Resources also have numbers— a unique number for each resource type in the file. Optionally, a resource may have a name, shown in quotes next to the resource type and number.

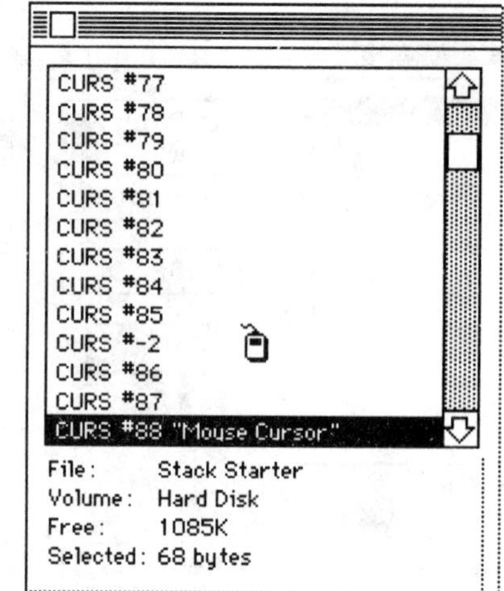


*Figure 54-2. Selecting a cursor resource changes ResCopy's cursor so you can try it out.*

When you select a CURS resource from the list (by clicking on it in the window), the active cursor changes to the cursor art of that resource so you can see what it's like to work with that cursor (Figure 10-2). Selecting an ICON resource displays the icon art in the dotted box in the center of the ResCopy window (Figure 54-3).

The type name for sound resources are the three lowercase letters "snd" and a space. In the list above, the space is represented by an underscore character. Resources of type snd_ actually come in two varieties, Format 1 and Format 2 (see chapter 25, Sound Resources, in my *HyperCard Developer's Guide* for an in-depth discussion of these formats). Only Format 2 sounds work in HyperCard. Such sounds may be tested from within ResCopy. Simply select a sound resource and click the Play button (Figure 54-4).

Any resource of any HyperCard stack may be renumbered or renamed with ResCopy. The Edit button is actually a pop-up menu, revealing two menu selections that lead you through renumbering or renaming a selected resource (Figure 54-5). While two resources of the same type may have the same name, they may not have the same number. Since some calls to resources, such as setting the cursor, may use names, you should avoid duplicate names of resources within the same resource type. As for assigning resource numbers, numbers below 129 are usually reserved for applications and Macintosh system use. To be on the safe side, specify numbers between 129 and 32767.

To copy a resource from one stack to another, open both stacks in their respective ResCopy windows. Select the file you wish to copy. The

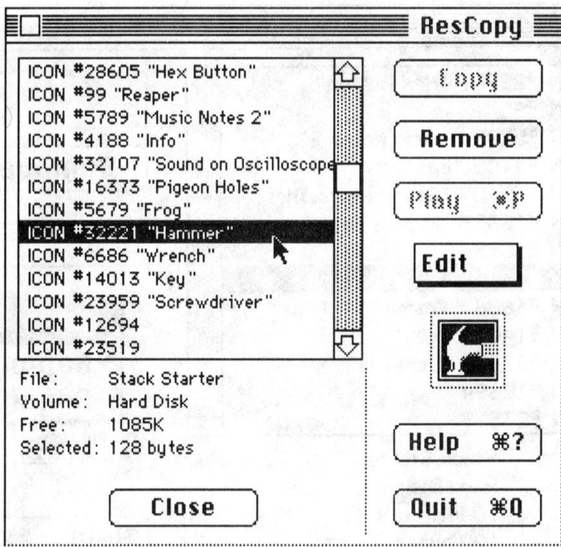


*Figure 54-3. Selecting a cursor resource in the small box below the Edit button.*

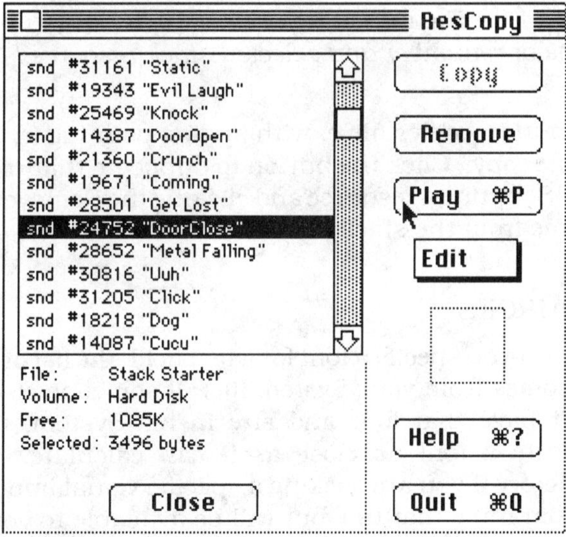


*Figure 54-4. You can play a sound resource within ResCopy by selecting it and clicking the Play button.*

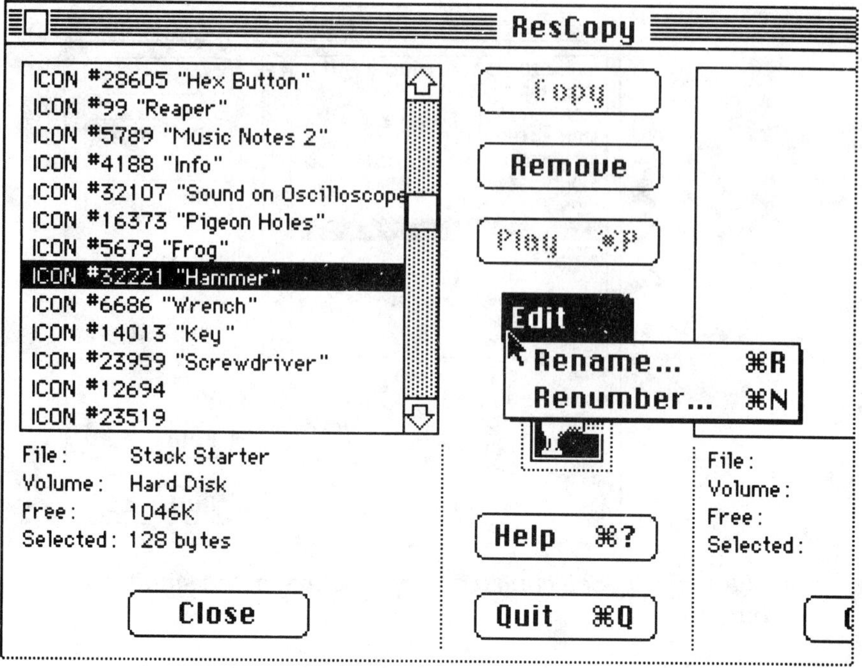


*Figure 54-5. The Edit button in ResCopy brings up two menu items to rename or renumber any selected stack resource.]*

Copy button comes alive, with arrows pointing in the direction of the possible copy. Click the button to duplicate that resource in the other stack. Selecting a resource and clicking the Remove button deletes that resource from the stack.

## FONT RESOURCES

Whenever you specify a font for a text field, the list of available fonts and sizes comes from your System file. If someone else using your stack doesn't have that font and size in his System, the Macintosh will substitute a font as close as it can calculate. This may not be satisfactory if you are seeking a specific visual impression with a font.

To guarantee that the font will be available to your stack, however, you may attach a font resource to the stack. That font will be available only for your stack, unless the user copies it to his System file.

These FONT resources are for screen fonts only, including screen versions of laser fonts. For the user to have laser quality text printout on a LaserWriter, he'll also need the laser font either in the printer's ROM or in his System Folder.

## CURSOR RESOURCES

A cursor resource is one of the simplest graphical resources on the Macintosh. It consists of information about pixels inside an 16-by-16 pixel square— the size of a standard Macintosh cursor. Those pixels are either black or white, and the pattern of those black and white pixels is what determines the shape of the cursor.

Creating or editing cursors takes some skill in understanding the interaction of what is called "mask" and "data" elements of the cursor graphic. The appropriate tool for editing cursors in an interactive way is ResEdit. You should be prepared to dig through *Inside Macintosh* a bit to see exactly how mask and data work to allow cursors to appear as they do on white, grey, and black backgrounds.

You don't have to know ResEdit, however, to copy an existing cursor resource into your own stack. Be sure it has a name, and then within handlers that don't exit to idle, set the cursor property to the name of the desired cursor. Recall that at idle time, HyperCard regains control of the cursor, returning it to the Browse or other chosen tool.

## ICON RESOURCES

Even though HyperCard comes with 101 icons for attaching to buttons, there is a strong desire among users to add icons. Common requests are for icons from applications programs or custom icons.

While ResEdit is a useful tool to create icons from bit-mapped graphics (see chapter 24, Icon Resources, in the *Developer's Guide*), a few commercial tools are also becoming available. An excellent tool for icon manipulation is *Icon Factory* (HyperPress Publishing Corporation, P.O. Box 8243, Foster City, CA 94404). It not only comes with a large library of good icon art, but you may also use its tools to grab art from a HyperCard picture and turn it into an icon for your own buttons. It also retrieves icons from external applications if you like. You may use Icon Factory or ResCopy to shift icons around your stacks once an icon resource has been created.

## SOUND RESOURCES

Adding to the hypermedia aspect of HyperCard is its abilities to play digitized, sampled sound that is in the format of a snd_ resource. Once a sound is in resource form, you may use the HyperTalk Play command to playback the sound at different pitches and durations. Digitized voices, especially for educational stacks, sound very real, compared to machine-sounding voice of MacinTalk.

The simplest method of creating sound resources is the HyperSound stack that comes with Farallon Computing's MacRecorder (Farallon

Computing, 2150 Kittredge Street, Berkeley, CA 94704). This stack lets you talk directly into the MacRecorder sound digitizer (a device about the size of a pack of cigarettes that plugs into the Macintosh modem port) or record other sounds either live or from prerecorded sources. The sound may then be instantly converted to the proper sound resource for HyperCard and copied to the stack. ResCopy may also play back and move those sound resources.

Sound resources typically take up a large amount of disk space—about 22 kilobytes per second of sound at the highest quality. That cute two- or three-second ditty can fatten a stack by 45 to 60K. I encourage the use and experimentation of sound in stacks, because it's a new medium that few of us have experience with. For extra tips on combining HyperCard visuals with sound resources in a playback sequence, see Appendix B, Interactive Sound in HyperCard by Tim Oren, in my the *Developer's Guide.*

## XCMDS

External commands and functions are essentially vocabulary words that you add to HyperTalk so that your stacks can do something that HyperTalk can't provide. The purpose of leaving HyperCard open ended (*extensible* is the technical term) is that a user can add a special purpose command or function which would not be of value to the mainstream HyperCard user. Rather than burden us all with loads of rarely used commands and functions, HyperCard offers us a broad-based vocabulary. When the special need arises, it can be added by attaching an XCMD resource to the stack.

XCMDs must be written in a language that can be compiled into a Macintosh code resource. Languages that qualify are LightSpeed Pascal, Borland's Turbo Pascal, LightSpeed C, MPW Pascal, C, or Assembler, and Mainstay's V.I.P. object oriented programming environment. As you might imagine, writing an XCMD is not as easy as writing a HyperTalk script. You must be familiar with the external language, Macintosh programming, and the inner workings of XCMDs and HyperCard.

Fortunately, there are dozens of XCMDs available from user groups and bulletin boards. A few collections of commercial XCMDs are also now available. You can use ResCopy to move these XCMDs into your stacks or into your Home stack. Because the commands and functions added by these external resources are viewed by HyperCard as new words in the vocabulary, they follow the object hierarchy just as HyperTalk commands and functions do. Therefore, if an XCMD is in the Home stack, it may be accessed by any stack; if the XCMD resource is in a single stack, that command is available only in that stack.

To use an XCMD or XFCN written by someone else, you must know its syntax, just like you need to know HyperTalk's vocabulary syntax. Most XCMDs require one or more arguments. All arguments must be separated by commas, just like HyperTalk command arguments. External function arguments must be in parentheses, just like user-defined functions in HyperTalk.

Most XCMDs that come from user groups or bulletin boards come in a stack that explains and demonstrates the XCMD. Inspect the HyperTalk code behind the sample button or other object. Watch what kind of arguments are passed to the XCMD and in what order the arguments appear. For instance, the ResCopy XCMD lets you copy resources directly with a HyperTalk command in lieu of the display window shown earlier. The syntax as noted in the ResCopy stack and in its help screen is this:

ResCopy "from file", "to file","resType",resource ID |
"resource name"

Notice one point in particular: the XCMD name, ResCopy in this case, is the command or function vocabulary word you use to access it. Thus, a sample resource copying command would be:

ResCopy "Home","My Stack","ICON","Left Arrow"

As in HyperTalk, any argument may be a string expression, including variables or other containers.

If you are proficient in Pascal, C, or Assembler, or have dabbled in these languages and want to learn more about XCMDs, consult Part Three of my *HyperCard Developer's Guide*. There you'll find an explanation about how HyperCard communicates with XCMDs and three examples of powerful XCMDs written by Chris Knepper, a member of Apple's Macintosh Developer Technical Support crew. They point the way to writing solid XCMD code in Pascal.

Working with resources in HyperCard is fun. Having ResCopy handy makes it even more so. The best way to use ResCopy is to copy it (and its own associated resources) to your Home stack. Then, no matter where you are in HyperCard, you can type *ResCopy* into the Message Box to start it up. You'll find that your stacks take on new powers and dimensions quickly.

## *Resources and Copyrights*

The ease with which ResCopy lets us copy and paste resources within HyperCard is seductive. In the ResCopy boxes, resources are mere items in a list. What we overlook, however, is that some individual created that resource and its contents. An artist may have designed the art for a cursor or icon; a musician may have recorded sound that is digitized into a snd_ resource; a programmer wrote the code for an XCMD. The real implication of this is that the person who created the source material owns the copyright to the work.

Even the most litigious copyright holder won't mind if you copy a legally-obtained resource and copy it into a stack you use. But if you intend to distribute that stack— even as free "public domain" software— you don't automatically have the right to include the resource in the stack. Most of the time, you can get permission from the creator to include the resource for free, but you must have that permission (preferably in writing). If the origin of resource is unknown, you'll be gambling that it may have been previously "lifted" from a copyrighted product.

In summary, just because HyperCard and ResCopy give us tools to freely borrow and adapt, let's not abuse the privilege.

# CHAPTER 55

# Interpreting "HyperCard Helper" Messages

YOU MAY HAVE EXPECTED THE TITLE OF THIS CHAPTER TO USE THE EXPRESSION "ERROR Messages," because the dialog boxes that present them are often an unpleasant sign. They indicate that something went wrong. They seem to imply that you made a mistake someplace.

I believe that is the wrong perspective. That you inadvertently left out a character from a HyperTalk script or didn't realize that your disk was filling up is hardly cause for anyone— much less a computer— to point a finger at you saying: "You are wrong." No one— including Bill Atkinson and Dan Winkler— is immune to a slipped digit or forgotten character.

But that's precisely why these messages are in HyperCard, and why they show up when something isn't perfect. They're not there to scold you, but to point out that something isn't quite right and needs your attention. Moreover, the wording of most messages is clear enough to direct you to the spot in a script or to your last manual operation so that they really help you figure out what needs investigation.

Therefore, I call these messages HyperCard Helpers. Use them as if they were suggestions from a kindly teacher. They won't solve the problem, but they guide you and prompt you to figure out what the missing character or word is. The purpose of this chapter, then, is to list the most common HyperCard Helpers, and explain why they occur and what to look for in solving the mystery—in other words, typical problems and typical solutions. Some Helpers from earlier HyperCard versions are now very rare, if not impossible to encounter. We focus here on Helpers you're most likely to encounter with HyperCard 1.2. They are presented in alphabetical order, so feel free to use this chapter as a reference when you're building stacks or experimenting with HyperCard.

## *A printing error has occurred; the print job cannot be completed.*

**Problem:** Something has happened at the printer end or in communication between printer and computer that tells HyperCard all is not well. A printing session in HyperCard is called a print job. When this message occurs, all printing activity ceases, and the print job is closed.

**Solution:** Check your ImageWriter for paper out conditions and make sure the printer is "on-line." LaserWriter printers usually provide their own clues in the AppleTalk window about printer problems, so you won't see this message as a result of paper out indications. Check that the Chooser is set to the correct printer, and double check all cabling between Macintosh and printer.

## *An error has occurred in the LaserWriter. Turning the printer off and back on again might clear up the problem.*

**Problem:** This message, specifically for the LaserWriter, lets you know that something has gone awry inside the memory or control circuitry of the LaserWriter. Sometimes, trying to print before the LaserWriter is ready causes the printer to "hang."

**Solution:** Do as the message says. Turning the printer off, waiting for about 5 or 10 seconds, and then turning it back on again usually clears up the problem. In the most severe case, you may also have to restart your Macintosh and the printer.

## *Bad data in card id #*

**Problem:** While compacting a stack, HyperCard regards text data in a card's field as corrupt.

**Solution:** There is no way to predict when this message will occur. In fact, there is no known way to make it happen. Somewhere along the way when entering text into a field or adjusting properties in an object, HyperCard made an internal error, which you cannot correct. You should, however, be able to open the card specified in the message. Copy the data to a new card, and delete the old one. Try compacting again. If the problem persists, try re-typing the text in a new card. Frequent compacting of a stack greatly reduces the likelihood of bad data.

## *Can't delete last card of protected background.*

**Problem:** You tried to delete the last card of a background whose Can't Delete Background box is checked in a background's Info dialog box.

**Solution:** If you wish to delete the last card of a protected background, first uncheck the setting of the Can't Delete Background checkbox in the background's Info dialog box.

## *Can't delete last card. Use delete stack instead.*

**Problem:** You are trying to delete the single card remaining in a stack. You cannot delete a stack by removing the last card, even if the card or background is unlocked.

**Solution:** Use Delete Stack to remove the stack from your disk. Delete Stack is not undoable.

## *Can't delete protected card.*

**Problem:** The Can't Delete Card checkbox in the card's Info dialog box is checked. The card is considered protected while that checkbox is checked.

**Solution:** To remove the card, first uncheck the setting of the Can't Delete Card checkbox in the card's Info dialog box.

## *Can't delete the home stack.*

**Problem:** You tried to delete the Home stack. Since HyperCard must have a stack named Home available to it, you may not remove it from within HyperCard.

**Solution:** Don't try deleting this stack. If the stack is a secondary (or false) home stack (i.e., there is another Home stack, which you want to be the real McCoy), quit HyperCard and delete the stack from the Finder. The Home stack that HyperCard finds on startup remains the "official" Home stack for the duration of the HyperCard session, even if you later open a second Home stack in a different folder.

## *Can't find menu item "".*

**Problem:** The name of a menu item specified in a DoMenu command is either misspelled or not available.

**Solution:** First, be sure the menu item is spelled correctly in your DoMenu command. Menu items with three periods after them must be represented in the argument to the DoMenu command with those three periods, as in doMenu "New Stack..." Next, check to make sure the user level setting gives you access to the menu. A userLevel of 2 (Typing), for instance, won't grant you or HyperTalk access to any menu item in the Objects menu nor to items left out of the shortened File and Edit menus at this user level. Finally, make sure the menu item specified in the command is not dimmed. A protected stack, for example, dims the Compact Stack and Delete Stack menu items in the File menu. When a menu item is dimmed, HyperCard cannot find it, even if you send the DoMenu command directly to HyperCard.

## *Can't get that property.*

**Problem:** You are attempting to retrieve a property setting that doesn't make sense to HyperCard, usually due to not specifying the correct object along with the property name.

**Solution:** If a property is a global or painting property, do not specify any object. The command would be something like *get userLevel* or get lineSize. If a property is a window, stack, background, card, field, or button property, use the appropriate object expression after the name of the property, as in *get scroll of field id 12* or *get script* of this stack. Also, be sure the property you're requesting for an object, is indeed a property of that object. Consult the property listings in Appendix B for quick reference.

## *Can't interpret that keyword in the message box.*

**Problem:** You tried to give HyperTalk a keyword (command) that can only be accepted from within a script.

**Solution:** It's a common practice to experiment with HyperTalk from the Message Box, but some items, particularly those in control structures, may not be tested this way. If-then and Repeat constructions or the Do keyword may not be used in the Message Box. Experiment with such constructions in mouseUp handlers of temporary buttons.

## *Can't modify this stack.*

**Problem:** The stack is protected, either physically (on locked media) or by property setting from HyperTalk or the Stack Info dialog box.

**Solution:** If the stack is on a CD-ROM, is locked on a local area network, or is on a locked diskette, you won't be able to modify the stack without changing the userModify property setting. If the stack is locked, and the UserModify property is set to true, you may make changes to a card, but those changes disappear the instant you go to another card or stack. If you must modify the stack, and it is neither password protected nor on a locked disk, then uncheck the Can't Modify Stack checkbox in the Protect Stack dialog box. If the stack is password protected, you will not have ready access to this dialog box without the password.

## *Can't open any more files.*

**Problem:** You attempted to open a fourth text file (for importing or exporting of text) while three others were already opened.

**Solution:** Limit the number of files currently open to three. If you are writing text out to many files, it will be more efficient to first accumulate the information (provided it's less than 30,000 characters per file) in local or global variables. When the text is ready to go, then open a file, write the contents to the file, and close the file before opening the next one. You cannot write to a file, close it, and then later automatically append additional text to that file. Reopening an existing file and writing text overwrites the original data in the file. You may, however, open a file, read the text into a HyperTalk variable, append new text to it, and then write the entire variable to the old file.

## *Can't read card or background id #*

**Problem:** HyperCard detects a corrupted card or background.

**Solution:** The cause of this problem has to do with HyperCard's internal management of objects and memory. Only when an object's space in the stack file gets "out of alignment" (i.e., it's not an even multiple of bytes required by HyperCard) does this message pop up. Frequent compacting greatly reduces the likelihood of corrupted cards and backgrounds. If you have a stack in its pristine form and can predictably cause this message to occur, Apple's HyperCard Team would like to see both versions of the stack.

To work around this problem, you'll need to create a new stack and copy as much as you can from the old to the new. If the problem is a bad card, use the following handler in the corrupted stack to copy cards on either side of the bad card to a new, empty stack you've created.

```
on transfer
  repeat with x = the number of this card to the number of cards
    go to card x
    put x -- shows you which card number you're on
    doMenu "Copy Card"
    push card
    go to last card of stack "Pyramid II"
    doMenu "Paste Card"
    pop card
  end repeat
end transfer
```

Run this handler until you reach the bad card (the handler will stop). Then go to the card after the bad one and restart the handler.

## *Can't rename the home stack.*

**Problem:** You attempted to rename the Home stack.

**Solution:** The first stack that HyperCard opens as the Home stack may not have its name changed from within HyperCard. From the Finder, HyperCard won't be the wiser, but remember that HyperCard must have a Home stack to open when it starts, even when you double-click on another stack icon from the Finder. While in HyperCard, you may name any other stack "Home," but HyperCard only recognizes the first Home stack it encountered in the session as the genuine article. Any secondary Home stack may be renamed at will without any intervention from HyperCard.

## *Can't set that button/field/card/bkgnd/stack/ HyperCard/window property.*

**Problem:** You attempted a) to set a property that doesn't belong to the named object or b) to set a property that may only be retrieved but not set.

**Solution:** Compare the arguments to your Set command against the property quick reference listings in Appendix B. Be sure that the property you are requesting is one of those available for the object you're specifying. For instance, you may not set the userLevel property of a stack, because that is a global property; similarly, you cannot set the script of HyperCard, because only stacks, background, cards, buttons, and fields have scripts. The other cause of this message is trying to set a read-only property. For instance, you may not adjust the rect of any window in HyperCard, so setting that property will result in this Help message.

## *Can't take the value of that expression.*

**Problem:** The Value function was unable to evaluate its argument.

**Solution:** Since the Value function expects to evaluate either an arithmetic expression or another HyperCard function, the argument to the Value function must be "evaluate-able." For example, if you take the value of 4*5, the function returns 20; if you take the value of "the long date," the function returns the current date from the Macintosh clock. In both cases, the arguments could evaluate to some other, more reduced form. But if you try to take the value of "Sydney," that text expression cannot be evaluated beyond what it is. To test whether a given expression can be evaluated, type it into the Message Box and press Return– HyperCard tries to evaluate any expression you type there.

## *Can't understand "".*

**Problem:** HyperCard doesn't recognize the first word of a statement line as a valid command or key word; HyperCard cannot evaluate a function because its argument is of an incorrect type.

**Solution:** Perhaps the most common HyperTalk help message, it also points directly to the source of difficulty: the first word of a HyperTalk statement or function.

For command words, usually the problem is a misspelling or a word that is not a HyperTalk command at all. Remember, all HyperTalk script statements begin with a HyperTalk (or XCMD) command verb. From the Message box, you may also type in functions, preceded by the word "the." But if the function name is misspelled, then the help message comes back saying it "Can't understand the."

Functions typed into the message box with improper arguments (e.g., text when a number is expected) generate this help message; inside a HyperTalk script, such mismatches generally produce the "Can't understand arguments" help message. Be sure that functions typed into the Message Box are functions, and not properties. Properties of all objects may be retrieved by typing their names (and objects) into the Message Box. Global property names by themselves result in this help message; but global names with the HyperCard object name (e.g., *userLevel of HyperCard*) return the property values to the Message Box without complaint.

## *Can't understand arguments of ""*
## *Can't understand arguments to command ""*

**Problem:** HyperCard does not recognize either a function's parameter as a valid type or something in a command line after the command name.

**Solution:** This is a more difficult problem to trace than the plain "Can't understand" message, unless you use the Script button in the help message's dialog box to point to the problem in a script. A command statement may have multiple arguments, as in a chunk expression (e.g., char 3 of word 2 of line 6 of field id 1982). Without a little help, you'll need to check each parameter very carefully for misspelling, missing spaces, or missing words. If there is a flaw in a HyperTalk script line, a click of the Script button from the Help dialog box will bring you to the location in the script where HyperCard balked. The text insertion pointer will be flashing immediately before or after the word HyperCard couldn't digest. In particular, look for incorrect adverbs (an "in" that should be an "into" or vice versa; literal text that requires quotes around it), missing arguments (forgetting the number or style to set a particular property), or missing object names (leaving out the field expression following a chunk expression; omitting an object name when getting or setting a property). If you still encounter difficulty, compare the arguments to the command of that line against the examples shown in the *Handbook* section for that command.

## *Can't understand what's after "".*

**Problem:** HyperCard has located something it does not recognize immediately after the designated character.

**Solution:** The designated character is usually a math operator (+, -, *, /, and left parenthesis) or a NOT Boolean. Basically, each of these operators expects a certain kind of expression immediately following them. For instance, the four arithmetic operators expect numbers after their symbols, provided HyperTalk has gotten that far (meaning that the character(s) before it was a valid number). Therefore, the expression "(3 - G)" would produce the help message "Can't understand what's after '-'," provided you did not have a variable named "G" previously defined with a number stored in it. Therefore, after an arithmetic operator, make sure the value expressed there either is or can be reduced to a number.

If the left parenthesis is the designated character, then check the contents of the parentheses for appropriate type. Chances are that as arguments to a command or function, the contents should be reducible to all numbers or all text, but not a mixture. Check the components of the items within parentheses to be sure they are of the correct type. Text may need to be in quotes, including text stored in variables (i.e., they must be stored in the variable with literal quotes, as in *put quote & "text" & quote into myVariable*).

When NOT is the designated character, it means that the following expression does not reduce to a Boolean True or False. Most often it's a case of a variable having some value other than True or False in it following the NOT operator. Test the value of the variable prior to that statement in the script by putting it into the Message Box, so you can see whether it's a Boolean or some other kind of value.

## *Can't use a reserved word as a variable name.*

**PROBLEM:** A script attempted to use a HyperTalk reserved word as a local or global variable name.

**SOLUTION:** To prevent confusion internally, HyperTalk prohibits users from naming variables the same as any reserved word. Not all words in the HyperTalk vocabulary are reserved for this purpose. Here is a list of words you may not use for variable names (a few are not reserved words in the true sense, but they may still not be used as variables, because their meaning is confused with valid containers or chunk expressions):

abbr
abbrev
abbreviated
after
and
any
before
char
character
contains
div
do
down
eight
eighth
else
empty
end
exit
false
fifth
four
fourth
global
if
into
is
item
last
line
lineFeed
long
me
message
mid
middle
mod
msg
next
nine
ninth
one
quote
repeat
return
second
selection
send
seven
seventh
short
six
sixth
space
tab
target
ten
tenth
then
third
three
true
two

| | | |
|---|---|---|
| first | or | up |
| five | pass | word |
| formFeed | pi | zero |

If you are trying to put a value into a variable with any of these names, choose a different name, one not on the list of reserved words.

## *Colon not allowed in name.*

**Problem:** You tried to rename a stack to a name containing a colon character.

**Solution:** Since colons are regarded as separator characters between branches down a pathname, a colon is not permitted in a file name. Omit the colon and choose another character, such as a period, bullet (Option-8), asterisk, or slash bar to carry the same meaning as the intended colon.

## *Destination does not contain a number.*

**Problem:** You are trying to perform an arithmetic operation on a container that evaluates to something other than a number.

**Solution:** Check the contents of the container to be sure that it holds a valid number before performing the arithmetic on it. If the container is a variable, it may be any expression that evaluates to a number. But you may not, for example, add a number to a field containing an alphabet character.

## *Existing file is not a HyperCard stack.*

**Problem:** You tried to save a copy of a stack or name a new stack with the same name as a non-HyperCard file.

**Solution:** Whenever you attempt to create a new stack or save a copy of the current stack, and the name you assign is the same as a file currently in the same folder on your disk, the Macintosh file system prompts with a dialog box whether you wish to replace the existing file with that name. HyperCard, like many Macintosh programs, won't allow you to overwrite a file unless it is the same file type as the one you're about to write. In other words, you can only overwrite a stack file with a new stack file. If the file with the same name is not a HyperCard stack file, you get this message, indicating that the save was not successful. Either delete the original file on the disk (in the Finder or via desk accessory products, such as CE Software's DiskTop) or re-do the operation, specifying a different file name.

## *Existing file is not a MacPaint document. Can't export paint to that file.*

**Problem:** You tried to export a HyperCard picture to a file with the same name as a non-MacPaint document on your disk.

**Solution:** Because exporting pictures from HyperCard creates a MacPaint document, you may overwrite only other MacPaint documents of the same name. Either delete the original file on the disk (in the Finder or via desk accessory products, such as CE Software's DiskTop) or re-do the operation, specifying a different file name.

## *Expected " " but found " ".*
## *Expected unsigned integer but found " ".*

**Problem:** HyperTalk was expecting a certain character or type of character in an argument, but encountered something else.

**Solution:** Before clicking the Script button when you see this Help message, pay close attention to what the message says it expected and what it found. The text insertion pointer will be showing you where the difficulty is (usually immediately after the expression it found unexpectedly). Most often, the missing character is a parenthesis in a math expression or the word "of" in a chunk expression. When HyperTalk expects an unsigned integer, it means that the expression at that point (usually an argument to a command or function) must be a positive, whole number with no decimal places. Among the solutions (depending on the nature of the expression that must be an unsigned integer) is to take the integer of the expression (use the Round or Trunc functions) prior to use or to set the numberFormat to "0" (if previously set to another format with places to the right of the decimal earlier in the handler) and add zero to the value prior to its use in the statement.

## *Expected end of line after "".*

**Problem:** HyperTalk expected a carriage return character where there was none.

**Solution:** Click on the Script button to see where HyperCard expected the carriage return. Most often, it's a case of commas missing between multiple command or function arguments. It may also be a case in which two commands are on the same line of a HyperTalk handler. Either repair the argument list or separate the two command lines, as needed.

## *External commands and functions cannot have more than 16 parameters.*

**Problem:** Your script is trying to pass more than 16 parameters to an XCMD or XFCN.

**Solution:** Since no XCMD or XFCN will ever be written to require more than 16 arguments, it is clearly a case of miscounting the number of arguments being passed along to the external code. Remember that arguments are separated by commas, and no argument may contain a comma unless the comma is inside quote marks.

## *Failed to create a new card.*
## *Failed to create a new stack.*
## *Failed to paste card.*
## *Failed to sort this stack.*

**Problem:** Insufficient disk space to accommodate creation of new card or stack or to write a sorted copy to disk.

**Solution:** Free up disk space on the current volume by deleting (or archiving) unneeded files, or save a copy to a floppy diskette and retry the procedure on the copy. If there isn't enough disk space to accommodate these operations, there certainly won't be enough to compact the stack to free up space.

## *Fields can't hold more than 30000 characters.*

**Problem:** You attempted to put more than 30,000 text characters into a field.

**Solution:** The exact number may vary by a few characters, but this is a limit that cannot be extended by compacting the stack. Divide the text into smaller chunks and distribute the text across multiple cards. Remember, too, that containers of all kinds have the same size limit.

## *File system error # while reading from the disk.*
## *File system error # while writing to the disk.*
## *File system error #*

**Problem:** The Macintosh File System is reporting difficulty reading or writing to the current disk volume. The error number is a Macintosh System error number.

**Solution:** These negative numbers in the range -33 to -61 relate disk problems not connected to HyperCard. Obvious problems, such as too many files open, are trapped by HyperCard and presented by way of its own Help messages, explained elsewhere in this chapter. For your reference, however, here are all possible File System errors and their numbers. If you see any of these errors, there may be a serious problem with your disk drive or diskette.

| Error Number | Error Indication |
|---|---|
| -33 | Directory full |
| -34 | Disk full |
| -35 | No such volume |
| -36 | I/O error |
| -37 | Bad name |
| -38 | File not open |
| -39 | End of file |
| -40 | Tried to position to before start of file |
| -41 | Memory full or file won't fit |
| -42 | Too many files open |
| -43 | File not found |
| -44 | Disk write protected |
| -45 | File is locked |
| -46 | Volume is locked |
| -47 | File is busy |
| -48 | Duplicate filename |

| | |
|---|---|
| -49 | File already open with write permission |
| -50 | Error in user parameter list |
| -51 | Refnum error |
| -52 | Get file position error |
| -53 | Volume not on line (was ejected) |
| -54 | Permission error |
| -55 | Drive volume already on-line at MountVol |
| -56 | No such drive |
| -57 | Not a Mac disk |
| -58 | Volume belongs to an external File System |
| -59 | File system 'system trouble' error |
| -60 | Bad master directory block |
| -61 | Write permission error |

If file system errors occur and you don't understand the nature of the error, it will be out of your control anyway. Disk problems may sometimes be remedied with the help of disk maintenance utility software, such as Symantec's Utilities for the Macintosh.

### *Found "else" without "then".*
### *Found "end if" without "if".*
### *Found "end repeat" without "repeat".*
### *Found "exit repeat" outside a repeat loop.*
### *Found "if" without "then".*
### *Found "next repeat" outside a repeat loop.*
### *Found "then" without "if".*

**Problem:** There is an imbalance in an if-then or repeat control structure.

**Solution:** With all control structures being of rather rigid structures (even within the wide latitude HyperTalk offers), HyperTalk can detect when an if-then-else construction is missing its "then," or when a statement tells it to exit a repeat structure when there is none. Typically, all the omissions indicated by these help messages can also be detected before running the handler, because HyperTalk won't be able to balance the entire handler. The End statement of the handler will not be flush left if any control structure in that handler is missing a crucial ingredient. Always press the Tab key when finished writing a handler, and check the End statement to make sure all is well within.

If not, look for the conditions indicated in this help messages. Even if you cannot locate the problem right away, you can test the handler and let the help message guide you to the trouble spot.

## *HyperCard does not have enough memory to continue.*

**Problem:** At idle time, HyperCard determined that there is insufficient memory to perform even simple HyperCard operations.

**Solution:** HyperCard "bails out" after this message, returning you to the Finder. Something happened to goggle up enough heap space to reduce the largest available block to less than 32K—an extremely low HeapSpace reading. Moving resources and aborting some XCMDs midstream can occasionally leave the heap so fragmented that no block is larger than 32K, causing this problem. Large desk accessories and INITs, like TOPS network software, or a large RAM cache can also contribute to the problem. Restarting HyperCard usually clears up memory problems. If the problem persists, turn off your RAM cache and restart your Macintosh without the memory-hungry DAs and INITs.

## *HyperCard requires more recent ROMS*

**Problem:** You tried to start HyperCard on a Macintosh that has the original ROM chips in it.

**Solution:** HyperCard in the minimum requires what are known as the 128K ROMs, ROM chips that were first used with the Macintosh Plus computer. If you are using an original Macintosh 512K with a memory upgrade to 1 megabyte, you still need the 128K ROMs to start HyperCard. HyperCard also runs on all ROMs since the Macintosh Plus ROMs. The 128K ROM upgrade is available only through authorized Apple dealers (it includes an 800K double-sided disk drive), but is increasingly difficult to locate as the years wear on.

## *"" is not the right type for "".*

**Problem:** HyperTalk expects an expression of a certain kind, but is not receiving it in the current statement.

**Solution:** While HyperTalk is not a "typed" language (i.e., you don't have to declare that a variable or other container hold only text or only integers), it still requires that certain arguments to commands and functions evaluate to the required types. For example, if you try the statement *put 3 + "howdy,"* a help message comes back saying that "howdy" is not the right type for "+," because the plus operator demands a number of some kind. Therefore, when this help message appears, study it closely to see what kind of expression it is looking for, and then check the point in the script to see how the expression that is in there is different from that expected type. Perhaps you're accidentally reusing a variable for text when it should be holding a number. You may always check the value of an expression inside a handler by putting that value into the Message Box on a trial run (e.g., if there is a variable called budget, insert a temporary line– *put budget*– before the problem line and watch the results in the Message Box).

## *Need true or false after "not" but got "".*

**Problem:** HyperTalk expects a Boolean True or False after the NOT operator, but encountered a different expression.

**Solution:** Test what the troublesome expression is to make sure that it is evaluating to either True or False. These Boolean values may be entered as either plain key words, or as literal strings (e.g., "True"). Either way, they evaluate to the Boolean expressions.

## *Never heard of "".*

**Problem:** HyperCard cannot locate a button, field, or background object named in a HyperTalk command.

**Solution:** This help message appears whether you call the object by number, ID number, or name, and specifies in its description the way it sought the object. One common mistake is to call an object by its ID number when you mean its number (or vice versa). It is also possible to misspell the name of an object if you're accessing it by name. Bear in mind when referring to objects by number or ID number in a Repeat loop (in which the counting variable is used to make up part of the object designation) that the number must be an integer. If the numberFormat property has been adjusted to something with places to the right of the decimal, HyperTalk will append the decimals to the Repeat loop counting variable when summoning the object, as in card ID 47.00. This will bring up the help message, and you'll see how HyperTalk is evaluating that counting variable to a non-integer.

## *No open file named "".*

**Problem:** In reading from or writing to a text file, the file name specified does not match a file currently open.

**Solution:** First check to make sure that the file of that name was opened earlier in the handler and has not been closed in the meantime. File messages like this one usually close all opened files, and they'll have to be reopened before they may be read from or written to. Second, be sure the name of the file you're reading from or writing to is identical (including pathname, if any) to the one opened earlier in the handler.

## *No such card.*

**Problem:** A command cited a card in the current stack by number, ID, or name that does not exist.

**Solution:** The first item to check is whether the card expression used to cite that card is entered correctly. If the reference is to a number, be sure you have your card number and ID numbers straight. Card numbers, recall, tend to change as the stack is sorted or has cards added to or removed from it. A card name may be misspelled. If you wish to go to a certain card and find it gone, that card may have been important enough to lock in its info dialog box so that it couldn't be accidentally deleted.

Importantly, this help message does not appear if a script attempts to go to a nonexistent card. Instead this message comes back as the Result of the Go command. Unless your scripts test for the result of a Go command, you won't be alerted that the card was not found.

## *Not a scrolling field.*

**Problem:** You tried to set the scroll of a field whose style is not scrolling.

**Solution:** If the field should be a scrolling field, then change its Style setting in its Info dialog box or its Style property with HyperTalk. If the field is not supposed to be a scrolling field, do not try to set this property. You won't be able to get the scroll property of a non-scrolling field, either.

## *Not enough disk space to compact.*

**Problem:** Compact Stack requires free space on the disk of approximately double the size of the current stack.

**Solution:** To compact the stack, you must remove or archive unused files on your disk to make space for the compaction process. HyperCard writes the compacted version of the stack to another part of the disk in a file with a temporary name, while the original version is still safely stored on disk. When the compact is successful, the new file is renamed to the old stack name, while the original file is removed from the disk directory.

## *Not enough ends.*

**Problem:** The handler has at least one more If or Repeat construction requiring an End statement than there are End statements.

**Solution:** When you click the Script button on the help message dialog box for this message, you may not be shown the location of the difficulty. Instead, the text insertion pointer will be flashing at the top of the script. It's up to you to locate where the extra End statement(s) is needed. In a complex handler with many nested if-then and Repeat constructions, look first to be sure that all Repeats have balancing End statements. Then look for If-then-else constructions to see if any ending Then or Else segments are more than one line long– these require End statements.

Typically, omissions of End statements can also be detected before running the handler, because HyperTalk won't be able to balance the entire handler. The End statement of the handler will not be flush left if any control structure in that handler is missing a crucial ingredient. Always press the Tab key when finished writing a handler, and check the End statement to make sure all is well within.

## *Not enough memory to read from file.*
## *Not enough memory to use the painting tools.*

**Problem:** There is not enough free memory to load information from an external text file or to choose any painting tool.

**Solution:** As with any insufficient memory condition, there are only a couple seemingly rash solutions. Insufficient memory for reading from a file or using the painting tools is often linked to having copied and pasted resources with in-HyperCard utilities such as ResCopy.

To free up memory space, you'll have to quit HyperCard. Restarting HyperCard from the Finder will start you out fresh. If you are running MultiFinder, be sure that you have allocated at least 750K of memory to HyperCard. It actually prefers 1000K. On 1 megabyte RAM Macintoshes, desk accessories and INIT files sometimes consume the safety margin built into HyperCard running on machines of that size. The TOPS network Desk Accessory and INIT, for instance consume nearly 100K. That can make the difference between there being enough memory for painting tools in stacks with many large global variables. Try restarting your system without these large Desk Accessories.

## *Nothing to copy. Try background.*

**Problem:** You tried to copy a card picture selection with nothing in the selection.

**Solution:** Often this message comes because you meant to be in background editing mode before choosing the Select painting tool to select part of a picture. Simply choose Background from the Edit menu before selecting the picture.

## *Out of memory.*

**Problem:** The Macintosh has insufficient memory to carry out a HyperTalk handler.

**Solution:** This problem occurs primarily on very large handlers— those nearing 30,000 characters, but sometimes with much smaller handlers in otherwise tight memory situations. To find out how large an object's script is, type the following into the Message Box (using the name of your object):

the length of script of <object expression>

This will reveal how many characters are in the entire script. If the number is above 20,000 consider breaking up the handler into smaller components. HyperCard loads the contents of an entire handler into a special section of memory, which has limits, even on multi-megabyte RAM Macintoshes. If you break up your handlers, that should prevent this memory condition.

Some large XCMD-based add-ons to HyperCard, such as Reports, occupy a great deal of memory while they are running. You may obtains Out of Memory indications while trying to print a report , or some handlers within Reports (like CardSelected and CardUpdate handlers) may indicate errors when in reality there isn't enough memory for them to carry out valid HyperTalk commands. Quit HyperCard and retry the printing. If the error persists, it means that you have some large INIT (like TOPS) or a large RAM cache, both of which should be turned off (and the machine restarted) to print your report.

## *Please select something first.*

**Problem:** In the Painting tools and with the powerKeys global property set to true (in the User Preferences card of the Home Stack), you pressed a PowerKey which activated an item in the Paint menu— but no picture was selected for the item to work.

**Solution:** This usually means that you intended to be in the Browse tool and were typing some command to go to another card or perform some other HyperTalk action. If one of the letters of the command was a PowerKey, this help message appears. Before carrying out the command, exit the Painting tools. The quickest way is to press Command-Tab, which chooses the Browse tool.

## *Save changes to script?*

**Problem:** You have "peeked" at an object script by the Option-Command keyboard shortcut, edited the script in some fashion, and are using the Option-Command shortcut to close the Script Editor.

**Solution:** This is merely a warning that you have made changes to the script while peeking at it. You can elect to save or discard changes. If you close the Script Editor by clicking on the Editor's OK or Cancel buttons, or press the Enter key, you do not receive this message.

## *Show Background Picture?* *Show card Picture?*

**Problem:** You are trying to edit a background or card layer picture while the ShowPict property of that picture is false.

**Solution:** You can choose any Painting tool while the picture of the current domain is hidden, but the instant you try to apply the tool to the picture, one of these messages appears. You must show the picture before you may add to that picture layer. If you elect not to show the picture from this message, you will not be able to draw on the picture layer. The layers are independent, so you may work on a background picture layer while the card picture is hidden.

## *Sorry, there isn't enough memory to print from Hyper-Card.*

**Problem:** There is insufficient memory to load the printer driver information.

**Solution:** See "Out of Memory" messages for solutions to such memory conditions.

## *Sort by what?*

**Problem:** The argument to the Sort command has been omitted or incorrectly stated.

**Solution:** The Sort command syntax includes the word "by" followed by optional modifiers (ascending/descending, and text/numeric/international/datetime) and an expression. Typically that expression is a field expression, but it may also be a background expression (to keep all cards of the same background together), a HyperTalk function (e.g., the length of a particular field) or even a user-defined function that establishes the sort key for each card "on the fly." If the expression is invalid, you'll receive this message: "" was not a valid expression for this card." Typically, the Sort by What message comes as the result of omitting the "by" of the syntax.

## *That disk is too full.*

**Problem:** The unlocked disk holding the current unlocked stack is too full to accommodate further changes to the stack or its fields.

**Solution:** You will either have to delete or archive files on the disk to free up room, or copy the current stack to a disk with breathing space and continue working with it there.

## *That tool is not available at the current user level.*

**Problem:** The UserLevel global property is set too low for the desired tool.

**Solution:** Even when a particular tool is set by a HyperTalk script, the UserLevel global property must be set to the level that supports that tool. The most typical hindrances come when a script needs to draw with the Painting tools, but the UserLevel is set to Typing (2). Before calling a Painting, button, or field tool, be sure the userLevel property is set correctly. This may be done in the openStack handler or just prior to using the tool.

## *Too many variables.*

**Problem:** Your scripts have created more variables than HyperTalk can track.

**Solution:** This was a problem primarily in HyperCard 1.0.1 and 1.1. The number of permissible variables has been greatly increased in version 1.2, making this message very rare.

## *Too much recursion.*

**Problem:** A handler or series of handlers is calling itself too many times, or may be in an infinite loop.

**Solution:** Recursion is like something that keeps folding back on itself. In a HyperTalk script, it could take the form a doMenu handler that traps for the "New Card" menu item. After performing some special extra preparation for creating a new card, it then uses the statement *doMenu New Card* in the hopes of actually creating the new card. This last statement, however, merely restarts the on doMenu handler all over again. This is caught in an infinite loop, and no new card ever gets created. Of course, HyperTalk recognizes this very quickly, and throws up this help message.

Tracing the point of recursion may not always be simple, especially if the recursion takes place across two or more handlers. In the case of the menu situation, above, the handler must *send "doMenu New Card to HyperCard"* to break out of the object hierarchy, and get the message to HyperCard where it belongs. In more complex situations, print out the handlers you suspect are in the way, and follow execution carefully line by line. If you find yourself coming 'round and 'round, you know you have a recursion problem, and must find a way out of it.

Experienced programmers may actually desire recursion under controlled circumstances for special kinds of math. For now, there is no way to turn off this recursion trapping that HyperTalk performs.

## *Unexpected end of line.*

**Problem:** HyperTalk encountered a carriage return in a script before a command line is finished.

**Solution:** An "end of line" character is simply a press of the Return key. Occasionally, HyperTalk will show this help message when a statement is incomplete. Compare the syntax of your command and functions against the listings in the *Handbook*.

## *Unexpected error #*

**Problem:** One of the hundreds of consistency checks that HyperCard performs on an ongoing basis has failed.

**Solution:** If you can recreate this problem on a stack (i.e., you have versions of the stack both before and after), the stacks would be of great interest to the HyperCard Team at Apple. When an unexpected error occurs, your stack is, unfortunately, corrupted. Until Apple completes a separate utility program that extracts data from corrupted stacks, you'll have to start from scratch. Frequent compacting during stack development can greatly reduce the likelihood of an unexpected error.

## *User level is too low to edit script.*

**Problem:** You are trying to gain access to an object's script while the UserLevel global variable is set to 4 or less.

**Solution:** As with accessing any tool, HyperCard must be set to the proper level before the Script Editor will open. Even if your own UserLevel setting (i.e., the setting in the User Preferences card of your Home stack) is set to 5, the author of the stack you're using may have locked the user level to below 5 to prevent you from looking into scripts. If access to a script of such a stack is important, remember that you can put the script of any object into a global variable and put the contents of that variable into a field of the same or other stack for perusal. There are also stack utilities that extract scripts and print them out for you. Script Report (from Heizer Software, P.O. Box 232019, Pleasant Hill, CA 94523) is an excellent tool for this purpose as well as checking your own stacks' scripts.

APPENDIX A

# Tips on Importing and Exporting Data

MOVING TEXT AND GRAPHICS INFORMATION BETWEEN HYPERCARD AND OTHER PROgrams is, if nothing else, flexible. Text transfers are accomplished by way of scripts, which can read or write text data in as many ways as there are formats. Graphics transfers benefit from the universal Macintosh bit-map formats that all paint-type programs share.

## *Text Transfers to HyperCard*

In chapter 27, we described the Read From File HyperTalk command and provided a sample script that can be used unmodified to import most database and spreadsheet information. The principles behind the format of information stored as text-only data are quite simple.

Microsoft Excel, for instance, stores information in cells along a row as individual text items with tab characters between them. The rightmost cell in a row, however, has a carriage return following it. Therefore, if you wish to import a row of numbers into fields of a single card, you must first prepare the card so there are enough fields for the number of cells in the row. Then write the import script in such a way that it reads until a tab (which puts the imported text into It) puts the contents of It into a particular field, and continues the reading and putting (but into subsequent fields on the card) until it reaches the return character at the end of the row. At that point, the import script should go to the next card in the stack and repeat the reading and putting process for that row and card.

Importing text from a database has a similar feel to it. In Helix, for instance, you can choose an export option (called Dump) that presents a dialog box of choices for field and record separators— the characters that indicate the end of each field and record. If you wish to have each field from the database form occupy one field of the HyperCard card, use Helix's default settings, which place a tab character between field data and a return character between records. This turns the text-only data into the same text-only format that Excel generates.

When importing text from a word processing document (presumably into a large or scrolling HyperCard field), you should first save the original document in a text-only format. HyperCard cannot read the custom file formats of word processors, but it does recognize the common language of Text Only (ASCII). If your word processor, like MacWrite, gives you a choice of saving with return characters at the end of each line or at the end of each paragraph, choose the paragraph setting. This will let the text attributes of your HyperCard fields take care of word wrapping and line lengths within the field. Then write a short HyperTalk script that reads text until a return character. That will put a single paragraph into a field.

If you want more than one paragraph per field, you may either read from the file for a fixed number of characters or read until HyperCard encounters an unusual keyboard character that you must insert at the end of the text-only document section. For example, if the text contains no special symbols, you can place an "@" symbol at the end of each block you wish to be read into a single HyperCard field. The script, then, would read from the file until that symbol. From there, the script may read another block into another field on the same card, or progress to the next card in the stack and read the next block— that depends on how you intend to manipulate the data in your stack.

## *Exporting Text*

The rules for exporting data are very similar to the rules for importing text. The important point to remember when writing your export script is how the program receiving the information expects the data to be formatted.

If the destination program is a spreadsheet, like Excel, then write tab characters at the end of each field's data— or data that will be going into a single spreadsheet cell. When the data is to go into the next row of the spreadsheet, write a return character before the next batch of tab-delimited data.

Databases are to be treated in the same way. They usually expect tabs between data that will be going into individual fields, and return characters between records. In the script line that actually writes the contents of a field to the file, you can concatenate a tab or return character like this:

write field 1 & tab to file "Transfer File"

When exporting long blocks of text that will go into a word processing document, all you need to do is write the field to the file. Observe, however, how subsequent fields will be written to the file. If you do not specify any return characters between fields, they will be run-on in the text file generated by HyperCard. To separate the fields by more traditional paragraph separation, write two return characters to the file after each block. Each return character you send advances the cursor one line down the destination document.

As with any text-only transfer in the Macintosh, none of the font attributes of the source document are stored with the characters. When you load the exported text into your word processing document, you may then assign font attributes as you see fit. Also, depending on the program you're using, you will probably have to save the document with a different name in the word processing program's own file format. Because the text-only document and the word processed document are different file types (something that the Finder keeps an eye on), you won't be able to save the specially formatted file to the same name as the text-only file you used for the transfer. Therefore, consider exporting documents to an intermediate file name you won't be needing later.

## *Graphics Transfers*

Whenever you choose a painting tool from the Tools palette, the File menu gains two new items, Import Paint and Export Paint. These menu items are your windows to bit-mapped graphics in other paint-type programs, like FullPaint and SuperPaint (when pictures are saved as MacPaint files).

To export a HyperCard screen, choose any painting tool and then Export Paint... from the File menu. You are presented with a standard file dialog box requesting a name for the MacPaint file you wish to create. This export picture includes not only the graphics layers of the card you're viewing, but also the contents of the fields. Field text, of course, will be converted into bit maps in the MacPaint document. Also, the picture will be placed in the upper left corner of the MacPaint document, just as a Command-Shift-3 screen dump is.

All painting programs can load MacPaint documents, so even if you have one of the newer graphics programs, you will still be able to load and modify the picture exported from HyperCard.

Importing MacPaint-formatted documents is just as simple. The one limitation you should be aware of is that the source graphics document must have its content in the upper left corner of the page. In other words, when HyperCard imports a picture, it takes a one-screenful bite from the top left corner—the same spot to which it exports pictures.

Don't forget, too, to watch the graphics layer into which the imported graphic is to go. Imported graphics generally come in as opaque graphics layers. If you wish it to be transparent—to let background fields and buttons on the card show through—immediately select the entire screen (use the A Power Key) and press the T Power Key for transparency.

One other method of importing graphics, especially sections of pictures that aren't in the upper left corner, is to use the inexpensive desk accessories, such as Paint Grabber and Artisto. Most Macintosh user groups have Artisto and similar paint-moving programs available at very low cost.

APPENDIX B

# HyperTalk Reference

EARLIER IN THE BOOK, COMMANDS AND FUNCTIONS WERE DIVIDED ACCORDING TO function. Here we present commands, functions, and properties in alphabetical order for quick reference. We also supply the form of any parameters that a command requires or that functions and properties return. In the parentheses to the right of each entry is the page number in the Handbook containing in-depth descriptions of the item. Page numbers in boldface are from this upgrade list.

## *Commands and Keywords*

| | | |
|---|---|---|
| **add** | <numeric expression> to <container> | (441) |
| **answer** | <question> [with <reply><br>[or <reply> [or <reply>]]] | (463) |
| **ask** | <question> [with <reply>] | (465) |
| **ask password** | <question> [with <reply>] | (465) |
| **beep** | [<number of beeps>] | (469) |
| **choose** | <tool name> tool | (429) |
| **click** | at <location> [with <modifier key>] | (430) |
| **close file** | <text file name> | (475) |
| **close printing** | | (439) |
| **convert** | <date expression> to <date format> | (446) |
| **delete** | <chunk expression> | (420) |
| **dial** | <phone number> [with [modem] | |

<modem commands>] (424)

**divide** <container> by <numeric expression> (445)

**do** <HyperTalk command statement> (428)

**doMenu** <menu item> (420)

**drag** from <point> to <point> (431)

**edit script** of <object> (458)

**exit** if | repeat (595)

**exit to HyperCard** (735)

**find** <search string> [ in <field expression>] (409)

**find char[acter]s**
<search string>
[ in <field expression>] (409)

**find string** <search string> [ in <field expression>] (746)

**find whole** <search string> [ in <field expression>] (746)

**find word** <search string> [ in <field expression>] (409)

**get** <any expression> (419)

**get** <property name> [ of <object> ] (454)

**global** <variable list> (457)

**go** [to] <card, background or stack expression> (407)

**help** (413)

**hide** menubar (449)

**hide** <window> (449)

**hide** <field or button expression> (449)

**hide** card | background picture (743)

**hide** picture of <card expression> | <background expression> (743)

**if-then-else** (586)

**lock screen** (744)

**multiply** <container> by <numeric expression> (444)

**next repeat** (594)

**open** [<document name> with] <application name> (436)

**open file** <text file name> (475)

**open printing** [ with dialog ] (439)

**pass** <handler name> (596)

**play** <sound resource name> [tempo <speed>] (470)
[ <"notes"> ] [# | b] [octave] [duration]

**pop card** [ into <container> ] (411)

**print** <document name> with <application name> (480)

**print** [ all | <number> cards ] | [ <card expression> ] (439)

**push** [ this | recent ] card (411)

**put** <any expression> [ into | after | before <container> ] (415)

**read** from file < text file name> until <delimiter character> | for <number of bytes> (476)

**repeat** [ forever | for | until | while | with ] (590)

**reset paint** (737)

**return** <function result> (561)

**select** <button expression> | <field expression> | me | target (738)

**select** [ before | after ] text | <chunk expression> of <field expression> (740)

**select empty**

**send** <HyperTalk message> to <object expression> (427)

**set** <property name > [ of <object> ] to <new setting> (454)

**show** [ <number> | all ] cards (451)

**show** menubar (451)

**show** <window> (451)

**show** <field or button expression> (451)

**show** card | background picture (743)

**show** picture of <card expression> | <background expression> (743)

**sort** [ ascending | descending ] [ text | numeric | international | datetime ] by <container or other expression> (434)

**subtract** <numeric expression> from <container> (442)

**type** <string expression> (433)

**unlock screen** [ with <visual effect> ] [<speed>] [to <color>] (744)

**visual** [effect] <effect name> [<speed>] [to <color>] (461)

**wait** [for] <quantity> ticks | seconds (422)

**wait until** <Boolean expression> (422)

**wait while** <Boolean expression> (422)

**write** <string expression> to file <text file name> (478)

## *Functions*

**the abbreviated | abbrev | abbr date** (523)

**the charToNum** of <character> (541)

| | | |
|---|---|---|
| **the clickH** | | (751) |
| **the clickLoc** | | (535) |
| **the clickV** | | (751) |
| **the commandKey** | | (531) |
| **the date** | | (523) |
| **the diskSpace** | | (750) |
| **the foundChunk** | | (754) |
| **the foundField** | | (754) |
| **the foundLine** | | (754) |
| **the foundText** | | (754) |
| **the heapSpace** | | (754) |
| **the length** | of <any expression> | (537) |
| **the long date** | | (523) |
| **the long time** | | (524) |
| **the long version** | | (757) |
| **the mouse** | | (534) |
| **the mouseclick** | | (534) |
| **the mouseH** | | (529) |
| **the mouseLoc** | | (529) |
| **the mouseV** | | (529) |
| **the number** | of <components> of <container> | (540) |
| **the number of buttons \| fields** | | (553) |
| **the number of cards** | [of <background expression> ] | (756) |
| **the numToChar** | of <ASCII value> | (541) |
| **offset** | (<match string> , <complete text>) | (538) |
| **the optionKey** | | (531) |
| **the param** | of <parameter number> | (558) |
| **the paramcount** | | (558) |
| **the params** | | (558) |
| **the random** | of <upper bound> | (545) |
| **the result** | | (555) |
| **the screenRect** | | (759) |
| **the seconds** | | (525) |
| **the secs** | | (525) |
| **the selectedChunk** | | (752) |
| **the selectedField** | | (752) |
| **the selectedLine** | | (752) |
| **the selectedText** | | (752) |
| **the shiftKey** | | (531) |
| **the sound** | | (556) |
| **the stackSpace** | | (749) |
| **the target** | | (557) |
| **the ticks** | | (526) |
| **the time** | | (524) |

| | | |
|---|---|---|
| **the value** | of <any expression> | (546) |
| **the version** | [ of HyperCard ] | (757) |
| **the version** | of <stack expression> | (757) |

## *Math Functions*

| | | |
|---|---|---|
| **abs** | (number) | (548) |
| **annuity** | (periodic rate, number of periods) | (548) |
| **atan** | (angle in radians) | (549) |
| **average** | (number list) | (549) |
| **compound** | (periodic rate, number of periods) | (549) |
| **cos** | (angle in radians) | (549) |
| **exp** | (number) | (549) |
| **exp1** | (number) | (550) |
| **exp2** | (number) | (550) |
| **ln** | (number) | (550) |
| **ln1** | (number) | (550) |
| **max** | (number list) | (550) |
| **min** | (number list) | (550) |
| **round** | (number) | (551) |
| **sin** | (angle in radians) | (551) |
| **sqrt** | (number) | (551) |
| **tan** | (angle in radians) | (551) |
| **trunc** | (number) | (551) |

## *Global Properties*

| | | |
|---|---|---|
| **blindTyping** | <true or false> | (484) |
| **cursor** | <id number or name><br>("hand" at idle time) | (485/766) |
| **dragSpeed** | <number> (zero at idle time) | (486) |
| **editBkgnd** | <true or false> | (487) |
| **language** | <language name> | (487) |
| **lockMessages** | <true or false> (false at idle time) | (761) |
| **lockRecent** | <true or false> (false at idle time) | (762) |
| **lockScreen** | <true or false> (false at idle time) | (488) |
| **numberFormat** | <format string><br>("0.######" at idle time) | (489) |
| **powerKeys** | <true or false> | (490) |
| **userLevel** | <1 to 5> | (491) |
| **userModify** | <true or false> (false after closing card) | (719) |

## *Window Properties*

| | | |
|---|---|---|
| **bottom** | <bottom> | (764) |
| **bot[tom]Right** | <right>,<bottom> | (764) |
| **height** | <height in pixels> | (764) |
| **left** | <left> | (764) |
| **loc[ation]** | <left>,<top> | (492) |
| **rect[angle]** | <left>,<top>,<right>,<bottom> | (493) |
| **right** | <right> | (764) |
| **top** | <top> | (764) |
| **topLeft** | <left>,<top> | (764) |
| **visible** | <true or false> | (494) |
| **width** | <width in pixels> | (764) |

## *Painting Properties*

| | | |
|---|---|---|
| **brush** | <brush number 1 to 42> | (494) |
| **centered** | <true or false> | (495) |
| **filled** | <true or false> | (495) |
| **grid** | <true or false> | (496) |
| **lineSize** | <line thickness 1 to 9 pixels> | (497) |
| **multiple** | <true or false> | (497) |
| **multiSpace** | <1 to 9> | (497) |
| **pattern** | <pattern number 1 to 40> | (498) |
| **polySides** | <number of polygon sides greater than zero > | (499) |
| **textAlign** | <left \| right \| center> | (499) |
| **textFont** | <font name> | (499) |
| **textHeight** | <leading> | (499) |
| **textSize** | <font size> | (499) |
| **textStyle** | <bold \| italic \| underline \| outline \| shadow \| condense \| extend \| plain> | (499) |

## *Stack Properties*

| | | |
|---|---|---|
| **cantDelete** | <true or false> | (767) |
| **cantModify** | <true or false> | (768) |
| **freeSize** | <number of bytes> | (763) |
| **long name** | stack <volume:[folders:] stack name> | (501) |
| **name** | stack <stack name> | (501) |
| **script** | <text of script> | (502) |

| | | |
|---|---|---|
| **short name** | <stack name only> | (501) |
| **size** | <number of bytes> | (763) |

## *Background Properties*

| | | |
|---|---|---|
| **cantDelete** | <true or false> | (767) |
| **id** | <unique ID number> | (122) |
| **long name** | bkgnd <id I background name><br>of stack <volume:[folders:] stack name> | (501) |
| **name** | bkgnd <id I background name> | (501) |
| **script** | <text of script> | (502) |
| **short name** | <background name only> | (501) |
| **showPict** | <true or false> | (771) |

## *Card Properties*

| | | |
|---|---|---|
| **cantDelete** | <true or false> | (770) |
| **id** | <unique ID number> | (125) |
| **long name** | card <id I card name><br>of stack <volume:[folders:] stack name> | (501) |
| **name** | card <id I card name> | (501) |
| **number** | <number relative to first card) | (125) |
| **script** | <text of script> | (502) |
| **short name** | <card name only> | (501) |
| **showPict** | <true or false> | (771) |

## *Field Properties*

| | | |
|---|---|---|
| **autoTab** | <true or false> | (770) |
| **bottom** | <bottom> | (764) |
| **bot[tom]Right** | <right>,<bottom> | (764) |
| **id** | <unique ID number> | (148) |
| **height** | <height in pixels> | (764) |
| **left** | <left> | (764) |
| **loc[ation]** | <left>,<top> | (503) |
| **lockText** | <true of false> | (504) |
| **long name** | card I bkgnd field <id I field name><br>of stack <volume:[folders:] stack name> | (504) |
| **name** | card I bkgnd field <id I field name> | (504) |
| **number** | <number in tabbing order> | (132) |

| | | |
|---|---|---|
| **rect[angle]** | <left>,<top>,<right>,<bottom> | (505) |
| **right** | <right> | (764) |
| **script** | <text of script> | (506) |
| **scroll** | <number of pixels> | (507) |
| **short name** | <field name only> | (504) |
| **showLines** | <true or false> | (504) |
| **style** | < transparent I opaque I rectangle I shadow I scrolling > | (507) |
| **textAlign** | <left I right I center> | (508) |
| **textFont** | <font name> | (508) |
| **textHeight** | <leading in pixels> | (508) |
| **textSize** | <font size> | (508) |
| **textStyle** | < bold I italic I underline I outline I shadow I condense I extend I plain> | (508) |
| **top** | <top> | (764) |
| **topLeft** | <left>,<top> | (764) |
| **visible** | <true or false> | (509) |
| **wideMargins** | <true of false> | (504) |
| **width** | <width in pixels> | (764) |

## *Button Properties*

| | | |
|---|---|---|
| **autoHilite** | <true or false> | (510) |
| **bottom** | <bottom> | (764) |
| **bot[tom]Right** | <right>,<bottom> | (764) |
| **height** | <height in pixels> | (764) |
| **hilite** | <true or false> | (510) |
| **icon** | <icon number> | (511) |
| **id** | <unique ID number> | (165) |
| **left** | <left> | (764) |
| **loc[ation]** | <left>,<top> | (512) |
| **long name** | card I bkgnd button <id I button name> of stack <volume:[folders:] stack name> | (513) |
| **name** | card I bkgnd button <id I button name> | (513) |
| **number** | <number in layer order> | (165) |
| **rect[angle]** | <left>,<top>,<right>,<bottom> | (514) |
| **right** | <right> | (764) |
| **script** | <text of script> | (514) |
| **short name** | <button name only> | (513) |
| **showName** | <true or false> | (510) |
| **style** | < transparent I opaque I rectangle I roundRect I checkBox I radioButton > | (515) |

| | | |
|---|---|---|
| **textAlign** | <left I right I center> | (516) |
| **textFont** | <font name> | (516) |
| **textHeight** | <leading in pixels> | (516) |
| **textSize** | <font size> | (516) |
| **textStyle** | < bold I italic I underline I outline I shadow I condense I extend I plain > | (516) |
| **top** | <top> | (764) |
| **topLeft** | <left>,<top> | (764) |
| **visible** | <true or false> | (517) |
| **width** | <width in pixels> | (764) |

# Index


Abbreviated date,
  date function, 523-524
Abbreviations, 707-708
Abs, math function, 548
Action commands, 415-440
  Choose command, 429-430
  Click command, 430-431
  Close Printing command, 439-440
  Delete command, 420
  Dial command, 424-427
  Do command, 428-429
  doMenu command, 420-422
  Drag command, 431-432
  Get command, 419
  Open command, 436-438
  Open Printing command, 439-440
  Put commands, 415-419
  Send command, 427-428
  Sort command, 434-436
  Type command, 433-434
  Wait command, 422-424
Add command, 441-442
  examples of, 442
  parameters of, 442
  purpose of, 441
  use of, 441-442
Advance handler, 707-708
After preposition, Put command, 418
Align handler, 782-783
And operator, 570-571, 585
Annuity, math function, 548
Answer command, 463-465
  examples of, 464-465
  parameters of, 464
  purpose of, 463
  use of, 463-464
Applications, 605-682
  conversion calculator, 651-662
  corporate directory, 605-615
  telephone logbook, 617-624
  time sheet, 625-633
  To Do list, 635-649
  visual outliner, 663-682
  See also specific applications.
Application Memory Size
  requirements, 699
Arithmetic commands, 441-447
  Add command, 441-442
  Convert command, 446-447
  Divide command, 445-446
  Multiply command, 444-445
  Subtract command, 442-444
ArrowKey, system messages, 389
Ask command, 465-467
  example of, 466-467
  parameters of, 466
  purpose of, 465
  use of, 465-466
Ask Password command, 465
  use of, 465-466
Atan, math function, 549
Authoring, 85-95
  backgrounds, 119-122
  buttons, 161-183
    background/card domains,
      changing domain, 180-182
    basic function of, 161
    Button tool, accessing, 162

card buttons, 164-165
cloning buttons, 177-180
Copying and Pasting, 182-183
HyperTalk, 175, 182
ID number, 165
moving, 176-177
newbuttons, creating, 175-177
order of, 165
resizing, 177
styles of, 166, 171-174
cards, 123-128
backgrnd/card relationship, 123
card names, 126
card numbers, 125
selection of, 126-128
design strategies, 120
blank backgrounds, 120-121
Info dialog box, 121-122
fields, 129-159
background/card domains, changing domain, 156-158
cloning fields, 152-156
copying/pasting between stacks, 158-159
field order, 132-138
Field tool, accessing, 130
font properties, 143-148
HyperTalk properties, 148-149
moving fields, 151
resizing fields, 152
styles of, 139-143
text fields, creating, 149
text versus graphics, 129
HyperTalk, 175, 182
layers, 109-117
background layer, 112-115
card layers, 115-116
heterogeneous stacks, 116-117
object layers, 109-111
linking, 185-192
button strategies, 191-192
hard links, 187-188
link scripts, 188-191
soft links, 188
to adjacent cards, 185-186
to different stacks, 186-187
to distant cards, 186
menus, 90
standard menus, 93
tear-off palettes, 93-94
Options menu, 259-276
painting, 193-199
background vs. card layers, 196-197
menus, 197-198
painting strategies, 277-280
painting tools, 201-243
paint menu, 245-257
undo, 199
versus drawing, 194-195
reasons for use, 86-89
compiling personal information, 86-87
distribution possibilities, 88-89
encouraging computer use, 87-88
screen, 92-93
9 inch screen, 92
large screens, 92-93
stacks, 97-108
creation of, 281-337
heterogeneous stack, 98-100
homogeneous stack, 98
new stack, creating, 100-105
protection, 105-108
See also specific topics.
autoHilite, button property, 510
Automatic diaang, 67
AutoTab, 702-703, 770-771
Average, math function, 549

Background
Background expression, 728
background fields
modifying
adding lines to card, 317-320
erasing field, 316-317
blank background, 120-121
Command-B, 24
empty space as, 24
foreground, 24
name property, 501
script property, 502-503
background graphics (modifying)
background text, 310
buttons, 311-316

card depth, 293-298
drop shadowing, 301-309
widening card, 299-301
background layer, 112-115
button layers, 113
graphics, adding, 113
icon buttons, 113
painting, 196
text field layers, 114-115
Batch processing, 4
Beachball cursor, 48
Beep command, 469-470
examples of, 470
parameters of, 470
purpose of, 469
use of, 469-470
Before preposition, Put command, 417-418
Bitmap Alignment, 71
Bit-mapped graphics, 194
and patterns, 271-272, 274
and Pickup Command, 249
Bitmap Printing, 70-71
Blank backgrounds, 120-121
blindTyping, global property, 484-485
Boolean
Boolean expression, 729
HyperTalk scripts, 365-366
Wait command, 423
Browsing environment, 17-81
backgrounds, 23-24
empty space as, 24
foreground, restoring, 24
browse tool, 43-44
getting tool, 44
buttons, 27-28
clicking on, 28
forms of, 27-28
cards, 24-28
adding to stack, 25
information on, 25
fields, 27
size of, 27
going back in time, 29
HomeStack, 28-32
cards in, 29
file preferences, 29-30
Home Card, 28-29
pathnames, 29-32
root directory, 29
linking, 65-67
automatic dialing, 67
Datebook linking, 67
and Message Box, 66-67
Message Box, 34-39
as calculator, 36-39
clearing of, 35
and close box, 34
and go address command, 36
and go commands, 35-36
and go home command, 36
moving of, 34
purpose of, 34
text display, 35
text pointer, disappearance of, 35
windows of, 34
printing, 68-81
Page Setup, 69-71
Print Card, 71
Print Report, 76-81
Print Stack, 71-72, 74
report formatting options, 76-81
Recent, 32-34
options to, 33
representations of cards, 32-33
stacks, 20
closing of, 22
opening of, 20-22
saving, 22
standard file dialog box, 20
Brush, painting property, 494-495
Brush shape, 268
Button properties, 510-517
autoHilite, 510
hilite, 510-511
icon, 511-512
loc[ation], 512
name, 513
rect[angle], 514
script, 515
showName, 510
textAlign, 516
textFont, 516
textHeight, 516
textSize, 516
textStyle, 516
visible, 517

Buttons
- adding
  - card layers, 115-116
  - to cards, 311-316
- background/card domains, 180-182
  - background layer, 113
- basic function of, 161
- Button tool, 162
- card buttons, 164-165
- check box buttons, 174
- clicking on, 28
- cloning buttons, 177-180
- Copying and Pasting, 182-183
- forms of, 27-28
- HyperTalk, 175, 182
- icon buttons, 166, 168-171
- ID number, 165
- and linking, 191-192
- names of, 171
- new buttons, 175-177
- opaque buttons, 173
- order of, 165
- radio buttons, 174
- rectangle button style, 174
- rounded rectangle button style, 174
- stack building
  - add background buttons, 321
  - card/button linking, 334-335
  - cloning buttons, 325-328
  - delete background buttons, 321
  - modification of, 321-324
  - stack button, 335-336
- transparent buttons, 171-172
- viewing locations of, 47
- See also Button properties; Button scripts.

Button scripts
- HyperTalk
  - Home button, 370, 374
  - Index button, 370, 375
- HyperTalk scripts, 372-376

Calculations
- automatic, 789-790
- Message Box, 36-39
  - example calculations, 37-38
  - order of calculations, 38
  - preprogrammed functions/ constants, 39
  - as scientific calculator, 38

Calculator, conversion calculator, application program, 651-662

CantDelete, 767-768

CantModify, 768-769

Card buttons, 164-165

Card expression, 726-727

Card layer, 115-116
- buttons, 115-116
- graphics, 116
  - adding graphics, 331-334
- modifying, 116
- painting, 196-197

Cards
- adding to stack, 25
- background/card relationship, 123
- card names, 126
- card numbers, 46, 125
- complete card, 128
- flipping through
  - with arrow keys, 45-46
  - cyclical nature of cards, 46-47
  - front of stack, 46
- Go command, 407-409
- information on, 25
- modifying background fields
  - adding lines to card, 317-320
  - erasing field, 316-317
- modifying background graphics
  - background text, 310
  - buttons, 311-316
  - card depth, 293-298
  - drop shadowing, 301-309
  - widening card, 299-301
- name property, 501
- new cards
  - creating, 61-62
  - saving, 62
- Pop command, 411-413
- Print stack, cards per page, 72
- Push command, 411-413
- script property, 502-503
- selection of, 126-128
  - Copy Card option, 126-127
  - Cut Card option, 126-127
  - placement in Clipboard, 127

stack building
card layer graphic, 331-334
linking to buttons, 334-335
new cards, 328-330
stack button, 335-336
CD-ROM, 791-797
explanation of, 792-793
interaction with HyperCard, 793
stack, getting onto CD-ROM, 794
Centered, painting property, 495
Characters, components of information, 403
charToNum, text function, 541-543
Check box buttons, 174
Choose command, 429-430
examples of, 430
parameters of, 430
purpose of, 429
use of, 429-430
Chunk expressions, 729-731
component of information, 405
Click command, 430-431
examples of, 431
parameters of, 431
purpose of, 430
use of, 430-431
The ClickH and ClickV, 751
clickLoc, mouse function, 535-536
Clipboard, 43
cards, placement in, 127
copying buttons onto, 182
Cloning buttons, 177-180
and stack building, 325-328
Cloning fields, 152-156
columns, 154-155
steps in, 153-154
Close Field, 368
Close File command, 475-476
examples of, 476
parameters of, 476
purpose of, 475
use of, 475-476
Close Printing command, 439-440
Columns, Print Report, 76-77
Command-2, flipping through cards, 45
Command-3, flipping through cards, 45
Command-4, user preferences, 17
Command-B, background, 24, 149
Command-F, text searches, 48, 49, 50, 56, 350, 409
Command-G, 350
Command-H, 350
user preferences, 17
Command-K, saving, 254
CommandKey
enhancement of
Eraser tool, 213-214
Lasso tool, 207
Paintbrush tool, 210
selection tool, 203
keyboard function, 531-534
paint tool, 221
shortcuts, Text tool, 234-235
Command-M, Message Box, 34, 35, 409
Command-P, 350
Command-R, 33
Commands (HyperTalk)
action commands, 415-440
Choose command, 429-430
Click command, 430-431
Close Printing command, 439-440
Delete command, 420
Dial command, 424-427
Do command, 428-429
doMenu command, 420-422
Drag command, 431-432
Get command, 419
Open command, 436-438
Open Printing command, 439-440
Put command, 415-419
Send command, 427-428
Sort command, 434-436
Type command, 433-434
Wait command, 422-424
arithmetic commands, 441-447
Add command, 441-442
Convert command, 446-447
Divide command, 445-446
Multiply command, 444-445
Subtract command, 442-444
containers, 400-405
components of information, 403-405
fields, 400-401
global variables, 402
local variables, 401

Message Box, 402
Selection, 400, 402
conventions related to, 398-399
file manipulation commands, 475-481
Close File command, 475-476
Open File command, 475-476
Print command, 480-481
Read From File command, 476-478
Write To File command, 478-480
navigation commands, 407-413
Find command, 409-411
Go command, 407-409
Help command, 413
Pop card command, 411-413
Push card command, 411-413
object manipulation commands, 449-459
Edit Script command, 458-459
Get command, 454-457
global variables, 457-458
Hide commands, 449-451
Set command, 454-457
Show command, 451-453
parameters of, 358, 398-399
screen manipulation commands, 461-467
Answer command, 463-465
Ask command, 465-467
Ask Password command, 465-467
Visual Effect command, 461-463
sound commands, 469-473
Beep command, 469-470
Play command, 470-473
words used, 360, 399
updated commands, 735-742
Exit to HyperCard, 735-737
Find, 736-737
Hide/show, 733-734
Lock/unlock screen, 734-736
Reset paint, 737-738
Select, 738-742
Components of information
characters, 403
chunk expressions, 405
concatenating components, 404-405
items, 403
lines, 403-404
words, 403-404
Compound, math function, 549
concatenate, &, math operator, 572-573
concatenate and space, &&, math operator, 572-573
Concatenating components of information, 404-405
Constants, 577-581
Down constant, 577-579
empty constant, 579
False constant, 577-579
formfeed constant, 580-581
linefeed constant, 580-581
quote constant, 579-580
return constant, 580
space constant, 580
tab constant, 580
True constant, 577-579
Up constant, 577-579
Containers, 400-405
Add command, 441-442
components of information in, 403-405
characters, 403
chunk expressions, 405
concatenating components, 404-405
items, 403
lines, 403-404
words, 403-404
Delete command, 420
Divide command, 445-46
Do command, 428-429
fields, 400-401
Get command, 419
global variables, 402
HyperTalk scripts, 365, 400-405
local variables, 401
Message Box, 402
Multiply command, 444-445
Put command, 415-419
Selection, 400, 402
Subtract command, 422-444
Contains operator, 573-575
ControlKey message, 709-710
Control structures, 583-597
if-then constructions, 584-588

if...then, 586-587
if...then...else, 587-588
nesting if-then-decisions, 589
structure of, 584-586
repeat constructions, 590-597
exit, 595-596
Exit If, 595-596
Exit Repeat, 595-596
Next Repeat, 594-595
pass, 596-597
Repeat For, 590-591
Repeat Until, 591-592
Repeat While, 592-593
Repeat With, 593-594
Conversion calculator, 651-662
overview of, 651-654
scripts/properties, 654-662
Convert command, 446-447
parameters of, 447
purpose of, 446
use of, 446-447
Copy Card, 126-127, 246
Copying and Pasting
buttons, 182-183
between stacks, 158-159
changing domains, 156-158
field between stacks, 158-159
Copyrights, fonts, 146
Corporate directory, 605-615
overview of, 605-608
scripts/properties, 608-615
streamlining of, 615
Cos, math function, 549
Current stack, search of, 48
Cursor, 766-767
Beachball cursor, 48
cursor resources 805
global property, 485-486
I-Beam text cursor, 55, 57, 58, 424, 425
styles of, 766-767
Curve tool
double-click shortcut, 231
Option key enhancement, 230-231
Cut Card option, 126-127

Darken, Paint menu, 250
Database software, 8-11
file management software, 8-9
and HyperCard, 10-11
relational databases, 9-10
Data fork, 800
Date
Convert command, 446-447
date function, 523-524
formats, U.S. version, 447
Datebook, and linking, 67
Default font, 150
Delete
deleting card, 62-63
deleting messages, 387-388
Delete command, 420
examples of, 420
parameters of, 420
purpose of, 420
use of, 420
Depth, card depth, reducing, 293-298
Destination
card destinations, 408
HyperTalk scripts, 365, 398
Dial command, 424-427
examples of, 426-427
parameters of, 425-426
purpose of, 424
use of, 67, 424-425
DiskSpace, The, 750
divide, /, math operator, 565-566
Divide command, 445-446
eemples of, 446
parameters of, 445-446
purpose of, 445
use of, 445
Do command, 428-429
examples of, 429
parameters of, 429
purpose of, 428
use of, 428
doMenu command, 420-422
examples of, 422
parameters of, 421
purpose of, 420
use of, 421
DoMenu message, system messages, 390
Dotted lines, Show Lines, 143
Double-click shortcut
Curve tool, 231

Eraser tool, 214
Irregular Polygon Tool, 241-242
Lasso tool, 207
Paintbrush tool, 211
Paint Bucket tool, 227-228
Patterns Palette, 243
Pencil tool, 209
Rectangle tool, 222
Regular Polygon tool, 237-238
selection tool, 205
Straight line tool, 216
Text tool, 233-234
Down constant, 577-579
Drag command, 431-432
examples of, 432
purpose of, 431
use of, 431-432
dragSpeed, global property, 486-487
Draw Centered, 224, 229, 274, 495
Draw Filled, 229, 231, 241, 274, 495
Drawing, versus painting, 194-195
Draw Multiple, 238, 275-276
Drop shadow effect, adding, 301-309

editBkgnd, global property, 487
Edit Pattern, 268
Edit Script command, 458-459
examples of, 459
parameters of, 459
purpose of, 458
use of, 458-459
Empty constant, 579
End mouseUp, 351, 363, 371, 374, 375
"End" statement, HyperTalk scripts, 351-352
Entering text, 57-62
cursor, I-Beam cursor, 57, 58
new card
creation of, 61-62
saving, 62
new stack, 104
text fields, 57
editing, 61
finding card's fields, 58-59
text entry, 59, 61
EnterInField, 710-712
EnterKey, system messages, 389
Entry point, messages, 376-378
equals, =, math operator, 566
Eraser tool
Command key enhancement, 213-214
double-click shortcut, 214
Shift key enhancement, 213
Error messages.See Helper messages
Exit, repeat construction, 595-596
Exit If, repeat construction, 595-596
Exit Repeat, repeat construction, 595-596
Exit to HyperCard, 735-737
exp1, math function, 550
exp2, math function, 550
Exp, math function, 549
Exporting text, 686-687
Open File/Close File commands, 475-476
Write To File Command, 478-480
Expressions, 725-733
background expression, 728
Boolean expression, 729
card expression, 726-727
chunk expression, 729-731
"do" and, 732
evaluating expressions, 727-728
most common expressions, 731
notation for, 732
stack expression, 728

False constant, 577-579
Fast Laser Printing, 71
FatBits, 196, 226
buttons, adding to cards, 311-316
Pencil tool, 209
scrolling in, 265
switching off, 264
switching on, 263-264
Field properties, 503-510
loc[ation], 503
lockText, 504
name, 504-505
rect[angle], 505-506
script, 506-507
scroll, 507
showLines, 504
style, 507-508
textAlign, 508-509

textFont, 508-509
textHeight, 508-509
textSize, 508-509
textStyle, 508-509
visible, 509-510
WideMargins, 504

Fields, 129-159
- background/card domains, 156-158
- cloning fields, 152-156
  - columns, 154-155
  - steps in, 153-154
- as container, 400-401
- copying/pasting between stacks, 158-159
- field order, 132-138
  - modifying, 134-137
  - Move Closer, 137
  - Move Farther, 137
  - new stack, example of, 132-134
- Field tool, 130
- font properties, 143-148
  - adjustment of, 144
  - copyrights, 146
  - limitations of, 143, 145
  - line height, 144
  - and resource editor, 146
  - reverse lettering, 147
  - shortcuts and, 147-148
  - and stacks, 146
  - standard fonts, listing of, 145
  - system fonts, 146
  - text alignment, 144
  - in text field, 143-144
- HyperTalk properties, 148-149
- moving fields, 151
- size of, 27
  - resizing fields, 152
- styles of, 139-143
  - Lock text, 142-143
  - opaque field, 140
  - rectangle field style, 141
  - scrolling field style, 142
  - shadow field style, 141-142
  - Show Lines, 143
  - transparent field, 139-140
  - Wide Margins, 143
- text fields, 149
- text versus graphics, 129

File management software, 8-9
- features of, 8-9

File manipulation commands, 475-481
- Close File command, 475-476
- Open File command, 475-476
- Print command, 480-481
- Read om File command, 476-478
- Write To File command, 478-480

Files
- data fork, 800
- resource fork, 800

File system errors/numbers, 822-823

Fill, Paint menu, 247

Filled, painting property, 495

Find command, 47-48, 409-411
- examples of, 410
- failure of, result function, 555
- parameters of, 410
- purpose of, 409
- use of, 409-410
- update, 700

Finding information, 41-56
- Browse tool, 43-44
  - getting tool, 44
- buttons, viewing locations of, 47
- Find command, 409-411
- flipping through cards, 45-47
  - with arrow keys, 45-46
  - cyclical nature of cards, 46-47
  - front of stack, 46
- retrieval environments, 42-43
  - HyperCard in Switcher, 42-43
  - stand-alone application, 42
- text searches, 47-56
  - Find, exercises with, 51-54
  - finding strings, 48, 49-50
  - and Message Box, 47-49
  - narrowing a search, 54-55
  - search-and-replace, 775-779

Find strings, 48, 49-50
- shortcuts, 50
- update, 700-701

Find Whole command, 701-702

Flipping
- through cards, 45-47
- with arrow keys, 45-46
- Command-2/Command-3, 45
- cyclical nature of cards, 46-47

front of stack, 46
Paint menu, 252-253
Font properties
Font properties
adjustment of, 144
copyrights, 146
default font, 150
fields, 143-148
limitations of, 143, 145
line height, 144
and resource editor, 146
reverse lettering, 147
shortcuts and, 147-148
and stacks, 146
standard fonts, 145
system fonts, 146
text alignment, 144
in text field, 143-144
Fonts
default font, 232
font resources, 804
font Substitution, 70
Text tool, 235
See also Font properties; Painting tools.
Foreground, restoring, 24
Foreign language versions, HyperTalk, 366
Formfeed constant, 580-581
FoundChunk, 754, 756
FoundField, 755
FoundLine, 755
FoundText, 754
FreeSize, 763-764
FunctionKey message, 709-710
Functions
HyperTalk scripts, 360-361
returns and, 360
keyboard/mouse functions
clickLoc, 535-536
commandKey, 531-534
mouse, 534-535
mouseClick, 534-535
mouseH, 529-531
mouseLoc, 529-531
mouseV, 529-531
optionKey, 531-534
shiftKey, 531-534
math functions
abs, 548
annuity, 548
atan, 549
average, 549
compound, 549
cos, 549
exp1, 550
exp2, 550
exp, 549
max, 550
min, 550
ln1, 550
ln, 550
random, 5445-546
round, 551
sin, 551
sqrt, 551
tan, 551
trunc, 551
value, 546-548
miscellaneous functions
number of cards/buttons/fields, 553-554
param, 558
paramcount, 558
params, 558-561
result, 555-556
sound, 556-557
target, 557-558
text functions
charToNum, 541-543
length, 537-538
number [of], 540-541
numToChar, 541-543
offset, 538-540
time/date functions
abbreviated date, 523-524
date, 523-524
long date, 523-524
long time, 524-525
seconds, 525
secs, 525
ticks, 526-527
time, 524
updates
the ClickH and ClickV, 751
the DiskSpace, 750

FoundChunk, 754,756
FoundField, 755
FoundLine, 755
FoundText, 754
HeapSpace, 749-750
Number of Cards, 756-757
ScreenRect, 759-760
SelectedChunk, 752-753
SelectedField, 752-753
SelectedLine, 752-753
SelectedText, 752-753
StackSpace, 749-750
Versions, 757-759
user-defined functions, 561-562

Get command, 419, 454-457
examples of, 419, 456-457
HyperTalk scripts, 365
parameters of, 454, 456
purpose of, 419, 454
use of, 419, 454
Global properties, 484-492
blindTyping, 484-485
cursor, 485-486
dragSpeed, 486-487
editBkgnd, 487
language, 487-488
lockScreen, 488-489
numberFormat, 489-490
powerKeys, 490-491
userLevel, 491-492
Global variables, 457-458
as container, 402
examples of, 457-458
HyperTalk scripts, 364, 402
parameters of, 457
purpose of, 457
use of, 457
Go command, 407-409
examples of, 408
failure of, result function, 555
parameters of, 408
purpose of, 407
use of, 407-408
Graphics
adding, card layers, 116
bit-mapping, 194
Graphics images
distortions on, 71
smoothing, 70
Graphics transfers, 687-688
Graphic text, versus fields, 129
greater than, >, math operator, 567-568
greater than/equal to, > =, math operator, 567-568
greater than/equal to) >, math operator, 567-568
Grid
painting property, 496-497
as time saver, 260

Handlers, scrolling handlers, 782-785
Hard links, 187-188
Header text, Print Stack, 74
HeapSpace, 749-750
Help command, 413
example of, 413
parameters of, 413
purpose of, 413
use of, 413
Helper messages
bad data in card id #, 811
can't delete the home stack, 812
can't delete last card of protected background, 811
can't delete last card. Use delete stack instead, 811
can't delete protected card, 811-812
can't find the menu item " " 811
can't get that property, 812-813
can't interpret that keyword in the message box, 813
can't modify this stack, 813
can't open any more files, 813-814
can't read card of background id#, 815
can't rename the home stack, 815
can't see that button/field/card/bkgnd/stack/HyperCard/window property, 815
can't take the value of that expression, 815-816
can't understand, " " 816
can't understand arguments of, " " 816-817

can't understand arguments of command ", " 816-817
can't understand what's after, 817-818
can't use a reserved word as a variable name, 818-819
colon not allowed in name, 819
destination does not contain a number, 819
an error has occurred in the LaserWriter. Turning the printer off and back on again might clear up the problem, 819
existing file is not a HyperCard stack, 819-820
existing file is not a MacPaint document. Can't export paint to that file, 820
expected " " but found " " 820
expected end of line after " " 821
expected unsigned integer but found " " 821
external commands and functions cannot have more than 10 parameters, 821
fields can't hold more than 30000 characters, 821-822
file system error #, 822-823
file system error # while reading from the disk, 822-823
file system error # while writing to the disk, 822-823
found "else" without "then", 823
found "end if" without "if", 823
found "end repeat" without "repeat", 823
found "exit repeat" outside a repeat loop, 823
found "if" without "then", 823
found "next repeat" outside a repeat loop, 823
found "then" without "if" 823
HyperCard does not have enough memory to continue, 824
HyperCard requires more recent ROMS, 824
" " is not the right type for " ", 824-825
need true or false after "not" but got " " 825
never heard of " ", 825
no open file named " ", 826
no such card, 826
not a scrolling field, 826
not enough disk space to compact, 827
not enough ends, 827
not enough memory to read from file, 827-828
not enough memory to use the painting tools, 827-828
nothing to copy. Try background, 828
out of memory,, 828-829
please select something first, 829
a printing error has occurred: the print job cannot be completed, 810
save changes to script? 829
show background picture, 829-830
show card picture? 829
sorry there isn't enough memory to print from HyperCard 830
sort by what?, 830
that disk is too full 830
that tool is not available from the current user level, 831
too many variables, 831
too much recursion, 831-832
unexpected end of line, 832
unexpected error #, 832
user level is too low to edit script, 832

Heterogeneous stacks, 98-100
  building from homogeneous stacks, 127-128
  and layers, 116-117
  organization of, 117
Hide command, 449-451
  examples of, 451
  parameters of, 450-451
  purpose of, 449
  use of, 449-450
Hide/show, 743-744
Hierarchy of HyperTalk scripts
  button scripts, 372-376

illustration of, 370, 372
workings of, 369-372
Highlighting
autoHilite property, 510
hilite property, 510-511
showName, property, 510
Home button, 370, 374
Home Card, 28-29
buttons, 29
HomeStack
cards in, 29
file preferences, 29-30
Home Card, 28-29
pathnames, 29-32
determining of, 31
listing of, 30
pathname rotation, 30
root directory, 29
userLevel, 491-492
User Preferences, 17-19
Homogeneous stack, 98
HyperCard
applications, 605-682
authoring, 85-95
Browsing environment, 17-81
card catalog model, 19
CD-ROM and, 791-797
compared to database software,10-11
entering text information, 56-63
exporting text, 686-687
finding information, 41-56
HyperTalk, 343-366
importance of, 11-12
importing text, 686
graphics transfers, 687-688
levels of
Browsing/Typing level, 13
Painting/Authoring level, 13, 14
Programming level, 13, 14
and Macintosh, 11-12
modularity of, 348-349
on networks, 794-797
limitations, 795-797
most efficient use, 795
queuing, 796-797
scripting for shared stack, 795-796
and programming, 12
properties, 483-517
button properties, 510-517
field properties, 503-510
global properties, 484-492
painting properties, 494-500
window properties, 492-494
resources, adding, 394
See also specific topics.
HyperCard with Switcher, memory needed, 42-43
retrieval, 42-43
uses of, 43
HyperTalk
abbreviations, 707-708
bugfixes (from version 1.2), 721-722
commands
Message Box commands, 345
Script commands, 345
constants, 577-581
control structures, 583-597
functions, 519-562
keyboard/mouse functions, 529-536
math functions, 545-551
miscellaneous functions, 553-562
text functions, 537-543
time/date functions, 523-527
use in scripts, 520-522
versus commands, 520
keyboard shortcuts, 713-714
choosing tools, 713
peeking at fields, 713-714
spreadsheet, 779
mathematics operators, 563-576
power of scripts, 346-347
and preprocessing, 344-345
programming, basis of, 348-349
properties of, 148-149
synonyms, 708-709
See also: Commands (Hypertalk).
See also specific topics.
HyperTalk scripts, 358-360
Boolean, 365-366
commands, 358-360
action commands, 415-440
arithmetic commands, 441-447
containers, 400-405
conventions related to, 398-399

file manipulation commands, 475-481
navigation commands, 407-413
object manipulation commands, 449-459
scope of, 358
screen manipulation commands, 461-467
sound commands, 469-473
containers, 365, 400-405
destination, 365, 398
foreign language versions, 366
functions, 360-361
returns and, 360
Get command, 365
hierarchy, 355, 368-376
button scripts, 372-376
illustration of, 370, 372
workings of, 369-372
messages, 355-358, 367-368
entry points, 376-378
generation of, 356-358
message handler, 356, 358, 368, 393-394
in object's script, 368
system messages, 383-394
modularity of, 349
objects, 352-355
hierarchial nature of, 355, 368
hotel analogy, 352-355
parameters, 361-362
Script Editor, 349-350
commands used, 350
features of, 349-350
structure of, 350-352
and syntax rules, 345
source in, 365
structure of
"end" statement, 351-352
"on" statement, 351-352
variables, 362-364
global variables, 364, 402
"it" local variable, 364-365
local variables, 364, 401
place in memory, 364
Wait command, 422224
See also Commands (HyperTalk); specific topics.
Hypertext concept, 172

I-Beam text cursor, 55, 57, 58, 424, 425
Icon buttons, 166, 168-171, 511-512
background layer, 113
Icon resources, 805
Idle handler, 391-392
Idle messages, system messages, 391-392
ID number, card, 165
If-then constructions
if...then, 586-587
if...then...else, 587-588
nesting if-then decisions, 589
structure of, 584-586
ImageWriter, 69, 216
Importing text, 686
graphics transfers, 687-688
Open File/Close File commands, 475-476
Read From File Command, 476-478
Index button, 370, 375
Information
database software, 8-11
historical view, 1-5
advertising agencies, 3
ancient times, 1-2
batch processing, 4
personal computers, 4-5
real time processing, 4
speed limitations, 2
steam locomotives, 2-3
telegraph, 3
information handler, 7
research links, 7
See also Components of information.
Into preposition, Put command, 416-417
Invert, Paint menu, 247-248
Irregular Polygon Tool
double-click shortcut, 241-242
Option key enhancement, 241
Shift key enhancement, 241
Items, component of information, 403
"It" local variable, HyperTalk scripts, 364-365

Keep, Paint menu, 254, 256
Keyboard
command/tilde key locations, 33
powerKeys property, 490-491

Keyboard/mouse functions
clickLoc, 535-536
commandKey, 531-534
mouse, 534-535
mouseClick, 534-535
mouseH, 529-531
mouseLoc, 529-531
mouseV, 529-531
optionKey, 531-534
shiftKey, 531-534
command/tilde key locations, 33
Keys property, 490-491
command/tilde key locations, 33
Keyboard/mouse functions
clickLoc, 535-536
commandKey, 531-534
mouse, 534-535
mouseClick, 534-535
mouseH, 529-531
mouseLoc, 529-531
mouseV, 529-531
optionKey, 531-534
shiftKey, 531-534
command/tilde key locations, 33

Language translation, global property, 487-488
LaserWriter, 69-71, 216, 233
Fast Laser Printing, 71
Lasso tool
Command key enhancement, 207
double-click shortcut, 207
Option key enhancement, 207
Shift key enhancement, 206
Layers
background layer, 112-115
button layers, 113
icon buttons, 113
text field layers, 114-115
two backgrounds in stack, 117
card layers, 115-116
buttons, adding, 115-116
graphics, adding, 116
modifying, 116
and heterogeneous stacks, 116-117
object layers, 109-111
background layer, graphics, adding, 113
opaque objects, 109-110
transparent objects, 109, 110-111
visible properties versus action properties, 111
Length, text function, 537-538
less than, <, math operator, 567-568
less than/equal to, < =, math operator, 567-568
less than/equal to, <, math operator, 567-568
Lighten, Paint menu, 250
Linefeed constant, 580-581
Line height, 144
Lines, as component of information, 403-404
lineSize, 268
painting property, 497
Linking, 188-191
automatic dialing, 67
button strategies, 191-192
to adjacent cards, 185-186
Datebook linking, 67
to different stacks, 186-187
to distant cards, 186
hard links, 187-188
and Message Box, 66-67
soft links, 188
to adjacent cards, 185-186
to different stacks, 186-187
to distant cards, 186
link scripts, 188-191
Local variables
as container, 401
HyperTalk scripts, 364, 401
"it" local variable, 364-365, 401
Loc[ation]
button property, 512
field property, 503
window property, 492-493
LockMessages, 761-762
LockRecent, 762-763
lockScreen, 485-486, 744-746
global property, 488-489
lockText, 142-143
field property, 504
Long date, date function, 523-524
Long time, time function, 524-525

Macintosh
  drawing, 194
    MacDraw, 195
  Open command, 436-433
    painting, MacPaint, 195
Macros, Send command, 427
Mailing labels, Print Reports, 80
Margins, Wide Margins, 143
Math calculation
  arithmetic commands
    Add, 441-442
    Convert, 446-447
    Divide, 445-446
    Multiply, 444-445
    Subtract, 442-444
  numberFormat, 489-490
Mathematics operators
  And operator, 570-571
  (concatenate) &, 572-573
  (concatenate and space) &&, 572-573
  contains operator, 573-575
  (divide) /, 565-566
  (equals) =, 566
  (greater than) >, 567-568
  (greater than/equal to) > =, 567-568
  (greater than/equal to) > ???, 567-568
  (less than) <, 567-568
  (less than/equal to) < =, 567-568
  (less than/equal to) <????, 567-568
  (minus) -, 564-565
  (multiply) *, 565
  (not equals) < >, =???, 566-567
  Not operator, 571-572
  Or operator, 571
  (plus) +, 563-564
  precedence, order of operations, 575-576
Math functions
  abs, 548
  annuity, 548
  atan, 549
  average, 549
  compound, 549
  cos, 549
  exp1, 550
  exp2, 550
  exp, 549
  max, 550
  min, 550
  ln1, 550
  ln, 550
  random, 545-546
  round, 551
  SANE functions, 548-551
  sin, 551
  sqrt, 551
  tan, 551
  trunc, 551
  value, 546-548
Max, math function, 550
Me function, 719-720
Menubar
  Hide command, 449-451
  Show command, 451-453
Menus
  authoring, 90
    standard menus, 93
    tear-off palettes, 93-94
  doMenu command, 420-422
  Options menu, 259-276
  painting, 197-198
  Paint menu, 245-257
  See also specific menus.
Message Box
  as calculator, 36-39
    example calculations, 37-38
    order of calculations, 38
    preprogrammed functions/
constants, 39
    as scientific calculator, 38
  clearing of, 35
  and close box, 34
  Command-M, 34, 35
  as container, 402
  and go address command, 36
  and go commands, 35-36
  and go home command, 36
  Hide command, 451
  and linking, 66-67
  moving of, 34
  purpose of, 34
  Show command, 451-453
  text display, 35
  text pointer, 35
  windows of, 34

Messages
hierarchy, examples of, 378-383
HyperTalk scripts, 355-358
generation of, 356-358
message handler, 356, 358, 368
in object's script, 368
message handler, placement of, 393-394
system messages
arrowKey, 389
creating messages, 387-388
deleting messages, 387-388
doMenu message, 390
enterKey, 389
idle messages, 391-392
mouseDown, 383-384
mouseenter, 387
mouseleave, 387
mouseStillDown, 384, 387
mouseUp, 384-386
mousewithin, 387, 391
open/close messages, 388-389
quit, 392
resume, 392-393
returnKey, 389
startUp, 392
suspend, 393-394
tabKey, 389
Min, math function, 550
minus, -, math operator, 564-565
Modem
Dial command, 426-427
Hayes compatible, 426
settings, registers, 426
Mouse
Click command, 430-431
Drag command, 431-433
mouse function, 534-535
See also Keyboard/mouse functions.
mouseClick, mouse function, 534-535
MouseDown, 367, 368
system messages, 383-384
Mouseenter, system messages, 387
mouseH, 529-531
Mouseleave, system messages, 387
Mouseloc, 453, 529-531
MouseStillDown,
system messages, 384, 387
update, 783-784
MouseUp, system messages, 384-386
mouseV, 529-531
Mousewithin, system messages, 387, 391
Move Closer, 137
Move Farther, 137
Moving fields, 151
Multifinder, 699, 721
Multiple, painting property, 497-498
multiply, *, math operator, 565
Multiply command, 444-445
examples of, 445
parameters of, 444
purpose of, 444
use of, 444
multiSpace, painting property, 497-498
Music, Play command, 470-473

Name
button property, 513
field property, 504-505
for stacks/backgrounds/cards, 501
Naming of cards, 126
card ID, 125
Navigation commands, 407-411
Find command, 409-411
Go command, 407-409
Help command, 413
Pop card command, 411-413
Push card command, 411-413
Nesting if-then decisions, 589
Next Repeat, repeat construction, 594-595
not equals, < >, math operator, 566-567
Not operator, 571-572, 585
numberFormat, global property, 489-490
Numbering, of cards, 125
Number [of], text function, 540-541
Number of cards/buttons/fields function, 553-554, 756-757
numToChar, text function, 541-543

Object layers, 109-111
Object manipulation commands, 449-459
Edit Script command, 458-459

Get command, 454-457
global variables, 457-458
Hide command, 449-451
Set command, 454-457
Show command, 451-453
Object properties
Get command, 454-457
Set command, 454-457
Objects
HyperTalk scripts, 352-355
hierarchial nature of, 355, 368
hotel analogy, 352-355
name property, 501-502
Send command, 427-428
Offset, text function, 538-540
1n1, math function, 550
1n, math function, 550
On mouseDown, 368
On mouseUp, 351, 363, 368, 369, 371, 374, 375
"On" statement, HyperTalk scripts, 351-352
Opaque
object layers, 109-110
Opaque buttons, 173
Opaque field, 140
Paint menu, 253-254
Open/close messages, system messages, 388-389
Open command, 436-438
examples of, 438
parameters of, 437-438
purpose of, 436
and special characters, 437
use of, 436-437
OpenField, 368
Open File command, 475-476
examples of, 476
parameters of, 476
purpose of, 475
use of, 475-476
Opening stack, 104-105
Open Printing command, 439-440
examples of, 439-440
parameters of, 439
purpose of, 439
use of, 439
optionKey
enhancement of
Curve tool, 230-231
Irregular Polygon Tool, 241
Lasso tool, 207
Rectangle tool, 222-223
Regular Polygon tool, 238-239
selection tool, 204
Straight line tool, 218
keyboard function, 531-534
Option shortcut, Pencil tool, 209
Options menu, 259-276
brush shape, 268
Draw Centered, 274
Draw Filled, 274
Draw Multiple, 275-276
Edit pattern, 268
FatBits, 262-265
scrolling in, 265
switching off, 264
switching on, 263-264
Grid, 259-262
as time saver, 260
line size, 268
polygon sides, 274
Power Keys, 266-268
listing of, 267
repeated pressing of, 268
Order of fields, See Fields, field order.
Or operator, 571, 585
Outlining, See Visual outliner.
Oval tool, semi-circles, 229

Page Setup
Bitmap Alignment, 71
Bitmap printing, 70-71
Font Substitution, 70
ImageWriter, 69
Larger Print Area, 71
LaserWriter, 69-71
and printer used, 69
and smoothing, 70
Paintbrush tool
Command key enhancement, 210
double-click shortcut, 211
Shift key enhancement, 210
Paint Bucket tool
double-click shortcut, 227-228
properties of, 226-227
Painting

background vs. card layers, 196-197
FatBits, 196
menus, 197-198
and pixels, 196
undo, 199
versus drawing, 194-195
See also Paint menu;
Painting properties;
Painting strategies; Painting tools.
Painting properties, 494-500
brush, 494-495
Centered, 495
filled, 495
Grid, 496-497
lineSize, 497
multiple, 497-498
multiSpace, 497-498
pattern, 498-499
polySides, 499
textAlign, 499-500
textFont, 499-500
textHeight, 499-500
textSize, 499-500
textStyle, 499-500
Painting strategies, 277-280
borrowing ideas, 277-278
menubar, need for, 279
sequential approach, 278-279
Painting tools, 201-243
Curve tool, 230-232
double-click shortcut, 231
Option key enhancement, 230-231
Eraser tool, 212-214
Command key enhancement, 213-214
double-click shortcut, 214
Shift keyynhancement, 213
Irregular Polygon Tool, 240-242
double-click shortcut, 241-242
Option key enhancement, 241
Shift key enhancement, 241
Lasso tool, 205-207
Command key enhancement, 207
double-click shortcut, 207
Option key enhancement, 207
Shift key enhancement, 206
Oval tool, 228-229
semi-circles, 229
Paintbrush tool, 209-212
Command key enhancement, 210
double-click shortcut, 211
Shift key enhancement, 210
Paint Bucket tool, 224-228
double-click shortcut, 227-228
properties of, 226-227
Patterns Palette, 242-243
double-click shortcut, 243
Pencil tool, 207-209
color and, 207
double-click shortcut, 209
FatBits, 209
Option shortcut, 209
Shift key enhancement, 208-209
Rectangle tool, 221-224
double-click shortcut, 222
Option key enhancement,222-223
Shift key enhancement, 223-224
Regular Polygon tool, 236-240
double-click shortcut, 237-238
Option key enhancement, 238-239
Shift key enhancement, 237
Rounded rectangle tool, 224
selection tool, 201-205
Command key enhancement, 203
double-click shortcut, 205
and Edit menu, 203
Option key enhancement, 204
rectangular area selection, 202
Shift key enhancement, 204
Spraypaint tool, 219-221
Command key enhancement, 221
Shift key enhancement, 220-221
Straight line tool, 214-218
double-click shortcut, 216
Option key enhancement, 218
resolution of printer and, 215-216
Shift key enhancement, 216-218
Text tool, 232-236
Command key shortcuts, 234-235
double-click shortcut, 233-234
fonts, choosing, 235
Shift key shortcuts, 234-235
text strategies, 235-236
Paint menu, 245-257
Darken, 250
fill, 247

flipping, vertical/horizontal, 252-253
Invert, 247-248
Keep, 254, 256
Lighten, 250
Opaque, 253-254
Pickup, 249
Revert, 256
Rotate Left, 252
Rotate Right, 252
Select, 246
Select All, 246-247
Trace Edges, 251
Transparent, 253-254
Palettes
patterns palette, 243
tear-off palette, 93-94
Paramcount function, 558
Parameters, HyperTalk scripts, 361-362
Param function, 558
Params function, 558-561
Pass, repeat construction, 596-597
Pathnames, 29-32
determining of, 31
listing of, 30
pathname rotation, 30
Pathways
Close File command, 475-476
Open File command, 475-476
Patterns, 268
and bit maps, 271-272, 274
inside patterns, 268, 270
painting property, 498-499
patterns palette, double-click shortcut, 243
Pencil tool
color and, 207
double-click shortcut, 209
FatBits, 209
Option shortcut, 209
Shift key enhancement, 208-209
Picking up text, 55-56
Pickup, Paint menu, 249
Pixels
Invert, 247-248
and painting, 196
Play command, 470-473
examples of, 473
note duration notation, 472
parameters of, 471-472
purpose of, 470
sound function, 556-557
tempo, 471
use of, 470-471
plus, +, math operator, 563-564
Polygon sides, 274
Polygon tools, See Irregular Polygon tool; Regular Polygon tool.
polySides, painting property, 499
Pop card command, 411-413
Pop command
examples of, 412-413
parameters of, 412
purpose of, 411
use of, 411-412
Power Keys
global property, 490-491
listing of, 267
repeated pressing of, 268
Precedence, order of operations, 575-576
Precision Bitmap Alignment, 234
Print command, 480-481
examples of, 481
parameters of, 480
purpose of, 480
use of, 480
Printing
Close Printing command, 439-440
Open Printing command, 439-440
Page Setup, 69-71
Print Card, 71
Print Report, 76-81
Print Stack, 71-72, 74
report formatting options, 76-81
See all specific topics.
Print Report, 76-81
formats, 76-81
backgrounds, text extraction, 78, 80
columns, 76-77
mailing labels, 80
rows, 78
Print Stack
cards per page, 72
front to back output, 74
header text, 74
size of cards, 72
speed factors, 71

Font Laser Printing, 71
split-page format, 72
standard format, 72
white space option, 74
Programming, 341-345
BASIC and, 342
and HyperCard, 12
and Macintosh, 342-343
and personal computers, 341-342
self-published software, 88-89
See also HyperTalk.
Properties
Properties
AutoTab, 770-771
button properties, 510-517
autoHilite, 510
hilite, 510-511
icon, 511-512
loc[ation], 512
name, 513
rect[angle], 514
script, 514-515
showName, 510
style, 515
textAlign, 516
textFont, 516
textHeight, 516
textSize, 516
textStyle, 516
visible, 517
CantDelete, 767-768
CantModify, 768-769
Cursor, 766-767
field properties, 503-510
loc[ation], 503
lockText, 504
name, 504-505
rect[angle], 505-506
script, 506-507
scroll, 507
showLines, 504
style, 507-508
textAlign, 508-509
textFont, 508-509
textHeight, 508-509
textSize, 508-509
textStyle, 508-509
visible, 509-510
WideMargins, 504
FreeSize, 763-764
Get command, 454-457
global properties, 484-492
blindTyping, 484-485
cursor, 485-486
dragSpeed, 486-487
editBkgnd, 487
language, 487-488
lockScreen, 488-489
numberFormat, 489-490
powerKeys, 490-491
userLevel, 491-492
LockMessages, 761-762
LockRecent, 762-763
painting properties, 494-500
brush, 494-495
Centered, 495
filled, 495
Grid, 496-497
lineSize, 497
multiple, 497-498
multiSpace, 497-498
pattern, 498-499
polySides, 499
textAlign, 499-500
textFont, 499-500
textHeight, 499-500
textSize, 499-500
textStyle, 499-500
Set command, 454-457
for stacks/backgrounds/cards, 500-503
name, 501
script, 502-503
ShowPict, 771-772
Size of Stack, 763
UserModify, 769-770
window properties, 492-494
loc[ation], 492-493
rect[angle], 493
visible, 494
Within, 772-773
Protection
stacks, 105-108
filtering out menu commands, 108
password-protection, 107-108
Private Access system, 107-108
Protect Stack, 106

Public domain stacks, 88
Push card command, 411-413
Push command
examples of, 412-413
parameters of, 412
purpose of, 411
use of, 411-412
Put command, 415-419
after preposition, 418
before preposition, 417-418
examples of, 418-419
into preposition, 416-417
parameters of, 416-418
purpose of, 415
use of, 415-416

Queuing, networks, 796-797
Quit, system messages, 392
Quote constant, 579-580

Radio buttons, 174
Random, math function, 545-546
Read From File Command, 476-478
examples of, 478
parameters of, 477-478
purpose of, 476
use of, 476-477
Real time processing, 4
Recent
Command-R, 33
options to, 33
representations of cards, 32-33
Rect[angle]
button property, 514
field property, 505-506
window property, 493
Rectangle button style, 174
Rectangle field style, 141
Rectangle tool
double-click shortcut, 222
Option key enhancement, 222-223
Shift key enhancement, 223-224
Regular Polygon tool
double-click shortcut, 237-238
Option key enhancement, 238-239
Shift key enhancement, 237
Relational databases, 9-10
features of, 9
Repeat constructions
Exit If, 595-596
Exit Repeat, 595-596
Next Repeat, 594-595
Repeat For, 590-591
Repeat Until, 591-592
Repeat While, 592-593
Repeat With, 593-594
Reports
Print Report, 76
formatting options, 76-81
See also Print Report.
ResCopy
copying into Home stack, advantage of, 807
copying resource from stack to stack, 802, 807
renumbering/renaming resources, 802
resource numbers, 801
standard resource names, 801
Reset paint, 737-738
Resizing buttons, 177
Resizing fields, 152
Resolution of printer, and Straight line tool, 215-216
Resource editor, 146
Resource fork, 800
Resources, 799-807
cursor resources, 805
font resources, 804
icon resources, 805
purposes of, 800
ResCopy, 800-804
sound resources, 805-806
Result funnion, 555-556
Resume, system messages, 392-393
Retrieval environments
HyperCard in Switcher, 42-43
stand-alone application, 42
Return constant, 580
ReturnInField, 710-712
ReturnKey, system messages, 389
Reverse lettering, 147
Revert, Paint menu, 256
Root directory, 29
Rotate Left, Paint menu, 252
Rotate Right, Paint menu, 252

Round, math function, 551
Rounded rectangle button style, 174
Rows, Print Report, 78

Saving
  Browsing environment, 22
  keep, 254
  new card, 62
Scientific calculator
  Message Box as, 38
  See also Calculations, Message Box.
Screen
  authoring
    9 inch screen, 92
    large screens, 92-93
  cursor property, 485-486
  Hide command, 449-451
  lockScreen property,
    488-489, 717-718
  Show command, 451-453
Screen manipulation commands,
  461-467
  Answer command, 463-465
  Ask command, 465-467
  Ask Password command, 465
  Visual Effect command, 461-463
ScreenRect, 759-760
Scripts
  button property, 514-515
  field property, 506-507
  foreign language versions, 366
  modularity of, 349
  for stacks/backgrounds/cards,
  502-503
  peeking at scripts, 714-715
  structure of, 350-352
  and syntax rules, 345
  See also HyperTalk scripts.
Script Editor, 349-350
  commands used, 350
  Edit Script command, 458-459
  features of, 349-350
Scroll
  FatBits, 265
  field property, 507
  scrolling field style, 142
Scrolling fields
  assembling fields, 780-781
  multiple, 780
  scroll control, 783-784
  scrolling handlers, 782-785
Search-and-replace, 775-779
Seconds, 628-629
  time function, 525
  and Wait command, 423
Secs, time function, 525
Select, 738-742
  Paint menu, 246
Select All, Paint menu, 246-247
SelectedChunk, 752-753
SelectedField, 752-753
SelectedLine, 752-753, 786
SelectedText, 752-753
Selection, as container, 400, 402
Selection tool
  Command key enhancement, 203
  double-click shortcut, 205
  and Edit menu, 203
  Option key enhancement, 204
  rectangular area selection, 202
  Shift key enhancement, 204
Self-published software, programming,
  88-89
Semi-circles, Oval tool, 229
Send command, 427-428
  examples of, 428
  parameters of, 428
  purpose of, 427
  use of, 427
Set command, 454-457
Shadow field style, 141-142
Shift key
  enhancement of
    Eraser tool, 213
    Irregular Polygon Tool, 241
    Lasso tool, 206
    Paintbrush tool, 210
    Pencil tool, 208-209
    Rectangle tool, 223-224
    Regular Polygon tool, 237
    selection tool, 204
    Spraypaint tool, 220-221
    Straight line tool, 216-218
  keyboard function, 531-534
  shortcuts, Text tool, 234-235
Show command, 451-453
  examples of, 453

parameters of, 452-453
purpose of, 451
use of, 452
Show Lines, 143
field property, 504
showName, button property, 510
ShowPict, 771-772
Sin, math function, 551
Size
of cards, Print Stack, 72
line size, 268
resizing buttons, 177
resizing fields, 152
of screen, 92-93
of stack, 763
Smoothing, effects of, 70
Soft links, 188
Software, self-published software, 88-89
Sort command, 434-436
examples of, 435-436
parameters of, 434-435
dateTime parameter, 435
international parameter, 435
number parameter, 435
purpose of, 434
use of, 434
Sorting, of cards, 46
Sound commands, 469-473
Beep command, 469-470
Play command, 470-473
Sound function, 556-557
Sound resources, 805-806
Space constant, 580
Speed, dragSpeed property, 486-487
Split-page format, Print Stack, 72
Spraypaint tool
Command key enhancement, 221
Shift key enhancement, 220-221
Spreadsheet
Selected Line function, 786
turning lines into calls, 786-789
Sqrt, math function, 551
Stack expression, 728
Stacks
applications corporate directory, 605-615
conversion calculator, 651-662
telephone logbook, 617-624
time sheet, 625-633
To Do list, 635-649
visual outliner, 663-682
buttons, 321-328
add background buttons, 321
cloning buttons, 325-328
delete background buttons, 321
modification of, 321-324
cards
card layer graphic, adding, 331-334
linking to buttons, 334-335
new cards, adding, 328-330
stack button, creating, 335-336
cloong of, 22
creation of, 281-337
approaches to, 282
preparation phase, 281
steps in, 284-293
and font properties, 146
Go command, 407-409
heterogeneous stack, 98-100
Home Stack button, creating, 602-603
homogeneous stack, 98
modifying background fields, 316-320
adding lines to card, 317-320
erasing field, 316-317
modifying background graphics, 293-316
background text, removing, 310
buttons, adding, 311-316
card depth, reducing, 293-298
drop shadowing, adding, 301-309
widening card, 299-301
name property, 501
new stack, 100-105
entering text, 104
opening stack, 104-105
opening of, 20-22
protection, 105-108
filtering out menu commands, 108
password-protection, 107-108
Private Access System, 107-108
Protect Stack, 106
saving, 22

script property, 502-503
Send command, 427-428
Sort command, 434-436
standard file dialog box, 20
use of, 337
Stand-alone application, retrieval, 42
Standard file dialog box, Browsing environment, 20
Standard format, Print Stack, 72
StartUp, system messages, 392
Straight line tool
double-click shortcut, 216
Option key enhancement, 218
resolution of printer and, 215-216
shift key enhancement, 216-218
Strings
Find strings, 48, 49-50
picking up text, 55
shortcuts, 50
Style
button property, 515
field property, 507-508
Subtract command, 442-444
examples of, 443-444
parameters of, 443
purpose of, 442
use of, 443
Suspend, system messages, 393-394
Symmetrical shapes, Flip commands, 252-253
Synonyms, 708-709
System fonts, 146
System messages, 383-393

Tab constant, 580
TabKey, system messages, 389
Tan, math function, 1
Target function, 557-558, 718-719
Tear-off palette, 198
Telephone dialing, Dial command, 424-427
Telephone logbook, 617-624
additions to, 624
overview of, 617-619
scripts/properties, 619-624
Text, picking up text, 55-56
Text alignment, 144
textAlign
button property, 516
field property, 508-509
painting property, 499-500
TextArrows, on/off, 697-699
Text fields
bugs, 785-786
creating, 149, 149-150
short method, 149
layers, background layer, 114-115
TextFont
button property, 516
keyboard shortcut, 705
field property, 508-509
painting property, 499-500
Text functions
charToNum, 541-543
length, 537-538
number [of], 540-541
numToChar, 541-543
offset, 538-540
TextHeight
button property, 516
field property, 508-509
painting property, 499-500
Text placement, Type command,433-434
Text response
Ask command, 465-467
Ask Password command, 465
Text searches, 47-56
Beachball cursor, 48
Command-F, 48, 49, 50, 56
Find, 51-54
Find command, 47-48
find strings, 48, 49-50
shortcuts, 50
and Message Box, 47-49
multiple matches, 48
narrowing a search, 54-55
quick searches, 48-49
TextSize
button property, 516
field property, 508-509
painting property, 499-500
Text strategies, Text tool, 235-236
TextStyle
button property, 516
field property, 508-509
painting property, 499-500

Text tool
  Command key shortcuts, 234-235
  double-click shortcut, 233-234
  fonts, 235
  Shift key shortcuts, 234-235
  text strategies, 235-236
Thickness of lines, lineSize, 497
Ticks
  time function, 526-527
  and Wait command, 423
Time
  Convert command, 446-447
  formats, 447
Time/date functions
  abbreviated date, 523-524
  date, 523-524
  long date, 523-524
  long time, 524-525
  seconds, 525
  secs, 525
  ticks, 526-527
  time, 524
Time sheet, 625-633
  computeBill handler, 629
  overview of, 625-626
  as relational database, 633
  scripts/properties, 627-633
To Do list, 635-649
  overview of, 635-638
  scripts/properties, 638-649
  yearly interrl routine, 649
Tools
  Browse tool, 43-44
  Tools palette, 44
Tools palette, Choose command, 429-430
Trace Edges, Paint menu, 251
Transparent, Paint menu, 253-254
Transparent buttons, 171-172
Transparent objects, object layers, 109, 110-111
True constant, 577-579
Trunc, math function, 551
Type command, 433-434
  examples of, 433-434
  purpose of, 433
  use of, 433
Typing
  blindTyping, 484-485
  Typing level, User Preferences, 18

Undo, 214
  key for, 199
Up constant, 577-579
Updates
  chronology of, 688-691
  steps for upgrading, 692-696
User-defined functions, 561-562
userLevel, global property, 491-492
UserModify, 769-770
User preferences, 18
  Command-4, 17
  Command-H, 17
  getting to options, 17
  levels of, 18
  Typing level, set to, 18
User-supported software, 88

Value, math function, 546-548
Variables
  HyperTalk scripts, 362-364
    global variables, 364, 402, 457-458
    "it" local variable, 364-365
    local variables, 364, 401
    place in memory, 364
  words not to be used for, 818-819
Versions, 716-717, 757-758
Visible
  button property, 517
  field property, 509-510
  window property, 494
Visual Effect command, 461-463
  effect names, list of, 462
  examples of, 463
  parameters of, 462
  purpose of, 461
  use of, 461
  visual effect techniques, 462-463
Visual outliner, 663-682
  adding features, 682
  overview of, 663-666
  scripts/properties, 667-682

Wait command, 422-424
examples of, 423-424
parameters of, 423
purpose of, 422
use of, 422-423
White space option, Print Stack, 74
Wide Margins, 143
field property, 504
Width, widening card, 299-301
Window properties, 492-494
Within, 772-773
Words, component of information, 403-404
Write To File command, 478-480
examples of, 479-480
parameters of, 479
purpose of, 478
use of, 478-479
Write protected disks, 705-706

XCMDs, 799, 801, 806-808
copyright aspects, 807-808
languages for writing, 806
sources of, 806
syntax factors, 807